CHRISTMAS/
BIRTHDAY 2020
We Love you Mom!

Denise & Suzanne

3002199

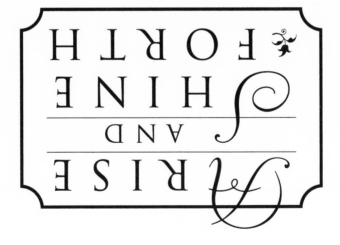

ARISE AND SHINE FORTH

TALKS FROM THE 2000 WOMEN'S CONFERENCE

SPONSORED BY BRIGHAM YOUNG UNIVERSITY AND THE RELIEF SOCIETY

BOOKCRAFT

Library of Congress Cataloging-in-Publication Data

Women's Conference (2000 : Brigham Young University)
  Arise and shine forth : talks from the 2000 Women's Conference sponsored by Brigham Young University and the Relief Society.
     p.   cm.
  Includes bibliographical references and index.
  ISBN 1-57345-909-7
  1. Women in the Mormon Church—Congresses. 2. Mormon women—Religious life—Congresses. I. Brigham Young University. II. Relief Society (Church of Jesus Christ of Latter-day Saints) III. Title.
BX8641 .W73 2000
267'.449332—dc21

00-067421

Printed in the United States of America   72082-6784

10   9   8   7   6   5   4   3   2   1

CONTENTS

HOW DO I? LESSONS IN ACCESSING THE LIGHT

CONVERSION: TASTING THE GOSPEL

FOR THEY THAT BE WISE

HOW DO I? LESSONS IN NURTURING

A WORKSHOP OF DAILY LIVING

HOW DO I? LESSONS IN APPLYING GOSPEL PRINCIPLES

TEMPLES: BUILDINGS AND BODIES

STANDING FOR TRUTH

PREFACE

꒰⌣꒱

This volume, the fifteenth in the series, is a collection of selected presentations from the 2000 Women's Conference, which was sponsored jointly by Brigham Young University and the Relief Society of The Church of Jesus Christ of Latter-day Saints. We are grateful for the energy, time, and prayer the authors put into preparing their presentations for the conference, and we are pleased that we can share a few of their ideas and feelings with an even greater audience through this volume.

The book has been divided into specific sections that will appeal to sisters throughout this worldwide church. In each section, sisters will find wonderful insights about personal worthiness, scripture study, temple worship, missionary work, parenting, and discovering joy, among other things.

We are grateful for the efforts of the conference planning committee, who made both the conference and this volume possible. We acknowledge the dedication and skill of our editorial team—Dawn Anderson, Suzanne Brady, Dlora Dalton, and Susette Green—who put this work together.

Our theme, found in Doctrine and Covenants 15:5, is a clarion to Relief Society sisters across the earth to "arise and shine forth, that thy light may be a standard for the nations." What an awesome and sacred responsibility! As you read this volume, may you catch the spirit of that call and stand with your sisters in the gospel throughout the world.

—Wendy L. Watson
Chair, 2000 Women's Conference

FOREWORD

꿎（ᵔ）ᵔ

Women's Conference 2000 was a bold beginning for the new millennium. More than twenty-two thousand women registered for the conference, and another two million in Canada, the Caribbean, Europe, and the British Isles viewed sessions by satellite. Ten sessions were broadcast over television.

This is the time to take to heart the Lord's call found in Doctrine and Covenants 115, the theme of this conference: "Arise and shine forth, that thy light may be a standard for the nations" (v. 5).

It is no coincidence that Women's Conference 2000 commenced on 26 April, the very day this revelation was given more than one hundred fifty years ago. On that date the Brigham Young University stadium was filled with sisters serving the Lord. They prepared newborn kits and school bags, they stuffed bunnies and bears for children, they extracted names for temple work, they sorted food, they gave blood—two thousand pints of blood—they made leper bandages and quilts. As I looked at quilts stretching from one goal post to the other, I thought that perhaps BYU football had met its match. You, the sisters of Relief Society, are indeed Saints—Latter-day Saints. Your lives are "a standard for the nations" (D&C 115:5).

The verse that follows our theme reads: "That the gathering together upon the land of Zion . . . may be for a defense, and for a refuge from the storm, and from wrath when it shall be poured out without mixture upon the whole earth" (D&C 115:6). Gathering at women's conference is part of that defense and refuge from the storm.

The service event, the blood drive in particular, drew my thoughts back to an experience I had in Rwanda when I was the presiding bishop. I had been serving in that assignment about a month when civil war broke out in that African nation. In Rwanda there is a constant clash between two tribes. One tribe runs the government and forces the other tribe out of the country. The outside group replenishes its arms until it can attack and take over. In April 1994, eight million people lived in Rwanda. By August four million were left. With almost a million killed and three million forced from their homes to camps outside the border, the situation was desperate.

The Church responded by shipping large quantities of humanitarian supplies to that part of Africa. I accompanied the delivery. As we drove down a road on the way to a prison, I kept seeing what appeared to be large splotches of oil. When I mentioned them, the driver slowed the car and said, "Bishop Bateman, that's not oil. That's blood."

We went first to a prison where we asked to deliver the blankets and soap personally to the prisoners. We wanted to make sure our relief supplies reached them. The prisoners looked like ordinary men to me—farmers, bakers, traders. Prisoners who had been condemned to death came up to us for a moment, raised their eyes, and then dropped them again. For a brief moment, I saw a light, a spark in their faces, and then it was gone. Do you know what it is like to look into eyes that have no hope? All we could do was leave them our kindness and our love. Into my mind came the words of Jesus Christ to his disciples, "I was in prison, and ye came unto me, [for] . . . inasmuch as ye have done it unto one of the least of these, . . . ye have done it unto me" (Matthew 25:36, 40). To "arise and shine forth," we must carry the light of Christ.

Our next stop was a maternity hospital where about eight hundred women waited to give birth or had just given birth. The hospital staff included only three nurses and two American doctors. Imagine so few to care for so many. The hospital wasn't just short on staff. Their storehouse was empty. There was no food, absolutely nothing. We had brought them some sugar, cereals, and powdered milk to keep them alive until more supplies arrived. Again the words of the Savior to those who serve, "I was an hungred, and ye gave me meat" (Matthew 25:35).

I think of the sisters preparing newborn kits during the conference, and I imagine the women in that hospital receiving them. I think of those who gave blood at the Red Cross station, and I imagine their pure blood saving someone's life. I think of the truths of the gospel that were taught from the pulpit, and I think of its power to blunt the wrath of the adversary "when it shall be poured out without mixture upon the whole earth" (D&C 115:6). Nothing in the world will match the light that shone forth from the BYU Women's Conference this year.

In this volume, sisters, is oil from that conference that you may take to fill your lamps. May you be filled with the Spirit of the Lord as you read, and may you draw that strength into your homes as a "defense and refuge" (D&C 115:6).

The Lord Jesus Christ is at the center of all you are doing. I am grateful for this conference, its influence on each of you, its influence on Relief Societies all over the world. Women's conference is an intellectually stimulating, spiritually enriching occasion. May your light shine forth.

—Merrill J. Bateman
President, Brigham Young University

"ARISE AND SHINE FORTH"

✠

Mary Ellen Smoot

More than ever you have demonstrated that we are a *Relief* Society. Look what can be accomplished when we unite in the sisterhood of Relief Society! Just yesterday, ten thousand Relief Society sisters were working together to bless countless lives. As I looked across the stadium and saw you stitching, stuffing, sorting, and serving in so many ways, I could hardly contain my excitement. If ever there was "a stadium of fire," it was yesterday afternoon and evening. The spirit of service has ignited our souls.

During the course of this year, you and other devoted sisters everywhere have made quilts and hygiene kits that have gone to Kosovo, Turkey, Mexico, Armenia, Georgia, Ukraine, Venezuela, Mozambique, Zimbabwe, Mongolia, and Moldova. You did it. You have found ways within the walls of your own homes and in Home, Family, and Personal Enrichment night to reach people in need around the world.

I had the privilege of looking into the faces of Kosovar refugees, hearing their stories, and witnessing the tremendous humanitarian efforts of the Church. You have no idea how many lives are being touched, how many burdens relieved, because you care enough to serve. How does that make you feel? Isn't it great to know you are saving a life, even while you live half a world away?

And in the process, think of how you have blessed the lives of those close to home. Your families and ward families have caught the

Mary Ellen Wood Smoot has served as Relief Society General President since April 1997. She loves family history and has written histories of parents, grandparents, and their local community. She served with her husband, Stanley M. Smoot, when he was called as a mission president in Ohio, and they later served together as directors of Church Hosting. They are the parents of seven children and the grandparents of forty-seven.

fire of service. Less-active members and nonmembers have found a place beside you in serving. Everywhere I go, I hear stories of reactivation and conversion in connection with these service projects. Also, Young Women, Scouts, and priesthood brethren have united with you.

Sisters, thank you! Mahalo! Gracias! Obragada! Please know how wonderful you are. The scope of your service is far and wide and deep. It encompasses not only material giving but also service in missionary efforts and family history and the examples you set in your everyday lives. As you turn to our Heavenly Father for guidance, follow the Spirit and serve as directed by the Holy Ghost.

During some of the darkest days of the Church, when the Saints were facing terrible persecution in Far West, Missouri, the Prophet Joseph Smith revealed the will of the Lord for the Saints then, and for you and me now: "Arise and shine forth, that thy light may be a standard for the nations" (D&C 115:5).

"Arise and shine forth." What hope this can give us. The Lord did not wait until the Saints in Missouri enjoyed more peace and prosperity, until they were settled in comfortable homes and friendly neighborhoods. He simply told them, and in turn each of us, to "let your light so shine" (Matthew 5:16).

You may be thinking, *You don't understand my situation*. I know that many sisters carry heavy burdens. Your sorrows, pains, and hardships are real; but with confidence and tender regard, I believe that each of you *can* "arise and shine forth." Not because I told you so but because our Lord and Savior arose on the third day and through his atoning sacrifice made it possible for each of us to find relief from the pains, sorrows, and limitations of mortality. In Christ's perfect life, each of us can find new life not only in the hereafter but also in the here and now.

At a recent general Relief Society meeting, President Gordon B. Hinckley, our prophet, gave us the charge: "If anyone can change the dismal situation into which we are sliding, it is you. Rise up, O women of Zion, rise to the great challenge which faces you."[1] He spoke to you and to me and to every sister in this great organization. We must rise up and be "a standard for the nations."

Reflect with me for a moment on how Mary Magdalene rose up that first Easter morning. Put yourself in the place of Mary when the Risen Lord visited her outside the empty tomb, and learn from her singular example.

Not three full days had passed since Mary witnessed the crucifixion of her Lord and God. She had "stood by the cross" (John 19:25) and watched the soldiers drive nails into his hands and feet. Mary had every reason to be at home grieving. But where was she on the morning of the third day? While "it was yet dark" (John 20:1), Mary arose and with the other women went to serve their Lord. They brought the "spices which they had prepared" (Luke 24:1) and went to anoint his body. The nature of their service was rather commonplace, a customary and thankless duty performed for the least among them. But it was an act of love, and in the performance of it, Mary would see the face of her risen Lord.

ARISE IN LOVING SERVICE

If we are to be a "standard to the nations," we must arise in loving service. The Relief Society Declaration reminds us that as Relief Society sisters we "delight in service and good works."[2] If we are to rise up and really serve others, we must understand and embrace the mission of Relief Society. Relief Society sisters are an integral part of our spiritual safety.

When the first twenty Relief Society sisters gathered in Nauvoo and were deciding on a name for their organization, Eliza R. Snow suggested the word *relief* because it implied service both common and extraordinary. Emma Smith, the newly set-apart president, liked the idea and said, "We expect extraordinary occasions and pressing calls."[3] The Prophet Joseph Smith was requested to be in attendance and he stated, "With the resources [the Relief Society sisters] will have at their command, they will fly to the relief of the stranger; they will pour in oil . . . to the wounded heart of the distressed; they will dry up the tears of the orphan and make the widow's heart to rejoice."[4]

We are seeing the fulfillment of this and other prophecies about the Relief Society organization. It was divinely inspired and organized. At the third meeting of the Relief Society, in a cabin about the size of your living room, the Prophet Joseph Smith said, "This society shall have power to command queens in their midst. . . . Queens of the earth shall come and pay their respects to this society. They shall come with their millions and shall contribute of their abundance for the relief of the poor. If you will be pure, nothing can hinder."[5]

As the tide of selfishness sends its waves so high in the world, we can determine to change that tide by being pure vessels of Christlike love and service. Service is the essence of Christ's gospel. Service is the antidote to the ills of our time. Service heals the wounded heart. President Hinckley observed: "Generally speaking, the most miserable people I know are those who are obsessed with themselves, the happiest people I know are those who lose themselves in the service of others. . . .

" . . . The most effective medicine for the sickness of self-pity is to lose ourselves in the service of others."[6]

In the first chapter of Alma, we read how the people become righteous and prosperous: "And thus, in their prosperous circumstances, they did not send away any who were naked, or that were hungry, or that were athirst, or that were sick, or that had not been nourished; and they did not set their hearts upon riches; therefore they were liberal to all, both old and young, both bond and free, both male and female, whether out of the church or in the church, having no respect to persons as to those who stood in need" (Alma 1:30).

No matter what your circumstances, "charity never faileth." This Relief Society motto and the new Relief Society Declaration are not just samplers that we hang on our walls; they must be inscribed in our hearts and become a way of life for us. Everything we do can be performed in a spirit of selfless love and service. Whether we are cleaning the house, shopping for groceries, talking with a friend, or visiting and teaching, we can be charitable.

One of the service captains who helped with the service project for this women's conference probably did not tell you how service has been a vital part of her healing process. Let me tell you her story. Not long ago, Sister Sherry Allen was diagnosed with breast cancer. Because she is a wife and the mother of several small children, this would be no small trial in and of itself. But she had recently adopted three foster children—each only one year old—and her seven-year-old daughter was diagnosed with a brain tumor shortly thereafter. Sister Allen, soon after her recovery, was called to the stake Relief Society presidency. She and her stake Relief Society president, Sister Nancy Howe, fasted and prayed often. They determined that they would stop focusing on their own troubles and reach out to help others. You see, Sister Howe's teenage son had been in a terrible accident that left him paralyzed from the neck down and on an oxygen vent. This faithful son really wanted to complete an Eagle project, so he began making arrangements to fund a large-scale service project for their Relief Society.

Their success was spectacular, and many in the community became involved. Though they were going through deep trials in their personal lives, these Relief Society sisters and this young man were determined to arise and shine forth. The service they rendered is worthwhile and impressive, but don't think you have to do exactly what they did. The circumstances of each of us are unique, and each of us has her own gifts to give. You do what you *can* do. Don't "run faster than [you have] strength" (Mosiah 4:27). The Spirit will guide you in your efforts, and you will remember that "all these things are done in wisdom and order" (Mosiah 4:27).

Relief Society sisters all around the world are serving in so many different ways. Let me highlight just a few. The sisters in Ukraine assist in making quilts for a local orphanage. Sisters in Austria assist the blind by making teaching kits and skill books for blind children. Relief Society members in England have an ongoing project of collecting food items for a homeless shelter. Sisters in South Africa gather supplies and make hand-knitted sweaters for sick children. And in the Philippines, sisters help train women in their community to sew, bake, and make dolls. Sisters in a Greeley, Colorado, stake are involved in literacy classes. The stake Relief Society president writes: "We began about eighteen months ago and are completing our fifth twelve-week session. Over fifty women have participated; more than half of them are nonmembers."[7] Special enrichment classes for the Spanish-speaking sisters are being held. The list goes on and on.

Loving service takes on so many different forms. Some of the most important services we ever perform are sharing the gospel of Jesus Christ and otherwise relieving spiritual suffering. The "casseroles" of faith and hope that we give to a friend, the "cookies" of kindness that we extend to our own families, the "coats" of charity that we gently place on others' shoulders when their hearts need spiritual warming— these are some of the most vital services. And many are performed within the walls of our own homes.

Whether as visiting teachers, member missionaries, family historians, or loving and devoted mothers, wives, sisters, and daughters, each of us needs to bring others to Christ.

ARISE AND BRING OTHERS WITH YOU

When you arise, bring others with you. Notice that Mary Magdalene didn't go to the Garden Tomb alone. Remember that "Joanna, and Mary the mother of James, and other women" (Luke 24:10) came with Mary to the sepulchre. Some of these women were probably members of her family; others were close friends. Perhaps some were those whom Mary had introduced to the Savior and brought unto him. May each of us reach out and feel the joy of bringing someone to the Savior.

Just like Mary, none of us walks the path that leads to the Savior without helping others along the way. "If any man [or woman] among you be strong in the Spirit, let him take with him him that is weak, that he may be edified in all meekness, that he may become strong also" (D&C 84:106).

When we are truly converted to the gospel of Jesus Christ, we reach out to others and help them find their way back to God, all of which secures our own grip on the iron rod. I have found that whenever we help someone else toward righteousness, our own faith is strengthened.

Are you actively seeking opportunities to share the gospel with your nonmember friends? When was the last time you bore your testimony to someone, including your family? Do your children and grandchildren know what you believe, how you came to believe as you do, and why your faith and testimony in Jesus Christ are central to your life?

The faithful mothers of Helaman's stripling warriors didn't just kind of think it was true or mostly believe—they knew it, and so must we! One of the most important things we can do as Relief Society sisters is strengthen ourselves spiritually and come to know that Jesus is the Christ, this is his kingdom on earth, and we are his servants. I'm not saying such a knowledge will keep us from heartaches and hardships, but I can assure you that it will carry you through.

President Joseph F. Smith often explained that his mother, Mary Fielding Smith, and his beloved "aunt" Emmeline B. Wells were able to remain so strong in the face of adversity because of their strong testimonies. He said: "Could you turn one of these women away from their convictions in the Church of Jesus Christ of Latter-day Saints? No, never in the world could you do it. Why? Because they knew it. God revealed it to them, and they understood it, and no power on earth could turn them from what they knew to be that truth. Death was nothing to them. Hardship was nothing. . . . All they felt and knew and desired was the triumph of the kingdom of God and the truth that the Lord had given to them.

"My soul, where are these women now?"[8]

I believe we can be such women. I know we can.

ARISE AND SEEK THE LORD

Mary Magdalene began to seek for Jesus long before she found the empty tomb. Her life had been one of following after him, listening and learning, believing and doing. He was her personal Redeemer, her Lord and Master. So when the resurrected Lord called her by name, she recognized his voice, "turned herself, and saith unto him, Rabboni; which is to say, Master" (John 20:16).

I believe that one of the ways we come to know the Master and hear his voice is by reading the scriptures. Whether you read two chapters or ten, one verse or twenty, when you read the scriptures every day, you open the windows of heaven. Those verses and thoughts stay with you and enlighten your perspective. They strengthen, protect, and inspire you—and your families.

Not long ago I learned of a Book of Mormon reading program that some Relief Society sisters in Pennsylvania had completed. Each of the sisters had made a personal commitment to read the Book of Mormon in forty days. They had an outpouring of the Spirit. They were blessed with missionary experiences, service opportunities, family togetherness, reactivation, and stronger testimonies simply because they had immersed themselves in the scriptures.

As Relief Society sisters, we "increase our testimonies of Jesus Christ through prayer and scripture study."[9] Sisters, take your scriptures to the meetings. Use the scriptures in your lessons. Read them in your families. If we are to be a "standard for the nations," we must "[feast] upon the word of Christ" (2 Nephi 31:20).

Arise and Be a Light

Arise and be a light, a standard to the nations. The Lord's words of comfort to Mary are for each of us as well. He simply said, "Woman, why weepest thou? whom seekest thou?" (John 20:15). All of her sorrows would be assuaged by the recognition of him as her Savior. And so will each of ours.

Once Mary Magdalene recognized the Lord and conversed with him, she "came and told the disciples that she had seen the Lord, and that he had spoken these things unto her" (John 20:18). In like manner, when we have felt his light and recognized his influence in our lives, we want to share that light with others.

Sometimes I think we forget what a glorious light is ours as members of The Church of Jesus Christ of Latter-day Saints. Not long ago, a national magazine did a feature article on a Latter-day Saint family with great artistic ability.[10] The photographers and writers spent three days with the Al and Nancy Young family, took more than eight hundred pictures, and ended up reporting at least as much about their family life as their artwork. The article featured the Youngs' interest in family history, food storage, and the activities they do together. It showed their daughter tracing the footsteps of her ancestors on a world globe.

Two quotations from the Doctrine and Covenants were included in the article. And one of Brother Young's lithographs was of a young woman named Charity, a woman whose basket is always filled with service and kindness.

Perhaps most interesting is the response this family is receiving from people all over the world. One person commented that the Youngs' values apply to everyone.

The world needs what the gospel gives us. Don't put your light "under a bushel." "Let your light so shine before men, that they may see your good works, and glorify your Father which is in heaven" (Matthew 5:15–16).

I was impressed with a recent article from the Northampton Stake in England: "Mormon Mum Makes Headlines."[11] The public affairs director set out to cover the organization of the Relief Society. A telephone interview with a mother of six included discussions on the family, morality, and religious beliefs and was followed by a visit to the family by a press photographer. The article ended up reflecting the importance of Relief Society in this sister's life and her emphasis on service. The article sparked an interest in how Latter-day Saints live, and local members have enjoyed missionary moments with friends and acquaintances who wanted to know more about this sister and the family-centered life the Church encourages.

In word, deed, thought, and song, the light we emanate truly can be a "standard for the nations" (D&C 115:5). I'll never forget when my husband and I traveled with the Mormon Tabernacle Choir to the

Holy Land. The choir sang what was in our hearts when we gathered at the Garden Tomb. And that is my testimony today:

> *Forbid it, Lord, that I should boast,*
> *Save in the death of Christ, my God;*
> *All the vain things that charm me most,*
> *I sacrifice them to His blood.*
> *Were the whole realm of nature mine,*
> *That were a present far too small;*
> *Love so amazing, so divine,*
> *Demands my soul, my life, my all."*[12]

If we give our all, everything else will fall into place. If we will arise in loving service, bring others with us, and seek the Lord for inspiration and knowledge, we will be a light in this world. "Choose ye this day, to serve the Lord God who made you" (Moses 6:33). We must not fail. We cannot fail.

Notes

1. Gordon B. Hinckley, "Walking in the Light of the Lord," *Ensign*, November 1998, 99.
2. Relief Society Declaration, *Ensign*, November 1999, 93.
3. "A Record of the Organization, and Proceedings of the Female Relief Society of Nauvoo," 17 March 1842, Archives of The Church of Jesus Christ of Latter-day Saints, Salt Lake City. Hereafter cited as Relief Society Minutes.
4. Joseph Smith, *History of The Church of Jesus Christ of Latter-day Saints*, ed. B. H. Roberts, 2d ed. rev., 7 vols. (Salt Lake City: The Church of Jesus Christ of Latter-day Saints, 1932–51), 4:567.
5. Relief Society Minutes, 28 April 1842; punctuation standardized. See also *The Words of Joseph Smith*, ed. Andrew F. Ehat and Lyndon W. Cook (Salt Lake City: Grandin Book, 1991), 117.
6. Gordon B. Hinckley, *Teachings of Gordon B. Hinckley* (Salt Lake City: Deseret Book, 1997), 589–90.
7. Letter in files of the general Relief Society office.
8. *Joseph F. Smith*, Teachings of Presidents of the Church series (Salt Lake City: The Church of Jesus Christ of Latter-day Saints, 1998), 189.
9. Relief Society Declaration, *Ensign*, November 1999, 92.

10. Colleen Heather Hogan, "For the Youngs of Utah: The Arts of Family Life," *Victoria* 14 (May 2000): 42–44.

11. "British Isles News," *Ensign,* March 2000, 4.

12. Isaac Watts, "When I Survey the Wondrous Cross," *Hymns and Spiritual Songs* (Leeds: John Binns, 1790).

"Be Thou an Example of the Believers"

✺⟨⟩✺

Virginia U. Jensen

As the new millennium dawned, I found myself in a hospital bed. It was 3 A.M. I had not been able to sleep the entire night. Thinking back to the previous week, I recalled how very ill I had been with what I thought was a terrible case of the flu. As my temperature soared, I began having trouble breathing. A trip to the doctor determined something was seriously wrong, and I was sent straight from his office to the hospital. The diagnosis was confirmed—a very large blood clot on my left lung had done considerable damage.

One of the doctors who had worked with me when I entered the hospital came into my room during that early-morning hour. She was surprised to find me awake and sat down to express some concerns. Laying out her clinical synopsis and its ramifications, she said, "I'm not sure you understand how serious your situation is. You could have died from this condition. People often have. And if you do get well, it could recur."

Her comments weren't exactly the sleep inducement I was hoping for. In the darkness, the good health I had taken for granted seemed like a priceless commodity, and life felt very precious. I began to consider the possibility that at what seemed the very young age of sixty,

---

Virginia U. Jensen has served as first counselor in the Relief Society General Presidency since April 1997. A homemaker, she and her husband, J. Rees Jensen, are the parents of four children and the grandparents of seven. She has served in numerous volunteer and Church service missionary assignments and enjoys gardening, grandchildren, and family activities.

still wanting to do much more with my life and longing to spend years of time with my family members, I might not be here.

I felt an overwhelming urgency to say things to all the people I love. I thought of picking up the phone and calling them right then. I ran through my mind how the conversation might go if I were to call my children. I would say, "Hi, it's Mom."

In a very sleepy voice, they would reply with alarm, "Mom, are you all right?"

"Yes," I would respond. "I was just thinking about you and wondering if you know how much I love you."

They would reply, "It's 3 A.M.!"

And I would say, "Well, I am sorry to wake you, but I must ask if you know what I believe in and what I stand for. Have I taught you all you need to know to get along well in life? Have I been the kind of example you need me to be?"

After a long pause, they would say, "Mom, what medication do they have you on?"

I decided not to call them right then.

The sobering medical facts I had learned and my own middle-of-the-night ponderings led me to consider that my life's example might have to speak for me. Our children, no matter what age, notice everything. They see the things we do. They form opinions, values, and beliefs based on what they observe in us.

I know the potent nature of example, and therefore I am struck by the value of Paul's admonition, "Be thou an example of the believers" (1 Timothy 4:12).

There is evidence all around us that the world desperately needs women who stand for something good and noble and righteous—even if that stand may not be popular. The world needs women who in their daily acts and deeds exemplify a higher standard. Women may not be the soldiers who lead our country into battle against evil forces, but every day they are at the front of the battle that Satan wages for souls. The example of a righteous woman—a woman who has made covenants with God and keeps them—is of paramount importance.

Others feel as strongly as I do about the power of example. Dr. Albert Schweitzer, the great humanitarian, phrased it this way, "Example is not the main thing in influencing others—it is the only thing!"[1]

I am especially touched by a sentiment expressed by President Howard W. Hunter: "Sincere believers in the gospel of Jesus Christ should proclaim its truth and show by example the power and peace of a righteous, gentle life."[2] I realized at that moment that the example I wanted to leave for my children was, as President Hunter stated, "a righteous, gentle life."

A believer is a person who learns of God's plan and lives his or her life in accordance with the requirements of that plan. The spot I found myself in during that hospital stay in January caused me to ponder on the effect that being a believer had had on my life. I thank my Heavenly Father that I was born of goodly parents who were believers, who taught me and set a good example for me. I was thankful at that moment for Primary teachers who had labored to teach me and Young Women leaders whose examples to this day guide me.

Being a believer had brought me a sense of direction. It had brought conviction that Jesus Christ is my Savior and my Exemplar. That conviction had brought amazing, beautiful peace to my life in the past, and certainly now, when my future seemed uncertain, it brought a powerful peace. I knew that, come what may, I would be just fine—and furthermore my family members, whom I cared about and worried about and loved so much, would be just fine. The example of the believers in my life had helped me become a believer as well, granting me the serenity I needed in that troubled hour.

Do we appreciate the power of our examples? Do we value the ability we as women have to bless so many others through the simple process of our daily living and what we believe in? In all our roles in the family, in professions and the community, in our neighborhoods and in our Church callings, our actions resonate as loudly as a calling voice booms through a narrow canyon.

Example echoes, especially in our homes, where we have the most profound influence on those around us. How we treat one another, how we demonstrate our belief, thunders without so much as a word being spoken. It is encouraging to know that we can influence others so vividly, that our daily actions can mean so much. It can also be sobering, even disconcerting, to think that what we do rings so loudly. The echoes of our actions can continue to sound through many years in the lives of those we influence. A favorite poem entitled "The Echo," by C. C. Miller, teaches us:

> 'Twas a sheep not a lamb
> That strayed away in the parable Jesus told,
> A grown-up sheep that strayed away
> From the ninety and nine in the fold.
>
> And why for the sheep should we seek
> And earnestly hope and pray?
> Because there is danger when sheep go wrong:
> They lead the lambs astray.
>
> Lambs will follow the sheep, you know,
> Wherever the sheep may stray.
> When sheep go wrong,
> It won't take long till the lambs are as wrong as they.
>
> And so with the sheep we earnestly plead
> For the sake of the lambs today,
> For when sheep are lost,
> What a terrible cost
> The lambs will have to pay. [3]

Every woman can bless the lives of others in countless ways when she puts into practice the principles she has learned and can learn in Relief Society. In fact, the virtues listed in the Relief Society Declaration, if incorporated into our lives, make us "an example of the believers." After all we can say, after all we can write, after all we can read, after all we can think, what remains is our example. How can we make certain that its influence is clear and true?

History provides many examples of good men and women, but even the best of mortals is flawed in some way or another. None could serve as a perfect model or an infallible pattern to follow, however well-intentioned that person might be. Only Christ can be our ideal, our "bright and morning star" (Revelation 22:16). Don't you love that description of the Savior? "Our bright and morning star." Have you ever noticed that problems, no matter their magnitude, seem much worse at night when it is dark and we are tired? The Savior is our bright and morning star to lead us away from darkness into the light, both literally and figuratively.

Only he can say without reservation: Follow me; learn of me; do the things you have seen me do. Drink of my water and eat of my bread. I am the way, the truth, and the life. I am the law and the light. Look unto me and ye shall live (Matthew 11:29; 16:24; John 4:13–14; 6:35, 51; 14:6; 2 Nephi 31:12; 3 Nephi 15:9).

What a consoling summary that is of why we look to Christ as the Author and Finisher of our faith. Only in following him, in striving to be like him, can we find hope that the dawn will yet break, no matter how dark and dreary the night.

I feel deep gratitude for my knowledge that Jesus Christ is our Savior and our Exemplar. He has beckoned us to follow his example. "What manner of men ought ye to be?" he asks. Then, answering his own question, he instructs, "Verily I say unto you, even as I am" (3 Nephi 27:27). Elder Neal A. Maxwell reminds us that "the clear requirement that the Father and Jesus have undeniably laid upon us as mortals is to strive, individually, to become like them."[4]

If we want to follow his blueprint for the kind of people we should be, then we must seriously set about developing the same qualities he has. This is hard work. It will take a lifetime. The straight and narrow path is not a speedway but rather a simple, sometimes obscure, path we walk along one step at a time. Sisters, we must keep walking. And, as the hymn suggests, "Let us in his footsteps tread."[5]

May I mention just two of the ways in which our Savior set the example for us.

First, we can follow Jesus' example of love. The Savior was effective in blessing lives because he loved everyone unconditionally. All through his ministry, he loved and ministered to all. He made no distinctions. He accepted, valued, included, and loved everyone.

He taught, "A new commandment I give unto you, That ye love one another; as I have loved you" (John 13:34).

He further taught: "This is my commandment, That ye love one another, as I have loved you" (John 15:12).

A lawyer tried to tempt the Savior by asking him, "Master, which is the great commandment in the law?" (Matthew 22:36).

Jesus answered, "Thou shalt love the Lord thy God with all thy heart, and with all thy soul, and with all thy mind. This is the first great commandment. And the second is like unto it, Thou shalt love thy neighbour as thyself" (Matthew 22:37–39).

There was a time, when I lived in a previous ward, that I felt like nobody liked me. My struggle with this feeling seemed to be reaching a high point about Christmastime. One evening I went to my mailbox, and there was a great surprise. Someone had left a small gift with a wonderful note expressing love and admiration for me.

I cannot begin to tell you my feelings from this act. These little surprises continued for eleven more days. I tried very hard to discover who was blessing my life. No matter how clever I was—even hiding in the snowy bushes one evening for what seemed like a very long time—I never learned the identity of this angel. Nevertheless, her kindness made me feel as if everyone loved me, and it brought a healing balm. If she is anywhere within the sound of my voice, let me now say, "Thank you, dear friend. You'll never know how much your love and kindness has meant to me."

This loving person in my ward was following Jesus' example. The Savior's unlimited love was evidenced even more by his example than by his words. He served people in places that others would not go. He was criticized for being a friend to publicans and sinners. He sought out those who were suffering from the effects of physical and spiritual deficiencies. He went among the people, forgiving them, healing them, feeding them, and showing all manner of love to them. To love one another as he loves us is a vast, encompassing directive.

Second, we can follow Jesus' example of obedience.

Obedience is the first law of heaven. From his high and holy perspective, the Savior knows we can be exalted only by obeying eternal laws and accepting his atonement. Even at the tender age of twelve, he knew he "must be about [his] Father's business" (Luke 2:49). From the start of his ministry, when he submitted himself to be baptized "to fulfil all righteousness" (Matthew 3:15), to the culminating act of the Atonement, when he cried from the depths of his agony, he perfectly exemplified the principle of obedience.

The atoning sacrifice of Jesus Christ is the most important event in all recorded history. We cannot possibly comprehend all the Savior experienced in Gethsemane and on Calvary's hill. We read about it, we talk of it, and we ponder it; but the suffering he experienced is beyond our comprehension.

When Jesus cried, "Father, all things are possible unto thee; take away this cup from me," his request was immediately followed by, "Nevertheless not what I will, but what thou wilt" (Mark 14:36). His sacrifice encompasses all of ours and exceeds them infinitely, yet he empathizes with our relatively small struggles, knowing that they seem great to us. Each act of obedience fortifies our faith and clarifies our vision of his plan for us. As we learn and live the gospel, line upon line and precept upon precept, we become increasingly sensitive to spiritual things. We can develop that habit of obedience which characterizes the life of a sincere believer.

Our wonderful Aunt Maude was in failing health when her grandson was about to leave on his mission. He realized that this would be the last time he would see his beloved grandmother alive on this earth. Because of that, he said to her, "Grandma, I don't want to go on this mission right now." With conviction borne of a lifetime of obedience, she replied, "Oh, Adam, you must go. It is our life. It is our faith."

Adam went on his mission. His grandmother passed on a few days later, leaving for her grandchildren a legacy of unwavering devotion.

Near the end of his suffering on the cross, Christ declared to his Father, "I have glorified thee on the earth: I have finished the work which thou gavest me to do" (John 17:4). And then in our behalf Jesus said, "Holy Father, keep . . . those whom thou hast given me, that they may be one, as we are" (John 17:11).

Whether we are building upon long years of righteous habits of love and obedience or have lately found our footing on the straight and narrow path, each of our lives can be blessed by renewed attention to Jesus' example. We can read of his washing his disciples' feet and grow in love and humble service. We can recall his utter submission to his Father's will and be moved to greater obedience. We can remember the Savior's promise in 3 Nephi, "Unto him that endureth to the end will I give eternal life" (3 Nephi 15:9), and find strength, as he did, to glorify our Father during our brief stay on earth and faithfully complete our earthly missions, whatever challenges they might hold.

When I think of following the Savior, I remember President Gordon B. Hinckley's response to a Protestant minister's query, "'If you do not use the cross [as a symbol of your religion, as do other Christian faiths], what is the symbol of your religion?'" President Hinckley replied, "The lives of our people must become the only meaningful expression of our faith and in fact, therefore, the symbol of our worship."[6]

The gospel is true. It will stand the test. We must consciously and deliberately choose the path of believers. The kingdom of God is moving forward with or without us. If we will move with it and be "an example of the believers," it will make all the difference in our happiness and peace of mind.

When a young woman from Singapore leaves her parents' home and begins to establish a home of her own, she presents her mother with a basket of gifts representing all the things her mother has taught her. In the basket will be found special foods, some of the daughter's handwork, paintings, or writings, as well as gifts that symbolize such virtues as patience and cheerfulness. Also included could be souvenirs from family experiences. Thus a mother from Singapore has a vivid display of how much influence her example has had in her daughter's life.

I'd like to have that tradition here. We might be surprised to know all the ways in which our examples have touched the hearts of others. I know that when I was in that hospital room a few months ago, I felt a new and poignant kind of gratitude for the many examples of the believers who had blessed my life. I felt an overwhelming gratitude for my Savior and Exemplar. I wanted each day of my life to be a gift of thanks to him.

I think I'll call my children now. I'll do it in the daytime so I won't disturb their sleep. I'll tell them how much I love them. I'll tell them how much I have loved being their mother. I'll tell them that I wish for them a righteous, gentle life. I'll remind them that that kind of life will bring them a powerful peace. I'll tell them if they will be "an example of the believers" and follow the Savior's pattern of "even as I am," that no matter how dark and sleepless their night, the bright and morning star will shine for them, and they will be just fine, come what may.

Notes

1. Albert Schweitzer, quoted by Delbert L. Stapley, Conference Report, April 1969, 46; also in "The Power of Example," *Improvement Era*, June 1969, 70.
2. Howard W. Hunter, Conference Report, October 1992, 22.
3. C. C. Miller, "The Echo," in *Best-Loved Poems of the LDS People*, ed. Jay A. Parry, Linda Ririe Gundry, Jack M. Lyon (Salt Lake City: Deseret Book, 1996), 312–13.
4. Neal A. Maxwell, *Even As I Am* (Salt Lake City: Deseret Book, 1982), 1.
5. "Come, Follow Me," *Hymns of The Church of Jesus Christ of Latter-day Saints* (Salt Lake City: The Church of Jesus Christ of Latter-day Saints, 1985), no. 116.
6. Gordon B. Hinckley, *Be Thou an Example* (Salt Lake City: Deseret Book, 1981), 85–86.

SHALL WE NOT GO FORWARD IN SO GREAT A CAUSE?

✧

Sheri L. Dew

Here we are at women's conference again. Another year has passed, and what a year it has been! We've welcomed in a new millennium—but not just any old millennium. This is the one foreseen by prophets from the beginning of time. What a magnificent time to take our turn in helping shoulder the glorious burden of the gospel kingdom!

I love the magnitude and the drama of it all, but then, I love drum rolls and bugles and big finishes and anything that stirs our souls and moves us to righteous action. That is just one reason I am drawn to the Prophet Joseph's exuberant declaration: "Now, what do we hear in the gospel which we have received? A voice of gladness! . . . Shall we not go on in so great a cause? Go forward and not backward. Courage, . . . and on . . . to the victory!" (D&C 128:19, 22).

Doesn't that just make you want to climb onto a rooftop or go on CNN and tell the whole world what you know and believe? We are engaged in the glorious cause of Jesus Christ. Nonetheless, standing firm in that cause is not always easy to do. When I was fifteen, I was invited to speak about the Church in my high school. Everyone knew I was LDS. Some of my friends had even come to Mutual with me. But as the only LDS girl in school, I often found myself trying to maintain that delicate balance between standing up for what I believed and not standing out. As the day of my presentation approached, I began to

Sheri L. Dew is the second counselor in the Relief Society General Presidency. She grew up in Ulysses, Kansas, and graduated from Brigham Young University with a degree in history. A popular speaker and writer, she is executive vice-president of publishing at Deseret Book Company.

panic. How would my friends react to the story about Joseph Smith and angels and gold plates? I am sorry to tell you that fear got the best of me, and I backed out. Afterwards I was so ashamed. I had let the Lord down. I had been more concerned about the praise of the in-crowd than the praise of the Lord. I had cared more about belonging to the "right" group than standing as a witness.

I imagine we have each had moments when we should have been more valiant in our testimonies of Jesus Christ, moments when in our desire to belong we have turned our backs on the Master. We each have a longing to belong—to feel that we fit in, to be part of something greater and grander than we are—so we often scurry about, chasing worldly distinctions that give us the illusion of importance and acceptance. But ironically, as the Lord's covenant people we already belong to an extraordinary in-crowd, and we have the potential of belonging to the most extraordinary group in time or eternity: the family of Christ. That depends, however, upon our willingness to go forward in the glorious cause of Christ.

In 1873 Eliza R. Snow stood in Jerusalem on the Mount of Olives, where she reflected on the Savior's sacrifice. As president of the Relief Society, she declared that the day would come when we would stand "at the head of the women of the world," because we had "greater and higher privileges than any other females upon the face of the earth."[1]

For as long as I can remember, I too have felt deeply about our role as sisters in the latter-day kingdom of God. Said President Joseph F. Smith: "He that sent His Only Begotten Son into the world to accomplish the mission which He did, also sent . . . every man and woman in the world, to accomplish a mission. . . . We [must] learn the obligation that we are under to God and to each other and . . . to the cause of Zion."[2]

I broach the subject with trepidation because after I spoke here last year, one sister wrote: "I did not like Sheri Dew's concluding remarks. She robbed life of all its joy and fun. . . . We need to be more casual about things. . . . I did not like being told all I needed to be and do. . . . Telling me the Lord expects valiant women did not help me. I don't want to be incredible. I want to be me." Frankly, I agonized over that letter, and I apologize to anyone whom I discouraged, but I dare not back away from what I said then or from what I am about to say now.

There are three things about which I am absolutely certain: Jesus is the Christ, his gospel has been restored to the earth, and every one of us has been foreordained to stand where we stand in the latter-day kingdom of God. We can't risk being casual about the Savior's work or about our role in it. No one else can fill my mission, and no one else can fill yours. This knowledge shouldn't increase our burden; it should only reconfirm that we are beloved spirit daughters of God, whose lives have meaning, purpose, and direction.

When Nephi saw our day in vision, he saw that the power of the Lamb of God descended upon the covenant people of the Lord, who "were armed with righteousness and with the power of God in great glory" (1 Nephi 14:14). During this culminating millennium, the influence of the righteous—that's you and me—will be far greater than our numbers or our natural ability if we go forward in this great cause.

Let us consider three principles from the Relief Society Declaration that teach us about standing joyfully where we have been foreordained to stand.

AS SISTERS, WE ARE UNITED IN OUR DEVOTION TO JESUS CHRIST

I have come to believe that whatever we really want, we'll probably get. If we really want money and status, we'll find a way to get them. By the same token, if we really want to overcome bad habits or cultivate integrity or become more pure so that we can better hear the voice of the Spirit, we'll find a way to do those things as well. Fifty years from now, what we have become shouldn't surprise us because we will have become what we have set our hearts upon.

Alma taught that the Lord "granteth unto men according to their desire" (Alma 29:4). And when asked to identify the first great commandment, the Savior said simply, "Thou shalt love the Lord thy God with all thy heart, and with all thy soul, and with all thy mind" (Matthew 22:37). It's no accident that our hearts were mentioned first.

Satan is also after our hearts, because he knows that if he can control our feelings and desires, he can control us—which is why he tries
to harden our hearts, puff up the pride of our hearts, and set our hearts
upon the vain things of the world (4 Nephi 1:28; 2 Nephi 33:2; 28:15;
Helaman 12:4). The Nephite civilization collapsed entirely once the
people were past feeling (Moroni 9:20). Likewise, we have been
warned that in the last days "men's hearts shall fail them" (D&C
88:91), and the nightly news verifies this sad reality: children killing
children, "spin doctors" celebrated for their articulate cunning rather
than censured for breaches of integrity, violence that knows no bounds.

No wonder we are commanded to "come unto the Lord with all
[our hearts]" (Mormon 9:27). No wonder the Lord "requireth the heart
and a willing mind" (D&C 64:34). Notice that he said nothing about
how gorgeous or thin, educated or affluent, we must be. He simply asks
for our hearts and our will, because that's all we have to give him.
Everything else is already his. Said Brigham Young, "The Lord must be
first and foremost in our affections; the building up of his cause and
kingdom demands our first consideration."[3] Ultimately we will become
what we give our hearts to, for we are shaped by what we desire and
seek after. If we love the Lord such that our hearts are changed, his
image will fill our countenances. But if we love the world more, we'll
slowly take upon us those characteristics. As Truman Madsen has
remarked, "In youth our face reveals genetics. At fifty, we have the face
we deserve."

I'll never forget a visit I made to the Missionary Training Center
when an instructor there said that the missionaries liked to refer to the
MTC as a concentration camp but that he thought of it as a consecration camp. Life is the ultimate consecration camp, where we learn to
turn our lives and our will over to the Lord. Only in giving all we have
may we receive all our Father has.

Not long ago I was in Africa, and the images of our beautiful
African sisters are still vivid in my heart and mind. Their countenances
reflect the image of Christ. When they pray, they *pray*. It's as though
they reach right through the veil and talk to a trusted Friend. And

despite severe temporal challenges, they are happy. By the world's measure, they have nothing—except happiness. By contrast, many of us have everything—except happiness. Their optimism springs from a bedrock faith in Jesus Christ, to whom they have given their hearts. I've found myself wondering who the Lord is most concerned about—those whose temporal challenges are extreme but whose hearts are fixed on him, or those who have more things of this world but who haven't offered their whole souls unto him (Omni 1:26). Hunger may be a problem in Africa, but our sisters there are not starving spiritually.

Whatever our temporal conditions may be, once we have turned our hearts over to the Lord and decided we want to be like him, the process of following him becomes one of joy rather than white-knuckled endurance.

That truth is crucial, because even as we turn our hearts to the Lord, we don't suddenly become perfect. We do have to endure to the end, and we'll all make mistakes and have lapses in judgment along the way. But when our hearts are changed, we have "no more disposition to do evil" (Mosiah 5:2), which means we no longer want to make mistakes. And the Lord judges not only our works but also our desires.

The question we might therefore want to ponder is simply this: What do we really want? And what are we willing to do to get it? When we were baptized, we said we wanted to come into the fold of God (Mosiah 18:8). But do we really? Do we delight in being called his people, though that probably means looking and acting and dressing differently from the rest of the world? If so, are we willing to yield our hearts to the Lord? Those who do will be born again as the sons and daughters of Christ (Mosiah 5:7). The choice is ours, for what we really want, we'll ultimately get.

WE ARE WOMEN OF CHARITY

I once attended a fireside at which a general authority asked, "How can you tell if someone is converted to Jesus Christ?" We gave dozens of answers about service and commitment and obedience, none of which satisfied him. Finally he said that though our comments were all good, he believed that the one sure measure of a person's conversion was how he or she treats others.

Frankly, I had expected something more profound, but his assertion so intrigued me that it drove me to the scriptures. There, after much study, I began to see how profound his message was: When we turn our hearts to the Lord, we instinctively open our hearts to others.

After Alma the Younger was converted, his thoughts turned immediately to his people, for he "could not bear that any human soul should perish" (Mosiah 28:3). After Enos's all-night conversion, he "began to feel a desire for the welfare of [his] brethren . . . ; wherefore, [he] did pour out [his] whole soul unto God for them" (Enos 1:9). The Savior taught Peter, simply: "When thou art converted, strengthen thy brethren" (Luke 22:32).

Almost every major scriptural sermon focuses on the way we treat each other. We are taught to turn the other cheek (Matthew 5:39), to be reconciled to each other (Matthew 5:24), to love our enemies and pray for those who despitefully use us (Matthew 5:44), to serve each other and avoid contention (Mosiah 2:17, 32). Said Joseph Smith, "The nearer we get to our heavenly Father, the more we are disposed to look with compassion on perishing souls."[4] He also said that "it is natural for females to have feelings of charity."[5]

Knowing this, Lucifer works hard at undermining our divine gift. All too often we fall into traps he has designed to estrange us from each other. He delights when we gossip and criticize and judge, when we stew over perceived offenses or measure ourselves against each other, or when we succumb to such envy that we even begrudge each other's successes. All of these spiritually debilitating behaviors wreak havoc in relationships. Let us not forget that Satan resents any righteous relationship—because he will never have even one. Thus his efforts to alienate us from one another are never-ending.

A while ago a woman approached me after a fireside and asked, "Don't you feel guilty for choosing a career over marriage?" Her words hurt, but I'm sure her comment would have been different if she had known my heart or if she had known how much time I've spent fasting and pleading with the Lord in the temple, seeking to understand his will for me. Only he knows how painful this process has been, but he also knows how grateful I am for the process, because it has sealed my heart to him.

How often have you and I made judgments that are equally unfair? Why can't we resist the urge to second-guess and evaluate each other? Why do we judge everything from the way we keep house to how many children we do or do not have? Sometimes I wonder if the final judgment will be a breeze compared with what we've put each other through here on earth!

The Spirit cannot dwell in a home, a ward, or a relationship where there is criticism. Contention neutralizes us spiritually. When we fail to champion one another, we in essence betray each other.

In the second meeting of the Relief Society, Emma Smith urged her sisters to "divest themselves of every jealousy and evil feeling toward each other."[6] And in a later meeting, the Prophet Joseph said, "Sisters of the society, shall there be strife among you? I will not have it—you must repent and get the love of God. Away with self-righteousness."[7]

It is simply not for us to judge each other. The Lord has reserved that right for himself, because only he knows our hearts and understands the varying circumstances of our lives. Principles and covenants are the same for all of us. But the application of those principles will differ from woman to woman. What we can do is encourage each other to constantly seek the direction of the Holy Ghost to help us make decisions and then to bless us with the reassurance that our lives are on course. Only when the Lord is directing our lives may we expect to feel peace about our choices. And his approval is so much more vital than that of the ward busybody.

Another kind of judging is more subtle but equally destructive. How often do we describe a sister with words like these: She's a convert. She's been inactive. She's a Utah Mormon. She's single. She's a stay-at-home mom.

When we label one another, we make judgments that divide us

from each other and inevitably alienate us from the Lord. The Nephites learned this lesson the hard way. After the Savior appeared on this continent, those converted to the gospel lived in harmony for two hundred years. Because they loved God, they also loved each other. And though previously there had been Nephites and Lamanites and Ishmaelites, there were now no "-ites," as the scriptures tell us (4 Nephi 1:17). They were one. The result? There was not "a happier people among all the people who had been created by the hand of God" (4 Nephi 1:16). It wasn't until they again divided into classes that Satan began to win many hearts. The Nephites never recovered spiritually.

Can't we get rid of the "-ites" among us? Can't we avoid this "hardening of the categories"? We gain nothing by segregating ourselves based on superficial differences. What we have in common—particularly our commitment to the same glorious cause—is so much more significant than any distinctions in our individual lives. I think again of our sisters in Africa. The fact that my life is completely different from theirs didn't matter. When we left that last meeting in Ghana, I wept because I felt such a bond with them. We are our sister's keeper. Heaven forbid that we would ever make even one sister feel left out. If there is any place in all the world where a woman should feel that she belongs, it is in this Church.

None of us needs one more person pointing out where we've fallen short. What we do need are each other's compassion, prayers, and support. What if we were to decide today that we would make just one assumption about each other—that we are each doing the best we can? And what if we were to try a little harder to help each other? Imagine the cumulative effect, not to mention the effect on ourselves spiritually. Followers of Christ who pray with all the energy of their hearts to be filled with his love, the pure love of Christ, will become like him (Moroni 7:48). As we are filled with this love, we no longer feel envy or think evil of others. That's because "charity never faileth" (Moroni 7:46). Charity is demonstrated when we give someone the benefit of the doubt, or readily accept an apology, or refuse to pass along a juicy piece of gossip. Might we this evening in prayer contemplate grudges we need to put behind us, jealousies we should let go, and relationships we could improve by simply laying our pride aside?

Said President Gordon B. Hinckley: "Do you want to be happy? Forget yourself and get lost in this great cause. Lend your efforts to helping people. . . . Work to lift and serve His sons and daughters. You will come to know a happiness that you have never known before. . . . Let's get the cankering, selfish attitude out of our lives . . . and stand a little taller . . . in the service of others."[8]

Let us keep in mind Lucy Mack Smith's classic statement that "we must cherish one another, watch over one another, [and] comfort one another . . . that we may all sit down in heaven together."[9] There isn't anything righteous we can't accomplish if we will stand together.

WE ARE A WORLDWIDE SISTERHOOD

We are members of the most significant community of women on this side of the veil—the Relief Society of The Church of Jesus Christ of Latter-day Saints.

When at age twenty-five I was called to serve as a ward Relief Society president, I wondered if my bishop was responding to inspiration or indigestion. I just didn't fit the Relief Society profile, which I saw as older, married, bread-baking women. But now, after more than twenty years of Relief Society service, my view of our organization has changed dramatically.

The story of Relief Society is the story of prophets who have believed in the divine nature of women. It is the story of an organization that elevates women in their stature, their behavior, and their influence—both in quiet, one-on-one ways, and in contributions that affect communities, countries, and even continents. It is a classic story of using the simple to confound the mighty and strong, for the Relief Society is the only organization for women on the face of the earth founded by a prophet and undergirded by the priesthood of God. Joseph Smith said that the "Church was never perfectly organized until the women were thus organized"[10] and that Relief Society was not only to "relieve the poor, but to save souls."[11]

President Joseph F. Smith later stated that this organization was "divinely ordained of God to minister for the salvation of the souls of women and of men."[12] He also said that it is not for us "to be led by the women of the world; it is for [us] . . . to lead the women of the world."[13]

Then President Spencer W. Kimball made this declaration: "There is a power in [the Relief Society] that has not yet been fully exercised to strengthen the homes of Zion and build the kingdom of God—nor will it be until both the sisters and the priesthood catch the vision of Relief Society."[14]

I take prophets at their word. I believe that we as sisters in Relief Society have a divine mandate to help save souls, to lead the women of the world, to strengthen the homes of Zion, and to build the kingdom of God. Shall we not go on in so great a cause? The cause of women of God is to help build the kingdom of God.

Imagine what would happen throughout the gospel kingdom if every morning 4.5 million of us got on our knees and asked our Father what he needed us to do that day to build the kingdom. And then imagine if we did it. When the sisters of this Church put their minds and hearts to something, the results are spectacular. It's as President Gordon B. Hinckley said about us in his recent address to the National Press Club: "People wonder what we do for our women. I'll tell you what we do. We get out of their way, and look with wonder at what they are accomplishing."[15] What a commendation!

Imagine what would happen if we turned our attention in force to the kinds of service that build the kingdom—such things as rearing righteous sons and daughters who themselves go forward in the strength of the Lord, or increasing our own spirituality so that we can strengthen others, or igniting missionary work by reaching out to investigators and inviting friends into our homes to talk with the missionaries, or befriending a newly baptized sister and helping ease her transition into the Church, or taking an interest in a child who needs extra attention, or helping a friend come back after years of being away, or making friends with a young woman who is beguiled by the world, or giving someone a copy of the Book of Mormon, or learning how to talk comfortably about the Church to our non-LDS neighbors. Imagine what would happen if we could mobilize the sisters of Relief Society to help build the kingdom of God.

We have just completed a historic general conference, the first held in the magnificent new Conference Center. Despite its vast capacity, thousands were still unable to get tickets. I half-expected President Hinckley to step to the podium and say, "This just goes to show that if we build it, they will come." If we rally our sisters to build the kind of sisterhood the Lord intends Relief Society to be, the women of the world will come. If we radiate the light of Jesus Christ because his Spirit shines in our eyes, because we tell the truth and teach our children to tell the truth, because we treat each other with gentleness, because we are modest but beautiful in the way we dress and speak and act, because we are quick to attribute benevolent intent to each other's actions, because we are armed with righteousness and with the power of God in great glory, and because we love Jesus Christ and are trying to follow him—the good women of the world will look to us in increasing numbers and increasing ways. Our influence will be penetrating and persuasive. Make no mistake about it: We have been foreordained to lead the women of the world. To borrow a phrase commonly applied to the British Empire, the sun never sets on the work of Relief Society. Shall we not go on in so great a cause?

Recently I and several other LDS women met with a group of wives of ambassadors to the United States. As we talked about the vital role of mothers and the family and the innate spirituality of women, several expressed curiosity about Relief Society. And when we exchanged good-byes, more than one ambassador's wife drew me aside and said, "There is such a wonderful feeling among your people. Could I find out more about your organization?"

If we build it, they will come. The time has come for us to arise as never before and to let our light be a standard for the nations. We are up to the challenge, for there is nothing more beautiful than a woman under the influence of the Holy Ghost. There is nothing more compelling than a woman who with gentle strength stands for righteousness, whether within the walls of her own home or before an international gathering of women.

The Lord needs every one of us. He needs those leading our children and our young women. He needs every eighteen- and eighty-eight-year-old, everyone who's been to college and everyone who hasn't, all who have borne children and all who delight in children, lifelong members and those baptized yesterday, those skilled at administering and those with a talent for ministering one-on-one, those who speak Vietnamese and those who speak Portuguese. He needs sisters who can testify of the doctrines of the kingdom, sisters who can receive personal inspiration and teach with the Spirit, sisters who show by their actions that their hearts are centered on him.

He needs every one of us to fulfill our foreordained mission. Shall we not, as women of God, go forward in so great a cause? Shall we not proclaim from the rooftops that the gospel is a gospel of gladness and that we are thrilled to be who we are?

I have reflected many times on the mistake I made in high school when I stumbled under the weight of popular opinion. But I won't do it again. I pledge to spend my life bearing witness of what I know to be true. Will you join with me? Let us stand together with our hearts devoted to the Lord and knit together in love one for another. If we will, the Relief Society will become a phenomenal force for good, a magnet and a beacon for those seeking truth, a haven for protecting the family and the nobility of womanhood. If we build a sisterhood filled with light, the women of the world will come. And we will become one of the greatest missionary forces this Church has ever seen. I repeat: The cause of women of God is to help build the kingdom of God. This is something we cannot be casual about. It is our stewardship, our privilege, our destiny.

Jesus Christ did not come in glory when he first came to earth, but when he comes again he will reign as Lord of lords and King of kings. The restored gospel will cover the earth. The Lord's kingdom will not fail, which means that for you and me there is just this question: Will we go forward in so great a cause? Today I declare with the apostle Paul what I wish I had said thirty years ago in high school: "I am not ashamed of the gospel of Christ" (Romans 1:16). He is our Advocate, our Deliverer, and our Redeemer. Of his divinity I bear witness, and to his work I pledge my life.

Notes

1. Eliza R. Snow, *The Evening News*, 15 January 1870.
2. Joseph F. Smith, Conference Report, October 1907, 4; punctuation standardized.
3. Brigham Young, *Deseret News Weekly*, 5 January 1854, 2.
4. Joseph Smith, *History of The Church of Jesus Christ of Latter-day Saints*, ed. B. H. Roberts, 2d ed. rev., 7 vols. (Salt Lake City: The Church of Jesus Christ of Latter-day Saints, 1932–51), 5:24.
5. Joseph Smith, "A Record of the Organization, and Proceedings of the Female Relief Society of Nauvoo, 28 April 1842, Archives of The Church of Jesus Christ of Latter-day Saints, Salt Lake City; hereafter cited as Nauvoo Minutes; see also Smith, *History of the Church*, 4:605.
6. Emma Smith, Nauvoo Minutes, 24 March 1842; see also Jill Mulvay Derr, Janath Russell Cannon, and Maureen Ursenbach Beecher, *Women of Covenant* (Salt Lake City: Deseret Book, 1992), 36.
7. Joseph Smith, Nauvoo Minutes, 9 June 1842; see also Smith, *History of the Church*, 5:25.
8. Gordon B. Hinckley, Liverpool England Fireside, 31 August 1995. Quoted in Mike Cannon, "Missionary Theme Was Pervasive during Visit of President Hinckley," *Deseret News*, 9 September 1995.
9. Lucy Mack Smith, Nauvoo Minutes, 24 March 1842; see also *Teachings of Gordon B. Hinckley* (Salt Lake City: Deseret Book, 1997), 545.
10. Joseph Smith, *Relief Society Magazine*, March 1919, 129; see also *Woman's Exponent* 12 (1 September 1883): 51.
11. Joseph Smith, Nauvoo Minutes, 9 June 1842. See also Smith, *History of the Church*, 5:25.
12. *Joseph F. Smith*, Teachings of Presidents of the Church series (Salt Lake City: The Church of Jesus Christ of Latter-day Saints, 1998), 184.
13. Joseph F. Smith, Minutes of the General Board of the Relief Society, 17 March 1914, 55–56, Archives of The Church of Jesus Christ of Latter-day Saints, Salt Lake City. See also *Joseph F. Smith*, 184.

14. Spencer W. Kimball, "Relief Society: Its Promise and Potential," *Ensign*, March 1976, 4.
15. Gordon B. Hinckley, quoted in "Church Leader Addresses Growth, Efforts to Improve People's Lives," *Church News*, 18 March 2000.

PRESSING FORWARD

꒰ ꒱

Ardeth G. Kapp

As a child in Primary, I remember standing and singing with my whole heart and soul, "Jesus wants me for a sunbeam, To shine for him each day."[1] I remember thinking that he really needed me. And I remember how I felt deep inside, singing, "I'll be a sunbeam for him," and then thinking, *I can if I but try.* He still needs us to shine for him each day, every day. We can if we but try. And we will try.

This is our time to "arise and shine forth, that [our] light may be a standard for the nations" (D&C 115:5). The heavens are very much open to women today. They are not closed unless we ourselves, by our choice, close them.

In a time past when the adversary sought to destroy the purposes of God and lead people astray, Captain Moroni raised the standard of liberty and fearlessly declared his position (Alma 46:12). With the same unrelenting courage can we in this day thwart the forces of evil now marshaled against the purposes of God? Can we press forward with steadfastness in Christ, having a perfect brightness of hope and a love of God and all men? The words of Nephi are very clear, "Ye [meaning you and me] must press forward" (2 Nephi 31:20). *Press forward* means to keep moving in the right direction with determination and boldness. In my mind I hear my mother's voice sending me off, "Ardeth, come straight home; do not dilly-dally by the wayside." This admonition had greater meaning years later when I read the words of President George Q.

Ardeth Greene Kapp, former general president of the Young Women organization, received a bachelor's degree from the University of Utah and a master's degree in education from Brigham Young University. A member of the BYU College of Education faculty, she has served on Church curriculum planning and correlation committees and is the author of twelve books. She is married to Heber B. Kapp.

Cannon, "You may dally by the wayside; you may fool away your time; you may be idle, indifferent and careless; but you only lose thereby the progress that you ought to make."[2]

Can we be a light to the nations in a darkening world? Shall we raise a standard by pressing forward with steadfastness in Christ? I testify to you that: we can—God has made it possible; we will—life has meaning, purpose, and direction; we must—we are women of covenant.

WE CAN PRESS FORWARD

First, we can press forward. Our Savior marked the path and led the way. Through the waters of baptism, we have entered the gate, and having received the Holy Ghost, we are on the path (2 Nephi 31:5). Our Father in Heaven wants us to be happy, supremely happy. He is our Father. The great plan of happiness of which Alma speaks is God's plan for us (Alma 42).

A faithful Bolivian woman, who drives her llama herd onto the Altiplano to forage for food each day, was visited one evening in her small home by two young missionaries, who taught her about the great plan of happiness, about the mission of the Savior, the doctrine of the Atonement, the resurrection, and the promise of eternal life. Her dark eyes widened, overflowing with tears, her heart flooded with hope, she whispered to the two young men, "You mean he did that for me?" To her earnest question, the Spirit bore immediate witness, and she again whispered, this time not in question but in reverent awe, "He did that for me." With that testimony burning in her soul, and in ours, as women of God we can press forward with steadfastness in Christ. We can press forward—all the way, every day. He made it possible.

When we determine to take a stand and commit to go the whole way, our whole lives, our Father in Heaven will be with us the whole way, our whole lives. Author C. S. Lewis suggests one analogy: When you go to the dentist to get rid of a toothache, that's all you really want—to be rid of the ache. But the dentist won't stop there. He grinds and grinds until all the decay is removed. Then Lewis adds, "This

Helper who will, in the long run, be satisfied with nothing less than absolute perfection, will also be delighted with the first feeble, stumbling effort you make tomorrow to do the simplest duty."[3]

The straight and narrow path and the rod of iron are not what cause the ache for most of us—we want to be good. It's the rough terrain, with its ups and downs, its trials and tests, that hurts. The pain and heartache, our fears and failures try our faith. At times we may think our Father in Heaven has forgotten us. Looking back we will realize he was with us all along.

> At the throne I intercede;
> For thee ever do I plead.
> I have loved thee as thy friend,
> With a love that cannot end.
> Be obedient, I implore,
> Prayerful, watchful, evermore,
> And be constant unto me,
> That thy Savior I may be.[4]

Shall we not press forward all the way?

WE WILL PRESS FORWARD

We can and we will. Our Relief Society Declaration reconfirms, "We are beloved spirit daughters of God, and our lives have meaning, purpose, and direction."[5] Once we understand our life's purpose, we begin to plan with a purpose what we are to do and also what we want as a result. That vision of our purpose fills us with life and light. The vision of our eternal possibilities lifts the burden, transforming the weariness of everyday doing to an exhilaration of accomplishing. And our greatest, most valuable accomplishments may well be invisible to the world. As Paul wrote to the Corinthians: "All things are for your sakes. . . . For our light affliction, which is but for a moment, worketh for us a far more exceeding and eternal weight of glory; . . . we look not at the things which are seen, but at the things which are not seen: for the things which are seen are temporal; but the things which are not seen are eternal" (2 Corinthians 4:15, 17–18).

In *The Little Prince*, the fox bids the Prince good-bye, saying: "And now here is my secret, a very simple secret: It is only with the heart that one can see rightly; what is essential is invisible to the eye."[6] When we press forward with steadfastness in Christ with a perfect brightness of hope, our lives have meaning. We begin not only to look but also to see, not only to talk but also to communicate. Our otherwise routine activities can become an offering on the altar of God. We don't just serve; we nurture. We don't just take our neighbor a loaf of bread; we share the bread of life. We're not just teaching a class; we're changing a life. Our gospel study goes beyond knowing about him to knowing him and striving to be filled, as he was, with the love of God. Our lives have meaning and purpose.

With a firm grip on the iron rod but without the vision of the tree of life, we sometimes focus on the blisters on our hands and forget his hands scarred with nail prints. Our vision of what we are working for, what we are living for, and what we want to happen in our lives elevates us to a higher level of living because it gives meaning to everything we are doing.

When we begin to understand, even in part, the magnitude of the promises of eternal life, then all the doings—the assignments, the calls, the programs, the activities, the dos and the don'ts, the peanut butter and jam smeared on the kitchen table, and yes, even the never-ending laundry—take on a whole new meaning. A burden ceases to be a burden once we see the purpose for it.

Our prayers being more purposeful, they become more answerable. Recently, my niece asked her little four-year-old son, Jake, to give the family prayer, to which he responded in his pure and childlike way, "Mom, I only do food prayers." What is sweet at age four would be truly sad at age forty. And we may still be doing just food prayers at forty unless we have a real purpose for our communication with God. Our Father in Heaven encourages our communication. He says over and over in the scriptures, Ask—ask in faith.

Some years ago when I was called to serve as the Young Women general president, I was searching for direction, for revelation, for comfort. More than I ever had before, I yearned to pray more effectively and listen more intensely. I sought to know how to pray with greater faith, desiring to hear the voice of the Lord in my mind and heart through the Holy Ghost. The guidance I sought came for me while "feasting on the word." I read Alma's counsel to his son Helaman about prayer. I noticed that Alma attends first to actions, then thoughts, then feelings: "Cry unto God for all thy support; yea, *let all thy doings* be unto the Lord, and whithersoever thou goest let it be in the Lord; yea, *let all thy thoughts* be directed unto the Lord; yea, *let the affections of thy heart* be placed upon the Lord forever." And then comes the promise: "Counsel with the Lord in all thy doings, and he will direct thee for good; yea, when thou liest down at night lie down unto the Lord, that he may watch over you in your sleep; and when thou risest in the morning let thy heart be full of thanks unto God; and if ye do these things, ye shall be lifted up at the last day" (Alma 37:36–37; emphasis added). This reminder of the availability of our Father in Heaven was the reassurance I needed.

When we pray with purpose, we have power in prayer. President Gordon B. Hinckley tells us, "Members can fight evil with prayer." Here are his words: "Believe in getting on your knees every morning and every night and talking to your Father in Heaven concerning the feelings of your hearts and the desires of your minds in righteousness. Believe in prayer. There is nothing like it. When all is said and done there is no power on the earth like the power of prayer."[7]

In answer to our prayers, our Father in Heaven will open doors for us, soften hearts, and heal wounds, spiritual and physical. Put simply, he will just make things better all around, because he wants us to be good and he wants us to be happy. And on occasion, he will direct us to be there in answer to someone else's prayer. Often I reflect on a tender message from a sister I met briefly at women's conference. She wrote in a card: "I was touched that you cared to ask who I am and spend your valuable time to look at me. I have found it so rare that anyone cares, but a stranger has given me hope." To look at her!

When we press forward in our sometimes stumbling ways, striving to share the love of God, I believe there are no little things. Through a note, a tap on the shoulder, a smile, yes, even in a look, God allows us to minister to one another.

Corrie ten Boom in *The Hiding Place* describes the horrible concentration camp at Ravensbruck. The hot miserable room where she and her sister Betsie were confined was infested with fleas. Corrie came to see it as a blessing because it kept the guards away and allowed her to share her scriptures with other inmates.[8] Hear her words: "Side by side, in the sanctuary of God's fleas, Betsie and I ministered the word of God to all in the room. We sat by deathbeds that became doorways to heaven. We watched women who had lost everything grow rich in hope. . . . We prayed beyond the concrete walls for the healing of Germany, of Europe, of the world—as Mama had once done from the prison of a crippled body."[9]

In our lives there will be opposition, trials, and tests of every kind, perhaps not as dramatic as those of Corrie and her sister Betsie, but in God's eyes equally significant, and from his perspective even heroic.

The last Mother's Day before my mom passed away, as I was pushing her in her wheelchair into the chapel, she whispered half to herself but loud enough for me to hear, "I never liked Mother's Day. It always reminds me of all the things I didn't do as a mother." Wanting to ease her mind, I leaned over and whispered, "Mom, I don't think you did so badly." She smiled.

When a hailstorm killed Dad's flocks of turkeys and more than once an early frost destroyed our crops of grain, Mom assured us children that all would be well. She still believed we could have a rich harvest. Dad moved an old granary next to our house, and Mom opened a small grocery store, where she worked her heart out while Dad worked in the fields. They didn't count the number of bushels to the acre, sure evidence of crop failure. They measured their harvest in other ways. Mom didn't teach my two sisters and me to sew and cook and other such things mothers often did, but by her side, in our little country store in Canada, she taught us that our customers from the Blood Indian Reservation, and the Hutterites from the nearby colonies, and the immigrants from across the river were not only our customers but also our friends who deserved our deepest respect and generosity. We needed them, and they needed us. "That's what makes good friends," Mom taught us.

I watched her many times tuck into a bag of groceries a sack of cookies from our meager resources that I noticed she never itemized on the customer's bill. I watched as a child would thoughtfully choose candy from the penny candy counter, have it in the sack and the top twisted, and then at the last minute have a change of mind. Mom never said, "Too late now, dear." It was never too late to help a child feel good. She was never too busy to be concerned for another human being. Would she not qualify as one pressing forward with steadfastness in Christ, having a perfect brightness of hope and a love of God and of all men? There is more than one way to model righteous mothering.

Hailstorms and crop failures will occur in our lives and in our families. Things don't always turn out the way we plan, but don't ever let what you haven't done eclipse all the good you have done and are doing. A hailstorm may destroy the crops, but with faith in God, I solemnly testify it need not prevent a rich harvest.

WE MUST PRESS FORWARD

Finally, in the words of Nephi, "Ye must press forward . . . in Christ" (2 Nephi 31:20). We are women of covenant, we have taken upon us his name, to always remember him and keep his commandments, that we may always have his Spirit to be with us.

Our testimonies, our commitments, and our covenants may lie deep inside, but until we take a stand and rid our lives of all of the distractions that obscure this treasure, we are not free to press forward in Christ. As long as we remain undecided, uncommitted, and uncovenanted, we remain unanchored, and every wind that blows becomes life threatening. Uncertainty will breed vacillation and confusion. Taking a stand and making a choice secures for us the gift of the Holy Ghost. That gift releases us from crippling doubt, indecision, and confusion. Once we take a stand, we then have access to power and blessings, so much so, that we will hardly be able to keep pace with our opportunities. Elder Bruce R. McConkie declared, "There is no price too high, no labor too onerous, no struggle too severe, no sacrifice too great, if out of it all we receive and enjoy the gift of the Holy Ghost."[10]

President Gordon B. Hinckley's words on the eve of the twenty-first century come as a call and a prayer: "May God bless us with a sense of our place in history and having been given that sense, with our need to stand tall and walk with resolution in a manner becoming the Saints of the Most High."[11]

The Lord, speaking through Joseph Smith, asserts, "There has been a day of calling, but the time has come for a day of choosing" (D&C 105:35). Eliza R. Snow, in her hymn "The Time Is Far Spent," echoes those same sentiments:

> *Be fixed in your purpose, for Satan will try you;*
> *The weight of your calling he perfectly knows.*
> *Your path may be thorny, but Jesus is nigh you;*
> *His arm is sufficient, tho demons oppose.*
> *His arm is sufficient, tho demons oppose.*[12]

Let us prepare ourselves that it might be said of us as Joseph F. Smith said of Eliza R. Snow, "She walked not in the borrowed light of others but faced the morning unafraid and invincible."[13] May God bless us not with borrowed light but with his light, and we shall press forward with vision, with renewed determination, with confidence and commitment.

> *True to the faith that our parents have cherished,*
> *True to the truth for which martyrs have perished,*
> *To God's command,*
> *Soul, heart, and hand,*
> *Faithful and true we will ever stand.*[14]

We can.

We will.

We must.

I know God lives. I testify of his promise in the words of Nephi, "Wherefore, if ye shall press forward, feasting upon the word of Christ, and endure to the end, behold thus saith the Father: Ye shall have eternal life" (2 Nephi 31:20).

Notes

1. "Jesus Wants Me for a Sunbeam," *Children's Songbook* (Salt Lake City: The Church of Jesus Christ of Latter-day Saints, 1989), 60.
2. George Q. Cannon, *Gospel Truth: Discourses and Writings of George Q. Cannon*, ed. Jerreld L. Newquist (Salt Lake City: Deseret Book, 1987), 19.
3. C. S. Lewis, *Mere Christianity* (New York: Macmillan, 1952), 171–72.
4. "Reverently and Meekly Now," *Hymns of The Church of Jesus Christ of Latter-day Saints* (Salt Lake City: The Church of Jesus Christ of Latter-day Saints, 1985), no. 185.
5. Relief Society Declaration, *Ensign*, November 1999, 92.
6. Antoine de Saint Exupéry, *The Little Prince*, trans. Katherine Woods (New York: Harcourt, Brace & World, 1943), 87.
7. Gordon B. Hinckley, "President Hinckley Addresses 15,000 in Laie," *LDS Church News*, 29 January 2000.
8. Corrie ten Boom, *The Hiding Place* (New York: Bantam Books, 1971), 198–99.
9. Ibid., 211.
10. Bruce R. McConkie, *A New Witness for the Articles of Faith* (Salt Lake City: Deseret Book, 1985), 253.
11. Gordon B. Hinckley, "At the Summit of the Ages," *Ensign*, November 1999, 74.
12. "The Time Is Far Spent," *Hymns*, no. 266.
13. Joseph F. Smith, as quoted in Susa Young Gates Papers, Miscellaneous History File, Archives of The Church of Jesus Christ of Latter-day Saints, Salt Lake City, Utah, 21; see also Carol Lynn Pearson, *Daughters of Light* (Provo, Utah: Trilogy Arts, 1973), 10.
14. "True to the Faith," *Hymns*, no. 254.

KEEPING THE SPIRIT AT THE CORE OF OUR SCRIPTURE STUDY

ᨒ

Coleen K. Menlove

When the Spirit is at the core of our scripture study, lives are changed. Think about that delicious and desirable fruit, the apple. If you were offered an apple, would you want a whole one or one that had been sliced and cored? You might select the cut apple because it is easier to eat, but is that the apple you would select to take on your way for an afternoon snack? In that case, you would probably choose the whole apple because it would keep longer and wouldn't become discolored or dehydrated. Which apple would you take if you were Johnny Appleseed and wanted to plant orchards of apples along your way? Probably the whole apple with its seeds safely stored within the core. The whole apple has greater potential for the future.

Compare these apples to scripture study in our homes. If we are not careful, we might offer our children just parts and pieces of knowledge that are easily taken but also easily forgotten. We might offer only isolated facts, stories, and ideas with little or no long-term impact. But when we strive to offer the whole fruit with its parts firmly attached to the core—the Spirit—then knowledge sinks deeper into our children's lives.

In family scripture studies, the Holy Ghost is the true teacher. It is

Coleen K. Menlove has served as Primary General President since October 1999. She received a bachelor's degree from the University of Utah and a master's degree from Brigham Young University. She has served on Church writing committees and the Young Women General Board. She and her husband, Dean W. Menlove, are the parents of seven children and grandparents of eight.

the Spirit that bears witness of the words, as promised in 2 Nephi 33:1, "The power of the Holy Ghost carrieth [the message] unto the hearts of the children of men." When the Spirit is at the center or core of our scripture study, lives are changed.

Let me share three suggestions that my husband and I received when we needed good counsel.

At that time, five of our seven children were between the ages of twelve and nineteen. With friends, a steady stream of cars coming and going, loud music, late-night and early-morning events, and a generally frantic level of activity, it would have been very difficult to determine who was the responsible party in our home.

In the midst of all the commotion, one of our sons was approaching missionary age, and he was not ready. Our family scripture study had been less than effective, and we knew he read his scriptures *only* to pass the letter of the law for seminary graduation. In fact, he had stopped doing many of the good things he had been doing. His behavior caused great anxiety for us and for his brothers and sisters. We were at a loss to know how to help him.

His seminary teacher gave us some advice. Opening his scriptures to Mosiah, he reminded us about Alma, who had great concerns for his son, Alma the Younger. He then counseled us to do three things to invite the Spirit to help.

First, he counseled us to do everything possible to invite and keep the Spirit in our home so this son and our other children would feel its presence. We wondered how a four-year seminary graduate, an Eagle Scout, and a son of ours could not know the workings of the Spirit. Perhaps we had been so "busy" rearing our children that we had crowded out some of the teachings and experiences we wanted most for them. Perhaps we hadn't left room for the Spirit to enter our home.

To create a spiritual atmosphere—to rid our homes of things that offend the Spirit—takes work. Such spiritual housecleaning requires us to empty out things. This emptying out is repentance. Repentance requires humility; humility then encourages the presence of the Spirit. Expressions of love and appreciation also invite the Spirit. When we express kindness and appreciation, children respond with kindness, and all family members become more sensitive to the Spirit. From Church meetings and temple experiences, we can bring the Spirit home with us. We can share what we have felt with our children. Uplifting, spiritual music, both sung and played, also invites the Spirit in wonderful ways.

Second, it was suggested that we, like Alma of old, fast and pray specifically for those things we felt our son needed. We prayed that he would begin reading the scriptures again, that he would read with real intent, and that through the power of the Holy Ghost he would find answers and direction in the scriptures.

Third, we were counseled to ask our son about his feelings and help him note how he felt obeying the promptings of the Holy Spirit and to compare that feeling with the dark feelings that arise from the temptations of Satan. Our children need to be able to clearly identify the difference.

We can ask our children what the Spirit feels like. Many children say it feels warm inside. One ten-year-old said, "It is a beautiful feeling. It feels like everything is right." Andrew, age eight, said, "When I can't feel the Spirit, I feel empty and sad inside."

When we ask, we need to listen as children share their thoughts and feelings. Parents must be in tune with the Spirit to know how best to respond. Remember that spiritual experiences are sacred, so they should not be shared casually, but "with care, and by constraint of the Spirit" (D&C 63:64).

We may wish to try new methods that will add variety and meet individual needs; however, in all we do, we need to remember that meaning will come only when the methods we use invite the Spirit to teach the minds and hearts of our children.

The ideas we received from the seminary teacher were good for all of us. As we work to create an atmosphere in our home where the Spirit can dwell, as we pray specifically for the Spirit to teach our children, as we identify and share feelings of the Spirit, the core of our family and individual scripture study will be the Spirit. That is what we want to have happen for our children—and for ourselves.

PREPARING THE SOIL

❧

Gayle M. Clegg

Not many years ago, our daughter Cheryl and her husband purchased their first home. They moved in June, when neighbors' homes were surrounded by summer blooms. Once she was settled into her new home, Cheryl went to work landscaping her yard, planting flowers, and pulling out weeds that had taken over the backyard. Some time later I asked her if she had had any success with her garden. A few herbs were doing beautifully, she replied, and she was looking forward to enjoying the flavor they would add to her recipes, but the flowerbeds were disastrous. She had more flowers in her grass than in her flower garden.

Working in the soil and looking forward to the fruits of a well-tended garden are much like diligently reading the scriptures and looking forward to the fruits of regular scripture study with our families. We have been promised blessings of increased testimony, peace, and less contention in our homes if we do so.

PREPARE THE SOIL FOR GOSPEL LEARNING

If we delight in the scriptures, ponder what we read, and record our feelings in the margins or in a journal, our children will know that we, like Nephi, delight "in the things of the Lord" (2 Nephi 4:16). This way we begin preparing the soil, so our children will want to explore, dig, and plant their own seeds of gospel learning.

Gayle M. Clegg, second counselor in the Primary General Presidency, graduated with a bachelor's degree in history from the University of Utah. She has taught classes in Utah, Brazil, and Argentina to students of all ages. She served with her husband, Calvin C. Clegg, when he was called as president of the Portugal Lisbon North Mission. They are the parents of five children and grandparents of nine.

A garden always needs attention, and often it takes time to see the results of our efforts. Sometimes we may be focusing so closely on the weeds that we don't really see the plants we are cultivating. One mother tried many times to begin a scripture study program but had little success: "It seemed that with trying to raise a family and fulfill my Church responsibilities, I never completely reached the goal. I would designate a certain time and place to study each day, only to have the schedule interrupted by the needs of children who were ill or with other immediate crises typical of a growing family. During that time of my life, I never really thought of myself as someone who was good at scripture study.

"Then one day, my mother visited my home. She looked at a large table covered with Church materials—among them my scriptures—and said, 'I love the way you are always reading your scriptures. They always seem to be open on one table or another.'

"Suddenly I had a new vision of myself. She was right. I was consistently into my scriptures, even though I had no formal study program. I loved the scriptures. They fed me. Scripture verses tacked to my kitchen walls lifted me as I worked, many of them scriptures I was helping my children memorize for talks they would give. I lived in a world of scripture reading, and I realized that I was being nourished abundantly."[1]

The second way to prepare the soil for gospel learning is to fill our homes with a spirit of love. Fortunately, my husband and I learned early that coercion never works in the long run. Sometimes when I have wondered, *Am I doing enough?* I remember Moroni 7:48 and realize that a sincere prayer asking the Lord to fill my heart with more love for my children is the answer: "Pray unto the Father with all the energy of heart, that ye may be filled with this love." When family members know they are loved unconditionally, they come more willingly to the gospel study hour.

When I asked our children how they gained a love for the scriptures, our daughter Tina said: "I remember sitting on the couch during those early mornings when our family lived in Argentina, watching

Dan lie on the floor pretending to be awake during our scripture study. I was frustrated by what I felt was your lack of action to my complaints about him. Now, as a parent, I recognize your valiant attempts to keep a spirit of love present during our scripture sessions. Of all of us, probably Dan developed the greatest love for the Book of Mormon that year; he went on to read it again on his own before he finished eighth grade."

START SMALL

Prepare a small plot first. Your plan should not be overwhelming, but it should help you be consistent in your gospel study. In other words, don't tackle the entire yard! One verse under the water glass at dinnertime may be enough to begin with. Sometimes just the goal of reading the Book of Mormon every day is enough, instead of setting an intimidating deadline such as finishing it by Christmas. Once the roots of opposition from one or two family members have been loved away, a specific time frame may become appropriate.

Try this great tip from the resource guide for gospel teaching: "Record your plan in a journal or notebook so you will not forget it."[2] You might include a step-by-step approach. If your plan is ambitious, perhaps step one is all you can stand to look at for a season.

DIFFERENT NEEDS REQUIRE DIFFERENT APPROACHES

Pray for insight into the needs and abilities of your children so each can participate. One day our son's second-grade teacher called me during the lunch hour to describe her disturbing day with our oldest child, Dan. I wanted to enlighten her about our precious son's endearing qualities, but I refrained. Later, when Dan came through the front door, I greeted him as usual: "How was your day?" Sensing my intense concern, he said, "Not so good." I asked why, and he responded, "Mommy, my body is in my desk, but my spirit is at recess."

We need to prepare the soil so that our active and busy children will come to our family gospel study time not only with their bodies but with their spirits too. All children hunger for light and truth, but their needs are different. We need to pray for insights about how each will best learn.

Some families keep to a scheduled time regardless of infertile soil. Others try a new brand of seeds. These might include going through the Book of Mormon chapter by chapter or by topics, reading a few verses and then relating the stories in their own words, using illustrated scripture readers, reading the same scripture assignment privately and then meeting to discuss it at another time. Even posting a scripture on the refrigerator and discussing it at breakfast constitutes family scripture study. I have put scriptures in the children's lunches, and then at dinner we have talked about them. Occasionally I have included a question about the scripture for them to ponder during their day.

Some of our children said studying the scriptures with music brought in the Spirit immediately. You might read and discuss the scriptural references to the music from the hymnbook or the *Children's Songbook*. One of our grandchildren, who prays no louder than a whisper and declines to volunteer an answer during a Sunbeam lesson, will sit alone at the piano playing and singing "I Am a Child of God" over and over again. (The accompaniment is original!)

Our daughter Cheryl managed to grow useful herbs despite repeated failures to plant flowers that would bloom. Why? Because Cheryl is a fabulous cook, and she loves creating new, delicious, healthy recipes. In other words, plants that filled a need flourished in her garden. What you are studying needs to move into your children's daily lives. As our children learn gospel principles, they need to learn how to live them. Daily scripture study does bring blessings, but the soil for gospel learning has to be prepared. "For my soul delighteth in the scriptures, and my heart pondereth them, and writeth them for the learning and the profit of my children" (2 Nephi 4:15).

Notes

1. *Teaching, No Greater Call: A Resource Guide for Gospel Teaching* (Salt Lake City: The Church of Jesus Christ of Latter-day Saints, 1999), 16.
2. Ibid., 16.

WHEN THE SCRIPTURES COME ALIVE

🔥

Sydney S. Reynolds

David and Goliath, Daniel and the lions' den, Nephi's quest to obtain the Brass Plates, Jesus' birth in Bethlehem—when stories like these are our introduction, how can we resist developing a love for the scriptures? The scriptures come alive when we realize that they are an account of the Lord's dealings with real people who lived in an actual time and place and whose messages have value for us today.

TAKING THE PEOPLE SERIOUSLY

When I was twelve years old, my bishop called me up out of the congregation to bear my testimony during ward conference. That's what they used to do in the old days. I remember saying something like, "I like the stories from the Book of Mormon, and someday I hope to read the whole book." The very next day I came down with German measles, and while I was out of school that week, I read the Book of Mormon. Reading it at one sitting like that made the people in the book come alive for me. The stories of the individuals sank into my heart and memory. I couldn't believe there was a man in the scriptures like Teancum—what a stout heart, what an adventurer! I loved the stories of Captain Moroni building fortifications around the cities he

Sydney Smith Reynolds, first counselor in the Primary General Presidency, received her bachelor's degree from Brigham Young University and did graduate studies in history and educational psychology. She is a member of the Timpanogos Storytelling Festival Board, and she wrote the Sharing Time page for the 1998 and 1999 issues of the Friend. She and her husband, Noel B. Reynolds, are the parents of eleven children and the grandparents of six.

would defend. I tried to lay out in my mind what it all must have looked like. Because my dad was a hunter in those days and an avid scripture reader, I identified with Enos going out on a hunt and having something touch his soul so powerfully that he prayed the whole day and night through. That was the beginning of my testimony of the Book of Mormon *and* of the Prophet Joseph Smith. The two are obviously intimately connected.

Two years ago, our stake president challenged us to read the Book of Mormon and write him a letter when we were finished. Again I read straight through, and once again the individuals stood out for me. I was moved to tears when I read the verses in which Moroni's voice begins. It is so different (in a literary sense) from Mormon's voice. Moroni is so alone, so very alone, and he had known only warfare all his days. The people in the Book of Mormon are real, and what they say to us— inscribing so laboriously at times (Jacob 4:1)—is true and valuable. We need to take those people, those prophets, seriously. They are real, and they are different, in the same way Elder Jeffrey R. Holland is different from Elder Dallin H. Oaks, who is different from Elder Henry B. Eyring. But they are just as real, and their inspired messages are aimed at us. They knew they were not writing solely for their own time.

TAKING THE PLACE SERIOUSLY

In the long run, to be sure, it doesn't matter where the land Bountiful is as long as we know that it really did exist. Yet knowing a probable location can enhance understanding and appreciation. Living in Jerusalem for a year, for instance, was an incredible experience for our family. To see the Valley of Elah, the Brook Kidron, the Temple Mount, the Sea of Galilee, and the Garden Tomb opened our eyes and touched our hearts.

Seeing can move the reality of what we are reading at least one step closer, but it isn't essential. One of the first Sabbaths we were there, a young man who had spent much of his youth in Israel bore his testimony and explained that he received his testimony of the Savior on his mission in Texas. Knowledge comes to those who invite the

Spirit to be with them as they read about those places and picture them in their mind. Then they *know* Jesus really did live, he really was resurrected from the dead, he lives today.

TAKING THE TEXT SERIOUSLY—AND WITH HUMILITY

When I was a college freshman, I had a religion teacher who asked us to memorize certain scriptures. That was in the 1960s before scripture mastery was a part of the seminary program. Some class members challenged him, "Can't we just tell you what the scripture says and what it means in general?" "No," he answered. "I want you to memorize each scripture word for word. Then its meaning will grow as your understanding grows"—in other words, we would not be stuck forever with our freshman interpretation of the meaning "in general."

I believe in taking the texts seriously, and at least two very different things happen as we do that. First, we benefit from the work of gospel scholars who enhance our understanding of the scriptures by pointing out the importance of language, structure, context, and so forth. Second, taking the scriptures seriously and searching them invites the Holy Ghost to be with us. We feel Nephi's courage and in turn are able to "go and do the things which the Lord hath commanded" (1 Nephi 3:7). We are comforted when the Lord says, "Be still and know that I am God" (D&C 101:16). We identify with Paul and Abinadi and renew our resolve to endure to the end. In other words, we liken the scriptures to ourselves (1 Nephi 19:23). And sometimes, as we read the scriptures, the Spirit sends messages straight to our own hearts. My friend Rochelle Anderson likes to say, "I go to the scriptures like I go to the mailbox—to see if there is a message for me."

As we ponder the scriptures and listen for the voice of the Spirit, we will understand not only what the Lord has done for generations past but also what he has done for us. I testify that he loves us and that the scriptures, read with faith and sincerity of heart, invite the sure witness of that fact.

WALKING IN THEIR SHOES

🦢

Gaye Strathearn

You've heard the adage that you can't know a person until you've walked a mile in his shoes. Something important happens to our scripture reading if we consciously attempt to walk *spiritually* in the shoes of the people we read about. The power of the scriptures, after all, comes not from reading about these people but from learning the lessons that they learned.

Sister Camilla Kimball was frequently asked, "What is it like to be married to an apostle?" Invariably her reply was, "Well, you know, I was married to him twenty-five years before he was one."[1] All of the prophets in the scriptures, to be sure, were foreordained to their callings, but none of them were born as prophets. All of them had to develop their relationships with deity; and to do so, they had to do the same kinds of things that you and I have to do. As we struggle to see these individuals as real people, we draw closer to them and better appreciate their teachings. Let me illustrate these ideas with a few experiences from a well-known and well-loved scriptural personality: Nephi.

As I ponder on Nephi, Sister Kimball's statement rings particularly strong. Nephi was an extraordinary man who eventually became both the Lord's prophet among the Nephites and their political leader; but Nephi was not always the prophet. As much as First and Second Nephi describe the physical journey of Nephi and his family as they left Jerusalem and traveled to the promised land, I think the more

---

Gaye Strathearn, an instructor in the Department of Ancient Scripture at Brigham Young University, is a doctoral candidate in the New Testament at Claremont Graduate University. She served a mission in Melbourne, Australia.

important journey these passages detail is Nephi's spiritual journey that prepared and enabled him to become the Lord's prophet.

Recall with me the first scripture many of us memorize as children: "I will go and do the things which the Lord hath commanded, for I know that the Lord giveth no commandments unto the children of men, save he shall prepare a way for them that they may accomplish the thing which he commandeth them" (1 Nephi 3:7). Children sing about this superb statement of faith in Primary, and undoubtedly it is one of the most often quoted passages in LDS scripture. Such bold statements help us formulate our image of Nephi. How old was Nephi when he made this declaration? In chapter 2, we learn that he was "exceedingly young" (v. 16) when his family left Jerusalem. Another question that surfaces is how someone who is "exceedingly young" can make such a bold declaration of faith, especially when his older brothers, Laman and Lemuel, could not do so. Certainly we know of other individuals who exhibit spiritual sensitivities at a young age, but Nephi's account offers some pretty explicit clues to how he developed such spiritual sensitivity. In 1 Nephi 2, while the family is camped in the valley of Lemuel, we first learn of Laman and Lemuel's displeasure over leaving Jerusalem (vv. 11–13), a displeasure that will be magnified over time and will be the source of many confrontations with both their father and with Nephi.

I find verse 16 interesting: "And it came to pass that I, Nephi, being exceedingly young, nevertheless being large in stature, and also having great desires to know of the mysteries of God, wherefore, I did cry unto the Lord; and behold he did visit me, and did soften my heart that I did believe the words which had been spoken by my father; wherefore I did not rebel against him like unto my brothers." Notice that Nephi had "great desires to know of the mysteries of God." At least on some level, leaving Jerusalem and all of their wealth and property at a moment's notice must have been something of a mystery to Lehi's family, including Nephi. It certainly was to Laman and Lemuel. Notice, however, that Nephi's reactions to this mystery are very different from Laman's and Lemuel's: while his brothers murmured against their father, Nephi "[cried] unto the Lord." This response is an important theme in Nephi's spiritual development: when faced with a situation that he doesn't understand, Nephi always turns to the Lord. And what does Nephi say happened in response to his prayer? The Lord "did visit me, and did soften my heart that I did believe all the words which had been spoken by my father."

What does this incident tell us of Nephi's feelings about leaving Jerusalem? He too was a little bewildered and had a propensity for rebelling against his father as well. Otherwise, why did the Lord need to soften his heart so that he did not rebel? For me, the critical difference between Nephi and his brothers is not their feelings about leaving home; it is the way they responded to those feelings. Is there a lesson there for me? I think so. Plenty of times in my life I bump up against things that don't make sense to me. In these situations I have two choices: I can complain, or I can turn to the Lord. We might try to make things more complicated than that, but that's really what it boils down to. Nephi also had to struggle with his father's decision to leave Jerusalem, but he chose a different path than his brothers.

Did you notice that Nephi receives this promise—"Inasmuch as ye shall keep my commandments, ye shall prosper" (1 Nephi 2:20)— before he boldly declares that he "will go and do the things which the Lord hath commanded"? I don't think that the sequence here is happenstance. I see a direct relationship between God's promise and Nephi's declaration.

Let us now turn to the confrontation between Nephi and Laban over the brass plates. Many of my students struggle with the legal or social ramifications of Nephi killing Laban; I'm more interested here in Nephi's inner struggle.[2] The whole reason behind Nephi's declaration back in chapter 3 was because the Lord had told Lehi to return to Jerusalem to get the plates. Nephi was assenting to that command in particular. The brothers made two failed attempts to get the plates. After each one, Laman and Lemuel were ready to give up and leave; but Nephi was committed to "go and do," not just "go and try." I have often thought about Nephi's commitment in this situation. It is one thing to make declarations of faith when you are in a position of relative safety, as he was with Lehi. It is another thing to maintain that commitment when you try and fail, try something different and fail again, and then get beaten up as a result of the second failure. When the angel came, he spoke to Laman and Lemuel and commanded *them* to "go up to Jerusalem again, and the Lord will deliver Laban into your hands" (1 Nephi 3:29). We all know, though, that it was Nephi, alone, who obeyed.

As Nephi entered the city, he "was led by the Spirit, not knowing beforehand the things which [he] should do" (1 Nephi 4:6). Is it possible that Nephi was willing to do that because of his experiences in chapters 2 and 3? I think so. He gained confidence in the Lord because he had turned to him in the past and received help. Surely Nephi had every right to expect the Lord to help him again. But this time the Lord's response was not simply a softening of his heart and a quiet assurance that his father was indeed a prophet. This time the Spirit was telling him to kill a man! Notice that there is no immediate declaration that he will "go and do the things which the Lord hath commanded." This time Nephi hesitates. "Never at any time have I shed the blood of man." He "shr[a]nk and would that [he] might not slay him" (1 Nephi 4:10). Can I be so bold as to suggest that I'm glad Nephi hesitated? How many people have been murdered throughout history and the culprits have claimed, "God told me to do it"?

Nephi knew how important it was to get the plates from Laban; he knew that the Lord had commanded his father to do so; he knew that an angel had reiterated the commandment. Nephi didn't have any doubt that the Lord would "prepare a way [that he might] accomplish the thing which [God] command[ed him]." But when the way was finally prepared for him, Nephi took a minute to weigh the consequences of what he was being asked to do. He needed to make sure that he was interpreting the still small voice accurately. For Nephi to carry out this commandment, he had to have a personal witness that what he was doing was indeed the will of God. Relying on his father's prophetic mantle in this instance would not be sufficient for what

Nephi would have to do. And so he listened more intently to the Spirit until he was satisfied that this was indeed the will of the Lord. Then, and only then, he obeyed.

There is an important lesson here for us. In our spiritual development, we all rely at times on the testimonies and spiritual insights of others. The Prophet Joseph learned through revelation that with the gifts of the Spirit "to some it is given . . . to know that Jesus Christ is the Son of God, and that he was crucified for the sins of the world" and "to others it is given to believe on their words" (D&C 46:13–14). To believe on the words of others is an important stepping-stone in our spiritual development, but it can never be the final destination. President Heber C. Kimball is reported to have said: "The time will come when no man nor woman will be able to endure on borrowed light. Each will have to be guided by the light within himself. If you do not have it, how can you stand?"[3] Ultimately, we need our own personal testimony of the divinity of Jesus Christ, the prophetic call of the Prophet Joseph, the inspired nature of the Book of Mormon, and our own witness that Gordon B. Hinckley is the Lord's anointed on the earth today. Ultimately, the testimonies of our parents, spouses, children, friends, or priesthood leaders will not bring us salvation until we make those testimonies our own.[4] If he hadn't realized that before, Nephi certainly came to that conclusion with Laban.

The impact of this lesson for Nephi becomes even more clear just a few chapters later. When the brothers returned to their parents with the plates, Lehi was ecstatic and immediately began poring over them (1 Nephi 5:9–16). Perhaps this searching of the plates acted as a catalyst for Lehi's great vision of the tree of life. But when Nephi heard his father's account of the vision and his subsequent teachings, he was not satisfied to sit back and rely on his father's testimony. Rather, he writes that he was "desirous also that [he] might see, and hear, and know of these things, by the power of the Holy Ghost" which is given to "all those who diligently seek him" (1 Nephi 10:17).

So Nephi did just that. "For it came to pass after I had desired to know the things that my father had seen, and believing that the Lord was able to make them known unto me, as I sat pondering in mine heart I was caught away in the Spirit of the Lord" (1 Nephi 11:1). Notice Nephi's formula here: first, he had a desire to know; second, he believed that the Lord would open his understanding (a principle that he had learned back in chapter 2); and third, he was willing to put forth every effort through pondering in his heart what he had heard his father teach. As a result of this process, the heavens were opened, and he was privy to one of the greatest visions ever recorded. The result might not have been the same if Lehi had received this vision in Jerusalem or shortly after embarking into the wilderness. Nephi's responses to earlier spiritual experiences had developed his spiritual sensitivity. Many years later Nephi taught his people, "For behold, thus saith the Lord God: I will give unto the children of men line upon line, precept upon precept, here a little and there a little; and blessed are those who hearken unto my precepts, and lend an ear unto my counsel, for they shall learn wisdom; for unto him that receiveth I will give more" (2 Nephi 28:30).

In contrast, remember how Laman and Lemuel responded to their father's vision and teachings. When Nephi returned from his visionary experience, he found his brothers "disputing one with another" (1 Nephi 15:2). So Nephi "spake unto [them]" and asked the "cause of their disputations" (1 Nephi 15:6). Note how they responded in verse 7, "Behold, we cannot understand the words which our father hath spoken." In return Nephi asked if they had "inquired of the Lord?" (v. 8). For Nephi, this was a natural reaction that he had been applying since chapter two. But that was not the case for his brothers: "We have not; for the Lord maketh no such thing known unto us" (1 Nephi 15:9). Why didn't the Lord do for Laman and Lemuel what he did for Nephi? The simple answer is: they never asked. Five hundred years later, Alma the Younger taught the same principle to Zeezrom. "It is given unto *many* to know the mysteries of God; nevertheless they are laid under a strict command that they shall not impart only according to the portion of his word which he doth grant unto the children of

men, *according to the heed and diligence which they give unto him*" (Alma
12:9; emphasis added).

We can approach the scriptures in many ways, all of which add
important dimensions to our experience. I have chosen just one that
has been fruitful for me. I have learned to love many of the individuals
described in the scriptures. Nephi is one of those, not so much because
he always chooses the right, even when his own father has a momentary lapse, but because I see in First and Second Nephi the metamor-
phosis of a young man, foreordained to great things, but who is still
learning to find his way spiritually. It is this side of Nephi that I relate
to as I face my own spiritual growing pains. I see in Nephi and others
the ideal of what is possible for me because I see them struggling with
the same spiritual struggles I have, and I see them initiate the same
spiritual steps that I know I must implement. This one tool for studying
the scriptures has made people become much, much more than mere
names on a page. They have become my inspiration. May they be so
for you also.

Notes

1. Caroline Eyring Miner and Edward L. Kimball, *Camilla: A Biography of
   Camilla Eyring Kimball* (Salt Lake City: Deseret Book, 1980), 172.
2. For an excellent discussion of the legal ramifications of this passage, see
   John W. Welch, "Legal Perspectives on the Slaying of Laban," *Journal of
   Book of Mormon Studies* 1 (Fall 1992): 119–41.
3. Orson F. Whitney, *Life of Heber C. Kimball, an Apostle: The Father and
   Founder of the British Mission* (1945; reprint, Salt Lake City: Bookcraft,
   1974), 450.
4. Note Elder Bruce R. McConkie's final, powerful address in general conference when, testifying of the Atonement, he said: "In speaking of these
   wondrous things I shall use my own words, though you may think they are
   the words of scripture, words spoken by other Apostles and prophets.

   "True it is they were first proclaimed by others, but they are now mine, for
   the Holy Spirit of God has borne witness to me that they are true, and it is
   now as though the Lord had revealed them to me in the first instance. I
   have thereby heard his voice and know his word" ("The Purifying Power
   of Gethsemane," *Ensign*, May 1985, 9).

The Woman at the Well

⋇⟨⟩⋇

Camille Fronk

As a child I attended the Tremonton First Ward in Tremonton, Utah. The ward still meets in the building that was constructed in 1928. The chapel is among the most beautiful I have ever seen: a large, bas-relief mural, spanning the entire front wall behind the podium, depicts the story of a Samaritan woman who came to know Jesus and his mercy at a well (John 4:1–43).

The artist was Torleif Knaphus, a Norwegian convert to the Church. He was commissioned to make the mural for the Tremonton chapel as his first replica of a relief he created for the Cardston Alberta Temple. Years later, a local Church member named Bob Macfarlane painted the mural, leaving one small portion (a disciple's satchel) the original hue of the clay.[1]

Every week at church I stared at that mural. I wondered what that woman had done to deserve such a prestigious place in our chapel. Because she had the Savior's complete attention, I figured she must have been pretty important and very righteous. I had yet to learn the mighty lessons inherent in her story. To begin, however, we need some background information.

Geographical Background

The event takes place in Samaria, a region just north of Judea and south of Galilee. This territory was the land inheritance given to the

---

Camille Fronk is an assistant professor of ancient scripture at Brigham Young University and a counselor in her stake Relief Society presidency. She has served as a member of the Young Women General Board, as dean of students at LDS Business College, and as a seminary and institute instructor.

two tribes of Joseph (Ephraim and Manasseh) when the children of Israel first conquered the land. At that time—centuries before the Samaritan woman met Jesus at the well—Joshua established the region as the first religious center for the Israelite nation. Mt. Ebal to the north and Mt. Gerizim to the south border the area.

Jacob's well is located near the foot of Mt. Gerizim, not far from the modern Palestinian city of Nablus. In New Testament times, the closest village was called Sychar, known in the Old Testament as Shechem. Here Jacob purchased land shortly after his favorable reunion with Esau, thereby giving the well its name. Strong Jewish, Christian, Muslim, and Samaritan traditions confirm this location as the site of Jacob's well. In fact, one scholar has suggested the site as the most authentic of all the holy places of Palestine.[2] The well is reportedly more than one hundred feet deep and seven feet wide. One can still draw sweet water from Jacob's well today.

HISTORICAL BACKGROUND

At the time of Christ, the region was inhabited by Samaritans, a people who had a nearly one-thousand-year history of contention with the Jews. Although both peoples descended from Jacob's twelve sons, a division occurred in about 975 B.C. when the Israelite nation split into two kingdoms, with two separate political and religious centers. The northern kingdom survived only until 722 B.C., when almost all of the inhabitants were scattered by the Assyrians. In 538 B.C., surviving Jews of the southern kingdom returned from Babylonian exile with permission from the Persian King Cyrus to rebuild the temple in Jerusalem. By that time, Jews viewed Samaritans as ritually unclean because of their gentile-tainted lineage. Samaritans were descendants from the residue of the ten northern tribes who had evaded deportation during the earlier Assyrian invasion and foreign colonists brought in by the Assyrians from other parts of the Assyrian empire.

The Mishnah, the compilation of oral law and rabbinical teaching which guides Jewish religious practice, warns: "He that eats the bread of the Samaritans is like to one that eats the flesh of swine."[3] The Jews, therefore, rejected the Samaritans' offer to assist them in reconstructing their temple. In retaliation, the Samaritans created obstacles that temporarily halted the work. Finally, in 128 B.C., the Jewish high priest sent troops to destroy the Samaritan temple on Mt. Gerizim. In the days of Christ, the enduring animosity between the Jews and the Samaritans encouraged most Jews to take an alternate route via the Jordan River Valley when traveling to Galilee from Jerusalem. By skirting the province of Samaria, Jews could avoid contact with the Samaritan people.

RELIGIOUS BACKGROUND

Samaritan beliefs were distinct from Jewish beliefs in notable ways. Samaritans anticipated the coming of a messianic figure, called the Taheb (meaning "restorer"), suggesting one who would restore true worship of God and the Samaritans to their rightful place in the house of Israel. Additional descriptions of this messiah were identified from the first five books of the Old Testament. These records, known as the Pentateuch, or the five books of Moses, were the only scripture accepted by the Samaritans. Most notable is the prophecy that the Messiah would be a prophet like unto Moses, as promised in Deuteronomy 18:18. Speaking to Moses, God said, "I will raise them up a Prophet from among their brethren, like unto thee, and will put my words in his mouth; and he shall speak unto them all that I shall command him." The Book of Mormon clarifies that this "Prophet like unto Moses" is Jesus Christ (1 Nephi 22:20–21; 3 Nephi 20:23).

CULTURAL BACKGROUND CONCERNING WOMEN IN FIRST-CENTURY PALESTINE

Every day, either morning or evening, or both, women went to the well to fetch water for their homes and families. This daily task required women to be physically strong and agile. Each woman walked the distance to the well carrying a lengthy rope and a leather or animal-skin vessel. These items were too valuable to be left by the well for public use. After manually drawing water from the well, each woman would carry her rope and now-heavy vessel back to her home, only to repeat the chore the next day.

Although they did much of the labor, women were generally ranked lowest in society. The Mishnah labels Samaritan women as "menstruants from their cradle," thereby making them regularly unclean.[4] Rabbinic literature also warned Jewish men against public association with women, including their own wives. "He that talks much with womankind," the passage reads, "brings evil upon himself and neglects the study of the Law and at the last will inherit Gehenna."[5]

Besides these reminders of rejection from religious leaders, the woman at the well faced additional censure. In John 4:18, we are told that she had been married to five different men in the past and was currently living with a man who was not her husband. Both the Jews and her own people would have ostracized her as a result. Perhaps that was the reason she went to the well during the "sixth hour," meaning six hours after sunrise, or about noon. The increased heat at midday would only add discomfort to her rigorous chore. Did the woman choose this unusual hour because it was the time she was least likely to meet other women? If men showed their disdain by ignoring her, women could be even more vicious with their judgmental gazes and whispers intended to be heard.

Jesus lived in this culture that discouraged public communication with women. Yet we find him at the public well, deep in theological discussion with a woman and a clearly imperfect one at that. Why? And why her?

A renowned Christian authority has observed, "The more unsavory the characters, the more at ease they seemed to feel around Jesus." He then poses a provocative question to church-going individuals: "Why don't sinners like being around us? . . . Somehow we have created a community of respectability. . . . How did Jesus, the only perfect person in history, manage to attract the notoriously imperfect? And what keeps us from following in his steps today?"[6] As remarkable as it may initially appear, this woman is the first person mentioned in the Gospels to hear Jesus identify himself as the Messiah. But that is at the end of the story. How did she come to receive such a profound blessing?

In the same manner that the Savior interacted with the woman at the well, he invites us to come unto him. Consider a four-part process that emerges from this New Testament text:

1. The Savior meets us where we are.
2. The Savior helps us to see our weaknesses.
3. The Savior leads us to recognize him.
4. The Savior invites us to leave our sins behind and bear testimony of him to others.

Let's explore each of these steps.

The Savior meets us where we are. Jesus went where he was certain to meet the woman, traveling right through the middle of Samaria rather than taking the alternate route. He also met her before she knew anything about him, either through his teachings or his miracles. He made no initial requirement that she be living a particular way. Through both his words and his actions, Jesus convincingly taught, "I am not come to call the righteous, but sinners to repentance" (Matthew 9:13). But the woman of Samaria knew none of this. She saw only a thirsty man at the well without equipment to draw up water to quench his thirst. He appealed to the woman, "Give me to drink" (John 4:7). Perhaps from his dialect or from the weave of his clothing, the woman recognized him as a Jew.

When she addressed him, her greeting was not only without any evidence of respect but communicated awareness of the deep animosity that separated her people from his. "How is it that thou, being a Jew, askest drink of me, which am a woman of Samaria? for the Jews have no dealings with the Samaritans" (John 4:9). Clearly the woman was on her home turf. The Jewish stranger was the one who was out of place. Initially, they did not communicate on the same level. But, just as he spoke with this woman, the Savior can speak in whatever language we understand.

She had come to the well seeking life-sustaining water. He offered her something better. He offered living water that sustains life eternally. Jesus said to her, "If thou knewest the gift of God, and who it is that saith to thee, Give me to drink; thou wouldest have asked of him, and he would have given thee living water" (John 4:10). As yet, the woman had no idea that she was conversing with the one Man who would suffer and die to make this miraculous living water obtainable. She did not yet realize the one she was facing had the power to give her eternal life. Her response shows, however, that she was gaining respect for the man and an interest in his proffered gift. For the first time she addressed him as "kyrie," translated from the Greek as "sir" or "lord." Beginning in verse 11 we read, "Sir, thou hast nothing to draw with, and the well is deep: from whence then hast thou that living water? Art thou greater than our father Jacob, which gave us the well . . . ?" (John 4:11–12).

In his answer, Jesus emphasized that the water he offered was not at all like the water in that well. No rope or leather bucket was necessary for his promised water. He alone supplies the gift. In reference to the water in Jacob's well, Jesus said, "Whosoever drinketh of this water shall thirst again: but whosoever drinketh of the water that I shall give him shall never thirst; but the water that I shall give him shall be in him a well of water springing up into everlasting life" (John 4:13–14). I'm certain that I don't understand all that is entailed in the Savior's gift of living water. Surely it must include complete forgiveness, personal revelation, and teachings that come through the witness of the Spirit and guide us back to God's presence. To Joseph Smith, the Lord revealed, "Unto him that keepeth my commandments I will give the mysteries of my kingdom, and the same shall be in him a well of living water, springing up unto everlasting life" (D&C 63:23).

The Samaritan woman was quick to respond to his explanation. Her interest in the gift was deepening, and the awe she was beginning to feel for this man increased. "Sir," she petitioned, "give me this water, that I thirst not, neither come hither to draw" (John 4:15). But one wonders what motivated her petition. Was she drawn by the thought of escaping the physical labor and social rejection associated with the well or by an inkling that there was a better life where thirst is eternally quenched? Was the woman beginning to see that there was hope—real hope—in her world so full of misery?

The Savior helps us see our weaknesses. Once we see the Lord's offer of a priceless gift that endures forever, we can face sins, shortcomings, and weaknesses that prevent us from wholly partaking of his offer. Note that Jesus did not begin his conversation with the woman by pointing out what she needed to change in order to come unto him. Rather he began by helping her see that he had a gift for her beyond anything she had ever yet experienced. When her problematic lifestyle was finally verbalized, she was not offended but reverenced him even more. "Go, call thy husband," Jesus invited, "and come hither" (John 4:16). She coyly answered, "I have no husband." Notice that Jesus first complimented her for telling the truth before spelling out the full story: "Thou hast well said, . . . for thou hast had five husbands; and he whom thou now hast is not thy husband" (John 4:17–18). "Sir," she immediately responded, "I perceive that thou art a prophet" (John 4:19). Again we wonder, How did Jesus, the only perfect person in history, manage to attract the notoriously imperfect?

Following the Savior's line of thought, we discover that he not only met her where she was physically but also spiritually. He knew that she was looking for a messiah who was a "prophet like unto Moses." After this interchange, she began to consider a greater identity for this man.

Her misconceptions, however, needed to be removed. Remembering that he was a Jew and she a Samaritan, she protested, "Our fathers worshipped in this mountain [meaning Mt. Gerizim]; and ye say, that in Jerusalem is the place where men ought to worship" (John 4:20). In the seventh century before Christ, King Hezekiah eradicated temple worship everywhere outside Jerusalem to curtail apostasy among the Israelites. At the time Jesus conversed with the woman at the well, the Jews were still adamant about centralized temple worship in Jerusalem. Again, the Samaritans were excluded.

In response, Jesus alluded to the temple in Jerusalem being destroyed just as the Samaritan temple on Mt. Gerizim had been. "Woman, believe me, the hour cometh, when ye shall neither in this mountain, nor yet at Jerusalem, worship the Father" (John 4:21). He wanted her to understand that specific location is not what is essential to worship, particularly when that location is not founded on truth. On the other hand, incorrect information about the object of our worship and how we worship will assuredly prevent true worship. To the correct aspects of Samaritan messianic expectation, Jesus therefore added detail concerning their anticipated "prophet's" mortal origins. "Ye worship ye know not what: we know what we worship: for salvation is of the Jews" (John 4:22). Jesus was a "Jew," born to the tribe of Judah. Surely salvation has come through the Jews!

The Savior leads us to recognize him. Scripture consistently teaches the one way to recognize Jesus as the Savior and Redeemer. Christ created an environment that enabled the woman to learn this truth just that way. In John 4:23 we read, "The hour cometh, and now is . . ." That opening phrase suggests both a future and a present application; there is only one true way to recognize the Christ, and it is the same in every era. The apostle Paul identified the way as clearly as any. He taught that no man can know that Jesus is the Lord except by the Holy Ghost (1 Corinthians 12:3).[7] To the woman, the Savior explained, "True worshippers shall worship the Father in spirit and in truth: for the Father seeketh such to worship him. For unto such hath God promised his Spirit. And they who worship him, must worship in spirit and in truth" (JST John 4:23, 26).

Learning in spirit and in truth necessitates the tutelage of the Holy Ghost. His mission is not to speak of himself but to bear witness of Christ and guide us to truth (John 16:13). And that is precisely what the Holy Ghost did for the woman at the well. She carefully listened to Jesus; but it was the Holy Ghost who revealed the messianic thread throughout his teachings. Once taught by the Spirit, she began to put it all together and professed, "I know that Messias cometh, which is called Christ: when he is come, he will tell us all things" (John 4:25).

Then, and only then, Jesus unequivocally declared himself the Messiah. The King James translation records the Savior's response in verse 26 as "I that speak unto thee am *he*," with the *he* in italics. Italics were used in that translation to indicate words that were added to the manuscript by the translators when clarification was deemed necessary. We are invited to consider the verse without the italicized word if the result gives us greater insight. In this case, I believe it does.

One of the Lord's titles is *Jehovah*, which is translated "I Am," as in The Always Existing One. In his gospel, John often records statements in which Jesus bears witness of himself as the great "I Am." In this verse, if we remove the italicized *he*, the Savior confirms his identity to the woman by saying, "I Am speaketh unto thee."

The Savior invites us to leave our sins behind and bear testimony of him to others. As soon as the woman received this confirming witness, she "left her waterpot, and went her way into the city, and saith to the men, Come, see a man, which told me all things that ever I did: is not this the Christ?" (John 4:28–29). Perhaps the abandoned water pot signifies the woman's former life—including her dependency on a sinful world to survive. He who is both the living water and the giver of the water eliminates the need for the world's formula for survival. One drinks living water; one does not carry it. A water pot is therefore unnecessary.

Now converted, the Samaritan woman's greatest desire was to share the good news with everyone in her village. She forgot about herself, her past, and her reputation. No doubt some of those who believed her message were individuals who previously had mistreated her. Furthermore, notice that she used an approach similar to the Savior's to introduce the truth to her neighbors. She met them where they were, both physically and spiritually. She went to them in the city and witnessed that she had found that "prophet, like unto Moses." "Come," she invited, "see a man, which told me all things that ever I did: is not this the Christ?" (John 4:29).

As a result of this woman's testimony, many came to know the true worship of God. Initially, they believed because of "the saying of the woman." But after having Jesus as a guest in their village two days, they knew by the Spirit. The converts proclaimed to the woman, "Now we believe, not because of thy saying: for we have heard him ourselves, and know that this is indeed the Christ, the Saviour of the world" (John 4:42). At a time when few Jews knew the true identity of Jesus, a little village in Samaria proclaimed the truth of truths, the declaration of declarations: "This is indeed the Christ, the Saviour of the world."

THE SAMARITAN WOMAN AND NICODEMUS

The story of the Samaritan woman at the well is not a parable. The event actually happened. The Savior met a Samaritan woman where she was, helped her to see her weaknesses, and created an environment in which she could learn his identity through the witness of the Holy Ghost. When filled with this knowledge, she abandoned her sins and became the catalyst who brought an entire village to Christ.

In nearly every way, the woman of Samaria contrasts with the stereotypical recipient of revelation. The exchange between Nicodemus and Jesus in the preceding chapter of John provides a nearly perfect opposite.

Nicodemus was a man—that fact alone establishes him in the upper echelons of Jewish society. The woman at the well was a woman *and* a Samaritan, a double reason to be labeled unclean by the Jews.

He was a Pharisee, well respected, among the best educated, and considered by many to be a master teacher. By contrast, she had an unsavory past and would have received no respect in any community. He was recognized as a singularly religious individual. She was among the gravest of sinners.

Nicodemus conversed with the Lord at night. No one would therefore see a prestigious rabbi being taught by a carpenter from Galilee. The Samaritan woman's exchange with Jesus was at midday in the midst of her daily chores.

Nicodemus sought to learn from the Savior after noting the many miracles Jesus had performed in Jerusalem. But he initially came on his terms, not the Lord's. On the other hand, Jesus met the woman where she was, without any show of miracles or previous introduction.

Nicodemus returned to his daily routine, presumably keeping his conversation with Jesus a secret. She left her water pot behind in her haste to spread the good news to all those who would hear her.

With all his power and position and opportunity for learning, Nicodemus could not see who stood before him. But the woman at the well saw. Isn't that the miracle? This woman who doesn't even have a name in our scriptures, this woman who would never be a standout in a crowd, is known by Jesus! She who has neither title, nor position, nor formal education, nor a stainless past *sees*—she actually sees the thirsty stranger as he truly is: the Savior and Redeemer of the world.

Life-changing revelation came to her, revelation as profound as we find in scripture. But her conversion was not in the dramatic fashion of Alma the Younger or Saul on the road to Damascus. In a quiet and contemplative way, the Samaritan woman received a clear witness while in the midst of doing ordinary housework. If she can recognize the Savior and overcome her shortcomings to follow him whole-heartedly, certainly there is hope and an invitation for you and me.

Whenever I return to the Tremonton First Ward, I still stare and marvel at that mural. The Samaritan woman is not only there at church every Sunday, but she is also in many of our temples. Why is she there? She who suffered from spiritual dehydration was offered and received living water. And ever since that day, she has been a "light unto the nations," inviting people in every land to come unto Christ. As we drink that same living water, I pray we will be like her—trusting in our Savior and acting upon the personal revelation he pours upon us. I bear witness that through his grace, we can then do and be all that he asks.

Notes

1. From the history of the Tremonton First Ward meetinghouse, written by Phyllis Christensen for the fiftieth anniversary of the building's construction, copy in possession of the author.

2. André Parrot, *Land of Christ*, trans. James H. Farley (Philadelphia: Fortress Press, 1968), 65.

3. Herbert Danby, trans., *The Mishnah* (London Oxford University, 1933), Shebiith 8:10.

4. Ibid., Niddah 4:1–3.

5. Ibid., Aboth 1:5.

6. Philip Yancey, *The Jesus I Never Knew*, Special Limited Ed. (Grand Rapids, Mich.: Zondervan, 1995), 147–48.

7. Joseph Smith, *Teachings of the Prophet Joseph Smith*, sel. Joseph Fielding Smith (Salt Lake City: Deseret Book, 1970), 223.

HOW CAN I IGNITE THE TRANSFORMING POWER OF THE SCRIPTURES?

꒰꒱

Jeanne Nebeker Jardine

Begin with faith. Our testimony of the scriptures may reflect our life's journey. My husband, for example, has never had serious doubts about the gospel, and he has always loved the scriptures. I, on the other hand, went through a period in my life when the scriptures seemed boring and unimportant. As I look back at my relationship to these sacred texts and think of how deeply I enjoy and find meaning in the scriptures today, I realize that the scriptures have stayed the same, but I have changed.

When I entered the University of Utah three decades ago, I registered myself as a nondenominational Christian rather than LDS. For a year or two, I struggled with whether or not the Church was true. Because I lacked a firm belief in Jesus Christ as my Savior and Joseph Smith as a prophet, the scriptures seemed irrelevant, and I looked for life-changing truth in secular texts. Each new philosophy I encountered had a wrenching appeal: one day I believed in the self-centered ideas of Ayn Rand, another day in Eastern meditation, and another day in Tolstoy's brand of Christianity. It was intellectually and spiritually exhausting to be without a foundation or core institution to hang on

Jeanne Nebeker Jardine received a master's degree in English from the University of Utah. A former magazine editor, she teaches English at Salt Lake Community College. Jeanne and her husband, Jim Jardine, are the parents of four children. She serves as a counselor in her ward Relief Society Presidency.

to. I have always related to Joseph Smith's sense of confusion before the First Vision.

Slowly I came back to a love for the Church and for Christ through the loving examples of friends and family and through the texts of the great Christian apologist C. S. Lewis. The logic, imagination, and beauty of Lewis's writing helped me begin to study the scriptures with a new appreciation. If we don't believe the scriptures to be the word of God, offering instruction, comfort, and, most of all, truth— they are just not that interesting. Because I have been without faith, I know its power and overarching potency.

Be eager to try out new ideas. "The best thing for being sad . . . is to learn something," advises the great mythic teacher and magician Merlyn. "That is the only thing that never fails. You may grow old and trembling in your anatomies, you may lie awake at night listening to the disorder of your veins, you may miss your only love, you may see the world about you devastated by evil lunatics, or know your honour trampled in the sewers of baser minds. There is only one thing for it then—to learn. Learn why the world wags and what wags it. That is the only thing which the mind can never exhaust, never alienate, never be tortured by, never fear or distrust, and never dream of regretting. Learning is the thing for you."[1]

My mother and her sisters have always been warm, creative, intellectual, and very unpredictable. As children we never knew exactly what a holiday party would be like because it changed a little every year at each aunt's house. My mother and aunts were always taking a class or reading a book that changed their ideas about what family gatherings should be. One year we'd all be historical characters from the first Thanksgiving and sing seventeenth-century Thanksgiving hymns. Another Thanksgiving we might have real dishes the Pilgrims feasted on. One Christmas all the cousins played chimes because Aunt Lucy was into English Christmas carols and chimes; another time we saw a slide show that celebrated our family heritage and honored loved ones we'd lost. Some families have traditions that never change; we had traditions that were always changing. This unpredictability and constant introduction of new ideas and traditions made holidays interesting and memorable.

My aunts brought this same eagerness to gospel studies. They pursued constant learning with dedicated passion. It wasn't until I became a mother and often felt too tired even to read a novel that I recognized how much energy and time that takes. Following in my aunts' footsteps, I returned to college in my early forties to finish a graduate degree in literature begun twenty years earlier. In my studies, I was assigned several works I had studied twenty years earlier. Some writers, like Shakespeare and Jane Austen, seemed more brilliant, wise, and engaging than I had remembered; others had lost some of their fascination for me. The literature was the same, but my life experiences led me to read and evaluate everything differently. After finishing the degree, I brought new skills to studying the scriptures. Like Shakespeare, these sacred texts contained more beauty, wisdom, and inspiration than I had remembered. They offered more to me spiritually and emotionally than they ever had before.

Deepen your desire to understand the scriptures. As a teacher and a parent, I have decided that a desire to acquire knowledge may be the single most important quality in someone's learning. I have seen my own children's academic progress shaped by desire. If a great teacher can ignite their desire to study art, music, or math, they respond. My youngest son, who thoroughly disliked reading in fourth grade, read and learned the complicated rules of football almost overnight. The rules to this game came easily because of his strong desire to learn.

Desire is the core of our agency. As much as we would like to as parents, relatives, or friends, we cannot change another's desire. We can force the scriptures on our family members, but they must desire to believe or the words of God will find no place in their hearts. We should also never underestimate the power of our desires on our own eternal exaltation. If we truly desire to access the light of the scriptures, they will be opened up to our understanding.

Cultivate humility as a tool to understand the scriptures. Another quality of the heart for meaningful scripture study is a virtue currently out of favor in our popular culture—meekness, humility, or submissiveness. Elder Neal A. Maxwell leads out the collection of essays *Learning in the Light of Faith* with his essay, "The Disciple-Scholar." He states, "The portions of the key attributes lacking in each of us vary from person to person. It is meekness which facilitates working on what is lacking."[2] Only when we have Christian humility can we go to the scriptures ready to learn and be transformed. If we think we are pretty smart—and so many of us do—going to the scriptures with a submissive and teachable attitude is difficult.

Professor and scholar James E. Talmage, author of *Jesus the Christ*, is a moving example of scholarship enhanced by humility. As one biographer observes, "Elder Talmage was a superb geologist who published in the leading scientific journals of his day. Yet he modeled in his life the qualities of meekness, humility, and submission to priesthood authority."[3] After Elder Talmage had finished writing *Jesus the Christ*, he read his work chapter by chapter to the First Presidency and the Twelve Apostles, seeking their suggestions and approval. That is remarkable. Some of the finest writers I have worked with as an editor would not allow me to change one word without calling them and begging for a different punctuation or phrase. Think of the submissiveness and desire for truth Elder Talmage must have possessed.

Faith in God, a desire for learning and truth, and submissiveness—these three spiritual qualities ignite the power of the scriptures to transform our lives.

Notes

1. T. H. White, *The Once and Future King* (New York: Berkley Publishing, 1966), 183.
2. Neal A. Maxwell, "The Disciple Scholar," in *Learning in the Light of Faith*, ed. Henry B. Eyring (Salt Lake City: Bookcraft, 1999), 12.
3. Paul Alan Cox, "Journey to City Creek: Adding Scholarship to Discipleship," in ibid., 28.

HOW DO I TEACH BEYOND WORDS?

✢༄ᴄ

Lori Budge Raymond

Turn words into flame. Primary children can tell you who Joseph Smith is. They can tell you who President Gordon B. Hinckley is. They can tell you about the Word of Wisdom. They can tell what it means to be honest or to pay tithing. Definitions are easy. But how do we turn the words—doctrine—into flame and inscribe it on the hearts of those we teach? We want our students to be able to say, as did Jeremiah, "[The Lord's] word was in mine heart as a burning fire shut up in my bones" (Jeremiah 20:9).

The answer is, of course, that *we* don't do it at all. The Spirit is the true teacher. Our responsibility is to take advantage of, produce, or make available any kind of situation that invites the Spirit so that he may do the true teaching. That is why the Church, I believe, encourages us to hold family home evening, to regularly study the scriptures, and to have family and personal prayer. This is why our leaders encourage us to listen to good music and speak to one another with tenderness and love. We must promote every opportunity possible to invite the Spirit, the true teacher, into our classrooms and homes, into our own and our children's daily lives.

Understand that we "see things feelingly." Shakespeare's play *King Lear* focuses on two main characters: King Lear and a nobleman

---

Lori Budge Raymond is a former member of the Church Teacher Improvement Curriculum Committee. She has served as a Webelos leader and Primary pianist and serves on the Relief Society Home, Family, and Personal Enrichment committee in her ward. She and her husband, Robert S. Raymond, are the parents of four daughters.

named Gloucester. Each man is a father who doesn't really know or understand his children. Because of their parental blindness, these men suffer a great deal at the hands of their children. King Lear is rejected by his wicked daughters, which rejection drives him mad. Gloucester is literally blinded at the hands of his evil son. Cast out on the moors, Lear and Gloucester meet and mourn together. "Do you see how the world goes?" Lear complains. And blind Gloucester, who sees clearly only after he has lost his eyes, says, "I see it feelingly."[1]

In Doctrine and Covenants 8:2 the Lord says: "Behold, I will tell you in your mind and in your heart, by the Holy Ghost." We also see things (with the mind) feelingly (with the heart). That is one of the ways the Spirit really converts us. When we teach with the Holy Ghost, we help others see the gospel feelingly. This understanding goes beyond words.

A few years ago, I was in the dressing room with my little eight-year-old who had just been baptized. I hurriedly stripped off her wet clothes and toweled her hair dry. I was keenly aware that people were waiting to have her confirmed and that two other wet little girls were waiting to use our dressing room.

Suddenly, in the middle of all this doing, my sweet child flung her arms around my waist and said, "Mom, do I smell clean?" I wrapped my arms around her damp little body and buried my nose in her wet hair. "Yes, Stephanie," I said, "you smell completely clean." And I *knew* in that moment that she truly was completely clean, that the ordinance she had just received was the symbol of everything we believe in. She had been buried, as Joseph F. Smith says, in the "liquid grave" and raised up to a new life.[2] She did smell clean. Completely. And I knew that if I lived worthy of that ordinance, that I too, even though I was forty years old and quite imperfect, could smell just as clean.

What I understood went far deeper than the words, deeper than the ordinance, far beyond what she said. For my eight-year-old daughter, "smelling clean" was the way the Spirit gave her expression. But her words brought me to an understanding that still defies my attempts to explain it. "When the Almighty reveals Himself unto man," stated

Joseph F. Smith, "He does it by the power of the Holy Ghost, and not through the natural eye or the natural ear. He speaks to man as if He were speaking to him independent of his body; He speaks to the Spirit . . . to the heart, to the living soul, to the eternal being of man."[3] Even now I cannot describe the profound feelings and the brimful heart that I experienced when my daughter asked me if she smelled clean. The Spirit touches each of us beyond the words, so that we "see it feelingly." Joseph F. Smith continued: "There are no words of man that can speak it. It can only be felt. It can only be understood by the immortal part of man."[4]

Wait upon the Spirit. Another phrase I have learned in my life is to "wait upon the Lord" (Isaiah 40:31), because, as Elder Dallin H. Oaks said, "You cannot force spiritual things."[5] There's no formula to ensure that the Spirit will attend our teaching. We know that certain things like singing hymns, saying prayers, and bearing testimonies invite the Spirit. But we cannot force him to be present. We must wait upon him. When he comes, it is a gift.

I learned this the hard way when I was asked to serve on the general Church committee that wrote materials to improve teaching. I'm in six car pools, I clean toilets and feed the dog, and they asked me to do this. I had—and still have—no titles behind my name. I was just—me.

I drove to Salt Lake every week to work with others on this assignment, and the task was daunting and overwhelming. I wanted so badly to be wonderful. I was overwhelmed thinking about writing anything that the whole Church was going to see, let alone my children. I did as we do when we undertake any challenging calling: spend many hours in deep and earnest prayer, pleading to be worthy of the responsibility, worthy of the blessing, worthy of the privilege of serving. In every thought, word, and action, I wanted the Spirit to guide me because this is the Lord's work. Many times, however, I turned in material that was not wonderful, and sometimes I didn't feel inspired at all. At times I labored under a "stupor of thought" (D&C 9:9). Other times the Spirit came when I least expected it—I said things I hadn't planned or even thought of.

I struggled mightily with one assignment. Facing a deadline, I had spent the entire day trying to write. I had fasted. I had gotten down on my knees in front of my computer four times that day: "Please tell me what I'm supposed to write!" I went upstairs to my husband, flung myself on the bed, and wailed, "It's not coming! Why isn't the Spirit telling me what I'm supposed to write?" Through all this I learned that I could not force the Spirit to attend me every time I felt the work needed it.

We cannot force the Spirit. All the Lord cares about in any call- ing we have is that we offer ourselves. So we do the best we can, con- secrating ourselves, our time, and our hearts, and we wait upon the Lord.

Notes

1. *King Lear*, 4.6.148–49.
2. *Joseph F. Smith*, Teachings of Presidents of the Church series (Salt Lake City: The Church of Jesus Christ of Latter-day Saints, 1998), 61.
3. Ibid., 6.
4. Ibid., 7.
5. Dallin H. Oaks, "Teaching and Learning by the Spirit," *Ensign*, March 1997, 11.

How Can the Scriptures
Help Me Handle Emotions?

⛤

Marian Shafer Bergin

Learn about emotions from the scriptures. The scriptures tutor us in the variety and legitimacy of the entire range of human emotions we experience. If we follow Nephi's admonition to read the scriptures and "liken them unto yourselves" (1 Nephi 19:24), we will find an infinite number of deeply felt emotions expressed that we can identify with or learn from.

Lehi, for example, felt *fear*. In fact, he "exceedingly feared" for the rebellious Laman and Lemuel. "Yea, he feared lest they should be cast off from the presence of the Lord" (1 Nephi 8:36). I too have feared for the eternal welfare of my children, and it has comforted me to know that one of the great prophets of the Lord had similar feelings.

Ammon felt *joy*. "Behold, my joy is full, yea, my heart is brim with joy, and I will rejoice in my God," he said (Alma 26:11). Do we let ourselves feel real joy? Alma describes a dramatic contrast of feelings: "There could be nothing so exquisite and so bitter as were my pains . . . on the other hand, there can be nothing so exquisite and sweet as was my joy" (Alma 36:21). I believe Alma would not have felt such joy if he had not experienced his bitter *pain*.

What about sorrow? Jeremiah felt *sorrow*. His words might help us

Marian Shafer Bergin received her master's of social work from Brigham Young University and is a clinical social worker in private practice. She has served on the Church Correlation Research and Evaluation Committee. She and her husband, Allen E. Bergin, are the parents of nine children and the grandparents of thirteen.

know we are not alone if we feel this emotion. "Is it nothing to you, all ye that pass by? behold, and see if there be any sorrow like unto my sorrow" (Lamentations 1:12).

In *tense* and *anxious* moments, we can remember the words of Christ to Martha: "Thou art careful and troubled about many things: but one thing is needful . . ." (Luke 10:41–42).

These are merely five examples from the wide range of emotions to be found in the scriptures. Our Savior fully experienced our world so "that he [would] know according to the flesh how to succor his people according to their infirmities" (Alma 7:12).

Don't turn off your feelings. Sooner or later most people have difficult, even tragic circumstances in their lives. Some days we may feel poked so full of holes that if we have to suffer one more thing, we will collapse in a useless heap like a layer cake when the oven door is opened at the wrong time. At such times, a profound source of help is easily and constantly accessible to us: the scriptures. You may believe that you have tried reading the scriptures and that they didn't help or inspire you. Or you may think you need to feel more spiritually inclined before you will try reading God's words. A few of you believe that God has abandoned you, and reading his words only triggers that feeling.

In my work as a therapist I hear much despair and despondency. I witness people crushed by emotional pain and confused by their lives. My heart and prayers go out to them. Some are suffering because of their own mistakes; others have been innocently wounded. Each is struggling to make sense of life. Sometimes the very nature of their affliction keeps them from trusting God enough to turn to him and his words: every time they trusted, they were hurt; any time they loved, they were betrayed. To claim a sense of control, some of these people stop trusting anyone, including God. Others, demoralized by their fears, put all their trust and faith in God but none in themselves.

Many who reach this rock-bottom place of hopelessness cope with life by turning off their feelings. If they allow themselves to feel, they reason, all they will feel is pain. So they shut down. The scriptures are full of feeling. To read them, then, is to risk feeling—often very deeply.

Those who don't want to feel are going to avoid the scriptures. Others don't read the scriptures because their feelings are hardened. They don't ever feel much of anything, so what they find in those blessed books seems meaningless.

I have found that a surprising number of people turn off their feelings, even among women. One young woman told me that part of getting ready for the day included turning off her feelings. In a workshop recently, I talked about how to manage feelings. As I related a tender experience, I became tearful. To my surprise, a sister near the front of the audience spoke out rather disdainfully, "See, it doesn't even work for you!" She took my tears as evidence that I didn't know how to manage my feelings. For her, feelings—especially if they led to tears—were not permitted.

Others of us know perfectly well how to cry but don't acknowledge feelings such as fear, anger, grief, or even doubt. I have found that when we deny our painful feelings, we sometimes also shut down our capacity to be spontaneous, excited, or joyful. Being open to our feelings does not mean we must act upon all of them. We should use them instead to understand ourselves and what is happening to us, and then to understand what we would like to change. We cannot work to change what we are not aware of.

Acknowledge your emotions to learn who you are. Without our feelings, we are like empty shells, going through life relying on external cues to tell us who we are. If we avoid the reality of our human condition, which is meant to be difficult, the positive self we present to the world may be false. While it is possible to be too negative, believing that we can correct that by denying our pain is a mistake. Rather we must seek and face the truth. Ultimately, if we are not willing to acknowledge our painful emotions, we cannot repent of our sins. We cannot come to Christ with a broken heart and a contrite spirit and feel his tender healing mercies, and we cannot claim his gift of eternal life.

An example is a woman I will call Sarah. Sarah suffered unspeakable abuse at the hands of two important women in her life. She is, nevertheless, a woman of great faith. In our sessions together, she had been unable to work through this trauma because the faces of these women in her memory so frightened her that she couldn't bear to fully acknowledge, even to herself, what had happened. If she couldn't review the events without terror, the abuse would continue to hold power over her, and she would never be free from feelings of power-lessness and worthlessness.

One day Sarah arrived, bursting to tell me about an experience. She had been trying to say her prayers, but every time she closed her eyes, her abusers' faces had appeared before her, frightening her and stopping her prayer. In desperation, she reached for her scriptures, which were by her side. She opened them, and the first words she read were these: "Be not afraid of their faces: for I am with thee to deliver thee, saith the Lord" (Jeremiah 1:8).

Imagine the power of reading these exact words at that precise moment. Being led to this scripture was like being handed cool water in a scorched desert. She felt instant relief and was renewed and strengthened in her endeavor to believe her life had meaning and purpose. Over time, Sarah worked through her fear and learned to love her life.

HOW CAN I TASTE THE SWEETNESS OF REMEMBERING?

꒰ ꒱

Sandra Rogers

Note how often the scriptures tell us to remember. The invitation to remember occurs often in the scriptures. Several hundred verses of scripture counsel us to remember or to "forget not." I invite you to consider turning your heart, might, mind, and strength to spiritual rememberings, for I promise you will find that remembering increases your faith, brings truth and light into your mind and heart, and answers life's daily problems. Can you hear his voice in your ears and mind and heart as he calls you to remember?

"Remember, remember that it is not the work of God that is frustrated, but the work of men" (D&C 3:3).

"Remember the sabbath day, to keep it holy" (Exodus 20:8; Mosiah 13:16).

"Remember that without faith you can do nothing; therefore ask in faith" (D&C 8:10).

"And now, . . . remember, remember that it is upon the rock of our Redeemer, who is Christ, the Son of God, that ye must build your foundation; that when the devil shall send forth his mighty winds, yea, . . . when all his hail and his mighty storm shall beat upon you, it shall have no power over you to drag you down" (Helaman 5:12).

"And now remember, remember. . . . that whosoever perisheth, perisheth unto himself; and whosoever doeth iniquity, doeth it unto himself; for behold, ye are free; ye are permitted to act for yourselves;

Sandra Rogers is associate academic vice-president for international, distance, and continuing education at Brigham Young University. She was a Welfare Services missionary in the Philippines and serves as the pianist in her ward Primary.

for behold, God hath given unto you a knowledge and he hath made you free" (Helaman 14:30).

I found only a few exhortations to forget. For example, we are counseled to forget the world, to come out of Babylon (D&C 133:7). We are also counseled to forget the reproach of our youth or widowhood (3 Nephi 22:4). Because I spent my teenage and young adult years as the resident wallflower of my high school, ward, and university, I took this counsel to heart. I understood it to mean that I should not dwell on past circumstances or hurts but rather trust in the Lord's promises to me.

In essence, we are told to remember the Light and long for it and to forget the darkness and to flee it quickly. Remembering light and truth gives us the inspiration, the hope, the momentum, the desire, and the confirmation to move forward in the Lord's work. It motivates us to be willing to make the sacrifices that qualify us for exaltation.

Remember Christ's atoning sacrifice. The essence of the covenant we renew with the Savior each week during the sacrament is to take his name, to always remember him, and to keep his commandments. The promised blessing is to have his Spirit, his light, and his truth with us always (D&C 20:75–79).

When our sacramental covenant asks us to "remember him," our thoughts turn to the Atonement, the central headline in the good news of the gospel. Christ overcame death and hell; there is no more glorious announcement to the world. As we take the bread and water of the sacrament, symbols of that atoning sacrifice, we remember that repentance is possible through the grace of our Savior. We can remember his sufferings for us in the Garden where incomprehensibly he took upon himself our sins, our sufferings, our pains, our afflictions, our sicknesses, our infirmities (Alma 7:11–12). We can remember his agony on the cross. We can remember that he conquered death three days later when he rose from the tomb. We can remember that he lives. Without a little light, a little sacred remembering, we might never be willing to remove from our lives the things that prevent us from enjoying and reflecting to others the Savior's light. Remembering helps us to humble ourselves. Each week our hearts are drawn to the Savior as we remember with gratitude his grace and mercy.

Practice faithful remembering. Remembering his atoning sacrifice, the most important event in the history of the world, is the gateway to faithful remembering of other important spiritual events in our own lives. Perhaps because of my advancing years, I treasure memory more than I have in the past. I have felt so moved by the sweetness of remembrance. The warmth of a tender memory comforts my soul. The women's conference service event brought to my mind a grand outpouring of the Spirit I experienced in the mission field. I believe such memories are reassurances of the Spirit.

During the last year, I received a new, challenging position at BYU. I had to develop new skills and talents and learn to understand complex and unfamiliar circumstances. My assignment especially required me to move forward in an area that was the exact expertise of the person I replaced but was something about which I knew absolutely nothing. Many times in the last year I felt pummeled by self doubt and the ever-increasing number of mistakes I felt I was making. I started comparing myself to others who I felt sure could do the job better than I was. I felt discouraged because I couldn't seem to learn fast enough or accomplish everything that needed to be done. I began to doubt that I had anything to offer. I even contemplated resigning. Then, one night, I read the words of the Lord to Oliver Cowdery, when he was feeling that he had little of importance to offer. The Lord said to Oliver, and to Sandi as I read the words, "Therefore this is thy gift; apply unto it, and blessed art thou" (D&C 8:4). I was reminded that perhaps I did have gifts I was overlooking. If I applied myself, those gifts could help me in my work. Not long after, I also read the words of Paul, when he reminded the Corinthians and the Ephesians to "remember" that they were *new* creatures in Christ (Ephesians 2:10–13 and 2 Corinthians 5:17). I was taught through this "remembering" that when I feel trapped by mortality and the weight of past sins and mistakes, the way is open through Christ to be new, to learn, and to change.

These were simple verses. Simple invitations to remember truth and light. Yet, what a strength they were to me. Sometimes the invitation to remember is for comfort, sometimes for counsel, and sometimes for reproof. In all occasions, these pleas to remember are evidence of God's goodness, his great love for us, and his desire to draw our hearts home to him and his light.

My uncle wrote a letter to his parents just before he was killed in Italy during World War II. He described the last time he came home before his unit was shipped to North Africa. It was a dark night. At last he drove over a hill and saw the little valley where he had been born and raised. His heart warmed when he saw lights in the kitchen window of his home. He told my grandparents there was no more beautiful sight than the lights of home, shining with love, warmth, and security in the darkness of that night. It is that same longing for the light of home that our Father in Heaven hopes our hearts will remember.

HOW CAN I LEAD A MORE SAINTLY LIFE?

❧

Tad Callister

Remember the power of the Atonement to lift as well as cleanse.
The Atonement seems to have at least four principal purposes: first, to
bring about the resurrection for all mankind; second, to temporarily
restore us to God's presence for judgment purposes—thus overcoming
what the scriptures call the first spiritual death; and, third, to create
the possibility of repentance, so that we might be cleansed from our
individual sins.

These three purposes help correct the "negative" conditions of the
Fall. They are largely redemptive in nature, but the Atonement was
designed to do more than restore us to the "starting line"—more than
just wipe the slate clean. It has a fourth and crowning purpose—to
endow us with power so that we might overcome each of our weaknesses and acquire the divine traits that would make us like God. The
Atonement was meant to be not only redemptive but exalting in its
nature. C. S. Lewis understood this principle: "For God is not merely
mending, not simply restoring a *status quo. Redeemed humanity is to be
something more glorious than unfallen humanity would have been,* more glorious than any unfallen race now is (if at this moment the night sky
conceals any such). . . . And this super-added glory will, with true
vicariousness, exalt all creatures."[1]

Some of us lose sight and hope of perfection and godhood, not

---

*Tad R. Callister works as an attorney in Glendale, California, and has written a
book on the Atonement. He has served as a bishop, stake president, area authority
seventy, seminary teacher, and counselor in a mission presidency. He and his wife,
Kathryn Saporiti Callister, are the parents of six children and grandparents of six.*

because of major sins but because of innocent mistakes or weaknesses. "I'm not a bad person," we say. "I just can't seem to overcome the weaknesses that so easily beset me and distance me from God. It's not the sins so much as the lack of talent, the lack of capability, the lack of strength that separate me from God." Those of us who fall within this category need to be reminded of the Atonement's lifting, as well as cleansing powers. Regardless of the depth or multiplicity of our individual weaknesses, the Atonement is always there. Therein lies its beauty and genius—it is never beyond our grasp. The Savior is always standing by, anxiously longing to endow us with those powers that will convert our every weakness to a strength. The LDS Bible Dictionary puts our need for this power in perspective: "Divine grace is needed by every soul in consequence of the fall of Adam and also because of man's weaknesses and shortcomings."[2]

Seek the gifts of the Spirit. How does the Atonement help us overcome our weaknesses and eventually perfect us? The reasoning may go something like this: First, through the ordinance of baptism, we are cleansed, not by the water, but through the atonement of Jesus Christ. Second, because of that cleansing, we are eligible to receive the gift of the Holy Ghost. Third, with the gift of the Holy Ghost comes the right to receive the gifts of the Spirit. Fourth, each of the gifts of the Spirit (such as faith, love, wisdom, patience, and so on) is an attribute of godliness. Thus, as we acquire the gifts of the Spirit, we acquire the attributes of God.

Gifts of the Spirit are intended to perfect the Saints. Orson Pratt clearly taught: "If there were no unbelievers on the earth, still there would be the same necessity for the miraculous gifts that there was among early Christians; *for if the whole world were believers in Christ they could not possibly be perfected without these gifts*."[3] That seems logical, for as we acquire the gifts of the Spirit we narrow the gap between man and God.

Is it any wonder the scriptures enjoin us to seek after these gifts? Elder Bruce R. McConkie joined in this heavenly mandate: "Faithful persons are expected to seek the gifts of the Spirit with all their hearts."[4]

President George Q. Cannon spoke of human shortcomings and then of the divine solution—the countermanding gift of strength to overcome each weakness: "No man ought to say, 'Oh, I cannot help this; it is my nature.' He is not justified in it, for . . . God has promised to give strength to correct these things, and to give gifts that will eradicate them. . . . He wants His Saints to be perfected in the truth. For this purpose He gives these gifts, and bestows them upon those who seek after them, in order that they may be a perfect people upon the face of the earth, notwithstanding their many weaknesses, because God has promised to give the gifts that are necessary for their perfection."[5] That is a sobering yet hope-filled pronouncement.

Earnestly pray for specific gifts of the Spirit. Hugh Nibley made this salient observation: "The [spiritual] gifts are not in evidence today, except one gift, which you notice the people ask for—the gift of healing. They ask for that with honest intent and with sincere hearts, and we really do have that gift. Because we are desperate and nobody else can help us, we ask with sincere hearts of our Lord. As for these other gifts—how often do we ask for them? How earnestly do we seek for them? *We could have them if we did ask, but we don't. 'Well, who denies them?' Anyone who doesn't ask for them.*"[6]

When is the last time we pled for one of the gifts of the Spirit in our prayers? Have we prayed for patience to confront a problem, wisdom to be better parents or leaders, increased faith to meet the challenges of life? These gifts are within our reach. The Atonement made it so.

One day when our daughter Angela was in the fourth grade, she came home from school distraught, her report card in hand. The teacher had placed a check under the column "Handwriting," indicating a need for improvement. That was hard for her sensitive soul to take. Teary-eyed and despondent, she felt like a failure. We tried to comfort her, but to little avail.

Finally, a kind Father in Heaven prompted struggling young parents. As we discussed possible solutions, a scripture came to mind—Ether 12:25, 27. We opened the Book of Mormon and read it with

Angela. Moroni, while abridging the plates of Ether, was lamenting to the Lord that the Gentiles would mock his writing. He was acknowledging a real weakness that was about to be exposed, perhaps even exploited. Moroni confessed, "When we write we behold our weakness, and stumble because of the placing of our words; and I fear lest the Gentiles shall mock at our words" (Ether 12:25). Then came the Lord's magnificent promise: "I give unto men weakness that they may be humble; and my grace is sufficient for all men that humble themselves before me; for if they humble themselves before me, and have faith in me, then will I make weak things become strong unto them" (Ether 12:27).

The Lord promised much more than an overcoming of our weaknesses; he promised they could become strengths in our lives. What a difference in perspective! What a difference in consequence!

As parents, we then discussed with Angela Moroni's experience. We knew, and she knew, the Lord would not make an idle promise. Accordingly, I gave her a father's blessing. This alone would not solve the problem, but it was one of many positive steps we could take. Angela made a poster inscribed with the Lord's promise to Moroni, which she placed prominently in her room, a constant reminder of her potential and the Lord's promise. She resolved that each day she would ask the Lord's help. That year she agreed to let us, her parents, review her homework each night. If her writing had not improved, she would redo it. My wife bought her a calligraphy set, which further whetted her appetite to improve. Two years later, when Angela was about to graduate from her elementary school, the principal announced that certificates would be given to the five finest handwriters in the school. Imagine our elation and surprise when he called out the name of Angela Callister. What might have been an abstract principle became a very real and personal testimony for this sweet little girl.

Allow the Lord to turn your weaknesses to strengths. Moses felt weighed down by a glaring weakness in his life. Although a prophet, he nonetheless complained, "O my Lord, I am not eloquent . . . but I am slow of speech, and of a slow tongue." It was as though he were saying,

"How can I lead this people when I have no fluency of speech, no gift of oratory?" The Lord answered his worries in this classic reply, "Who hath made man's mouth?" As I understand it, he was saying to Moses, "I, who made man and worlds without end, certainly have the ability to correct the simple problem of one man's mouth. Just have faith in me and I will solve this minor problem." Then the Lord gave Moses this promise, "Now therefore go, and I will be with thy mouth, and teach thee what thou shalt say." That should have solved the problem. But Moses, great as he was, lacked faith this one time, for he could not believe his speech problems could thus be solved; instead he sought his own solution—a spokesman. How did the Lord react? "And the anger of the Lord was kindled against Moses" (Exodus 4:10–14). In consequence, Moses got his spokesman, but a weakness failed to become the strength it might have been.

Contrast Moses' experience with that of Enoch. The initial facts were almost identical. Enoch, too, called to be a prophet, had a glaring speech impediment: "Why is it that I have found favor in thy sight, and am but a lad, and all the people hate me; for I am slow of speech; wherefore am I thy servant?" (Moses 6:31). The Lord's response to Enoch was similar to his advice to Moses, "Open thy mouth, and it shall be filled, and I will give thee utterance" (Moses 6:32). It is here, however, that the scripts part company. There is no suggestion in the scriptural record that Enoch doubted the Lord's promise. The scriptures then reveal the awesome power of God's grace: "And as Enoch spake forth the words of God, the people trembled, and could not stand in his presence" (Moses 6:47). The scriptural record continues: "And so great was the faith of Enoch that . . . he spake the word of the Lord, and the earth trembled, and the mountains fled, even according to his command; and the rivers of water were turned out of their course . . . *and all nations feared greatly, so powerful was the word of Enoch, and so great was the power of the language which God had given him*" (Moses 7:13; emphasis added). His weakness had become a mighty strength.

Don't accept the spiritual status quo. Benjamin Franklin wrote about his pursuit of perfection. He recalled his frequent relapses to old ways, his lack of progress, and finally the near resolution "to give up the attempt, and content myself with a faulty character." Then he thought of the man who brought an axe to a neighboring blacksmith and "desired to have the whole of its surface as bright as the edge." Franklin relates: "The smith consented to grind it bright for him if he [the neighbor] would turn the wheel; the neighbor turned, while the smith pressed the broad face of the ax hard and heavily on the stone, which made the turning of it very fatiguing." The neighbor would stop every so often to see how close to done they were. Progress was slow and eventually he said to the smith that he would take his axe as it was without further grinding. "'No,' said the smith, 'turn on, turn on; we shall have it bright by-and-by; as yet, it is only speckled.' 'Yes,' says the man, *'but I think I like a speckled ax best.'"*[7]

Perhaps some have reconciled themselves to a speckled life, have found it easier to accept a spiritual status quo than exert the required effort to make the whole of their lives bright. No doubt there are some who believe they possess irrevocable weaknesses and shortcomings. Many such good souls have "plateaued out" spiritually. "It is my nature," they say. But it is not. May the words of the Lord to Moses echo in our minds: "Who hath made man's mouth?" (Exodus 4:11). Cannot God, the creator of all, fashion, shape, add to, modify, and help the faithful overcome any weakness? That was the promise of the Atoning One.

Notes

1. C. S. Lewis, *Miracles* (New York: Macmillan, 1978), 122–23; emphasis added.
2. LDS Bible Dictionary, s.v. "grace," 697.
3. Orson Pratt, *Orson Pratt's Works,* (Salt Lake City: Deseret News Press, 1945), 96–97; emphasis added.
4. Bruce R. McConkie, *Mormon Doctrine,* 2d ed. (Salt Lake City: Bookcraft, 1966), 314.
5. George Q. Cannon, as quoted in Marvin J. Ashton, *The Measure of Our Hearts* (Salt Lake City: Deseret Book, 1991), 24–25.
6. Hugh Nibley, *Approaching Zion,* ed. Don E. Norton (Salt Lake City: Deseret Book, 1989), 90.

7. Benjamin Franklin, *Benjamin Franklin His Life As He Wrote It,* ed. Esmond Wright (Cambridge, Mass.: Harvard University Press, 1990), 83.

Song Forgotten, Song Remembered

꒰ C ꒱

Vesna Gruppman

I grew up in Yugoslavia, which in my lifetime was first a communist and then a socialist country. To speak about God brought ridicule
and danger. My father was a music teacher, and my mother taught
school. In their teaching, they could never mention God. My mother,
nevertheless, did believe in God and in Jesus Christ. I remember when
she would be in despair and very depressed, she would pray to the Lord,
and she wasn't shy to do it in front of me. I often wondered, *Who is this
incredible being that she is praying to? Who is this being who hears her when
there is nobody around and yet answers her prayers?*

Very soon my mother died. I was ten years old, and I was left alone
with no brothers or sisters, only a father who grieved so much that he
barely could take care of me. This time was probably the most difficult
of my life. But my mother left something so valuable with me: her faith
in the Lord Jesus Christ. From the early days of my childhood, the
desire to know this Lord, this Jesus Christ, grew in me like a seed.

I was a child prodigy in my country. I won numerous violin competitions year after year and performed on radio and television. People
knew me so much that they would come from different parts of the
country to hear me. That put incredible pressure on me as a child, pressure to be the best all the time. This expectation distracted me from

---

*Vesna Gruppman, a native of Yugoslavia, is a convert to the Church. She teaches
violin and viola at Brigham Young University. She has been the concertmaster for
the San Diego Opera and an associate professor of music art at California State
University, Los Angeles. She and her husband, Igor Gruppman, have performed
around the world.*

really realizing at the time why I am on this earth and what my mission is.

I received a special scholarship to study music in the Soviet Union when I was only fourteen years old. I had to leave my father, my friends, my schoolmates and go to Russia. I considered it a privilege because I was the first person in Yugoslavia to receive such a scholarship. I felt that this sacrifice was worth making.

I entered a country fundamentally different from the one I had left. I didn't know the language. I was placed in the pupils' house, a dormitory for children. Life there was terribly difficult. I slept in a room with twelve or sixteen beds. We took baths only once a week, and the food was so horrible that very soon I developed an ulcer. I was miserable and thought about going home, but there was no way back. My whole country looked up to me and expected me to be the best; how could I give up? Especially after the great honor they invested in me, the scholarship they gave me, I felt it wasn't right. So I stayed, and I had moments when I wanted to end my life. One day I was in the sleeping room by myself, and I was thinking, *Should I jump through this window?* This is a very sacred thing to me, but I am impressed to tell you. A response came, "You can't do this. This is going against God." I didn't know then what it was, but now I know it was my first experience with the Holy Ghost. I was confused, but the impression was so strong I couldn't ignore it. And so I didn't act on those thoughts. I know now that the Spirit of the Lord prevented me from ending my life.

In spite of these difficulties, my teachers in Russia were wonderful. I was happy to work hard through challenges and difficulties to learn music, which was so dear to my heart. I felt that my mission in life was to be a musician and share this glorious gift with others. During the time of my worst depression and despair, I had incredible visions about music. From that experience, I realized that there must be some higher power, some God who was with me, who prevented me from ending my life and who tried to help me every day. I began to look for that being who was my guide and helper. My desire to know the Lord grew strong in my heart.

When I finished school and went to the conservatory, I received a roommate from Kiev, in Ukraine, who believed in God and had been baptized into her church despite the danger of persecution. I admired her greatly for her courage, sincerity, and love for the Lord Jesus Christ, and I decided to be baptized into her church. I loved the wonderful, sincere people but felt something was missing. I read the New Testament and knew that this church was not exactly like the one in the days of Jesus Christ. I spoke to the Lord and made an oath that wherever I went, I would search for the truth. Whenever I performed in Europe, I would look for the truth, sure that when I found it, I would recognize it.

As I traveled to perform concerts, I didn't miss an opportunity to attend different churches. I found wonderful people, all sincere in their beliefs, and I know that the Lord takes their righteousness into account. But no church felt exactly right.

In 1980 I decided to come to the United States. A year earlier, my Jewish friend, also a musician, and his family had emigrated from Russia. We had wanted to get married in Russia but we couldn't because being married to a foreigner would be a great danger for him. He would be denied a career and wouldn't be allowed to participate in competitions. When I finished my post-graduate studies, I visited him in America, and we decided to get married. But how? I wanted to get married in a Christian church, and his parents wanted him to get married in a synagogue. Instead, we had a civil marriage. We had conversations about God and about how wonderful it would be to find a church where Jew and Christian would be one, where we could raise children of two different faiths and yet be accepted in the church. Our neighbor, also a Russian immigrant, said to us one evening, "You know, I have these friends who are Mormons. They claim that they have a prophet and his name is Joseph Smith. I don't know all the details, but it's an interesting story. He prayed to God and was told not to join any church because they were all churches of men and not of God."

I felt that there was something true about this story because her words were planted so strongly in my heart that day. I decided to investigate this Mormon church. However, I did not speak English very well yet—actually I spoke poorly—and I would be so shy. It was my first year in the states, and I didn't even drive a car. How could I go to a Mormon church? But the Lord knew my heart. Three days later, missionaries stood at my door, two sisters—one elderly, the other younger. Incredibly, the older one looked to me as if I had known her all my life. *How can this be possible?* I wondered. I asked her where she was from and she said Idaho Falls. How could I possibly know her? I'm from another continent. Yet I felt as if I did. I felt that two angels were standing at my door at that particular moment, sent right from heaven.

They told me glorious things about Jesus Christ being not only the Savior but also the creator of the universe, creator of earth and heaven, our creator. That thought shook me—I felt I had always known it. It was like a song I had in my heart, but had forgotten and then remembered. I decided to investigate, to really study what they told me, but I gave them a hard time. I asked them many difficult questions. The older sister, who spent all her life washing clothes to make a living, couldn't answer all my questions, but she told me, "If I didn't know that this is the true church of God, I wouldn't be here today. The Church is everything to me." This is what actually converted me: I saw tears in her eyes and I knew that she was telling me the truth, that she was absolutely sincere. This certainty can come only from God. I did as they told me. I read the scripture in Moroni about praying and asking in faith and receiving. (I prayed in my bathroom because I didn't have a closet as they told me.) I didn't expect thunder and lightning or signs, but I felt in my heart that if there were any percent of a chance that this might be true, I did not want to miss that chance

I was very insecure about reading the scriptures. Though my husband wasn't there when the missionaries presented me with the Book of Mormon, he secretly read the book every day. Then he asked me hard questions and told me to go ask this and go ask that. I was baptized, and wonderful people fellowshipped me and took me to church every Sunday. My Sunday School teacher, Tom Nibley, the son of Hugh Nibley, was wonderful. I learned so much about the gospel, and I loved every minute of it.

A year later, we moved to San Diego. I did not know if my husband was ready, but I knew he was reading the Book of Mormon, so I asked the stake missionaries to come. Apparently my husband had been ready all the time, but he had a terrible smoking habit, begun at age thirteen, which is common in Russia. He thought he needed to be perfect before he joined the Church. (Little did he know that baptism is just the start!) The stake missionaries blessed him by the power of the priesthood that on the day of his baptism, he would wake with no memory of smoking and would have no desire to smoke a cigarette again. And, indeed, that has happened.

The Lord has blessed my husband and me so much. He has poured love upon us. Miraculous things have happened in our lives. Of course, my life has not been the happiest song all the time. I have difficult moments, and growing in the gospel is not an easy path. But the Lord has blessed us. Let me share one experience that opened our eyes, my husband's and mine.

We were scheduled to perform in Jerusalem, but sadly President Sacrabin had been assassinated that day. Our performance was canceled, so we took a tour following the footsteps of Jesus Christ. In front of the tomb where the Savior was buried, I tried to contemplate the moment of his resurrection, and I asked the question, *How did Mary feel to see the resurrected Savior first? How did the apostles feel?* I longed to feel only a little bit of what she felt when she saw the resurrected Savior. Then an amazing feeling came upon me, not only of Mary, but of all of us, all the hosts of heaven, everyone who has ever lived in heaven and who has not been born, and those who have died. Everybody had the opportunity to witness the resurrection of Jesus Christ. We all shouted for joy. It was an absolutely incredible moment, the most wondrous music and art were conceived in the heavens at that instant as a result of the joy of our Savior's resurrection. What we hear now and what we perform is just a glimpse of that glorious music created as a result of Jesus Christ's resurrection.

I teach my students that they should perform with an eye single to the glory of God, instead of worrying whether somebody likes them or not, if they miss a note, or if they play in tune. Their homework is to work hard so that once they are on stage, they can feel that they are doing the glorious work of the Lord, transmitting that same glorious moment that we felt in the premortal existence, in the spirit world, when we witnessed the resurrection of the Savior. That alone makes me feel so blessed to be a musician and performer.

Ten years ago I translated the temple ordinances into Serbian. I translated for two weeks and had only one day left to finish working on the sealing prayers. I worked all night alone. Usually a group of people work together, but I was the only endowed person in my country, so I worked on this alone. I prayed that I would be able to finish the work that night. Miraculously, the moment I looked at the text in English, immediately the full knowledge of how it should be translated into Serbian came to me. It was almost like somebody had dictated to me. I am grateful for this experience. I know that great work is being done on the other side—after all, there are more on the other side than on this side, and temple work is incredibly important.

I have a great testimony of the Savior, Jesus Christ, and of his love for us, all of us, in the Church and out. He watches over us all the time. I have a living testimony that his mercy blankets all the world—God loved the world so much that he gave his only begotten Son to save the world, every race, every nation, every person.

I am going through another difficult time in my life. I injured my hands and don't know whether I will be able to perform ever again. But I know that the Lord is here and knows my pain. He has never left me alone. He has never left you alone. If you look at your life, even the moments when you didn't see him or when you felt nothing around you but the adversary, he has still been with you. He descended below us all to know all of our pain, to know everything that we will ever go through, to understand it fully, and to have mercy. Find your own miracles. Search your life and see how wonderful it is that the Lord has been with you every moment. Whether you are a member of the Church or not, even when you are doing something wrong, he is with you. We may lose the capacity to feel his presence for a moment, but he never leaves us alone.

DECISIONS AND MIRACLES: AND NOW I SEE

❧

Irina Kratzer

There was a time in my life when I was touched by love and the light of Christ. My life has since changed forever.

I know how it is to live without the gospel. I lived that way for thirty years. I was born in Russia of goodly parents. They gave me tender love and care and an opportunity to have a good education. They did their best for me to be happy. For most of my life, I lived in Siberia. When I grew up, I got married and gave birth to a lovely baby girl. Soon I successfully graduated from the university and got a job I really liked. And yet, regardless of everything, I was far from being happy.

From the beginning, my marriage did not seem to work and gradually fell apart. Economic situations in Russia were getting worse every day. I was hardly able to provide simple food for my daughter and me. I sinned. I made one wrong choice after another. Hunger, depression, and poor decisions made my life miserable. I was blaming bad fortune, not realizing that in many ways I was suffering the natural consequences of my sins. But how could I know that? Sin did not exist according to what I had been taught. Let me explain.

Religion in Russia was prohibited after the Communist revolution in 1917. I was taught from kindergarten that there is no such thing as God and that only the Communist party and Grandpa Lenin could bring happiness to the Russian people. Religious people were badly

---

Irina Kratzer, a native of Siberia, Russia, is a recent convert to the Church. A cardiologist in her own country, she is taking the medical boards to practice in the United States. She and her husband, Tay Kratzer, have a blended family of four children. She serves as a Relief Society teacher in her ward.

persecuted in our society. Believers lost their jobs, were not allowed to go to school, and were labeled "crazy." Everybody was required to take atheism classes at the university, where we proved that God does not exist. Although over time socialism in our country collapsed, and communist ideology proved to be not viable, atheism still lived in people's minds. It had deep roots in my mind also. I just did not think of God. Yet I felt pain deep in my heart about my poor choices. Later I would learn that the pain I felt was the Light of Christ giving me a sense of conscience to tell right from wrong. But society opposed my feelings of pain. In other people's eyes, I was not doing anything particularly bad.

Elder M. Russell Ballard said: "The standards of the world have shifted like the sands of a wind-blown desert. That which was once unheard of or unacceptable is now commonplace."[1] That's how I lived. If there is no God, there is no sin; if there is no sin, it is absolutely up to you what you do with your life. Enjoy it. Take advantage of it. Because when you are gone, everything else will be gone also.

In the Book of Mormon, I have read about this same philosophy taught by the anti-Christ, Korihor: there is "no atonement made for the sins of men, but every man fare[s] in this life according to the management of the creature; therefore every man prosper[s] according to his genius, and . . . every man conquer[s] according to his strength; and whatsoever a man [does is] no crime" (Alma 30:17).

This philosophy appealed to me at first, but after a while, life seemed to me like a dark tunnel with only the grave at the end. I felt I was slowly dying. It is written in the scriptures that men are to have joy (2 Nephi 2:25). We came to this earth with the instinct to seek happiness, no matter where we live—in Russia, Africa, or blessed America. I did not know how to pray, so I dreamed. I am a big dreamer. I dreamed that one day I would run away from everything miserable in my life and would start again from the beginning—happy and bright. I wanted so much for my daughter to have a better life than I did. I dreamed about America. Somehow Russian people, and probably many other people in the world, associate America with a good life, success, and happiness.

Even when we do not know God's ways, he knows our hearts and listens to our dreams. One day a retired American doctor came to visit my city in Siberia. His name was Dr. Woodmansee, and he was a Mormon from Utah. All I'd heard about Mormons was that they did not drink tea and coffee, and that seemed strange. I was assigned to show Dr. Woodmansee around the hospital where I worked. At the end of our fifteen-minute visit he asked me, "Would you come to America to continue your education if I helped you?" Later he told me that in coming to Russia he never planned to make such an offer, but he followed a sudden prompting of the Spirit.

After that, for ten long months I corresponded with Dr. Woodmansee as we arranged for my coming to America. His acquaintance, Brother Ray Beckett, helped us communicate through the Internet and proved to be the best LDS missionary I've ever known. Very often he shared his testimony with me. In one of his letters he promised me that my coming to America would change my life forever. He saw God's hand in what was going on in my life. He also arranged to send my documents through the Church mail system, so that I could pick them up at the Novosibirsk mission office in Siberia. That's how I met the LDS missionaries, who gave me a Book of Mormon. I was not interested in reading this book and put it somewhere on the shelf. During my next visit to the Novosibirsk mission home, I was given an *Ensign*. I was trying to learn English at that time so I was very glad to receive such a present. It would help me in my English studies. The first article I read was about how the Book of Mormon had changed the lives of so many people, bringing them happiness and peace. These stories intrigued me and I decided to look closer into this book.

That is how the Book of Mormon came into my life. I read one chapter every morning before I went to work. Reading this book, I learned that God lives, that Jesus is his Son, and that he came to this earth to help sinners like me. The more I read this book, the more I saw the gap between the teachings of Christ and the way I lived. I learned that was why my life was so miserable. I felt pain and I had a great desire to change.

In 1997 President Thomas S. Monson said: "The decision to change one's life and come unto Christ is, perhaps, the most important decision of mortality. Such a dramatic change is taking place daily throughout the world."[2] At this time in my life, I received a new vision and understanding of life and could no longer live the way I had before. I was ready for a dramatic change. I will always remember the night in Russia when I cried the whole night through, realizing that my life was not good, that my poor decisions had hurt people I loved the most. It was the most painful experience of my life. I sobbed and pled the whole night, "Lord, please, help me!" By the end of the night I was exhausted and had no more tears. When the first morning light broke through, peace and relief came to me. I heard the words: "Here is my hand. I will lead you and guide you. But you have to promise me that you will change." And I did; I promised. I wanted this guidance and help more than anything else.

Alma the Younger related a similar experience to his son Helaman:

"But I was racked with eternal torment, for my soul was harrowed up to the greatest degree and racked with all my sins.

"Yea, I did remember all my sins and iniquities, . . . and that I had not kept his holy commandments. . . .

"And . . . while I was harrowed up by the memory of my many sins, behold, I remembered also to have heard my father prophesy unto the people concerning the coming of one Jesus Christ, a Son of God, to atone for the sins of the world.

"Now, as my mind caught hold upon this thought, I cried within my heart: O Jesus, thou Son of God, have mercy on me, who am in the gall of bitterness, and am encircled about by the everlasting chains of death.

"And now, behold, when I thought this, I could remember my pains no more; yea, I was harrowed up by the memory of my sins no more.

"And oh, what joy, and what marvelous light I did behold; yea, my soul was filled with joy as exceeding as was my pain!

"Yea, I say unto you, my son, that there could be nothing so exquisite and so bitter as were my pains. Yea, and again I say unto you, my son, that on the other hand, there can be nothing so exquisite and sweet as was my joy" (Alma 36:12–13, 17–21).

I did not know, on that painful and joyous night in Russia, how great Christ's promises are. I did not know then that in just a little while I would travel to America where I would learn more about the gospel, and I would soon be baptized. I did not know that in less than a year from that eventful night, I would marry a wonderful man with three beautiful little children, a man who is so precious to my heart now, and with whom I want to live forever. I did not know that my daughter would come to America to join us in happiness with our newly formed family. Oh, I did not know then how great his promises are.

Now I know how much every soul is important to God. For me to get baptized, he took me out of cold Siberia and put me in sunny Utah to warm up my heart with friendly and kind people. He gave me so many miracles that I did not have even a little chance to doubt his divine hand in my life. I agree with President Monson. The decision to get baptized was the most important decision in my life, and my conversion was the biggest miracle for me.

But what about after my baptism? Do miracles still happen? Yes, they do! The fact that I no longer live with pain but with joy is the miracle that I have now daily. Like everybody else, I have my up and down days, but I have found true happiness on this earth. I was looking for it for thirty years, but I searched in all the wrong places, following the directions of the world and not knowing the Spirit.

Many other miracles, small and great, have come about in my life. And what matters most is what I have learned from them. First, I have learned that almost every miracle I have experienced since my baptism has come as a result of prayer and effort. God requires effort and faith on our part. Second, I have learned that the faith and testimony we gain require constant nourishment. Daily scripture study helps us to do that. Without effort on our part, our testimonies will fade, and the feelings of joy will fade also. If we don't go forward, we will go back. The third lesson I learned was that to receive daily miracles, we need to ask for them and then recognize them when they come. We recognize them not only to thank God, but to bring to our own awareness the ways in which God has blessed us. This process builds further faith.

Now in my dreams and in my letters, I return to Russia, to my friends, to people I love, and ask them: "Do you know who you are? Do you know where you come from? Please, listen. Listen to what I've learned." The fire burns in my soul day and night. The fire of joy, the fire of love, the fire of gratitude. And I cannot be still. I need to tell the whole world what I know now. Once I was blind, and now I see. Once I lived in darkness, and now I live in the brightest light.

Walk with Christ! Hold onto his hand! Feast upon his word. Drink in his light with your every pore, with all your soul. In times of hardships, you won't be left in a dark tunnel but in the light of his love with brighter light always ahead of you.

Notes

1. M. Russell Ballard, "Like a Flame Unquenchable," Ensign, May 1999, 85.
2. Thomas S. Monson, "They Will Come," Ensign, May 1997, 44.

TRUTH AND RIGHTEOUSNESS WILL SWEEP THE EARTH

※⟨⟩⟫

Merrill J. Bateman

A few years ago, I listened to a young Hispanic sister recount her conversion story in the Saturday evening session of a stake conference. "When the missionaries knocked on my door," she said, "I saw the smile on their faces and felt the firm grip of their handshakes. They asked if they could take a few moments and share a message that would bring happiness into my life. At the conclusion of their visit, they turned to Moroni's promise in the Book of Mormon and invited me to pray and exercise my faith to obtain a witness of the book's truthfulness and Joseph Smith's first vision.

"I was surprised! They were asking me to find out for myself, to learn that the Holy Ghost would speak to me, that I was not just to believe their words. Later, as I listened to the missionaries explain the plan of salvation, I suddenly felt a confirming witness that I was more than a speck in the universe. My life was important not only to me but to a loving Heavenly Father and his Son. They knew me! There is a purpose to life, and they have a plan for me to achieve that purpose. I could never feel worthless again!"

The truth of the young sister's testimony burned in me that evening. I too have felt the touch of the Master's hand and know there is purpose to life, that every person is of infinite worth, that there is a plan. Not only are innumerable earths known to the Father and the

Merrill J. Bateman, a member of the First Quorum of the Seventy, serves as president of Brigham Young University. He has served as presiding bishop of the Church and as dean of the College of Business and School of Management at BYU. He and his wife, Marilyn, are the parents of seven children and the grandparents of twenty.

Son (Moses 1:35), but more important, the Father and Son know each of us individually. The Son not only died for our sins but in some incomprehensible way in the garden and on the cross received power to give us all "life and godliness" if we are obedient (2 Peter 1:3).

Before the foundation of the world, the Lord instructed his children regarding the plan for their eternal development. The blueprint for our growth and happiness called for a period of time outside his presence during which memories of our earlier spirit life would be veiled. Agency and opposition were part of the plan because they are essential elements of human development. Earth life would be a time to receive a physical body to overcome tendencies toward sin. It would be a time to receive instruction regarding the principles by which we should live and then be tested regarding our will to obey. It would be a time to discover who we are and the potential within us. We would discover these things by exercising faith in Jesus Christ, by repenting, and by entering into his ordinances and covenants. Through the atoning sacrifice of the Only Begotten, *everyone* could be made new and exalted to a higher plane. Everyone could receive immortality and eternal life (Abraham 3:22–26; 2 Corinthians 5:17; Moses 1:39).

The time outside the Lord's presence is a probationary period divided into two parts—a relatively short period in mortality followed by a longer span in a world of spirits. To protect agency and righteousness, no one is forced to accept truth. If adults reject eternal principles, they may lead their children and future generations astray. Since many do not receive the full blueprint in mortality, missionary work continues in the spirit world (1 Peter 3:18–20; 4:6).

We should not procrastinate living the righteous principles taught us in this life. In Amulek's words: "This life is the time for men to prepare to meet God; . . . for that same spirit which doth possess your bodies at the time that ye go out of this life, that same spirit will have power to possess your body in that eternal world" (Alma 34:32, 34). The plan calls for those who receive the gospel to share it with others, to be exemplars and teachers of righteousness, both here and, for some, on the other side of the veil. This plan applies to all of the Father's family. Only one set of truths leads to a fulness of light, a fulness of joy. Jesus Christ and the truths taught by him are the "way, the truth, and the life" (John 14:6).

The gospel plan was given to Adam and Eve (Moses 5:4–9). But even they saw apostasies. From the beginning of time, the Lord's servants have been commissioned to search out those who fall by the wayside, to teach them the gospel and help them to return to the fold. Following the Savior's earthly ministry, a time of apostasy occurred, when "the heavens [were] darkened, and a veil of darkness [covered] the earth"—a period of "great tribulations" (Moses 7:61). Nearly all of the apostles were killed within forty years following the Savior's crucifixion, and as Paul foretold, Church members turned away from the truth, unable to "endure sound doctrine" as "grievous wolves enter[ed] in . . . not sparing the flock" (2 Timothy 4:3; Acts 20:29).

TRUTH AND RIGHTEOUSNESS WILL SWEEP THE EARTH

Following the great Apostasy, a time of refreshing was foretold, when "righteousness [would come] down out of heaven; and truth [would come] forth out of the earth, to bear testimony of [the] Only Begotten." In the day of refreshing, "righteousness and truth will I cause to sweep the earth as with a flood, to gather out mine elect from the four quarters of the earth" (Moses 7:62).

Righteousness descending from the heavens was fulfilled in the revelations received by the Prophet Joseph Smith, including the Savior's appearance in the Kirtland Temple followed by Old Testament prophets delivering priesthood keys. Truth coming forth out of the earth was fulfilled by the publication of the Book of Mormon. Missionary work and Church growth in many nations fulfills the Lord's promise that "righteousness and truth will I cause to sweep the earth."

How pervasive will the flood of righteousness be? Is it a period in which all of the Father's earthly children will embrace the gospel? If not all, will most or a majority of his children enter the Kingdom? A vision received by the prophet Nephi helps answer these questions. Nephi records that in the last days, although members of the Church will be scattered upon all the face of the earth, they will be small in number (1 Nephi 14:12). Today the Church numbers eleven million— less than 1 percent of the earth's six billion. Sociologists forecast that the Church's population near the end of this next century may number as high as 280 million. Although large, this number will still be less than 1 percent of the earth's expected total.[1]

THE INFLUENCE OF A RIGHTEOUS PEOPLE

Nephi indicates that the Saints' influence will be well beyond their proportionately small numbers. In the last few years, observers have witnessed the Church's rise out of obscurity and an increase in its influence. Churchwide humanitarian service is one manifestation of the "righteousness and power" referred to in Nephi's vision. These efforts manifest the great power of the Lamb, as gospel principles and the Holy Spirit cloak the Saints with the strength and will to reach out and help those in need "across the street, across the world and across the veil."[2]

As the presiding bishop a few years ago, I learned that almost three-fourths of the volunteers that appeared in Miami on the first weekend to clean up after Hurricane Andrew were LDS. Not only did they appear in significant numbers, they were organized. Eighteen-wheeler truckloads of supplies from the Atlanta regional storehouse carried plywood, nails, hammers, blankets, food, medicinal supplies, and other materials to relieve suffering and rebuild the city.

Following the floods in Central Georgia a few years later, approximately six thousand of the eight thousand volunteers who came to clean out homes were LDS, even though Church membership in Georgia makes up less than 1 percent of the state population. Oklahoma, Texas, and California have seen similar responses during recent catastrophes. In the mid-1990s, the president of the American Red Cross, having learned of our Church members' relief efforts, asked to meet with Church officials to establish a set of protocols for future emergencies. Truth and righteousness are sweeping the earth, and although our numbers are few, there is power in the principles by which we live.

EARLY STAGES OF MISSIONARY WORK

For a moment let's look back through the pages of history and review the Lord's missionary program, remembering that agency is a paramount principle. Missionary effort has existed from earliest times. In the beginning, the gospel was declared and taught to Adam, Eve, and their children by the Lord's own voice, by angels sent from his presence, and through the gift of the Holy Ghost (Moses 5:58–59). In turn, Adam and Eve were given responsibility to teach their children and reach out to those who left the fold (Moses 5:12, 26–27; 6:4–6). Enoch was called to preach repentance and was successful in converting his people, but Noah, with the same commission, was unsuccessful except for his own family. Old Testament prophets were called to reclaim a city, a people, or a nation.

The first organized missionary effort occurred in the meridian of time, when the Savior called and gave power to the Twelve to preach the gospel to the lost sheep of the House of Israel (Matthew 10). The program was extended when the Seventies were called, given the same commission as the Twelve, and sent two by two "into every city and place, whither [Christ] himself would come" (Luke 10:1).

During one of the Redeemer's last appearances following his resurrection, the Savior expanded the Twelve's calling: they were now to "Go . . . into all the world, and preach the gospel to every creature"— to "teach all nations" (Mark 16:15; Matthew 28:19). The Twelve were no longer restricted to the house of Israel. They may not have fully understood the new injunction; missionary work remained focused on the Jewish nation until Peter received a revelation that emphatically opened the door for the Gentiles (Acts 10:1–35). Through a vision which prepared Peter to teach the gospel to a Roman centurion, Peter learned that God is no respecter of persons, that he should not consider any man "common or unclean" (Acts 10:14). It was time to take the gospel to every nation.

The Savior assigned the ancient apostolic missions prior to his ascension. Tradition holds that the Twelve canvassed the known world of their day. Peter served in Syria and Rome. John served in Asia Minor and was eventually banished to the Isle of Patmos. James the Greater went to the far reaches of Western Europe, while Philip served in Turkey and Andrew in Russia. Scriptural references indicate that James the Just remained in Jerusalem, while tradition holds that Simon the Zealot was assigned Persia, and Bartholomew went to the lands east of the Caspian Sea. Mark served with Peter in Rome and then visited Egypt after Peter's death and founded the Church of Alexandria.[3] One of the more interesting assignments was given to Thomas. Tradition states that he was sent to India where he taught along the southwest coast, experienced considerable success, and died as a martyr in A.D. 68.[4] Today millions of "Thomas Christians" in India trace their gospel origins to St. Thomas the Apostle.[5]

Ancient documents indicate that all of the apostles, except John and perhaps Matthew, died as martyrs within forty years of Christ's death. Soon priesthood keys were gone, and doctrines and ordinances were changed or lost. The apostasy became a reality. In the 1500s to 1600s, reformers appeared on the scene and light penetrated the veil once more. The time of refreshing shown in vision was not complete, however, until a total restoration occurred.

TRUTH SWEEPING THE EARTH IN THE LAST DAYS

With the call of the Prophet Joseph Smith and the restoration of priesthood keys, the foundation was laid to once again initiate missionary work across the earth. As early as September 1830, the Lord told Joseph: "Ye are called to bring to pass the gathering of mine elect" (D&C 29:7). In October 1830, the Lord instructed Joseph that the elect would be gathered from the "four quarters of the earth" (D&C 33:6). In January 1831, with only 280 members, the Lord told Joseph that missionaries would be sent to every nation (D&C 39:15).

Eighteen months after the Church was organized, with membership at only a few hundred, Joseph received the Lord's preface or introduction to the Doctrine and Covenants, which is today the first section. If the Church were the work of human hands and minds, it is doubtful that anyone would have had the audacity to issue this proclamation: "Hearken ye people from afar; and ye that are upon the islands of the sea, listen together. For verily the voice of the Lord is unto all men . . . ; and there is no eye that shall not see, neither ear that shall not hear, neither heart that shall not be penetrated. . . . And the voice of warning shall be unto all people, by the mouths of my disciples, whom I have chosen in these last days" (D&C 1:1–2, 4).

In 1834, with Church membership near four thousand, Joseph Smith told a small gathering of priesthood brethren: "I want to say to you before the Lord, that you know no more concerning the destinies of this church and kingdom than a babe upon its mother's lap. You don't comprehend it. It is only a little handful of Priesthood you see here tonight, but this church will fill North and South America—it will fill the world."[6]

The formation of the Church and the beginning of missionary work were almost simultaneous. Samuel Smith, brother of Joseph, was the first missionary. In April 1830, shortly after the Church was organized, he filled a knapsack with copies of the Book of Mormon and traveled from community to community in upstate New York introducing the book and the story of the Restoration.[7]

The tiny seed planted in upstate New York has now spread to more than 160 countries. How has that happened? Truth and righteousness are sweeping the earth in three phases. The first is missionary work, which introduces the gospel. With success, small branches are formed with limited priesthood keys. As the Church grows in an area, branches become wards, which then become stakes. Stakes represent the second phase. Stakes are centers of strength and denote additional priesthood keys. The presence of a stake indicates that the gospel has taken root and a mature membership exists. Temples represent the third phase. A temple in an area signifies a number of stakes within close proximity and a spiritual maturity worthy of higher ordinances and covenants.

Temples in the Latter Days

The highest ordinances and covenants available to God's children are given only in buildings dedicated as houses of the Lord. President Hinckley has announced that there will be at least one hundred operating temples at the end of the year 2000.

Of the temple ordinances, President Brigham Young said: "To accomplish this work there will have to be not only one temple but thousands of them, and thousands and tens of thousands of men and women will go into those temples and officiate for people who have lived as far back as the Lord shall reveal."[8] For years I thought President Young's statement would be fulfilled in the Millennium. Perhaps it will, but we are living in a day when it has become apparent that thousands of temples will dot the earth.

I recall sitting in the upper room of the Salt Lake Temple in March 1996 during a general authority meeting. The Church was preparing to dedicate its fiftieth operating temple after 166 years of this dispensation. At the end of the meeting, President Gordon B. Hinckley stated that he hoped there would be at least one hundred temples operating before he completed his ministry. I sat there stunned. He was in his eighty-sixth year. It had taken 166 years for the first fifty temples. How could another fifty temples be built in the remaining years of his life?

About eighteen months later, in another meeting in the Salt Lake Temple, President Hinckley revealed the concept of the small temple. On a long summer trip returning from the Mormon colonies in Mexico, he learned through revelation how small temples should be constructed. The temples would be of the finest materials and constructed to last for hundreds of years. Many of them would be built next to stake centers in fulfillment of Doctrine and Covenants 124:36, which associates temple work and stakes. In the year 2000, we stand on the summit of the centuries and can view the Lord's miracle of the last 170 years. Where will it go from here? Again we turn to the Prophet Joseph Smith for the answer: "No unhallowed hand can stop the work from progressing; persecutions may rage, mobs may combine, armies may assemble, calumny may defame, but the truth of God will go forth boldly, nobly, and independent, till it has penetrated every continent, visited every clime, swept every country, and sounded in every ear, till the purposes of God shall be accomplished, and the Great Jehovah shall say the work is done."[9]

Joseph's words will be fulfilled. Truth and righteousness are sweeping the earth, evidenced by the spread of missionary work, the formation of stakes, and the building of temples. May the Lord bless us that we may be faithful participants in his great work.

Notes

1. Rodney Stark, as cited in Carrie A. Moore, "Pres. Hinckley Wants Temples Just a Day Away," *Deseret News*, 6 October 2000, A1.

2. Wendy L. Watson, as quoted in Sarah Jane Weaver, "BYU Women's Conference Expected to Attract 30,000," *Church News*, 1 April 2000.

3. LDS Bible Dictionary, s.v. "Mark," 728.

4. *The World Book Encyclopedia*, 26 vols. (Chicago: Field Enterprises Educational Corp., 1974), s.v. "Thomas," 19:201.

5. Franklin Hamblin Littell, *The Macmillan Atlas History of Christianity* (New York: Macmillan, 1976), 12.

6. Joseph Smith Jr., as quoted by Wilford Woodruff, Conference Report, April 1898, 57.

7. *Encyclopedia of Mormonism*, 4 vols. (New York: MacMillan, 1992), s.v. "missions," 2:916. One book sold to Phineas Young was passed on to his father, sister, and then to his brother, Brigham. In 1832, after two years of study and soul-searching, Brigham, moved by the testimony of a Mormon elder, joined the Church. For an overview of the spread of missionary work in the last days, see *Encyclopedia of Mormonism*, s.v. "Young, Brigham"; Bruce A. Van Orden, *Building Zion: The Latter-day Saints in Europe* (Salt Lake City: Deseret Book, 1993); and R. Lanier Britsch, *Unto the Islands of the Sea* (Salt Lake City: Deseret Book Company, 1986).

8. *Discourses of Brigham Young*, sel. John A. Widtsoe (Salt Lake City: Deseret Book, 1954), 394.

9. Joseph Smith Jr., *History of The Church of Jesus Christ of Latter-day Saints*, ed. B. H. Roberts, 7 vols. 2d ed. rev. (Salt Lake City: The Church of Jesus Christ of Latter-day Saints, 1932–51), 4:540.

"FOR THEY THAT ARE WISE"

❧

Jolene Merica

My thoughts on parenting are positioned within a parable that has come to symbolize my hopes and dreams not only for myself but also for my children. In thirteen short verses in the book of Matthew, we find the account of the ten virgins. "And five of them were wise, and five were foolish" (Matthew 25:2). Given by the Savior during his mortal ministry, the parable of the ten virgins teaches of his second coming, the coming we await and are hopefully anxiously engaged in preparing for. A large part of my preparation for his coming is in the rearing of righteous sons—sons only because that is what I have been blessed with. In rearing these sons, I have at times been foolish, and I have at times been wise.

I

I have been a foolish virgin when I have allowed others to convince me that I parent alone; I am wise when I truly understand that the Lord "will be on [my] right hand and on [my] left," that his spirit will be in my heart and his "angels round about [me] to bear [me] up" (D&C 84:88).

One day as I graded papers, the words in a student's essay, *coming from a broken home*, jumped out at me. I spoke with the student and asked her to help me understand her use of the phrase "broken home." She explained that a text in another class described homes with only one parent as broken. My student had been offended, angered by this

---

Jolene Merica is a program administrator for BYU Conferences and Workshops. She is parenting singly her two sons and teaches Sunday School in her ward.

negative label that others used to describe her reality, yet at the same time she had chosen this same phrase to describe her family to me. I wondered if my own children viewed our home as broken. I wondered at the power of a phrase to label my reality.

The phrase "broken home" emphasizes what a home is missing, overlooking the fact that even the presence of two parents does not assure wholeness. "Brokenness" is a label unworthy of our adoption. I also dislike the label "single parent." Women who introduce themselves as *single* parents, limit themselves. As President Gordon B. Hinckley has said: "Somehow we have put a badge on this large group. It reads 'singles.' I wish we would not do that. You are individuals, men and women, sons and daughters of God, not a mass of 'look-alikes' or 'do-alikes.' Because you do not happen to be married does not make you essentially different from others."[1]

Single parent implies difference for me, so I choose to describe my situation as *parenting singly*. In using this term I am defining not what I am but how I do things. Parenting singly does not imply being less than whole but rather states how I am accomplishing my stewardship as a parent. I parent singly. But, even with this enlightened taxonomy, I err. Heavenly Father has taught me that even though I have not had a partner in the rearing of my sons, I have *never* been alone. He has surrounded me with a wonderful family and ward; he has encircled me in his arms (D&C 6:20) and enabled me to deal with the stresses of rearing children, working, and furthering my education. My reliance on my Father in Heaven and my Savior Jesus Christ has helped me to see that *single parenting* is a phenomenon experienced by those who've lost their faith in God. It is through my faith in God that I have been able to move beyond coping, to creating the kind of life that will put my family on the straight and narrow path. I trust in the words of Paul that the trials of our faith are "more precious than of gold" (1 Peter 1:7) and in the counsel of the great prophet Alma to his son Helaman "that whosoever shall put their trust in God shall be supported in their trials, and their troubles, and their afflictions, and shall be lifted up at the last day" (Alma 36:3).

The Lord has given us a remedy for loneliness and self-pity: "Wherefore, my beloved brethren [and sisters], pray unto the Father with all the energy of heart, that ye may be filled with this love" (Moroni 7:48). By asking to feel and be filled with the love of our Father in Heaven and our Savior Jesus Christ, we are less likely to fall prey to the adversary, who would have us believe that in our parenting and in our individual lives we have been left alone. In asking to feel the love of God, we receive his assurance that we are not alone, that he reaches our reaching, that with him all things are possible.

II

I have been like a foolish virgin in my attempts to control my children's choices; I have been wise in trying to allow them their right to choose.

In 2 Nephi, Lehi teaches his children: "For there is a God, and he hath created all things, both the heavens and the earth, and all things that in them are, both things to act and things to be acted upon. . . . Wherefore, the Lord God gave unto man that he should act for himself. Wherefore, man could not act for himself save it should be that he was enticed by the one or the other" (2 Nephi 2:14, 16).

Some of the most important concepts our children can ever learn are how to act and what to do when acted upon. In the Doctrine and Covenants we read, "It must needs be that the devil should tempt the children of men [meaning my children as well as yours], or they could not be agents unto themselves; for if they never should have bitter they could not know the sweet" (D&C 29:39). If we speak to our children for their profit and learning, we will teach them that "being enticed," being tempted, is an integral part of God's eternal plan. When our children, or we ourselves, are bombarded by the darts of the adversary (1 Nephi 15:24; D&C 3:8), we need to remember that our response to bitterness makes possible an eternal sweet.

The scriptures are clear about the necessity of opposition in our lives, and children seem to understand this bittersweet concept. Equally understood is the principle of being agents unto themselves.

While one of my greatest roles as a parent is to guide my children as they learn to be agents, one of my greatest struggles as a parent is allowing them to choose.

Several weeks ago as we sat down to dinner, my sons complained about what I had prepared. Irritated at their pickiness, I said what any good mother would say: "If I hear one more complaint, you will leave this table and have nothing to eat for the rest of the day." Silence. Then the process of labored eating began—a fork in one hand and a glass of water in the other. The short-lived silence was broken when my fourteen-year-old announced that he was going to write a book entitled *Growing Up in a Communist House* or *My Mother, the Communist.* My parenting style was being likened to a political system where the equal distribution of economic goods is achieved by "dictatorial means."[2] In this case, both boys were being required to eat an undesirable entree!

Trying not to laugh, I asked exactly what he meant by *communist.* My twelve-year-old replied, "Well, we have no free will." While I know this dinner conversation was in jest and that many foods have become favorites as the result of communistic table tactics, I couldn't help but reflect on the times when in an effort to push my children along the straight and narrow path, I have made dictatorial decisions that have overridden their agency.

Granted there are times when, as parents, we are required to override personal choice for the safety and protection of a child. At other times, however, we have to allow a child freedom to choose—*without* allowing them freedom from the consequences of their choices. Overriding a child to protect him is easy; meting out consequences with consistency is more tough; but actually allowing a child to choose is often most difficult.

I learned firsthand about overriding a child's choice when my youngest son was awarded an honorable mention in an essay contest. He had written the essay while I was away on a trip and had refused his grandmother's offer to act as an editor. This truly was his work. Being the proud parent that I can sometimes be, I volunteered my son to read

his essay in Relief Society. When I informed him of this great opportunity, he said he wouldn't do it. I told him he had to read his essay
because the Relief Society instructor was counting on him, and I had
promised that he would. With tears in his eyes, he looked at me and
said, "But Mom, you stole my choice."

On the following Sunday, my son sat silently by my side awaiting
his part in the lesson. Halfway through the reading of his first page, he
broke into tears. I left my chair on the front row and stood behind him
at the podium. I asked if I could read his essay for him. He shook his
head no, choked back his tears, and finished reading as fast as he could.
We left the Relief Society room together, and the weight of my taking
away his choice was heavy on my mind. I gave him a hug, asked if he
was all right, and offered to take him home. He opted to go to Primary;
and as he left me in the hallway said, "Mom, it's hard to be the only
guy in a room." It is hard to stand alone. It's also hard to be a mother
who realizes she did something a heavenly parent would never do—
take away one's right to choose.

III

I have been a foolish virgin in my attempts to solve my children's
problems and provide all the answers; I have been wise in encouraging
them to ask, to seek, and to find.

"What things soever ye desire, when ye pray, believe that ye
receive them, and ye shall have them" (Mark 11:24).

C. S. Lewis wrote the following about this passage: "The New
Testament contains embarrassing promises that what we pray for with
faith we shall receive. Mark 11:24 is the most staggering. Whatever we
ask for, believing that we'll get it, we'll get. No question, it seems, of
confining it to spiritual gifts; *whatever* we ask for. No question of a
merely general faith in God, but a belief that you will get the particular
thing you ask."[3]

Lewis concluded that such answers to prayer—getting whatever is
asked for—come only to the most believing, requiring a faith that few
can attain. My own personal testimony, having "tried the experiment,

and planted the seed" (Alma 32:33), is that receiving answers to prayer, receiving personal revelation, is not held for the few, but is available to all who are willing to ask.

In 1835, Bronson Alcott, father of *Little Women* author Louisa May Alcott, founded the Temple School in Boston. Alcott engaged his young students, ranging in ages from five to twelve, in weekly conversations on the four Gospels. The following discussion took place after the students had read a passage in the book of John:

Mr. Alcott: Where did Jesus get his knowledge? . . .

[Student]:   Jesus knew what was in man, because God told him.

Mr. Alcott: In a different way from what he tells you?

[Student]:   No; but Jesus was better, and God told him more.

Mr. Alcott: Does God's telling depend on you or on God?

[Student]:   God tells us all we ought to know always.[4]

Both this master teacher's question ("Does God's telling depend on you or on God?") and his pupil's insightful answer ("God tells us all we ought to know always") teach important eternal truths. In the April 2000 general conference, President Boyd K. Packer taught that our ability to receive promptings from the Holy Ghost "is awakened with prayer and cultivated 'by obedience to the laws and ordinances of the Gospel.'"[5] God's telling does depend on us. Does "God tell us all we ought to know always?" President Packer recently encouraged young adults in the Church to "begin asking for the gift of the Holy Ghost." He shared how the scriptures contain more than seven hundred admonitions to ask. "The message that is most repeated in all revelation is said in many ways but said simply 'Ask and ye shall receive.'"[6]

Our Heavenly Father will tell us all things, and his telling depends not only on our personal righteousness but also on our willingness to ask. One of my greatest challenges as a parent is teaching my children not only how to "ask" but also how to discern what it is they have received. Both asking and discerning involve internal, private processes that are not readily seen.

I received a potted plant for Mother's Day several years ago.

I admired my small son's artwork on the pot and asked for an interpretation. He pointed out a campfire, a tent, and me scaling what appeared to be the Swiss Alps. While I occasionally speak of my love for mountains and hiking, I was touched by a small son's ability to capture a passion that is talked about but rarely seen. Children do learn through example, but this simple gift taught me that children also internalize even our most briefly expressed hopes and dreams. Each time I water this plant, I reflect upon the message of the pot. Can simple expressions of how I involve the Spirit in my life leave mountain-like impressions?

While I was preparing this essay, my boys continually checked on my progress, asking, "Mom, how is it coming?" During one such progress interview, I skirted their question and asked, "Do you know how I'll make my presentation better?" One of my son's experiences in writing led him to answer, "Well, in writing and rewriting and rewriting." I affirmed his comment, then pointed my finger up toward the sky. What followed was a short, but understanding reply, "Ohhh, the Lord." My son left the room; end of interruption—or a teaching moment disguised as an interruption.

This brief conversation allowed me to spread some eternal seeds; but merely acknowledging my willingness to ask will not be enough to swell, sprout, and grow the seeds. I constantly seek moments to share with my sons how I try to allow the Holy Ghost to be my guide.

A minor misdemeanor with honesty provided one such opportunity. The guilty party was called in for a chat, we reviewed the steps of the repentance process, and I told him I needed some time to decide what the consequence package would contain. Fortunately we were charting new territory, so I didn't have a solution already in the bag. I sat down at my desk and made a list of possible consequences. Items at the top of the list were rather severe, but my anger seemed to flow out and away through my pen. As I continued to brainstorm, the severity of my ideas ebbed. At twenty-five possible punishments, I had partially reestablished my emotional equilibrium. With my pet punishments selected—the most severe on the list, of course—I was ready to act as judge and jury. I wanted this to be a lesson my son would grow old telling his children about, if, in fact, he ever grew old!

Knowing that those in heaven had a keen interest in this young man who was about to feel the wrath of a telestially tormented mother, I prayed to my Heavenly Father to know the right course of action. I started at the top of my list and asked, "Is this an appropriate punishment?" I did not feel the Spirit in the way he most often communicates with me. This stupor was, in and of itself, my answer; but I wanted to make sure I hadn't "heard" incorrectly. So, I rephrased the question and asked, "This isn't an appropriate punishment?" Wham! I received a strong confirmation of the Spirit that my most severe, my most prized, punishment had just fallen out of the top twenty-five. I proceeded to ask about each item on the list, allowing the Spirit to guide me to the action my Father in Heaven would have me take. In the end, only three of my twenty-five punishments remained; and as you can probably guess, a loving Heavenly Father was much kinder than a mother with telestial vision.

I called my son in to discuss the consequences of his choice, and I shared with him the list of potential punishments, the majority of which had lines drawn through them. I explained how I had asked the Lord to help me know what would best teach this important lesson in honesty. I shared my process of asking specific questions that required yes or no answers. A yes answer acknowledged by a confirmation from the Holy Ghost in the way he manifests himself to me; a no answer resulting in a stupor of thought or no clear sense of direction. We then talked about how my son feels the Spirit and ended this teaching moment with the charge for him to experiment with the process and allow the Holy Ghost to be his guide.

This first lesson, and all that have followed since, cannot make my sons ask. My hope, however, is that with review, they will remember in times when they "are tempted to make the wrong choice" to take a moment and ask, "Is this an appropriate action?" If they don't receive a confirmation from the Holy Ghost in the way the Spirit speaks to them, they will know they can rephrase the question and ask, "Is this not an appropriate action?"

If our children see our trust in the Lord and our willingness to lean on him instead of our own understanding (Proverbs 3:5), they will be more willing to put their trust in him. The process of taking the Holy Spirit for our guide is not easy. Elder Neal A. Maxwell helps us understand why: "When we speak about teaching by the Spirit it is not about a mystical process which removes responsibility from the missionary or teacher [and I'll add parent] for prayerful and pondering preparation. Teaching by the Spirit [learning by the Spirit] is not the lazy equivalent of going on 'automatic pilot.' We still need a carefully worked out 'flight plan.' Studying out something in one's own mind is, in itself, an invitation to the Spirit in our preparations as well as in our presentations. We must not err, like Oliver Cowdery, by taking no thought except to ask God for His Spirit (D&C 9:7). The Lord is especially willing to take the lead of an already informed mind in which things have been 'studied out.'"[7]

I wish I always had the Spirit and that I was always willing to ask. But I am not. My desires to do my will, instead of the will of the Father, often prevent his companionship. I know that the Holy Ghost can show us *all* things that we should do (2 Nephi 32:5), whether it be at home or at work or at school. But first we must study things out in our minds, come to a decision, and then ask for a confirmation of the Spirit. We must *do* this, not just talk about it. I cannot imprint my children, without first being imprinted myself.

IV

"They that were foolish took their lamps, and took no oil with them: [they that were wise] took oil in their vessels with their lamps" (Matthew 25:3).

We are like the wise virgins when we set aside the world's labels and fill our hearts with the love of God. We are like wise virgins as we come to understand agency and our tendency as parents to control our children's choices. Further, we contribute to the wisdom of our children by teaching them how to seek the Spirit and take him as their guide.

Brigham Young University professor Joseph Fielding McConkie explains, "In the parable of the ten virgins, the five virgins who are pre-pared to meet the bridegroom are those whose lamps are full of oil, or whose lives are full of the Holy Ghost. These are they who are 'wise and have received the truth, and have taken the Holy Spirit for their guide' (D&C 45:56–57; Matt. 25:1–13)."[8]

In understanding this parable's representation of the Holy Ghost as oil, we see anew the importance of teaching our children about this most precious gift. Just as the wise virgins could not share their oil with the foolish ones, we cannot give our gift of the Holy Ghost to our chil-dren. But, we can share the light that his presence brings. We can use the Holy Ghost as our guide and assist our children in trimming their lamps.

We live in a world where almost everything is fueled by self-interest and self-gratification—agency gone awry. As we teach agency to our children, it must be coupled with a knowledge that we are here to do the will of the Father, to help bring about Zion, to see if we will not only be agents unto ourselves but, more important, unto God.

The parable of the ten virgins tells of the second coming of Christ. If our lamps are not trimmed, if our children's lamps are not trimmed, burning brightly with oil, we will not be ready to meet the Bridegroom.

"And at that day, when I shall come in my glory, shall the parable be fulfilled which I spake concerning the ten virgins.

"For they that are wise and have received the truth, and have taken the Holy Spirit for their guide, and have not been deceived—verily I say unto you, they shall not be hewn down and cast into the fire, but shall abide the day" (D&C 45:56–57).

The oil in the virgins' lamps represents the Spirit that must fill each of us, so that Christ's Spirit may in turn fill the earth. Not until we are filled will we be able to arise and shine forth that our lights and the lights of our children may be standards to the nations.

Notes

1. Gordon B. Hinckley, as quoted in Kellene Ricks, "Reach Out to Others, LDS Singles Urged," *Church News*, 4 March 1989.
2. *Webster's New World Dictionary*, 3d College Ed. (New York: Simon & Schuster, 1994).
3. C. S. Lewis, *The Joyful Christian: 127 Readings*, 1st Touchstone ed. (1977; reprint, New York: Simon & Schuster, 1996), 95–96.
4. A. Bronson Alcott, *How Like an Angel Came I Down: Conversations with Children on the Gospels* (Hudson, N.Y.: Lindisfarne Press, 1991), 180.
5. Boyd K. Packer, "The Cloven Tongues of Fire," *Ensign*, May 2000, 9.
6. Boyd K. Packer, CES Fireside, quoted in Emily Cannon, "Elder Packer Urges Young LDS to Understand Gift of the Holy Ghost," BYU NewsNet, 5 March 2000, Provo, Utah.
7. Neal A. Maxwell, *The Neal A. Maxwell Quote Book*, ed. Cory H. Maxwell (Salt Lake City: Bookcraft, 1997), 337–38.
8. Joseph Fielding McConkie and Donald W. Parry, *A Guide to Scriptural Symbols* (Salt Lake City: Bookcraft, 1990), s.v. "olive oil."

WHO SWEEPS A ROOM

❦

Nancy Young

My husband once paid me a compliment that I am sure could be said of any Latter-day Saint woman. As I recall, I was headed off to run some errands. Al wondered how long I would be gone, and with my characteristic sense of time I said, "an hour," which generally means three. "Please don't be gone very long," he said. "When you leave, so does home."

Almost two thousand years ago, in a tender and telling New Testament story, the Savior taught us of the magical nature of home as he created for his disciples an impromptu refuge on an obscure shore. This very familiar story takes place at that critical period when the disciples experienced not only the unprecedented agony of Gethsemane and the betrayal and crucifixion but the unspeakable joy of embracing the resurrected Lord.

What happens now? seems to have been the pervasive atmosphere of their world. A little lost, they returned to the pursuits and prospects they had left, without a backward glance, three years before. "Peter saith unto them, I go a fishing. They say unto him, We also go with thee. They went forth, and entered into a ship immediately; and that night they caught nothing" (John 21:3).

Imagine the weariness and discouragement of men whose arms have cast and recast nets, only to draw them back empty again and again. Famished and exhausted, they headed back towards shore. "But when the morning was now come, Jesus stood on the shore: but the disciples knew not that it was Jesus. Then Jesus saith unto them,

---

Nancy Young is a wife, mother, and homemaker. She and her husband, the artist and writer Al Young, are the parents of three children. She serves as a Sunday School teacher in her ward.

Children, have ye any meat? They answered him, No. And he said unto them, Cast the net on the right side of the ship, and ye shall find. They cast therefore, and now they were not able to draw it for the multitude of fishes. Therefore that disciple whom Jesus loved saith unto Peter, It is the Lord. Now when Simon Peter heard that it was the Lord, he girt his fisher's coat unto him, . . . and did cast himself into the sea. And the other disciples came in a little ship, . . . dragging the net with fishes. As soon then as they were come to land, they saw a fire of coals there, and fish laid thereon, and bread. . . . Jesus saith unto them, Come and dine. . . . Jesus then cometh, and taketh bread, and giveth them, and fish likewise" (John 21:4–9, 12–13).

While the disciples were struggling and striving, wavering between hope and despair, the Savior of the world was creating a little, temporary home for them—a place where they could be refreshed and renewed, and later instructed. It was a home first and foremost because he was there. It was a home, too, because like a loving wife or mother, he was considering their needs and pleasures, their comforts and joys—and meting his services to their heartaches and yearnings.

I am reminded of the account of Elrond's house from the stories of Tolkien: "His house was perfect, whether you liked food, or sleep, or work, or story-telling, or singing, or just sitting and thinking best, or a pleasant mixture of them all. Evil things did not come into that valley.

"I wish I had time to tell you even a few of the tales or one or two of the songs they heard in that house. All of them . . . grew refreshed and strong in a few days there. Their clothes were mended as well as their bruises, their tempers and their hopes. Their bags were filled with provisions light to carry but strong to bring them over the mountain passes. Their plans were improved with the best advice."[1]

The Savior's little home on that shore also puts me in mind of the sweet homemaker's verse: "All day I did the little things, the little things that do not show; I brought the kindling for the fire, I put the candles in a row, I filled a bowl with marigolds, the shallow bowl you love the best—and made the house a pleasant place where weariness might take its rest."[2]

The meal the Savior prepared for his disciples was a simple one. Have you ever wondered at that? This was, after all, the resurrected Lord. He could have produced any food from any corner of the planet and from any period of time. It could have been paté, peach cobbler, or pressed duck. Instead, the risen Christ—with hands bearing our wounds—prepared a sweet, simple, familiar meal for his weary followers. And it is upon the simplicity of that meal that I would like to focus particularly. For the Lord was celebrating something we seem to avoid in our culture; he was celebrating the mundane, the repetitive, the ritual.

In a recent essay, Pacific News Service journalist Richard Rodriguez observed that troops returning from the Second World War came home "famished, . . . not for a hero's parade of tape and confetti—but famished for the mundane."[3] There is great reassurance for us and for our loved ones in the mundane rituals of our everyday lives. They truly are one eternal round. They always lead us back—we know how to begin and we are reassured to know where they will end. They free our minds to meditate and ponder. They include the sights, sounds, and smells that recall for us our sweetest sensations and dearest emotions.

So often the mundane consists of things that virtually everyone can afford, yet things that make us feel rich—flowers from the garden, tomatoes from the vine, bread from the oven, kisses from toddlers, and words from the scriptures.

Laura Fronty said of her French grandmother: "My childhood home was the home of a woman with a genius for inventing daily life, who found happiness in the simplest of gestures."[4]

Somewhere along the way, we have lost that sense of honor and privilege in serving those within our own homes. We have failed to "[find] happiness in the simplest of gestures"—changing sheets, plumping cushions, polishing silver, or dusting cookies with powdered sugar.

My own Swiss mother tells of the women of her small town cleaning house, then getting flowers each Saturday in the open-air markets so that their homes could be delightful and fresh in honor of the Sabbath.

One of my greatest heroes from the Old Testament was such a homemaker. Referred to simply as "the Shunammite," she used her wealth to create a wonderful room for the prophet Elisha—a home where he could stay whenever he passed through her city. She entreated her husband: "Let us make a little chamber, I pray thee, on the wall; and let us set for him there a bed, and a table, and a stool, and a candlestick: and it shall be, that when he cometh to us, that he shall turn in thither" (2 Kings 4:10).

This account is remarkable for several reasons. The furnishings of the room tell of thoughtful comforts; what we would probably call "a genius for everyday living." The "little chamber on the wall" was generally the best room in the house because it was above the noise and dirt of the street, and was somewhat open to catch the breezes. Biblical scholars tell us that the term "stool" may perhaps be better translated as "throne." And the table and candlestick provided Elisha a comfortable place to eat and study, as well as a sense of independence and privacy.

At our home, we have attempted to implement the Shunammite's plan for virtually every room in our house. The approach is a simple one but provides pleasure. Whatever the primary function of a room—be it a kitchen, a study, or a bedroom—we try to add those same elements: a place to eat, a place to study and write, and a comfortable place to read. Because the approach is not costly, it has endured, particularly since most of our treasures have come to us because they were another's castoffs. But it makes rooms comfortable and welcoming.

Another remarkable aspect of this Old Testament story is that the Shunammite seems to have turned to the temple for at least some of her inspiration. The defining elements of the sanctuary in Solomon's Temple were precisely tables and candlesticks.

We too can benefit from turning to the temple as we make our homes. Much could be said about this, but I would like to dwell on just one way home may be like the temple. One of the great blessings of frequent temple attendance is the sense of what President Ezra Taft

Benson called being "unrushed."[5] The temple beckons us not to rush, sometimes in a way that feels almost unnatural in our harried existence. The temple slows us to the cadences of heaven. The rituals performed there are done thoughtfully and mindfully. Dignity and meaning pervade the simplest of acts.

We can draw heaven closer by approaching the rituals of home in the same manner.

I am a youngest child; therefore, I learned to bathe a baby, not from watching younger brothers or sisters being bathed, but from watching my mother bathe and dress my own newborns. Every motion she performed was purposeful and loving. The method and care were precise and repeatable. There was no rush. There were no phones, doorbells, or news stories. There was time for each element: from washing hair and lotioning toes, to dressing the baby in something fresh and sweet and new.

So many acts in our home can bear the stamp of loving care and mindfulness; and our hearts and spirits can be refreshed and blessed by such service. Anthony Lawlor says it this way in *A Home for the Soul:* "The most immediate way of deepening soulfulness in a home is through cleaning and repair. Housework, however, is denigrated in our society, and we usually overlook the power of purification and maintenance in fostering soul. The intent of most spiritual practices, in fact, is the transformation of disorder into order. . . . The word *cleaning* conveys this spiritual connotation. The roots of the word *clean* suggest the purity conferred by a ceremonial anointing with oil. Cleaning in this sense bestows a blessing on a house or apartment. It makes whole the life of the house."[6]

"Who sweeps a room as for Thy law, makes it and th' action fine."[7] Or expressed in a more earthy way, "You can praise God by peeling a spud, if you do it to perfection."[8]

Perfection, however, is a sticky wicket. I have visited many model homes over the years. They are generally impressive, sometimes downright intimidating. Their beauty, however, often arises from the fact that they are not lived in. My favorite homes are beautiful precisely because they are lived in. Like a variation on the Shaker proverb, "If you would have a lovely home, live a lovely life."

A lived-in home will never be perfect in the sense of a model home. Things are in flux; there is always something to be done, or something to be done better. In this regard, we do well to remember that the Savior was not correcting Martha because she loved order and was careful, nor was he commending Mary because she was a slovenly intellectual. What Mary possessed was the gift of being present to the moment. As the Lord pointed out, it would "not be taken away from her" because she was experiencing a fleeting moment to its fullest and creating an eternal memory (Luke 10:38–42).

Anthony Lawlor emphasizes this idea: "Cleaning does not imply the compulsive work of creating a sterile environment. It is the artful care of objects that supports the needs and dreams of the soul, as this story about the Japanese tea master Sen no Rikyu implies. One day Rikyu asked his son Do-an to clean the path leading through the tea garden. Do-an swept and scrubbed each stepping-stone with the greatest of care and then asked his father to inspect the work. 'Not complete' was the master's response. Do-an repeated the task with even greater mindfulness until each speck of dust and pine needle was washed away. He called his father a second time to look over his work, and again it was not accepted. After a third cleaning, Do-an was certain that the path was in perfect condition, but [his father] just shook his head. In desperation the son threw up his hands and shouted, 'Well, you show me how to do it, then!' The tea master walked to a small maple tree near the path, grabbed the trunk, and gave it a vigorous shake. A rain of autumn leaves sprinkled the path with an array of dazzling colors. 'Now the garden is perfect,' he said."[9]

And so, returning to the Old Testament and the Shunammite woman's preparations for Elisha, we read Elisha's awe-struck response: "Thou hast been careful for us with all this care" (2 Kings 4:13).

When I ponder Elisha's exclamation, I think of the Victorian and Edwardian children's books our family loves to read and their descriptions of "careful care." There is in those stories from another time and place a sense of preciousness and delight in blessing the lives of others—especially children. The feelings I experience in reading those descriptions of careful care remind me of a delightful couplet from John Masefield: "And he who gives a child a treat makes joy-bells ring in Heaven's street."[10]

I recall the accounts of Bobbie's birthday party in *The Railway Children*, Mole's comfortable home from *The Wind in the Willows*, Rebecca's white muslin graduation dress in *Rebecca of Sunnybrook Farm*, the description of Elnora Comstock's lunchbox and its contents from *A Girl of the Limberlost*. These and dozens more speak volumes about loving, careful care and the joy of creating it.

I also think of how the Shunammite shared in the actions of heaven as she bestowed "tender mercies" on Elisha and his servant. Recently I had to find a way to reduce that phrase "tender mercies" to its most basic any-child-could-comprehend-it elements. *Tender* comes from the Latin verb "to stretch"—hence the concept of reaching forth, such as tendering change, or tendering a resignation. There is also the concept of stretching until something is delicate as well as vulnerable. Even used as an adjective, some of the meaning of the verb root lingers in the idea of tenderness: reaching forth, delicate, vulnerable.

In speaking of *mercy*, we could speak of such sophisticated concepts as clemency and justice, but reduced to its simplest form, mercy is simply being kinder than what's required. The Shunammite was already feeding the prophet whenever he came to her city. It was not incumbent on her to lodge him in a room kept ever ready for that sole purpose. She was stretching forth delicate kindnesses, far greater than what might have been required. She was giving her cloak, as well as her coat, and cheerfully spanning the second mile.

I know your lives are filled with similar "tender mercies." You are the women who, though bone-tired, tuck a child in and tell a story; who take to a recuperating neighbor a better meal than you will eat yourself; who purchase for your daughter the new sweater you'd like to have; who mend hearts while yours is breaking.

Perhaps, in fact, you feel that it is your arms that ache from forever casting and recasting nets, and who are weary and hollow. Such feelings come. My sister is the mother of five boys, and there are days—not a few—when she raises her hand and in her best playground holler cries out, "I choose not to be the mother today!" On such days, the remedy is the same: look to the Savior, cast in our nets one more time on the right side, and commence pulling up blessings so great we may not be able to draw them in, but must drag them to the feet of the Savior to thank and bless him.

Such was the fate of the Shunammite. The full text of Elisha's exclamation is: "Behold, thou hast been careful for us with all this care; what is to be done for thee?" (2 Kings 4:13). She asks for nothing but is blessed with everything. She is barren, yet within a year she and her good husband are blessed with a son. The son dies as a child. Elisha responds to her pleas and literally breathes life back into him. A famine comes to Israel. Elisha warns the Shunammite to flee with her household. She removes to Philistia for the seven years of the famine. When she returns to Shunem, although her lands have become confiscate to the crown, the king restores her property as well as everything that would have grown on her land during her absence.

Now, may I conclude with an observation from one of our favorite books, *Mother Carey's Chickens*. This delightful story by Kate Douglas Wiggin includes this phrase: "One real home always makes others, I am sure of that!"[11]

Our Heavenly Father prepares a heavenly home for us, while we wander and wonder here below. While we labor in weariness upon the darkness of the deep, he prepares our exquisite rest. He fills that future home with every comfort and with every joy. And to guide us on our homeward way, he sent his Son to show us how to succor those we love. Like the Savior, the touch of our hands can make even the simple splendid. Our presence can define home.

One real home always makes another, *I* am sure of that.

Notes

1. J. R. R. Tolkien, *The Hobbit*; rev. ed. (New York: Ballantine, 1937), 61.

2. Blanche Bane Kuder, "The Blue Bowl," in *The Best Loved Poems of the American People*, sel. Hazel Felleman (Garden City, N.Y.: Doubleday & Company, 1936), 376; line breaks and capitalization omitted.

3. Richard Rodriguez, quoted in "A Tale of Time," Online NewsHour, 30 December 1999, http://www./pbs.org/newshour/essays/2000_essays/Rodriguez_2000.html

4. Laura Fronty, quoted in "Old Fashioned Advice: Good and Simple," *Victoria* 14, no. 1 (January 2000): 67.

5. Ezra Taft Benson, *Come, Listen to a Prophet's Voice* (Salt Lake City: Deseret Book, 1990), 32.

6. Anthony Lawlor, *A Home for the Soul: A Guide for Dwelling with Spirit and Imagination* (New York: Clarkson Potter, 1997), 38.

7. George Herbert, "The Elixir," quoted in *Dictionary of Quotations*, ed. Alison Jones (New York: Chambers, 1997), 475.

8. *Chariots of Fire*, dir. Hugh Hudson, written by Colin Welland, Warner Bros. Film, 1981.

9. Lawlor, *A Home for the Soul*, 41.

10. John Masefield, "The Everlasting Mercy," in *Poems* (New York: Macmillan, 1913), 98; line break and capitalization omitted.

11. Kate Douglas Wiggin, *Mother Carey's Chickens* (New York: Grosset & Dunlap, 1910), 139.

SUPPER WITH MEATLOAF AND MORONI

꒜ꕥ꒪

Stephen D. Nadauld and Margaret D. Nadauld

SDN: Who hasn't wanted to be better at working with and understanding young people, at teaching and touching the hearts and lives of children, especially in the vulnerable teenage years?

MDN: Today's children face such major issues as changing gender roles; preparing for future responsibilities; moral purity; peer pressure; modesty in behavior, speech, and appearance; and staying close to family and the Church. Our children can be stronger if we help them know where to find encouragement and strength to face their challenges. We want to focus on four important sources available to them: doctrine and principles, parents, leaders, and the Lord.

LOOK TO DOCTRINE AND PRINCIPLES

SDN: First, our children can find strength and safety in doctrine and true principles. Elder Boyd K. Packer has observed, "True doctrine, understood, changes attitudes and behaviors."[1]

Margaret D. Nadauld and Stephen D. Nadauld are the parents of seven and grandparents of five. Margaret serves as the Young Women General President and is a member of the board of trustees of Brigham Young University. She has taught high school English and served as a member of the Relief Society General Board. Stephen, a former member of the Second Quorum of the Seventy and the Young Men General Presidency, is a professor at the Marriott School of Management at Brigham Young University. He is an author, speaker, business consultant, and former president of Weber State University in Ogden, Utah.

Today's young people were once mature spirits. They have been taught by God himself, and it wasn't that long ago. They don't need any more fluff and nonsense in their lives; the world already gives them more than they need. What they can use is a better understanding of gospel truths. As President J. Reuben Clark said many years ago, they "are hungry for the things of the spirit; they are eager to learn the Gospel, and they want it straight, undiluted.

" . . . You do not have to sneak up behind [them] and whisper religion in [their] ears. . . . You can bring these truths [out] openly."[2]

Most children want to be successful. They want to be respected, have influence, and amount to something. In an age of situational ethics, of microwave, pushbutton, and instant everything, with books promising quick fixes to every problem, teens can easily become confused about life's best processes. They need to be taught to look to doctrine and principles for strength, power, safety, and enduring value.

MDN: Jay Evensen in a *Deseret News* editorial discussed a 1998 review of forty separate studies of young people's religious worship and its relationship to criminal behavior. He concludes: "Many people who commit crimes or become drug addicts report that they stopped going to church when they became adolescents. These studies show religious people have lower crime rates, lower levels of sexual promiscuity, better health, and a better chance of escaping poverty and despair than people who don't actively believe in a God. Yet, other studies also have found that social scientists tend to discount this relationship."[3]

SDN: In Helaman 5:4 we learn that "Nephi had become weary because of [the people's] iniquity; and he yielded up the judgment-seat, and took it upon him to preach the word of God all the remainder of his days, and his brother Lehi also, all the remainder of his days." Here is a very important pedagogical concept at work. Perhaps the most effective way to change behavior is to teach *doctrine*, from which emerge *principles*, which, when understood, lead to *behavior*.

Elder Boyd K. Packer states, "The study of the doctrines of the gospel will improve behavior quicker than a study of behavior will improve behavior."[4] Parents and sometimes leaders, usually out of frustration, spend time and energy chiding, hectoring, and railing on the behavior of their children. When they transfer their attention to principles and doctrine, they obtain better long-term results—not to mention lower blood pressure.

LOOK TO PARENTS

MDN: A story may illustrate our second point. One evening a family was sitting around the family room, the little children playing at the feet of their parents, when the three-year-old, out of the blue, said, "3 Nephi, chapter 11, verse 33." Startled, the father asked, "What did you say, Son?" The little boy repeated the reference. The mother checked her Book of Mormon and found this scripture: "And whoso believeth in me, and is baptized, the same shall be saved; and they are they who shall inherit the kingdom of God."

The parents, at first puzzled, decided he must have learned it in Primary. They might have smiled and gone on with what they were doing. Instead, they stopped to gather all their children and talk with them about the doctrine of baptism. These parents nourished the seed planted in a Sunbeam class. They didn't wait or leave it to the Primary teacher. The Lord instructs, "And again, inasmuch as parents have children in Zion, or in any of her stakes which are organized, that teach them not to understand the doctrine of repentance, faith in Christ the Son of the living God, and of baptism and the gift of the Holy Ghost by the laying on of the hands, when eight years old, the sin be upon the heads of the parents" (D&C 68:25).

SDN: In our family of seven boys, each son took a turn reading the scriptures. One morning we were in the Beatitudes. Our little first-grader tried to sound out each word with lots of help. He read, "Blessed are the merciful for they shall . . ." and then without any help at all he finished, "orbit Mercury!" We all burst into laughter at his creative translation of "obtain mercy," and he joined us as we hugged him and cheered his efforts.

MDN: Years later, when he studied this scripture as a missionary, we hope for a fleeting moment his mind and heart went back to the happy day he and his family read the Beatitudes together.

SDN: It's not always easy to get children in a mood to join in family scripture reading. We would say: Keep it happy, keep it light. Serious times come soon enough.

MDN: We've tried every way we could think of: early morning on Mom and Dad's bed, or at supper with meatloaf and Moroni. Many times we read with friends joining in. We tried on Sundays, on Mondays, sometimes awake, sometimes not.

It wasn't always a pretty, orderly sight, but at least all the boys were there. Sometimes it took us a long time to finish one of the books because we discussed what we read, and sometimes our reading was short to match attention spans. In fact, we remember saying good-bye to a missionary son and promising him we'd try to finish the Book of Mormon by the time he returned.

SDN: We weren't perfect in our scripture reading. We wanted to be and we tried lots of ways to be perfect in it, but we did the best we could under the circumstances.

Parents should be a child's first teacher of correct principles. But that is not all we must do. We have chosen to highlight three other important responsibilities. The first is *example*.

MDN: Example is the foundation upon which parents build testimony in their children. Parents teach the gospel through their actions. And our children should feel safe as they look to our examples. What a blessing it is when parents speak kindly, treating their children with respect. Harsh, coarse words should not be part of our vocabulary.

SDN: President Gordon B. Hinckley, in speaking of his father, said that "more religion is caught than is taught."[5] What we are doing as parents is contagious. Let our example of integrity and temple attendance, of love and gospel living, be one that youth can and will want to follow. We cannot afford to be indifferent or wavering or weak. We must speak up for right in happy and appealing ways and with a strong voice.

MDN: We must help our young men and our young women to

value family above career, above social or political concerns, above all else. Elder Neal A. Maxwell has said: "When the real history of mankind is fully disclosed, will it feature the echoes of gunfire or the shaping sound of lullabies? The great armistices made by military men or the peacemaking of women in homes and in neighborhoods? Will what happens in cradles and kitchens prove to be more controlling than what happened in congresses? When the surf of the centuries has made the great pyramids so much sand, the everlasting family will still be standing."[6]

SDN: Let us keep in mind what Jean Paul Richter once said, "What a father [and, may I add, a mother] says to [their] children is not heard by the world, but it will be heard by posterity."[7]

In addition to example, children need to look to their parents to be taught *how to work*. This important ethic should be taught early and taught in the family. Children need to know that they are part of the family engine and not part of the baggage. In earlier rural times, work was a natural part of everyday family life. The pioneers would never have made it across the plains if the teenagers had ridden in the wagons. Learning to work together as a family is more of a challenge in our modern society. Yet it is no less important to our children's success.

As our boys were growing up, we tried very hard to keep them working. They love to remind us that at times we were quite creative. One Saturday morning as Margaret and I were leaving to go to an assignment, the boys were imagining a whole Saturday of unsupervised free time. Before we left, a huge dump truck drove up to our home, dumped an enormous load of dirt on our driveway, and pulled away. The boys' version of the story is that I gathered all of them around that huge pile of dirt and said, "Boys, we need to raise the level of the back-yard six inches. Please have this dirt hauled out there and spread around by the time your mother and I get back."

MDN: As important as learning how to work, is learning *how to play*. Have fun with your family. Play together.

Our family home evenings when the boys were young followed a definite pattern. We sang, prayed, paid allowances, praised each boy for something wonderful he had done (like a good spelling test, making his bed, or something), timed them while they ran to do forgotten chores, had a short message, and then went down to the local college playing field for a game of family soccer. Every week! We must have liked soccer. The boys chose what would be fun, and it was always the same. I'd love to know what a family of girls or a mixture of sons and daughters would choose.

With another family, we bought an old, used boat. One time we took it and the children (they were usually happy to go boating) out into the middle of a nearby lake. Steve turned off the engine, and as we floated for a few minutes, no escape possible, we passed around the licorice, and then he said, "You know, boys, there is something I've been wanting to talk to you about." Then he taught them. But he was brief. Short lessons were the key in our family of active boys.

SDN: You do what it takes to love, teach, have fun, work, and build unity in a family. Children must know to what source they may look—and parents are the scripturally mandated source! "And ye will not suffer your children that they go hungry, or naked; neither will ye suffer that they transgress the laws of God, and fight and quarrel one with another, and serve the devil, who is the master of sin. . . . But ye will teach them to walk in the ways of truth and soberness; ye will teach them to love one another, and to serve one another" (Mosiah 4:14–15).

LOOK TO THEIR LEADERS

MDN: Now to our third point: children need to *look to their leaders*. At the opening of a children's exhibit at the Museum of Church History and Art, one small child recognized President Howard W. Hunter as he was leaving in his wheelchair. The boy ran after President Hunter, singing, "Follow the prophet, follow the prophet!" We hope as he grows to manhood that small boy will continue to look to a living prophet as a source of guidance.

SDN: President David O. McKay was the prophet of our youth. How we loved him! President Gordon B. Hinckley describes him as "a tall and handsome man, physically robust, he loved the contest, his mind was scintillating and his wit delightful. His was a buoyant personality, he was always encouraging, lifting up, seeing the bright side of things, and challenging others to move forward."[8]

MDN: I once had a personal meeting with President McKay. As part of a group of college students, I was thrilled to be invited to meet with the president of the Church. I felt unprepared for such an interview, but I also remember thinking how marvelous it would be if I could sit close to him and receive his personal counsel to me.

I was determined to be as spiritually prepared as possible. With a prayer in my heart, I read my scriptures all the way from Provo to Salt Lake City, "cramming" like the college student I was. When we arrived at President McKay's apartment in the Hotel Utah, several of the apostles were leaving, and they stopped to greet us. Then I met President McKay. He invited us to sit with him on the couch, and he kept my youthful hand in his large, warm prophet's hand during the entire meeting. I will forever remember the great warmth and love I felt in his presence as he talked with us.

All too soon the visit ended, and I realized he had given no personal advice to me or any of us. In fact, I no longer remember what he said, but certain feelings are still very clear. I had heard President McKay teach principles from the pulpit many times, and on this day I understood in a new way that when the prophet speaks, he *is* speaking to me—to each of us—personally. Ever since then, I have listened carefully to our prophets for that sure guidance.

Our children too can find guidance from a living prophet, from his counselors in the First Presidency, and from the Quorum of the Twelve Apostles, whom we sustain as prophets, seers, and revelators. In following their counsel, we can find safety and peace.

We think the greatest blessing leaders can give to young people is a vision of who they are and what they can become. It is not by accident that young women worldwide are encouraged to stand each Sunday to recite the Young Women theme, which begins, "We are daughters of our Heavenly Father who loves us, and we love Him."[9]

SDN: The statement of Aaronic Priesthood purposes provides a similarly strong vision to young men so that they too know clearly who they are and what is expected of them.

Let us tell you a quick story. It was Sunday morning, and there, about twenty-five feet up in the top of the very large tree in our front yard was a big, strong, eighteen-year-old boy. He was wearing his Sunday clothes—white shirt, tie, nice pants. He was surrounded on nearby limbs by six or seven others in similar attire. Their most prominent features were big grins. I have no idea what our nonmember neighbors thought. It looked like a flock of very strange birds had swooped out of the sky and landed in our tree. They were having just as much fun taking the fifteen rolls of toilet paper out of the tree as they undoubtedly had had hurling them into the tree the night before.

This was not our first experience with that particular flock of priests. I had been the Young Men president and their quorum advisor for several years and had come to know them as an energetic, playful, and altogether typical group of sixteen- to eighteen-year-old boys. Indeed, as I looked at the boy highest in the tree, I remembered a remark I had made to Margaret several years earlier, something about why didn't this boy's parents do a little better job with him? Of course, our own boys were then three and four years old, so we were in the best possible position to render an expert opinion on these matters. With seven teenage sons of our own, you can only imagine how many times Margaret and I have eaten those words.

In 1997, nearly twenty-five years later, we saw that flock of priests again. One of them organized a reunion for us all at general conference time. There was the former bishop and his wife, Margaret and I, and eighteen of the nicest Melchizedek Priesthood holders you have ever seen. They came from California, Oregon, Washington, Idaho, and Louisiana. They were scoutmasters, bishops, and elders quorum presidents, fathers, and husbands. They loved the gospel and they loved the Lord, and oh, how they loved their families.

The boy highest in the tree? The ringleader? The one about whom I had said to Margaret, "He's a nice-looking boy, honey, but I think he's just a scatter-brained football player"? Yes, he was there. I knew he would be. Three years before, I had visited a stake in Louisiana with the assignment of reorganizing the stake presidency. I was told about a wonderful young counselor in the stake presidency who would have made a great stake president had he not just moved. He had been a professor at the university, had a national reputation in his field, and had been recruited by other universities around the country. I asked his name. I asked it again. I said, "Naw, it couldn't be," but it was! That big bird, the football player, had his Ph.D., was a nationally renowned scientist, and had recently served in a stake presidency.

Oh yes, he was there at the reunion with his wife and family. I threw my arms around him, and he hugged me so hard it about broke my back.

MDN: We had a joyous reunion, a grand celebration. We celebrated Aaronic Priesthood boys becoming Melchizedek Priesthood men. We celebrated a bishop who never gave up. We celebrated parents who really had taught correct principles. We celebrated Leo, who had driven all night from California and parked his eighteen-wheeler the full length of our residential lot.

SDN: I don't know how they did it (I didn't help them), but that Saturday night as I sat on the stand in the Tabernacle looking out, there they all were, seated on the front row. I wondered where these ingenious boys had gotten tickets! Who could have imagined that that group of boys would one day all be seated together on the front row of the Tabernacle for a general priesthood meeting? That weekend we laughed together, we cried, we hugged, we talked, we ate together, and we prayed together.

The morning after they left, Margaret and I awoke, still basking in the glow of that experience. We walked out onto our front porch, and there we saw that each of our little new trees that could hardly hold leaves had been delicately and lovingly adorned with one carefully placed strand of white toilet paper.[10]

MDN: Parents and leaders need to believe in our youth and to share with them a vision of who they really are and the great contributions they can make as they become future leaders of the Church.

Leaders also can help children by being a cadre of caring adults. Suppose a bishop gathered together all the adults in the ward—youthful adults, middle-aged adults, and senior adults and said something like this:

"Brothers and sisters, we have gathered you all together, old and young alike, for a specific purpose. We have wonderful young people in our ward. They have great promise, we love them, and we wish to see them realize all their God-given potential, but we need your help. We need to make up our collective minds—all of us together—that we are not going to lose a single young person. We invite you to become a part of our ward cadre of caring adults. Please smile at and call a teenager in our ward by name. Inquire about his or her interests. Attend a choir concert, ball game, or dance recital. Invite a young person to dinner, tell him or her about your job, your hobby, or your glory days as a high school athlete. Hire them to work in your yard or in your house and talk to them while they do it. Grandmothers and grandfathers have wisdom and love to share. Young marrieds have enthusiasm and vitality to share. Let's try this for three months and see what happens. Do just one thing a week—one interaction in the hall at church, one visit in the neighborhood, one invitation to dinner. Together we can make a huge difference."[11]

LOOK TO THE LORD

SDN: The ultimate success for our children, as well for us as parents, depends on how well we teach them to look to the Lord. Nephi clearly understood this important instruction. That is why he repeated for emphasis, "And we talk of Christ, we rejoice in Christ, we preach of Christ, we prophesy of Christ, and we write according to our prophecies, that our children may know to what source they may look for a remission of their sins" (2 Nephi 25:26).

Teaching children to look to the Lord ought to be foremost as we consider sacrament meeting programs, conduct Sunday School classes, and plan activities. But it turns out that the real heavy lifting for this task is not institutional. A study of Latter-day Saint young men concluded some years ago by the Church Evaluation Division analyzed the behavior of young men in the Church—their attendance at meetings, participation in priesthood assignments, relationship with advisers, and so on. The conclusions of the study were found to hold true for young women as well in subsequent work done by BYU professors Brent L. Top and Bruce Chadwick.

The results are quite revealing. The best predictors of missionary service for young men and temple marriage for young women and young men is *private religious observance*. It is not attendance at meetings. It is not participation in girls camp or super activities or stake athletic programs. Those things are important but only if they bring the Spirit and strengthen testimonies. The number one predictor is private religious observance or, in other words, looking to the Lord on an individual basis. Private religious observance is what goes on in the home—personal prayer, family prayer, scripture reading, tithe paying, and Sabbath day observance. It is in these simple, private religious activities that our children really come to know the Lord, to know of his goodness and mercy and love.

The object of our children's religious experience ought to be to learn to love the Lord. Our zeal for teaching, training, and requiring of our children must not result in resentment of the Church because of our awkwardness or heavy-handedness.

MDN: I love the story Stephen tells about a time in his teenage years. He and a friend, Richard Sharp, were shooting hoops on the driveway of Richard's home one beautiful Sunday afternoon in Idaho Falls. Eventually President John Sharp, Richard's father, drove up to the house, after a meeting of the stake presidency. He leaned against the car and watched the boys playing. They eagerly coaxed him to shoot a few baskets with them. His reply was simply, "Well, I don't think so, boys. I guess I'll just watch you today." That was all. He didn't berate them for not properly honoring the Sabbath Day. He didn't shame Richard for not setting a good example as the son of a member of the stake presidency. He didn't scold them for knowing better than they were behaving.

SDN: He didn't belittle me, the neighbor boy, for leading his boy astray on the driveway with a basketball or any of the many other things he could have said. He just loved us both. We knew it. We felt it as he stood there and just watched and taught by his example. We felt no resentment. We did feel loved and understood.

MDN: In time these very good boys came to understand what the example of that good and kind man had taught them. And they followed it. Each boy served a mission and continued in lives of Church service, always with love for the Lord and his commandments foremost in their hearts, never with feelings of resentment.

SDN: In a new millennium, the Christian world unites in faith to commemorate two thousand years since the birth of our Savior, the Son of God. It is truly remarkable that the world still remembers that little baby boy born in Bethlehem so long ago. He grew from boy to man.

MDN: He lived a life that we still try to follow. He showed us the way. He performed miracles. He taught by parables. He taught truths that are still true after two millennia; they are the truths of heaven. He willingly suffered for our sins because he loved us so completely. Through his atonement, he gave us the right to repent. And he gave his life that we might be resurrected and live again after death. When our children know this for themselves, they will know the true Source to which they may look every day of their lives.

Notes

1. Boyd K. Packer, "Little Children," *Ensign*, November 1986, 17.
2. J. Reuben Clark Jr., "The Charted Course of the Church in Education," address to religious educators, Brigham Young University Summer School, Aspen Grove, Utah, 8 August 1938; also in Boyd K. Packer, *Teach Ye Diligently* (Salt Lake City: Deseret Book, 1977), 310, 317.
3. Jay Evensen, "Religion Can Combat a Parent's Worst Nightmare," *Deseret News*, 9 April 2000, editorial page.
4. Packer, *Ensign*, November 1986, 17.

5. Gordon B. Hinckley, *Teachings of Gordon B. Hinckley* (Salt Lake City: Deseret Book, 1997), 184.

6. Neal A. Maxwell, "The Women of God," *Ensign*, May 1978, 10–11.

7. Quoted in Hinckley, *Teachings of Gordon B. Hinckley*, 386.

8. Hinckley, *Teachings of Gordon B. Hinckley*, 523–24.

9. *Church Handbook of Instructions, Book 2: Priesthood and Auxiliary Leaders, Section 4: Young Women* (Salt Lake City: The Church of Jesus Christ of Latter-day Saints, 1998), 211.

10. Also told in Stephen D. Nadauld, *Principles of Priesthood Leadership* (Salt Lake City: Bookcraft, 1999), 76–78.

11. Also told in ibid., 99.

How Do I Grandmother in This New Millennium?

⁓

Margaret Lifferth

Be prepared to move out of the central role. When I became a grandmother, I thought I already knew everything I needed to know to be one. I knew a lot about babies and toddlers and even teenagers. But I had a lot to learn—especially about relationships with sons- or daughters-in-law and their families.

When a child marries, a mother's role shifts dramatically. That marriage creates a new family unit, and we mothers become a peripheral part of that unit—not the center. This shift is not easy, since we are accustomed to being the center of our family unit and a key person in our children's lives. This is both a time of letting go of our own child and of accepting a new son- or daughter-in-law, who will bring new perspectives, priorities, and traditions, and different expectations that sometimes can be at odds with our own.

Our child and the new spouse must adjust, decide on priorities, and define the foundations of a new family. It is a mother's job to validate, support, and encourage. Remember, our children want to succeed, they want us to be proud of them, and they still need our affirmation.

Support new family relationships. *Hold your tongue.* Realize that you will not always approve of everything the new couple does. But you can and must find different ways to teach besides criticizing, demanding, or giving unasked-for advice. We grandparents must avoid

---

Margaret Lifferth serves as a Church service missionary at the Church Museum of History and Art and is a member of the Primary General Board. She and her husband, Dennis Lifferth, are the parents of seven children and the grandparents of eight.

contention and never cause it. The simplest way I know to do that, and the most difficult, is to know when and how to hold my tongue. We can yield—even when we know we are right.

Appreciate new allies. Accept your new son- or daughter-in-law's parents as allies. Focus on their strengths and be grateful that they support your children. Don't undermine their influence or the time they will want to spend with the family. Resist the temptation to try to position yourself as the "favorite grandmother." Women can get secret satisfaction from that. My friend teasingly calls the other grandmother "the other woman." Do what you can to make every relationship in your children's and grandchildren's lives positive and edifying. One grandmother, when told by her grandchild that her other grandmother took her shopping for new clothes, exclaimed, "Aren't you lucky you have a shopping grandmother? I guess I'm the story-telling grandmother, and don't we have fun reading stories together." She effectively diffused any attempt to compete and defined an area they could enjoy together.

Create good times. Work at creating good times with a son- and daughter-in-law as diligently as you worked at creating good times with your children. In her biography, *Glimpses*, Sister Marjorie Hinckley talks about the personal phone calls she makes to each of her daughters and daughters-in-law on a regular basis for "girl talk."[1]

Avoid "spoiling" the grandchildren. Grandparents often joke about how fun it is to spoil the grandchildren. Temper that a little by supporting the parents in upholding the rules that their family has defined. If they don't want their children to eat half an hour before dinnertime, think twice before you offer candy or ice cream. One of the nice things about being a grandmother is that I am not the disciplinarian, but I am appreciated more if I follow the family rules.

Don't fall into the mythical supergrandma role. What kind of grandmother do you want to be? Ask yourself some questions: What can I contribute? What are my strengths? What do I enjoy? How much time do I have? How good is my health and how much energy do I have? Answers to these questions, which are different for each of us, will help us avoid trying to fill the role of that mythical ideal grand-mother. Remember how we all nearly killed ourselves trying to be the "ideal mother," only to find out that there was no such thing? The same is true of being a grandmother. Whatever our health, energy, or talents, let's approach this season of our lives sensibly, also realizing that we can be a powerful influence for good.

I was young when my grandmothers died, and I did not have much insight into their lives. But one of my grandmothers left a written per-sonal history for her family, and one did not. Because of her history, I know about her parents, her courtship, the family life of my mother, and most important, her testimony. We may forge the link between the past and the future in many ways. For instance, label family heirlooms and record the stories of who owned them and why they are important. Label old family photographs. Saved letters, too, can be a record of family histories.

Re-evaluate family traditions. Grandmothers are in a special posi-tion to pass on family traditions. Remember, however, that the in-laws' families, traditions, and schedules must be considered. This means that traditions should have real meaning, should be flexible, and may some-times need to be re-evaluated. I think my children all breathed a sigh of relief when we finally decided to host Thanksgiving only every other year, giving them uninterrupted Thanksgiving time with the other side of their families. Last Christmas we were at my mother-in-law's house, when my daughter arrived with her children. Little Josh came up to me with his eyes glazed over and said, "This is the fifth grandma's we have been to today." What he really wanted—and needed—was an hour to play with his new toys. Perhaps that tradition should be re-evaluated.

Also consider whether a tradition can (or should) be sustained over the years. Last fall my oldest grandchild was baptized, and I wanted to do something special to commemorate that event. I consid-ered different possibilities. Then I thought about the potential number of grandchildren I could have with seven of my own children. I had to choose something that I could repeat for each one, considering both cost and time. I decided to purchase a small book to take to his baptism and then invite all the guests to write their testimonies in. I kept it for another week or two to gather testimonies from missionary cousins or others who were not able to attend. That little book has the testimonies of both of his grandmothers and three of his great-grandmothers. Josh included his own feelings about that day and then rarely looked at it again. His mother put it away, and I hope that as he grows, and sometimes stumbles trying to find his way, that the book will prove to be a very personal source of strength to him.

Be an anchor in a world of shifting values. "Now to you grandmothers and great-grandmothers may I say a word," said President Gordon B. Hinckley. "Tremendous has been your experience. Tremendous is your understanding. You can be as an anchor in a world of shifting values. You have lived long, buffed and polished by the adversities of life through which you have passed. Quiet are your ways, deliberate your counsel."[2]

By example we can teach love, family prayer, scripture study, integrity, cheerfulness, love of education, hard work, and testimony. Some of us may serve missions. My neighbor recently lost an adult son in a drowning accident. She and her husband were the primary source of emotional support for his wife and children for many months after the accident. The little family was not doing well. Nevertheless, the bishop called her and her husband on a mission. Desperately worried about their daughter-in-law and grandchildren, they accepted the call purely as an act of faith. They remembered President Ezra Taft Benson's counsel that they would have more influence if they fulfilled a mission than if they stayed home.[3] They put that little family in the Lord's hands and went to England. My friend wrote a separate letter to each grandchild every week. In those seven handwritten letters a week, she told them about England and about their activities as missionaries, about the young people in their branch and the challenges LDS youth faced living in the mission field. She assured them of her love and of her testimony. During those months, her grandchildren continued to heal, strengthened by her love and example of service.

Our children may have other difficult circumstances that make our role of example and teacher critical. How do you share your testimony with your grandchildren if their parents are inactive? When you have the chance, take them to church and other places where they will be influenced by gospel. I volunteer at the Museum of Church History and Art. One day last winter, a couple brought their young granddaughter to the museum to see a puppet show depicting the stories of Jesus. They explained that she didn't have the chance to go to Primary and they took every opportunity to expose her to gospel truth. Another grandmother takes a more direct approach. Her divorced son adores his children, but has not included the Church in their lives. She calls him occasionally and asks, "Brad, what are you doing to teach your children the gospel?" She knows that he knows it is important and nudges him toward his stewardship.

Notes

1. Virginia H. Pearce, ed., *Glimpses into the Life and Heart of Marjorie Pay Hinckley* (Salt Lake City: Deseret Book, 1999), 115–16.
2. Gordon B. Hinckley, "Stand Strong against the Wiles of the World," *Ensign*, November 1995, 100.
3. Ezra Taft Benson, "Our Commission to Take the Gospel to the World," *Ensign*, May 1984, 45.

How Can I Be a Polar Star Parent?

Karen Warner

Provide both light and lightness. "You parents," taught President Gordon B. Hinckley, "you fathers and mothers, live the kind of exemplary lives before your children that they will find in you the polar star to which they can look as they shape their own lives."[1] Have you ever gazed up into the night sky and pinpointed Polaris, the polar star? We must provide the kind of example and teaching for our children that will be as constant as the position of the polar star in pointing their lives toward Christ.

As we become a *light* in spiritual guidance, we must also assume a *lightness* as sunshine-weather makers in our homes. Remember, sunshine comes from a star, too, the one nearest us. President Heber C. Kimball once said, "I am perfectly satisfied that my Father and my God is a cheerful, pleasant, lively, and good-natured Being. . . . He is a jovial, lively person, and a beautiful man."[2]

Promote, don't police, family values. Once upon a time in our home, we had perfect, rigidly structured family home evening lessons. The children sat up, were quiet, paid attention, and participated only when scripted. Then we heard institute teacher and author George Durrant say that in his family the kids rolled on the floor, ate popcorn *during* the lesson, and sometimes even threw a little of it. Our family home evening lessons are for *our* families, Brother Durrant suggested, and we can even close the curtains and not worry about what the

---

Karen Warner received her bachelor's degree in elementary education. She is a former member of the Provo Cable TV advisory committee. She and her husband, Paul Warner, are the parents of six children and grandparents of fifteen. She serves as a stake Young Women president.

neighbors think.[3] In our case, the new policy made for less tension, more interest, and a better learning environment.

In general, where there is no immediate moral danger, an attitude of *lightness* can make our *light*, or guidance, more effective. How about a sign on the kitchen counter to remind the family it's fast Sunday? This puts us in the role of fasting promoter, not fasting police.

Our example can be another light approach. Sister Larkin, the wife of our stake's area authority, said on occasion she used to notice her mother praying when her bedroom door was ajar. She was always filled with curiosity about what in the world her mother could be saying for so long. It was an effective lesson on prayer without preaching.

Examine family rules. Well-meaning but rigid family rules can sometimes generate counterproductive feelings. A good rule of thumb is to ask ourselves if we've ever seen or heard a general authority give similar counsel or example. Do their wives forswear makeup or stylish clothes? Do they refuse to own a television? Do they practice or promote extensions to the Word of Wisdom, such as vegetarianism or no chocolate or any of the health food programs? I'll never forget the rumble in Provo many years ago when Elder Bruce R. McConkie advised the students at a BYU six-stake priesthood leadership conference that they *could* be doing their homework on Sunday and *should not* be praying together on dates.[4] Mormons do have a pharisaic tendency to invent more rules and practices than are necessary. This anonymous verse may capture how our youth feel about rules:

> My parents told me not to smoke. I don't.
> Or listen to a naughty joke. I don't.
> They made it plain I mustn't wink. I don't.
> Or think about intoxicating drink. I don't.
> To dance and flirt is very wrong. I don't.
> I kiss no girls; not even one.
> Some folks may think I have no fun.
> I don't.

Brigham Young said, "When parents whip their children for reading novels, and never let them go to the theater, or any place of recreation and amusement, but bind them to the moral law, until duty becomes loathsome to them; when they are freed by age from the rigorous training of their parents, they are more fit for companions to devils, than to be the children of such religious parents."[5]

Don't be afraid to say no. If we are not oppressive in general matters, our children will be able to accept some no's on critical moral issues such as "No, you can't date until sixteen." Or "No, you can't watch that R-rated movie, or any other vulgar, immoral, or suggestive video for that matter. Who says? Good question. Let's make that our topic for family home evening this week." "No, you can't wear it if it's too short, too tight, or too revealing." "No, you can't do body piercing."[6]

It's my observation that the most underaddressed issue regarding our youth is not whether *they* can handle being told no but whether *parents* have the courage to say no. How can we expect our sons and daughters to have courage to tell their friends, their peers, "No, I can't," or "No, I won't," if we can't say no to our children? Our children learn their courage from the way *we* deal with *them*.

Oh, if we could all be like the mothers of the two thousand stripling warriors—unified in what we teach and what we expect. Do you suppose those stripling warriors went to their mothers on the eve of their first battle, whining, "I know the Lamanites are restless tonight, but, hey, I wanna go hang out in Bountiful with my friends. I hear it's rockin'! And Mom, everybody's doing it!" The stripling warriors didn't say that, for one thing, because no one else *was* doing it. Those mothers were unified in their teachings, standards, and expectations. The stripling warriors faced a righteous cause with courage because their mothers faced those causes with courage (Alma 56:46–48). Stripling mothers, can we make sure our lights are always pointing toward the Savior and then band together with other mothers, open dialogue between us, compare information, and trench in?

Notes

1. Gordon B. Hinckley, as quoted in "Families: Fundamental Units of Society," *Church News*, 4 March 2000, 10.
2. Heber C. Kimball, *Journal of Discourses*, 26 vols. (London: Latter-day Saints' Book Depot, 1854–86), 4:222.
3. George D. Durrant, *Love at Home—Starring Father* (Salt Lake City: Bookcraft, 1976), 41–49.
4. Bruce R. McConkie, BYU six-stake priesthood leadership conference, 31 October 1981, Provo, Utah, no transcript (verified by telephone conversation with Joseph F. McConkie, 12 October 2000).
5. Brigham Young, *Journal of Discourses*, 2:94; see also Brigham Young, *Discourses of Brigham Young*, sel. John A. Widtsoe (Salt Lake City: Deseret Book, 1954), 209.
6. To review the standards endorsed by the First Presidency and the Quorum of the Twelve, see *For the Strength of Youth* (pamphlet) Salt Lake City: The Church of Jesus Christ of Latter-day Saints, 1990.

How Do I Become a "Mother in Israel"?

✺⟨⟩✺

Josephine R. Bay

Several months ago a friend told me a "grandpa story." He and his wife were visiting their son's family in Austin, Texas. Their oldest grandchild, Madeline, affectionately called "Maddy," is two. One Sunday, Maddy insisted that her grandparents walk her to the nursery. Grandpa and Grandma wanted to hold her hand while she walked between them, but she insisted, "No. I lead the way." As she walked a step ahead of them, her grandparents heard Maddy saying to herself, "I not going to cry. I not going to cry. I not going to cry." She repeated these words all the way to the nursery. Her grandfather promised he would pick her up when nursery was over, and in she went. Walking away was as much a trial for those grandparents as it was for little Maddy. Two hours later when her grandfather returned, Maddy's eyes were all aglow, her smile bright, and with outstretched arms she proudly announced, "Grandpa, I not cry."

For me, three truths emerge from Maddy's story. First is the power of determination; Maddy was determined not to cry. Second is the power of repetition; Maddy told herself over and over, "I not going to cry." Third, Maddy taught me the value of return and report; Maddy was eager to report her success to her grandfather.

The power of determination. Mothers in Israel are determined to fulfil the charge given them by the Lord: "Arise and shine forth, that

---

Josephine Rudd Bay is a native of England raised in Canada. She works as a marriage and family therapist. She and her husband, Thomas D. Bay are the parents of one daughter, Tiffiny Bay. She serves as a temple ordinance worker and is the stake Relief Society president.

thy light may be a standard for the nations" (D&C 115:5). I am impressed with the vision of women today who go the extra mile, determined to influence their families for righteousness sake. One grandmother who has an inactive son and wife diligently takes her two grandchildren, who live nearby, to church every Sunday. She has done so since they were babies. One is now in Young Women and the other in his last year of Primary. She remains prayerful that her son and his wife may return to full fellowship in the gospel.

My mother was a determined and inventive teacher. The most memorable lesson about the law of tithing I've ever had came through a botched Sears catalogue order. Mom had ordered a few articles of clothing, carefully selected after a session of armchair shopping with us. The package arrived in the mail, and my sisters and I were eager for Mom to open the parcel. On top of the package, however, was a note: "Dear Sears customer, Thank you for your order. We are temporarily out of item number 246, but have sent a replacement of greater value. We trust this will be acceptable." As always, Mom took care opening the packages, comparing the contents to her order. Item 246 turned out to be Jennifer's pajamas. We girls fell silent, wondering, *Did we get a good deal or not?* Then Mom spoke, "Oh girls, a tithing blessing from the Lord!" We didn't have time to be disappointed. Who could argue with a tangible gift from the Lord? And every time Jennifer wore those pajamas, I thought about the blessings of paying tithing. Mom could have complained or expressed disappointment at the substitution. Instead she framed a teaching moment to encourage gospel learning. Throughout our childhood, my mother kept gospel principles our foremost concern. What a fine example of determination not to let secular agendas matter more than spiritual growth.

Let me introduce you to another family. The parents appear to follow the Savior; they are good people. However, they struggle intensely with one of their four children. Their plea to me when they brought him in for counseling was, "Fix this kid." They described an out-of-control thirteen-year-old who terrorized his family with violent outbursts of anger and relentlessly taunted and teased his siblings and mother. When asked, the mom acknowledged feeling depressed most of the time. Depression is typically anger turned inward. She feels alone and helpless to change things. Her husband is also stymied by his son's behavior and, not knowing how to cope, disappears when his son starts raging. He's fed up and wants a quick fix. To him that means medication or a foster home. Rather than learn new skills, these parents have fallen into the "if only" trap. If only this boy would be like his siblings, then peace would be restored to their home. But it's when our children are troubled that we need to be most determined to stay the course.

Unfortunately for this family, the parents seemed to lack faith—faith in their ability to change the situation, faith in their son's innate worth—and determination to work on solutions. I urged them not to mistake conformity for growth. Let us rejoice in the gift of a challenging child; for it is through their unwitting behavior that we learn to be more effective parents and grow toward building better homes.

The power of repetition. Our church is replete with practices of repetition. We repeat sacramental prayers to ourselves as we hear them each Sunday. We repeat sacred temple covenants—covenants of promise made available through our righteousness. Primary children repeat the Articles of Faith; our daughters repeat the Young Women values. Some women have memorized the Proclamation on the Family and the Relief Society Declaration. Repeating these inspired words encourages us to be better women.

Holding regular family home evening is another example of the power of a repeated practice. One Monday night, my sister's children wanted to watch a hockey game. "Mom," they begged, "can we just have a short lesson tonight?" That question speaks volumes, doesn't it? They did not say, "Mom, do we have to have family home evening tonight?" They were in the habit. She said, "Sure"; she believes in being flexible. They had their short family home evening, and the kids went down to watch the hockey game. In her cupboard, Jennifer had little two-inch ice cream cones. She put about a tablespoon of ice cream in each one and took them down. "Hey kids, here's a short treat for a short lesson." Of course, as Jennifer knows, the length of a lesson isn't what counts. What reinforces learning and conviction is regular repetition.

Besides repeating gospel principles, repeatedly paying attention to good behavior is a powerful parenting tool. Dr. Glenn Latham states: "There is absolutely no substitute for positive and pleasant interactions between parents and their children! When children are in a good mood, playing nicely together, pleasant to be around, doing their chores as instructed, getting their homework completed, and generally behaving appropriately, these behaviors should be acknowledged. . . . Smiles, a pat on the back, and sincere verbal acknowledgement are all things you can do to positively acknowledge appropriate behaviors."[1] The mother who wanted me to "fix" her son complained, "I just can't find anything good about him. I don't know what to say as a compliment." "Why don't you start with his hair?" I suggested. "His hair is absolutely beautiful." Once we get out of a critical mode, finding positive statements isn't difficult. I remember hearing Mary Ellen Edmunds, in her lighthearted way, suggest some ideas for compliments: "Oh, I just love the way you are breathing. It's so smooth. It's so constant." Dr. Latham comments, "I recommend there *never* be more than one negative interaction for eight to ten positive interactions."[2]

Avoid vain repetition. Consider the scriptural admonition to avoid vain repetitions in prayers (Matthew 6:7). Should this caution be applied to other practices? Isn't it vain repetition to regularly yell at our children or pay attention only to their mistakes? Habitually being critical, disapproving, and scornful will undo all the good of regular family scripture study, prayer, and home evening. How about "vain repetition" in watching television, reading magazines, and poring over catalogues?

The power of return and report. Returning and reporting encourages accountability in various aspects of our lives, both as Church and as family members. For example, our Church leaders hold stewardship interviews. In temple recommend interviews, we account for our worthiness.

I like to reminisce on my family's practice of returning and reporting after coming home from an evening out, a pattern I learned from the example of my older sisters. When we arrived home, we would go to our parents' bedroom and let them know we were home safe. My mother would always say, "Oh good, Jo, you're home. Did you have a nice time?" Dad would say in his English accent, "E-hey, you're home. What time is it?" It didn't matter if it was early or late, that was his standard question. It is a fond memory. Taking time in the evening hours with your children to listen to their day's events can be a "great connector" between parent and child as are also those bedtime routines of stories, lullabies, hugs and kisses, and the inevitable "Just one more thing, Mom."

The ultimate return and report is to our Lord and Savior. It is to him, our advocate with the Father, that we account for our comings and goings. Alma says, "Counsel with the Lord in all thy doings, and he will direct thee for good; yea, when thou liest down at night lie down unto the Lord, that he may watch over you in your sleep; and when thou risest in the morning let they heart be full of thanks unto God; and if ye do these things, ye shall be lifted up at the last day" (Alma 37:37).

One mother's four-year-old son was extremely ill with croup. In a desperate hour, she knelt to offer a mother's pleading prayer that her son's breathing would ease. Meanwhile, her older daughter stood listening by her brother's bedroom door. During the mother's prayer, the daughter could not hear the boy's labored breathing. Soon the mother joined her and both listened. Hearing nothing and fearing the worst, they entered the room and approached the bed. The sweet sound of this child's restful, easy breathing filled their hearts with joy. It was an immediate answer to prayer. The grateful mother turned to her daughter and said, "There is yet another prayer to offer." She and her daughter knelt in prayer and offered gratitude to the Lord. This type of returning and reporting pleases the Lord. "And in nothing doth man offend God, . . . save those who confess not his hand in all things" (D&C 59:21). A child was healed, another child stood by to witness a mother's faith and thankfulness. What greater gift can a Mother in Israel offer her children than to feel her faith, experience her determination and reliance on the Lord, and join with her often in prayers of gratitude.

Notes

1. Glenn I. Latham, *The Power of Positive Parenting: A Wonderful Way to Raise Children*, rev. ed. (Logan, Ut.: P&T ink, 1994), 372.
2. Ibid., 373.

CELESTIAL THERAPY

⁂

Wendy L. Watson

The other evening, a friend called on her cell phone to tell me she was stuck in traffic.

"Where are you?" I asked.

"I can't really tell," she said in despair. Then suddenly she relaxed. "Oh, just a minute. Where's the temple?" She got her bearings by noting where she was in relation to the temple.

"Where's the temple?" What a marvelous question for us to ask to keep our bearings as we journey through life. This question is absolutely crucial to ask when we are stuck in the traffic problems of daily living—or stalled in our marriage and family relationships.

Where is the temple? And where are we in relation to it?

The prime location of any temple is not a matter of geography. It is a matter of our faith and focus. The very best location of any temple is at the center of our lives. When the temple is at the center of our lives, our marriages and families are organized around temple covenants and worship, temple service, truths, and blessings.

Where is the temple in our lives? As endowed women, did we "go through" the temple—or did the temple, as it really should, "go through" us? Is the temple in our cells and in our souls? It needs to be.

When we are weary, worried, in despair, restless, lonely, misunderstood, indecisive, discouraged, overlooked, overweight, overwhelmed, overwrought, underappreciated, underemployed, or undernourished

---

Wendy L. Watson holds a Ph.D. in family therapy and gerontology from the University of Calgary in Calgary, Alberta, Canada, and also holds degrees in nursing and psychology. She is a professor of marriage and family therapy in the School of Family Life at Brigham Young University and served as chair for the 2000 BYU Women's Conference.

with love, is our immediate question, "Where is the temple?" For women of covenant, it *needs* to be. An apostle of the Lord recently warned, "As the forces around us increase in intensity, whatever spiritual strength was once sufficient will not be enough."[1] I'm grateful for Elder Henry B. Eyring's words. They have haunted me ever since I first heard them.

Forces around us are wreaking havoc with our marriages and families—and we as women are often the first to identify the problems. But what then? What do we do about the problems in our lives once we discover them?

As we look for solutions to our problems, far too many of us are far too content to live far beneath our privileges as women of covenant. *Arise* is a holy and familiar word for covenant-making women. As we seek to heal our hearts and homes, it's time to arise and benefit from the privileges of the temple. In fact, it's time for each of us to make sure we are engaged in what could be called "Celestial Therapy."

CELESTIAL THERAPY OFFERED TO EVERYONE EXCLUSIVELY IN THE HOUSE OF THE LORD

"There is only one aristocracy that God recognizes," said President George Albert Smith, "and that is the aristocracy of righteousness."[2] No one is turned away who is willing to comply with the Lord's rules for admission. He, himself, has set the requirements. His injunction is very simple: "Keep my commandments" (John 14:15). The Lord welcomes *everyone* whose actions show a readiness for Celestial Therapy.

The Savior waits with open arms to help us overcome those problems that are to be overcome—and to endure those that are to be endured. He is waiting to help. What are we waiting for?

The Lord is the Master Healer. And what an assurance it is to seek help from one who knows us better than we know ourselves. He knows our names and struggles, our minds and hearts; he knows our friends and those who seem raised up to test us. He knows our spouses—even though we may not; and our children—even those we have not yet borne. He knows *everything* about us and *everything* about this earth, galaxy, universe . . . and beyond.

Because the Savior loves us, he wants to offer us all he knows. The glory of God *is* intelligence. He offers us his eternal laws and ordinances with their accompanying joy and peace. The more laws we know, and more important, the more laws we live, the more joy and peace we experience.

Our telestial choices keep us from celestial healing. The laws the Lord offers us in his temple bring us out of the world. As we live them, we rise above telestial living, that kind of living which predictably brings grief and darkness into our lives.

Celestial Therapy brings us blessings we can neither quite fully comprehend nor deny. In Doctrine and Covenants 109:22, the Lord tells us of four priesthood blessings that accompany faithful keeping of temple covenants. He promises that when we go forth from his house we can leave

1. armed with his power,
2. with his name upon us,
3. with his glory round about us, and
4. with his angels having charge over us.

What difference can these promised temple blessings make in our lives? Through these blessings, we can do the otherwise impossible in our lives. Let's consider how the Lord's power and his name may influence a woman and her family who are suffering from years of her chronic rage and perpetual criticism. She feels rejected and misunderstood. Her husband feels worthless and alone. Her children, now adults, show impatience with themselves and others; they habitually flog themselves with the soul-searing memory of their mother's verbally and emotionally abusive voice of authority.

What happens as this mother commences regular temple worship? According to the Lord's promises, she has the opportunity to access his power. Armed with the Lord's power, this woman has the power to see herself perhaps as she has never seen herself before. When she reads

Jacob 2:35, perhaps she now reads it this way: "Ye have broken the heart of your tender husband, and lost the confidence of your children, because of your bad example before them." The house of the Lord is indeed a house of revelation.

This woman could also plead for and be given power to cast away contention, which prohibits the Spirit of the Lord from being present. The Spirit is the messenger of love. Through temple experiences she now knows that when the Spirit flees because of contention, so does the perception of love. That's why even though she *feels* love for her family, they have not *experienced* her love. Now, however, with new understanding and armed with the power of the Lord, this woman can learn to do what she previously could not, namely, apologize, commend, forgive, and express love.

How can the second promise of the Lord—that his name will be upon us as we leave his house—help this woman? What happens when she leaves the temple and remembers that every action of hers is now done in the name of the Lord? What happens when in the midst of yelling and raging, this woman catches herself with the thought, *As an endowed mother, I am now yelling and calling my children names—in the name of the Lord! Is this really the way I want to represent the Lord?* Now that's "Kolob shock therapy."

As this woman applies her sacred covenants day by day, her heart will be turned to her husband and children. Her concern will be to do everything she can do to enliven her husband's spirit and to strengthen her children's hearts. Her desire will be to breathe life into her family members rather than to knock the wind out of them.

One or two trips to the temple won't bring these results; but as this woman continues to immerse herself in temple worship, she will experience unprecedented power and Christ's protection. Through him, she will withstand impulses to retaliate and will win her fight against fighting. She will be able to contend against contention. "Her children arise up, and call her blessed; her husband also, and he praiseth her" (Proverbs 31:28).

And what is true for this woman and her anger, is true for:

- a woman and her procrastination.
- a man and his lying.
- a woman and her unforgiveness.
- a man and his struggle with pornography.
- a woman and her battle with weight.
- a man and his indecisiveness.
- a woman and her grief.

And what is true for all these women and men is true for you and for me. Through temple experiences, *each* of us can access the Lord's power and other blessings of the priesthood.

THE LORD'S ALTAR AND SYMBOLS ARE PART OF CELESTIAL THERAPY

Celestial Therapy heals with the help of the Lord's altar. The Lord can *alter* whatever we are willing to put on his *altar*. A woman struggled with chronic bitterness toward her husband. With a longing for change, she fasted and prayed. With power and knowledge gained through temple worship, she laid her bitterness on the Lord's altar. Almost immediately her husband noticed a difference. She was able to reach out to him in ways she had not done for many years. And he responded in kind.

Celestial Therapy also heals with the help of symbols. The temple is filled with symbols. As we wrap our minds and hearts around the mighty symbols of the temple, we ask the Lord earnestly and ourselves reflexively: "What does this symbol mean for me now? What message is the Lord trying to give me through that symbol?" Truman Madsen asks himself two other questions: "Do I understand the symbol the way I should?" and "Do I feel about the symbol the way I should?" The unlayering of possible meaning in temple symbols invites us to dig for deeper meaning in our own lives.

One woman found herself using this type of "temple symbol meaning" question to help her with her family relationships: "What does my daughter's withdrawal really mean?" "What message is the Lord trying to give me through this experience with my husband?" Temple symbols invite us to consider that there are many ways to interpret something.

She found, through Celestial Therapy, that the meanings discovered with her *temple* eyes were increasingly benevolent—and very different from her initial beliefs.

A husband had been hiding a habit of lying, more from himself than from his wife. He became a man of integrity the day Celestial Therapy helped him recognize the meaning his wife attributed to his habit. For her, his lies symbolized the message: "I don't really love you or our children, and I don't really want to be with you through the eternities. I love these lies more than I love you."

Faced with this chilling symbolic meaning, the man called upon the power and blessings of the temple through prayer. He pleaded with the Lord to help him fight this habit. Graced with new strength and power, he wrote a heartfelt letter of apology to his wife about his years of dishonesty.

Now the challenge: How does a husband who has lied for years, and *lied about lying*, win his wife's trust when he finally apologizes? As a symbol of his sincerity, he offered his apology in a place where he knew she would believe him: the celestial room of the temple. This symbolic act strengthened his resolve and his wife's confidence in him. He reports that he is now enjoying "the best relationship I've ever had with my wife and children."

For *every* problem in life, there is power and knowledge in the temple to help us. One sister said, "As covenant women of God, our motto should be: Got a problem? Go to the temple!"

I offer three ways Celestial Therapy heals our hearts and homes:

1. It frees us.
2. It reveals to us things we have never before considered about ourselves and others.
3. It comforts us.

CELESTIAL THERAPY HEALS US AS IT FREES US

After commencing Celestial Therapy, many ideas, projects, and passions that previously held us hostage, consuming our time, energy, and financial resources, are no longer on our "wanna do," "gotta do" lists. Celestial Therapy can even change the way we determine when enough is enough.

Celestial Therapy can also free us and save us time and energy by turning many "hot issues" of the world into "non-issues" for us. Try this Celestial Therapy prescription: Take one world "hot issue." Immerse it in temple truths. What is the result? Most often, a non-issue; at the very least, an abundance of eternal clarity that reduces prolonged debate to a Post-it-Note-sized comment.

Celestial Therapy can free us *and* our ancestors. I am fascinated with the Lord's economy. We vicariously bring to women who no longer live in this world the saving ordinances they absolutely need to be freed from spiritual death and the chains of hell. And in the process, *we* are freed. We are freer when we leave the temple than when we entered. Freer to do what the Lord requires of us and to discern good from evil. Freer to fill the measure of our creation and experience joy. Freer to solve our problems and freer to give our will to the Lord. We are also freer to put aside telestial relationship behaviors that shrink our spirits and grieve the Spirit.

Eliza R. Snow and Zina Diantha Huntington Young were great advocates of temple worship for women. Was it Zina's temple experiences that allowed her to respond so lovingly to an emotionally cruel comment? Zina had been told by an informant that a certain woman didn't like her. Her response? "Well, I love *her* . . . and she can't help herself."[3] When someone is unkind, judges us unfairly, and persistently undermines our best efforts, can we respond as Zina did? Through Celestial Therapy we can.

CELESTIAL THERAPY CAN HEAL US THROUGH WHAT IT REVEALS TO US

Celestial Therapy can give us new insights into ourselves and others, sometimes clarifying what we should do in difficult situations. The Lord generously manifests to us those things we are seeking—just as soon as he perceives we are ready. At times we get more than we requested.

During her temple worship, one woman fervently prayed for further purifying so she could fill the measure of her creation. To her chagrin, during the proxy endowment session and for a full week following, the whisperings of the Spirit invited her to become a "pride detective" in her life. She was embarrassed to discover obvious pride manifested in judging others and in unforgiveness. But truly dramatic changes began for her when through her temple lenses she saw that pride was the hidden root of many other things she struggled with—from feeling left out to being overweight.

Pride had invited her to believe that the Lord's laws of health really didn't apply to her. She didn't have to exercise and eat healthfully to stay healthy and fit. Pride made her believe she was above that, and thus pride invited excessive pounds and ill health to become part of her life.

This woman also found that on occasions when she felt left out, it was really her pride telling her that others should be more interested in her. Pride's myopic stance isolated her. A major revelation for this woman was that feelings of low self-worth, selfishness, and pride are a tragic trio.

Another woman was continually in emotional upheaval and even despair because of a very difficult relationship with her mother-in-law. By immersing herself in intensive Celestial Therapy, she was able to give up defending herself and criticizing her supposed enemy. How? One day, as this woman reflected on this anguishing situation in the light of her temple covenants, a question came to her mind: "How would I respond to her gross misinterpretations of everything I do were I to discover that one of my mother-in-law's premortal assignments was to help me prove myself to the Lord and, in the process, truly come to know myself?"

These celestial thoughts totally changed her view of her mother-in-law's difficult behavior and freed this woman's mind and heart, allowing her to extend kindness and love, even in the midst of continuing accusations from her mother-in-law.

CELESTIAL THERAPY CAN HEAL US BY COMFORTING US

One source of comfort is anticipatory joy. Celestial Therapy was the healing balm for a barren woman devastated by the pain of childlessness, by the grief of believing both she and her body had somehow betrayed her loving husband, and by judgmental remarks from her neighbors who cruelly questioned her devotion to home and family.

One day in temple worship she received the comforting thought that her children were indeed waiting on the other side of the veil for her. Friends had offered similar suggestions before, but she had passed them off as a trite way to dismiss and even negate her pain. But, in the temple that day, this thought came to her as a personal truth mercifully given by the Lord who *really* knew. As she contemplated this truth, she felt impressed that her children so wanted to have her as their mother that they were willing to wait until the next life.

Her pain and grief fell away, and from then on she began to groom herself into a great mother in this life by nurturing and bearing with others—even in their most unlovable moments. With confidence borne of celestial tutoring, she continues to move through her life, blessing others and no longer shrinking from the violets offered on Mother's Day.

Celestial Therapy can indeed heal us as it frees, reveals, and comforts. Inside the temple, the Lord's altar and symbols are part of Celestial Therapy. When we depart from the temple, Celestial Therapy continues as we leave with the Lord's power and name upon us and with his glory and angels round about us.

Through Celestial Therapy the Savior's atoning sacrifice becomes real to us in a manner we have never before experienced. We come to know *him*, not just know about him. And we come to *love* him—above everyone and everything else. As he named and blessed his newborn son, one young father prayed, "Pedro, you will know your wife because she will love the Lord *more* than she loves you." When we want to live closer to the Lord than we ever have, closer to him than to anyone else, he brings us closer to everyone else. We experience through temple worship an anchoring and a direction in all our other relation-ships.

May we always know where the temple of the Lord is and where we stand in relation to it. May we stand in these holy places and seek Celestial Therapy to solve our problems. And as we do so, may we arise and shine forth as women of light.

Notes

1. Henry B. Eyring, "Always," *Ensign*, October 1999, 9.
2. George Albert Smith, *Sharing the Gospel with Others* (Salt Lake City: Deseret Book, 1948), 198.
3. In Susa Young Gates, Diary, 25 July 1879, holograph, Archives of The Church of Jesus Christ of Latter-day Saints, Salt Lake City. See also Janet Peterson and LaRene Gaunt, *Elect Ladies* (Salt Lake City: Deseret Book, 1990), 57.

THE UNSPEAKABLE GIFT

꒛

Sally H. Barlow

We have been taught that "God shall give unto you knowledge by his Holy Spirit, yea, by the unspeakable gift of the Holy Ghost, that has not been revealed since the world was until now; which our fore-fathers have awaited with anxious expectation to be revealed in the last times, which their minds were pointed to by the angels, as held in reserve for the fulness of their glory; a time to come in the which nothing shall be withheld" (D&C 121:26–28).

Our beloved prophet, President Gordon B. Hinckley, spoke at a recent general conference about the gradual evolution of his testimony.[1] It took root at the age of five with a tender blessing by his father along with a salt poultice prepared by his mother that freed him from the pain of a terrible earache. Next, a sense of peace lingered one cold winter night after he had knelt to pray alongside his brother in their unheated bedroom. Later gospel study quickened his testimony as he served a mission in the British Isles. His experiences continued, each building on the previous one, toward an unshakable foundation. His story illustrates the gradual growth process we go through to be both sharpened and softened by the Holy Ghost. This gracious development of life's most important communication is sometimes bestowed "like the dews of heaven" and sometimes like a bolt of lightning. These at times simple, at times spectacular communications are from the Holy Ghost.[2]

I love being in President Hinckley's presence, even if it's only electronically. When he said, "You've probably heard enough from me!" at

Sally H. Barlow, a clinical psychologist, is a professor of psychology at Brigham Young University. She serves as the Gospel Doctrine teacher in her ward. She is a single mother to one son who is currently serving a mission in Colombia.

175

the close of the 170th general conference, I shouted from my living room, "No, we haven't!" The best moments of my life have been like these, when I have been in the presence of truth, goodness, beauty. I have been cataloging those moments:

> struggling with a difficult concept and finally understanding it
> lingering over the scent of a flower
> seeing a Minerva Teichert painting
> standing outside the nursery window looking at my newborn son
> listening to a Brahms symphony
> watching a client struggle with a serious mental illness and triumph
> feeling the clear spiritual witness of the Holy Ghost

These moments defy description; though I know what they all have in common: namely, I am no longer inside myself looking out but instead, I am one with the moment in an inexplicable rush of joy. The psychologist Abraham Maslow labels these moments "peak experiences."[3] We all seek them in some way or another. Unlike fads or fancies of culture, true beauty points us to God. Yet the experience lasts only a few precious seconds. I treasure these moments, and I often seek to recreate them. I can go to art galleries; as a psychologist I can continue to see new patients and hope we reach the ground of good health together; I can bury my nose in the spring flowers. I can always listen to Brahms—all I have to do is flip a switch. In other words, there is something about these experiences I can control.

Matters of the Spirit are more complex. We cannot simply flip a switch to encounter a witness of the Holy Spirit. I have wrestled with this dilemma all my life and have made many wrong turns trying to control the Holy Ghost. As the scientist John Haught stated, "Religious revelation can be encountered only by allowing oneself to be grasped by it, not by grasping it."[4] Earlier in my life's journey, in my frustration at not being able to control the Holy Ghost, I sought counterfeit ecstasies until I finally realized that this path was a dead-end. Little by little I have learned about and felt the Lord's love, as his grand communicator, the Holy Spirit, has taught me patience and submission to God's will.

For most of us, cultivating the gift of the Comforter alternates between spurts and starts and steady lessons. Why is the Holy Ghost so important? Different parts of me answer in different ways. The psychologist in me thinks anything that activates the higher mental processes of our brains is better than mere appetite. The mother in me needs the Holy Ghost's help prompting me to be patient. As a neighbor, I am thankful to be reminded not to yell at the neighbor kids when they break my window or trample my flowers. The list goes on. You could say, "Well, that's just good common-sense, civilized behavior." True. Still, we know that everything good comes from God. And somewhere in that mix of my doing the right thing and the prompting of the Holy Ghost exists the very real influence of Jesus Christ and, in helping, guiding, and comforting us, the Holy Ghost testifies of him.

The Spirit gives us what we need, not merely what we may think we want. Symphonies and roses never correct us, but the Spirit can, and frequently does, gently chastise us while still loving us. A friend has given me permission to share this experience. "For the last seventeen years, I have always had a child with me. I have been fortunate in finding pleasure in my children's company. As they grew, I felt myself mourning the loss of their daily association. I wanted to be comforted, and I didn't want change, even though I knew that it was coming. I was driving—one of my favorite quiet times—and I felt the gentle impression of the Spirit tell me to look to my left. I saw a bed of newly blossoming daffodils. The question came to my mind, 'What do you see?' I thought to myself, *Beautiful flowers*. Then the question, 'Did you see them there last week?' *No*, I thought. Then the sweet, gentle chastisement, 'Couldn't you be a little more like mother earth that moves so gracefully from one season to another?' I felt comforted, enlightened, challenged, all at the same time."

Truth found only in beauty does not offer the fulness of the gospel. The painting *Carnation, Lily, Lily, Rose* by John Singer Sargent partially illustrates this principle.[5] One night at twilight Sargent saw two girls playing with lanterns in a garden. Entranced by the light, he determined to paint it. But try as he might, he could not capture the image.

After many failures, he finally invited the two girls to pose for him for fifteen minutes every night at twilight for two years. Many love the innocence and light of the resultant painting and are grateful to Mr. Sargent for patiently seeking a way to capture a transforming moment in his life. This beauty, as great as it is, can fail us, however, but the pattern Sargent followed—his patient, determined search for artistic inspiration—illustrates the way to the beauty and power that will never fail. Try as I might to recapture the awe of the Holy Ghost's illuminating Spirit, all I can do is practice patiently by reading God's words, fulfilling my callings, and repenting of my sins. I can count experiences of visitations of the Spirit on one hand. But I am learning to count the preparation time more steadily.

LDS women are a sisterhood of individuals from different nations and races, young and old, single/married/widowed/divorced, in a mind-boggling array of differing circumstances. Our eleven million members stretch across all geographical borders and psychological boundaries. Our experiences with the Holy Ghost, testifying to us individually, allow for our spiritual unity. No individual circumstance detracts from that. The only requirement is our willing discipleship.

When women come together to learn and share truths of the Spirit, we bring to life Doctrine and Covenants 108:7: "Strengthen your [sisters] in all your conversation, in all your prayers, in all your exhortations, and in all your doings." But to sustain these feelings of well-being and camaraderie, we must go home and study and pray and put into practice the admonitions of the Savior. Then, when we are weary of the world, we can call to remembrance the good feelings we had together, and carry on. If I am so enchanted by one painting of Sargent's, might I be even more enveloped and transcended by the true manifestations of God's artistry? As Nephi said, "I glory in my Jesus" (2 Nephi 33:6).

THE HOLY GHOST

Who is this remarkable personage of Spirit, whom Luke names fifty-seven times in Acts alone, "which . . . filleth with hope and perfect love"? (Moroni 8:26). Elder James E. Talmage boldly states that the Holy Ghost manages everything![6] As the third member of the Godhead, the Holy Ghost has been referred to by the familiar names of Holy Spirit or Holy Ghost, as well as others. The Hebrew and Greek translations are *ruach,* or "wind," and *pneuma,* or "breath." The Holy Ghost has been known variously in emblematic form as fire, living water, oil, a dove, rain, and dew (see Table 1, page 186). The Holy Ghost transforms us from within (Jeremiah 31:33–34; Hebrews 8:8–10; Ephesians 1:13; Mosiah 5:12). In a slow, often painful, process we become new.

For thousands of years, from Adam to Moses to Christ, God carefully orchestrated this hope of internal revolution. Certainly the Holy Ghost visited prophets of old as Jehovah spoke to them promising to give them a "new heart . . . and a new spirit" (Ezekiel 36:26). But his death brought his mission to a whole new level of hope by bestowing the regenerating power of the Holy Ghost that works within, as Paul said, a "circumcision . . . of the heart" (Romans 2:29).

Given the many wonderful functions of the Holy Ghost, what keeps us from his company? Many in the world simply do not believe in the divinity of Jesus Christ. The Holy Ghost's main function is to testify of Jesus. What about those of us who believe and yet still can't seem to find his company? We might be troubled by a number of things in Christianity that seem contradictory: prosperity of the wicked, adversity for the righteous, the suffering of innocents, and other issues. Numerous examples of each can be found in the scriptures. And perhaps even more troubling is the apparent silence of God. Why does he not speak to us through the Holy Ghost whenever we experience need, when we are desperate, afraid, indecisive?

If the Holy Ghost spoke to us every minute, we would not develop true faith. God's plan is brilliant, and we cannot quite grasp with our mortal minds just how intricately we are to be remade into new creatures. As I watched the building of the new Conference Center in downtown Salt Lake City, the immensity of the project, from the vaulted ceiling to the pipes of the organ, amazed me. Are not our eternal identities even more complex undertakings? Will it not take steel girders, concrete, the removal of thousands of yards of dirt, delicate carvings in our inner parts to truly craft us in his image?

How do we hone this gift so that through the years we learn to distinguish the soft whispering of truth from the whining of the world? We must fine-tune our bodies—physically, emotionally, and mentally—so that our spirits can flourish.

FINE-TUNING OUR BODIES

Our midbrain regulates appetites—hunger, thirst, sex. We need to learn to control those appetites rather than let them control us. In Romans 8:9, we are told that a man without a spirit is one who follows natural instincts. Our brains are built for anger, lust, gluttony. Why would God create our brains in this fashion? Why not just make us nice from the beginning? Perhaps because unearned niceness is as tasteless as many grocery store tomatoes. Every day, in every way, every time we face our faults, our impulsive flare-ups of anger, lust, or unrighteous power, we begin a dialogue between our midbrain and our forebrain that slowly but surely creates the templates which allow God gradually to transform us through his grace into beings of light, new creatures who can eventually stand in the very presence of the God of glory. Still, those conversations between our midbrain and forebrain can be hard work. When we are feeling discomfort or cravings, our midbrain appetites usually communicate something like this:

"I am so (tired, depressed, sleepy, angry, despairing, flustered). I think some (heroin, cocaine, speed, marijuana, cigarettes, alcohol, junk food, stimulating drinks, misuse of prescription drugs, binging and purging, sex outside the covenant) would help me get through this (day with the kids, class, test, meeting, the night shift, homesickness, horrible divorce). But I am trying not to give in to that. How am I going to get through the next four hours? Why can't God just help me out here! [Long but not contemplative or listening prayer.] See, I knew he wouldn't help me. Might as well use what I know I can count on any time . . . (drugs, binging and purging, etc.)."

That I have listed certain substances and certain circumstances side by side may be uncomfortable. Obviously some items on this list are far worse than others, but our ultimate goal is to rely in all things on God, not on the arm of flesh. Many of these outlets—from cocoa to cocaine—place a barrier between us and God. That is not to say that physical and mental suffering aren't devastating. Often the intensity of some experiences draws us into addictions we would never have thought possible—and away from God. But we are promised that, through Christ, no affliction or iniquity is beyond consolation (Alma 36:18–19).

Elder Neal A. Maxwell has suggested that whatever our circumstances, we must strive for true contentment to accept our mortal allotment without self-pity.[7] All around us are women who yearn for children and have none, who long for formal education and have no access to it, who struggle with dire illnesses and long for health, who wish to be married and are not, who are desperately poor, who are missing limbs or sense organs. The list goes on. Certainly we should do all we can to remedy these circumstances, but we must also accept some things. As Paul stated, "There was given to me a thorn in the flesh." He then asked three times, Why me? God responded, "My grace is sufficient for thee: for my strength is made perfect in weakness" (2 Corinthians 12:7, 9).

Elder Maxwell continues, "Life's necessary defining moments come within our allotments. . . . Sufficient unto each life are the tests thereof!" He suggests further that "deprivation can [be] excavations that make room for greatly enlarged souls. . . . Our trusting contentment lets the Holy Ghost have precious time in which to do His special work. When spiritually aligned, a poise can come, even when we do not know 'the meaning of all things' (1 Ne. 11:17)."[8]

In her essay "That's How the Light Gets In," poet Nancy Hanks Baird writes poignantly of her own struggle with stuttering: "Where—I stamp my foot as do all human beings who have had pieces of their life stolen—where is there comfort and peace for me? Has not my heart been broken enough? I believe the balm of Gilead, that resin of regeneration, must come from within, from achieving a perfect inner harmony with oneself and the Spirit of God. I have found this place a few precious times, and so I know what it feels like, to be so grounded in God's Spirit that nothing, no pain in this world, can shake you. . . . O to be there always! . . . There are paths to that place. . . . We all have wounds, cracks in the perfect surfaces of our lives. That is how our hearts are broken and through which [they] may be filled with light. That is how we know our strength."[9]

We all have difficulties to overcome, some of our own making, some not. The only reliable partner in this endeavor is Jesus. Where do we seek him? How does he communicate with us? Through his holy words in the scriptures, the prompting of the Holy Ghost, and our constant prayers to the Father. If I take a drink, scream at my son, stray from the path of Christ, I can depend on the temporary relief of the adversary. To give up these soothing habits by putting my faith in God often creates an immediate unknown, but an eventual reality. "For now we see through a glass, darkly; . . . but then shall [we] know even as also [we are] known" (1 Corinthians 13:12).

Mental and physical health enables our spirits to thrive. Maimonides, the physician and rabbi, wrote, "Since it is impossible to have any understanding or knowledge of the Creator when one is sick, it is one's duty to avoid whatever is injurious to the body and to cultivate habits that promote health and vigor."[10] Sometimes achieving health is, however, beyond our capacity. Joseph Smith in *Lectures on Faith* talks about the ravages of mental illness, for instance.[11] Certainly, mental illness is just one example of when we may not have the capacity to rise above our infirmities and reach for God. We may, in fact, confuse the Holy Ghost with our own troubling thoughts. Fortunately, the Lord has enlightened many of the sciences about the ways our minds and bodies work, and at these times, we should seek others to hold up our arms that hang down, friends or professionals who have the ability to discern what is truly best for us. Their help can help us to eventually restore our relationship with God.

FINE-TUNING OUR SPIRITUAL SELVES

Elder F. Enzio Busche has said: "I have seen tragedies happen when members professed that they had prayed about a certain direction and then, assuming that they had received answers, ran right into disaster. There seems to be, inside of us, the capability to be spiritually illiterate. . . . We must never forget that our enemy, the adversary, is a spiritual being. . . . Occasionally we may even feel a certain reluctance to deal with matters of a spiritual nature because of our insecurity in discerning the difference between the influence from the Spirit of God and the promptings that may come from the liar and deceiver. Every faithful Latter-day Saint will see the influence of the adversary in blunt and blatant appearances, but it seems easy to become confused when the influence of the adversary comes as a subtle deception, as he is the master of disguise."[12] How may we avoid these subtle deceptions? Galatians 5:22–23 offers the key: "But the fruit of the Spirit is love, joy, peace, longsuffering, gentleness, goodness, faith, meekness, temperance." If the communication you receive yields fruits that are opposite—hatred, contention, ill-temper, impatience, meanness, cold selfishness—then you may know it is not from the Holy Ghost. The Lord has given us the skills to determine the source of our inspiration (D&C 52:14, 19; Luke 14:33).

As we call on the Spirit more and more, we will be able to use one of the gifts of the Spirit, discernment, to ferret out the true Spirit from our own mortal and sometimes fallible emotions.

Elder Busche also said, "In my humble understanding, . . . there are only two elements that separate us from the Holy Spirit. First, our lack of desire to repent, and, second, our lack of desire to forgive."[13] Our conscious efforts to draw near to God (through prayer, supplication, service to others, and contemplative scripture study) are most effective when we live the principles of forgiveness and repentance. As President Gordon B. Hinckley taught: "There is no peace in reflecting on the pain of old wounds. There is peace only in repentance and forgiveness. This is the sweet peace of the Christ, who said, 'Blessed are

the peacemakers: for they shall be called the children of God.'
(Matthew 5:9)."[14]

Constant busyness can also distance us from God. Elder Boyd K.
Packer recently stated that he worries about how busy we are, so busy
that we may not be able to hear the Holy Ghost as his influence is
mostly felt—"a thought put into your heart."[15]

The Holy Ghost brings peace, the one feeling Satan cannot duplicate. He can duplicate pleasure, momentary happiness, and many other
feelings. But he cannot duplicate pure joy and peace. Across the spectrum from these is worry, an activity women are particularly good at.
We worry about important things, to be sure: the state of the world, the
future of children, relationships. Our brains are wired for fear and its
stepchild, worry. As Dr. Edward M. Hallowell said: "Virtually every cell
in our bodies and every one of our physiological systems can contribute
in one way or another to the human response of fear. . . . Hormones,
nerve cells, neurotransmitters, great chunks of the brain, sensors in the
skin, reflex arcs, involuntary muscles, even hearts—all these stand on
alert twenty-four hours a day. . . . As far as nature is concerned, happiness doesn't really matter. Survival does."[16]

Life floods us with constant tensions, but perhaps we can learn to
see and experience them differently. For instance, I have wondered
why, when I could finally be a really good mother, now that I've figured out a lot of things, I no longer have a young child at home to parent. (I have also wondered why, now that I am old enough and experienced enough to do a better job as a teacher, my mind is starting to go
to pot!) Because my son is no longer a child, I must resist spending my
energy worrying about the mistakes I made with him. All I can do is
repent, ask for forgiveness, and move on. I can then help others with
their children instead of constantly worrying over or lamenting the loss
of my own. Most women experience similar tensions about parenting.
Perhaps God intends to introduce us to the notion of limitation so that
we need always to rely on him, as well as upon others. This reliance
creates true empathy, patience, and love. These tensions might be,
then, a way of keeping us "theotropically" aligned—always searching

for the Light of Christ. Just as plants stretch their leaves toward the sun's light, we must reach out for God's light. And, from every beautiful spiritual experience I've been blessed to know, the clear message has been, "Do not worry."

The story of Leah Widtsoe, granddaughter of Brigham Young, illustrates how the Holy Ghost can help us understand mortal actualities and awaken us to spiritual possibilities. Leah's mother, Susa Young Gates, filed for divorce when Leah was only four, and she lived most of her childhood with her alcoholic father. She might have said, "Why me?" and let herself be limited by resentments and despair, but she chose to follow other promptings. She recounted later: "During my lonely childhood I promised myself that if the Lord would ever grant me my great desire and let me be a mother in the flesh to some of His spirits that I would give my all to make for them a happy home where they should be loved and understood which at times is better than love." When she and her mother reconciled in Leah's teenage years, Leah set aside past hurts and embraced her mother. Her wish finally came true, too. She went on to be married—by all accounts in a happy union with John A. Widtsoe—and they had children. Leah also tirelessly worked to promote the national and international movement of family education. Certainly in her youth she would have been justified in harboring anger at being abandoned by her mother to an alcoholic father. But she chose the higher road of sanctification that comes from cracks in our souls, weaknesses made strong, the strength we are given when we forgive and move on.[17]

Let us awake to patterns of behavior in ourselves, such as contention, worry, busyness, and resentments, that separate us from the God of love. We are poised in a position to learn about ourselves and our loving Father as we repent. I am grateful for mortal experience, grateful for the inner transformation available to me if I keep the commandments. I am grateful for a "new heart . . . and a new spirit" (Ezekial 36:26) and the regenerating power of the Holy Ghost that works within to craft us in his image.

TABLE

NAMES, FUNCTIONS, AND FORMS OF THE HOLY GHOST

Bible Names of the Holy Ghost

Breath of the Almighty—Job 33:4

Comforter—John 14:16

Eternal Spirit—Hebrews 9:14

Good Spirit—Nehemiah 9:20

Holy Spirit—Luke 11:13

Spirit of knowledge—Isaiah 11:2

Spirit of truth—John 14:17

Spirit of holiness—Romans 1:4

Spirit of burning—Isaiah 4:4

Spirit of revelation—Ephesians 1:17

Spirit of Christ—Romans 8:9

Spirit of prophecy—Revelation 19:10

Spirit of wisdom—Isaiah 11:2

Spirit of understanding—Isaiah 11:2

Forms of the Holy Ghost

Fire—Matthew 3:11; 2 Nephi
31:13–14

Living water—Isaiah 44:3

Oil—Luke 4:18

Dove—Matthew 3:16; 2 Nephi 31:8

Rain and dew—Psalm 133:3

Functions of the Holy Ghost

Testifies of Christ—John 15:26

Dwells within us—John 14:17

Brings to remembrance—
John 14:26

Reproves the world of sin—
John 16:8

Guides, speaks, declares—
John 16:13, 15

Yields fruit of the Spirit—Galatians
5:22, 23

Inspires the scriptures—Acts 1:16

Speaks to his servants—Acts 8:29

Forbids certain activities—
Acts 16:6–7

Intercedes—Romans 8:26

Shows the new way—Luke 24:49

Enables apostles to persevere—
John 16:20, 33

Prophesies—Luke 1:67

Gives joy—Romans 14:17

Fills with hope and love—
Moroni 8:26

Guides missionaries on travels—
D&C 31:11

Unfolds mysteries of God—
1 Nephi 10:19

Notes

1. Gordon B. Hinckley, "My Testimony," *Ensign*, May 2000, 69–71.

2. Witness the conversion of Paul in the old world and Alma the Younger in the new world approximately a hundred years earlier versus the less dramatic conversions of many others.

3. Abraham Maslow, "Self-Actualizing and Beyond," in *The Pleasures of Psychology* (New York: New American Library, 1986), 299.

4. John F. Haught, *God after Darwin: A Theology of Evolution* (Boulder, Colo.: Westview Press, 2000), 8.

5. John Singer Sargent, 1856–1925, *Carnation, Lily, Lily, Rose,* Tate Gallery, London.

6. James E. Talmage, *Articles of Faith,* 12th ed. (Salt Lake City: The Church of Jesus Christ of Latter-day Saints, 1924), 159–62.

7. Neal A. Maxwell, "Content with the Things Allotted unto Us," *Ensign,* May 2000, 72.

8. Ibid., 72–74.

9. Nancy Baird, "That's How the Light Gets In," in *Clothed in Charity,* ed. Dawn Hall Anderson, Susette Fletcher Green, and Dlora Hall Dalton (Salt Lake City: Deseret Book, 1997), 211, 214.

10. Maimonides (1135–1204), quoted in Benjamin Blech, *Understanding Judaism* (New York: Macmillan, 1999), 21.

11. Joseph Smith, *Lectures on Faith* (Salt Lake City: Deseret Book, 1985), 1:10.

12. F. Enzio Busche, "Unleashing the Dormant Spirit," in *Brigham Young University Speeches* (Provo: BYU Press, 1996), 221–22.

13. Ibid., 226.

14. Gordon B. Hinckley, "Of You It Is Required to Forgive," *Ensign,* June 1991, 2, 5. Our beloved prophet also said in this talk: "We see the need for [forgiveness] in the homes of the people, where tiny molehills of mis-understanding are fanned into mountains of argument. We see it among neighbors, where insignificant differences lead to undying bitterness. We see it in business associates who quarrel and refuse to compromise and for-give when, in most instances, if there were a willingness to sit down together and speak quietly one to another, the matter could be resolved to the blessing of all. Rather, they spend their days nurturing grudges and planning retribution."

15. Boyd K. Packer, "The Cloven Tongues of Fire," *Ensign,* May 2000, 8.

16. Edward M. Hallowell, *Worry: Controlling It and Using It Wisely* (New York: Ballantine Books, 1997), 57–58. Worry and anxiety can be constant com-panions. We are told to be good stewards. We are given a long list of things to do every conference—from gardening, to supporting our neigh-borhoods and communities, to providing the constant attention we need to give to our families. Is this what is really meant by always being engaged in a good cause? It likely doesn't mean the fretfulness and worry and anxi-ety that many of us experience.

17. In Mary Jane Woodger, "Leah Widtsoe: Pioneer in Healthy Lifestyle Family Education," *Family and Consumer Science* 92, 1 (2000): 50–54.

AND SHE SAID, "LET THERE BE MOLEHILLS"

꠵ᏟᏗᏟ

Emily Bennett Watts

The unexpected letter inviting me to speak at BYU Women's Conference arrived several months before the event was to take place. As I considered the opportunity, one of the first things that popped into my head was the question, "How much weight can I lose by April?" I knew it to be a shallow thought, unworthy of the charity I had experienced among the women at women's conference, but that was how I felt.

Just how well I was doing with this goal became evident a few weeks before the conference when the young man at the grocery checkout handed me, along with the receipt, a strip of stickers "for the little one." Because there were no little ones with me, I must have looked confused and perhaps a little hesitant. He gestured toward my stomach, indicating that he thought I was not merely pregnant but in imminent danger of delivering a child who would soon need stickers to amuse him.

Now, I was not pregnant. I had not been pregnant for eight years. I will likely never be pregnant again in this lifetime. But because I have been pregnant five times, and because I haven't done a sit-up in twenty years, and because I love chocolate and lead a sedentary life and have a penchant for the sort of flowing dresses that pregnant women wear, I am often mistaken for one of their number. My friend Janette Rallison

---

Emily Bennett Watts is director of the Bookcraft imprint at Deseret Book Company. She has served as a Gospel Doctrine teacher, a counselor in ward Primary and Young Women presidencies, and as ward Relief Society president. She and her husband, Larry, are the parents of five children.

from Arizona gave me a line that someday I'm going to be brave enough to use when this happens. She says, "I'm not a pregnant woman, but I play one on TV." I'm going to say that sometime—but usually I just smile and say thank you, take the stickers, and get out of the store.

The fact is, I have learned that—for me, anyway—losing weight takes a tremendous amount of emotional energy. I have chosen to invest my emotional energy in other places right now. And so what I have to do is treat that aspect of my life with humor. As Marjorie Hinckley says, "You either have to laugh or cry. I prefer to laugh. Crying gives me a headache."[1]

A sense of humor can be an incredibly valuable asset in life. When, as conference participants, we were invited to consider where in Jerusalem we might stand to deliver our messages, I couldn't imagine that applying to my topic of humor until a slide came up of the Wailing Wall. Immediately I thought, *What better place would there be to stand and say, "Weeping may endure for a night, but joy cometh in the morning"* (Psalm 30:5), *or "Someday you will be able to smile, perhaps even laugh again, and when you do, you will know that you are on your way to healing."*

That is easy for me to say because I don't have problems that require a wailing wall. What I need is more like a whining wall. Little things build up. It's not the great big problems that are most troubling, because I know enough to seek the Lord in those times, but the little accretions of every day just glom onto me, building up even when I don't quite realize it's happening. Those are the things that get me down. Those are the times when an appropriate sense of humor would help. Notice the word *appropriate*. Humor matters, and I've discovered a great key to distinguishing between a helpful sense of humor and a harmful sense of humor.

In the scriptures, when the word *laughter* is used, it is generally associated with being scornful. "All they that see me laugh me to scorn" (Psalm 22:7) is a typical reference. On the other hand, the scriptures frequently encourage us to be of good cheer (John 16:33; 3 Nephi

1:13; D&C 61:36). Does that mean we are to be of good cheer but keep it all inside and never laugh? Impossible. But clearly there is a difference between humor that mocks and humor that lifts.

We can stay clear about that difference by remembering one of the main effects of humor: Humor trivializes things. Understanding that effect provides a good handle on how to use it appropriately. We don't laugh about sacred things because humor trivializes, and sacred things ought not to be trivialized. People, also, ought not be trivialized, so we don't make fun of people. Yet many other aspects of mortality should be trivialized—in fact, would do better trivialized. Some mountains would be better if they were considered molehills.

After twenty-two years of marriage and five children, I can tell you, you're never going to be finished with the laundry. Never in your life is every dish in your house going to be clean, unless you live alone. Maybe then you will achieve this celestial goal of clutter-free kitchen counters and a completely empty dishwasher. There's never going to be enough time for all that you want to do. And there's never going to be enough money. But you know what? Somebody paid the price of there being not enough. Somebody gave us the grace that says, "Do what you can, and I will make it enough."

A sense of humor can help us trivialize those things that need to be diminished in our lives. With that effect firmly in mind, I'd like to discuss several other qualities of humor that can lighten our burdens as we toil through this life.

1. Humor builds bridges. As a child I was captivated by the ancient custom described in the *Arabian Nights* that if you ate salt with someone you could do him no harm. It was a great plot device. Could the warrior get his enemy to eat salt with him so he couldn't kill him?

Have you ever noticed that it's difficult to be mad at somebody you have laughed with? Laughing with someone is like eating salt with that person in the Arab world. Humor builds those bridges. How many times have you heard President Hinckley say, "Well, we have been here a long time," or "Well, you've sat through a lot." Humor acknowledges shared experience: he knows that sitting in the Tabernacle or in the

Conference Center for a long time can be wearing. Humor helps us recognize and acknowledge what each other is going through. It builds a bridge between us. That's the first effect.

2. Humor helps us to keep things in perspective. When my children were little, sometimes they would get hopping mad. If you've had a toddler, you've probably seen that little face screwed up and ready to burst into tears in frustration. In our house, when a child is in that state, we usually say, "Don't laugh." Because their emotions are so close to the surface anyway, it's easy to switch them over to the laugh track. Sometimes you have to say it two or three times: "Don't laugh . . . ah-ah-ah, I see a laugh coming . . . oh oh, here it comes!" They try hard to keep frowning, but pretty soon they laugh. Whatever they were mad about has been forgotten. I remember being extremely frustrated with my two-year-old daughter. I don't remember now what she had done, but I do remember her looking up at me with her big, green eyes and saying, "Don't laugh, Mom." It worked! I couldn't be mad at her anymore; I couldn't be frustrated. It was a moment of perspective for me.

A similar moment came when I was Relief Society president in my ward (in itself a cause of humor for some). I was pregnant and had a big maternity coat. This was a large coat. This coat could have served as our family's emergency preparedness tent. One homemaking night, I hung my coat on the rack in the ward house—and it got stolen. I was perplexed. Why on earth would anybody steal what was obviously not a highly fashionable coat?

When I got home and poured out my sad tale, my husband pointed out that a person could shoplift half of Albertson's under that coat—a twenty-five-pound turkey could have been hidden in its folds, and nobody would have noticed. Somehow, that knowledge failed to make me feel better. Whatever the reason for the theft, I had no maternity-size coat. I was upset, and being pregnant, I cried a lot more than I cry normally. Observing this, my two-year-old son got a very determined look and volunteered, "I will get mad at them for you, Mom." The thought of my small son going out to battle the hooligans who had filched my coat settled me down enough to restore some perspective.

This loss was not the end of the world. I didn't want that coat any-way—and after the baby was born, I wasn't going to wear it again ever—so it was all right. That mountain shrank back down to its proper molehill size.

3. Humor releases pressure so we can resolve problems. When I was a child I had a healthy fear of my mother's pressure cooker. I don't think we use pressure cookers as much anymore now that there are microwave ovens; in fact, I don't even own one. In case you aren't familiar with them, a pressure cooker is a massive, heavy pot with a lid that locks in place to keep the lid on as pressure builds. When steam starts to emerge from the vent pipe, you put a small weight over the opening, and the air vent whistles and sputters as the steam escapes. It sounded scary to my young ears, and Mom would always caution, "Don't *ever* take the lid off the pressure cooker until you have run cold water on it to bring the pressure down or it will explode." I always feared that one day the pressure cooker would explode all over the house. (It never did.) Here's the point: Humor is like the cold water you put on the pressure cooker that brings down the heat so that you can open it up and solve your problems.

For a few months while we were engaged, my future husband lived in Cedar City and I lived in Salt Lake City. One week my family trav-eled down to Cedar City to attend the Shakespeare Festival and also to give me a chance to see him. During this trip, he took us to Mammoth Cave, which isn't a cave like Timpanogos or Carlsbad Caverns with beautiful rock formations and tour guides. It might more aptly have been named "Mammoth Hole in the Ground." You climb down into the mouth of it on your own with flashlights. The tunnel, a little lava flow, gets progressively smaller and narrower until you come out of the cave at the other end. He thought it would be an adventure for us, so in we climbed: my parents, my brothers, my fiancé, and me.

Being somewhat cautious and not at all sure footed, I was the last one to get through the cave, and when I finally got to the climbing-out part, I got stuck. My husband-to-be stood outside Mammoth Cave and laughed and laughed and laughed. That sounds unchivalrous, maybe even mean, but it would have been meaner for him to come over and say, "Oh my goodness, oh my gosh, what are we going to do?" I was having visions of Winnie the Pooh, being stuck there until I thinned out enough that they could pop me out. Because he was laughing, the pressure was off, and I felt confident that there must be a solution. Sure enough, my kind younger brother assessed the situation and instructed me how to untangle my feet and my legs so that I could wriggle out of Mammoth Cave and carry on with my life.

Now, humor was not the solution. I want to make that clear. Sometimes humor is not the solution to the problem; humor is what releases the pressure and gives us perspective so that we can *find* the solution to the problem.

So if humor is that great a thing to have, how do we find it? We have to look for it. We have to cultivate it. I cut out comics. When I was a little girl, my parents bought Bill Cosby records to listen to. I read jokes on the Internet, though I never remember one long enough to tell it.

I often find humor in words. For example, preparing to come to women's conference, I bought a large quantity of pantyhose at the outlet center, thinking I'd like to have five or six reserve pairs in case I got runs in four or five on my way to the Smith Fieldhouse. As I was pulling them out to pack them, I noticed that the package said "size 3X, slightly irregular." I had to laugh; that seemed a reasonably accurate description of my body.

Another thing we can do to cultivate humor is to save some things to laugh at later. Some events that really aren't very funny right now might indeed be funny in a few weeks or a few months. For instance, I have a son for whom it was virtually impossible to sit still in church or to walk reverently down the halls when he was little. We even used to take him over to the ward building on weeknights so he could practice folding his arms and walking quietly; he usually managed about three or four steps before he was off and running.

I spent a lot of time in the foyer in those days. In fact, I despaired of ever being able to sit through an entire meeting again. One particularly trying Sunday, when another beleaguered mother and I were doing our best to corral our little ones, I smiled at her and said, "Someday we'll be telling about this at their missionary farewells."

That rambunctious son of mine is eighteen years old now. His mission farewell will be next year, and I can't wait to tell this story. It won't just be my way of getting back at him; it will be my opportunity to say that this was a joyous time of our lives, a time we can look back on with laughter and remember with fondness.

I have a friend who says, "If it can be wiped up or rubbed off, it's not worth fussing about." I have a picture of my daughter at about age one with indelible, blue marker scrawls all over her stomach. At the time, I wasn't particularly amused, but I was farsighted enough to recognize that it would be funny someday. So I took a picture, which not only allows me to laugh now but gives me leverage for when I want her to do something. I remind her that she sometimes brings around young men who might just be interested in our family photo album . . .

There are evidences all around us that our God is a personage of cheer. Go to Temple Square and count how many different kinds of tulips there are. Think of sunsets. Think of animals. Think of all the wonderful, cheerful things there are in this world. Then look in your Topical Guide, not under *laughter* but under *cheer* and *cheerfulness* and *glad* and *happy* and *joy* and *merry*, and you will see that our God intends us to be a happy people. One of my favorites of his scriptures is, "If thou art merry, praise the Lord with singing" (D&C 136:28). My colleagues tell me that sometimes when I come into the office I *am* singing. "Why are you so happy?" they want to know. And I stop and wonder, *Am I singing because I'm happy, or am I happy because I am singing?* I don't know which came first, but it makes me appreciate the words of the Shaker hymn, the last verse of which goes:

> *I lift mine eyes; the cloud grows thin;*
> *I see the blue above it;*
> *And day by day this pathway smooths*
> *Since first I learned to love it:*
> *The peace of God makes fresh my heart,*

Though sorrow forth is springing:
All things are mine since I am His—
How can I keep from singing?
—James Lowry, 1860

I pray that we will know that we shouldn't keep from singing. We should lift our hearts and be glad. We should know that our Father in Heaven wants us to have joy here and now. With a good sense of humor, appropriately applied, we can find a way to that joy.

Note

1. Marjorie Pay Hinckley, *Glimpses into the Life and Heart of Marjorie Pay Hinckley,* ed. Virginia H. Pearce (Salt Lake City: Deseret Book, 1999), 107.

HEY, GUYS, I'M HAPPY

꒰ ꒱

Emma Lou Thayne

On a quick visit to our house, our two-year-old (born on my birthday and named Emma Grace) climbed into her car seat, looked around,
and said, "Hey, guys, I'm happy!" This is the baby who at five days old
meditated—I'm sure of it—looking contentedly for thirty minutes at a
time at a white wall, holding, I know, to the trailing clouds of glory.

So why not at two the declaration, "Hey, guys, I'm happy"? Oh, my
little honey, my sprite of a namesake, keep being that. It is intelligent
to be happy—not as a mood, but as a mode. Not to wallow in self-pity,
not to cling to bad times, but to set about finding help even in what
might seem like tragedy. Sometimes, if we're open to it, peace can find
us.

We will win, we will lose; we'll hit winners, we'll make errors. We
must celebrate the temporary to buffer us for anything to come, but we
must hold to the great constancy, the presence of Jesus Christ in every
winning or losing. It has nothing to do with status.

A most moving moment in scripture for me is in John, which
records the Savior's last moments: "Jesus therefore saw his mother, and
the disciple standing by, whom he loved, he saith unto his mother,
Woman, behold thy son! Then said he to the disciple, Behold thy
mother! And from that hour that disciple took her unto his own home"
(John 19:26–27). We know nothing more. Where was Joseph? Was

---

*Emma Lou Thayne, poet and author of more than thirteen books, has been a part-
time English teacher at the University of Utah for thirty years. She has also served as
a member of the YWMIA General Board and the Deseret News Board. With her
husband, Melvin E. Thayne, she has a family of five daughters, five sons-in-law,
and nineteen grandchildren. She considers her present Church calling the best ever:
a greeter in her ward.*

that disciple, John, married? Did he have a family? All we know is that Jesus cared enough about each one alone to want them to have each other when he was gone. That caring is what makes Jesus the one we can turn to, especially in adversity.

One of the problems with adversity—as if it needed any problems—is that we expect it, sometimes even wait for it. "Anticipatory anxiety," I kid my daughters when they worry without reason about what is yet to come. Anticipatory anxiety. How it trips off the tongue. And how easy it is to indulge it. How we get caught up in it. Take, for instance, New Year's Eve 2000. Remember Y2K? The dire predictions of calamity, of evil, of dread foulups of our computers, terrorist takeovers, threat of shortages. Instead, what? A worldwide celebration of light—as if the Savior himself traveled the globe to welcome a new millennium. In our watching, it started in Lapland in a hotel of ice. Surrounded by friends in furs, a Lapland couple dressed also in furs walked an aisle of ice. I could not understand a word the priest said until first the groom and then the bride answered a hearty "Yah!" Then the kiss that went on and on. (The kind to which Mel, as a sealer in the temple, has to say, "That will do.") Then laughter and cheering as they walked back up the aisle of ice, the first marriage of a new century.

Delight! From there to New Zealand, where opera diva Kiri Te Kanewa sang the beat of her Maori kinsmen, to Paris and the Eiffel Tower, which was bursting with fireworks, around the globe over and over again, the light, the warmth, the unity, the universal celebration, the peace on earth, ending of all places in Las Vegas on the infamous Strip where the lofty fountains of the extravagant new Bellagio Hotel and Casino rose and throbbed in time to—imagine!—the "Hallelujah Chorus" of Handel's *Messiah*. Glory indeed. The happiness multiplying back in Salt Lake that year as Mel and I each turned seventy-five and celebrated our fiftieth anniversary with all five of our daughters and their husbands on a five-day holiday in California—golf, tennis, beach, a movie, eating eating eating, visiting into the night, lots of hugs, and, of course, laughing. Hey guys, we were happy.

Then the jagged course. Back home, three dear friends in desperate trouble. Still bright but with macular degeneration and far from steady legs, Edith Shepherd—the last of her generation for me, my friend to visit on Sundays ever since our days on the YWMIA General Board, still in her ninetieth year and determined to live alone, maintain her precious independence, but having falls and pains. Debbie Bell—forty-five, sweet, energetic, for ten years the meticulous rescuer of my home with deep housekeeping and bright conversation once a month—suddenly doubled over upon leaving after a day of cheerful cleaning. No doctor; insurance questionable. Emergency surgery—ovarian cancer. And my pal, amazing DeAnn Evans, fifty-nine, only female managing editor of *The Deseret News,* there when I was for seventeen years the only woman on the board of directors, the two of us friends and coadvocates for staff, readers, and women. More recently she was a beloved professor of journalism at the University of Utah, my buddy in the world of words and music—and she just died. Cardiac arrest at fifty-nine. Ten years ago I gave her two kittens for Christmas. I have now brought them home, meowing their displacement, Luciano and Violetta, so named for our mutual love of opera. I could hear my salty friend saying about the pets she adored, "Now the damn cats are yours, Emma Lou." And so they have become, lolling on Mel's lap as well as mine and purring like I'd like to be able to again as I ask "Where can I turn for peace?" in every prayer.

Each of these three remarkable women was living her life as "one": Edith widowed, Debbie divorced, DeAnn never married. Credible, loving, loved women, central to extended families, though living alone. Linked as we are—or not—in a household, each of us was born as one, will die as one, hurt as one, and heal as one. We matter as one.

Remember the woman with the flow of blood for twelve years. Imagine such an affliction! She "had spent all her living upon physicians, neither could be healed of any, came behind him, and touched the border of his garment: and immediately her issue of blood stanched. And Jesus said, Who touched me? When all denied, Peter and they that were with him said, Master, the multitude throng thee and press thee, and sayest thou, Who touched me? And Jesus said, Somebody hath touched me: for I perceive that virtue is gone out of me. And when the woman saw that she was not hid, she came trembling, and falling down before him, she declared unto him before all the people for what cause she had touched him, and how she was healed immediately. And he said unto her, Daughter, be of good comfort: thy faith hath made thee whole; go in peace" (Luke 8:43–48).

Was the woman married? Did she have children? Was she single? How old was she? Was she rich or poor? Without sin or weakness? All we know is that she was one person—in a throng—reaching with childlike faith. It could be Edith or Debbie or me trying to deal with pain and DeAnn's death. Over and over, Jesus said, "My peace I give unto you: not as the world giveth, give I unto you" (John 14: 27). Each of us is eligible as we try hard, play fair, and have fun. But we must pray at night and *expect* that peace. We must allow ourselves the honor of receiving in celebration or in grief—to let the vacancies fill as they refine and mellow us. And we must be willing to move on.

In 1970, our oldest daughter at nineteen was caught in the agony of manic depression, bulimia, and anorexia, when few knew anything about any of those perils, least of all us, her very bewildered parents. For three years she—we—struggled in by far the most bleak time of our lives. No day or night was without anxiety, anger, extremities of love and desperation.

Becky healed. Thanks to prayer and knowing where to turn, and thanks to the gracious professional help of a doctor and medication, together with the love of Paul, who was to become her husband and the father of her three sons, she was able to reenter the life she had left. Twenty years after her bout with her illness and after helping girls in Young Women in her ward, she told me she wanted us to write her story—together. "Mothers suffer as much as the girls do," she told me. So we wrote a book entitled *Hope and Recovery*. Recovery. Becky and I both testify to the moving on and finding in the layers, not in the litter, the way to say, "Hey, guys, I'm happy."

May I suggest ten ways to find happiness through finding peace:

1. Know that life is a jagged course, a kaleidoscope, that this too—whatever it is, joy or pain—will pass.
2. Expect the healing. Pray at night, listen, and then plan in the morning.
3. Remember the Serenity Prayer: God, grant me the serenity to accept the things I cannot change, the courage to change the things I can, and the wisdom to know the difference.
4. Move out of bitterness—not to be defeated twice, once by circumstances and again by self.
5. Don't try to fix everything. Only God can do that.
6. Remember in any relationship: I can love you with all my heart, but not with all my time.
7. Pass the baton. Let someone else take it up.
8. You don't have to do all you used to do. Enjoy vicariously. Going slow is a gift.
9. Maintain your own life. Keep track of yourself as a person so you can be part of the answer instead of part of the problem.
10. Know with assurance that the sun will come up—and come up with it.

Perhaps my final route to peace in these later years is to offer myself the privilege of receiving. I have watched my girls grow, take on their own struggles, sometimes searing, call on me and their dad when they have needed to but emerge as five strong women married to five strong men. They are for the most part—cross your fingers with me—happy women who along the jagged course find openings to laugh in, never forgetting to laugh.

Martriarch

Center of the wheel, matrix, she will not be gone.
Her hands that warmed the other hands,
shook salt into sameness,
rubbed shine into what had to be done
are far from cold.

Her eyes that stayed open for other eyes,
knew tears and how to give hers
to take others' away are seeing.

Her feet that sprang to run down
a hungering, to trample a threat
quietly go about their business.

Her breath that breathed sun
into trying and green into discouragement
touches where it's needed.

Her ears that drew sadness
away from what was left
are denied no hearing,
still give laughing audience to laughing.

Her heart will not be closed on
its numberless passions
and indignations,
her amazing head has not
gone off with its secrets.

Her soul, transparent, will not be replaced
by a vacant moon.
No, I will not hold to how she filled her spaces,
recognize her in the strong fingers of a daughter
finding the right note,
see her in the run of a grandson heading out,
feel her in a friend weeping in private.
I will follow her abundunce into aromas
of pinyon and cinnamon,
the ripe cold of spring.

Her house will not be empty.
Band-Aids and soup,
peppermints and a paintbrush,
much-handled books
will speak for her.

God will send autumn and Christmas
then of course summer
and let us hear her singing us home.

And someone will be carrying on.

—Emma Lou Thayne

LETTING THE LIGHT IN

꒰ ꒱

Janet S. Scharman

Mary Elizabeth Lightner was just twelve years old and a recent convert to the Church in Kirtland, Ohio, when she heard that a copy of the "golden Bible," or Book of Mormon, had been sent from Joseph Smith to Brother Isaac Morley, the elder presiding over her branch. She raced to his house and asked to see it. Recounting this event in her autobiography some years later, she told of her overwhelming desire to read the book once it was placed in her hands. She begged Brother Morley to allow her to take it with her for just one night. He hesitantly agreed on condition that she take great care with it and bring it back early the next morning. Mary said that she was "perfectly happy in the possession of [this] coveted treasure."[1] The following day Brother Morley was surprised to learn that this twelve-year-old girl had read and studied a good portion of the text throughout the night. He allowed her to keep the book a little longer and encouraged her to keep reading. A short time later, the Prophet Joseph himself came to Kirtland. He was touched when he heard the story of Mary and the book. Mary vividly recalled her first meeting with the true and living prophet: "When he saw me he looked at me so earnestly, I felt almost afraid. After a moment or two he came and put his hands on my head and gave me a great blessing, the first I ever received, and made me a present of the book, and said he would give Brother Morley another."[2]

Over the following decades, Mary's faith grew. As an elderly woman in 1905, she bore a fervent, unwavering testimony of the gospel's truthfulness to a group at Brigham Young University: "Every principle that has been given in the Church by the prophet is true. I

Janet S. Scharman is the dean of students and assistant student life vice-president at Brigham Young University. She and her husband, Brent, have a blended family of one son and nine daughters. She serves as Gospel Doctrine teacher in her ward.

know whereon I stand, I know what I believe, I know what I know and I know what I testify to you is the living truth."[3]

This passionate testimony comes as no surprise given the very spiritual nature of Mary's introduction to the Church. She had heard the words of a living prophet, received a blessing of God through his hands, and read the truest book ever written. Here is just a sample of what else is recorded in her autobiography: "I have been in almost every mob. I have been driven about and told I would be shot and had a gun pointed at me. . . . I was there in all the tribulations and trials. I have been in the houses that have been stoned. . . . I have seen the brethren shot and ruined for life. I saw the first martyr dead. . . . I have seen our bishop tarred and feathered in the streets of Missouri, my husband did not belong to the Church. I begged him and pled with him to join, but he would not."[4]

Yet despite all that, at age eighty-seven she was able to say with conviction, "I know what I know."

Jane Manning James was another great woman of light who was touched with the spirit of God. Born a free black woman in Connecticut, she had to contend with the many challenges that blacks faced at the time, yet Jane was able to look beyond the prejudices and dream bigger dreams. As had Mary Lightner, she joined the Church during its early days. Feeling compelled to unite with other Saints in Nauvoo, she and a few members of her family began the long trek. Authorities denied them passage on the Erie Canal in Buffalo, New York, and so the little group began the eight-hundred-mile journey on foot. Jane's trunk, carrying all her personal possessions, disappeared en route, and she was left with nothing but the clothes on her back. She later recounted how they walked until their "feet became sore and cracked open and bled until you could see the whole print of our feet with the blood on the ground."[5] This would have pushed most to the point of despair, but she continues: "We stopped and united in prayer to the Lord. We asked God the Eternal Father to heal our feet and our prayers were answered and our feet were healed forthwith."

Jane lived for a time with Joseph Smith and his family, and she knew Brigham Young personally. Highly respected by the entire Salt Lake community, she was one of few who enjoyed a prime reserved seat in the Tabernacle for Sunday services. Joseph F. Smith was one of several Church officials who spoke at her funeral.

But life in general was very challenging for Jane. She experienced the hardships and deprivations of all who crossed the plains, and her early years in the Salt Lake Valley seem almost unbearable. Her journal recounts the devastation of the crickets and grasshoppers, which left the Saints with almost nothing. Just as they began to rebuild, her husband, Isaac James, deserted her and their children, and she struggled desperately to provide for her family. She outlived all but two of her seven children, and six of her fourteen grandchildren died before reaching the age of four. During her later years, Jane's health failed and she could barely see. Of all her hardships, perhaps the most painful for her was her ineligiblity as a black woman to receive the temple ordinances.[6]

Mary and Jane represent to me models of great strength, courage, and character. They loved the Lord and wanted to serve him. Why did they experience so much heartache? Why did even their righteous desires go unfulfilled? Why was Jane denied in her lifetime the blessings of temple ordinances? Why was Mary unable to ever bring her husband to accept the gospel? I don't know.

I am often drawn to the words of Nephi, who was privileged to see our day, and who understood much more than he was permitted to share with us. Even with that knowledge he said, "I do not know the meaning of all things" (1 Nephi 11:17). If he were speaking to us today, he might say, "I don't know why righteous mothers sometimes have to watch their children suffer—physically or spiritually. I don't know why some who want children desperately are not blessed, while at the same time the out-of-wedlock pregnancy rate throughout the world is soaring to an all-time high. I don't know why some children are abused, some employers are unfair, or why some political agendas have the momentum to sever the very fiber of our moral values." Then I go back to that very same verse in which Nephi also says, "Nevertheless, I know that he [meaning our Heavenly Father] loveth his children."

These words move me to the real question about Mary Elizabeth Lightner and Jane Manning James. Despite all their trials, how were they able to go on in righteousness and goodness, never criticizing or attacking their Church or their God? I do have an answer for that question. I believe they, like Nephi, knew beyond any doubt of Heavenly Father's love for them. The Spirit had witnessed to them this profound truth so powerfully that they could never deny it, regardless of the hardships and disappointments that came their way. At times in their lives, they must have wondered why they were given such trials to bear. Their questions didn't have ready answers, just as ours don't. Trusting in the Savior's love and watchful care through good times and bad and knowing that their experiences would ultimately be for their benefit propelled them to greater resolve and commitment.

We can have that same witness. That unmistakable knowledge of his love and light is a gift "bestowed upon all who are true followers of his Son" (Moroni 7:48). It is a gift freely given. Our task is not so much to earn it, for in truth we can never do enough. Rather, we are only asked to look to and acknowledge the source of that power and gift and then be willing to accept it—to humble ourselves enough to let God's love into our lives.

That sounds simple enough, and it is. Unfortunately, the adversary is working overtime to confuse, tempt, and lead us away from light into darkness. His message is that life is unfair and that we have been left on our own to do the best we can.

It wasn't always that way. President James E. Faust reminds us that "[Satan] was not always the devil. Initially, he was not the perpetrator of evil." He was, in those premortal councils, "an angel of God who was in authority in the presence of God" (D&C 76:25). President Faust goes on: "Satan became the devil by seeking glory, power, and dominion by force. . . .

"Because of his rebellion, Lucifer was cast out and became Satan, the devil, 'the father of all lies, to deceive and to blind men, and to lead them captive at his will.' . . . And so this personage who was an angel of God and in authority, even in the presence of God, was removed from the presence of God and his Son. . . . This caused great sadness in the heavens, 'for the heavens wept over him—he was Lucifer, a son of the morning.'"[7]

Satan and his followers were not cast out because they were no longer loved. They were not the victims of bad luck or recipients of unfair punishment. They suffer a consequence based on a choice freely made. Cast out because they refused to acknowledge the source of their light and strength, they now entice as many others of their brothers and sisters as they can to deny the light as well. Guatemala City Temple president Ernest L. Hatch notes, "The devil is not smart because he is the devil; he is smart because he is old."[8] He has been around, and he knows human frailties, those things most likely to cause us to deviate from the path which leads us back home.

My Salt Lake City stake provides ecclesiastical support for some of the LDS branches at the Utah State Prison. Many inmates there are serving long terms for heinous crimes, atrocities that I try not to even imagine. And yet, from those whom I have met in a church setting, I sense a tenderness, a desire to do better, to make a connection with their Father in Heaven. Ray F. Smith, formerly an LDS chaplain at the prison, told of meeting the mother of one inmate. "You know," she had said, "he is a good boy." Brother Smith commented, "I think of our Heavenly Father looking down upon His spiritual children . . . I think He says, 'Just a few years ago they were good boys. They were here in my heavenly home. In fact, they were so good I held them in reserve. I didn't send them to earth until the gospel was there.'"[9]

We are daughters of God, also given knowledge, talents, experiences, and opportunities to contribute to God's plan and held in reserve for this day when the gospel has been restored. But we have vulnerabilities, and, over centuries and even millennia, Satan has become well aware of them. While he may be unable to tempt us to choices that would lead us to prison, Satan has learned how to demoralize us—to focus us on our inadequacies, to encourage us to feel overwhelmed, and to distract us from remembering that Christ is the true power behind all that we are able to do. The adversary knows how to draw us away from the light, and no one—not even prophets—are exempt from his meddling.

I remember President Spencer W. Kimball as a man of resolve, ready to tackle any worthy task head-on. "Do it," read the sign on his desk. It's hard to imagine him shrinking from any assignment or challenge, and yet consider his immediate response when called to be an apostle: "The predominant thought was my own limitations and incapacities and weaknesses and I was overcome. The tears came then, an inexhaustible flood . . . I wept and wept . . . I was in convulsions of sobbing."[10] These words, so inconsistent with my image of President Kimball, well express sentiments recorded in any number of places in my own journal. Somehow it comforts me to know that even the choicest of God's children have struggled with similar feelings to my own. Only days after being sustained as president of the Church, President Gordon B. Hinckley commented, "I have, during these past few days, been overwhelmed with feelings of inadequacy. . . . I do not know why this mantle has fallen upon my shoulders. I suppose some of you may also wonder. But we are here."[11]

These men were valiant soldiers during the war in heaven, called by God to be prophets in our day and sustained by the councils of heaven. But here, with the veil drawn, they are human beings with human emotions, experiencing the uncertainties that often accompany tremendous responsibility. For much lesser causes, I have felt similar feelings. These emotions shouldn't surprise or frighten us. What we do with them is what counts.

Elder Jeffrey R. Holland addressed the issue of self-doubt and Satan's role in it. "Beware the temptation to retreat from a good thing. If it was right when you prayed about it and trusted it and lived for it, it is right now. Don't give up when the pressure mounts. *Certainly don't give in to that being who is bent on the destruction of your happiness.* Face your doubts. Master your fears."[12]

Elder Holland continued, "Fighting through darkness and despair and pleading for the light is what opened this dispensation. It is what keeps it going, and it is what will keep you going." The Lord assures us in Doctrine and Covenants 50:24–25: "That which is of God is light; and he that receiveth light, and continueth in God, receiveth more light; and that light groweth brighter and brighter until the perfect day. And . . . I say unto you, and I say it that you may know the truth, that you may chase darkness from among you." That is the promise God has given us. We have the power to chase darkness away from us. Satan *is* powerful, but as Joseph Smith taught, "The devil has no power over us only as we permit him."[13] He will try and try and try again, but as we receive light, and continue in light, it grows brighter and brighter, giving us the power we need so that we can do as Mary Elizabeth Lightner and Jane Manning James did. They chased away the darkness that could have consumed them.

Without question there are times when despite our sincere pleading for light, it may seem as though nothing is happening, at least not the way we expect it. Elder Boyd K. Packer reminds us: "You cannot force spiritual things. . . . You can no more force the Spirit to respond than you can force a bean to sprout, or an egg to hatch before its time."[14] But there are things we can do to ready ourselves to receive the Spirit, and these things *are* within our control. Besides the essentials of prayer, fasting, and scripture reading, let me suggest three other things we can do to develop spiritual strength.

First, be willing to respond to promptings, however small, and then remember to thank the Lord for them. Some months ago I misplaced my only pair of glasses, and I needed to prepare a lesson for a class the next day. I am at that point in my life when I can't squint hard enough or hold papers far enough away to decipher anything without my glasses. I searched the house from top to bottom. I examined every corner again and again, retracing my steps numerous times. I enlisted the help of my husband, who went through the same routine but with no better success. I simply did not know what to do. Finally, I offered a modest but sincere prayer to my Heavenly Father: "I know you know where these glasses are," I prayed. "I also know that it is my fault that they are lost and that I may not be particularly deserving of your help right now. But I don't want to let my students down by being unprepared. Please help me." Immediately I felt impressed to go outside. I did not receive a vision or voices from heaven—just a thought. It was dark outside and there, in the driveway, on the top of the car sat my glasses, probably the only time in my life I have ever put them there. Then I remembered taking them off earlier as I was doing yard work. This may seem minor, but it was exactly the miracle I needed that night. Numerous times I have been guided in small but significant ways for my own needs, as well as for the needs of others, and I have learned to heed and be grateful for these promptings.

Second, learn to have realistic expectations for yourself and others. Working hard is important, but, as the saying goes, "Even if you win the rat race, you're still a rat." We need to stay out of the rat race as much as possible. This means being very clear about what is truly important and then being willing to let go of some less important things that consume our time and energy.

I know a woman who every morning dutifully created a "to do" list for the day and took great satisfaction in being able to cross off the items on her list. It was important to her to be organized and productive and feel that she was doing her best. The problem was, she had a few complications that didn't fit neatly into this organized structure: several small children, a demanding Church calling, and a husband who needed her help with his new business. Predictably, she never seemed to have enough time to get to the tasks at the bottom of the list, especially that last item, "scrub the floor." She became very discouraged. Finally late one night she decided not to go to bed until she had devised a plan that would not leave her feeling exhausted and inadequate at the end of every day. She thought and calculated and reworked various plans, but there seemed to be no solution. Then, as if by inspiration, the answer came to her. She dropped "scrub the floor" off her list. No longer printed in black and white, broadcasting her inadequacies, she could ignore the floor and feel better about reading a book to her children or sitting down for a few minutes to rest.

This worked for her. Another solution may work better for you. Of course, things of eternal importance should never be dropped from our lists. The point is, we can determine what is essential in this life and what will best help us achieve that end. When we feel calm and in control, even if everything isn't exactly perfect, we are much more likely to be receptive to the Spirit. We need energy to tackle problems, and we also need to feel that we are doing well enough to invite the Lord's spirit into our lives.

A third way to develop spiritual strength came to me as I participated in the "pass the torch" event at Brigham Young University, where the current student body officers hand over their responsibilities to the next year's officers. As part of the ceremony, the president lights a candle and then with that candle lights candles held by individuals on either side of him. They, in turn, light the candle of the person next to them, and so on. In that process, the original candle dims for just a moment as the next candle takes flame. Then both candles immediately come to full brightness, producing twice the light. It is a simple but nonetheless true concept that one way to increase our light, and ultimately feel better about ourselves, is to share it with another.

The resurrected Christ, speaking to the Nephites, said, "Behold I am the light which ye shall hold up" (3 Nephi 18:24). What we are really feeling when we serve others is the spirit of Christ within us. It's not always easy to consider another's needs, and initially we may even fear losing what we have if we give it away. Experience shows us, however, that if we share with someone else, even just a little, we will be blessed. How does all this work? As Nephi said, there are many things I don't know; but I do know this: Heavenly Father loves his children. I know he wants us to be happy, and if we make our best efforts to qualify for his spirit, I know that Christ will acknowledge the goodness in our hearts and give his light to us. Like Mary Elizabeth Lightner, I also know what I know: His love is his light.

Notes

1. "Mary Elizabeth Rollins Lightner," autobiography, *Utah Genealogical and Historical Magazine* 17 (July 1926): 194.

2. Ibid., 194–95.

3. Mary Lightner, address to Brigham Young University, 14 April 1905, typescript, BYU Archives and Manuscripts, Harold B. Lee Library, Brigham Young University, Provo, Utah, 2.

4. "Lightner," 196–260.

5. In Linda King Newell and Valeen Tippetts Avery, "Jane Manning James, Black Saint, 1847 Pioneer," Ensign, August 1979, 26.

6. Henry J. Wolfinger, "Jane Manning James: A Test of Faith," in Worth Their Salt: Notable but Often Unnoted Women of Utah, ed. Colleen Whitley (Logan, Utah: Utah State University Press, 1996), 14–30.

7. James E. Faust, "The Great Imitator," Ensign, November 1987, 35.

8. Ibid., 35.

9. Ray F. Smith, address given at Brigham Young University, 5 February 1957; copy in possession of author.

10. Edward L. Kimball and Andrew E. Kimball Jr., Spencer W. Kimball (Salt Lake City: Bookcraft, 1977), 191.

11. Gordon B. Hinckley, "This Is the Work of the Master," Ensign, May 1995, 69.

12. Jeffrey R. Holland, "Cast Not Away Therefore Your Confidence," Speeches: Brigham Young University 1999–2000 (Provo, Brigham Young University Press, 2000); see also Ensign, March 2000, 8–9.

13. Joseph Smith, Teachings of the Prophet Joseph Smith, sel. Joseph Fielding Smith (Salt Lake City: Deseret Book, 1976), 181.

14. Boyd K. Packer, "The Candle of the Lord," Ensign, January 1983, 53; see also "That All May Be Edified": Talks, Sermons, and Commentary by Boyd K. Packer (Salt Lake City: Bookcraft, 1982), 338.

HOW CAN I FEEL JOY?

❧

John Bytheway

Don't let life's ups and downs "interrupt your rejoicings." Do you remember the story of Korihor, who taught the people that there would be no Christ? I have always appreciated the first question put to Korihor by Giddonah, the high priest: "Why do ye teach this people that there shall be no Christ, to interrupt their rejoicings?" (Alma 30:22). Our knowledge of Jesus Christ and his saving mission should cause us to *continually* rejoice. When our hearts are plagued with feelings of guilt and inadequacy, these may be Satan's attempts to "interrupt our rejoicings."

Life rarely unfolds the way we plan, but we can trust the Savior that "all things shall work together for [our] good" (D&C 100:15). Our joy in life comes because of him. Elder M. Russell Ballard said: "The best thing about living a Christ-centered life . . . is how it makes you feel—inside. It's hard to have a negative attitude about things if and when your life is focused on the Prince of Peace. There will still be problems. Everyone has them. But faith in the Lord Jesus Christ is a power to be reckoned with in the universe and in individual lives."[1] Faith in Christ is real power to deal with life. Why? Because it gives us perspective. The history of the world has already been written. John, Nephi, and many other prophets saw it from start to finish. We know the final outcome, and we know that the Lord will reign triumphant. Our job is to keep our covenants and keep the faith!

Take off your blinders. Elder Boyd K. Packer once compared the

John G. Bytheway, a popular speaker and writer, is a part-time instructor of religious education at Brigham Young University. He and his wife, Kimberly Loveridge Bytheway, are the parents of two children. John serves as the elders quorum president in his ward.

plan of salvation to a three-act play. Our premortal life he called act one. We don't remember our performance there, and the curtain has been drawn. We are now in act two. This is the hard part. Act two, Elder Packer taught, is characterized by tests, trials, temptations, and tragedies. Nowhere in act two appears the line "happily ever after." That phrase is reserved only for act three.[2]

A few years ago, my creative wife "kidnapped" me on my birthday and took me horseback riding. I noticed then that some of the horses in the corral wore blinders to keep them focused on only what was right in front of them. Blinders are useful for horses; but if we wear blinders and focus only on act two—the tests, trials, temptations, and tragedies—our joy may be interrupted.

We say it so often: "Have an eternal perspective." Taking off those blinders and opening our eyes to the entire plan of salvation helps us see all our difficulties in context. We need to remember that there was an act one (and I suspect we got rave reviews), and there will be an act three.

On Brigham Young University's campus is a building called the Testing Center. If you took a peek inside, you'd see a huge room filled with students focusing intensely on their tests. You could cut the tension with a knife in that place. One semester I sat there for five hours while taking a statistics final. I was exhausted when I left, and I felt like I had just been let out of prison. I've never seen anyone about to burst with joy in the Testing Center. Of course not, it's a place to take tests.

Life is often like a testing center; and the tests are difficult, with lots of unexpected questions. But our loving and merciful grader is not as concerned about our answer sheets as he is about our hearts. None of us will ace this test! The Lord knows that, and he asks us to take our tests with joy and faith. Jesus taught, "Wherefore, fear not even unto death; for in this world [act two, the testing center] your joy is not full, but *in me your joy is full*" (D&C 101:36; emphasis added).

You've likely heard or read President David O. McKay quote the phrase, "No other success can compensate for failure in the home." Some of us feel like we have failed that test, but it's not because we haven't tried. Listen to the whole context of the quotation: "When one puts business or pleasure above his home, he that moment starts on the downgrade to soul-weakness. When the club becomes more attractive to any man than his home, it is time for him to confess in bitter shame that he has failed to measure up to the supreme opportunity of his life and flunked in the final test of true manhood. No other success can compensate for failure in the home. The poorest shack in which love prevails over a united family is of greater value to God and future humanity than any other riches. In such a home God can work miracles and will work miracles."[3]

Did you catch the context? Failures come when we put business or pleasure above the home. The real failure is the failure to try. Laman and Lemuel and Nephi came from the same home, and we know that Lehi and Sariah tried. Would we call them failures? I suspect that, like Lehi and Sariah, many parents struggle and work and pray, and their children still have problems. If you're worried about some of your children, may I suggest that you find your May 1992 *Ensign* and reread President Boyd K. Packer's talk, "Our Moral Environment." He says that because we live in such a corrupt environment, it would be unfair to judge parents solely on how their children turned out. His conviction is that someday the evil forces of our corrupt environment will be overruled.[4]

I'd also recommend another book, *When a Child Wanders*, by Robert L. Millet, dean of Religious Education at BYU. Listen to this experience from Brother Millet:

"Several years ago my wife and I were struggling with how best to build faith in all of our children and how to entice wandering souls back into Church activity. A caring colleague, sensing the weight of my burden, happened into my office one day and asked, 'Do you think our heavenly parents wander through the heavens in morose agony over their straying children?' Startled, I thought for a moment and said, 'No, I don't think so. I know they feel pain, but I honestly can't picture them living in eternal misery.' My friend responded, 'Ask yourself why they do not do so, and it will make a difference in your life.' I didn't get much work done the rest of the day because I spent many hours pondering the question." Brother Millet discussed this question with his wife, Shauna, that evening, and together they "set about a prayerful quest . . . to understand how our eternal Father and Mother deal with their pain."

He said that "in time it began to dawn on us. . . . Perspective. PER-SPECTIVE. That was the answer. God deals with pain through and by virtue of his infinite and perfect perspective. He not only knows what we have done and what we are doing, but he also knows what we will do in the future. If, as the prophets have taught, many who are heirs to the blessings of the covenant made with Abraham, Isaac, and Jacob will either in time or in eternity be reconciled to the covenant family, then all we need to do for the time being is to seek through fasting and prayer for a portion of God's perspective."[5]

Turn it over to the Lord. Many of us have a strange hearing problem. We've heard the verse in Moses 1:39, "Behold, this is my work and my glory—to bring to pass the immortality and eternal life of man." But some of us who are parents hear it this way, "Behold, this is your job and your glory to bring to pass the immortality and eternal life of your children." The Lord says it is *his* work, and in another place he says, "I am able to do mine own work" (2 Nephi 27:20). Go through the scriptures one day and search for the words *willing* and *able*. You'll notice that the Lord asks us to be willing, but he is able. He requires the heart and a willing mind (D&C 64:34). When we take the sacrament, we witness that we are willing to take upon ourselves the name of the Son. As with many things in life, we are not always able, not perfectly anyway; but the Lord wants our hearts. We can be willing. We must do the best we can, knowing that he is able.

Use your imagination to exercise faith. While serving as a zone leader on my mission in the Philippines, I had the opportunity to go tracting with two sister missionaries. I saw what they had to go through, the places they had to go, the drunk men who harassed them, and other dangers in their particular area. I went back to my area and spent many hours worrying about those sisters. One day it dawned on me that I had a choice. I could either worry about them, which would do no good at all, or I could exercise faith in the Lord on their behalf. (It's interesting that we use the phrase "exercise faith," because keeping your thoughts positive and faithful is definitely an exertion). Every time a negative thought or a "what if" crept into my head, I told myself, "Nope, I'm not going to do that. I won't worry. Instead, I will keep the faith." Every one of us has been given an imagination, and most of us use it for exactly the wrong thing, continually acting out worst-case scenarios of what might go wrong. Perhaps we were given an imagination to exercise faith and to think of what might go right. So in my thoughts and prayers I exercised faith that the sisters would be in the Lord's hands, and they would be protected. And do you know what? They were.

In the final hours of Jesus' life, he said to his apostles: "Peace I leave with you, my peace I give unto you." Then, because that saying Shalom—was so common in his time, he added, "My peace I give unto you: not as the world giveth, give I unto you. Let not your heart be troubled, neither let it be afraid" (John 14:27). Elder Jeffrey R. Holland has commented:

"I submit to you that [John 14:27] may be one of the Savior's commandments that is, even in the hearts of otherwise faithful Latter-day Saints, almost universally disobeyed; and yet I wonder whether our resistance to this invitation can be any more grievous to the Lord's merciful heart. I can tell you this as a parent: As concerned as I would be if somewhere in their lives one of my children were seriously troubled or unhappy or disobedient, nevertheless I would be infinitely more devastated if I felt that at such a time that child could not trust me to help, or should feel his or her interest were unimportant to me or unsafe in my care. In that same spirit, I am convinced that none of us can appreciate how deeply it wounds the loving heart of the Savior of the world when he finds that his people do not feel confident in his care or secure in his hands or trust in his commandments."[6]

After hearing Elder Holland's talk, I understood that scripture in a new way. I had not considered that when I let my heart become troubled or afraid, I may be demonstrating a lack of faith in the Savior. It is my hope that we will lift up our hearts. That we will exercise faith. As Joseph Smith wrote, from a testing center called Liberty Jail, "Therefore . . . let us cheerfully do all things that lie in our power; and then may we stand still, with the utmost assurance, to see the salvation of God, and for his arm to be revealed" (D&C 123:17). Jesus has overcome the world! He has overcome death! We will see our deceased loved ones again! We can be cleansed from our sins and freed from our past! Men and women are, that they might have joy, and with our hearts and our minds focused on the Savior of the world, we have the best defense available for anything that may attempt to interrupt our rejoicings.

Notes

1. M. Russell Ballard, *Our Search for Happiness: An Invitation to Understand The Church of Jesus Christ of Latter-day Saints* (Salt Lake City: Deseret Book, 1993), 15.
2. Boyd K. Packer, "The Play and the Plan," Church Educational System Fireside, 7 May 1995; see also "President Packer Tells of 'Drama of all Ages,'" *Church News*, 13 May 1995, Z3.
3. David O. McKay, Conference Report, April 1964, 5; see also "What a Person Does Practically Believe Determines His Character," *Improvement Era* 67 (June 1964): 445.
4. Boyd K. Packer, "Our Moral Environment," *Ensign*, May 1992, 66–68.
5. Robert L. Millet, *When a Child Wanders* (Salt Lake City: Deseret Book, 1996), 153–54.
6. Jeffrey R. Holland, "Come Unto Me," *Brigham Young University Speeches, 1996–97* (Provo: Brigham Young University, 1997), 190.

WHAT IS THE PERFECT LIFE?

✺

Ann Crane Santini

Revamp your understanding of the word *perfect.* If God is perfect and all his works are perfect, how do we explain famine, disease, war, earthquakes? How can there be such imperfection in a perfect world? Imagine with me a conversation between Saint Peter and a newcomer to the afterlife.

SAINT PETER: Good morning, Sister Brown. Welcome to heaven. Did you enjoy your perfect life?

SISTER BROWN: What do you mean, "my perfect life"? You must have me mixed up with someone else—someone who never had any problems—you know, the ones who lived up on the hill.

SAINT PETER: Actually, Sister Brown, I've just reviewed the record of your life. It's right here. And no, I don't have you mixed up with anyone else.

SISTER BROWN: Now wait just a minute. My life was a lot of things, but one thing it certainly *wasn't* was perfect! In fact, I had more problems than almost anybody I knew. What about that traffic accident and the multiple surgeries my little Susan had to endure afterwards? She was only ten, you know. Or how about when my husband lost his job? Little Jimmy had just been born, and we lost our house and everything we'd been working toward. And that's just for starters!

SAINT PETER: Sister Brown, I think you're under the impression that "perfect" means "easy." In reality, "perfect" means "whole." How

Ann Crane Santini, a graduate of the University of Nevada in Las Vegas, is the manager of international relations for the Church in Washington, D. C., where she hosts events with foreign ambassadors and embassy diplomats. She and her husband, Jim Santini, are the parents of four children, and the grandparents of eight.

could you have a whole life without struggling? How could you gain the experience to identify with the rest of humanity if you just coasted along? Your husband's lost job brought many challenges, but look what it drew forth from you—renewed faith and endurance. And you learned that worldly goods were not so important after all. Look how united you became as a family, sharing responsibilities, loving one another, and all of you drawing closer to your Heavenly Father. Do you recall the scripture, "Whom the Lord loveth he chasteneth"? (Hebrews 12:6). You may remember that my death was by crucifixion, upside down. Now would you call *that* an easy experience? Strange as it may seem to say so, that death was a privilege for me.

SISTER BROWN: I'm so sorry. I had forgotten about that, Saint Peter. How you must have suffered! So what you are saying is that my life, with all its troubles, is perfect for me? To teach me, to bring me to Christ—to perfect me. Is that right?

SAINT PETER: Exactly, Sister Brown.

Accept your perfect problems. It was 1978. For four years my husband, Jim, had been serving in the United States Congress, representing the state of Nevada, when his work brought us to Salt Lake City to conference with Church leaders. By phone, our hosts had politely asked what I would like to do while in Salt Lake. I didn't hesitate. I wanted to get my less-than-idyllic life fixed. I was really tired of all the problems coming my way, way more than my fair share. And who was I going to get to fix things up? Why, the prophet, of course—President Spencer W. Kimball. He had the power to make things better. "Thank you so much," I said politely. "I would love for my family to meet and share some time with President Kimball." "That can be arranged," I was told.

Looking forward to that meeting, I started preparing my problem shopping list. Let me give you some background. Mark Santini, my spina-bifida-disabled but absolutely terrific son, was six years old. He had already endured ten surgeries and had spent more time in the hospital than at home. He had survived spinal meningitis and a hit-and-run accident at age three; a shunt in his head controlled his hydrocephalus; a urinary diversion called an ileostomy kept his kidneys from further deteriorating; he had endured surgeries to correct his club feet and curved leg bones; and numerous operations loomed on the horizon.

As Mark's mother and protector, I was not only dealing with a very precarious and uncertain future for him but I also had to consider the needs of Lisa, fifteen, and Lori, thirteen. They were teenagers (need I say more?). On top of this, political life from a wife's perspective is awful and wonderful, depending on what day of the week you are talking about. I had a big role to play in the upcoming reelection process. To these responsibilities, add a personal sadness that I was trying to work through, and there you have it.

I needed some help. I saw no way to solve all these problems by myself. Do you have any idea how much I wanted to lay at the feet of President Kimball in this one meeting? I wanted President Kimball to lay his hands on Mark's head and take away his pain and suffering—to make him walk right out of that wheelchair. I wanted President Kimball somehow to command Lisa and Lori not to act like teenagers. I wanted him to make *everything* all right again.

The day finally came. President Kimball, in my mind, was always bigger than life, so I was very surprised when I could look him straight in the eye. We were the same height! And how could anyone grasp his hand and not feel his goodness? As he spoke, I noticed his raspy voice and remembered stories about his battle with throat cancer. He knew, too, what operations and pain were all about. Then it struck me: maybe he hadn't had a perfect life either. But how could that be? He was a prophet!

As if he could read my thoughts, he began to talk about his own physical problems, speaking directly to Mark and embracing his shoulders. "So this is the lad I have heard about," he began. He talked about many things during the hour we spent with him, and at its end, I asked him if he would give Mark a blessing. "Of course," he responded. "I am glad you asked." It was a wonderful blessing, full of hope and love.

As we were leaving, he handed me a pamphlet entitled *Tragedy or*

Destiny? and said "J e just finish vriting this, and I think you will like it. It will sw ei .. ir questions." Then he smiled knowingly and hugged me

Don't rail, resist, or run away. How many times have you prayed, asking the Lord to fix your life, to remove whatever pain or suffering or injustice you've stumbled into? How much time do we spend asking Heavenly Father to "let this cup pass from me"? (Matthew 26:39). Like Adam and Eve, we must come to know that the cup is necessary.

Saint Peter defined it to Sister Brown, I believe, accurately: a perfect life is a *whole* life. Do you doubt there is a wholeness about a woman who knows who she is and accepts what she can and cannot do? There is a wholeness about a woman who can give her time, her energy, her talents, her compassion, and her strength to others and not feel diminished. There is a wholeness about a woman who can lose someone through death, through estrangement, and still feel complete. Blessed is the woman who has endured her pain and come through it whole.

We cannot teach others of Christ, preach to others of Christ, or rejoice in Christ ourselves if we don't understand the way Christ's plan works. We cannot rail against the plan, resist the plan, or run away from life's sufferings. We certainly can't blame our Heavenly Father for the very problems that would perfect us. God loves us; he wants us all to return to his presence perfected in righteousness. Our royal birthright as God's children endows us with the ability to learn from and triumph over the challenges we face.

"In the world ye shall have tribulation: but be of good cheer; I have overcome the world" (John 16:33).

Note

1. Spencer W. Kimball, *Tragedy or Destiny?* (Salt Lake City: Deseret Book, 1977).

How Can I Make the Sabbath a Delight?

❧

Karen Bradshaw Maxwell

When I was a young mother with two children under age two, I abandoned any effort to take my children into the absolute stillness of the sacrament meeting at the singles' ward where my husband was a counselor in the bishopric. I didn't attend for a month, but that was all I could stand. I remember looking with incredulity at the other counselor's wife, sitting with eight children who were as still as the proverbial church mice, and thinking there was some secret I obviously had not caught onto.

I have caught on now; it's called age. It is easier to have eight children over age three than to have two under that same age. We may wonder why we even attend, only to spend our time in the hall, in the nursing room, changing diapers, getting drinks, and dispensing that hallmark of determined church attendance—Cheerios à la Tupperware. Why go when we only occasionally hear a scripture quoted and never actually read one, when we are grateful for the respite a heartily sung hymn provides from the "hush" we hope will not hang eternally on our lips?

Maintain a pattern of Church attendance and be patient. Sometimes our only comfort is that we are maintaining a pattern of attendance and hoping a little bit of the Spirit will rub off if we don't become too frustrated with our kids. If this is true for you, may I reassure you that this is "just a stage" and that you *are* the righteous that

---

Karen Bradshaw Maxwell is the recipient of invaluable advice from parents and in-laws. She directs sixth-grade Shakespeare plays and serves as a counselor in her ward Relief Society presidency. She and her husband, Cory H. Maxwell, are the parents of eight children.

Isaiah says should be praised (Isaiah 3:10; 24:16; 60:21). Someday you too may, as Isaiah also says, "call the sabbath a delight" (Isaiah 58:13). Actually, it wasn't so bad to hold a baby on one hip and the scriptures on the other—perhaps a little hard to read well while bouncing in a quieting rhythm—but it was a rewarding balancing act in the end. Young mothers, especially, can have a core hunger to hear the word of the Lord and an adult voice speaking words of peace and truth and testimony. Surely the Sabbath is a delight and a feast for those who so hunger, for they shall be filled (3 Nephi 12:6).

The promises of observing the Sabbath day are joyful, marvelous blessings worthy of our best efforts (D&C 59). If it means we need to offer a reward for attendance, or actually make a quiet book, or do a "Let's Make a Deal" transaction with teenagers by placing the car keys behind door number one, or get rid of an encroaching job, or go to church even when we've been on the night shift—either at the office or with toddlers—the promises are real and will be fulfilled.

Seek the love in the Sabbath. Some believe that Christ fulfilled the law of the Sabbath and that, other than attending meetings, there need be no proscriptions on Sabbath activity. They see our observances as so many constricting don'ts. To some outside observers, we may appear almost pharisaical. In one great scene of *As You Like It*, Shakespeare contrasts several ways of looking at life. His character Jaques, who would no doubt be one of those accusing us of being pharisaical about Sabbath observance, talks about all the world being a stage. He then dwells on the negative in each stage of life, beginning with the infant "mewling and puking in the nurse's arms" and ending in old age "sans teeth, sans eyes, sans taste, sans everything."[1] Just at that moment, young Orlando appears, carrying his eighty-year-old servant who has sacrificed everything—his savings, his home, and his very life—to follow his young master into exile. Orlando tenderly puts down this ancient of days (whose name is Adam) and, with great love, helps revive him. In this touching scene, Shakespeare lets us see that it is love that changes even the very difficult end of life to something sweet and admirable.

It is love that changes the Sabbath from a day "sans everything" to a day that is most rewarding and precious. It is a feast and a fountain of living waters. On this day, those who longingly seek the Savior's love will find it, as in the words of the hymn:

> Come, ye disconsolate, where e're ye languish;
> Come to the mercy seat, fervently kneel. . . .
>
> Here see the Bread of Life; see waters flowing . . .
> Come to the feast of love; come ever knowing
> Earth has no sorrow but heav'n can remove.[2]

Those tender, wounded parts of us can bind us closely to the Lord on his Sabbath as we take the sacrament. This uplifting and solemn ordinance is the part of our worship services we can hold up to the world as a candle in darkness, the part of our meetings I would most want an investigator or less active friend to witness. I am always moved by it and am grateful for its beautiful simplicity.

To keep the Sabbath, set your heart apart. I have heard Truman Madsen say that the Sabbath has kept the Jews. They regard it as the queen of days—the bride—and mankind, as the bridegroom, dresses up and prepares all things to meet the bride. Some even regard every failure to enjoy the Sabbath as a sin. Their honoring of the Sabbath has united them as a people and brought them through historical holocausts, widescale scatterings, and rough reintegration in the Holy Land.

The Sabbath can do even more for us. It can get us through reintegrations and the holocausts and scatterings of everyday evils. How? Setting this day apart sets the heart apart as belonging to the Lord. It allows a change of focus. The Sabbath is truly made *for* man—not as just an arbitrary hurdle—to focus our worship in more intense, concentrated ways on the subjects of our love and adoration: our Heavenly Father and his Son, Jesus Christ. A day of rest? Busy Latter-day Saints may find the idea amusing while attending to all their Sabbath duties, but if not a formal rest, a change, a respite, a break in worldly routine, a focus on the family, an exercise of different spiritual muscles, and an opportunity to do good.

Consider the words of Elder Mark E. Peterson: "We constantly talk about the worldliness of the present day and speak of the fact that our young people face more serious temptations than did those of a generation ago, and this is probably true. Also, more parents seem to be caught up in the worldliness of today than was the case a generation ago.

"What can we do to protect ourselves under these hazardous circumstances? How can we better help our young people to remain unspotted from the world?

"The Lord gives us the answer, and says that it can be done by sincerely observing the Sabbath day. Most people have never thought of it in this way, but note the words of the Lord in this regard: 'That thou mayest more fully keep thyself unspotted from the world'—note these words—'that thou mayest more fully keep thyself unspotted from the world, thou shalt go to the house of prayer and offer up thy sacraments upon my holy day.'

"Think about that for a moment. . . .

"The Lord knows what he is talking about. Sabbath observance will help us to more fully remain unspotted from the world."[3]

Ask the Father what he would have you do. Have you ever played "Mother, May I?" We used to every Sunday evening in our neighborhood—sometimes we still do. I don't think the Pharisees ever played it, let alone on the Sabbath. Perhaps if they followed the pattern of the game, they would have thought to ask, "Father, may I?" about what to do on the Sabbath. And perhaps Heavenly Father would have given them giant steps or leap frogs instead of mere baby steps. Perhaps they would have gotten into the spirit of things and, finding what a joyful, loving Father he is, basked in their time with his Son. But perhaps they thought as Laman and Lemuel, "The Lord maketh no such thing known unto us" (1 Nephi 15:9). My guess is that they were simply not interested in God's will for his own day. They seem not to have been interested in much except exclusionary rules they could use to elevate themselves and abase others.

Thinking about the Savior and his Sabbath is not enough. Like Mary at the empty tomb, we must turn to his voice, hear him on the

Sabbath, and call him Master (John 20:16). Like John the Beloved, we should run toward the good news, the desire of our hearts (John 20:3–4), and like Peter, jump in when we know "it is the Lord" (John 21:7). We must show loving-kindness to our neighbor, gather with our families, feast on his word, and pray with all the energy of our hearts. We must hunger for the Bread of Life and thirst for the Fountain of Living Waters that is to be found at the center of the Lord's Sabbath. May we begin and maintain traditions of Sabbath observance that will bless us and our families, hold up a standard to the nations, and secure for us the riches of eternity.

Notes

1. William Shakespeare, *As You Like It*, 2.7.139–65.
2. "Come, Ye Disconsolate," *Hymns of The Church of Jesus Christ of Latter-day Saints* (Salt Lake City: The Church of Jesus Christ of Latter-day Saints, 1985), no. 115.
3. Mark E. Peterson, "The Sabbath Day," *Ensign*, May 1975, 47–48.

"Ye Are the Temple of God"

⚜

LaNae Valentine

Not so long ago I believed that only unmarried women experience feelings of loneliness and isolation. In fact, I had convinced myself that marriage was the key to feeling whole and complete, to filling any emotional void. I have since learned from my work as a therapist that marriage and children do not guarantee peace and contentment. Many women feel a sadness they cannot name. Though we accomplish much, something seems to be missing from our lives. Each of us might have a different idea about what that is. One woman told me that her life would be perfect if she didn't have to worry about finances and weight—if only she could have more money and less fat.

This "less fat" wish is a common one for women.[1] We live in a culture that brainwashes us into believing we should be thinner, prettier, firmer, younger, and thus in all ways better. These attitudes and beliefs are reflected in a $33-billion-a-year diet industry, a $20-billion-a-year cosmetics industry, and a $300-million-a-year cosmetic surgery industry.[2]

We set out to correct our physical imperfections, thinking that will transform our lives. Many of our young people can't even distinguish between the *possible* body and the dream body they see portrayed in the media. They don't care that models are airbrushed and digitally altered. They look and think, "This is what I must be," and long to achieve that "right" look. As Tessa Meyer Santiago notes, "[Many women] think that because our bodies do not look a certain, supposedly desirable, way, they are not worth having at all. Thus, we enter into a war with our bodies, hating the very tabernacle our Father has given us,

---

LaNae Valentine is a clinical practitioner specializing in women's issues and eating disorders. She is coordinator of Women's Services and Resources at Brigham Young University. She serves as the humanitarian leader in her ward.

despising the flesh. If Satan can get us to fixate on our bodies, either in vanity or self-loathing, then he has caused us to misunderstand completely the role our bodies play in our salvation."[3]

If I were to ask any Latter-day Saint why we are here on earth, one likely response would be, "To get a body." Joseph Smith taught that to receive a body is essential to our growth and progression. Yet, Latter-day Saints are as prone as anyone to act as if our bodies are more of a burden than a blessing. LDS men and women have been seduced by worldly attitudes and standards—manifested by growing epidemics of eating disorders, binge dieting, steroid use, and obsessive attention given to "fixing" our bodies. We of all people must resist ensnarement and repent of these worldly attitudes.

Among other faiths, some people believe the body is a sinful, disgusting, often decrepit hindrance that we must strive to transcend and hopefully discard some day. Others adopt a *carpe diem* philosophy, believing we must use our bodies' capacities for enjoyment to the fullest. One non-LDS man, grappling with concerns about the body-building, body-worshipping phenomenon in our society, noted, "All of us have to decide essentially what the body is for beyond just building it. Are we building it for a purpose? Are we building it just to be beautiful? Is being beautiful the purpose—or is being in control the purpose? . . . It seems to me the real issue we face in the world . . . as we grow older is how to be generative, how to use our bodies and our real selves for something that . . . has true value in the world."[4]

As I listen to people struggling to understand the purpose of their bodies, I'm more and more impressed by how gospel teachings can protect us from false traditions of our culture and its distortions and lies. The gospel makes clear who we are and the role of our body in our salvation. If we Latter-day Saints loathe the divine body that Heavenly Father has given us, what does this say about us? If we hate our bodies then we hate ourselves—our very essence—because our bodies are part of who we are. The word *hate* comes from the Greek word *kedos*, meaning grief. What might we be grieving for? Perhaps a loss of who we are.

Practically every woman I know suffers in varying degrees from this loss of identity. Having left our "royal courts on high,"[5] where we were nurtured by our Heavenly Father's side, we are not unlike deposed royal families who find themselves in exile. Studies of such deposed royal families reveal that their sense of who they are becomes distorted, and they become confused and disoriented. In the same way, as our sense of who we are becomes distorted, we forget our limitless potential and become confused and disoriented about our mission in life. In other words, we lose our inner and outer bearings. We forget that we are children of God. We misplace our royal crowns. Once we've lost them, how can we hope to rediscover them?

Hugh Nibley writes, "[The temple] is a scale model of the universe, for teaching purposes and for the purpose of taking our bearings on the universe and in the eternities, both in time and in space. . . . That is what a *templum* is—a place where you take your bearings on things."[6] The temple calls us back to our senses, reminds us who we really are.

The apostle Paul teaches, "Know ye not that ye are the temple of God, and that the Spirit of God dwelleth in you?" (1 Corinthians 3:16). Surely, this search for identity, this quest to find our bearings can be found within ourselves, for we too, as the apostle testifies, are temples. We must not be deceived into believing we can find ourselves in the perfect figure, an academic degree, professional status, or the perfect relationship. Instead of searching fruitlessly "out there" for answers, we must turn inward and listen to the promptings of the Spirit, which will always confirm who we are and tell us all things that we should do. Hearing those promptings may be difficult for those accustomed to listening to a horde of louder outside voices clamoring for our attention. Our eternal progression, however, requires us to hold still and listen to the still, small voice within—a voice that we *feel* more than we hear.[7]

Our temple buildings offer the keys after which to pattern our temple bodies. By attending our temple buildings and attending *to* our temple bodies, we can find our misplaced crowns. We can find them by comparing temple buildings to our temple bodies.

Comparison 1: Each temple is unique and beautiful. All of our temple buildings are beautiful and unique. Even though some may seem more grand than others, the benefit we receive from attending temples has nothing to do with their external structure. Nor does the exterior beauty change the value of what occurs inside each temple. Those attending the Salt Lake Temple do not get a better endowment or marriage ceremony than someone attending a smaller, less majestic temple. Just as it is ludicrous to value our temples by their outward appearance, it is ridiculous to value our bodies on external appearance.

Heavenly Father has made each one of us unique and authentic. As Patricia Holland states: "The Lord has created us with different personalities, as well as with differing degrees of energy, interest, health, talent and opportunity. So long as we are committed to righteousness and living a life of faithful devotion, we should celebrate these divine differences, knowing that they are a gift from God."[8] Comparisons and competition have no place in the kingdom of God. We must not worry so much about pleasing and performing for others that we lose our own uniqueness. We must not try so hard to fit in that we copy and clone others. Perhaps we were not meant to fit in, but to stand out. Our task is to fulfill the measure of *our* creation, not that of someone else.

Elder Henry D. Moyle said: "I have a conviction deep in my heart that we are exactly what we should be, each one of us. . . . I have convinced myself that we all have those peculiar attributes, characteristics, and abilities which are essential for us to possess in order that we may fulfill the purpose of our creation here upon the earth.

" . . . That allotment which has come to us from God is a sacred allotment. It is something of which we should be proud, each one of us in our own right, and not wish that we had somebody else's allotment. Our greatest success comes from being ourselves."[9]

Comparison 2: The temple is kept physically clean inside and out. We are commanded to keep our physical bodies the same way. The temple is carefully maintained, just as we should maintain our bodies. A guard at the temple door restrains those who are unworthy from entering, just as we should have a guard at our door to keep out unworthy thoughts, desires, and appetites. Elder Russell M. Nelson said, "As children of God, we should not let anything enter the body that might defile it. To allow sensors of sight, touch, or hearing to supply the brain with unclean memories is a sacrilege."[10]

The Word of Wisdom admonishes us to refrain from using or eating harmful food or substances. Obedience to this law brings more than a promise of physical health. We are promised great treasures of knowledge—even hidden treasures—and that the destroying angel shall pass us by (D&C 89:19–21). Apparently, the health of the body affects the spirit, or the Lord would never have revealed the Word of Wisdom.

I once read that our society is overfed but undernourished. Much of what we eat satisfies emotional, not physical hunger. Sometimes, when we are tired, lonely, depressed, or stressed, we turn to inappropriate foods or entertainment to comfort and distract us. Sometimes we use inappropriate substances and behaviors to avoid problems and challenges, which, if faced, could aid our spiritual growth. Habit-forming substances or behaviors interfere with delicate spiritual communication, our true source of comfort. We must have a guard at the door ever mindful and watchful that we entertain only nourishing and life-sustaining experiences.

Comparison 3: The temple is holy ground. Temples are built on consecrated land, and temple buildings themselves are consecrated and dedicated to be houses of the Lord. We enter our temples with an attitude of reverence and respect. Yet, in remarks at a temple dedication, President Joseph Fielding Smith taught, "It is not really temples that we dedicate, for temples are merely mortar and stone; it is people that we dedicate or rededicate to the purposes of the Lord."[11]

Spirits and bodies inseparably connected in human form are the true temples of God; our glorious temple buildings are mere representations. We are the eternal temple, consecrated and dedicated to the work of the Lord. Do we understand this? Do we understand that *we* are holy ground? Would we ever disrespect our temple buildings like we sometimes abuse our bodies? Would we ever refer to temple buildings in the derogatory and denigrating ways we sometimes refer to our bodies? We are living in a tabernacle of flesh, but our destiny is to become temples of holiness. Temple buildings may stand for hundreds or thousands of years, but we will stand forever.

Disrespectful, abusive behaviors such as overeating, starving, purging, overworking, taking stimulants to stay awake, denying the body movement and expression, and engaging in addictive habits commonly deaden our feelings, leaving us cut off from our bodies. This is a more serious condition than many of us realize. Joseph F. Smith saw in vision that the dead look upon the absence of the body as a joyless state of bondage (D&C 138:17, 50).[12] The Lord has revealed that "spirit and element, inseparably connected, receive a fulness of joy; and when separated, man cannot receive a fulness of joy" (D&C 93:33–34).

Even in life, when we split ourselves from our physical reality, we put ourselves in a state of bondage and reduce our capacity to experience joy. Surely, Satan would like nothing better. He has taken great pains not only to tempt us physically but to mislead us intellectually and spiritually so that we misunderstand the body's role in our salvation.

Perhaps the most compelling reason for reverencing our bodies is to provide a home for the Holy Ghost. If our bodies are numbed and deadened by addictions, starvation, or abuse we cannot feel the workings of the Spirit. Elder Boyd K. Packer teaches: "There are two parts to your nature—your temporal body born of mortal parents, and your immortal spirit within. . . . But if you learn by reason only, you will never understand the Spirit and how it works—regardless of how much you learn about other things." He further teaches that "Your body is the instrument of your mind. In your emotions, the spirit and the body come closest to being one. *What you learn spiritually depends, to a degree, on how you treat your body.*"[13]

Comparison 4: Our temples teach about order and balance. An Indian proverb says that everyone is a house with four rooms: a physical, a mental, an emotional, and a spiritual. We tend to live in one room most of the time; but unless we go into every room every day, even if only to keep it aired, we are not complete. Certainly, focusing too intensely on our physical appearance or any other one aspect of our lives keeps us from being complete. A complete person is a holy person. The word *holy* comes from the Old English word *hale*, the common root to such words as *whole, healthy, heal, and holy*. Patricia Holland states: "We need so much for body, mind, and spirit to unite in one healthy, stable soul. Surely God is well balanced, so perhaps we are just that much closer to him when we are."[14]

Our temples teach us about such holiness or wholeness. Temples have many rooms, each serving a particular function. The different aspects of being human compare to the various rooms. Each complete person will have a creative aspect to life—a garden room for reflection; a world room for practical, everyday affairs; a terrestrial room for study; and a celestial room for high devotion, where prayer and repentance can wash away the burdens of our past failures, allowing us to start each day renewed and cleansed. Thus, we become living temples with the words "Holiness to the Lord" written on our foreheads.

When the scriptures speak of our standing in holy places in the last days, they do not mean all worthy Saints will be crowded into the temples. Rather, people's lives will be dedicated to holiness. When every internal home is patterned after the order of the temple—"even a house of prayer, a house of fasting, a house of faith, a house of learning, a house of glory, a house of order, a house of God" (D&C 109:8)—the kingdom of God will come.

Comparison 5: The kingdom of God is within. Just as all the necessary ordinances for our salvation are contained within our temple buildings, our temple bodies contain all the ingredients of deity. Elder Gene R. Cook states, "Somehow the Latter-day Saints have the mistaken notion that in the end, when the day comes that the Lord will make them gods or goddesses, [then] someone lays their hands on their heads and, as it were, says to them, You have now all that you need to be a God—go ahead." Elder Cook emphasizes that this notion is not true; we *already* have within us all we need. "Your job is to take those crude elements within you and refine them."[15]

The scriptures teach us that all things have their likeness and all things are created and made to bear record of our Heavenly Father and of our divine identity, "both things which are temporal, and things which are spiritual; things which are in the heavens above, and things which are in the earth . . . : all things bear record of me" (Moses 6:63). In other words, everything around us bears witness of our divine path. The caterpillar becomes a butterfly, the tadpole becomes a frog, a bud becomes a rose, a seed becomes a tree, and humans, the greatest of all, become gods and goddesses.

We must remember the divine promise, "The kingdom of God is within you" (Luke 17:21). When we give too much attention to our flimsy, unstable outer world, we tend to forget the glorious possibility within our own souls. As we receive a fulness of the Holy Ghost, our bodies and spirits become sanctified. Our celestial spirit unfolds and awakens us to memories of our immortal soul. Those memories enlighten our whole being. Godliness, holiness—our true identity is within. As poet Carol Lynn Pearson suggests, we needn't look for it anywhere else:

WITHIN

I read a map once
Saying the kingdom of God
Was within me,
But I never trusted
Such unlikely ground.

I went out.
I scoured schools
And libraries
And chapels and temples
And other people's eyes
And the skies and the rocks,
And I found treasures
From the kingdom's treasury,
But not the kingdom.

Finally
I came in quiet
For a rest

And turned on the light.
And there
Just like a surprise party,
Was all the smiling royalty,
King, Queen, court.

People have been
Locked up for less, I know.
But I tell you
Something marvelous
Is bordered by this skin:

I am a castle
and the kingdom of God
Is within.[16]

Notes

1. In a *Glamour* magazine 1984 survey, 33,000 American women reported they would rather lose ten to fifteen pounds than achieve any other goal in life, including success at work or in love (cited by Naomi Wolf, "Hunger," in *Feminist Perspectives on Eating Disorders*, ed. Patricia Fallon, Melanie A. Katzman, Susan C. Wooley [New York: Guilford Press, 1994], 96).

2. Naomi Wolf, *The Beauty Myth: How Images of Beauty Are Used against Women* (New York: Morrow, 1991), 17.

3. Tessa Meyer Santiago, "Latter-day Deceits," in *May Christ Lift Thee Up* (Salt Lake City: Deseret Book, 1998), 208–9.

4. David Groff, cited in "Our Relationship with the Millennial Body," *Weekend Edition with Scott Simon*, 12 February 2000, National Public Radio, transcript by Burrelle's Information Services, Box 7, Livingston, New Jersey, 07039.

5. "O My Father," *Hymns of The Church of Jesus Christ of Latter-day Saints* (Salt Lake City: The Church of Jesus Christ of Latter-day Saints, 1985), no. 292.

6. Hugh Nibley, *Temple and Cosmos* (Salt Lake City: Deseret Book, 1992), 14, 19.

7. Boyd K. Packer, "The Spirit of Revelation," *Ensign*, November 1999, 24.

8. Jeffrey R. and Patricia T. Holland, *On Earth As It Is in Heaven* (Salt Lake City: Deseret Book, 1989), 84.

9. Henry D. Moyle, *Improvement Era*, December 1952, 34.

10. Russell M. Nelson, "We Are Children of God," *Ensign*, November 1998, 87.

11. Quoted by Joseph Fielding McConkie, *The Spirit of Revelation* (Salt Lake City: Deseret Book, 1984), 28–29.

12. Joseph F. Smith, *Gospel Doctrine* (Salt Lake City: Deseret Book, 1986), 475.

13. Boyd K. Packer, "Personal Revelation: The Gift, the Test, and the Promise," *Ensign*, November 1994, 59, 61; emphasis added.

14. Holland, *On Earth*, 88.

15. Gene R. Cook, *Living by the Power of Faith* (Salt Lake City: Deseret Book, 1985), 91.

16. Carol Lynn Pearson, *A Widening View* (Salt Lake City: Bookcraft, 1983), 32–33.

TEMPLES SHALL DOT THE LAND

✦

Paul Koelliker

In 1833, just three years after the Church was organized, came the revelation and direction to build the Kirtland Temple. The Church has been on an interesting path ever since. I am sure those who built the first temple of the Restoration felt some of the same things we feel about timetables. In fact, the Prophet Joseph was chastised for not moving fast enough in building the Kirtland Temple. He increased his pace, and in three years the temple was completed.

Consider the following words of the prophets as they have spoken with regard to the work of temples on the earth and a summary of temple building in the latter days.

Joseph Smith presided over the construction of two temples and the abandonment of one of them during his tenure as president of the Church. "From what we now witness," he said, "we are led to look forward with pleasing anticipation to the future, and soon expect to see . . . temples for the worship of our God erected in various parts, and great peace resting upon Israel."[1] He also said, "We need the temple more than anything else."[2]

President Brigham Young lost one temple and built one more. He said, "To accomplish this work there will have to be not only one temple but thousands of them, and thousands and tens of thousands of men and women will go into those temples and officiate for people who have lived as far back as the Lord shall reveal."[3]

John Taylor added another temple, bringing the number back up

---

Paul E. Koelliker is the managing director of the Church Temple Department and serves as a sealer in the Salt Lake Temple. He and his wife, Ann N. Koelliker are the parents of seven children and the grandparents of six.

to two. He said, "We expect to build hundreds of [temples] yet, and to administer in them in carrying out the work of God."[4]

Wilford Woodruff, responsible for dedicating two more temples—bringing the total to four—said, "When the Savior comes, a thousand years will be devoted to this work of redemption, and Temples will appear all over this land of Joseph—North and South America—and also in Europe and elsewhere."[5]

Lorenzo Snow, with no temples dedicated during his service, said, "The time will come when there will be Temples established over every portion of the land and we will go into these Temples and work for our kindred dead night and day."[6]

Joseph F. Smith, with no temples dedicated during his presidency, was quoted by Elder LeGrand Richards: "I heard President Joseph F. Smith say in Rotterdam in 1906 that the day would come when temples of the Lord would dot that whole land of Europe."[7]

Heber J. Grant dedicated three temples during his service, bringing the total to seven. "I have no doubt in my mind," he said, "that Temples of the Lord will be erected in Europe."[8]

President George Albert Smith, with one temple dedicated during his service, brought the total to eight. In 1943, President Smith, in setting apart Lorin F. Jones as the president of the Spanish American Mission, declared: "You will see marvelous things transpire as affecting the Lamanite people. . . . These will be history-making events in the Church."[9] In 1945, two years later, President Smith and the First Presidency authorized the translation of the temple ordinances into Spanish—the first time they were translated into another language. The temple endowment has now been translated into more than sixty-one languages, with many more translations in progress.

President David O. McKay, responsible for five temples being dedicated—bringing the total to thirteen—said, "I envision that someday there will be a temple in the south seas to which you and your children may go to receive the blessings of the House of the Lord."[10]

President Joseph Fielding Smith, with two temples dedicated during his presidency—bringing the total to fifteen—said, "The great work of the millennium shall be performed in the temples which shall cover all parts of the land."[11]

President Harold B. Lee, whose tenure as president was very short, added no temples during his service. He said, "Remember, it is the Lord that decides where a temple shall be built. And when He inspires the President of the Church, that's where the temple will be built. . . . We will build them when and where the Lord wants his temples and their influence to be established."[12]

President Spencer W. Kimball, with twenty-one temples dedicated during his service—bringing the total to thirty-six—said, "Five other temples are in varying stages of construction, and more are in contemplation toward fulfilling the prediction of latter-day prophets that holy temples will dot this and other lands from end to end."[13]

President Ezra Taft Benson, with nine temples dedicated during his service, brought the total to forty-five. "If this redemptive work is to be done on the scale it must be," he declared, "hundreds of temples will be needed."[14]

President Howard W. Hunter dedicated two temples during his presidency, bringing the total to forty-seven. "Let us be a temple-attending people," he urged. "We desire to bring the temples closer to our people."[15]

That significant statement embodies the vision that President Gordon B. Hinckley is building into reality—to bring the temples to the people.

President Hinckley, with thirty-four temples dedicated so far, bringing the total to eighty-one as of the end of April 2000, said, "This is the greatest era of temple building in all the history of the world. But it is not enough. We must continue to pursue it until we have a dedicated temple within the reach of our faithful people everywhere."[16]

Compare what has been promised with what has come to pass: 121 temples are currently operating, announced, or in the process of construction. At the beginning of 1998, fifty-one temples were in operation. By the end of December 2000, just thirty-six months later, fifty-one more temples will have been completed. That is incredible. I bear testimony that this is the work of heaven as revealed to the prophets of God and expressed to us by each one over time.

President Hinckley has said, "Every temple, be it large or small, old or new, is an expression of our testimony that life beyond the grave is as real and certain as is mortality."[17] I had never thought of temples quite that way. Temples are here to bless our lives. Temples are here to strengthen us.

Many are unable to enjoy the blessings of the temple for economic reasons. There is a way you can help those Saints. You can contribute to the Temple Patrons Assistance Fund, which is available to people all over the world to help them come to the temple. In Bogotá, Colombia, I stood at the window of the housing complex at 5 A.M. and looked out as Saints lined up along the sidewalk. This was not for the dedication. That had been held the day before. This was for the opening of the temple, and they were there to receive their endowments. They had come by busloads from all over. Many of them had waited years. Many had sacrificed much. Many had wanted to come to the temple sooner and could not afford to. Through the contributions, kindness, and generosity of many of you who live here in this land of plenty, nearly 350 people received their endowments in the first half of the day. Then another three busloads showed up, bringing another 150 people. I watched the temple president as he worked from 6 A.M. until after midnight, sealing people at the altars of the temple. This is a sacred work. This is God's work.

President George Q. Cannon indicated what we must understand about temples: "Every foundation stone that is laid for a temple and every temple completed lessens the power of Satan on earth and increases the power of God and godliness, moves the heavens in mighty power on our behalf, invokes and calls down upon us the blessings of eternal gods and those who reside in their presence."[18] The adversary is trying to thwart the work, of course, but he will fail. The Lord will prevail. The work will go on.

Notes

1. Joseph Smith, *History of The Church of Jesus Christ of Latter-day Saints*, ed. B. H. Roberts, 2d ed. rev., 7 vols. (Salt Lake City: The Church of Jesus Christ of Latter-day Saints, 1932–51), 4:338–39; *Teachings of the Prophet Joseph Smith*, sel. Joseph Fielding Smith (Salt Lake City: Deseret Book, 1976), 186.

2. Smith, *History of the Church*, 6:230.

3. *Discourses of Brigham Young*, sel. John A. Widtsoe (Salt Lake City: Deseret Book, 1954), 394.

4. John Taylor, *Journal of Discourses*, 26 vols. (London: Latter-day Saints' Book Depot, 1854–86), 18:201.

5. Wilford Woodruff, *Journal of Discourses*, 19:230.

6. Lorenzo Snow, *Millennial Star*, 31 August 1899, 546; Hoyt W. Brewster Jr., *Behold, I Come Quickly: The Last Days and Beyond* (Salt Lake City: Deseret Book, 1994), 212.

7. LeGrand Richards, "'God Moves in a Mysterious Way,'" *Improvement Era*, December 1970, 70.

8. Heber J. Grant, as cited in Richard O. Cowan, *Temples to Dot the Earth* (Salt Lake City: Bookcraft, 1989), 157.

9. George Albert Smith, as cited in ibid., 148.

10. David O. McKay, in *Cherished Experiences from the Writings of David O. McKay*, comp. Clare Middlemiss (Salt Lake City: Deseret Book, 1976), 129.

11. Joseph Fielding Smith, *Doctrines of Salvation*, comp. Bruce R. McConkie, 3 vols. (Salt Lake City: Bookcraft, 1954–56), 2:252.

12. Harold B. Lee, Fifth Annual Genealogical Seminar Address, 7 August 1970; Harold B. Lee, *The Teachings of Harold B. Lee*, ed. Clyde J. Williams (Salt Lake City: Bookcraft, 1966), 583.

13. Spencer W. Kimball, *Ensign*, May 1979, 4.

14. Ezra Taft Benson, *The Teachings of Ezra Taft Benson* (Salt Lake City: Bookcraft, 1988), 247.

15. Howard W. Hunter, *Ensign*, November 1994, 8.

16. Gordon B. Hinckley, *Teachings of Gordon B. Hinckley* (Salt Lake City: Deseret Book, 1997), 629.

17. Gordon B. Hinckley, *Ensign*, May 1993, 74; Gordon B. Hinckley, *Teachings of Gordon B. Hinckley*, 636.

18. George Q. Cannon, *Gospel Truth: Discourses and Writings of George Q. Cannon*, sel. Jerreld L. Newquist (Salt Lake City: Deseret Book, 1987), 366.

INCOMINGS AND OUTGOINGS

꒰⊶꒱

S. Michael Wilcox

Early in the Restoration, the Lord commanded Joseph Smith to build a temple, "that your incomings . . . [and] your outgoings may be in the name of the Lord" (D&C 88:120). A temple is a symbol that the Lord desires to dwell with his people, for he has required his house to be built in their midst. It is also our sign to the Lord that we desire him to dwell with us, for we have constructed a house for him. He is always home. The pillar of fire by night over the ancient Hebrew tabernacle and the cloud by day suggested his presence, just as smoke coming from a chimney during the day and a light shining through the windows at night (Numbers 14:14) indicate that a person is home. The Lord desires our visits and extends to us an open invitation. We go into the temple as invited guests; we go out "in the name of the Lord," representing the Savior.

More than thirty years ago, as a newly called missionary, I experienced my first incoming and outgoing from the temple. I went in somewhat unprepared, and I came out with a degree of bewilderment and unease. Now, after more than thirty years of attending the temple, I join my voice with that of David, who wrote, "One thing have I desired of the Lord, that will I seek after; that I may dwell in the house of the Lord all the days of my life, to behold the beauty of the Lord, and to enquire in his temple" (Psalm 27:4).

What has made the difference between my first outgoing and my present ones? Through my deepest ponderings, I have learned how to

---

S. Michael Wilcox, a popular speaker and author, is an instructor at the institute of religion at the University of Utah. He received his Ph.D. at the University of Colorado. He and his wife, Laura L. Chipman, are the parents of five children. He serves as an ordinance worker in the Jordan River Temple.

feel the deeper love of our Father in Heaven and our Savior contained in the ordinances of the house of the Lord.

A friend of mine was leaving for the temple when his small son asked him where he was going. "We're going to the temple," was the reply. "Well, when you get there," the son said, "will you tell my friend Jesus hi?" "I don't think we'll see him there," the mother answered. With the spiritual insight of a child, the son said, "Oh, I think you'll find him if you look hard."

Doing the temple work for my own ancestors has been perhaps the most critical factor in helping me discover the love of our Father in Heaven and his Son. An ordinance worker once told our family, as we prepared to be baptized for individuals whose names we had researched ourselves, "Many of those for whom you will be baptized today lived difficult lives; many of them died wondering if God had forgotten them. Today you will show them he has not forgotten them. He never forgets a single child. For the first time in many, many years, their names will be spoken again, here in the Lord's house, and they will know of their Father's eternal love."

INCOMINGS IN THE NAME OF THE LORD

To bring the love and peace of the temple with us as we leave, our incomings must be done properly. When Jacob returned to the land of Canaan with his family, he was commanded to take them to a mountain called Beth-el. *Beth-el* in Hebrew means "the house of God." Twenty years earlier Jacob had dreamed there of a ladder or stairway descending to the earth whose top reached into heaven. Angels ascended and descended on this stairway, and God stood above it. What better description could there be of a temple?

Jacob asked his family to do three things before they went up to Beth-el. "Put away the strange gods that are among you, and be clean, and change your garments: and let us arise, and go up to Beth-el" (Genesis 35:2–3). Rachel and Leah, our ancient mothers, were among those who went up to Beth-el. "And they gave unto Jacob all the strange gods which were in their hand, and all their earrings which were in their ears; and Jacob hid them under the oak which was by Shechem" (Genesis 35:4).

The "strange gods" and "earrings" this devoted family considered inappropriate were for them, and represent for us, the things of the world. Before we go to the house of the Lord to make covenants and to receive eternal blessings, we must first put away the things of the world. Notice the great lesson inherent in the words: "and Jacob hid them under the oak which was by Shechem." When they left Beth-el, they did not pick up the strange gods and trappings of the world. They left them buried by the oak of Shechem. To maintain the calming serenity of the temple, our outgoings must be the same.

One of the saddest things I experience in my present Church assignment is to see good members of the Church, whom we love, give up the "strange gods" and "earrings" of the world with their incomings to the temple only to pick them up again as they leave. These strange gods may be bad habits, unwillingness to pay tithes and offerings, love of material things, inappropriate forms of entertainment or environments, or grooming and clothing styles that compromise the sacredness of what we receive in the temple and are instructed to take with us as a reminder of the beautiful symbols and sacred covenants of the temple. Everything associated with the temple should be kept sacred, covered, and should not be revealed outside temple walls. Please, let the Lord's respect and honor for what takes place in the temple guide our regard for that sacred article of clothing we wear day and night.

We are told in Genesis that God protected Jacob's family as they left Beth-el and journeyed in the dangerous world of Canaan. If we follow their example, if we give up the "strange gods" of this world, we also are assured of the Lord's protection. The scriptures teach that the temple is a house of refuge and safety. When my children were approaching their teens, I went to the temple one afternoon to seek guidance as a father. I told the Lord I was willing to offer any sacrifice if he would protect my children from worldly temptations and bless them with his Spirit. Many of you have offered such a prayer in behalf of your children, grandchildren, nieces, and nephews.

I felt the Spirit whisper, "This is the sacrifice I ask of you. Be in this house frequently, constantly, and consistently, and the promised protection of this house will be extended to those you love." This promise is not exclusive to me; it is a promise made to all of us. I knew the Lord was not promising all my children would grow up without problems. Rather, this was the promise of a powerful influence in their lives. If we are true to our covenants, our outgoings from the temple will carry a protective shield for our families.

STAND IN HOLY PLACES

The Lord counsels us to "stand . . . in holy places, and be not moved" when we face the destructive influences of the world (D&C 87:8, 45:32, 101:22). "Be not moved" means more than staying in one place; it also means "don't be afraid." "To stand" is active rather than passive. It means "to make a stand" or "to fight." "Stand in holy places, and be not moved," counsels the Lord, or in other words, make your stand against the world's influences in holy places, and don't be afraid.

Contemplating today's world many centuries ago, Isaiah told of the three holy places where the Latter-day Saints will take a stand against the forces of the world and prevail. "And the Lord will create *upon every dwelling-place* of mount Zion, and *upon her assemblies,* a cloud and smoke by day and the shining of a flaming fire by night; for upon all the glory of Zion shall be a defence" (2 Nephi 14:5; emphasis added). Just as the pillar of fire was over the tabernacle while the children of Israel wandered in the wilderness, so in the latter days the Lord's Spirit as a pillar of fire will rest over the homes and the gatherings of those true to their covenants.

Isaiah then speaks of the protective power of the temple. "And there shall be a tabernacle for a shadow in the daytime from the heat, and for a place of refuge, and a covert from storm and from rain" (2 Nephi 14:6). Isaiah also indicated that the temple was God's hearth, his fireside, his home (Isaiah 29:1, n. b). When the forces of the world bear down on us like a hot summer's day, pushing us to the limits of our endurance, the Lord seems to say, "Come home. Sit in the shade of my house. Feel the breezes of my Spirit. Be refreshed. Drink from my fountain of truth, and swim in my healing river. Now, your outgoings can be with greater strength and you can face the heat of the day."

As we take our places in the great latter-day battle between good and evil, sometimes all the forces of temptation and worldliness threaten to overwhelm us. We feel isolated and afraid. At such times the Lord is, in essence, calling to us, "Come home. No stinging hail penetrates the shingles of my house. The flood waters cannot sweep away its foundations. No worldly wind can chill your spirit here. Sit by my hearth and listen to my truths. Feast at my table. Learn here of the great battle for the souls of men and women begun before the world was. Receive instruction on how to hold firm against the adversary. Be warmed by the love of your Eternal Father. Now, your outgoings into the storms of life can be without hesitation, without fear."

Within the sacred triangle of home, stake, and temple, we can take our stand.

AT THE LORD'S TABLE

The Lord revealed to Joseph Smith that He would prepare a feast of the finest things, "yea, a supper of the house of the Lord, well prepared, unto which all nations shall be invited" (D&C 58:9). The feast of the temple consists of the richest doctrines, the most nourishing truths, the most life-sustaining covenants and ordinances. During his earthly ministry, Jesus spoke of this feast in a parable:

"A certain man made a great supper, and bade many: and sent his servant at supper time to say to them that were bidden, Come; for all things are now ready. And they all with one consent began to make excuse. The first said unto him, I have bought a piece of ground, and I must needs go and see it: I pray thee have me excused. And another said, I have bought five yoke of oxen, and I go to prove them: I pray thee have me excused. And another said, I have married a wife, and therefore I cannot come. . . . And the lord said unto the servant, Go out into the highways and hedges, and compel them to come in, that my house may be filled" (Luke 14:16–20, 23).

Sometimes our lives become so busy that we realize it's been quite some time since we've been to the temple. We know the feast is waiting, and we sense our need for its spiritual nourishment, but there is ground to see and oxen to prove and we ask to be excused. Yet the parable testifies that the Lord truly desires that his house be "filled."

We find ourselves often making bricks without straw. When Moses first appeared in Pharaoh's court, he simply asked that the Israelites be allowed "three days' journey into the desert" to offer sacrifice to the Lord. In other words, in the midst of their brick-making for Pharaoh, they needed time off for worship. "Get you unto your burdens," Pharaoh said. "They be idle; therefore they cry, saying, Let us go and sacrifice to our God. Let there more work be laid upon the men, that they may labour therein; and let them not regard vain words" (Exodus 5:3–4, 8–9). He then withheld the needed straw for the making of bricks.

Does life sometimes treat you that way? Does it demand so much of your time and energy that there is nothing left for feasting and sacrifice? Part of the adversary's plan is to see that we have no time left for feasting. The daily "tale" of bricks must not be diminished until, eventually, without that essential nourishment, like the overworked Israelites, we "[hearken] not . . . for anguish of spirit, and for cruel bondage" (Exodus 6:9).

Jesus' parable of the supper was introduced by these words, "And when one of them that sat at meat with him heard these things, he said unto him, Blessed is he that shall eat bread in the kingdom of God" (Luke 14:15). We look forward to our celestial feast in the Lord's eternal kingdom. But the Savior seems to be telling us that we need not wait for the kingdom of God to enjoy the feast. We can "eat bread" with the Savior now, in his house, if we will not make excuse.

The bread of the temple endowment is like the five barley loaves Jesus used to feed the five thousand. At first the loaves did not seem sufficient to satisfy the needs of so many, but Jesus blessed it, and all could eat "as much as they would" until "they were filled." When the feast was finished, they "filled twelve baskets with the fragments . . . , which remained over and above unto them that had eaten" (John 6:11–13). The symbolic nature of temple ordinances enables us to return again and again to the twelve baskets that remain, for symbols offer many meanings to nourish us during the ever-changing circumstances of our lives.

OUTGOINGS IN THE NAME OF THE LORD

We live in a wonderful time. The scriptures mention only a handful of temples. We now have one hundred. In ancient Israel only one man, the high priest, a descendant of Aaron, could pass through the veil of the temple into its most holy place and only on one day a year. We can enter the celestial room as often as we desire. Every race and nationality, both men and women, can pass through the veil. What wonder must the ancients feel as they see thousands of women daily entering into the temples and sitting in its most hallowed places? If we understand that, our outgoings will always be full of gratitude.

The Lord tells us that his house is a house of learning. He desires that our outgoings be filled with knowledge. Because we are taught through symbols in the temple, we may not understand and receive all the truth the Lord desires we obtain. We must discover how to learn through symbols. Let me suggest a formula for temple worship that may help you. Much of our ability to receive the power of the temple depends on what we do when we are outside its walls.

We find this formula in 3 Nephi 17. Jesus had spent the day teaching the Nephites and Lamanites. At the day's conclusion he said, "I perceive that ye are weak, that ye cannot understand all my words which I am commanded of the Father to speak unto you at this time" (3 Nephi 17:2). Do you ever feel this way as you leave the temple? You just don't understand all you've experienced and been taught? The Savior understands and teaches us what to do. He does not want us to be discouraged, doubtful, or apathetic but to do five things: "[1] Go ye unto your homes, and [2] ponder upon the things which I have said, and [3] ask of the Father, in my name, that ye may understand, and [4] prepare your minds for the morrow, and [5] I come unto you again" (3 Nephi 17:3).

Often we do only the first of the Savior's suggestions—go home. Yet, if we want our next incoming to the temple to be more powerful, we must ponder, deeply reflect, upon our temple experience. We must show the Lord our desire to receive the full benefits of his teaching by sincerely asking him for understanding. Perhaps the best way to prepare our minds to receive the Lord's teaching is to go to the temple hungering after insight and knowledge. I know how wonderful it is to teach a class of students who hunger for truth. The temple uses "teacher" words to help us prepare our minds to learn. We must be alert, and attentive, and reverent. If these words reflect our attitude, we are prepared to receive. Last of all, we must return, as frequently as our circumstances allow, yearning toward his promise: "and I come unto you again."

A beautiful prophecy in Ezekiel tells us what accompanies our outgoings from the Lord's house. Ezekiel is shown in a vision a temple in Jerusalem. From its eastern doors, which face the bleak, barren Judean wilderness and the Dead Sea, a river begins to flow. The river brings life to the desert, and Ezekiel sees "very many trees" on both sides of the river. He is promised that "every thing that liveth, which moveth, whithersoever the rivers shall come, shall live" (Ezekiel 47:7, 9). The pure temple waters flow into the Dead Sea and heal it. Fish begin to swim there, and Ezekiel is shown fishermen spreading their nets all along its shores. Each time Ezekiel wades into the river, it is deeper, until finally it becomes "a river that I could not pass over: for the waters were risen, waters to swim in, a river that could not be passed over" (Ezekiel 47:5).

Whenever I read this marvelous prophecy, the Spirit seems to whisper, "What is true of this prophetic temple is true of all my temples." From the doors of every temple, a pure river flows. We cannot see these rivers with our natural eyes, but they are there just the same. They are rivers of truth, light, and love. We can be assured that they will give life to and heal "everything that liveth." They will give life to marriages and to parent-child relationships. They will heal families and bring life to branches, wards, and stakes. They will heal a parched life, rendered dry by the dust storms of trial and heartbreak. One day the combined flow from all the temples will bathe the world in love and light and bring a final healing peace.

Rivers of faithful, radiant Latter-day Saints, women and men, flow from the temple, endowed with the power of love and inner peace, secure in their covenants, enlightened by revelation and eternal perspective, trusting in promised protection, confident that families are eternal units, assured of a Father and a Savior's great plan of happiness.

May your outgoings from the temple help to heal and give life to the spiritual deserts and Dead Seas of the world, until one day you meet your Father in Heaven at the doorway of his eternal celestial kingdom, where he will lead you by the hand to your final home. Then, as the scriptures promise, there will be no more outgoings forever (Revelation 3:12).

BRINGING THE TEMPLE
TO OUR CHILDREN

Ann N. Madsen, Emily Madsen Reynolds, Cindy Anderson Madsen, and Mindy Madsen Davis

Ann: On Thanksgiving weekend a year ago, we had a family snow holiday in the mountains. While the grandchildren built a wonderful igloo outside, I asked our grown, married children, "Why do you love the temple?"

They each said, "You loved the temple. You loved ironing your temple clothes. You would come home from the temple all aglow, and we could feel it."

Orson Pratt, in describing our day, said, "In the latter days there will be a people so pure . . . that God will manifest himself, not only in their Temple[s], . . . but . . . when they retire to their [homes], behold

---

Ann Nicholls Madsen, Isaiah scholar and poet, has taught ancient scripture at Brigham Young University for more than twenty years. She and her husband, Truman G. Madsen, are the parents of three children and a Navajo foster son and the grandparents of sixteen.

Emily Madsen Reynolds received her master's degree in psychology and has taught at BYU. She serves as a counselor in her ward Relief Society. She and her husband, Mark, are the parents of seven children.

Cynthia Anderson Madsen received her bachelor's degree from Brigham Young University in English. She has lived all over the world and was converted to the Church in Belgium. She serves as the Primary chorister in her ward. She and her husband, Barnard N. Madsen, are the parents of four children.

Mindy Madsen Davis received her bachelor's degree from Brigham Young University and works as an office manager for her husband's medical practice. She serves as literacy specialist in her ward and as an institute teacher in the Church Educational System. She and her husband, J. Grant Davis, are the parents of three children.

each [home] will be lighted up by the glory of God."[1] Is that possible? Can we be that people? Can our homes be lighted by the glory of God?

Perhaps this bringing the light home is the whole point of temple worship. Mothers in Zion throughout the world have the privilege of joining with prophets as we accept the responsibility of preparing our children to go up in worthiness to meet the Lord in his holy house. To prepare our children for the temple, we can ready them to make specific temple covenants. We prepare them by the way we live each day.

1. See the big picture.

Cindy: An important part of the big picture is to understand that God is a creator. That essential divine trait needs to become an intrinsic part of each of us. This life may be compared to a chrysalis stage in which we are preparing to become in all ways like our heavenly parents. We need to do *now* what we will be doing *then*, which is creating. Too often we and our children live in the passive voice where creation is concerned. For entertainment we watch someone else act on television, listen to someone else create music on the radio, play a game within someone else's parameters on the computer. We eat bread made by the sweat of someone else's brow and wear clothes made by another's hands. Whenever possible, we should assert our own active voice of creation. Remember, you do not need to be an expert to be a creator. The prophets counsel us to be self-reliant, not experts. President Mary Ellen Smoot said, "Be patient, ask in faith, and you will receive guidance in your creative efforts."[2]

Emily: Seeing the big picture also means paying attention to symbols, types, and metaphors. More symbolism and ceremony is found in the temple than in any other Latter-day Saint worship. Sometimes that is a shock because we have been too casual about baptism, the sacrament, and the laying on of hands. We can prepare new temple goers for temple symbols by teaching them reverence for our sacred ordinances and by never speaking lightly of sacred things. We can also teach them to see the many types, symbols, and metaphors in the scriptures as we read them together. And we can talk about the symbolism of what we are doing as we partake of the broken bread, raise the right arm to the square in a baptism or sustaining, or circle an infant to give a name and a father's blessing.

2. Understand that the temple is the most important destination of our lives.

Mindy: Through the ordinances of the temple, we begin, as President David O. McKay said, a "step-by-step ascent into the Eternal Presence."[3] Temples are the way back home. We teach our children to go to the temple by going ourselves. Teach them the song "I Love to See the Temple" and take them there so the song will be real to them. If you can, bring your children to temple grounds often: at Christmas to talk about the baby Jesus, at Easter to talk about the resurrected Lord, on birthdays for teaching moments. My friend makes a special book about the law of chastity and gives it to each child on the temple grounds where she teaches them about remaining clean and pure to enter the temple. Even if you don't live close to a temple, a picture of one in your home will foster a love in your children for the temple.

Emily: In this era of extensive temple building, it is comparatively easy to participate in groundbreakings, cornerstone layings, open houses, and dedications. Several months before the Provo Temple was dedicated, when I was about seventeen, a member of our stake presidency challenged us to be prepared to participate in the unique spiritual experience of the dedication.

The temple became the topic of several family home evenings, and we laid careful plans, which included a fast and a beautiful celebration feast to break our fast when the dedication was over. The day of the dedication I don't remember doing anything but getting ready. We set the table early in the day with the very nicest dishes we had. We showered and dressed with extra care. Then we went to the dedication. It was, in fact, a remarkable experience that deepened my desire to enter the temple.

That's one way it can go. But let me give you another example, this one involving the Palmyra Temple dedication. Delete all the careful preparations of my previous example and replace them with our oldest son's wedding in the works, a mom also getting ready for a presentation at Women's Conference, a dad whose business was suddenly requiring much more attention and a lot of travel, as well as two teenage boys who forgot to schedule interviews with the bishop to get their tickets until the day before the dedication. Then, to add insult to absent-mindedness, those same two teenagers shot baskets until so close to time for the dedication that I am sorry to report they went without showering.

Just before we went out the door, one of our sons—by then crabby and disgruntled—asked a question that began with, "Why do I have to . . . ?" and I responded, "Try to *remember* that a temple dedication isn't just *anything,* you know." Immediately the thought came, *He's supposed to know that after the way this day has gone?*

On the way home from the dedication, my husband asked the kids to talk about what had impressed them. I expected dead silence, feeling that we deserved it, but my fifteen-year-old piped up, "Well, I can tell you the moment when I got little tingles over my entire body. It was when we started to sing 'The Spirit of God.'"

For me the point of this story is that, in spite of all the good things I didn't do, there *was* such a moment for him, and he will long remember it. I have no doubt that had we been better prepared it would have been a richer experience for all of us, but I stand as a witness that our Father is merciful and loving and that if we participate in the events surrounding the building of a temple, in whatever ways we are able, our children—and we—will be blessed.

Ann: The temple is a bridge of love between this world and the next. Our loved ones at times reach across the veil and assist us in our journey. We can teach our children and grandchildren the reality of their relatives by preserving family stories. Write them down. Tell them at bedtime, at the table, in talks, in teaching moments so that *their* goodness can reach down the years to influence *your* children.

My great-grandmother Anna found the Church in Sweden, where it was against the law at the time to join, but she did. I can see her stubborn faith replicated in myself, my children, and my grandchildren. She wouldn't marry her sweetheart until they could be sealed in the

Endowment House, so she traveled by wagon train, which included her sister, Charlotte, to the valley of the Great Salt Lake. Her journal records: "Charlotte was sick today, so I carried her." She left no written complaint—only the bare fact of what she had done. "When the load seems heavy I am called to bear,"[4] who do you think reaches out her hand to me through that thin veil that separates us? My great-grandmother Anna.

3. Show love, but not as the world loves.

Ann: The temple is a house of love—it's where we can feel God's love. We can prepare our children by loving them beyond anything they have known in the world. Let them know that their Heavenly Father and Jesus love them even *more* than we do. Help them learn charity—a love that *never* stops. Then they will understand a little about the everlasting love that will crown their temple experience in a sealing room one day. Prepare them for that moment at a sacred altar, not just for a lavish reception.

Mindy: Plan to communicate love. A few years ago, I started a Valentine tradition of writing a letter to my husband and each of my children telling them why I love them. When Max was eleven, I wrote: "Your face is bright and handsome. I love the angles in your jaw that are showing up as you mature. I look forward to seeing that handsome face ready to serve a mission. We'll miss you this summer when you're away from us at camps. Thanks for being the oldest. I love you. You are my joy and my delight!"

My Valentine letter to Max in 1999 was dated April 16. (It was a bad year.) Here's part of what I wrote: "I felt so loved this morning when you really hugged me before you left for school. You have been such a wonderful son. You are growing up so well! I like to write you every Valentine's Day and tell you why I love you. But this year I didn't do it—too busy, I thought. But this is much more important than anything else I was doing. I wish I'd done it sooner."

4. Be comfortable with being different.

Cindy: We can let our children know that Latter-day Saints are different and that's okay. The temple is a holy place, a place of revelation where the Lord can show us great things—things that make us different. The Lord instructed Nephi to build a ship that was not after the manner of men (1Nephi 17:7–8). In the temple, we are given a basic pattern for how to construct our lives. If I go often to the temple and plead for guidance, the Lord will also show me the unique way I am to build my individual life so that I can fulfill the specific mission he intends for me.

The same is true for each one of us. Our lives will not be patterned after the world but after the manner of the Lord. The world will have Lamans and Lemuels who will scoff at the way we are framing our lives. Our lifestyles will differ from what others are doing, seeming "curious," perhaps. But in the end they will be "exceedingly fine" and will carry us to the promised land (1 Nephi 18:1, 4).

Emily: The temple is a place that reminds us to be different, to be in the world but not of it. It is a safe haven: many things from the world simply cannot be found within the walls of a temple. Our homes should be the same. If we don't let certain things in, our children will know by experience what it takes to maintain a sacred space. This will teach them how to go about *standing in holy places*. They can learn from us to turn off a video in the middle, get rid of an inappropriate book or Website, or abandon a conversation that has turned contentious. Our homes can be safe havens from the evil that increasingly surrounds and assails us; they can be places where we can feel the Spirit. If these things happen, our children will find a familiar, comfortable feeling when they enter the doors of the temple.

Cindy: Even the conversations in our homes should be different. What do you discuss around *your* dinner table? I must admit that most of our dinner conversations are fairly mundane. But laced among the soccer games, latest dating crises, stress of work, and spilled milk, we need to consciously make room at our tables for spiritual applications to present problems. Besides our gratitude for the gospel and our belief in it, we need to bear testimony to our children of how the gospel pertains in practical ways to our everyday lives. It provides solutions to our daily problems. It provides clear standards by which to judge current events, cultural attitudes, and their influence on us.

Mindy: Wearing garments is a daily reminder of our commitment to be different. President Carlos E. Asay taught that the garment is the one tangible thing we can take with us from our temple experience.[5] One morning my little daughter was talking to me as I was getting dressed, and I realized I had never expressed how I feel about my garments. So I told her how much I love wearing them, that I think they are beautiful. Our children only know how we feel if we tell them. I once heard a temple worker say to a group of young women, "Instead of finding excuses to take *off* your garments, find excuses to keep them on."

5. Expect Satan to oppose our efforts.

Emily: Both God and Satan teach us by way of messengers, not face to face—and everyone is a messenger. That is one of the tricky things about mortality. It is therefore critical for children to understand, as Adam and Eve did, that not all messengers tell the truth. On the subject of sex, for instance, I tell my children up front that everything they see or hear about sex outside our family is probably wrong or at least distorted. If they think they hear something true, they can always ask me. On other subjects, the line may not be so clear, but my basic message to them is the same: Be wary. Not all information is equal; no one knows everything; the popular argument may not have a single truth in it. When we are surrounded with lies, we wait for messengers from our Heavenly Father to teach us.

Cindy: We live in a world overrun with advice. Talk show hosts on the television and radio editorialize about what to eat, wear, read, and watch. We see the world through the lens of a news camera and hear events interpreted through a reporter's bias. The scope and breadth of self-help books appears to be limitless. This deluge of "stuff" coming at us is staggering. For our children, this daily bombardment can be confusing, even numbing. There are so many voices.

In the temple, we are instructed to listen to people we can trust. Our children need to know whose voice to listen to; *who* speaks the truth; *who* are the true messengers of our Heavenly Father. Our Savior said, "I am the way, the truth, and the life" (John 14:6). He shows us the way in the scriptures. Our children need to know, love, and trust the voice of the scriptures. They need to understand that the scriptures are pertinent right now.

"Come, listen to a prophet's voice and hear the word of God."[6] Our children need to know, love, and trust the words of the prophet. They need to feel reverence, respect, and confidence in those who lead the Church. We should be very careful about how we speak of those in authority so that we do not undermine or dull our children's faith in them. Out of a cacophony of voices, they need to know how to discern the soft whisperings of the Spirit, "even the Spirit of truth; whom the world cannot receive, because it seeth him not, neither knoweth him: but ye know him; for he dwelleth with you, and shall be in you" (John 14:17).

Ann: A dear friend told me not long ago, "The temple is a house of revelation and we must teach our children to recognize revelation in our homes." We need to teach our children and grandchildren how to recognize the Holy Ghost in their daily lives. They can feel the Spirit in so many settings. For example, right after each general conference our family gathers and, beginning with the youngest grandchild, we take turns telling what we have learned, ending with the testimony of the patriarch of our family. Each time we do this we feel the Spirit together. We can translate for our children at times like this by saying, "What you are feeling right now is the Holy Ghost."

6. Let temple preparation be a lifelong process.

Ann: So where do we begin? To find out what our children and grandchildren really know about the temple, we can simply ask them. Not long ago, as we snuggled in bed early one morning at our cabin, our six-year-old grandson, Gabe, gave me this extended answer when I asked him, "What is the temple?" At first I thought he had misunderstood the question. He said, "Joseph Smith prayed to know which church is right and he saw the Father and the Son and they told him none of them and then later that he should build a house. The temple is Heavenly Father's house." If you ask, "What happens in the temple?" or "What will you do when you go to the temple?" they will probably answer: be baptized or get married. Then *you* could begin to explain what a tender experience it is to be a proxy or stand-in for someone who has died and could *never* do this for her or himself. Your children will begin to glimpse what is really waiting for them in the temple.

Pray and you will know what and when to teach each of your children who are journeying toward the truths of the temple. It takes a lifetime of prayers, which will be answered with blessings we can scarcely comprehend.

The temple helps us access the blessings of Abraham. A Jewish legend tells that when Abraham asked, "Will I ever have children?" the Lord said, "Look down at the sands where you stand. You will have children, numerous as the sands." Then Abraham cried out, "But what will they be like?" And the Lord answered, "Look up, Abraham, your children will be full of light, like the stars." Our children are the stars that Abraham saw. You are the stars Abraham saw. Let us lead our children to the Light that can be found only in the house of the Lord. I testify that it is there.

Notes

1. Orson Pratt, *Journal of Discourses*, 26 vols. (London: Latter-day Saints' Book Depot, 1854–86), 16:83.
2. Mary Ellen Smoot, "We Are Creators," *Ensign*, April 2000, 65.
3. David O. McKay, cited in Truman G. Madsen, *The Highest in Us* (Salt Lake City: Bookcraft, 1978), 102–3.
4. "Count Your Blessings," *Hymns of The Church of Jesus Christ of Latter-day Saints* (Salt Lake City: The Church of Jesus Christ of Latter-day Saints, 1985), no. 241.
5. Carlos E. Asay, "The Temple Garment," *Ensign*, August 1997, 22.
6. "Come, Listen to a Prophet's Voice," *Hymns*, no. 21.

"I WILL MANIFEST MYSELF TO MY PEOPLE"

꒰ ꒱

Virginia H. Pearce

Eighteen hundred and twenty. One hundred and seventy years ago. A grove of trees. A fourteen-year-old boy with a question. We don't know the day of the week or the number on the calendar, but we do know it was spring—spring in every sense of the word, when truth that slept, seemingly lifeless, began to wake up, to send forth vibrant shoots that would change the world.

On that glorious spring day, the die was cast. An obscure farm boy would spend his life—all of his spiritual, intellectual, physical, emotional, and social energy—bent toward one purpose: understanding and putting in place, piece by piece, the restored gospel of Jesus Christ. Joseph would finally finish miles and miles from Palmyra—on a bend in the Mississippi River, above a red brick store in the year 1844, just weeks before his death. On that April day, he said to his associates: "Now if they kill me you have [got] all the keys, and all the ordinances, and you can confer them upon others, and the hosts of Satan will not be able to tear down the kingdom as fast as you will be able to build it up."[1] From a fourteen-year-old boy to a thirty-nine-year-old prophet. From Palmyra, New York, to Nauvoo, Illinois. From a simple prayer in a grove of trees to the highest ordinances of the Holy Temple.

And now another spring. The awakening time of a millennial year. A dedicated temple, with all of the keys and all of the ordinances

---

Virginia Hinckley Pearce received a master's degree in social work from the University of Utah. She and her husband, Dr. James R. Pearce, are the parents of six and the grandparents of twelve. A former first counselor in the Young Women General Presidency, she serves as the Relief Society president in her ward.

looking down on that quiet grove of trees in Palmyra. A sacred grove. A sacred temple. Only the ancient word *hosanna* comes near to expressing what we feel. We are assured that because of temples and what they mean, Satan will not be able to tear down the kingdom of God as fast as we will be able to build it up. From temples we go forth . . . armed with his power, his name upon us, his glory round about us, and his angels over us (D&C 109:22).

Temples are an expression of the Savior's love and mercy—his outstretched hand—offering us a way to return to the presence of the Father in spite of our sins and shortcomings. The ordinances of the temple invite us and all our kindred dead to receive the fullness. When we have a temple, we have everything the Father has to offer us on this earth.

I am filled with the wonder of temple after temple being built and dedicated in great cities and isolated towns. Surely, they are evidence of the hastening of the work promised by the Lord (D&C 88:73).

In a very personal way, I have wanted to think more, know more, and do more about temples. In the past few months, I have taken my first wobbly steps into family history. When I have attended the temple, I have felt more attentive and alive to the ordinances. In the *Church News* I have read and reread dedicatory prayers. In short, I have felt compelled to understand everything I can about the temple—the final piece of Joseph Smith's mission of restoration. With that in mind, it occurred to me how little I knew about the Kirtland and Nauvoo temples, and so I embarked on a wonderful, personal-study adventure. I have read pages and pages about the Kirtland and the Nauvoo temples, believing that as I understand more about these foundation temples—the first two of the Restoration—I will understand more about temples today.

I have not been disappointed—just frustrated with the limitations of time and space to share what I have learned.

Oh, well.

Let me divide my time between Kirtland and Nauvoo and then consider them in relation to the present. Watch for recurrent themes

that surfaced in my study: sacrifice, personal purity, preparation, protection, and power.

KIRTLAND, JANUARY 1836

Oh, what a happy and bustling community of enthusiastic Saints.
They were on fire with the unfolding truths of the gospel. The School
of the Prophets was flourishing—preparing priesthood holders for missionary work. Participants in the school stretched their minds, learning about the wonders of the universe, studying Hebrew, geography,
astronomy, and delving deeply into the plan of God. The local stone
quarry hummed as the temple walls rose higher, the printing office was
operating, Father Smith was giving patriarchal blessings, and the town
buzzed with marriages, meetings, choir rehearsals, spinning, sewing,
and rejoicing. Missionaries were called home to receive an endowment.
Housing was cramped as new converts arrived daily. A spirit of open
doors and open hearts abounded as newcomers crowded in with those
who had homes. Even with a growing number of apostates within and
the persecution from without, even with painful family separations as
individuals left behind loved ones who would not follow Mormonism,
even with poverty and constant sacrifice, there was an exuberance
about this community as the temple approached completion.

Caroline Barnes Crosby, convert and newlywed of just one year,
wrote: "We reached Kirtland the 7th of January, [1836]. The first person that we saw was . . . one of the young men who first brought the
gospel to Mass[achusetts] at the time my husband was baptized. He
assisted us in getting our wagon up the hill near the temple. . . . [We]
were soon introduced to a score of brethren and sisters, who made us
welcome among them. I ever felt myself quite at home in their society."[2]

Although the temple would not be dedicated until the end of
March, Joseph began giving the promised endowment on 21 January
1836. After doing so, he reported that "the heavens were opened upon
us," and he "beheld the celestial kingdom of God, and the glory
thereof." He saw the "blazing throne of God, whereon was seated the

Father and the Son." Others also saw the face of the Savior and were ministered unto by holy angels.[3] "Roger Orton reported that he saw 'a mighty angel riding upon a horse of fire, with a flaming sword in his hand, followed by five others, [who] encircled the [temple], and protected the Saints . . . from the power of Satan and a host of evil spirits.'"[4] These were just a few of the Pentecostal outpourings experienced in the weeks before and after the dedication of the temple. W. W. Phelps penned the stirring anthem "The Spirit of God Like a Fire Is Burning," sung at the dedicatory service on March 27. The Savior himself appeared on April 3, the Sunday following the dedication (D&C 110). The faithful rejoiced in the season—knowing it was a time of preparation for spreading the glad news abroad. The first mission abroad would begin with Heber C. Kimball in 1837.

Caroline wrote: "I well recollect the sensations with which my mind was actuated when I learned the fact that my husband had been called and ordained to the Melchi[z]edek priesthood and would undoubtedly be required to travel and preach the gospel to the nations of the earth. I realized in some degree the immense responsibility of the office, and besought the Lord for grace and wisdom to be given him that he might be able to magnify his high and holy calling."[5]

Amid all of the activity of the day, preparation of the temple and individual preparation were of prime importance. Lucy Mack Smith noted: "There was but one mainspring to all our thoughts and actions, and that was, the building of the Lord's house."[6]

In my studies, I learned that the Kirtland endowment was not the same as that which would be given in Nauvoo and in subsequent temples. It was a preparatory or initiatory endowment, given only to men preparatory to missionary service. It promised needed protection and blessings upon the heads of those who would leave without purse or scrip. In his charge to the Twelve, Oliver Cowdery told the brethren: "You will see what you never expected to see; you will need the mind of Enoch or Elijah, and the faith of the brother of Jared; you must be prepared to walk by faith, however appalling the prospect to human view."[7]

In a powerful statement, Joseph Smith described one of the purposes of the endowment: "It is calculated to unite our hearts, that we may be one in feeling and sentiment, and that our faith may be strong, so that Satan cannot overthrow us, nor have any power over us."[8]

Despite this wonderful possibility, even those who had received the endowment would be among Joseph's most bitter apostates as they reacted to the bank failure the next year. Persecution from within and without increased. Joseph fled to Missouri. The faithful followed, abandoning the temple to those who would soon use the dedicated building to shelter their animals. Hay and animals on the pulpits of the priesthood!

In summary, no full endowments were given in the Kirtland Temple; no marriages or sealings were performed; and no baptisms for the dead or other vicarious work for the dead occurred. From our viewpoint might we say, "What? Three years of incredibly difficult work, $60,000 raised from a poverty-stricken people, for only a preparatory endowment given to the men? Why this huge effort for a building that would be used for less than two years before apostasy and other problems forced abandonment?"

That was not the reaction of the faithful. So let's look again. Could there possibly be too much work, too much money, too much sacrifice, or too little use for a temple where the mortal world and the heavens would meet; where the veil over the earth would burst; where individuals would receive knowledge and power to resist Satan; where Elijah would restore keys that would eventually allow work to go forward for those beyond the veil; where the Savior himself would come, saying, "Behold, I have accepted this house, and my name shall be here; and I will manifest myself to my people in mercy in this house" (D&C 110:7)?

NAUVOO

Now jump across time and space—across Missouri and on to Nauvoo. Here the Saints found an unhealthy climate, poverty, persecution, and the continuing challenge and excitement of a constant stream of new converts. In the midst of this, the Lord said to his people: "Come ye, with all your gold, and your silver, and your precious stones . . . with iron, with copper, and with brass, and with zinc, and with all your precious things of the earth; and build a house to my name, for the Most High to dwell therein. For there is not a place found on earth that he may come to and restore again that which was lost unto you, or which he hath taken away, even the fulness of the priesthood" (D&C 124:26–28).

In Kirtland the preparatory endowment was offered only to the living, and then only to Melchizedek Priesthood holders. But I learned something else about temple beginnings. Elijah came to Kirtland. Now, in Nauvoo, Joseph began to teach baptisms for the dead. In contrast to Kirtland, the Nauvoo Temple would have a baptismal font—on the backs of twelve oxen. The Saints rejoiced as they were baptized for their dead.

Nauvoo would not see a single grand dedication as had occurred in Kirtland. The times were too chaotic, the Saints too beset by persecutors. Rather, the Prophet Joseph oversaw a series of dedications: first the baptismal font, then subsequent floors, then a secret dedication, followed by a public one. Joseph administered the complete endowment to his associates—above the Red Brick Store, before the temple could be used. In contrast to Kirtland, women were included, Emma being the first, with others joyously following. The new and everlasting covenant of marriage was revealed, and husbands and wives were sealed together. The joy of the Saints knew no bounds.

In April 1844, before the temple was completed and two months before he was martyred, Joseph Smith met with the Twelve above the Red Brick Store and carefully instructed them, giving them the keys to administer all of the ordinances of the temple. With this act, Joseph Smith finished his work. His desire to see the temple itself completed would not be granted. None of us knows why he was denied this, but looking back, it is clear that finishing the temple provided a rallying point for a people who might have disintegrated with the martyrdom of their beloved leader. The temple provided a holy, urgent, and immediate goal—something consuming and uniting they could do with their grief: finish the temple; complete the mandate of their beloved Joseph. At the same time, they knew that receiving their own endowments would prepare them for the exodus to the West—they would have the protection and power they needed to face the challenge ahead. They wanted to receive the "things which have been kept hid from before the foundation of the world, things that pertain to the dispensation of the fulness of times" (D&C 124:41). They wanted this so desperately that Brigham Young acquiesced to their pleas and kept the temple open, ministering night and day. On February 7, more than 600 received the ordinances. At the close of that session, the doors were closed, never to open again for that type of temple service.[9] Of the following day, Brigham Young later wrote: "We knelt around the altar, and dedicated the building to the Most High. We asked his blessing upon our intended move to the west; also asked him to enable us some day to finish the Temple, and dedicate it to him, and we would leave it in his hands to do as he pleased."[10]

It took five years to build the Nauvoo Temple, costing the beleaguered Saints one million dollars. It would be thirty-one long years before the Saints would worship in another dedicated temple. In Utah, the final piece would be put into place, as the Saints received instruction to extend initiatory work, endowments, and sealings to the dead. Elijah came to Kirtland, baptisms for the dead were instituted in Nauvoo, and the other ordinances for the dead were instituted in Utah. The keys Elijah brought in 1836 were finally in full operation.

TODAY

Today the work continues. Temples fill our thoughts and call us to action. It is difficult to put into words the unity members of the Church feel as we play our parts. Surely we felt that unity as we joined together in the dedication of the Palmyra Temple on 6 April 2000.

Think of the words associated with temples—the ones I mentioned earlier: *sacrifice, purity of heart, preparation, protection, power.* We hear them echo in Kirtland and Nauvoo. How do we hear them today, in our own temple worship?

Sacrifice. What does it mean to us? We aren't the women of Nauvoo sewing shirts for the men who worked on the temple. We don't spin, weave, or give our china to be crushed and mixed with the plaster in Kirtland. But we tithe our income. One of the great blessings of developing the habit of paying tithing—particularly if you started doing it as a small child—is that you simply don't miss it, don't even think about it. And yet, our tithing is our spinning and weaving. It is certainly one way we sacrifice. In the past few months I have stopped myself when I contemplate an item that I would like to buy but can't afford. I have said: "Actually, I could afford that if we hadn't paid tithing this month." Then I have the thrill of saying: "I would much rather pay tithing than have that item!" This may seem silly to you, but it has increased my awareness of the joy of paying tithing.

When our daughter, Amy, was very young, we walked her over to the bishop's house to pay her tithing one Sunday afternoon. On the way over she wanted to know what tithing was used for. Among other things, her father told her that it is used to build temples. Later that week, reading the newspaper, we commented that a new temple in Taiwan had been announced. She looked up delightedly and said, "They got my money just in time!" That's an exclamation we can all make every time a temple is announced.

Temple worship requires much more of sacrifice. Is there a more precious commodity in our day than time? Whether it be a temple trip requiring days or a drive across town with a total time of three hours—it is time, and as such, a personal sacrifice.

Purity of heart. It is impossible to talk about sacrifice without talking about purity of heart. A pure heart is both the antecedent and consequence of sacrifice. We make sacrifices out of the purity of our hearts. We purify our hearts through sacrifice.

President Gordon B. Hinckley has said that we have not partaken of the gospel fully unless we have served vicariously for others. This work more nearly approaches the work of the Savior than any other.

We give a gift without a possibility of receiving thanks—at least in this life—from the recipient. Doing work for the dead is sacred and sanctifying work.[11]

Preparation. With our historical hindsight, we can surmise that the Kirtland endowment prepared the brethren to go forth and spread the gospel as missionaries. Similarly, the endowment in Nauvoo prepared the Saints for their grueling exodus west. What does the endowment prepare you and me for? I don't know, but I have some ideas. Each of us undoubtedly has a grueling experience or two in our future, more than one event or circumstance that will require vision and faith and eternal perspective. Eternal perspective is what the temple offers us—and it offers it to us again and again as we are given the privilege of time after time standing proxy for others. The temple is a constant refresher of the great and meaningful things of life. Do you think that eternal perspective kept the Saints going when they fled Kirtland and Missouri and Nauvoo? It made all the difference. Does it makes a difference now? The more clear our understanding of the big picture, the more energy we will have to live the details. Temples remind us of the great and meaningful things of life. They help us to sift through the clutter. Do we need this in an age of information overload? I do.

Protection. We are prepared for the future as we understand more completely the plan. This understanding offers us protection. What kind of protection? There is no limit, I believe. Certainly the knowledge and understanding offered us in the temple protect us from Satan's cunning traps. Our very worthiness to enter the house of the Lord indicates that we are protected from the ravages of drugs, alcohol, immorality, and other assaults. The temple recommend we carry is an indication of our faith and works—and faith and works bring with them their own blessings of protection.

Power. Our worthiness allows us in our extremities to call down the powers of heaven. We pause in the celestial room, hearts open in prayer, knowing that God knows who we are, knows each sorrow, each heartache, each weakness, and yet he loves us completely. In the temple we approach him who has the power to forgive. The temple *is a* house of forgiveness. In Solomon's ancient dedicatory prayer, he speaks movingly of this. Read it again in Chronicles and be inspired by it (2 Chronicles 6). This dedicatory prayer helps us understand that the temple is a place where we come to look inward and find our own shortcomings. We can rise above them and stand tall, and he will forgive our sins. Each time we go to the temple it can be a time of repentance, an opportunity to turn our lives around. Does this give us power? Yes. It gives me the power to leave yesterday behind, get up in the morning, and try again. To keep going forward. To know that I can be better. It has been said that through the ordinances of the temple our natures actually change to become like God. As we grow in spiritual power through temple participation, we will have more peace in our homes and love in our relationships.

President Hinckley has said: "Keep the temple as busy or busier than it has been. The Lord will bless you and you will be happier. I make a promise to you that every time you come to the temple you will be a better man or woman when you leave than you were when you came. That is a promise. I believe it with all my heart."[12]

Keep thinking *power.* As you watch the downward spiral of our society as evidenced in the media, do you feel helpless? George Q. Cannon taught that the construction of temples "lessens the power of Satan on the earth and increases the power of God and Godliness, [and] moves the heavens in mighty power in our behalf."[13]

That means that with every announcement of and dedication of a temple reported in the newspaper, we can know that we are making headway against the forces of evil.

Sacrifice, purity of heart, preparation, protection, power, and much, much more. There is no end, because temples are the apex of our earthly experience, and so, within them we find the whole gospel. They represent the complete restoration—Joseph's mission—which in essence was a restoration of the mission of Jesus Christ. When we stand in temples, we stand by Joseph. And when we stand by Joseph, we stand by the Lord, Jesus Christ.

I close with expressions of gratitude to my Savior. Through the temple he has extended to me the highest and most sacred blessings available on this earth—at any time in the history of the earth. With each dedication of this multitude of new temples, I desire to rededicate myself to the purposes of the Lord—to prepare myself and do my part in preparing the earth for his triumphal return, when we shall greet him with the Hosanna Shout, expressing our love, reverence, and respect for God and the Lamb.[14]

Notes

1. Joseph Smith, *Times and Seasons* 5, 19 (2 October 1844): 651. See also John Jacques, "The Life and Labors of Sidney Rigdon," *Improvement Era* 3, no. 8 (June 1900).
2. In Kenneth W. Godfrey, Audrey M. Godfrey, Jill Mulvay Derr, *Women's Voices: An Untold History of the Latter-day Saints, 1830–1900* (Salt Lake City: Deseret Book, 1982), 46.
3. Milton V. Backman Jr., *The Heavens Resound* (Salt Lake City: Deseret Book, 1983), 287–89.
4. In ibid., 292.
5. In Godfrey, *Women's Voices*, 48.
6. Lucy Mack Smith, *History of Joseph Smith by His Mother Lucy Mack Smith*, ed. Preston Nibley (Salt Lake City: Bookcraft, 1958), 231.
7. In Joseph Smith, *History of The Church of Jesus Christ of Latter-day Saints*, ed. B. H. Roberts, 2d ed. rev., 7 vols. (Salt Lake City: The Church of Jesus Christ of Latter-day Saints, 1932–51), 2:197.
8. In Backman, *Heavens Resound*, 301.
9. E. Cecil McGavin, *The Nauvoo Temple* (Salt Lake City: Deseret Book, 1962), 69; see also Smith, *History of the Church*, 7:579–80.
10. In ibid., 70; see also Smith, *History of the Church*, 7:580.
11. Gordon B. Hinckley, *Teachings of Gordon B. Hinckley* (Salt Lake City: Deseret Book, 1997), 366; see also *Church News*, 19 November 1994.
12. In "President Hinckley Addresses 15,000 in Laie," *Church News*, 28 February 2000.
13. George Q. Cannon, *Gospel Truths*, ed. Jerreld L. Newquist (Salt Lake City: Deseret Book, 1987), 366.
14. "President Lorenzo Snow taught that this shout will herald the Messiah when he comes in the glory of the Father" (*Encyclopedia of Mormonism*, ed. Daniel H. Ludlow, 4 vols. [New York: Macmillan, 1992], s.v. "Hosanna Shout," 2:659).

LETTING THE LIGHT WITHIN SHINE FORTH

⁊℃

Kathleen H. Barnes

I *love* being a Latter-day Saint woman. I love knowing that I am a spirit daughter of God and that my life has meaning, purpose, and direction. Like the prophet Alma, I too have wished that I could tell those around me—in a way that they could hear—that life for them could be more wonderful (Alma 29:1–2). "I do not glory of myself," Alma explained, "but I glory in that which the Lord hath commanded me; . . . that perhaps I may be an instrument in the hands of God to bring some soul to repentance; and this is my joy" (Alma 29:9). To be, as Alma says, an instrument in the hands of God is our task and our joy. To allow our light to shine by virtue of righteousness is our privilege.

The light I speak of is hard to define. If you are like me, when you look in the mirror you don't always see a radiant glow. And yet, that light is with us in some form. Not long ago, a friend and I were walking through a very large department store in a country far from home. In such settings, I realize that Latter-day women are but a mere speck on the surface of the earth. That day as we strolled slowly up and down the aisles, a woman approached us and asked in English, "Where are you from?" When we responded, "Utah," her eyes lit up. "Are you here to attend the Mormon conference tonight?" I don't know why she approached us. I was in travel-worn clothes, weary from jet lag, and I

Kathleen Hinckley Barnes, a daughter of President Gordon B. and Marjorie Pay Hinckley, received her bachelor's degree in education and is a self-taught business and community leader. She and her husband, Alan Barnes, are the parents of five children, and the grandparents of eleven.

can't think there was any glow about me, but maybe, just maybe, there was a glimmer of that light.

As sisters in God's great kingdom, we have opportunities to let our light shine, to serve, to bless, to perform. We don't stand on rooftops and beam our light into the sky. But we go to work and make a difference, as Elder Neal A. Maxwell has stated, "within our allotted 'acreage.'"[1] As our daily lives intertwine with those around us, we create an atmosphere where love can be nurtured and flourish. We make decisions based on principles. We teach by our words and our actions. We increase the light in our personal spheres by reaching out, by doing and by being.

Let me relate the experience of a young Latter-day Saint mother living in Japan. Her neighborhood is an eclectic mix of people from around the world. For the most part, they are families who are raising children and trying to create stability in a turbulent environment. Because of the likelihood of earthquakes in Japan, this mother decided to invite her neighbors to an emergency preparedness gathering. She took a simple approach. She contacted the designated local shelter and arranged a tour. She then produced a small flyer on her computer, and she and her children walked the neighborhood distributing flyers on doorsteps. Her children were rather skeptical. "What if no one comes?" they asked. "It won't matter," their mother replied. "Then we will go on the tour by ourselves." The following Saturday morning, fifty-two people showed up. They walked together to the shelter where they received information on procedures and supplies. These neighbors became so enthusiastic that they began to meet on a regular basis. The neighborhood welcomed an opportunity to rally together, to increase their friendship, and to improve their surroundings.

This mother was simply working within her allotted acreage, which was her neighborhood, using skills she had learned in a gospel setting. What she did involved relatively little work or time. It was a small extension of life as she knows it. President Hinckley, at a National Press Club interview in Washington, D.C., said, "People wonder what we do for our women. I will tell you what we do. We get out of their way, and look with wonder at what they are accomplishing."[2]

Our neighborhoods are a great place to start letting our light shine forth. President Spencer W. Kimball told the women of the Church, "We desire women to develop social refinements because these are very real dimensions of keeping the second great commandment—to love one's neighbor as oneself."[3] Part of that social refinement is learning to be articulate. As LDS women, we need to articulate the gospel in a righteous way. Again President Kimball has said, "We should be as concerned with the woman's capacity to communicate as we are to have her sew and preserve food. Good women are articulate as well as affectionate."[4]

During recent focus groups held in Arizona, stake and ward mission leaders were asked to identify what prevented them from sharing the gospel with their nonmember friends. The overwhelming response was *fear*. Fear of losing a friendship, fear of sounding self-righteous, fear of not being able to explain questions of doctrine.

Women by nature love to share. We share recipes; we share books and movies; we share information on child-rearing, on husband-endearing (or enduring as the case might be), on planting flowers, or cleaning our showers. But when it comes to sharing the thing which brings us the most happiness and creates deep joy that arises from the very core of our souls, we become fearful, or, at the least, timid. But God is not the author of these feelings: "For God hath not given us the spirit of fear; but of power, and of love, and of a sound mind" (2 Timothy 1:7).

One day while I was standing on a Salt Lake City street, a woman approached me, asked a couple of questions, and then launched a verbal attack, beginning with her opinion that Mormon women are brainwashed and subservient. She accused us of coercing our children and stripping them of their abilities to make independent decisions. (She obviously didn't know some of our children.) She claimed we forced others to our way of thinking. She implied that Mormon women were illiterate and mindless. She had clearly formed a judgment against

Latter-day Saint women so comprehensive, angry, and misinformed that I knew I could not turn it around. Frankly, I didn't dare try because she was a hefty woman, much larger than I am, and I was certain that if I provoked a blow, I would soon find myself a blob on the sidewalk.

So I listened and let her unload. After what seemed endless minutes of ugly verbage, she appeared satisfied that she had sufficiently impacted me with her message, and she fell silent, glaring at me, waiting for me to respond. We speak of fear; but I can tell you that I *knew* fear at that moment. I felt physically threatened as well as wounded by her words.

I began to respond, saying the only thing that came into my mind. "Someday," I said, "you may open your door to some young Latter-day Saint missionaries. Before you slam it, please remember that somewhere they have a mother just like you and just like me, who is praying for them and for those they meet. Then you might want to say, 'I met a Mormon woman once, and she told me that she was the happiest person alive. She said her happiness did not come from riches or fame. Her happiness was rooted deeply in her heart and came from a rich understanding of life and her connection to her Savior. She said she lived with a kind of joy and peace that comes from God. She said she wished that I, too, could know that kind of joy.' And then at that point, if you want to, you can tell those young missionaries, 'Thank you, but I am not interested in your message.'" To my surprise, the woman hung her head for a moment, muttered, "Thanks," then turned and walked away.

That day I learned that a simple expression of feelings can often diffuse an attack. So when all else fails, just speak from your heart. We need not be timid, nor do we need to defend ourselves

Mary was saying good-bye to a wonderful neighbor. On a number of occasions, Mary had tried to share the gospel with this dear friend, and though her neighbor was cordial, she did not appear to be interested. Mary wondered what she could give as a going away gift. A Book of Mormon seemed bold, but it felt right. So Mary got a book and inside the front cover inscribed, "I wanted to give you something that was nearest and dearest to my heart, but I didn't think you would like five more children. So instead I am giving you the other thing that means the most to me." Her friend wept as she read it. It was a gift given in love and received in love.

"Be not afraid, only believe," said the Savior (Mark 5:36).

A young woman recently greeted missionaries of another faith at her door. A returned missionary herself, she felt empathy for what they were doing. Ordinarily she would have thanked them and sent them on their way, but this day she put aside her disinterest and brightened her light just a bit by extending herself a little further. She talked with them and acknowledged their work. She commended them for their faith and then expressed her own faith in a living prophet who speaks in God's behalf. When they encouraged her to accept their literature, she suggested that they trade literature. A conversation that began rather coldly, ended with warmth, each knowing a little more about the other's faith.

For the most part, Latter-day Saint women do not lack in belief, but sometimes we lack the confidence to express our beliefs in forthright but accepting ways. Our convictions will not always be echoed in others, of course, but they will generally be met with respect if stated with confidence and simple honesty.

Heather's seven-year-old daughter fell in love with Irish dancing. The competitions associated with this new-found love call for many extra rehearsals. When the first rehearsal schedule was distributed, several were scheduled on Sundays. Heather explained to her daughter's dance teacher that Sunday was their family day. They attended church services and discouraged any family participation in organized sports or other events on Sunday. The teacher listened respectfully, but made no changes to the schedule. Some days later, when Heather was not there, the schedule was again discussed. Another parent, one of Heather's non-LDS friends, explained simply, "Heather and her family are Mormons, and it is against their religion to do these kinds of things on Sunday. They believe in the commandment of keeping the Sabbath day holy." The teacher brightened. "I did not understand that it was a religious commitment. In that case," she said, "we will reschedule the Sunday rehearsals."

Heather later stated, "In my effort not to offend or to appear self-righteous, I skirted the issues. I did not state my position with confidence and clarity."

In a Gallup "Twenty-four Hour Spiritual Practice Survey," 91 percent of the respondents stated that they believe in God, 82 percent experienced in their lives a need for spiritual growth, 80 percent had a personal relationship with God, and 75 percent said they pray daily.[5]

In research done by Wirthlin Worldwide, women were asked to rate the things they considered most important in their lives.[6] At the top of the list were:

Having a successful marriage
Raising a family
Developing personal relationships
Growing spiritually

Clearly, the stage is set. Women across this world want the knowledge that can bring them peace, spiritual growth, and strong, viable family values. We can help them find it. We can listen to them. We can talk with them. We can acknowledge their feelings and offer understanding and acceptance.

Sometimes it is difficult. One day I sat at a lunch table with a group of women I did not know. The conversation turned to men and soon deteriorated into some ugly generalizations. *All* men, they concluded, were sinister and evil, and those who professed otherwise were liars. These blanket accusations upset me. For days, I brooded and grew more angry. One day it dawned on me that their words and feelings reflected their experiences. They had, unfortunately, each been the victim of a man who lacks integrity; each had lost trust and respect for men. Once I understood that, I felt compassion, not anger.

President Hinckley's counsel to us has been very specific: "Let us as Latter-day Saints reach out to others not of our faith. Let us never act in a spirit of arrogance or with a holier-than-thou attitude. Rather, may we show love and respect and helpfulness toward them. We are greatly misunderstood, and I fear that much of it is of our own making. We can be more tolerant, more neighborly, more friendly, more of an example than we have been in the past. Let us teach our children to treat others with friendship, respect, love, and admiration. That will yield a far better result than will an attitude of egotism and arrogance."[7]

My dear friend Mary Kay is a good Jewish woman. The week following the Palmyra Temple dedication, Mary Kay asked me about it. "Oh, it was wonderful," I said. "In fact, it was so glorious I could hardly stand it." And then, quite spontaneously, I added, "Oh, Mary Kay, I love this church *so* much!" She answered by saying, "I know you do, and I think your church is lucky to have you."

And do you know what? I think this church *is* lucky to have us, and we are lucky to have this church. Because we love it, we can express this love in ways that can be heard and felt.

If we want to be a part of this latter-day work, we must move with confidence and assurance that the Lord is on our side and will use us to accomplish his purposes. We are the believers. And we have a solemn responsibility to articulate our beliefs in word and action and in a spirit of love and acceptance. Individually and collectively, we must put our fears aside and let the light within shine forth. We must speak with convicton and clarity. We must listen with love and understanding.

Not long ago, I recounted to my father an afternoon I had spent working with women who engaged in some Mormon bashing during the course of the day. They launched slanderous innuendoes at the Church and Church leaders. In relating this experience, I said to my father, "I didn't like being there. I don't want to be with them again!" His answer was quiet but sure, "The only way to change them is to make them your friends."

To that I add my simple testimony, and do so in the words of Alma: "O that I were an angel, . . . that I might . . . speak with the trump of God. . . .

"But behold, I am a [woman], and . . . I do not glory of myself, but

I glory in that which the Lord hath commanded me; . . . that perhaps I may be an instrument in the hands of God to bring some soul to repentance; and this is my joy" (Alma 29: 1, 3, 9).

Notes

1. Neal A. Maxwell, "Content with the Things Allotted unto Us," *Ensign*, May 2000, 72.
2. Gordon B. Hinckley, as quoted in "Church Leader Addresses Growth, Efforts to Improve People's Lives," *Church News*, 18 March 2000.
3. Spencer W. Kimball, "Privileges and Responsibilities," *Ensign*, November 1978, 104–5.
4. Ibid., 104.
5. George Gallup Jr. and Timothy Jones, *The Next American Spirituality: Finding God in the Twenty-first Century* (Colorado Springs: Cook Communications, 2000).
6. "1006 adults surveyed in the U.S.," Wirthlin Worldwide, August 1996; personal conversation with Cathy Chamberlin, senior research executive of Wirthlin Worldwide.
7. Gordon B. Hinckley, "A Time of New Beginnings," *Ensign*, May 2000, 87.

WHERE HE NEEDS US

⁂

Carole Mikita

In Palmyra, the not-quite-spring day began with weather best described as bleak. Nearby communities had heavy rain showers, even sleet. In spite of cold temperatures and wind, President and Sister Hinckley were among the early arrivals at the new Palmyra Temple, and as they entered, the weather began gradually to settle. As one seasoned journalist noted, "Well, the President must be here. Just wait, by the time he comes outside in that white suit he wears, the clouds will part and the sun will shine."

Sure enough, that's exactly what happened. "It's almost a miracle," he said. "It is a miracle; it's wonderful." Was he speaking of the weather? Or perhaps of the fact that we were witnesses to a completed circle: a temple about to be dedicated as a house of the Lord, in Palmyra, where it all began.

Down the hill and across the street sat the tiny log home where Joseph Smith learned from an angel of his role in the restoration of the gospel. Before that, he had wandered into a grove of nearby trees and prayed to know the truth. There he received an answer: light and knowledge in a vision of both the Father and the Son. But it would be decades after the Church was established and its few members pushed out that any would return to settle in this tiny upstate New York community, not welcomed but determined to stay.

Let me tell you how I received the light. I brought to my eventual conversion the simple faith of a child. From my earliest recollections, I knew God lived. Not only that, I knew he was my friend. I knew I

Carole Mikita, news anchor and arts and religion reporter for KSL-TV in Salt Lake City, is a convert to the Church. She and her husband, Neil York, are the parents of two daughters. She teaches the sixteen- and seventeen-year-olds in her ward Sunday School.

could talk to him about anything. I learned this from my parents and from a children's book in our home about God and the power of prayer.

When missionaries came to our Ohio door in 1960 when I was nine years old, it was as if I had heard their words before. I wasn't surprised that my mother responded to their message by asking to be baptized. She told me about a book she was reading, the Book of Mormon, which came with a promise that if you read it and prayed for an answer, you would receive one, just as Joseph Smith had.

I looked at that thick book and instantly decided that it was too long and complicated for a nine-year-old. *Someday*, I thought. *The Lord will understand. After all, he knows me and my abilities. I'll just explain.* So I talked to my Father in Heaven, apologizing for not reading it, but telling him that I believed he would still answer my prayer, a child's simple, straightforward request. And, yes, I received my answer . . . powerful, undeniable. I never forgot that witness. Though I was not baptized until the age of twenty-one, I knew the gospel was true at age nine. Do not underestimate the testimony that springs from an innocent believer.

When our daughter Caitlin turned eight, she was excited to be baptized. Her Primary teachers had prepared her well, and our stake held a wonderful meeting for all the children who would make that decision within the coming months. She looked on her baptism as a graduation into the gospel, something she really wanted. Naturally, she wanted all of her friends and neighbors to share it with her. Unbeknownst to me, and with the help of her older sister, she made invitations announcing the big event and suggesting everyone come to our house afterwards for a party. After all, this was surely something to celebrate. She hand delivered her invitations to just a few ward members. After all, as Cate explained, they already knew about baptism. Then, boldly I might add and armed with a smile and a child's confidence that they would come, she took the invitations to friends of other faiths.

Her baptism day arrived, and I was very nervous; I did not want her to be disappointed. I stored up several excuses—but I didn't have to use them. Shortly after we arrived, the chapel began to fill with members of our ward, family members of the two other children being baptized, and then one by one all of the people Caitlin had invited—her teacher at school, the other carpool mom, her husband and two children, the next-door neighbors, and then the ones up the street (the mother and two children in that family are now members of the Church)—all of the important people in her daily life. She wanted them to be there. I had the job of speaking about the Holy Spirit, and I remember looking into those faces smiling back at me from the pews; they were happy to be there for our daughter. We have the picture of Cate and all of her friends standing around a baptism cake in our home. Her huge smile seems to say, *See, Mom, I told you.* I thought to myself, *Oh, ye of little faith.*

Mormon women need to move forward into the twenty-first century with the kind of confidence that Cate displayed. We can take courage and inspiration from our prophet, President Gordon B. Hinckley: "The future of this church is assured. . . . There isn't any question in my mind about that. . . . The patterns of the past become the pattern of the future and that will go on. . . . It will increase. . . . There isn't any question at all in my mind about that. The Church will grow."[1]

It occurred to me recently that spreading the gospel is not something that we *do*; it's simply who and what we are. We must live our beliefs every day, then be prepared, be knowledgeable, and live with the Spirit to alert us to the opportunities.

A few years ago, my husband, Neil, and I had just completed a four-and-a-half year stint as Gospel Doctrine teachers. The experience had been glorious, and we felt mentally prepared for whatever the bishop needed us to do next. Or so we thought, until we heard the words "activities chairmen." Considering that we had never attended any of our ward's activities, I wondered how serious he could be. I left his office in tears. Could I do this? Maybe. Did I want to do this? Definitely not. Neil, his usual stoic self, just shook his head and tried to comfort me. I actually went back to the bishop's office the next day and asked, "Do I look like a social director to you?" He laughed and said, "No, you are an arts person. We need someone in tune with that, who will bring a little culture into our ward and reach out to the neighbors not of our faith, as well. Go forth and do good. We'll call people who will help you, I promise."

I prayed hard and came away with several goals for every activity. I wanted each in some way to be spiritually uplifting, helpful to others, and, yes, to include nonmembers. I was also determined to have food only if absolutely necessary and not to spend any church money.

When I was a little girl attending the Episcopal Church, my father always made sure that I had a quarter tucked into my white glove for the collection plate. I was very happy to contribute. Our minister would put that plate with everyone's money on the altar. I figured the angels came after we left and took it with them back to heaven for the building up of the kingdom. I have since learned that this is the Lord's kingdom on earth, and we need the money here. But, when I was in charge of activities, there would be no money spent on food or decorations.

The bishop kept his word and called talented members to our committee. For every activity we created invitations that our children helped deliver to each house within our ward boundaries. The first was a winter fireside, featuring my friend, colleague, and immensely popular television anchor, Dick Nourse. He drew a crowd, and he had lots to say about his life and newfound direction in the Church. He was everything he needed to be . . . and, yes, nonmembers came.

In the spring our ward had signed up to help clean a section of This Is the Place State Park in Salt Lake City, where a pioneer village was being constructed. When we arrived with tools in hand, those in charge directed us to an outdoor amphitheater. They needed us to clear the hillside, remove branches and debris from the stage area, and clear the dirt where the audience sits. We had a great crew and worked quickly, but I just kept asking, *Where are the nonmembers going to come from?* By afternoon, we found out. A wedding party from one of the Greek Orthodox churches in the valley would hold its ceremony there that evening. As they showed up, we introduced ourselves and helped them set up chairs and a gazebo for their priest, bride, and groom. As a final touch, we all tossed flower petals on the path where they would walk.

Our fall activity was a neighborhood concert. We held auditions and said no to some offers, like an Elvis impersonator. We wanted a serious musical production with ushers, programs, and an intermission. It turned out to be a wonderful evening, and once again, nonmembers shared their talents with us. I hoped that they would feel welcome in our building, and they did.

At Christmas, members of our committee came up with the idea for a giving tree. We decorated the tree in our foyer with paper ornaments, which had dollar amounts on them (twenty-five and fifty cents for the children). Ward families then took whichever ornaments they could match with a donation. We also encouraged members to bring canned goods and wrapped toys, so that we could help with the needs of our stake. For our gathering, we asked each family to bring a plate of cookies or fruit and a blanket to sit on. We had music, sang Christmas carols together, listened to a message from our bishop, and, yes, people of other faiths donated and attended. It was classic pandemonium with children running everywhere and crumbs all over the floor. Clean up was not nearly as much fun as decorating with donated trees, lights, wreaths, and ribbons had been. I went home feeling unsure of what we had accomplished. But the following Monday our stake president called to thank us for what he called an incredible effort. Our bishop's office had been piled to the ceiling with food and gifts. Our ward had donated nearly half the money the stake needed to take care of people who needed help. The seven little girls who wanted baby dolls for Christmas, but whose families couldn't afford them, would each now receive one.

As a church and as individuals, we are a powerful force for good. The Lord knows where he needs each of us and will place us there with the help to get the job done. Our lives are changed for the better whenever we are engaged in his work.

On a recent visit to Poland, his homeland, Pope John Paul II told the crowd who had come to hear him speak, "Do not be afraid to be saints. . . . Today's world needs the holiness of Christians who, in the ordinary conditions of family and professional life, take on their proper daily duties . . . in the spirit of love of God and neighbor."[2]

In Jerusalem last September, I witnessed a miracle of music with Utah's Millenium Choir and Lex and Peggy de Azevedo's magnificent video titled *Gloria: The Life of Christ.* Ina Esther Joost, from the Jerusalem Symphony Orchestra, said, "I think it's a wonderful idea to join the Jerusalem Symphony Orchestra, which is the orchestra of the radio of Israel, together with this American Mormon Choir, and in the year 2000 to sing a glory to our God of Israel."[3]

While there I had the opportunity to observe women of other faiths going about their daily tasks and, especially, worshipping. The Dome of the Rock Mosque is considered the third most sacred site of Islam in the world. Tens of thousands of Muslims arrive for prayers each Friday, Holy Day, and on their way home they pick up household and food items at the bazaar near the Damascus Gate of the ancient walled city. Closer to the mosque, pilgrims from Mecca were dressed in white. White clothing signifies purity, and before entering they also wash their hands and feet in the fountains outside to signify cleanliness. Inside the mosque, with its rich mosaics and gold, is the rock upon which Mohammed is said to have ascended into heaven.

I felt the Spirit there. The people were righteous, praying sincerely for help, guidance, and forgiveness. They had their families uppermost in their minds. We have this in common. If we understand and respect other people's faith, they in turn will respect ours. We are all brothers and sisters. Abraham Abul Elhawa, our dear guide and friend from Mt. of Olives Travel & Taxi Service, would often say, "Mormons and Muslims, we are very close."

The Western Wall, or Wailing Wall, sacred to the Jews, is all that is left of Herod's Temple, which was destroyed in 70 A.D. Men and women who worship there are separated by a curtain. Individually they approach the wall with reverence. They stop to read scriptures on nearby tables. They pray silently, usually chanting or rocking to help their concentration. I was there on a Friday. When the sun set, the Jewish Sabbath would begin. To the Orthodox Jews, all preparations for that twenty-four-hour period had to be completed by then—the stores closed, the shopping finished and meals prepared, and only a single candle lighted in each home. Just before dark, the men actually blocked the streets, so no traffic would disturb the spiritual songs and thoughts.

It was a spiritual experience to watch a young Jewish mother backing away from the wall in reverence, teaching her two young daughters about the sacred nature of this place and why they should honor it. Here was another righteous woman, obeying the commandments, loving her children and the Lord.

We are on a journey toward perfection in a very imperfect world, where it is easy to stumble and lose our way and our spiritual life. How hard it is sometimes to maintain our spiritual equilibrium in an ever-changing world. To do this we must understand something as pure and simple as the gospel itself—that truth does not change. The Lord is "the same yesterday, today, and forever" (Mormon 9:9). Gospel principles are entrenched, eternal, and will work in all walks of life—and emerge victorious. Our Heavenly Father understands our hearts, our trials, our current temptations, our foes, our weaknesses . . . and he is always available to us. He is a concerned parent. He wants us to succeed, to be our best, to return to him one day glorious, exalted beings. Perhaps we will be here when his son comes again in glory! "Then we which are alive and remain shall be caught up together with them in the clouds, to meet the Lord in the air: and so shall we ever be with the Lord" (1 Thessalonians 4:17).

In these crucial latter days, we are the standard bearers, the nurturers, the keepers of the faith. Children watch every move we make, listen to every word we say. The world inspects our behavior. Some find it hard to believe we have raised our bar so high! Let me repeat, the Lord knows where he needs each of us and he will place us there with whatever help we need to get the job done. Do not look at yourself for

an instant as an outsider but as one who very much belongs in the fore-
front, a woman with a mission to be true to her heart and mind and to
her Lord. We are in a world that needs our spiritual refinement and
unshakeable faith.

We belong to The Church of Jesus Christ of Latter-day Saints. My
mother loved to say the name; I do as well; so should you. When you
speak, use it. It is incumbent upon us to live our faith in the world, in
the most polished, confident, articulate way we can. "For I am not
ashamed of the gospel of Christ: for it is the power of God unto salvation to every one that believeth" (Romans 1:16).

Notes

1. Gordon B. Hinckley, from personal interview with President Hinckley for
   KSL-TV, February 2000.
2. Pope John Paul II, as quoted by the Associated Press, spring 2000.
3. Ina Esther Joost, videotape interview, September 1999, tape in possession
   of KSL-TV Eyewitness News, Salt Lake City.

"Stand by My Servant Joseph"

⚜

Heidi S. Swinton

They called him Brother Joseph, the Saints from the eastern seaboard, Canada, and an ocean away in England. For fourteen years, Joseph Smith led this Church born on American soil. He did not emerge from the great New England universities or seminaries, nor did he preach before a highly acclaimed congregation. He was a farmer who lived on the edge of civilization but at the center of a holy war— a war fought for the hearts and souls of all our Father's children.

It all began in a grove in upstate New York. Joseph recounted, "I saw two Personages, whose brightness and glory defy all description, standing above me in the air. One of them spake unto me, calling me by name and said, pointing to the other—*This is My Beloved Son. Hear Him!*" (JS–H 1:17).

That singular experience affects us all.

Five years ago, I too was in upstate New York visiting the Peter Whitmer farmhouse in Fayette. To the world, it is simply a small frame building in the middle of rolling fields. To members of the Church, it is much more. Here, in an upstairs room, Joseph Smith finished translating the Book of Mormon from the gold plates. Here, on the grounds, an angel showed Mary Whitmer the sacred plates. Here, in the main floor room, Joseph Smith and a handful of believers gathered on 6 April 1830, to establish the Church.

During my visit, the missionary sister assigned to the home spoke with great reverence to our group about those significant early days.

Heidi S. Swinton, a graduate of the University of Utah, has written several documentaries on Church subjects, including American Prophet: The Story of Joseph Smith, *and has contributed to many others. She and her husband, Jeffrey, are the parents of four sons. Heidi serves as a member of one of the Church's curriculum writing committees.*

She bore testimony of the truths of the gospel of Jesus Christ and of her love for the Prophet Joseph. As we were ushered out of the home and onto the back lawn, I felt impressed to step away from the crowd. At the edge of the grass, I leaned up against a fence to take in the setting. It was a beautiful day; the tall corn in the field behind me brushed my shoulders.

I was thinking about my family when into my mind came thoughts so clearly defined they seemed to be words: "Heidi, the Church was established here, just like she said. Joseph Smith was a prophet of God, and you need to know that." I remember thinking, *I know that. Everyone knows that. I have heard people bear that testimony since I was a child.* Immediately the words came again: "The Church was established here just like she said. And Joseph Smith was and is a prophet of God . . . and someday you will need to know that."

The word *someday* stood out in my mind. *Someday.* What did that mean? And then immediately I asked myself, "Why would I need to know that?"

I understand now why I needed that witness.

For the past two and a half years I have worked on a project about Joseph Smith. I wrote the script for a nationally televised PBS documentary and its companion book that put before the world the life of this great prophet. Joseph Smith was the essence of faith and goodness, determination and devotion. To capture his life and words, I needed a strong testimony that he was a prophet of God.

The writing task was daunting. The story had to speak to both a Mormon and non-Mormon audience. I call it being bilingual. Those of us whose belief is founded in faith understand how the Lord uses angels and revelation. We are grateful for the power of the priesthood. But for those who do not share that faith, miraculous events so central to Joseph's work are difficult to grasp. Add to the events the fact that many of our angels have names. At one point, the sponsoring public television station suggested showing the gold plates on screen to authenticate the visit of Moroni. Imagine explaining that Joseph gave the plates back to Moroni, who took them back to heaven or buried them, perhaps in another hill.

In the process of writing dozens of drafts, I often looked back on that bright summer day at the Peter Whitmer farmhouse, and I remembered the statement of the Book of Mormon prophet Jacob: "I had heard the voice of the Lord speaking unto me in very word, . . . wherefore, I could not be shaken" (Jacob 7:5).

Every one of us can receive that witness. It is not predicated on a writing project or years of study. It is a product of our willingness to have ears to hear. You may be saying to yourself what I said when I heard those words, "Why would I need to know that?"

Here's why.

In Doctrine and Covenants 76, Joseph Smith and Sidney Rigdon describe seeing a vision when Joseph was working on revisions of the Bible: "We beheld the glory of the Son, on the right hand of the Father, and received of his fulness;

"And saw the holy angels, and them who are sanctified before his throne, worshiping God, and the Lamb. . . .

"And now, after the many testimonies which have been given of him, this is the testimony, last of all, which we give of him: That he lives!

"For we saw him, even on the right hand of God; and we heard the voice bearing record that he is the Only Begotten of the Father—

"That by him, and through him, and of him, the worlds are and were created, and the inhabitants thereof are begotten sons and daughters unto God" (vv. 20–24).

That's why we need to know that Joseph Smith was a prophet of God. Because of his witness of the Savior. Joseph Smith saw Jesus Christ. He saw him in the grove; he saw him in Hiram; he saw him in Kirtland. He talked with him. Joseph Smith was prepared before the world was to be the prophet of these last days. He was called by Jesus Christ to lead the Restoration and gather the Saints.

Everything about Joseph Smith points to Jesus Christ. When Joseph states, "He lives," I hear those words from the hymn, "He lives, he lives, who once was dead. He lives, my ever-living head."[1] And everything about Jesus Christ points to our Father in Heaven.

When I began intensive research on the Prophet Joseph, I read stacks of books, journals, articles, papers, and commentaries. I found that many who have written about him do not understand the significance of his prophetic mantle. They place him in earth time but not in God's time. From the moment Joseph Smith visited the grove as a fourteen-year-old boy, the veil thinned. His life cannot be cast in sequence, nor can a writer necessarily explain that this happened and then this and this. So much of historical analysis is trying to make sense of context: date, time, and place. Yet Joseph worked beyond our mortal understanding and his own historical setting to gain his knowledge. He received his power from those who held keys anciently. He spoke with messengers of our Lord, not once but often. Put simply, his life is not linear. It does not sit down comfortably on a chronological chart. He sits now in the timeless councils of heaven and waits for us to join him in our Father's kingdom.

That is so important to understand. For when Joseph Smith stated in 1843, "No man knows my history," I think he was not talking about concealed facts but about misunderstood perspectives.[2] He saw angels. He received priesthood authority from John the Baptist and Peter, James, and John. Moses brought him the keys of the gathering of Israel, and Elijah the keys of this dispensation. That's why his brother Hyrum said of him, "Joseph has the spirit and power of all the prophets."[3] Joseph's grasp of history reached before this world and beyond it.

If Joseph Smith is a casual reference in your testimony, now is the time to strengthen your witness. Consider how a scripture in Doctrine and Covenants 6 may help you. But, first, let me put it in context. This revelation was received when Joseph, living in Harmony, Pennsylvania, was translating the plates. Oliver Cowdery served as his scribe. The headnote to section 6 states that Oliver had already received a divine manifestation of the truth of the Prophet's testimony respecting the plates, and he must have believed that Joseph was chosen to restore the gospel. I imagine that Oliver wanted to know what the Lord had in mind for him to do, just as we so often ponder what the Lord would have us do. Like so many revelations to the early Saints, each of us can "hear" our own name for the one given, for as the Lord said to Emma, "I say unto you, that this is my voice unto all" (D&C 25:16).

In Doctrine and Covenants 6:18 the Lord counsels Oliver, "Be diligent; stand by my servant Joseph, faithfully, in whatsoever difficult circumstances he may be for the word's sake." "Be diligent" is a clear call to do all we can. Work hard. Do everything within your power and your reach. Then what does he ask of Oliver—and of each of us? "Stand by my servant Joseph, faithfully." What does that mean?

Joseph Smith bears witness of Jesus Christ: "That he lives." When we "stand by Joseph, faithfully," we do the same. We add our testimony to Joseph's testimony that Jesus Christ is the Savior and Redeemer of the world. "That he lives." We—like Joseph—commit to work in the kingdom of God on earth. Not just when it is convenient or fits our schedule, but "in whatsoever difficult circumstances," the Lord says. "Faithfully," he says. To stand by Joseph means to stand firm in our faith in the gospel of Jesus Christ and in our willingness to share our testimony with the world. Joseph said, "I will always maintain a true principle, even if I stand alone in it."[4]

Where do you stand? Do you stand by Joseph? He said of his own efforts, "I am a lover of the cause of Christ . . . and an upright steady course of conduct and a holy walk."[5] If we are to stand by him, what should be our course of conduct? Is ours a "holy walk"? Sometimes the pavement isn't smooth, nor is the path lined with flowers. Joseph knew about difficulty. In Liberty Jail, he petitioned the Lord, "Where art thou?" For the Church and for Joseph, this was a time of crisis. Have you cried out to the Lord with the same plea? And what is the Lord's answer? "Peace be unto thy soul; thine adversity and thine afflictions shall be but a small moment" (D&C 121:7). When we stand by Joseph, we stand confident, come what may, knowing our Savior has promised us "angels round about . . . to bear [us] up" (D&C 84:88).

At another point Joseph describes his efforts, saying, "All I can offer the world is a good heart and a good hand."⁶ Do we offer the same? Or have we allowed our earthly assignment to become complicated and blurred with too much of the world?

We can learn a great deal from those who joined the Church in the early days and chose to stand by Joseph. Their contributions were like most of ours: quiet, often done in secret, and rarely of the magnitude heralded by the world. They would not have been noted on any chronology that earns a place on the shelves of world history, but in the Lamb's Book of Life, they stand out as valiant.

Of all the accounts that speak of standing by Joseph, my favorite is from the journal of Joseph Knight Sr., who gained a witness of the young prophet in the earliest days of Joseph's ministry. Consider what he teaches us.

One day Joseph Knight felt impressed to take some supplies to the Smiths down in Harmony, a quiet little community on the banks of the Susquehanna River. In those waters Joseph had baptized Oliver, and Oliver had then baptized Joseph, the two having received the holy priesthood from John the Baptist. This is a sacred place.

Busy translating the gold plates, Joseph had little time to farm or make a living. Joseph Knight wrote in his journal, "I bought a Barrel of Mackerel and some lined paper for writing . . . nine or ten Bushels of grain and five or six Bushels [of] taters and a pound of tea, and I went Down to see him and they [were] in want."⁷

Listen closely. He took fish, grain, and some potatoes. The food was important, but what strikes me is what was sandwiched between the mackerel and the bushels of grain—"some lined paper for writing." Every time I pick up my Book of Mormon I like to imagine that some of the words of one of those great prophets—Nephi, Jacob, Benjamin, or Helaman—were translated onto that "lined paper for writing." Perhaps it is the writer in me that loves the image so much, but I don't think so. I think it's the image of an older man, the age of Joseph's father, hearing the prompting to take what was needed for the work to go forward.

It isn't dramatic. No one has built a statue or named a building to recognize Joseph Knight's contributions. But he heard the prompting of the Spirit. And he acted upon it. What does this say to all of us who quietly load the wagon each morning, who prepare food for those in need, our families in particular, who do the work that brings no glory here because the "glory be to the Father" (D&C 19:19)? The glory of God is to see his children anxiously engaged in a good cause; Joseph Smith called it "the cause of Christ."[8]

Joseph Knight Sr. did not stand alone. In 1836 when Joseph Smith called Heber C. Kimball to serve a mission in England, Heber did not leave with a suitcase full of Mr. Mac suits nor was he prepared in the MTC with a diet of Lucky Charms and a plane ticket from the Church travel office. At that time, apostasy was rampant in Kirtland. Members were turning on the Prophet in droves, and it would have made sense for Heber to remain in Kirtland to defend the Church. Instead, he left his wife, Vilate, and a small family with no definite return date to do what the Lord had commanded. Why? Because he knew that Jesus Christ lives and that Joseph Smith was his servant on the earth chosen to unfold the gospel. Heber left Joseph's side, but he stood by him, though his destination was thousands of miles across the Atlantic. His part was to bring the blood of Israel to Zion.

Vilate Kimball, Heber's wife, wrote in her journal: "It was June 13th. . . .

"At nine o'clock in the morning of this never-to-be-forgotten day. . . . Heber bade adieu to his brethren and friends and started without purse or scrip to preach the gospel in a foreign land."

Just imagine. Vilate didn't know how long he was going to be gone. She didn't ask who was going to provide for them. She "stood by Joseph," offering her husband to the Lord.

Vilate continues in her journal, "Sister Mary Fielding, who became afterwards the wife of Hyrum Smith, gave him five dollars with which Heber paid the passage of himself and Brother Hyde to Buffalo."[9]

Mary Fielding was new to the community, not part of the inner circle of Kirtland. Money was scarce. Imagine reaching in her pocket and pulling out five dollars. That's what she had to give, and she gave it freely. "In whatsoever difficult circumstance," the revelation says. No matter what, "stand by Joseph." For, as in the days of Nephi, "by small means the Lord can bring about great things" (1 Nephi 16:29).

In one of the most desperate periods in Mormon history, when the Saints were being driven from their Missouri homes in the middle of winter and Joseph was locked in Liberty Jail unable to help them, Emma Smith wrote to her husband: "[Dear Joseph] No one but God, knows the reflections of my mind and the feelings of my heart when I left our house and home, and allmost all of every thing that we possessed excepting our little children, and took my journey out of the State of Missouri, leaving you shut up in that lonesome prison . . . I hope there [are] better days to come to us yet."[10]

Emma walked across the frozen Mississippi to refuge in Quincy, Illinois. Sewn into the underskirts of her dress were Joseph Smith's revisions of the Bible. She carried in her arms their infant; by her side walked their small children. With each step she stood by Joseph. She didn't know if she would ever see him again. With hope for "better days," she carried on in the most difficult circumstances. She was seemingly alone.

Have you, like Emma, walked on carrying problems that seem insurmountable? Remember the Lord's promise if we are faithful: "I will go before your face. I will be on your right hand and on your left" (D&C 84:88).

W. W. Phelps, on the other hand, had to learn about really being alone. Here was a man who at age forty chose to do the will of the Lord. He moved to Kirtland and devoted himself to the work. When the Kirtland Temple was dedicated, the congregation sang the stirring anthem chorused at every temple dedication since: "The Spirit of God like a fire is burning!"[11] Written by William Wines Phelps, the words came from his heart.

Wouldn't you think that here was a disciple Joseph could count on? Don't you feel that way about yourself when you have sung "We'll sing and we'll shout with the armies of heaven"?[12]

But Phelps didn't stand by Joseph. In fact, he contributed to one of the most desperate times in Joseph's life. Phelps stepped away in Missouri when tensions were high among the non-Mormons and the cry to kill the Prophet was heard from the highest ranks of the military. Joseph was arrested and jailed. Who signed his name to those trumped-up charges? Who spoke against the Prophet? W. W. Phelps. He had fallen into apostasy and joined with the adversary.

Joseph spent the winter in a dark, dirty prison, separated from his people and the work he loved. Did he shake his fist at the sky and call down the powers of heaven on Phelps or the others trying to thwart the work of the Lord? No, he understood the atonement of Jesus Christ. He petitioned the Lord for comfort and guidance. What was the Lord's response? "Thy God shall stand by thee forever and ever" (D&C 122:4). What a promise. And then he reminded Joseph, "The Son of Man hath descended below them all"(D&C 122:8). Clearly, the atonement of Jesus Christ had paid for the sins of W. W. Phelps.

Joseph was allowed to escape from jail. He and Hyrum—who stood by him at all times, even in death—made their way to Illinois where the Saints had fled, and Joseph began to build a city from a swamp on the banks of the Mississippi. "No unhallowed hand can stop the work from progressing," Joseph told the people.[13] He knew the Lord was in charge; he is in charge today.

Phelps's betrayal didn't stop the work, and he soon came to realize that he had made an enormous mistake. To his credit, he wrote Joseph and begged for forgiveness and for his friendship. You see, Phelps was standing alone. The adversary doesn't stay with anyone after they have done his bidding; he leaves them to loneliness and despair. Phelps was no exception.

Joseph wrote back: "The cup of gall, already full enough for mortals to drink, was indeed filled to overflowing when you turned against us. . . . 'had it been an enemy, we could have borne it.' . . .

"However, the cup has been drunk, the will of our Father has been done, and we are yet alive, for which we thank the Lord. . . .

"Believing your confession to be real, and your repentance

genuine, I shall be happy once again to give you the right hand of fellowship, and rejoice over the returning prodigal.

"'Come on, dear brother, since the war is past,

"'For friends at first, are friends again at last.'"[14]

What a tender reminder of the pure love of Christ.

How is it with us? Is the war past, or are we carrying around wrongs we can't quite "forgive," mistakes we can't quite forget? Some of them are our own. Are there friends on the other side of the fence who need our hand of fellowship? To "stand by . . . Joseph" means to follow his example, embracing one another, no matter the hurt or the circumstance. "For friends at first, are friends again at last."

W. W. Phelps had a change of heart so dramatic that when Joseph Smith was martyred, Phelps wrote the stirring tribute: "Praise to the man who communed with Jehovah! Jesus anointed that Prophet and seer."[15] God's work didn't stop with Joseph Smith. The Lord has called each one of us to do our part to "arise and shine forth, that thy light may be a standard for the nations" (D&C 115:5).

In the eternal plan, each barrel of mackerel, each sheet of lined paper, each five-dollar bill, each hymn of praise put willingly and lovingly on the altar is counted for our good. And the good of all our brothers and sisters. When Joseph Smith described his efforts, he said, "All I can offer the world is a good heart and a good hand."[16] We must do the same. For Joseph prophesied that "the truth of God will go forth boldly, nobly, and independent, till it has penetrated every continent, visited every clime, swept every country, and sounded in every ear, till the purposes of God shall be accomplished, and the Great Jehovah shall say the work is done."[17]

That's why we need to know that Joseph Smith is a prophet of God: because he is a lover of the cause of Christ. What is that cause? To do the will of the Father.

Consider how our prophet today has reiterated the call to stand. Said President Gordon B. Hinckley at the concluding conference of a century: "We stand on the summit of the ages, awed by a great and solemn sense of history. This is the last and final dispensation toward which all in the past has pointed. . . .

"May God bless us with a sense of our place in history and, having been given that sense, with our need to stand tall and walk with resolution in a manner becoming the Saints of the Most High."[18]

Stand tall. Stand by Joseph. No matter where you are or what you are asked to do. By a fence near a farmhouse or on your knees by the bed. At church, in the community, or with your family—most of all, with your family. In doing so, your witness will testify that Jesus Christ lives.

And this is the Lord's promise: "Be of good cheer, and do not fear, for I the Lord am with you, and will stand by you; and ye shall bear record of me, even Jesus Christ, that I am the Son of the living God, that I was, that I am, and that I am to come" (D&C 68:6).

Notes

1. "I Know That My Redeemer Lives," Hymns of The Church of Jesus Christ of Latter-day Saints" (Salt Lake City: Deseret Book, 1985), no. 136.
2. Joseph Smith, History of the Church of Jesus Christ of Latter-day Saints, ed. B. H. Roberts, 2d ed. rev., 7 vols. (Salt Lake City, The Church of Jesus Christ of Latter-day Saints, 1932–51), 6:317.
3. Ibid., 6:346.
4. Ibid., 6:223.
5. The Personal Writings of Joseph Smith, ed. Dean C. Jessee (Salt Lake City: Deseret Book, 1984), 246.
6. Joseph Smith, Teachings of the Prophet Joseph Smith, sel. Joseph Fielding Smith (Salt Lake City: Deseret Book, 1938), 313.
7. Joseph Knight Sr., Joseph Knight Reminiscences [n.d.], Archives of The Church of Jesus Christ of Latter-day Saints, Salt Lake City, 6; see also Heidi S. Swinton, American Prophet: The Story of Joseph Smith (Salt Lake City: Deseret Book, 1999), 57.
8. Jessee, Personal Writings of Joseph Smith, 246.
9. Quoted in Edward W. Tullidge, Women of Mormondom (New York: Tullidge and Crandall, 1877), 114–15; see also Karl Rick Anderson, Joseph Smith's Kirtland (Salt Lake City: Deseret Book, 1989), 86.
10. Emma Smith to Joseph Smith, 7 March 1839, manuscript, Joseph Smith Letterbook, 2, 37, LDS Church Archives; see also The Personal Writings of

Joseph Smith, ed. Dean C. Jessee (Salt Lake City: Deseret Book, 1984), 388–89.

11. "The Spirit of God," *Hymns*, no. 2.

12. Ibid.

13. Smith, *History of the Church*, 4:540.

14. Smith, *Teachings of the Prophet Joseph Smith*, 165–66.

15. "Praise to the Man," *Hymns*, no. 27.

16. Smith, *Teachings of the Prophet Joseph Smith*, 313.

17. Smith, *History of the Church*, 4:540.

18. Gordon B. Hinckley, "At the Summit of the Ages," *Ensign*, October 1999, 74.

THE ONE WHO KEEPS HIS PROMISES

Sharon G. Larsen

Some years ago I was hustling around lining up baby-sitters and chauffeurs for my children so I could attend the BYU Women's Conference. Even thinking about going seemed a fantasy, but my husband agreed that I should go—on one condition: that upon my return I would not try to program him. Now that was revealing! There loomed the possibility that I had done such a thing in the past. I was shocked! Program him? Who would ever presume such a project?

On closer inspection, I have to plead guilty to soaking up the ideal and returning home to "boot camp" my family into becoming perfect by hook and by the book. I was exercising my agency all right, but I was stifling my family's freedom to choose and act for themselves. Sometimes in weaker moments, I have thought that Satan's way had its points. I have even tried some of those points on a difficult child— manipulation, coercion, bribery, threats. Impatience might also fall into this category. Sad to say, in exercising my agency, I was not always wise enough to see that I was infringing on my son's right to choose. I justified my actions because of my fears—fear of what lay ahead for him, fear of what he might do to himself or others, fear that his mistakes would have untold ramifications, none of them good.

I found myself pleading with the Lord to change my son, to validate my efforts to *make* him compliant. Over a period of long years, the

---

Sharon Greene Larsen serves as second counselor in the Young Women General Presidency. She has taught in the public schools, on educational television, in seminary, and in institute. She and her husband, Ralph Thomas Larsen, are the parents of two children and the grandparents of three.

Lord has tutored me about moral agency and freedom and what he means when he says, "You are free" (meaning *all* of his children, including mine). All of us "are permitted to act for [ourselves]; for behold, God hath given unto [us] a knowledge and he hath made [us] free"— free to think, choose, and act (Helaman 14:30). This magnificent gift from God comes with endless opportunities, accompanied by responsibility and consequences. Making good choices and acting on them increases our capacity to exercise our agency. Making bad choices and acting on them limits that capacity, even though we still possess our agency. Our choices and their consequences are inseparably connected.

With careful use of our agency, we can arise as women of God, even though the world around us makes it difficult to commit our agency to God. Faithful sisters may vacillate and equivocate while trying to walk the "strait and narrow path" past that great and spacious building where all the fun seems to be happening. Sometimes we become confused by an overload of messages and choices and stumble over the rock Helaman told his sons to build on (Helaman 5:12). Nephi warned us about those who would tell us we could have freedom without consequences. They would say, "Eat, drink, and be merry; nevertheless, fear God—he will justify in committing a little sin; . . . there is no harm in this; . . . and if it so be that we are guilty, God will beat us with a few stripes, and at last we shall be saved in the kingdom of God" (2 Nephi 28:8). The temptation to delay commitment to the Lord is a lie that comes from Satan.

Did you hear about the two chubby ladies who realized they needed to lose weight, but weren't quite ready to commit to a diet? Standing in front of the bakery window, admiring the calorie-laden goodies, one woman turned to the other and said, "Let's just go inside and see what happens."

There was never any question about Joshua's choice. Near the end of his life, he gathered the tribes of Israel together and reminded them of all the blessings their Father in Heaven had given them. After reciting the goodness of God, Joshua said, "Choose you this day whom ye will serve; . . . but *as for me* and my house, we will serve the Lord" (Joshua 24:15; emphasis added).

President Boyd K. Packer, a modern-day Joshua, has said, "I am not ashamed to say that . . . I want to be good. . . . This was established between me and the Lord so that I knew that He knew which way I had committed my agency."[1] When we use our agency to wholly and freely turn ourselves over to God, we will rise as his—free and unburdened.

I am grateful that my great-grandmother Susan Kent chose to serve the Lord when her heart desperately wished for something else. My great-grandmother was engaged to be married to a man she loved with all her heart when she heard about the Mormon Church. After study and prayer, she knew the Church was true and wanted to be baptized. She pleaded with her betrothed to study and pray about the Church to find out for himself, but he refused and told Susan she would have to choose between him and the Church. With faith and a firm testimony of the Church, she turned her life over to the Lord and broke the engagement. That renunciation was not easy for her. For days she would not eat or see anyone. She became ill, and her family feared she was dying of a broken heart, but after several days, she managed to take nourishment and in time, her heart healed. Later she met and married Evan Molbourne Greene, a righteous man whose mother was Brigham Young's sister. Evan and Susan were promised in a blessing that their posterity would have "believing blood." Her conscious commitment to choose God's will, his agenda over hers, brought about unmistakable spiritual consequences not only for herself but for her posterity—six generations, so far.

The cycle of choice, action, consequence, choice, action, consequence affects our character and our life experiences. Every day and every decision determines the next. In time we will look back at what may seem like disconnected, independent pieces of our lives and better understand what God is trying to make of us. You remember the analogy quoted by C. S. Lewis: "Imagine yourself as a living house. God comes in to rebuild that house. At first, perhaps, you can understand what He is doing. He is getting the drains right and stopping the leaks in the roof and so on: you knew that those jobs needed doing and so you are not surprised. But presently he starts knocking the house about in a way that hurts abominably and does not seem to make sense. What on earth is He up to? The explanation is that He is building quite a different house from the one you thought of—throwing out a new wing here, putting on an extra floor there, running up towers, making courtyards. You thought you were going to be made into a decent little cottage: but He is building a palace."[2]

God can make much more out of our lives than we can—if we will let him.

Choosing righteously helps us grow up. Using agency in harmony with God's will teaches us what the Lord already knows about ourselves. In the Garden of Eden, God asked Adam where he was because *Adam* needed to know where he was (Genesis 3:9; Moses 4:15).

Do you learn something about yourself when you spend hours crocheting leper bandages or tying quilts for those in need? What do you learn about yourself from the movies and videos you watch or when you choose to read a story to your three-year-old instead of watching a favorite TV show? Returning the grocery cart and voting on propositions that affect your community tells something about you. Obedience to God's laws, which were given out of love, leads to more freedom and greater peace. Disobedience limits our capacity to exercise agency. Nothing can free us spiritually more than obedience to God's laws. Just as a car was invented to run on gasoline so were we created to feast on the "fuel" the Lord offers. Yet too often we resist his outstretched arm. Isn't it incredible—we have the freedom to reject the God who gives us that freedom?

Christ wept over the rebellion of Jerusalem and her people. "O Jerusalem, Jerusalem, . . . how often would I have gathered thy children together, even as a hen gathereth her chickens under her wings, and ye would not!" (Matthew 23:37). Those four words, "and ye would not," are a sad indictment. Elder Neal A. Maxwell has said we can trust that God will never send legions of angels to force or compel us. "He wants conversion without intimidation."[3]

Through the chain of life's choices, actions, and consequences, are you choosing, either consciously or subconsciously, to become a victim? According to Elder Maxwell, some pools of self-pity are Olympic size![4] Because of a rebellious family member, other circumstances beyond our control, or even our own guilt, have we felt victimized by others' misdeeds? We can all find plenty of fodder to be hapless victims. Let me illustrate.

My sister Ardeth Kapp has been my hero all my life, and she still is. In Church circles she is quite well-known, and until recently, I have not had a name—I have always been introduced simply as her sister. In the past couple of years, I have taken several trips in connection with Church assignments with Sheri Dew, and in about six weeks of togetherness, we've gotten to know each other pretty well. Every place we go, sisters rush up to Sheri to tell her how much they love her and how her talks have changed their lives. No matter where we are, Latter-day Saint women know and love Sheri Dew. On one of our trips, Sheri, who is unmarried, turned to me and said, "You know, I've always been the bridesmaid."

I seized my opportunity. "Give it up, Sheri," I said. "All my life I've been Ardeth Kapp's sister, and now I'm Sheri Dew's traveling companion. *I* am the one who's the bridesmaid!" I wasn't going to let Sheri be the victim on this one!

Many of you have legitimate reasons to feel like the victim, because you have been. Jewish psychiatrist Viktor Frankl endured years of unspeakable horror in Nazi death camps. He said: "Everything can be taken from a man but one thing: the last of the human freedoms—to choose one's attitude in any given set of circumstances, to choose one's own way.

" . . . Fundamentally . . . any [one] can, even under such circumstances, decide what shall become of him—mentally and spiritually."[5]

It may be difficult, but we never *have* to be the victims. And choosing not to be victims affects more than just ourselves. As sisters in

Zion, our choices affect many lives. How good are our choices for others? We shape the world in more ways than we know. Consider these possibilities in the ordinary, everyday present. A baby who is physically comfortable, fed, and clean is more likely to be a happy baby. A growing boy needs a parent to be there for him. An empathetic listener can help a daughter discover her potential and vent her fears and frustrations. Families flourish in an atmosphere of stability, comfort, and warmth. We can choose to help these things happen.

One wise use of agency leads to another. When we've set our course, the Lord will help us set our priorities. The Holy Ghost will be our constant companion. The routine patterns of life will take on new meaning, and we will be spending time on things that really matter— like our families.

When our daughter reached kindergarten age, I wasn't quite ready to let her go. I made an agreement with her. We had walked in the rain together since she was old enough to walk, so I said, "How will it be if I walk you to school every day it rains?" She thought that sounded fun, and so did I. But invariably the rainy mornings were the ones when I was supposed to be three places at once. I was always tempted to say, "We'll do it next time." Sometimes breakfast dishes were washed with the supper dishes that night and urgent errands postponed to the next day, but we walked to school in the rain. Friends would stop to offer rides, but we were building memories. We did that for seven years. Then came junior high. I woke up one rainy morning and poked my head into Shelly's room. "We get to walk to school; it's raining." She said, "Oh, Mom, I can't walk in the rain today. We're having a dance after school. But would you drive me so my hair doesn't get messed up?" So drive her I did. I was a little sad that our rainy day walks were over, but I was grateful I had walked with her when I could. After she went away to college, she wrote me the kind of loving, appreciative letter every mother hopes for. Among other things, she said, "How can I get my children to love the rain like I do?"

Now that she's away, with a family of her own, I have never said,

"Oh darn! I wish I hadn't spent so much time walking in the rain with Shelly!"

There is not time to live out all our hopes, dreams, and opportunities. We can't spend time with every person we would like to spend time with. Some concerts, plays, and movies will have to go unheard and unseen. We must choose to give up some experiences for those we want more. Each choosing can help us know and trust our choices more.

The Lord warned us about spending money for things of no worth or our energies for that which cannot satisfy (2 Nephi 9:51). Obeying the promptings of the Holy Ghost will develop our tastes and desires for life on a higher plane, one that satisfies and brings us peace.

My daughter, Shelly, now the mother of three little boys, brought treats to sacrament meeting to pacify her sons. As the sacrament tray of bread was passed down our row, Jake, then three, whispered in my ear, "Tell them we don't need that bread. We brought our own treats." To a three-year-old, the treats from home looked much more inviting than the pieces of broken bread. Jake did not yet understand the sacred symbolism of the bread. But what about those of us who do understand? Do we fill our lives with so many of our own treats that we have no appetite for the Bread of Life that will sustain us? Why do we pass up the banquet the Lord has prepared for us and choose instead a "mess of pottage" without any essential nutrients?

Evils and designs do exist in the hearts of conspiring people (D&C 89:4). *Imaginary* evil seems to be exciting and fanciful, full of mystery and life; *imaginary* good appears boring and lifeless. *Real* evil is stagnant and redundant; *real* good is always exhilarating, fresh, and inspiring.

It takes faith to choose the good. Exercising faith in the Lord and his plan for us is spiritual calisthenics. Every day we have opportunity to improve our skills so we will not be deceived. As women of God, we can feel the Lord's love and strength daily. Even though we are trying our best, however, we will all slip. We must then pick ourselves up and try again; the Lord will be there to dust us off. Some of us carry heavy burdens. Loving God does not free us from tribulation or weighty loads. But I testify, because I know, that he will make us strong to carry whatever burdens we must. Let him heal your broken heart and broken dreams.

President George Q. Cannon reminds us, "No matter how serious the trial, how deep the distress, how great the affliction, [God] will never desert us. He never has, and He never will. . . . We have made Him our friend, by obeying His gospel; and He will stand by us. . . . We shall emerge from all [our] trials and difficulties the better and purer for them, if we only trust in our God and keep His commandments."[6]

We can arise as women of God when we choose to trust him and keep his commandments. This reassuring song, "Come unto Him," speaks for us.

> *I wander through the still of night,*
> *When solitude is ev'rywhere—*
> *Alone, beneath the starry light,*
> *And yet I know that God is there.*
> *I kneel upon the grass and pray;*
> *An answer comes without a voice.*
> *It takes my burden all away*
> *And makes my aching heart rejoice.*
>
> *It matters not what may befall,*
> *What threat'ning hand hangs over me;*
> *He is my rampart through it all,*
> *My refuge from mine enemy.*
> *Come unto him all ye depressed,*
> *Ye erring souls whose eyes are dim,*
> *Ye weary ones who long for rest.*
> *Come unto him! Come unto him!*[7]

Choose ye this day whom ye will serve. As for me, I will serve the One who keeps his promises and has never left me alone.

Notes

1. Boyd K. Packer, *"That All May Be Edified": Talks, Sermons & Commentary by Boyd K. Packer* (Salt Lake City: Bookcraft, 1982), 272.

2. C. S. Lewis, *Mere Christianity* (New York: Macmillan, 1952), 174.

3. Neal A. Maxwell, "Content with the Things Alotted unto Us," *Ensign*, May 2000, 74.

4. Ibid.

5. Viktor E. Frankl, *Man's Search for Meaning* (New York: Washington Square Press, 1984), 87.

6. George Q. Cannon, "Freedom of the Saints," in *Collected Discourses*, comp. Brian H. Stuy, 5 vols. (Burbank, Calif.: B. H. Publishing, 1988), 2:185; also quoted in Patricia T. Holland, "Filled With All the Fulness of God," *Clothed with Charity*, ed. Dawn Hall Anderson, Susette Fletcher Green, Dlora Hall Dalton (Salt Lake City: Deseret Book, 1997), 3.

7. "Come unto Him," *Hymns of The Church of Jesus Christ of Latter-day Saints* (Salt Lake City: The Church of Jesus Christ of Latter-day Saints, 1985), no. 114.

INDEX

Contents

The author and publishers are grateful to the following for
permission to use copyright photographic material:

Section One:

1 photograph © Mike Forster/Solo Syndication; 2 © Solo Syndication;
3, 4, 5, 8, 10, 13, 14 © Rex Features; 6 © PA News Photo Library;
7 © Popperfoto; 9, 16 photographs by Tim Graham; 11 © Alpha;
12 © Wakehams; 15 photograph by Les Chudzicki

Section Two:

1 photograph by Tim Graham; 2, 4, 10 © UK Press; 3, 6, 7, 9, 12, 14
© Rex Features; 4 © Solo Syndication; 8 photograph © Mike
Forster/Solo Syndication; 11 photograph © Adrian Sherratt/South
West News Service; 13 photograph © Darren Fletcher/South West
News Service; 15 photograph © John Giles/PA News Photo Library;
16 photograph © Chuck Stoody/Associated Press; 17 photograph
© Paul Ashton/South West News Service

Acknowledgements

This book could not have been written without the huge generosity of so many people who gave up their time to talk to me. I will not list them, since some spoke in confidence, but simply say thank you to each and every one of them. I would also like to thank the people, who again must remain nameless, who read the manuscript and corrected errors. Thanks are also due to so many people at St James's Palace, particularly in the Prince of Wales's press office, who were so helpful in finding me the information I needed.

My agent, Jane Turnbull, has been quite fantastic throughout, a huge support and fount of encouragement, as has Eddie Bell, Executive Chairman and Publisher at HarperCollins. They both believed in an idea at a very early stage, and kept faith even when the outcome was by no means certain. Everyone at HarperCollins has been a very great pleasure to work with, and I owe a particular debt of gratitude to Val Hudson and Andrea Henry, who worked magic on my manuscript in what must be record time. Other people that warrant particular mention are Adrian Bourne, Adrian Laing, Kim Dawe, Heather Rogers, Katie Fulford, Rachel Smyth, Mel Haselden and James Annal.

Photographer, Les Wilson, has also been a star. The quality of illustrations are entirely down to his encyclopedic knowledge of royal photographs and where to find them – and, like everyone, he has worked with astonishing speed and with great good humour.

I am grateful to one or two friends who have been amazing in their support and help. And last, but by no means least, I thank my family without whom...

~

Books Consulted
There are two books in particular from which I have drawn: *Diana – Her True Story/In Her Own Words* by Andrew Morton (Michael O'Mara Books, 1997), and *The Prince of Wales* by Jonathan Dimbleby (Little, Brown, 1994). Both provided unique source material, and I am grateful to the authors and publishers.

Other books include: *The Monarchy and the Constitution* by Vernon Bogdanor (Clarendon Press, 1995); *Highgrove, Portrait of an Estate* by HRH The Prince of Wales and Charles Clover (Chapmans Publishers, 1993); *A Greater Love, Charles and Camilla* by Christopher Wilson (Headline Book Publishing, 1995); *The Royal Encyclopedia* edited by Roland Allison and Sarah Riddell (Macmillan Press, 1991); *Diana in Private: The Princess Nobody Knows* by Lady Colin Campbell (Smith Gryphon, 1992).

List of Illustrations

14 The Prince of Wales and Mrs Camilla Parker Bowles.

15 The Princess of Wales and Major James Hewitt.

16 The Prince and Princess of Wales and their two sons at Highgrove.

Section Two

1 The Prince of Wales with his dog, Harvey.

2 The Prince and Princess of Wales on their Korean tour.

3 The Princess of Wales and Prince Harry at Thorpe Park.

4 The Princess of Wales carrying the ashes of her father, Earl Spencer.

5 The Princess of Wales's last official engagement.

6 The Prince of Wales and Mrs Camilla Parker Bowles leave Balmoral.

7 The Princess of Wales greets Carolyn Bartholomew.

8 The Prince of Wales with his arm in a sling.

9 The Princess of Wales on 'Panorama'.

10 Diana appears for her public on the evening of Prince Charles's Dimbleby programme.

11 Mrs Camilla Parker Bowles with the Beaufort Hunt.

12 The first public sighting of Mrs Camilla Parker Bowles following her divorce.

13 Mrs Camilla Parker Bowles arrives at Highgrove for her fiftieth birthday party.

14 Diana, Princess of Wales, on holiday in the South of France with Mohamed al Fayed and his daughter Jasmin al Fayed, Prince William and Prince Harry.

15 The Prince of Wales playing basketball at his first official engagement following the death of Diana, Princess of Wales.

16 The Prince of Wales wearing a hat from the Canadian Olympic team.

17 Mrs Camilla Parker Bowles and her daughter Laura.

Introduction

Opinion polls suggest that the reputation of the Prince of Wales is beginning to recover after the emotional turmoil of Diana's death in August 1997. It had not been good before she died, largely because of his relationship with Camilla Parker Bowles, but in the days that followed the fatal crash it plumbed new depths, as the nation's anger at the loss of the Princess it loved so dearly turned on the monarchy and, more particularly, the heir to the throne. When Diana's brother, Charles Spencer, gave his address at her funeral, and said that he would rescue her sons from the clutches of the Royal Family, the nation cheered – literally – as his voice was relayed to those inside and outside Westminster Abbey.

The Prince's new-found popularity is no doubt gratifying, and has much to do with the way he has been seen to care for his children in the wake of their mother's death. A significant percentage of the population would even sanction his marriage to Camilla Parker Bowles. However, a popular misconception undermines this growing acceptance: the belief that the Prince always loved Camilla and made no attempt during his years of marriage to Diana to shut his mistress out of his life.

Few would deny that it takes two to make a marriage, and two to break it. Yet millions of people the world over have been led to believe that the Prince of Wales destroyed his marriage, alone and unaided, because of his obsession with Mrs Parker Bowles. In 1992,

Andrew Morton told Diana's story – one side of the story – in a book that brought about the end of the 'fairytale' marriage. *Diana – Her True Story*, which was reissued after Diana's death and renamed *In Her Own Words*, gave a picture of Charles and Diana's life together and the part his mistress had to play in it, which is not quite what those who knew both Charles and Diana best remember.

So far, no one has attempted to tell the complete story. While Diana was alive the Prince would never allow it because he didn't want to hurt either her or their children. In all their years together and apart, and despite intense provocation, he never spoke ill of her in any way. Now that she is dead Charles is even more determined that he will not defend himself and that history alone shall be his judge. If that means waiting until he is long dead, so be it. He has no qualms about meeting his maker. The evidence to support what really happened – letters, diaries, tapes, medical records, which explain the true nature of the relationship – is under lock and key at the Royal Family Archive at Windsor. One day in the future, when they are released, the whole truth will be told.

In the meantime, a number of his family and friends feel he has suffered enough and believe there should be some attempt to correct at least some of the misconceptions.

Diana said some terrible things about Charles, which she later regretted quite bitterly. Not, however, before millions of people were led to believe that she was taken 'like a lamb to the slaughter' into a loveless union, in order to produce an heir for a man who had no intention of honouring his marriage vows. On the strength of Diana's words, there are many who believe that he carried on an affair with his mistress throughout his marriage, even sleeping with her the night before his wedding and resuming their affair immediately after the honeymoon. They believe Charles was a cold and insensitive husband and a cold and insensitive father, who only now, after Diana's death, is beginning to show a little affection for his children. Some people even blame Charles for Diana's death. And, because Diana said so on prime time television, in an interview for 'Panorama' in 1995, many believe he is not fit to be king.

It is hard to imagine Prince Charles's emotions as he walked behind Diana's cortège that September morning, their sons by his side, bravely fighting back their tears. Never had there been such public outpourings of love and grief for someone so few had ever met. The world had loved her, admired her, worshipped her. He had rejected her, divorced her. Why?

Charles: Victim or Villain? tries to explain what really happened in that marriage; to give a more objective view than Diana's, and reveal more clearly than ever before the part Camilla Parker Bowles played in it. Not for the sake of the Prince of Wales – who, like Diana, is not entirely blameless – but for the sake of the millions of people who have lived through this royal soap opera and have never had an alternative account of what happened on which to form a judgement for themselves. At the moment there is only Diana's account, which is flawed and inevitably partial, as even her friends will admit in private.

It is an attempt to describe why Charles married Diana, what life was like for them both, and what went so badly wrong that she felt compelled to tell the world and take very public revenge on her husband. What possessed Charles to confess his infidelity on camera – as he did to Jonathan Dimbleby in a two-and-a-half-hour documentary about his life in June 1994 – and how did he feel when he faced the public after the embarrassment of the Camillagate tapes that exposed his late-night ramblings on the telephone to his mistress?

The two young princes, William and Harry, have lived through it all – the embarrassment, the affairs, the divorce and, finally, the traumatic death of their mother. How are they faring as a family today? What do they think of Mrs Parker Bowles? What is the future likely to hold for them all?

This is a portrait of the Prince of Wales at fifty. A very private man, with a public role, in an intrusive media world. A single parent and future king, a man emotionally handcuffed by his upbringing and damaged by the failure of his marriage. He is a man who inspires great love and loyalty, but a man of contradictions. He can be the greatest company or the most sombre; the kindest, most considerate of human beings or the most selfish. He has warmth and charisma, and a wicked sense of fun but, when he doesn't get what he wants, a fearsome temper that in fifty years he has never learnt to control. He is a man who cares about the disadvantaged, and the sick and dying, no less than the planet we pass on to future generations and the English we teach our children. A man who is cocooned from the real world, who has butlers and valets, helicopters and fast cars, yet who has seen more deprivation and who understands despair better than most politicians. A man whose life has been given over to duty to the institution he was born into, and who longs to modernise it, but who is thwarted by the very people his wife called 'the enemy' – the courtiers who rule royal life – and who must wait for the death of the mother he loves before he can begin his task. He is a man who cares above all else – even above his own happiness – for the future well being of his sons. While they are children he can protect them, but he knows that as they come of age he will be powerless to stop the intrusion, the criticism and pressure that very nearly destroyed him.

ONE

Death of a Princess

'They tell me there's been an accident. What's going on?'
Charles in the early hours of 31 August 1997

The first call alerting the Royal Family to Diana's accident came through to Sir Robin Janvrin, the Queen's deputy private secretary, at one o'clock on the morning of Sunday 31 August. He was asleep in his house on the Balmoral estate in Aberdeenshire. It was from the British ambassador in Paris, who had only sketchy news. There had been a car crash. Dodi Fayed, it seemed, had been killed, although there was no confirmation yet. The Princess of Wales, who had been travelling with him, was injured but no one knew how badly. Their car had smashed into the support pillars of a tunnel under the Seine. It had been travelling at high speed while trying to escape a group of paparazzi in hot pursuit on motorbikes.

Janvrin immediately telephoned the Queen and the Prince of Wales in their rooms at the castle. He then telephoned the Prince's assistant private secretary, Nick Archer, who was staying in another house on the estate; also the Queen's equerry and protection officers. They all agreed to meet in the offices at the castle, where they set up an operations room and manned the phones throughout the night.

Meanwhile, in London, the Prince's team were being woken and told the news, ironically, by the tabloid press. The first call to Mark Bolland, the Prince's deputy private secretary, came at 1 a.m. from the *News of the World*. Having gone to bed at his flat in the City after a very good dinner party, he let the answering machine take the call, and when he heard something about an accident in Paris dismissed it as the usual Saturday night fantasy. It was not until he heard the voice of Stuart Higgins, then editor of the *Sun*, a paper not published on a Sunday, speaking into the machine ten minutes later, that he realised something very odd was going on and picked up the phone. Higgins had much the same news as the Embassy. The reports were conflicting but it sounded as though Dodi had been killed and Diana injured.

The Prince's press secretary, Sandy Henney, had also just gone to bed at her home in Surrey, having seen the last guest out after a fortieth birthday party for her sister-in-law. She too was woken by a journalist with a very similar story. The media, getting news directly from the emergency services, were in many ways better informed than the Embassy that night and provided a real service to the Prince's staff.

Mark Bolland immediately rang Stephen Lamport, the Prince's private secretary, at his home in west London, then Sandy Henney, and within minutes the phone lines across the capital and between London and Scotland were buzzing.

The Prince telephoned Bolland in London. 'Robin tells me there's been an accident. What's going on?'

He wanted details. Shocked and unable to believe what he was hearing, he asked the same questions over and over again: What had caused the accident? What had Diana been doing in that situation? Who was driving? Where had it happened? Why had it happened? Questions to which, for the time being, there were no answers. They spoke for almost an hour.

There was no more concrete news. Reports one minute said Diana was seriously hurt, and the next suggested she had walked away with superficial injuries.

The Queen was also awake in her suite of rooms next door to her son's on the first floor of the castle. Her private secretary, Sir Robert Fellowes, was on holiday in Norfolk, but like the Prince's staff her own people were in constant touch with one another. The Prince's private secretary on duty in Scotland was Nick Archer, but it was

Stephen Lamport and Mark Bolland in London who were calling the shots.

Bolland telephoned Robin Janvrin to tell him that the Prince would be flying to Paris later that day to visit Diana in hospital, and needed a plane. 'He's going,' he said. 'This is not a matter for discussion. He is going to see his ex-wife.'

His request did not go down well initially. Was it the right thing to do? wondered Janvrin. An aeroplane of the Queen's Flight couldn't be ordered without the Queen's specific agreement, and that was unlikely to be forthcoming.

'Okay, fine,' said Bolland. 'We'll take a scheduled flight from Aberdeen.' The Queen would be irritated, no doubt, that yet again Diana was disrupting everyone's lives. She had lost patience with Diana long ago, and as the week wore on she was confirmed in her belief that everything to do with her former daughter-in-law was always extraordinarily complicated.

Unbelievably, although the Queen and Prince Charles were just feet away from one another in their separate rooms, divided by paper-thin walls, it was their staff who were discussing the rights and wrongs of asking the Queen's permission for Charles to use her aeroplane. Never was the true nature of this mother–son relationship more starkly demonstrated. Closely knit though the family appears, there is very little real communication between them. The Prince loves his parents dearly but they don't talk. The Queen and the Duke of Edinburgh had not known quite how serious the problems with their son's marriage had been until 1987, when two friends wrote to the Queen, having decided independently and simultaneously that she ought to know what was going on. Their letters landed on her desk on the same day. They had witnessed some odd incidents, like Diana falling down the stairs at Sandringham, and Diana had told them on one occasion that her life with the Prince was impossible because of Mrs Parker Bowles, but they had not discussed the problems with their son.

That Sunday, Charles, William and Harry had all been planning to fly to London. The boys' summer holiday was almost over and they were due to meet up with their mother, who was flying back from Paris. Diana always had the children for the last few days before they went back to school at the start of a new term, so that she could get everything ready and make sure they had the right kit. The Prince would spend a few days at Highgrove, his home in Gloucestershire, before heading for Provence, in the South of France, his habitual haunt in early September.

The Prince was in no doubt that he wanted to go and see Diana in Paris that morning, but uncertain whether he should take the children. He was worried that her injuries would be too upsetting for them. Clearly no decision could be made until they knew how bad her injuries were. And as the hours crept painfully past, he talked about the Princess, whom he still loved and prayed for every night, despite the failure of their marriage, despite the hurt that had existed between them.

'I always thought it would end like this,' he said, 'with me having to nurse Diana through some terrible injury or illness. I always thought she'd come back to me and I would spend the rest of my time looking after her.'

The walls in Balmoral are so thin that there is no keeping of secrets. One regular visitor says that if you want to have a private conversation you have to put the plug in the wash basin and talk quietly, or it will be all round the castle. Inevitably, with this kind of drama going on, most of the family were by now awake and watching the television or listening to the radio, which was already given over to news of the accident. The Duke of York was staying in the castle at the time, also Princess Anne's son Peter Phillips, then aged nineteen, two friends of the Queen and Princess Margaret, the Queen's sister. William and Harry were asleep and it became a priority to get their radios out of their bedrooms and the television out of the nursery, to prevent them waking up and switching one of them on.

At about 3.30 a.m., Mark Bolland rang Robin Janvrin again to find out how he was doing with the plane, and whether he had woken up the people at RAF Northolt, in Greater London, where it was based. In the middle of the conversation, at 3.45, they were interrupted by a telephone call that came through from the Embassy in Paris for Janvrin, and he put Bolland on to Nick Archer while he took the call.

'We can't muck about with his plane,' Bolland was saying. 'Make sure Robin is quite clear what is going to happen ...'

'Oh, Mark, I think we're going to have a change of plan.'

In the background Archer could hear Robin Janvrin breaking the news to the Prince of Wales on the telephone. 'Sir, I'm very sorry to have to tell you, I've just had the Ambassador on the phone. The Princess died a short time ago.'

The announcement that went out at 4.30 a.m. said she had died at four o'clock. It had actually been earlier.

The Prince immediately rang Mark. 'Robin has just told me she's dead, Mark, is this true? What happened? What on earth was she doing there? How could this have happened? They're all going to blame me, aren't they? What do I do? What does this mean?'

Mark's first reaction was to ring Camilla Parker Bowles to tell her that Diana had died, and warn her that she could expect a call at any moment from the Prince, in a state of serious distress. He had rung a number of close friends that night, and Camilla and the Prince had already spoken several times. She was shocked to the core by the news that Diana was dead, and utterly devastated for the boys; also terrified for the Prince, of what would happen to him, what people's reaction would be.

Diana's death came as a terrible shock to everyone. All the news had indicated that she had survived the crash, and with some reports having suggested she had walked away from the car, people were totally unprepared. The truth was that she had sustained terrible chest and head injuries. She had lost consciousness very soon after the impact, and never regained it. She had been treated in the wreckage of the Mercedes at the scene for about an hour and was then taken to the Pitié-Salpêtrière hospital four miles away, where surgeons had fought for a further two hours to save her life, but in vain. The reaction was total horror and disbelief.

The Prince's first thought was for the children. Should he wake them and tell them or let them sleep and tell them in the morning? He was absolutely dreading it, and didn't know what to do for the best. The Queen felt strongly that they should be left to sleep and he took her advice and didn't wake them up until 7.15. William had had a difficult night's sleep and had woken many times. He had known, he said, that something awful was going to happen.

The Prince, like Camilla, realised only too well what the public reaction might be, and what the media would say. 'They're all going to blame me,' he said. 'The world's going to go completely mad, isn't it? We're going to see a reaction that we've never seen before. And it could destroy everything. It could destroy the monarchy.'

'Yes, sir, I think it could,' said Lamport with brutal honesty. 'It's going to be very difficult for your mother, sir. She's going to have to do things she may not want to do, or feel comfortable doing, but if she doesn't do them, then that's the end of it.'

The Queen's first difficulty was upon her before dawn had broken. The Prince decided he should be the one to go to Paris to collect Diana's body, but the Queen was against the idea and was strongly supported by her private secretary. The Princess was no longer a member of the Royal Family, argued Sir Robert Fellowes; it would be wrong to make too much fuss.

Robin Janvrin came up with the remark that clinched it. 'What would you rather, Ma'am,' he said; 'that she came back in a Harrods' van?' There was no further argument.

Diana's love affair with Dodi Fayed had been a source of deep concern to everyone at court, not least the Prince of Wales. Not because he resented her happiness – it was his deepest wish that Diana would find happiness – but because he feared it would end in disaster. He feared that Diana was in danger of being used by the al Fayed publicity machine. Dodi's father, Mohamed al Fayed, the high-profile Egyptian owner of Harrods, was a controversial figure. Long denied British citizenship, he had tried relentlessly to ingratiate himself with the establishment. He had done some inspired matchmaking that summer between his playboy son and the Princess of Wales in the South of France, and had milked it for all it was worth. He had scarcely been out of the news for a month: he had been photographed with William and Harry, the Queen's grandsons, who had been his guests on board his yacht, and was hoping for the greatest coup of all, to secure the mother of a future king of England as a daughter-in-law.

Dodi was a serious member of the international jet set, a kind and gentle man, but with more money than intellect, and a string of conquests to his name amongst the world's most beautiful women. While he was busy wooing Diana, another woman thought she was engaged to marry him. He dabbled in the film business, but was essentially financed by his rich father, who denied him nothing. Dodi and Diana did appear to be in love, and may well have gone on to marry had things turned out differently. She would have been the biggest catch in the world for him. He would have provided the wealth she needed, even after her divorce settlement, to finance her enormously expensive lifestyle, and it would have been the ultimate two-fingered gesture to the Royal Family she so despised.

The boys had not enjoyed their holiday on board al Fayed's yacht. They had not taken to Dodi or his father and had hated the publicity – as a result William had had a terrible row with his mother – and the whole trip had been extremely uncomfortable. And to add insult to injury, at the end of their stay, their two royal protection officers were taken aside by a Fayed aide, and handed a brown envelope each, stuffed with notes. 'Mr al Fayed would like to thank you for all you have done,' he said. In a panic, they immediately telephoned Colin Trimming, the Prince's detective and head of the royal protection squad, and told him what had happened. 'You've got to give it back,' he said.

'We've tried,' they said, 'but we were told that Mr al Fayed would be very upset if we didn't accept it.' The money went back.

The mention of Harrods to the Queen was enough to trigger Operation Overlord – the plan, which had been in existence for many years but never previously needed, to return the body of a member of the Royal Family to London. There is a BAe146 plane ear-marked for the purpose, which can be airborne at short notice from RAF Northolt. It had always been thought the Queen Mother might be its first passenger, which given she was then ninety-seven years old was not unreasonable. No one in their wildest dreams could have guessed it would be used for Diana, still so young and beautiful, super-fit and brimming with health and vitality.

The plane left Northolt at 10 a.m. that Sunday morning, bound for Aberdeen, with Stephen Lamport, Mark Bolland and Sandy Henney on board. First stop was RAF Wittering in Rutland, where it collected Diana's sisters, Lady Sarah McCorquodale, who lived nearby, and Lady Jane Fellowes. It was Robert Fellowes who had broken the news to Diana's family, and the Prince had telephoned Sarah to suggest they might like to go with him to collect the body, whereupon Jane had driven up from Norfolk to join her sister. From Wittering they flew to Aberdeen, where they collected the Prince of Wales, and then on to Paris. The Prince had decided this was not a trip for the children and so they stayed at Balmoral with Tiggy Legge-Bourke, who, as the Queen said, 'by the grace of God' had just arrived in Scotland ready to take the Princes down to London to meet their mother. She and their cousin Peter Phillips were utterly brilliant with William and Harry that day and for the remainder of the week.

Diana's sisters spent most of the flight to Paris in tears. The Prince was controlled but clearly very shaken. Stephen Lamport took everyone through what would happen at the other end. There was a possibility, he warned Sarah and Jane, that Mohamed al Fayed might be at the hospital and if he was the Prince would have to speak to him; how did they feel about that? Both sisters were adamant they wanted nothing to do with Mr al Fayed; they didn't even want to see him.

In the event he wasn't there. By the time the Prince's party arrived al Fayed had already taken his son's body home for prayers in Regent's Park Mosque, followed by a Muslim burial that night at a cemetery in Woking, Surrey. On arrival at the hospital the Prince was met by President Chirac, who had come in person to express his nation's great sadness at the death of the Princess.

With protocol observed, the Prince and the two sisters were taken to see Diana's body. A doctor accompanied them into the small room on the first floor of the hospital, as well as a priest, whom they had specifically asked for. It was a distressing sight for which none of them was adequately prepared. Diana's body was laid out in a coffin which had been flown to Paris earlier that morning on a Hercules from RAF Brize Norton in Oxfordshire. Levertons, the north London family firm of undertakers, were an integral part of Operation Overlord. The Princess had been embalmed and was wearing a dress that her butler, Paul Burrell, had flown out with earlier, but the body that lay so still and cold and empty looked nothing like the Diana they had known. Her head had been badly damaged in the crash and her face was distorted. The Prince told Diana's sisters how glad he was that he had not taken William and Harry to Paris with him. It would have been much too distressing for them.

They stayed with Diana's body for seven minutes. Sarah and Jane were sobbing helplessly when they left and were taken to a room for some privacy while they recovered. The Prince was not crying when he came back into the corridor, but it was obvious that he had been, and was visibly very distressed. His eyes were quite red, his face racked with pain. A small crowd was waiting in the corridor, most of them hospital staff, and also a number of men in dark suits. The Prince came out of the door, stopped, closed his eyes and bit his lip. Then after a moment's pause, while he fought to regain his composure, he set off down the corridor, a private man no longer, to shake hands with the doctors and nurses and thank them for all they had done. As someone watching remarked, 'He went from human being to Windsor' – as nearly fifty years of training ensured he would. Duty above all else. When he heard that the parents of the Welsh bodyguard, Trevor Rees-Jones, employed by the al Fayeds, who had been the sole survivor in the accident, were at the hospital, he immediately said he must talk to them.

Moments later the coffin, by now closed and draped with the maroon and yellow of the Royal Standard, was carried out of the room. It was suddenly obvious that the men in dark suits were the undertakers, and without a word needing to be said, everyone in the corridor spontaneously formed two lines and silently bowed their heads as the coffin passed between them and down the stairs into a waiting Renault Espace.

There were thousands of people in the streets outside. The whole of Paris seemed to know who was in the Espace and what was going on. To a man, woman and child they were silent. As the motorcade made its way slowly through the city and out on to the périphérique towards the airport, the people on the pavements bowed their heads in silence, people in street cafés stood up as the cars passed, each one flanked by two large motorbikes on either side, and no one made a sound. The Prince was deeply moved, and in the silence that enveloped the aircraft on the flight home, with everyone wrapped up in their own thoughts and emotions, he said, 'Wasn't it wonderful that everybody stood up.'

But if the tribute paid to Diana by the Parisians had been moving, the arrangements that had been made unbeknownst to him for the next stage of her journey enraged him. While Sarah and Jane disappeared into another part of the cabin to have a cigarette, the Prince asked what arrangements had been made after they touched down at Northolt. The Prime Minister, Tony Blair, would be there, he knew, also the Lord Chamberlain, Lord Airlie, who is the most senior member of the Queen's household. He wanted to know how many RAF people would be there to carry the coffin, whether the flowers he had said he wanted had been sorted out, whether there would be a proper hearse to carry the coffin, and where they were planning to take Diana's body. The answer to that final question was the mortuary in Fulham, commonly used by the Royal Coroner.

'Who decided that? Nobody asked me. Diana is going to the Chapel Royal at St James's Palace. Sort it. I don't care who has made this decision. She is going to the Chapel Royal.'

Sandy Henney spent much of the remainder of the flight on the plane's telephone ensuring that the Prince's instructions were carried out to the last detail.

The decision had almost certainly been made by Robert Fellowes, doing what he imagined the Queen would have wanted, without actually asking her, but his second guessing was not far off the mark. There is no doubt that in the course of the days leading up to Diana's funeral, the hostility that both the Queen and the Duke of Edinburgh had felt towards their erstwhile daughter-in-law came dangerously close to the surface on several occasions. She had caused nothing but trouble and embarrassment over the years, and here she was, in death, still managing to cause mayhem.

The Prince's relationship with Diana had been turbulent and troubled and they were no longer man and wife, but Diana was still the mother of his children and, in a way, he still loved her. He wanted her treated with the dignity she deserved. After Sandy's hasty and heated phone calls from the plane, the plan about the mortuary was changed and it was agreed that the Princess of Wales would be taken to the Chapel Royal at St James's Palace, just yards from the office they shared so disastrously until their divorce. She was also to have outriders. And while he was at it, her sisters Sarah and Jane were to be given a plane to take them wherever they wanted to go, and if they wanted to go with the body into London first, then so be it. So at the Prince's bidding, the plane which had brought the Prime Minister from his constituency to Northolt to meet the returning party was kept on hold, but in the end was not required. The sisters accompanied the body into London and chose to make their own ways home.

The plane carrying the coffin touched down at Northolt and taxied out of sight of the reception party, where it came to a halt. One of the crew climbed out and opened up the cargo hatch, and the group onboard listened in silence to the bolts holding the coffin in place being loosened beneath them. The plane then taxied on and came to a halt in front of the airport building where Tony Blair, David Airlie and 150 or so photographers and pressmen were waiting quietly on the tarmac. In silence the coffin was unloaded and carried to the waiting hearse. The only sound to be heard was the Royal Standard flapping in the breeze.

Wrapped in thought, his emotions in turmoil, the Prince of Wales climbed back aboard the aircraft, accompanied by Stephen Lamport, to fly back to Balmoral and be with his grieving sons, while the hearse made its way slowly down the A40 into west London.

It was only then that the real enormity of what had happened began to dawn on the Palace staff. The motorway, the bridges and embankments – and when they ran out, the roads and pavements – were full of cars and people who had come to watch and weep as Diana's coffin passed by. Tributes had started pouring in from all over the world, and flowers were being laid at the gate of every building with which Diana was associated.

This, they realised, was going to be unlike anything anyone had ever seen before.

TWO

A Nation Mourns

'A girl given the name of the ancient goddess of hunting was, in the end, the most hunted person of the modern age.'
Charles Spencer

In the days following Diana's death, the future of the monarchy hung perilously in the balance. As the mountain of flowers outside her Kensington Palace home grew ever higher, spreading further and further into the park, the people of Britain, stunned, shocked and numb with grief, looked for someone to blame for their awesome sense of loss.

The national reaction to Diana's death bordered on hysteria. Few of the people who mourned had ever met the Princess, yet her compassion and vulnerability had touched a chord deep in the public psyche. Everyone grieved for the stranger whom they felt they knew, with a depth of feeling never before shown for a public figure. Months later, counsellors were still treating people who had been unable to come to terms with their grief. In a rather studied tribute, the Prime Minister, Tony Blair, called her 'the people's Princess', and it was the perfect epithet: the people felt she cared and spoke for them, and in a curious way she probably took greater comfort from her relationship with strangers than with almost anyone else.

'I feel like everyone else in this country,' said Tony Blair. 'I am utterly devastated. We are a nation in a state of shock, in mourning, in grief. It is so deeply painful for us. She was a wonderful and a warm human being. Though her own life was often sadly touched by tragedy, she touched the lives of so many others in Britain and through the world, with joy and with comfort. She was the people's

Princess and that is how she will remain in our hearts and memories for ever.'

Whatever the psychological and sociological explanations for the nation's reaction to her death might be, there was not only grief, but also anger on the streets of London – anger directed in very large part at the Royal Family. As Charles had instinctively feared would happen, some went so far as to suggest that he was responsible for her death. Had he loved her instead of his mistress, they said, this would never have happened. They would still have been married and she would never have been in a car racing through the streets of Paris with Dodi Fayed. Yet at the same time others were leaving tributes to both of them outside Kensington and all the other palaces, 'To Diana and Dodi, together for ever', and paying eulogies to the man who had brought Diana true love and happiness.

There was also anger at the tabloid press, which encouraged the paparazzi by paying such huge sums of money for photographs and stories. In the weeks before her death, the red-top papers, and some of the broadsheets too, had been full of long-lens photographs of Diana and Dodi canoodling on his father's yacht in the South of France. Diana's brother, Earl Spencer, had not held back when he heard the news at his home in South Africa. 'I always believed the press would kill her in the end,' he said. 'But not even I could imagine that they would take such a direct hand in her death as seems to be the case.' At that time it was thought the paparazzi were entirely responsible for the accident; and he said that the editors and proprietors of every newspaper which had paid money for intrusive pictures of his sister had 'blood on their hands'. The public, of course, had not been slow to buy these newspapers, all of which argued a vicious circle of supply and demand. But this was not the time to draw too much attention to hypocrisy.

Strangely, no blame was ever levelled at Dodi, or even his father, who had provided the car they were travelling in, and who also employed the driver, Henri Paul. He had not been the regular driver and, it soon transpired, he had been several times over the drink-driving limit that night. The proper driver had been sent off in a decoy car. It was an elaborate attempt to try to foil the paparazzi, who were all waiting outside the Ritz Hotel, where they had had dinner that night, ready to follow them home. Yet Dodi failed to make the driver slow down, and he was doing well over 100 mph when he ploughed into the underpass. Almost overnight, the paparazzi ceased to be seen as the sole cause of the accident. Afraid that the tables might turn and that, as Henri Paul's employer, he might find himself liable, Mohamed al Fayed shared his own private theory about the crash with the press. It was, he suggested, a conspiracy cooked up by the Queen and the security services to assassinate Diana so that she would not marry Dodi; such a marriage would have given William, second in line to the throne of England, a Muslim and Egyptian step-father. It was a ludicrous notion invented by a man who had spent the months since his son's death telling lies about Diana's last words, which medical evidence suggested could never have been uttered. Yet in the spring of 1998 he was given airtime on Channel 4 television to explain why he believed the Queen had murdered Diana and Dodi. His words were picked up not only in Britain but in Egypt, and as a result the Queen's life is now at risk. Her security arrangements have necessarily been stepped up considerably, so much so that a friend whom she was visiting recently said over dinner, 'Ma'am, I thought things were supposed to be better with the IRA these days.'

'No,' the Queen replied. 'They think there's a good chance I'm going to be killed by a Muslim.'

The Queen would no doubt have been horrified by a marriage between Diana and Dodi, and William and Harry no less appalled. And they would not have been alone. Millions of people were shocked by the overtly sexual nature of the relationship, which Diana seemed to be flaunting so brazenly to the press. No one was labouring under the illusion that she was still the shy, blushing innocent Princess. Her various well-documented affairs had put an end to that. Apart from the much publicised revelations about James Hewitt, she had been publicly blamed by the wife of rugby player Will Carling for destroying their marriage. In his autobiograpy, published in October 1998, Carling was coy about the relationship, saying, 'I was attracted to her but I never made a pass at her. To be honest, if I had had a sexual relationship with her I wouldn't say I had. I don't think that would be right.' At the time, however, he boasted quite openly to his friends about the sexual nature of his relationship with Diana.

The press was becoming increasingly critical of Diana's conduct. She had subjected her boys to Dodi and, worse still, to his father, and she was paying the price.

'The sight of a paunchy playboy groping a scantily-dressed Diana must appal and humiliate Prince William ...' wrote Lynda Lee-Potter in the *Daily Mail* on 27 August. 'As the mother of two young sons she ought to have more decorum and sense.'

'Princess Diana's press relations are now clearly established,' wrote Bernard Ingham for the 31 August edition of the *Express*. 'Any publicity is good publicity ... I'm told she and Dodi are made for each other, both having more brass than brains.'

On the same day, Chris Hutchins wrote in the *Sunday Mirror*, 'Just when Diana began to believe that her current romance with likeable playboy Dodi Fayed had wiped out her past liaisons, a new tape recording is doing the rounds of Belgravia dinner parties. And this one is hot, hot, hot! I must remember to take it up with Diana next time we find ourselves on adjacent running machines at our west London gym.'

But then, suddenly, the music stopped and, as in the party game, all those who were still moving were caught out. Overnight, Diana found instant beatification; pity those columnists who had committed their thoughts to print on the Saturday afternoon, little knowing that their target would be a saint by the time their words hit the streets on Sunday.

'She was the butterfly who shone with the light of glamour which illuminated all our lives,' wrote Ross Benson in the *Express*; 'A beacon of light has been extinguished,' said Lady Thatcher, the former Prime Minister; 'A comet streaked across the sky of public life and entranced the world,' wrote Simon Jenkins in *The Times*; and

Paul Johnson in the *Daily Mail* called her 'A gem of purest ray serene.'

Her love affair with Dodi was given new status: she had found 'true love at last', and the couple may very well have been on the brink of announcing their engagement. It was a week of instant judgements and media saturation, and while one pundit after another filled the airwaves or the column inches on the loss to the nation, the nation itself displayed its distress on the streets of every town and city. People of all ages and from all walks of life wept openly and clasped one another for comfort. They queued, in some places for hours, to sign books of condolence, and in many instances people sat down and wrote in the books for half an hour. In London, they pilgrimaged from one royal palace to another to lay flowers with messages to Diana and Dodi.

Meanwhile the Royal Family sat, stoic and silent, in Scotland, and the nation's anger grew. It was assumed they didn't care about the nation's grief. If they had cared – the received wisdom went – they would have come to London to be with the people. There had been no statement about Diana's death, so it was assumed they didn't care about that either. Instead, it was business as usual. That the family had even gone to church on the morning of Diana's death – just hours after hearing the news – and taken the boys with them, and that there was not so much as a quivering lower lip to be seen, provoked more outrage. What further proof could there be that everything the Princess had said about this cold, heartless family she had married into was absolutely true?

Yet in the privacy of their own home there had been plenty of tears. The Prince of Wales is an emotional man, and does cry, but he was brought up to keep emotion of all sorts to himself: a characteristic which, in a less touchy-feely, emotionally transparent society, was never questioned. Indeed, to keep one's grief to oneself was a sign of strength. Yet in 1997 it was taken as a sign of insensitivity. It is not a cold heartless family, as close friends know, but it is rare for anyone outside that charmed inner circle to see a display of either emotion or affection.

In a more religious age, taking a grief-stricken family to church

31

would have been seen as the natural thing to do. In the material nineties it was seen as insensitive and unfeeling. In fact, they had gone to church that Sunday before Charles set out for Paris because Prince William had specifically said that he would like to 'talk to Mummy'. It was a week in which the children were given choices about everything, when their needs came before public relations. Church has always been a central part of the family routine and in the emotional turmoil of that Sunday, the familiarity, routine and permanence of a church service was comforting to them all.

God is very much a part of the Prince's life and his thinking and philosophy. He doesn't wear it on his sleeve, but he is a sincere believer that having a spiritual dimension to life, having faith of some sort or another – whether it is in God, Mohammed, Buddha or anyone else – is important to the human soul. He also believes that religious and cultural diversity is a real strength, and fears for Scotland and Wales breaking away from the rest of the UK for much the same reason.

His own choice of religion is Prayer Book Church of England, and he is a regular churchgoer no matter where he is. When he is at Highgrove on a Sunday, he will attend one of five village churches run by Chris Mulholland, vicar of the neighbouring village of Leighterton, who holds services in rotation. He has boycotted Tetbury Church ever since the vicar, John Hawthorne, denounced the Prince in the pages of most national newspapers for his adultery with Mrs Parker Bowles. It did not endear him to the Prince, particularly as Charles had given his support to a number of Tetbury Church fundraising initiatives.

Among the Prince's great loves are old churches – an enthusiasm he discovered he shared with Matthew Butler, his assistant private secretary, who introduced him to one or two he had never seen before. Fitting an old church or two into the schedule at the end of a day was a great treat for the Prince and when, at the end of his secondment, Matthew returned to his career in business and was awarded an MVO, he chose to receive it in Cardiff Castle, which was unusual for someone used to working in London and who lived in Tetbury. 'Matthew, what are you doing here?' asked the Prince as he ceremoniously handed over the medal. He explained that having organised the Prince's twenty-fifth anniversary tour of Wales it seemed more appropriate than Buckingham Palace. 'Oh, I suppose so,' said the Prince, then, suddenly lighting up, 'Matthew, I saw this wonderful church the other day ...'

Of the churches they visited together, there was one in Staunton Harold in Leicestershire which the Prince found particularly poignant. It had been built by Sir Robert Shirley, Baronet, a Royalist, and ancestor of the present Earl of Ferrers, during the Commonwealth in 1649, after the turbulent reign of Charles I. Like the King, he was beheaded for his pains. There was an inscription over the door, which the Prince seemed to take to heart:

'All things sacred were throughout the nation either demolished or profaned.'

With his religious conviction running deep, the Prince firmly believes in life after death. He talks about death being 'the next great journey in our existence', and is dismayed that as westerners we have become separated from the cycles of Nature, and what they have to teach us. Speaking at a Macmillan Fund anniversary a few years ago, he said, 'The seasons of the year provided for our ancestors a lesson which could not be ignored; that life is surely followed by death, but also that death can be seen as a doorway to renewed life. In Christianity the message is seen in the mystery of resurrection, and in the picture of Christ as a seed dying in the ground in order to produce the new life that supplies bread, and sustenance.'

The subject of death has fascinated the Prince for a long time. He has suffered great personal loss on a number of occasions – most notably the death of his cousin Prince William of Gloucester in an air crash in 1972, and the brutal murder of Lord Mountbatten, Nicholas Knatchbull and others by the IRA in 1979. Despite the difference in age, his great-uncle Mountbatten was closer to him than anybody else, and the news that he had been suddenly and mercilessly blown to bits by a terrorist bomb while out fishing with his family in Ireland had been completely devastating. Charles was also with his friend Major Hugh Lindsay when he was killed in a horrifying skiing accident in Switzerland in 1988. He has watched friends die, and the children of friends, and visited hospices and hospitals and talked to strangers about their experiences of death, as Diana herself did so sympathetically.

For Charles, death is a mystery and a painful parting, but not something to fear, and Diana had much the same view. She too believed in life after death and frequently consulted mediums and clairvoyants. She was quite certain that her paternal grandmother, Cynthia, Lady Spencer, who had died in 1972 when Diana was a child, kept guard over her in the spirit world.

Balmoral is the Royal Family's spiritual home, the place where they instinctively feel relaxed and at ease, where they adopt an informality that is not seen in any of the Queen's other residences. They had stayed there because it was the most sensible place for the boys to be, and that week William and Harry were the top priority. They love Balmoral like the rest of the Royal Family. They love the freedom, the walking, the fishing, the stalking, riding, go-karting; and in that week when their entire world had been turned upside down, they needed the comfort and familiarity of home. Buckingham Palace is little more than the Royal Family's institutional headquarters, and to have brought the boys to London would have been to imprison them within four walls. At Balmoral they could be certain of some privacy in which to begin to take in the enormity of what had happened, and to prepare for their mother's funeral and the most traumatic ordeal of their young lives.

Yet in London, the anger was mounting. People wanted a public display of grief. 'They're up in bloody Scotland,' was the common cry. 'They should be here. Those children should be down here.'

The whole Royal Family was well aware of the negative atmosphere building up in the south. They could see for themselves what was going on in the media and there was also a constant stream of news, views and advice coming in from politicians, friends, historians and VIPs from all over the world. But the Prince recognised it was not for him to take the lead. There was nothing he could usefully say which could have helped anyone. He had brought Diana's body home from Paris; but if he also made a statement about how very saddened he was by her death, the public would have called him a hypocrite.

The *Daily Mail* headline on Tuesday morning – 'Charles weeps bitter tears of guilt' – only exacerbated the problem. It was an obscene headline over a picture of Charles taken some months before which the newspaper swiftly recognised had been a mis-judgement. The Royal Family was appalled, and from that morning onwards stopped putting the newspapers out on display for everyone to read at Balmoral, as they previously had. It seemed that the Prince's only option was to keep a low profile and look after his sons, but by the middle of the week, when his mother's advisers still saw no need to put on a public display of emotion, he became more forceful.

Meanwhile arrangements were underway for the funeral, and once again, there was fierce disagreement between the Prince's office at St James's Palace and the Queen's at Buckingham Palace. Robert Fellowes was in an unenviable position. He was torn between duty to his wife, whom he adored, and his employer. Jane was very deeply distressed by the death of her sister and, like the rest of the Spencer family, had very definite ideas about how Diana's funeral should be handled. While wanting to respect her wishes, Fellowes also had to think of what was the best course of action for the monarchy. The Spencer family wanted a very small, private funeral, and the Queen, inclined to agree to a minimum of fuss, strongly supported this wish to keep it small and for family only. The Prince, however, felt very strongly that Diana should have nothing less than a full royal funeral at Westminster Abbey, and had told Sarah and Jane on the plane coming back from Paris that he thought it would be impossible to do anything else. Although reluctant at first, once they saw the public reaction they began to realise that this was no family affair; they couldn't keep it to themselves. There were bitter exchanges between the two camps. Even once a state funeral had been agreed upon, Earl

Spencer and Sir Robert Fellowes thought that it should only be Spencers who walked behind the cortège. The Prince disagreed, and the question was not to be resolved until the last minute.

There were yet more rows over who should sit on the Funeral Committee, set up on the day of Diana's death, chaired by Lord Airlie, the Lord Chamberlain, which met throughout the week in the Chinese Room at Buckingham Palace. The Prince of Wales wanted Downing Street represented on the committee, as did Tony Blair. The Queen didn't, and it was left to Robin Janvrin to persuade Robert Fellowes that they needed help from Number 10.

As the week progressed, the absence of a flag flying at half mast at Buckingham Palace became another issue, upon which much of the public's anger and emotion was focused. Outside the Palace, the piles of flowers grew ever more mountainous; flags were flying at half mast all over the country, and yet none of the Queen's men could reach a decision about Palace protocol. The Royal Standard never flies at half mast over Buckingham Palace because the sovereign is never dead. The minute one dies, he or she is immediately succeeded by another: 'The King is dead, long live the King.'

This was one occasion, however, where it was clear that the people of Britain didn't give a damn about protocol. They wanted to see some feeling, some indication that the Royal Family was affected by the death of the Princess, and there appeared to be no such feeling. None of them had spoken publicly, none of them had been seen, and the most elementary of gestures, the lowering of a flag, had not been observed. To the press and to the nation this embodied everything that was irrelevant and out of touch about the monarchy in the nineties, and stood in stark contrast to the warmth and compassion of the Princess, which the public had so admired. It caused a furious row internally and, in the heat of the moment, it was suggested that Sir Robert Fellowes might 'impale himself on his own flag staff'.

Finally Stephen Lamport spoke to Prince Charles. 'You've got to talk to your mother. You've got to make her understand. You're the only person who can do it.'

The Queen and the Duke of Edinburgh were entirely taken aback by the reaction to Diana's death, and were not pleased at being told how to behave in order to appease public opinion. The Queen was so often castigated for being a remote mother who always put the country before her children. Now, on the one occasion on which she was putting her grieving grandchildren first, she was being castigated for not being in London when her country needed her. After discussing the matter with David Airlie, the Queen was persuaded that a public sign of grief was required and agreed on the Thursday that a Union Flag would fly at half mast from Buckingham Palace.

That same day the family ventured out of the gates of Balmoral for the first time since the morning of Diana's death, as a means of gently preparing William and Harry for the funeral that was to be held two days later. The Prince of Wales had asked Sandy Henney, his press secretary, to come and have a chat with them. She had been in London for most of the week and witnessed what was going on there. She had felt the mood, and was one of the many people who had been feeding information up to Scotland all week, saying, 'You can't read about this, you can't even see it on television. There is real hatred building up here, and the public is incensed by your silence.'

She took the children aside. 'Mummy's death has had the most amazing impact on people,' she said. 'They really miss her, and when you go down to London you will see something you will never ever see again and it may come as a bit of a shock. We want you to know about it so you will be ready for it.'

Flowers had been piling up outside the gates of Balmoral, although in nothing like the quantity at Buckingham Palace, St James's or Kensington Palace in London. So the following day, when the children expressed the desire to go to church again, the Prince of Wales took the opportunity to give them a taster of what was awaiting them in the capital, and let them walk amongst the bouquets, reading the messages.

About sixty members of the press were waiting outside the gates of Balmoral that day, yet they uttered not a single word as the

Queen, the Duke of Edinburgh, Peter Phillips, the Prince of Wales, William and Harry climbed out of their cars to look at the flowers and tributes. The only sound to be heard, apart from the clicking of the camera shutters, were the voices of the royal party. Five days after their mother's death, the country had its first view of the boys, and it was a touching scene. All three Princes, father and sons, were visibly moved by what they saw and taken aback by the messages attached to most bouquets.

'Look at this one, Papa,' said Harry, grabbing hold of his father's hand and pulling him down. 'Read this one.'

Captured on film, the gesture sent shock waves around the world. The Prince of Wales did seem to have a heart after all. He actually held his son's hand, something no one could ever have imagined before. He also seemed to have aged.

Of all the criticism Diana threw at the Prince during their bitter war of words and television, that he was unfeeling and cold was the one that hurt him most. It was demonstrably untrue, as anyone who has seen Charles with his children knows very well. Diana knew it too, and later regretted her words.

The sight of the Prince of Wales and his sons did much to soften the public mood, and when the Queen made a surprising live television broadcast that Friday evening before the funeral, the mood softened further. The fact that it was only the second time during her reign that she had broadcast to the nation other than at Christmas – the first being during the Gulf War – made it an additionally impressive gesture.

'Since last Sunday's dreadful news we have seen, throughout Britain and around the world, an overwhelming expression of sadness at Diana's death.

'We have all been trying in our different ways to cope. It is not easy to express a sense of loss, since the initial shock is often succeeded by a mixture of other feelings: disbelief, incomprehension, anger – and concern for all who remain.

'We have all felt those emotions in these last few days. So

what I say to you now, as your Queen and as a grandmother, I say from my heart.

'First, I want to pay tribute to Diana myself. She was an exceptional and gifted human being. In good times and bad, she never lost her capacity to smile and laugh, nor to inspire others with her warmth and kindness.

'I admired and respected her – for her energy and commitment to others, and especially for her devotion to her two boys.

'This week at Balmoral, we have all been trying to help William and Harry come to terms with the devastating loss that they and the rest of us have suffered.

'No one who knew Diana will ever forget her. Millions of others who never met her, but felt they knew her, will remember her.

'I for one believe that there are lessons to be drawn from her life and from the extraordinary and moving reaction to her death.'

The Queen's words were delivered in the nick of time.

The decision about who should walk behind the cortège was not made until the very last moment. The Prince of Wales wanted to walk as a mark of respect to the Princess, who despite everything had been his wife for fifteen years, and he wanted his sons to walk too. He felt intuitively that this was something they should do for their mother and that it would aid the grieving process. Earl Spencer, backed by Sir Robert Fellowes, had been against it. He had wanted to walk behind his sister's cortège on his own. There was a bitter exchange on the telephone between the Prince and the Earl in which Earl Spencer hung up on the Prince of Wales. Over dinner on the Friday night, when the whole Royal Family was together at Buckingham Palace, the Duke of Edinburgh put an end to the argument by saying that he would walk too. The next morning Earl Spencer was told what was going to happen, and the three men and two boys all walked together.

It was a long walk from St James's Palace, where they joined the cortège, to Westminster Abbey, with every bite of the lip and tremble of the chin exposed to the world's media and the millions of people lining the route. Some threw flowers, some cried, some wailed. It was an ordeal that called for huge courage from the boys, and they did their mother – and their nation – proud. They walked slowly and steadily, struggling at times to hold back tears, but their composure never wavered, until they were inside the Abbey, when at times the music, the poetry and the oratory were too much for them. But by then the cameras were off them, forbidden to focus on the family. The boys displayed maturity beyond their years, which touched everyone. It was an ordeal for the Prince too, worrying as he was about whether the boys would be all right, but at the same time knowing that so many of the people weeping for Diana blamed him for her death. Fears that he might have been booed by the crowd were unfounded.

There were millions of people in London that Saturday and many millions more watching all over the world. Many of those in the capital had walked the streets for much of the night, or held candle-lit vigils in the park – even Diana's mother had been walking quietly amongst the mourners. Some had brought sleeping bags and had been soaked through by torrential rain the afternoon before. They did not care. United in their grief, strangers talked to strangers, as they had seventeen years before, when the Royal Wedding united them in joy.

Earlier in the week, around the royal parks and palaces the atmosphere had not been so good humoured, and felt almost intimidating at times, but by the morning of the funeral, the sun shone gloriously and although emotions were still very raw, there were tears but there was laughter too.

The funeral itself was immensely moving, and a masterpiece of organisation – the British doing what they do best: the precision timing, the military professionalism, the ceremonial pageantry, but mixed with a refreshingly human touch so perfect for Diana. Tony Blair gave a rather ham reading of 1 Corinthians 13, and Elton John sang a specially re-written version of 'Candle in the Wind' which left not a dry eye. An American film cameraman outside Kensington Palace, watching on a television monitor, said that in the silence before Elton John began to play, a sudden gust of wind, in an otherwise perfectly still morning, whipped through the millions of flowers laid at the gates, rustling the cellophane wrappings. It then disappeared just as suddenly as it had come, at the very moment Elton hit the opening chords. At the same time a small grey cloud hung over Buckingham Palace, leaving this hardened cameraman distinctly unnerved.

The denouement of the service, which no tabloid editor had been allowed to attend, was Earl Spencer's tribute to his sister. Grievously insulting to the Royal Family sitting just feet away from him, it was applauded by those within the Abbey and cheered loudly by the thousands listening on the sound relay outside.

'Diana was the very essence of compassion, of duty, of style, of beauty. All over the world she was a symbol of selfless human-ity. All over the world she was the standard bearer for the rights of the truly downtrodden, a very British girl who transcended nationality. Someone with a natural nobility who was classless and who proved in the last year that she needed no royal title to continue to generate her particular brand of magic.

'There is a rush to canonise your memory; there is no need to do so. You stand tall enough as a human being of unique qualities not to need to be seen as a saint. Indeed to sanctify your memory would be to miss out on the very core of your being, your wonderfully mischievous sense of humour with a laugh that bent you double.

'Diana explained to me once that it was her innermost feel-ings of suffering that made it possible for her to connect with her constituency of the rejected.

'And here we come to another truth about her. For all the status, the glamour, the applause, Diana remained throughout a very insecure person at heart, almost childlike in her desire to do good for others so she could release herself from deep feelings of unworthiness, of which her eating disorders were merely a symptom.

'She talked endlessly about getting away from England, mainly because of the treatment that she received at the hands of the newspapers. I don't think she ever understood why her genuinely good intentions were sneered at by the media, why there appeared to be a permanent quest on their behalf to bring her down. It is baffling.

'My own and only explanation is that genuine goodness is threatening to those at the opposite end of the moral spectrum. It is a point to remember that, of all the ironies about Diana, perhaps the greatest was this – a girl given the name of the ancient goddess of hunting was, in the end, the most hunted person of the modern age.

'She would want us today to pledge ourselves to protecting her beloved boys William and Harry from a similar fate, and I do this here, Diana, on your behalf. We will not allow them to suffer the anguish that used regularly to drive you to tearful despair.

'And beyond that, on behalf of your mother and sisters, I pledge that we, your blood family, will do all we can to continue the imaginative way in which you were steering these two exceptional young men so that their souls are not simply immersed by duty and tradition but can sing openly as you planned.'

It was a deeply moving tribute, bravely delivered as the Earl struggled against his own tears. But the last sentence was a shocking kick in the teeth to the Prince of Wales; it was thoroughly insensitive of the Earl to have criticised William and Harry's father and grandparents – indeed, one half of their relatives – in front of them on the day they buried their mother.

What really offended the Prince, however, was being forced to sit and be lectured about parental responsibility by a man who had a disastrous marriage of his own: four young children, a wife who had been ill-treated for years, and a history of adultery – all of which became very public during a bitter divorce some months later. What is more, Spencer had the gall to bring his latest mistress, Josie Borain, to the funeral. She sat beside him in the Abbey and accompanied him – on the royal train with the Prince of Wales – to the Spencer family home in Northamptonshire, Althorp, for Diana's interment immediately afterwards. Diana was buried on an island in the middle of a lake in the grounds, not in the family crypt as she had requested. It was thought that the small village churchyard would be unable to cope with the number of people that might come to visit her grave.

Charles Spencer and Diana had not been particularly close in recent years. The relationship had been up and down, as it was with most of her family. She was particularly upset that after her divorce her brother told her she could not have a particular cottage she wanted to move into on the Althorp estate. Charles, who had inherited Althorp after their father's death in 1991, said she couldn't have the cottage she wanted because it was near the gates of the estate and he was worried about the media interest she would attract. He had offered her others to choose from but Diana had set her heart on this particular cottage and felt badly let down.

Ironically, in burying Diana on the island, the Earl has turned the estate into a Mecca. He has created a museum in memory of his sister in the old stable block at Althorp, where all the hundreds of books of condolence, her dresses and various other bits of memorabilia are housed, and where videos of her, both as a child and a Princess, play constantly throughout the day. Visitors are taken around a small section of the house and then herded out to the lake, and to the shrine to the Princess that has been built on the water's edge. Some of her words are inscribed on it, and some of his from his funeral tribute.

There is a rumour, however, that Diana is not there. A very select group was invited to attend the burial, and many people believe that her body is actually in the family crypt at the churchyard in the village of Great Brington, alongside the remains of her father, the eighth Earl, and the grandmother she so adored, Cynthia Spencer, who had been her guide, she always felt, in the spirit world.

THREE

The Young Prince

'I've fallen in love with all sorts of girls …'
Charles

Nothing could have been further from the truth than the *Daily Mail*'s claim that Charles had wept 'bitter tears of guilt' as he walked the lonely moors in the immediate hours after Diana's death. He wept bitterly for the loss of the girl he had once loved, whose life had been so sad, he wept bitterly for his children, whose grief he knew would be unimaginable. He was terrified about having to break the news to them. But there was no guilt, either about Diana's death or about his affair with Camilla Parker Bowles. He knew that he was not responsible in any way for what had happened in that Parisian tunnel. Although he had failed, he knew that he had done everything in his power to make his marriage to Diana work; and he knew that no headline writer could ever begin to understand the reasons why.

If the Prince of Wales felt at all guilty, it was because of all the emotions he felt about Diana's death, the principal one was relief. Relief that the pain and the suffering was now over, that his children would no longer be torn in opposite directions, confused and upset by their mother's bizarre behaviour, and that he would no longer be spied upon – she had always tried to find out what he was doing, who he was seeing, where he was going – but be free to get on with his life. He wept bitterly because of the sheer tragedy of it all. Their life together had begun with such promise and such joy, but had ended in such acrimony and anger. But mostly he wept for William and Harry, whose lives would never be the same again, who would

44

never have the comforting arms of their mother around them and who would carry that loss for the rest of their lives. No one, he knew, would ever be able to take away their pain.

He understood. He knew the numbing, hopeless, gnawing emptiness of grief. He had known it when Lord Mountbatten was murdered. Learning to make sense of living without this mainstay in his life had seemed impossible. How much worse for William and Harry, still so young and vulnerable, to lose their mother.

So he cried for them, and he cried for his failure to help Diana. He had tried desperately, but she had been beyond any help he had been able to provide. And he cried for the failure of his marriage – as he had done many times before. He cried for all the people they had let down, and for all the lost hopes that they both had cherished in the early days, to create a secure, happy and loving home for each other and their children.

He had wanted this, just as much as she had. They had both passionately believed in the importance of family. He wanted Diana to be the person with whom he might share his life and interests, who could be friend, companion and lover. Sadly, neither he nor Diana knew what a happy home was. Neither of them had grown up with a normal loving relationship to observe, on which they might base theirs; and both were crippled by low self-esteem and lack of confidence, and a desperate need to be loved.

By 1980 the pressure on the Prince of Wales to find a wife had been intense. Guessing who it might be had been an international obsession during the seventies, which reached the height of absurdity one summer's day when the *Daily Express* announced his imminent engagement to Princess Marie-Astrid of Luxembourg, whom he had never even met. Dubbed Action Man, Charles cut a very dashing figure, particularly on the polo field, and he had had a string of attractive girlfriends, some suitably aristocratic, others glamorous and highly unsuitable starlets. The press followed every romance with fascination, especially the French and German magazines, and it was they who began the long-lens paparazzi style of photography that came to make everyone's life such a misery.

The Prince had never been short of pretty female company, but he was always handicapped because of his position. No one ever behaved normally in his company, and there was always a danger that he was attractive to women for no better reason than because they wanted to be seen with the Prince of Wales. When this was the case he was never the best person to spot it. He had always been shy and awkward and, with little opportunity to gain experience, he was ignorant about women and how to treat them. He had been to ordinary schools and university, and he had done a spell in the Navy, but most of his life had been spent in a rarefied atmosphere. With a handful of exceptions, men and women alike bowed and curtsied when they met him and called him 'sir'. Even Diana called him 'sir' until they were engaged. It is as much a mark of respect for the title as it is for the individual, but it is enough to keep a very strong barrier between him and the real world.

Charles would take girlfriends to watch him play polo at Smiths Lawn, or he would take them to the opera or the ballet and bring them home to his apartment at Buckingham Palace for supper afterwards. But there was little room for spontaneity, and certainly none for privacy. He couldn't even be alone with them in his car. Ever since a gunman ambushed Princess Anne as she was being driven down the Mall in 1974, security for all the family has been tight – and on any journey there will be a detective in the car and a backup car behind. The Prince's staff would make the arrangements and girls were usually brought to wherever he happened to be, which understandably made encounters awkward and forced. And if the formality didn't kill a burgeoning relationship, then the other hazard of dating the Prince of Wales – being splashed all over the gossip columns – usually did.

Lord Mountbatten had encouraged Charles to take girlfriends to his Hampshire estate – he was a great believer that the Prince should 'sow his wild oats' before settling down – and Broadlands afforded greater privacy (as well as the chance for Mountbatten to vet the latest conquest), but it was still an unhappy situation, and one from which most suitable girls ran a mile. Far more relaxing, Charles discovered, was the company of married women. There was no pressure on him, no expectation from them, and best of all the press left him alone. This was how he became so friendly with Camilla Parker Bowles, although she was only one of several he was close to.

He had first got to know Camilla Shand, as she then was, in 1972, when he was in the Navy. She was single at the time, but she had been going out with Andrew Parker Bowles for six years. He was a cavalry officer, nine years older than her, and hugely attractive, but hopelessly faithless. He had swept her off her feet when she was just eighteen – as he swept many girls before and since, including Princess Anne – and she hoped he would marry her, but he took her for granted, and treated her badly, knowing that she would always be there to take him back.

It was while he was stationed in Germany and their relationship was going through an off patch that Camilla and the Prince of Wales had a brief affair in the autumn of 1972. The Prince fell in love with Camilla. She was the most wonderful girl he had ever met. She was pretty and bubbly and laughed easily, and at the same sort of puerile dirty jokes he enjoyed. She loved the Goons and silly voices and put on accents that made him laugh, and she had no pretensions or guile of any sort. She loved horses and hunting, loved watching polo, loved the countryside, and was relaxed and exciting to be with.

He saw a lot of her at the end of that year and fell ever more deeply in love. He even began to think that he might have found someone he could share his life with. To his great joy she seemed to feel the same way about him, but he was only just twenty-four and too reticent to say anything to her – and certainly too reticent to discuss the possibility of any future together. Three weeks before Christmas their time together came to an enforced end. Duty called, and he went off to join the frigate HMS *Minerva*, as Acting Sub Lieutenant, which was due to set sail for the Caribbean in the New Year, and would keep him away for eight months. Before he left, Camilla came down to have lunch on the ship, once with Lord Mountbatten, with whom she had stayed with Charles at Broadlands, and on another weekend on her own.

By the time Charles came back Camilla had married Andrew Parker Bowles. They had become engaged in March, two months after he set sail, and were married at the Guards Chapel in London in July. This was what she had been waiting seven years for. He was one of the most attractive and desirable men in England and she adored him. When Charles heard of the engagement he was deeply upset. As he wrote to a friend, it seemed particularly cruel that after 'such a blissful, peaceful and mutually happy relationship' fate had decreed that it should last no more than six months. 'I suppose the feeling of emptiness will pass eventually.'

Despite the bitter disappointment, he and Camilla remained friends, and during the next seven years, when he was dating other girls with enthusiasm, she was someone he could talk to. When the Parker Bowles's first child, Tom, was born in 1975, Camilla asked Charles to be his godfather. For many years there was nothing sexual in their relationship, but because they had had such a happy and intimate affair during those six months, there remained a closeness and trust and friendship that was special. He confided in Camilla and spent a lot of time on the telephone to her. They also met at polo, parties and royal gatherings – Andrew Parker Bowles's mother had been a friend of the Queen and he was distantly related to the Queen Mother. Camilla and her family had also been on the periphery of royalty. Her father, Bruce Shand, was a wealthy wine merchant and businessman, and her mother, Rosalind, a member of the hugely rich Cubitt family – her father was Baron Ashcombe. Camilla's great-grandmother, Alice Keppel, had been mistress to King Edward VII, who was the Prince's great-great-grandfather, and Camilla enjoyed the idea of history repeating itself. She and Andrew were frequently invited to stay at Sandringham, Windsor and Balmoral, and Charles went to spend weekends with Camilla and Andrew and the children in Wiltshire. Their daughter Laura was born in 1979.

The friendship only became physical again after Laura's birth, long after Camilla realised that the philanderer she had pursued for seven years before their marriage had continued in much the same way after marriage. What was so hurtful was that as often as not the women Andrew bedded were friends of hers. As time passed, she spent a lot of time on her own in the country, looking after the children and horses, while Andrew lived in London, where he escorted other women quite openly. Under those circumstances, who was to mind if she had a fling with the Prince of Wales? It was not serious, it couldn't go anywhere, it was just a bit of fun, and although there were occasional references to Camilla in the satirical magazine *Private Eye*, and the odd gossip column, it was the Prince's single starlets that attracted the headlines.

The Duke of Edinburgh disapproved of the playboy image that the Prince was acquiring, and when he passed his thirtieth birthday, and still showed no signs of settling down, told him what he thought. Charles knew it was his duty to provide an heir for the future security and stability of the monarchy, but he wanted to find the right wife and had repeatedly spoken about choosing someone who would know what she was letting herself in for.

'I've fallen in love with all sorts of girls and I fully intend to go on doing so, but I've made sure I haven't married the first person I've fallen in love with. I think one's got to be aware of the fact that falling madly in love with someone is not necessarily the starting point to getting married,' he once said. '[Marriage] is basically a very strong friendship ... I think you are lucky if you find the person attractive in the physical and the mental sense ... To me marriage seems to be the biggest and most responsible step to be taken in one's life.

'Whatever your place in life, when you marry you are forming a partnership which you hope will last for fifty years. So I'd want to marry someone whose interests I could share. A woman not only marries a man; she marries into a way of life – a job. She's got to have some knowledge of it, some sense of it, otherwise she wouldn't have a clue about whether she's going to like it. If I'm deciding on whom I want to live with for fifty years – well, that's the last decision on which I want my head to be ruled by my heart.'

Despite the girlfriends, the Prince was fundamentally lonely and longed to find someone to share his life with. He wanted to settle down, be domestic, have a garden and dogs and children, and all the things that his friends had. He had spent his life in search of love and reassurance and was dogged by a sense of worthlessness, which his parents had done nothing to help him overcome. They are not demonstrative people, and praise for one another's achievements is not something that comes naturally in the Royal Family.

Those who have known the family since Charles was a child say that the Queen adores her eldest son, as she adores all her children – there is no doubting the affection – but sadly it is not in her nature to be overtly affectionate. Some remember her sitting him on her knee at afternoon tea when he was small, and playing games with him, but that physical closeness disappeared as he grew older. The Queen inherited the throne when he was three years old on the death of her father, George VI, and her duties as monarch inevitably competed with motherhood, taking her away more than she would have chosen. She made it a rule to be with her children at bath and bedtime, whenever possible, and to be at home during the school holidays, but day to day care was left to much-loved nannies, which was normal in upper-class families of that period. The one time she was away for a sustained period was for the Coronation tour in 1953–54, when she and the Duke of Edinburgh were gone for six months, including Christmas. It was then that Charles saw so much of the Queen Mother and, although the Prince adores his mother, the relationship never developed the real warmth or intimacy that he shares with his grandmother.

Even on the night Diana died, when his mother was on the other side of a thin partition wall, he sat and talked and worried not with her, but with his friends and his advisers. When he thought Diana was injured and was undecided about whether to get on a plane and go to Paris, he didn't ask his mother's advice, he asked his private secretary; and in the arranging of the plane, his advisers spoke to her advisers. This is no ordinary mother–son relationship: Charles has been in awe of her all his life and, even at fifty, is still delighted beyond reason when she compliments him on something she has noticed he has done well.

His father is equally loving and proud of his eldest son, but no less sparing in showing it. He was rough with Charles as a child and witnesses say he frequently reduced the boy to tears. Charles was a sensitive, shy and uncertain little boy, in contrast to his sister Anne, who was tough and sure of herself and could do no wrong. The Duke probably thought this kind of treatment would make a man of Charles, but it only served to undermine his confidence still further. Charles was frightened of his father, and desperate for his approval, but try as he might to please him, he seldom could.

There are not many men of fifty, with independent means, who are still trying so hard to please their parents – certainly not men with the kind of physical courage that the Prince of Wales indisputably has. But the family that Charles was born into is not like any other family in Britain and he was conditioned to accept, without question, a way of life that normal people would find quite intolerable. Duty to Queen and country comes before any other consideration. Charles is never entirely alone: a detective is within earshot twenty-four hours a day. He never goes anywhere without someone knowing. He has no privacy, therefore, and is dependent upon the discretion of the men who shadow him.

There is no heart to the family: it is a business, an institution, and participation is not an option, it is duty. There is very little communication between members of the family. When there is, it is often by memo, or via private secretaries. And, except for holidays and ceremonial fixtures, there is very little contact between them. Their lives are run to a formula, from which there is no deviation or spontaneity, and the formality with which the Queen runs her household is from another age.

Apart from the companionship, which he craved, Charles had no need for a wife. His life was ordered: his meals were cooked; his clothes bought, laundered and laid out for him; his every whim catered for; his friends numerous, understanding and sufficiently fawning; his office compliant; his love life exciting; and his sporting activities and holidays strategically organised from one year to the next to fit in around official fixtures, functions and the call of duty.

He had houses in the country and convenient apartments at Buckingham Palace; he had horses, dogs and cars, and a fleet of royal helicopters, planes and trains, not to mention the royal yacht at his disposal, plus holiday homes in all the places he most liked to be. He only had to click his fingers and what he wanted arrived or was fixed. The only benefit a wife could bring, which he could get nowhere else, was an heir.

By an accident of birth the Prince of Wales was cursed with a life in which his waking hours are mapped out six months in advance, and there are fixtures in his diary which will be there on the same day every year for the rest of his life. He is surrounded by people who tell him what they think he wants to hear; he is paraded like a performing poodle on high days and holidays, and his every twitch and grunt recorded and analysed by the tabloid press. His right to exist is debated regularly, as though he had some say in the matter, and his character and physique considered fair game for whoever fancies taking a passing punch. This is how it has been since he was three years old, when his mother became Queen.

He is an uneasy mix of old and new, half expecting the deference, service and lifestyle of another era, and half wanting to be a modern man of the people in an egalitarian age. But he is hampered by being kept at one remove from the life modern man leads. Diana had one huge advantage over the Prince: she did understand how the other half lived, because she had grown up in the real world. The Prince, try as he might, has never been given a chance. He has wanted to meet people in their own environment, but he is always cushioned. Try as he might to empathise, he will never know what it is like to queue for hours in a hospital casualty department or have petty bureaucrats be rude to him. He will never be elbowed out of the way in the rush for the first bus to appear in twenty minutes, know the frustrations of a train being cancelled, or have to hang around an overcrowded airport lounge. And if it starts to rain, someone will appear with an umbrella to keep him dry.

When he was forty minutes late for an Order of the Bath ceremony at Westminster Abbey with the Queen not long ago, he was incandescent with rage. The helicopter had been unable to land at Highgrove because of fog, so he was told to drive to RAF Lyneham nearby, only to discover that the fog was just as bad and the helicopter couldn't land there either. There was no alternative but to drive all the way to London, which made him late. Some unfortunate person had got it wrong, and he hit the roof. When his staff once failed to organise his supper menu on the royal train because they had been working exceptionally hard on a very tricky weekend of engagements that had gone like clockwork, he was furious. The chef said he could do him one of three dishes: some salmon, a salad or steak and kidney pie. He petulantly said he didn't like any of them. When a member of staff once failed to call him 'sir' or 'Your Royal Highness' – terrified by the experience of meeting the Prince for the first time – he said, 'Do you think you could ask that chap to call me something when he meets me?' Friends will say, 'He only lets people know who he is when they forget,' but it evidently depends upon what sort of mood he is in, and during the difficult times in his marriage, his moods were highly unpredictable.

Employees see this side of the Prince more than friends, which perhaps makes it all the more reprehensible.

Yet at other times he is relaxed and will laugh when things go wrong. A trip to the United World College in Trieste some years ago fell during the transition period between two private secretaries. The one who had done the recce – when the precise details are worked out of where HRH will go, who he will speak to, and how long it will all take – was not the one there on the day. Thus with great élan, but no certainty about where they were going, the Prince and accompanying entourage were led off down an alley way, only to discover it was a dead end which led to the dustbins. Covered in confusion the party did a swift U-turn and with photographers swarming around them beat a hasty retreat. The incoming private secretary, Major-General Sir Christopher Airy, a highly efficient man, was mortified, but the Prince simply laughed.

He was also amused by an encounter with Chris Eubank, the champion boxer, who had been running a fitness workshop at a

Prince's Trust residential course in Brighton. He was standing at the end of a line-up to meet the Prince and was obviously very nervous, so the private secretary went across to try and calm him down. 'Don't worry,' he said, 'the Prince is very easy to talk to, just enjoy it.'

After they had met, he went up to Eubank to see how it had gone. 'Yes, of course it was okay,' said Eubank. 'I wasn't frightened. If you've been in the ring with Nigel Benn you're not frightened of the Prince of Wales. So it was absolutely fine.'

The private secretary beat a retreat. A little later Eubank called him back. 'Anyway, I hope I did the right thing. I called him Mr Windsor. I'm Chris Eubank, so I'm Mr Eubank. He's Charles Windsor, so he must be Mr Windsor. Right?'

'Yes,' said the private secretary, fearing for his profile. 'That's absolutely fine.'

Charles does have a sense of humour and a great sense of the absurd, but anyone who knows him well knows how important it is to judge his mood before ever presuming familiarity. His children are the exception; they can say and do what they like to him and if he starts to get testy or pompous about it, they simply tease him out of it. They are sensitive enough, though, to know who not to tease him in front of.

One other person who can stop the Prince taking himself too seriously, and get away with it, is Mrs Parker Bowles; but she too picks her moments and would never embarrass the Prince in front of anyone other than his closest friends. They all acknowledge she has a miraculous effect on him, and whenever invitations to dinner at Highgrove are issued, they desperately hope Camilla will be there. If she is, the evening will be relaxed and good fun, with a great deal of gossip, jokes and giggling. Without her, the Prince is likely be serious and if he's feeling down – which without her he often is – he can be fairly leaden company.

Thousands of young people whom he has helped during the course of the last twenty-one years rightly regard him as someone very special: without him they might never have had a chance in life. He has helped when no bank manager would have considered their application – even if they had known how to apply for a loan. He believed in their potential and has put time, thought, effort and money into helping through the Prince's Trust and its various offshoots. The Prince's Trust was just the beginning. He has spread himself over a wide range of interests and concerns, and he has done a huge amount of good in his fifty years, much of it unrecognised by the majority of the population. He has exploited his privilege and his position to very good ends, and there is no doubt that he is an extremely sensitive man, who cares desperately and sincerely. Yet he remains intrinsically very selfish and very spoilt.

The problem is that Charles has no social equal, and few people have ever been brave enough over the years to say what needed to be said. There have been a few exceptions, and whenever rebuked for behaving in an inconsiderate manner to someone, the Prince has always been deeply ashamed. On one occasion, speaking at a Queen's Silver Jubilee Trust dinner, the Prince made some rather barbed remarks about a couple of people in the room who were dragging their feet about taking up one of his ideas. At the end of the evening, Michael Colborne told the Prince he thought he had been unnecessarily harsh on the two individuals. Colborne had known the Prince during his time in the Navy and joined his staff in 1974. He felt so strongly that over the following weekend he sat down and put his feelings on paper, and sent the letter to the Prince, who was by then staying on a Duchy farm. A week later Charles was back at Highgrove, and called Colborne into his office.

'You know that letter you wrote me?' he said. 'Do you know what I did with it? I read it and I screwed it up into a ball and I kicked it round the bedroom.'

'Oh you did, did you, sir?' said Colborne with a slight smile. 'Why was that?'

'Because unfortunately you were right. I wasn't very nice to those two men that night.'

FOUR

The Discovery of Diana

'She was a sort of wonderful English schoolgirl
who was game for anything.'
Friend of Prince Charles

When Charles first met Diana she was a nondescript schoolgirl of sixteen – his girlfriend's little sister. He was in the midst of a lengthy and enjoyable relationship with Sarah, and they met at Althorp, where he had been invited to a shoot. Diana was nothing more than a slightly plump, noisy teenager, but he made a profound impression on this particular teenager and Diana secretly set her heart on him then and there and determined that she would become Princess of Wales.

Sarah's romance with Charles came to an end when she spoke candidly to the press about it, saying, 'I wouldn't marry anyone I didn't love, whether it was the dustman or the King of England. If he asked me I would turn him down.' But they remained friends, and the Prince invited Sarah and Diana to his thirtieth birthday party at Buckingham Palace a year later, and a few months after that, in January 1979, they were both invited as guests of the Queen to a shooting weekend at Sandringham. That very weekend, their father, Earl Spencer, had come out of hospital following a brain haemorrhage that very nearly killed him.

Later that year Diana was staying with her sister, Jane Fellowes, in her house at Balmoral to help with Jane's new baby, while the Royal Family was in residence at the castle. But the first time Charles saw her as anything more than a jolly and bouncy young girl whom he enjoyed taking out from time to time as one of a group to make up numbers was in July 1980, when they were both invited to a weekend party with mutual friends in Sussex. He had just had a dramatic and humiliating bust up with his latest passion, Anna Wallace, and he and Diana were sitting side by side on a hay bale while their hosts prepared a barbecue, when the conversation turned to Mountbatten, who had died the previous August. What Diana said touched the Prince deeply – as she knew it would.

'You looked so sad when you walked up the aisle at Lord Mountbatten's funeral,' she said. 'It was the most tragic thing I've ever seen. My heart bled for you when I watched. I thought, "It's wrong, you're lonely – you should be with somebody to look after you."'

It is ironic that her sensitivity about Lord Mountbatten should have triggered Charles's interest in Diana as a future bride, for Mountbatten would not have approved of the match. In losing his beloved great-uncle, his 'Honorary Grandfather', the Prince had lost his mentor; also, for a considerable time, he had lost his way in life. Mountbatten would have applauded Diana's sweet nature, her youth, her beauty, her nobility and her virginity; but he would have seen that the pair had too little in common to sustain them through fifty years of marriage. He might also have spotted her acute vulnerability and the damage sustained by her painful start in life, and known that the Prince, with his own vulnerability and insecurity, was not the right man to cope with her needs.

Mountbatten's murder had an unimaginable impact on the Prince's life; it knocked him entirely off-balance. As he wrote in his journal on the evening he heard the news, 'Life has to go on, I suppose, but this afternoon I must confess I wanted it to stop. I felt supremely useless and powerless ...

'I have lost someone infinitely special in my life; someone who showed enormous affection, who told me unpleasant things I didn't particularly want to hear, who gave praise where it was due as well as criticism; someone to whom I knew I could confide anything and from whom I would receive the wisest of counsel and advice.'

Mountbatten had criticised the Prince of Wales, most notably for his selfishness, but he also made him feel he was loved and valued, which neither of his parents had ever been able to do. Where his father had cut the ground from under his feet, Mountbatten had built him up, listened to his doubts and his fears, rebuked him when he felt he had behaved badly, encouraged him, cajoled him, provided a sounding board for his wackier ideas, a shoulder to cry on, and given him some much needed confidence. There was no one else in his life at that time who could do this.

From the time when Charles was so touched by their exchange on the hay bale, to the announcement of their engagement, the romance was brief – less than seven months – and their moments alone were rare, but throughout the course of the relationship, Diana was in charge. She knew what she wanted and she went all out to get it. She had cherished her dream of marrying the Prince since their first meeting three years before, and with great cunning ensured her dream came true. She had always said since she was a small child that when she grew up she was going to be someone special. Her siblings called her 'Duch' – because she was determined to be a duchess at the very least. When the opportunity arose, she threw herself at the Prince, quite blatantly and brazenly. Yet it was only the more astute of Charles's friends who realised what was going on. He didn't appear to notice. Like most men he was easily flattered, particularly by a pretty young woman who professed great interest in everything he said and did, and manifested great sympathy and understanding for the trials and tribulations of his life. He found her quite intoxicating, and she was willing and amenable to do whatever might please him. She slotted neatly into whatever plans he already had, she talked about her love of the country and of shooting and her interest in taking up horse riding, and she liked his friends. And crucially, she made him laugh. She was fun.

But it was all a sham. Diana didn't like any of these things. She hated the countryside, had no interest in shooting or horses, or dogs, and she didn't even really like his friends. She found them old, boring and sycophantic. What she enjoyed was the city. She liked shopping in expensive Knightsbridge department stores, and lunching in smart London restaurants. She liked cinema and pop music.

Diana was a victim, who needed love and attention and constant reassurance – needs she carried to an exaggerated degree from her childhood. Her mother, Frances Shand Kydd, had run away from a violent and unhappy marriage when Diana was six years old and the experience of that loss – her feeling of rejection that followed when her mother disappeared – left deep scars in Diana's psyche.

Frances Shand Kydd has been unfairly maligned for deserting her children, not least by Mohamed al Fayed when they attended an investigative meeting in Paris in June 1998 about the crash that killed both their children. He lashed out at her, saying, 'She didn't give a damn about her daughter ... If you leave a child when she's six years old how can you call yourself a good mother?'

Whatever her qualities as a mother, Frances had every expectation when she left home for good just before Christmas in 1967 that it would be a temporary separation. She intended to sue her husband for divorce on the grounds of cruelty, and it was unthinkable for a mother in these circumstances not to be given custody of young children. Her husband, Johnnie Althorp, who later became the eighth Earl Spencer on his father's death, was a well-respected, genial, if rather dim, member of the aristocracy. He had been an equerry to George VI, then to Queen Elizabeth II.

Abuse ran in the Spencer family marriages and their thirteen years together had not been happy. To compound her misery, Frances had lost a child, a baby boy called John, born after Jane and Sarah, in January 1960, who only lived for ten hours. Diana was born eighteen months later, and then in May 1964 Frances gave birth to another boy, Charles, the son and heir her husband so badly wanted.

Shortly afterwards she met and fell in love with Peter Shand Kydd, a wealthy married businessman. Their affair broke up both marriages, and Frances seized the opportunity to escape. In the autumn of 1967 she and Johnnie had a trial separation, and at

Christmas it became permanent and she left the family home. But her plans to sue for cruelty went badly awry. Shand Kydd's wife, Janet, sued him for divorce on the grounds of his adultery with Frances. With that proven, Frances had no defence when Johnnie also sued for divorce because of their adultery. The cruelty suit was thrown out, and in the custody proceedings that followed, he brought some of the most influential people in the land to speak up for him – including her own mother, Ruth, Lady Fermoy, a considerable snob, who was said to have been appalled that her daughter had run off with a man 'in trade' – albeit a millionaire.

As a result, custody of Jane, Sarah, Diana and Charles was given to their father, who employed a string of itinerant nannies to take care of them. Frances was only allowed to have them on specified weekends and parts of the school holidays.

Diana said, 'It was a very unhappy childhood ... Always seeing my mother crying ... I remember Mummy crying an awful lot and every Saturday when we went up for weekends, every Saturday night, standard procedure, she would start crying. On Saturday we would both see her crying. "What's the matter, Mummy?" "Oh, I don't want you to leave tomorrow."'

One of Diana's other early memories was hearing her younger brother Charles sobbing in his bed at the other end of the house from her room, crying for their mother. She understood none of what had gone on between her parents. All she could see, like any small child in a similar situation, was that her mother didn't want her any more. She told Andrew Morton that she began to think she was a nuisance, and then worked out that because she was born after her dead brother, she must have been a huge disappointment to her parents. 'Both were crazy to have a son and heir and there comes a third daughter. "What a bore, we're going to have to try again." I've recognised that now. I've been aware of it and now I recognise it and that's fine. I accept it.'

Rightly or wrongly, Diana felt rejected, worthless and unwanted. Those were the feelings she nursed throughout her childhood and teenage years and, three weeks after her twentieth birthday, took with her into marriage. She was still desperately seeking love and reassurance.

Her mother's departure was not the end of the trauma in Diana's young life. In June 1975, shortly before her fourteenth birthday, her paternal grandfather died and her father inherited the title and the ancestral home, Althorp. It meant an upheaval from Norfolk, where she had friends and roots, to Northamptonshire, where she knew no one. Worse still, her father, whom the children had had more or less to themselves for the last eight years, had taken up with a formidable woman, Raine, Countess of Dartmouth, daughter of the romantic novelist, Barbara Cartland, mother of four and former member of Westminster City Council, the London County Council and the Greater London Council. To the children's horror, the couple were married just over a year later, and the woman one of her friends described as 'not a person but an experience' took over Althorp and all who lived in it.

Diana's education was poor. After prep school at Riddlesworth Hall in Norfolk, she followed her sisters to West Heath, another boarding school in Kent, where she passed no O-Levels, despite two attempts, and left in December 1977 at the age of sixteen. She went from there to finishing school in Switzerland but didn't enjoy it; she came home after six weeks and refused to go back. She did some brief nannying jobs, learnt to drive, did a short cookery course, and briefly worked as a student teacher at Betti Vacani's children's dancing school in Knightsbridge. But that too she gave up. One day she simply didn't arrive for work, and when she was telephoned and asked what the problem was, she said she had hurt her leg. The truth was that whenever the going got tough, Diana quit. After that she did cleaning jobs for her sister and any friends who wanted their flats vacuuming or their laundry done. She had been obsessively clean and tidy ever since she was a small child. At school she had done far more washing than anyone else. It was the one thing she was prepared to stick at.

On 1 July 1979, her eighteenth birthday, Diana came into money which had been left in trust for the Spencer children by her American great-grandmother, Frances Work, and was encouraged by her mother, as her sisters had been before her, to buy a flat with some of the money. The flat she bought was 60 Coleherne Court, said to have cost £50,000, which she shared initially with two friends. By the time she began seeing the Prince of Wales, she had three flatmates, Carolyn Pride, Virginia Pitman and Anne Bolton; and was working three afternoons a week as an assistant at the Young England Kindergarten in Pimlico, run by the sister of a schoolfriend of Jane.

Diana's problem was that she had had no discipline in her life. Like so many children of divorced parents, she had been indulged. She was an extremely rich, extremely spoilt young woman, who was used to getting her own way. In marrying the Prince of Wales she was taking on one of the most disciplined ways of life in Britain.

The Prince of Wales was quite besotted by Diana at the time he asked her to marry him, and when she came to Balmoral in the late summer of 1980 everyone fell in love with her. She was a fresh, delightful, funny girl, with a podgy face and pudding basin haircut, who told jokes, had no clothes so borrowed everyone else's, asked daft questions, knew nothing about anything, and made everyone helpless with laughter. Charles couldn't believe his luck, that this lovely girl, whom all his friends seemed to find so attractive and engaging, said she loved *him*.

Charles's excitement at finding Diana, who seemed to be perfect in every way, was quite touching. In public, the mask behind which he hides is impenetrable. In private, he has never been able to hide his emotions, and since he was a small child, if asked, he has always blurted out everything he is thinking and feeling. He has no guile, and over the years most of these thoughts and emotions have been committed to paper in letters and notes to friends and relations. As his feelings for Diana began to run away with him, his older and wiser friends told him that he should slow down and keep his cool, lest he blow it.

In August 1980, several of Charles's friends were with him on board the royal yacht *Britannia* for Cowes Week on the Isle of

Wight, the oldest yachting regatta in the world and one of the great events of the social season. He invited Diana, and confided to one of his friends that he had met the girl he intended to marry. Oliver Everett, an assistant private secretary, who had accompanied her to the yacht, returned to his colleagues in the office saying, 'I think this is serious.' In September the Prince invited her to Balmoral, again with his friends. By then he was confessing that he was not yet in love with her, but felt that because she was so lovable and warm-hearted, he very soon could be. The friends could see no objection. At nineteen she was younger than most of them by many years, but she was friendly and easy company and most of them warmed to her. She was fun and bubbly, and told Charles how completely at home she was in the country. As one of his friends said, 'We went walking together, we got hot, we got tired, she fell into a bog, she got covered in mud, laughed her head off, got puce in the face, hair glued to her forehead because it was pouring with rain ... She was a sort of wonderful English schoolgirl who was game for anything, naturally young but sweet and clearly determined and enthusiastic about him, very much wanted him.'

The Prince taught Diana to fish on the River Dee, and it was while she was out alone with him one afternoon that she was spotted by James Whitaker, at that time royal correspondent of the *Daily Star*, who had been pursuing Charles for many years to secure the scoop of the decade – the girl who would be Queen – and his tenacity can only be marvelled at. It was a matter of hours before Diana's name, address and pedigree were all over Fleet Street and her flat in Coleherne Court in Chelsea was under siege by seldom fewer than thirty photographers. They followed her every move, telephoned her at all hours of the day and night, pointed long lenses at her bedroom window from the building opposite, and made her life totally intolerable until the engagement was announced five months later and she was able to move into the sanctuary of Buckingham Palace.

Charles was badly smitten, but his decision to ask Diana to marry him in February was not born out of spontaneity or conviction.

It was a pitiful combination of poor communication, media manipulation and pressure that he no longer had the strength to resist. Diana was clearly suitable and in every way might have been tailor made. She came from a family that had been connected to the Royal Family for years, she understood the protocol, she was comfortable around them all. She was sexy, pretty and fun to be with. She was interested in all the things he was interested in, and young enough to fit in with his lifestyle without too much difficulty. The newspapers loved Diana, and the country wanted him to marry her.

It was still early days, but because the media had reached fever pitch – not entirely discouraged by Diana, who developed quite a warm relationship with people like James Whitaker during that time – Charles was forced into making a decision that he was not yet ready to make. Everyone wanted him to find a wife. The pressure from inside and outside the family was intense, and there were not many candidates by the 1980s who fitted the job description. Diana seemed as close to perfect as he had known. She appeared to love him very much, so, hoping for the best, the Prince allowed himself to be led by others.

There was one other decisive factor. It was one of the most inexplicable episodes, which has remained a mystery ever since and probably always will. In November, a story appeared in the *Sunday Mirror* entitled 'Love in the Sidings', which claimed that a blonde woman of Diana's description had driven from London in the middle of the night, and been secreted on to the royal train for a few hours with the Prince while it was parked at a siding in Wiltshire. She had been telephoned and asked for a comment and said the story was quite untrue. Bob Edwards, the editor, was so convinced it was true that he published anyway, and was shocked by the unprecedented reaction from the Queen's press secretary, Michael Shea. He demanded a retraction, calling the story 'total fabrication'. Some years later, Edwards had a Christmas card from his friend Woodrow Wyatt which simply said, 'It must have been Camilla.' Camilla and the Prince both say the incident never happened –

Camilla has never been on board the royal train – and neither they, nor any of the Prince's staff who were around at the time have ever been able to get to the bottom of where the story could possibly have come from. The royal train is heavily guarded by British Transport police – it is their big moment – and when it stops overnight, there are patrols walking up and down both sides of the train, men on bridges, cars everywhere, plus a large crew on board. It is inconceivable that anyone could have been smuggled on to the train undetected, and if someone had seen a blonde woman smuggled into the Prince's compartment, whether Camilla or not, the story would have been out long ago.

However, it was pivotal to Charles and Diana's relationship, and it would not have been beyond the cunning of Diana to have tipped off the *Sunday Mirror* herself – nor some years later, consumed with jealousy for Camilla, suggested the blonde was Camilla.

The clear implication from the story was that Diana had slept with the Prince, which cast doubt on her virtue. The fact that the Queen should have been so quick to protect her virtue gave Diana a special status. She had not stepped in to protect any of the other women the Prince had been with. It further fuelled speculation that this one would become his bride.

Diana's mother wrote to *The Times* appealing for an end to it all. 'In recent weeks,' she wrote, 'many articles have been labelled "exclusive quotes", when the plain truth is that my daughter has not spoken the words attributed to her. Fanciful speculation, if it is in good taste, is one thing, but this can be embarrassing. Lies are quite another matter, and by their very nature, hurtful and inexcusable … May I ask the editors of Fleet Street, whether, in the execution of their jobs, they consider it necessary or fair to harass my daughter daily from dawn until well after dusk? Is it fair to ask any human being, regardless of circumstances, to be treated in this way? The freedom of the press was granted by law, by public demand, for very good reasons. But when these privileges are abused, can the press command any respect, or expect to be shown any respect?'

Sixty MPs tabled a motion in the House of Commons 'deploring the manner in which Lady Diana Spencer is treated by the media' and 'calling upon those responsible to have more concern for individual privacy'. Fleet Street editors met senior members of the Press Council to discuss the situation. It was the first time in its twenty-seven-year history that such an extraordinary meeting had been convened, but it did nothing to stop the harassment.

It was against this background that the Duke of Edinburgh wrote to his son saying that he must make up his mind about Diana. In all the media madness, it was not fair to keep the girl dangling on a string. She had been seen without a chaperone at Balmoral and her reputation was in danger of being tarnished. If he was going to marry her, he should get on and do it; if not, he must end it. The Prince of Wales read the letter as an ultimatum from his father to marry Diana.

Others to whom he has shown the letter believe that the Prince misinterpreted what his father wrote, and that to have laid the ultimate blame for his failed marriage on his bullying father is unfair. There was obviously an ambiguity that was never resolved verbally. The two men did not sit down and talk – indeed, they cannot sit down and talk, which is a great sadness to both.

The Prince was faced with an impossible choice. To ask Diana to marry him before he was quite sure she was the right girl, or to risk letting her go when she was so perfect in so many ways and things were looking so promising.

'It all seems so ridiculous because I do very much want to do the right thing for this country and for my family – but I'm terrified sometimes of making a promise and then perhaps living to regret it.'

He allowed himself to be pushed into a marriage that he was uncertain in his own mind was a good idea. He confessed to one friend that he was in a 'confused and anxious state of mind'. To another he said, 'It is just a matter of taking an unusual plunge into some rather unknown circumstances that inevitably disturbs me but I expect it will be the right thing in the end.'

He knew he wasn't in love with her, but he liked her very much, and he knew there was a good chance he would grow to love her.

Mountbatten had told him to find a young girl and mould her to his way of life. Wasn't someone like Diana precisely what he meant? More importantly, given the hysteria that Diana had caused in the media, what other girl would ever dare be seen with him, if this was the likely consequence? Convinced that his father was telling him to marry Diana, he decided to go with that decision and hope for the best.

Had Lord Mountbatten been alive Charles would have turned to him for help; and Mountbatten would in all probability have told him not to marry Diana. Yes, he had a duty to marry, but it was imperative for the Prince of Wales above all people, who could not contemplate divorce, to be quite certain he had found the right woman.

In Mountbatten's absence, Charles consulted his official advisers, friends and family, most of whom were eager to approve. It is the curse of the Prince of Wales to be surrounded by friends and advisers, most of whom tell him what they think he wants to hear. Few have the courage to say what they think he needs to be told for fear that it might put an end to their friendship or employment. The Queen offered no opinion whatsoever. The Queen Mother, a hugely influential figure within the Royal Family to this day, was strongly in favour of the match. Lady Diana was, after all, the granddaughter of her good friend and lady-in-waiting, Ruth, Lady Fermoy. And Ruth, Lady Fermoy, who knew that Diana had emotional problems, which would make the match extremely unwise, failed to speak up.

Two of Charles's close friends, Nicholas Soames and Penny Romsey, advised against marriage. Soames thought that the pair had too little in common, and saw an intellectual gap of giant proportions. Penny Romsey was similarly worried about the intellectual mismatch, but she was also very concerned that Diana was in love with the notion of being Princess of Wales without any real understanding of what it would involve. Penny told the Prince of her worries some weeks before the engagement, and persuaded her husband Norton, the Prince's cousin, to do the same. Norton's principal concern, like that of Nicholas Soames, was the intellectual gulf, which he predicted would lead to silent evenings, resentment and friction. All three were deeply suspicious about the way in which Diana had gone after the Prince so single-mindedly. They had seen how she controlled the relationship. She had wanted the Prince of Wales, she had flirted and flattered and been everything that he wanted, and she had got him. Romsey tackled the Prince on more than one occasion, becoming blunter with every attempt. The Prince didn't want to hear, and he was angrily told to mind his own business.

Although he often seeks solitude, the Prince has a network of close friends upon whom he is very dependent and confides in, as they do in him. He is a tactile man, and he pours out love and affection to them, both male and female, although he has always tended to be closer to women. He speaks to them on the phone, writes long, soul-baring letters, and asks their opinion on every subject that interests or worries him. He confides far more than is probably wise, and is completely open and honest with them. In return they protect his trust absolutely. It is a tightly knit bunch, mostly older than him, and includes the Palmer-Tomkinsons, the van Cutsems, the Keswicks, the Paravicinis, the Wards, the Romseys, the Brabournes, the Devonshires, the Shelburnes and Nicholas Soames. They wield great influence with the Prince and are fiercely jealous of their friendship. Most of them have plenty of money, which is inherited, and not a great deal of sensitivity about how the other half lives. None of them shares the Prince's enthusiasm for hunting but they indulge in all the other sporting activities of the British upper classes. They shoot grouse in either Yorkshire or Scotland, from 12 August through to December; shoot pheasant and partridge from October to February, and duck from a month earlier. They fish for salmon on any of the great rivers, mostly in Scotland or Iceland. They have large country houses, which the Prince visits, and in return they enjoy invitations to his family homes, to weekend shooting parties at Sandringham, and stalking and fishing holidays at Balmoral.

The Prince of Wales thought he had found the girl of his dreams, the girl whom the country would find acceptable, and who would be able to share his job and his life. He had not reached this judgement alone. He was not a normal man wanting a normal wife to live a normal life. He had waited a long time to find the right person, and he was now thirty-two years old. It was important for the country that he make the right decision, and he wanted to be reassured by his friends and advisers that he was correct in his selection. But though he canvassed opinion about Diana before he asked her to marry him, and he relied upon friends to bolster his resolve, once she had accepted his proposal, the subject was closed. He had made his decision, and was not receptive to advice, warning or criticism. He was determined that the decision to marry Diana was the right one, and when doubts began to creep into his mind during the five months before the wedding, he kept them to himself.

'I do believe I am very lucky that someone as special as Diana seems to love me so much,' he wrote to two of his friends. 'I am already discovering how nice it is to have someone round to share things with ... Other people's happiness and enthusiasm at the whole thing is also a most "encouraging" element and it makes me so proud that so many people have such admiration and affection for Diana.'

The truth was rather different; but when his friends told him they had serious doubts about the suitability of the match, he refused to listen. When he himself began to have serious doubts about Diana, he refused to talk about it. He went ahead knowing that there was a question mark over the future. To have called off the wedding would have been horrendous and humiliating for everyone, and the headlines and public castigation could only be imagined, but with hindsight, it would have been infinitely less painful and less damaging to everyone concerned, particularly the monarchy, if he had had the courage to do it.

There are some close to the Prince who believe he had a duty at least to have discussed it. A relative goes so far as to say that his failure to do so was his big mistake.

'In his position he bloody well should have spoken to people because he had to think of the constitutional side as well as the private side. He had chosen Diana with both sides in mind, but equally he needed to think of the consequences for both, if it was going to go wrong.'

FIVE

The Fairytale Fiancée

'Such exciting news ...'
Camilla

The Prince of Wales proposed in early February, just after his annual skiing holiday with the Palmer-Tomkinsons in the Swiss resort of Klosters. He had phoned Diana from Switzerland and told her he had something to ask her when he got back the next day. Knowing full well what the question was likely to be, she laughed when he said, 'Will you marry me?' But was not slow to reply, 'Yeah, okay.'

Then she laughed some more. He was thrilled.

'You do realise that one day you will be Queen,' he said.

'Yes,' she said. 'I love you so much, I love you so much.'

According to Diana, he then coined that most memorable phrase, 'Whatever love is', and ran upstairs to telephone his mother with the news.

Diana rushed back home to tell her flatmates, and they screamed and howled and went for a drive around London with their secret. Meanwhile, the Prince rang a few of his closest confidants to let them know how he had got on, one of whom was Camilla Parker Bowles. Not because she was his lover – that had ended when he started to fall for Diana's charms – but because she was his best friend, as she is today. She had played a key role in helping and advising Charles in his relationship with Diana. She and Andrew had been at Balmoral in September, and he had taken Diana to spend weekends at their house in Wiltshire several times. They had been racing at Ludlow together from there, when Charles was riding his racehorse, Allibar; he had first taken Diana to see Highgrove while staying with the Parker Bowles; and he and Andrew had been hunting together on a couple of occasions, leaving Diana and Camilla together at home. Camilla had known he was planning to propose to Diana that day and, like so many others, was eager to have a progress report.

The Prince had also told Michael Colborne, secretary to the Prince of Wales's office, about his marriage plans the day after the proposal. He had come into Colborne's office in Buckingham Palace, sat down in an armchair and told Michael to shut the door.

'I've got something to tell you,' he said. 'Other than Her Majesty, and Papa and a few others, nobody knows. This is between you and me. I've asked Lady Diana to marry me, and she said yes straight away, but I've asked her to think about it and she's going to Australia to stay with the Shand Kydds. We've got a very busy period in front of us and we've got a tour coming up ...'

Michael was thunderstruck. 'Congratulations, sir,' he said.

The Prince smiled. 'Well, we'll see what happens.'

Michael Colborne knew the Prince better than most, and was to play an important part in Diana's early years at court. The two men had met aboard HMS *Norfolk* when the Prince was a sub-lieutenant and Colborne a non-commissioned officer, and he was one of the few people who were not afraid to tell the Prince what he thought. They struck up a good friendship and, when the Prince left the Navy and needed to set up an office in London, he invited Colborne to join it. Officially in charge of his financial affairs, he became the Prince's right-hand man, and remained with him for ten years, providing many valuable lessons about what life was like beyond the ocean of privilege in which the Prince swam. He was the only member of his staff at the time who was not in the public school, officer training college or Foreign Office mould, and he viewed all those who were with a healthy disdain. The Prince liked his straightforward approach. In offering Colborne the job he had made him promise that he would never change. 'If you don't agree with something, you say so,' he had said, and over the years Michael had spoken his mind. Charles didn't always like what he heard and became extremely angry on several memorable occasions, but it was an exceptionally warm relationship nonetheless.

That same day, Diana went to Australia for a holiday with her mother and stepfather, Peter Shand Kydd. As Charles put it, 'to think if it was all going to be too awful'. For three weeks they hid from the press and kept Diana's whereabouts such a guarded secret that even the Prince of Wales had difficulty getting through to her when he telephoned.

'I rang up on one occasion,' he said in a television interview after the engagement had been announced, and I said, "Can I speak?" And they said, "No, we're not taking any calls." So I said, "It's the Prince of Wales speaking." "How do I know it's the Prince of Wales?" was the reply. I said, "You don't. But I am," in a rage. And eventually ... I mean, I got the number because they were staying somewhere else. They said the phones were tapped or something – which I found highly unlikely ...'

When Diana arrived back in London the Prince told Michael Colborne that he wanted the biggest, smelliest bunch of flowers possible delivered to Diana's flat, and gave him a hand-written note to be delivered with the flowers. Knowing that her flat would be under siege, Colborne telephoned ahead to warn Diana that some flowers were on their way and a very sleepy voice answered the phone. 'Okay,' she said, 'I'll look out for them.'

Sergeant Ron Lewis was duly dispatched to deliver the flowers and note to Coleherne Court that morning, but Diana's memory of the incident was sadly different from the facts. Ten years later she said, 'I came back from Australia, someone knocks on my door – someone from his office with a bunch of flowers and I knew that they hadn't come from Charles because there was no note. It was just somebody being very tactful in the office.'

Michael didn't meet Diana until shortly after she returned from Australia, when the Prince asked him to look after her for the afternoon. She had been to watch Charles ride out his racehorse, Allibar, along the gallops at Lamborne early one morning. He was in training for a race at Chepstow the following weekend, and having completed seven furlongs, they were walking quietly home for breakfast, when Allibar had suddenly collapsed with a massive heart attack and died in his arms. The Prince refused to leave the horse until a vet arrived, and was so distraught that he couldn't drive. It was his detective, unusually, who drove them back to Highgrove.

It was obvious as soon as the car arrived back at the house that something was wrong, and Diana went into the kitchen with Michael to explain what had happened, while the Prince went off to be alone for a moment. But the treadmill of his life pauses for neither courtship nor grief. That afternoon, a helicopter arrived at two o'clock sharp to take him to an engagement in Swansea. Meanwhile Diana and Michael Colborne went into the drawing room for the first of many lengthy heart-to-hearts. Later, as they wandered around the garden together, Diana told him all about herself, her family, her parents' divorce, her father's illness and her stepmother. The relationship between them was cemented. He was struck by how young she was – she had puppy fat and quite ruddy cheeks – and how badly educated. He also realised how little discipline she had had in her life, and wondered if she had any idea what she was taking on. Twenty-seven years her senior, he felt like a father to her and became one of her closest friends in the Palace. They shared an office in the run-up to the wedding and he tried hard to help her understand and prepare her for what lay ahead, but knew it was going to be difficult.

'Is it all right if I call you Michael, like His Royal Highness does?' she asked, to which he said, 'Of course.'

'Will you call me "Diana"?'

'No,' said Colborne. 'Certainly not. I appreciate what you've just said, but if it all works out you're going to be the Princess of Wales and I'll have to call you Ma'am then, so we might as well start now.'

Two days later the engagement was officially announced and Diana was swept into the royal system. The idea was to rescue her from the media that had made her life so impossible. She had certainly found the attention extremely frightening at times and was pleased to be rescued. But the effect was to make her lonely and insecure. Buckingham Palace is not a home by any normal standards, and not even members of the Royal Family would describe it as such. Over 200 people work there, from the Lord Chamberlain to the telephone operators who man the switchboard. There was no alternative place to take her, but with hindsight, nobody – least of all her fiancé – had thought through the implications of removing a nineteen-year-old from a flat full of jolly giggly girls and setting her down in a suite of impersonal rooms with no one of her own age for company, and a fiancé who was always busy.

Diana told Andrew Morton that it was during the first week of her engagement that her bulimia started. One of Diana's flatmates said, 'She went to live at Buckingham Palace and then the tears started. This little thing got so thin. She wasn't happy, she was suddenly plunged into all this pressure and it was a nightmare for her.'

In fact she was initially treated not for bulimia but for anorexia nervosa, which was the same eating disorder that her sister Sarah had when she first met the Prince of Wales in 1977, shortly after breaking up with a previous boyfriend. Desperate to find ways of encouraging Sarah to eat, her family would refuse to let her speak to the Prince on the telephone unless she put on weight. In the end she sought professional help in a London nursing home, and she recovered.

The two conditions are similar in that the root cause of both disorders is an upset in childhood, but the trigger is some sort of emotional stress in the present, and teenage girls are the most commonly affected. Bulimia involves binge eating followed by self-induced vomiting, whereas anorexics go to ingenious lengths to avoid food. Secrecy is a key element, and also denial. Both result in dangerous weight loss, and a host of related medical problems, and both can be fatal.

Shortly before the engagement Diana started taking the contraceptive pill and, as so many women do, put on a lot of weight. Her reaction was to stop eating, and her weight loss was dramatic. The blue Harrods suit she wore for the engagement photograph was a size fourteen. In the five months to the wedding in July, her waist measurement fell from twenty-nine inches to twenty-three and a half, and it continued to diminish.

Diana's memory of the events as told to Andrew Morton are repeatedly at odds with what others remember. Her first night at Clarence House, the Queen Mother's London home, is a case in point. She told Morton that there was no one there to welcome her. In fact, she had dinner that evening with both the Queen Mother and the Prince of Wales, and the next day moved to Buckingham Palace, where she was greeted with open arms by many of the Queen's household who had known Diana and her family for years. A particular friend was Lady Susan Hussey, a lady-in-waiting, who had known Diana all her life, and in the coming months spent hour upon hour with her. She had a son almost exactly the same age as Diana, and was like a mother to her. She thought Diana was quite adorable, and was thrilled for the Prince whom she also adored. She and Diana went shopping for clothes together and prepared for the wedding and talked about all Diana's hopes and fears.

There were others in the Palace whom Diana loved in those early days and who were deeply fond of her. Lt.Col. Blair Stewart-Wilson, the deputy master of the household, was one, whom Diana kissed on the station platform on her wedding day to his utter confusion; Sir Johnny Johnston in the Lord Chamberlain's office another, and Sir William Heseltine, the Queen's deputy private secretary. She used to go into their offices and sit on their desks and talk to them, or invite them to lunch or to drinks. And she was forever popping in to see the ladies-in-waiting and the helpers who had been taken on to deal with everything that needed to be organised for the wedding. She would pop in to chat or to giggle about some extraordinary present that had arrived, or to show off clothes that she had bought. Her sister Jane was with her a lot, her mother too, and she frequently met friends for lunch. Yet she said she was unhappy and lonely.

One of Diana's fears at that time, which she often talked about, was the Prince's former girlfriends. Charles had made no secret to Diana of his previous love affairs, and possibly with his fatal compulsion to tell the whole truth when half would be kinder or more sensible, he told Diana everything. He had never experienced jealousy himself, and had no understanding of how a young girl might feel, knowing that he had loved other women, particularly those who were still friends that he saw regularly. It didn't cross his mind that there might be a problem. From her perspective, at nineteen with precious little education, no accomplishments, no sense of style and no knowledge of the world, they were grown up, clever, smart and sophisticated, and they made Diana feel desperately insecure. One of the Queen's ladies-in-waiting had also married a man much older than herself when she was nineteen, and she and others repeatedly told Diana she must forget about these other women. Yes, of course the Prince had had girlfriends and some quite serious relationships in his time, which at thirty-two years old was to be expected; and yes, they were older and more sophisticated than she was, but the Prince hadn't married any of *them* – the one he wanted to marry was *her*.

Jealousy and insecurity nonetheless gnawed away at her. She was even jealous of the Prince's relationship with his mother. He put letters and memos that came from the Queen into a safe to ensure no one could copy or steal them. He had always done it as a matter of course, but Diana was suspicious that the Queen was writing about her and that Charles was deliberately keeping it from her. 'Why don't you just ask me about the things that are worrying you?' Charles would say, but she never would. When she arrived at Clarence House there was a letter waiting on her bed from Camilla Parker Bowles. It was dated two days previously and said, 'Such exciting news about the engagement. Do let's have lunch soon when the Prince of Wales goes to Australia and New Zealand. He's going to be away for three weeks. I'd love to see the ring. Lots of love, Camilla.' It was a friendly note sent with the best of intentions. She and Diana had seen a lot of each other during the previous few months, and Camilla thought they were friends. She thought Diana was young, but good fun, as most of his friends did.

Diana told Andrew Morton she thought 'Wow' and organised

lunch, 'bearing in mind that I was so immature, I didn't know about jealousy or depressions or anything like that ... So we had lunch. Very tricky indeed. She said, "You are not going to hunt, are you?" I said, "On what?" She said, "Horse. You are not going to hunt when you go and live at Highgrove, are you?" I said, "No." She said, "I just wanted to know," and I thought as far as she was concerned that was her communication route. Still too immature to understand all the messages coming my way.'

Camilla remembers the lunch as being entirely friendly. Diana was extremely excited, showed off her ring with glee.

Camilla had been one of the girlfriends the Prince of Wales had told Diana about, and Diana had made him give her a solemn promise that there was no longer anyone else in his life, and that there would never be any other women in his life. He had happily given his promise on both counts. His mistake was thinking this was all he needed to say. He was telling the truth – he intended to be entirely monogamous – and as a man of honour, he expected Diana to accept his word as the truth. Similarly, as a man of honour, when Diana asked him whether he still loved Camilla he said 'yes', which was also the truth. Camilla was very special to him, but so were a number of other women. He loved and still loves them all, and no doubt always will.

The Prince of Wales is a thinker and a philosopher, a spiritual and religious man, and love to him bears little relationship to the two-dimensional 'love' discussed on the pages of romantic novels and women's magazines. This is why he used that dreadful phrase 'whatever love means' when asked by a television reporter about his feelings for Diana on the day of his engagement. He is too honest for his own good; he can't give the simple answer that everyone is waiting for, because for him the matter is not simple.

It didn't occur to him that a white lie would have been kinder. He didn't put himself into Diana's position, didn't ask himself how this nineteen-year-old girl might be feeling or whether she might need greater reassurance. Most young people are intrinsically jealous, and the notion that someone can love more than one person without diminishing their feelings for another only comes with age and experience. For an intelligent man, there are astonishing gaps in his awareness.

What he didn't realise at the time was that Diana was a particularly vulnerable nineteen-year-old, with an abnormally pronounced sense of suspicion and insecurity, and a strong feeling that people were conspiring against her. This had not been apparent during their courtship, but immediately after the engagement was announced the Prince sensed a change in Diana which he didn't understand. Where before she had been so happy and easygoing, she became moody and wilful. She displayed a terrible temper, which he had never seen before; it came from nowhere, along with hysterical tears, and could be gone as quickly as it came. She suddenly turned against people she had appeared to like and said they were out to get her, to undermine her, or spy on her.

He was not the only one to notice the change and to be worried about her. But Charles put it down to nerves and the stress she had been under during the past few months, which he assumed would all disappear once the wedding was behind them.

Diana hated being left alone. She wanted the Prince to be with her all the time and couldn't understand why his work had to take precedence over their being together. His days then, as now, were a relentless round of public engagements, meetings, paper work and sporting commitments from early in the morning until late at night, often taking him out of London. Almost immediately after the engagement was announced, he left on a tour of Australia, which had been fixed long before, and there was a very tearful and loving farewell at the airport.

During Charles's various absences Diana was looked after by whichever members of his staff were not accompanying him. The Prince's private secretary at that time was the Hon. Edward Adeane, a brilliant barrister, Eton and Cambridge educated, whose father and grandfather had been private secretaries before him. The Prince's assistant private secretary, Francis Cornish, came from the Foreign Office. His predecessor, Oliver Everett, was also ex-Foreign

Office and had returned there in 1980, but was invited back specifically to help Diana before the wedding, and afterwards became her official private secretary. It was an intellectually high-powered team, who were all at least twice her age. Sympathetic as they might have been, and flattered by her charm and giggly girlishness, they had no idea of how to handle someone so young, whose experience and education were so severely limited. They were astonished when, for example, she asked where Dorset was, or confessed she didn't know the capital of Australia.

Diana had no inhibitions about her ignorance and laughed such moments off carelessly, but it was an awkward situation for them all. Socially, she had much in common with the private secretaries, but she found their intellect threatening. She was more comfortable with Michael Colborne, a former grammar school boy, whose office she shared. He could see how lost she was and would spend hours talking to her, which was all she wanted to do. The Prince's staff were not prepared for this. They would never have expected to sit and idly chatter with the Prince, and found it hard to do so with Diana. He was the Boss, and the relationship between employer and employees was always strictly professional. They expected it to be the same with Lady Diana Spencer.

But Diana was scarcely more than a child. She had never employed anyone in her life. She had never had much of a job, never worked in an office. She had no idea what was expected of her and no idea of what she was taking on in marrying into the Royal Family. Her concept of what lay before her was little more than a romantic notion.

Like thousands of girls of a similar age, who devoured Barbara Cartland novels and soap operas on television, she had no interest in a career. All she wanted was to be loved, looked after, have babies and live happily ever after. She thought she had found a man who would provide all of this and more. In the excitement and thrill of the chase she had visualised none of the reality.

She could be forgiven. There had been no Princess of Wales for over seventy years – when the future George V was created Prince of Wales in 1901 and his wife, Princess May of Teck, became Princess

– and there was no job specification to guide either Diana or her courtiers. There was no one she could consult who had experience of her predicament. No commoner had married into the Royal Family at such a senior level this century, not even the Queen Mother. Her husband became George VI, but at the time of their marriage he was Duke of York, and only second in line to the throne.

Several people did try to give Diana some help, Michael Colborne and Susan Hussey amongst them, but Diana was not altogether receptive. She didn't want to be told what to do and when. In the past when she had not wanted to do something, with the indulgence of divorced parents, she had never been coerced. Accepting the discipline of royal life did not come easily.

The Family and their courtiers all took what they did so much for granted, they assumed that, being a Spencer, Diana would have no problems and would know what to expect. She was, after all, a member of one of the most aristocratic families in Britain and had lived from the age of thirteen in one of the most traditionally run stately homes in England. Her brother is the Queen's godson, one of her sisters is the Duke of Kent's goddaughter. Her father had been equerry to the Queen. Both her grandmothers had been ladies-in-waiting to the Queen Mother; and both the Spencers and the Fermoys had been close friends of the Royal Family for several generations. It was not an unreasonable assumption that Diana would know what royal life was all about. That was partly why she had seemed so tailor-made for the role. But she was lost, and no one realised.

When she went to spend the weekend at Royal Lodge at Windsor, for example, no one had thought to tell her that if she wanted to go out for a walk in the Great Park she had to tell someone where she was going. She returned to find the whole place in turmoil, alarms going and her policeman on the verge of heart failure. The following Monday morning she told Colborne what had happened and said she didn't know how she was going to cope.

'This is going to be your life,' he said. 'You're never going to be on your own again. And you're going to change. In four to five years you're going to be an absolute bitch, not through any fault of your own, but because of the circumstances in which you live. If you want four boiled eggs for breakfast, you'll have them. If you want the car brought round to the front door a minute ago, you'll have it. It's going to change you. Your life is going to be organised. You open your diary now and you can put down Trooping the Colour, the Cenotaph service, Cowes Week, the Ascots. You can write your diary for five years ahead, ten years, twenty years.'

Gradually the truth began to dawn and Diana recognised that what he was saying was true, and from that moment she began to look increasingly apprehensive. But she was on a giant roller coaster with the wedding just weeks away and preparations to be made before then. There were also presents to be acknowledged and people thanked. They were pouring into Michael Colborne's office from all over the world, and Diana wrote most of the thank you letters herself, in her distinctive large, rounded hand.

One Friday afternoon, about two weeks before the wedding, a package was delivered to the Privy Purse door, which the footman brought up to Michael Colborne's office. He opened it and found a number of things he had ordered on the Prince's behalf to give as gifts to various friends. The Prince has always been a great giver of presents, particularly jewellery, as a means of thanking people. Amongst various pieces, one of which was for Dale, Lady Tryon, and another for Lady Susan Keswick, and another for Lady Cecil Cameron – all good friends – was a bracelet for Camilla Parker Bowles. It was a gold chain with a blue enamel plate, engraved with the initials GF. They stood for Girl Friday, which was the Prince's nickname for Camilla.

As Colborne was examining the contents, the buzzer went, calling him into Edward Adeane's office. He left the package on his desk and went next door. While he was out of the room Diana came in and, suspicious of everyone, must have had a look through the things on Colborne's desk. She saw everything that came into the office, and he had no reason to hide this or anything else from her. As far as he was concerned this bracelet held no special significance. Camilla, like a number of the Prince's other very close friends, had been an emotional mainstay during his bachelor years, and given him house-space on innumerable occasions, as well as advice and help during his courtship. He wanted to thank them, and saw each of them individually to hand over their presents and say goodbye to the bachelor life they had all supported him through in one way and another.

Colborne finished his conversation with Adeane and, instead of going straight back to his desk, went into the main office. Adeane, suddenly remembering there was something more he wanted to say, went into Colborne's office, thinking he would find him there, and was almost knocked clean off his feet by Diana rushing out at top speed.

'What on earth have you done to Lady Diana?' he said when he finally found Colborne. 'She nearly bowled me over and was really upset.'

When Colborne got back to his office he realised what had happened. The package had been opened up and the lid was off the box with the bracelet inside. He didn't see Diana again until Monday morning, when she confessed to having had a look at what was on his desk, but said nothing more about it. Her account of that incident appeared in *Diana – Her True Story*, but like so much of the book, with a twist that gave it a different interpretation.

'Anyway, somebody in his office told me that my husband had had a bracelet made for her which she wears to this day. It's a gold chain bracelet with a blue enamel disc. It's got "G and F" entwined in it, "Gladys" and "Fred" – they were their nicknames. I walked into this man's office one day and said: "Oh, what's in that parcel?" He said: "Oh, you shouldn't look at that." I said: "Well, I'm going to look at it." I opened it and there was a bracelet and I said: "I know where this is going." I was devastated. This was about two weeks before we got married. He said: "Well, he's going to give it to her tonight." So rage, rage, rage! "Why can't you be honest with me?" But, no, he cut me absolutely dead. It's as if he had made his decision, and if it wasn't going to work, it wasn't going to work. He'd found the virgin, the sacrificial lamb, and in a way he was obsessed with

83

me. But it was hot and cold, hot and cold. You never knew what mood it was going to be, up and down, up and down.'

Diana later harboured another destructive fantasy about the Prince and Camilla, which ate away at her. She became convinced about ten years after their marriage that Charles and Camilla had slept together in Buckingham Palace two nights before the wedding, which took place on Wednesday 29 July. On the Monday night the Queen had given a dinner party for Diana's mother and father with their respective spouses, and family and close friends. That was followed by a huge reception and dance, to which Camilla and her husband, also her sister Annabel and her husband, Simon Elliot, were all invited. The ball went on until the small hours of the morning, when the Royal Family all had to see their guests, including most of the crowned heads of Europe, into coaches to take them to Windsor Castle, where they were staying, as there was insufficient room at Buckingham Palace. When the last coach had gone, Charles and Diana climbed into their beds in their separate suites of rooms at Buckingham Palace, both exhausted.

The Tuesday night is the only one when Diana was sleeping else-where, and when it might have been possible, in theory, for Charles to have seen Camilla. Diana stayed at Clarence House, in keeping with the tradition of not seeing the groom the night before the wedding, and he spent the evening along with the rest of the Royal Family and half a million of the public at a fantastic fireworks display in Hyde Park. The display was a copy of celebrations held two hundred years earlier for the Peace of Aix-la-Chapelle. Rockets whizzed into the air, multi-coloured stars burst over the city's skyline, the massed bands of the household musicians struck up, and the Morrison Orpheus Choir and the Choir of the Welsh Guards burst into song. Above the noise of it all, the Royal Horse Artillery fired salvoes from the guns of the King's Troop.

It was an extraordinary night of happiness and celebration. Beacons were alight and parties in full swing all over the country. Millions of people had arrived in the capital in preparation; hundreds had been camping along the route to St Paul's Cathedral for days, and had come equipped with sleeping bags and supplies of sandwiches, beer and Champagne. Strangers talked to strangers, there was no ugliness, no crime, and real life was suspended for a while. The weather was balmy, and the excitement was electrifying. It was to be the wedding of the decade, a glorious musical extravaganza, a gathering of most of the Kings and Queens of Europe, Africa, the Middle East and Asia, along with 160 foreign presidents and prime ministers. It truly was, as the Archbishop of Canterbury declared, 'the stuff of which fairy tales are made'.

Once the fireworks were over, the Prince went home to Buckingham Palace in a highly emotional state for his last night as a single man, to contemplate the enormity and nagging uncertainty of the step he was about to take in the morning. He sat up chatting for a while to Lady Susan Hussey, whose rooms were adjacent to his own. She had been a friend, confidante, shoulder to cry on and tower of strength to him for many years and had known him since he was twelve years old, when she became a lady-in-waiting to the Queen. She knew the whole family extremely well and there was scarcely a secret Charles had not shared with her. Soon after midnight, they said goodnight and went to their beds.

About half an hour later, Lady Susan heard a knock at her door. It was the Prince saying he couldn't sleep. She had not been able to sleep either, and so they went into her sitting room and, dressed in their night clothes, stood looking from her window down on the Mall, at all the activity going on below, and the music and the excitement, with tears streaming down both their faces. Some time after 2 a.m. she insisted he go to bed or he would be hopeless in the morning, and persuaded him to take an Aspirin to help him sleep. Camilla was a long way away.

SIX

The Honeymoon Period

'I seem to do nothing but collect flowers
these days; I know my role.'
Charles

With hindsight, the plans for the honeymoon could not have been worse. The Prince should have taken Diana to some sun-drenched island with no memories of his past, no royal connections, and no obligations to entertain others or be on duty in any way. After the stress and scrutiny they had both been under in the months leading up to the wedding, they needed time together on their own, to get to know each other better, to have some fun doing things they both enjoyed, and discover what marriage and sharing your life with someone else was all about.

Instead it was an inauspicious beginning. They spent three nights at Broadlands, Lord Mountbatten's former estate in Hampshire, now owned by his grandson, Norton Romsey, and his wife Penny. The Romseys had moved out to give them some privacy, but it was where Charles had taken most of his previous girlfriends, and by the second night, according to Diana, he had buried himself in the first of seven Laurens van der Post novels he had brought with him. Having the time to sit and read was a pleasure and a luxury for the Prince, but for Diana, who was not a great reader, it was a monumental slight. She concluded he was more interested in his books than in her. To make matters worse, when she did have his attention, he talked about what he had read: 'He read them and we had to analyse them over lunch every day.'

From Broadlands they flew to Gibraltar to join the royal yacht for a couple of weeks in the Mediterranean and Aegean seas, where they sailed, swam and sunbathed, and wrote warm letters of thanks to their staff and everyone who had helped make their wedding day such a huge success. Both of them wrote about their happiness at being together, although the Prince admitted that 'Diana dashes about chatting up all the sailors and the cooks in the galley, while I sit hermit-like on the verandah deck, sunk with pure joy into one of Laurens van der Post's books.'

But with twenty-one naval officers and a crew of 256 men, a valet, a private secretary and an equerry, it was hardly the romantic cruise either of them might have hoped for. It was a grave disappointment and a tough introduction for Diana to the very public way members of the Royal Family have to live their lives if they are not to cause offence to all and sundry. They were hardly ever alone. When they weren't entertaining dignitaries, including the President of Egypt, Anwar Sadat, and his wife in Port Said, the candle-lit dinner they sat down to at night was shared with the officers and a band of the Royal Marines. Had they borrowed some friend's private yacht things might have been different, but if a member of the family is on board *Britannia*, they cannot visit foreign soil without being met and greeted by local dignitaries. Similarly, when they travel around Britain, unless a visit is entirely private, the local Lord-Lieutenants, mayors and councillors expect to be involved when members of the Family come on to their patch.

'By then,' Diana told Morton, 'the bulimia was appalling, absolutely appalling. It was rife, four times a day on the yacht. Anything I could find I would gobble up and be sick two minutes later – very tired. So of course, that slightly got the mood swings going in the sense that one minute one would be happy, next blubbing one's eyes out.'

There were two particular incidents which Diana remembered very clearly: one when a photograph of Camilla fell out of the Prince's diary, and the second when, dressed for a white-tie dinner with the Sadats, the Prince wore a pair of gold cufflinks, engraved with interwoven Cs. 'Got it in one,' said Diana. 'Knew exactly.

"Camilla gave you those, didn't she?" He said: "Yes, so what's wrong? They're a present from a friend." And, boy, did we have a row. Jealousy, total jealousy ...'

Their rows were usually very one-sided. Diana screamed and shouted and burst into tears. The Prince – though perfectly capable of losing his temper and shouting at the people who work for him and even throwing ornaments – had never experienced anyone shouting at him before, with the possible exception of his father, and was completely nonplussed. Her rage was quite terrifying, and he soon discovered that when she was in this condition, nothing he could say appeared to calm her. Indeed, trying to argue with her or justify himself only made matters worse. On these occasions he refused to engage, which made her even more furious.

The third and final stage of the honeymoon was spent at Balmoral with the in-laws and the rest of the Royal Family, which congregates there traditionally between August and October. Once again, not the most sensitive way to treat a young bride; and for Diana, it was another brutal introduction to the life she had signed up for without fully understanding what marriage to the Prince of Wales and to the job would really mean. Although they were not staying with the Queen, they dined with her and the rest of the family, also the lady-in-waiting and equerry, who always eat with the family, several times a week. This was either at the castle, when official guests like the Prime Minister came to stay, or more often in one of the lodges on the estate, built by Prince Albert, Queen Victoria's husband, for deer stalking. In a rare show of informality, they pack food for a barbecue into the cars and, dressed in slacks or jeans, and with the Queen in a tweed skirt, take off with no servants to a different lodge each night for supper. The Queen's job is to lay and then clear the table, the Duke of Edinburgh is the cook, and the Prince of Wales and the equerry between them traditionally hand round the drinks.

Balmoral is probably the Prince's favourite place in all the world. It's the one place where he can be entirely on his own – or rather, where police presence is minimal – where he can walk for miles without seeing another human being, and where he can indulge his passion for stalking and fishing, or sitting on a craggy hillside with his sketch pad and watercolours. He hoped Diana would share his enthusiasm, as she had seemed to the summer before. Then, she had joined in. She had appeared thoroughly to enjoy the place, which was one of the things that so endeared her to him and made him feel they were so compatible. But now she had hated it. Hated the countryside and hated the Royal Family's obsession with horses and dogs. She hated the rain that poured down remorselessly, and the feeling that the Prince was avoiding intimate contact. The anorexia had entirely taken hold and she was still suffering terrible mood swings and losing weight at an alarming rate. The Prince had no idea what the problem was. He couldn't understand why she wouldn't eat and did everything to try and tempt her. 'Come on, Darling,' he would say, 'try just a little bit of this, it's delicious.'

If she was disappointed by her first taste of marriage, so was he. He was a romantic. He had had visions of his life being enhanced by a wife. She would be a friend and confidante, boost his morale, massage his ego, share his bed and fit comfortably into his life. What he imagined, however, like many men perhaps, was that all this would happen without him having to change one iota of his routine.

Diana had an equally romantic view of matrimony. She had visions of a man who would devote himself to her and want to spend every minute by her side, who would love and cherish her, give her beautiful children and be there to protect and look after her, to give her confidence and a secure family unit. Both their expectations were equally unrealistic. They had married the wrong person to give them even a fraction of what they needed.

At Balmoral this conflict was polarised. Charles didn't alter the routine of his days to accommodate his wife. He slipped straight into the Balmoral lifestyle that he had adored since childhood, imagining that Diana would want to join in. But now that she was married, she wanted no part in any of it. His friends came to stay, as they always had done, and he went off for hours at a time engaged in one of his solitary or sporting pursuits. Diana, younger than his friends by far and longing to have her husband to herself, quickly became cross and bored, and her friends, summoned to Balmoral to keep her company and try to cheer her up, failed to do any good.

Amongst those asked to help was Michael Colborne, who was solid and dependable and enormously fond of both Charles and Diana. He was enjoying a weekend at home when the phone rang on the Saturday night and the Prince said he wanted him to take the sleeper train from King's Cross the next night to Aberdeen, where a car would meet him and take him to Craigowan Lodge, the small house on the estate where the Prince and Princess were staying. 'I will be out stalking that day,' he said, 'but I will see you before I go and I'd like you to spend the day with the Princess.'

On Monday morning he was sitting in the kitchen at Craigowan, eating a hearty breakfast which the chef had just prepared for him, when the Prince arrived and thanked him for coming. 'I'll see you when I get back,' he said, with no further explanation, and with that disappeared for the day along with his house guest, Norton Romsey.

A little later Penny Romsey came into the room and, seeing Michael said, 'What are you doing up here? Are you working today?'

Colborne explained that the Prince of Wales had asked him to come up. 'I think I'm going to spend the day with the Princess of Wales.'

'Oh, that's strange,' said Lady Romsey. 'The Princess and I were going out for a walk in a minute.'

A moment later Diana put her head round the door and, without a word to Penny Romsey, said, 'Oh, Michael, come on.' He followed her down the corridor into the drawing room. 'Did you have a good journey up?' she asked, but wouldn't look at him. He sensed she didn't really want to talk. He had learnt long ago with the Prince that sometimes he would not want to talk, often for very long stretches, and had become accustomed to sitting in silence. So he was not uncomfortable sitting in the room with the Princess saying nothing, and this was how they sat for about fifteen minutes. Then suddenly she began to cry, and through the tears she told him how unhappy she was, how she hated Balmoral, hated stalking, hated the rain.

Then she fell silent, and so they sat until she began again; pacing around the room this time, angrily kicking the furniture and raging furiously against everything and everybody – the place, the Royal Family, the friends, the weeks she was going to be stuck there, the boredom, the things they wanted her to do. Nothing he could say seemed to help, and then she stopped as suddenly as she had started. And so the day passed, with tears, anger and brooding silence, from ten to nine in the morning until five past four in the afternoon. He sat and watched the hands of a large clock on the wall creep slowly forward, with a plate of sandwiches brought in at lunchtime the only distraction. At five past four the Princess suddenly said, 'I'm going upstairs,' and left the room.

Shocked, distressed and utterly drained, Michael Colborne borrowed a pair of wellington boots, and despite the pouring rain, which had not let up all day, took himself off for a long walk. When he returned, there was a note from the Prince saying he wanted to see him. How had he got on? he wanted to know.

'I haven't had a very good day, sir,' said Colborne.

'I understand,' said the Prince. 'I'll see you later.'

At eight o'clock that evening they were due to drive to Aberdeen to board the royal train. The Prince had a regimental engagement in Aldershot the following day. At eight o'clock sharp Colborne, the Prince's detective, John Maclean, and valet, Ken Stronach, were standing about on the gravel outside the front door of the house, waiting for the Prince. A brand new Range Rover which had been delivered that morning was packed and ready to go. It was pitch dark outside and a single lamp hung over the door.

As they stood by the car they could hear the Prince and Princess having a fearsome row on the other side of the closed door. All of a sudden the door flew open, the Prince came shooting out, said, 'Michael!' and threw something at him. It was Diana's wedding ring, made of twenty-two carat Welsh gold, from the same nugget used to make wedding rings for the Queen Mother, the Queen, Princess Margaret and Princess Anne. By some miracle Colborne caught it before it vanished into the gravel. Diana had become so thin it no longer fitted and she wanted him to take it back to London to be made smaller.

They began to get into the car. The Prince always drives with his detective by his side. 'Sit in the front, Michael,' said the Prince. Michael ignored him purposefully and climbed into the back. They travelled down the winding road to Crathie Church in absolute silence. When they reached the main road the Prince began to attack Colborne verbally. He called him all the names under the sun because the new Range Rover was not exactly as he had specified. He had not wanted carpet in the back because he wanted to be able to put deer carcasses there, and Michael hadn't taken any notice of what he had asked. In fact, Colborne had written the Prince a note telling him that, in response to his request, Range Rover had given him a special carpet with press-studs, so that it could be very easily removed. It was clear that the Prince had not read the note. All the way to Aberdeen, the Prince laid into Colborne for one failing after another. Having just had a bloody day with his wife, Michael was not prepared to engage. He simply stared out of the window until they drove on to the station platform soon after nine o'clock. On board the train he ordered himself a treble gin and tonic.

It had not yet arrived when there was a bellow from down the corridor. 'Michael!' He ambled slowly down the train in no great hurry for once to join the Prince of Wales. The Prince offered him a drink. 'Tonight, Michael,' he said, 'you displayed the best traditions of the silent service. You didn't say a word.'

'Firstly,' said Colborne, 'you never gave me a chance to say anything because you just went on and on. And secondly, if you had read your notes you would understand that the press-studs in the back can be taken out by anyone. They are very simple to do.'

'I hear you've had a rough day,' said the Prince.

'Yes,' said Michael, 'I've had an awful day.'

For the next five hours or more, they talked about Charles's marriage to Diana. The Prince was baffled and despondent, and quite at a loss to know what had gone wrong or how to cope.

Diana came to London soon afterwards. 'All the analysts and

psychiatrists you could ever dream of came plodding in trying to sort me out. Put me on high doses of Valium and everything else. But the Diana that was still very much there had decided it was just time; patience and adapting were all that were needed. It was me telling them what I needed. They were telling me "pills"! That was going to keep them happy – they could go to bed at night and sleep, knowing the Princess of Wales wasn't going to stab anyone.'

Back in London, however, they had no home of their own to go to – another thing not properly or sensitively thought through. The Prince had bought Highgrove in 1980 but the new décor had not been completely finished and, at that stage, his office was at Buckingham Palace and all his work was done from London. Apartments in Kensington Palace had been earmarked but they were not ready until shortly before William was born the following year. And so Charles and Diana moved into the Prince's bachelor apartment at the top of Buckingham Palace. He had no household staff of his own, no butler, no footman, or chef: living in his mother's house he had not needed them. For nearly nine months of marriage, therefore, they were dependent upon the Queen. It was rather like living in a hotel above the office, with the in-laws along the corridor. It wasn't a home, and for Diana, who had been used to her own flat, where she did everything herself and was surrounded by her own things and furnishings, it wasn't a real life. She didn't need to shop or cook or even instruct the chef or talk to the housekeeper, and although there was a lot to learn and plenty going on, she felt very bored and lonely.

No one had thought through what her public role would be. All these things which seem so obvious are perhaps only obvious with the benefit of hindsight. No one had considered how she might be affected by the public's adulation, and what demands it would put upon her, although it is true to say that no one expected the adulation to continue beyond the wedding. No one was prepared for the extraordinary way in which her popularity grew over the years, not even Fleet Street. No one had reckoned on her star quality, and her unique ability to touch the hearts and minds of the people she spoke to in the crowds. She was a natural from her very first tour in October, which, fittingly, was to Wales. The Prince proudly presented her to the principality. It was a baptism by fire for both Diana and her newly appointed and only full-time lady-in-waiting, Anne Beckwith-Smith. But the people of Wales were knocked out by the Princess, and Charles was delighted.

Diana had been told how to cope if someone in the crowd grabbed or attacked her, but she had no idea about the simple logistics of accompanying her husband. How, for example, would the Prince and Princess walk into a room together? Would she walk beside or behind her husband? The Prince of Wales had had a mother, father and grandmother to watch over the years, and had grown up with the cameras and the crowds; but even he at almost thirty-three was unsure of his role in life. Diana came to it completely cold, and at twenty had to make up the rules as she went along. Charles was very worried about how she would cope with the crowds and the cameras, particularly given her state of health, and he was very encouraging in the early days when, sick with fear, she had to be cajoled out of the car at each stop.

But it was virgin territory, and no one knew quite what a modern day Princess of Wales should do. If anyone had thought to try and help, the title HRH had elevated Diana to such a level of seniority that friendly words of advice, unless she was in a particularly receptive mood, were difficult to deliver. Certain members of the Queen's household did try to make suggestions, but Diana was suspicious of everyone's motives.

Like every member of the Royal Family Charles was accustomed to being the star and the focus of attention at home as well as out and about. They operate in isolation from one another and they don't like being upstaged by anyone else. They now have what is called a Way Ahead Group, which the Duke of Edinburgh suggested. Senior members of the family get together with their private secretaries to discuss what they are all doing, so they don't double up, but this is an innovation. There is no mutual support, no thrashing out of ideas, no discussing problems, no real interest in one another's work, and no handing out of praise. Because of who they are and how they have been brought up, surrounded by deferential courtiers and deferential friends, they are all intrin-sically selfish. They are also all fundamentally jealous of one another's success. One of the accepted wisdoms passed on to new members of the household is that they should never try to get members of the Royal Family to appear at the same event. Apart from the traditional events like Trooping the Colour and the remembrance ceremony at the Cenotaph, they very seldom appear together.

As his wife, Diana was the Prince's equal, but he was very set in his ways and it didn't come easily to have to consider someone else when planning his day. Diana, in her youthful naiveté, was equally unprepared to accommodate someone else's needs. She had no better idea of what the give and take of married life involved than he did. Her vague, traditional vision of marriage was gleaned mostly from novels and magazines and, in her determination to become Charles's wife, she had not wanted to see or be told that the Prince was by no means a normal man. She could never have done the cooking, shopping and ironing, and been the epicentre of his existence. He was already committed from birth to a life of courtiers, butlers, valets and, above all, duty. He belonged to his country, to the people who would one day be his subjects, who already felt an ownership of him in some small way, and the right to his time. His life was not his own to give wholeheartedly to any woman, and could never have accommodated the kind of marriage Diana, in her girlish, idealistic way, dreamed of.

She didn't understand why he flirted so brazenly with danger, worked himself so hard, or in idle moments took such pleasure in being entirely by himself, away from everyone. She wasn't interested in his needs. She wanted him to pay attention to her one hundred per cent of the time, and couldn't bear it if he was wrapped up in a book, even if he was by her side the while.

Yet the marriage was not all disaster. There were certainly occasions when they had a wonderful time together, and made each other roar with laughter, and their happiness was a pleasure to see.

There were moments of pure unalloyed joy when she was feeling happy, and some very vigorous and enthusiastic sex. Their mutual love of Highgrove in the very early years, and of William and Harry, brought them significantly closer for a while. Friends remember going to lunches with them at Kensington Palace where they would giggle and joke throughout. They remember arriving to go to the theatre with them in the evening, and Diana saying to Charles, 'Come on, let's go and say goodnight to the children – I'll race you to the top of the stairs!' The pair of them would run up the stairs and collapse at the top in a heap of laughter.

But it was all froth. There was never any depth to the relationship or to their understanding of each other. Diana couldn't be the soul mate he wanted in a wife. She didn't share his enthusiasm for books or horses or gardening, or opera or any of the dozens of things which she had pretended to be so interested in at the outset. She was not the one to cure the loneliness and uncertainty of his life, or give him the unconditional love and support and reassurance he needed to make him a confident and happy man – because she desperately needed all of those things herself. Diana was yet another example in the long list of characters he had misjudged.

Charles is no great intellectual, and some people would say he doesn't always use the intellect he has to full capacity, but he does know a huge amount about a vast number of different subjects. He reads extensively, listens to experts in every field and soaks up what he hears. He has a curiosity about everything that goes on around him. Diana had none of that, and if they had had more time together before Charles was rushed into becoming engaged, he might have discovered this.

What Diana did have was an extraordinary instinct for what made people tick; she always knew what to say to make them feel on top of the world, and a warmth and compassion and sense of fun. She was also extremely sexy. It was an irresistible combination for a brief encounter, as so many of the people who fell under her spell discovered, but not for life. The pity was that the Prince of Wales did not discover this until the ring was on her finger.

t Diana's funeral, nothing was
more heartbreaking than the
and-written note to 'Mummy'.

It was the Duke of Edinburgh
who settled the argument
between the Prince of Wales and
Charles Spencer about who
should walk behind Diana's
cortege. In the end, they all did.

Diana and Charles met for the very first time on a shoot at Althorp in November 1977.

To begin with Diana was perfectly friendly towards Camilla. But later, to use Camilla's words, 'Diana went Tonto'.

Diana outside the kindergarten where she worked. The photograph caused a huge stir, and made Diana realise just how effectively she could use the cameras.

Charles couldn't believe his luck. Here was a gorgeous, funny, delightful girl whom everyone seemed to adore and approve of, and she loved *him*.

'Here is the stuff of which fairytales are made,' declared the Archbishop of Canterbury as he made them man and wife. The crowds basked in the romance of it all, but the fairytale was already in question.

In retrospect, Balmoral was not the best place to choose for such a large part of the honeymoon.

Diana's first walkabout in Wales, in October 1981. Although Charles was proud of the way she handled the crowds and the cameras, it was the first time he had had to share the limelight, and it was uncomfortable for him.

Leaving hospital with Prince William, June 1982. For Diana, already debilitated with anorexia, it was the start of crippling post-natal depression.

Diana made Charle[s] laugh and when times were good, they were very, very good – as they were on a visit to Pinewood film studios when she hi[t] him over the head with a fake bottle.

Mother and son, sovereign and heir. There is great love, but no real communication.

An exuberant Diana running to win the mothers' race at William and Harry's school sports day.

harles and Camilla
arker Bowles in 1979.
he had been his first
al love and his best
iend. There was an
timacy and an easiness
hich made them enjoy
ich other's company.

Diana with James
Hewitt in 1987. Their
affair lasted many
years and she admitted
she had adored him,
but he let her down.
He felt that Diana had
discarded him.

The family at Highgrove, in the wild flower
meadow Charles created. They were already
leading separate lives, but put on a show of
togetherness for the sake of the children, the
country and the cameras.

In marrying, the Prince would have to share the stage, on which he had been a solo player for all his adult life, with his bride, and initially he was proud to do so, and delighted by the public's enthusiasm. In Wales thousands upon thousands of people turned out to catch a glimpse of her, undaunted by the pouring rain, and he was touched. He was even quite amused when people handed him bunches of flowers to give to his wife. 'I seem to do nothing but collect flowers these days,' he said. 'I know my role.'

What he had not bargained on, however, was this role becoming permanent. As time passed, it became increasingly obvious that in their enthusiasm for Diana, the public was losing interest in him. It had been amusing for three days in Wales but when he realised that this was his future, always to be eclipsed by his wife – albeit at that time quite unintentionally – he became distinctly humourless. The Princess of Wales was supposed to be his consort, not his leading lady.

The public's fascination with Diana grew and grew. She was photogenic, she began to wear glamorous clothes and dazzling jewellery. Gone were the borrowed skirts that had made everyone laugh and love her so much in the early days. She was young and modern, and she was a Princess who loved to spend money and dress the part. Newspapers sold millions more copies than usual if they had a photograph of Diana on the front page, so the pressure was on to get those pictures. Photographers besieged her wherever she went; long lenses sought her out even in what she had assumed was the privacy of her own home. There was no distinction between the public and private Princess. They even followed her to a private beach on the island of Eleuthera in the Bahamas where, unknown to her, they took photographs of her five months pregnant wearing a bikini. And with the photographs went commentary, acres of newsprint devoted to analysing every look and gesture she made, to speculating on her state of health, or possible pregnancy, her hairstyle, her clothes and which designer was in the ascendant. The Prince was scarcely mentioned and when he was it was usually to congratulate Diana on having successfully changed his hairstyle or his wardrobe.

When he delivered speeches on matters which he thought important and had put time and effort into preparing, his words were
largely dismissed, and the focus fell instead on his wife. Diana had
not sought the coverage and at that time was quite intimidated by
the attentions of the press; but at the same time she loved to read
about herself in the newspapers, and as the media obsession with her
grew, so too did her obsession with the media.

In November 1981, Diana announced she was pregnant and they
were both thrilled. The Prince rang all his friends, including Camilla
Parker Bowles, to tell them the good news. He was overjoyed, not
because Diana might be carrying his heir but because for years he
had longed for children, as his friends well knew. He had lots of
godchildren, whom he loved visiting and playing with, and whenever friends of his had babies he always wrote effusive letters. He
had heard the news about one baby while he was confined to his
bunk on board HMS *Minerva*.

'For some time I *entirely* forgot that I was meant to be feeling sick
and had a headache, and leapt about in my bunk with joy and
squeaks feeling incredibly happy for you both ... By the time you
receive this I expect you will be out of hospital and beginning to
wonder how on earth you're going to cope with a small screaming
thing that requires feeding every four hours.'

He had thoroughly enjoyed his brothers, Andrew and Edward,
eleven and fifteen years younger than him, and at the age of twenty
sat down and wrote a book for their bedtime reading called *The Old
Man of Lochnagar*.

It was a difficult pregnancy. Diana suffered from morning sickness. She was tired, though she was still carrying out engagements.
She was under pressure, and the anorexia was a constant factor. She
said she felt that she was 'a nuisance to the set up'. They spent their
first Christmas together at Sandringham.

'We've had such a lovely Christmas – the two of us,' wrote
Charles to a friend on Boxing Day. 'It has been extraordinarily
happy and cosy and being able to share it together ... Next year will,
I feel sure, be even nicer with a small one to join in as well.'

Days later Diana fell down the stairs in what she later claimed was the first of a series of cries for help. 'I threw myself down the stairs. I said I felt so desperate and I was crying my eyes out and he said: "I'm not going to listen. You're always doing this to me. I'm going riding now." So I threw myself down the stairs. The Queen comes out, absolutely horrified, shaking – she was so frightened ... Charles went out riding and when he came back, you know, it was just dismissal, total dismissal. He just carried on out of the door.'

Other witnesses to that particular incident believe that the Princess fell by accident, and are convinced that she would have done nothing to endanger the baby she was carrying. But there were other 'cries for help', which are not so open to interpretation. On one occasion, she told Morton, 'I wanted to talk to Charles about something. He wouldn't listen to me, he said I was crying wolf. So I picked up his penknife off his dressing table and scratched myself heavily down my chest and both thighs. There was a lot of blood and he hadn't made any reaction whatsoever.' Another time she hurled herself at a glass cabinet, and on yet another occasion she cut herself with a serrated lemon knife.

These were not the actions of a rational mind. In her desperation to make the Prince pay her more attention, she was doing the very things that were guaranteed to drive him away. The first few times she had become hysterical, he had been very seriously alarmed. However, as he heard the threats again and again, as he listened to the hysterics and the screaming, the shouting and the tears, and as time passed, he did just walk away when it happened. He was baffled and frightened by the strength of her emotion; he didn't understand what caused it, nor did he know how to help. It was like being with a complete stranger, a different woman entirely from the sweet gentle girl he had fallen in love with, and his instinct was to turn and run.

Diana said Camilla Parker Bowles was responsible for all her years of unhappiness. It was her husband's obsession with his friend from the beginning that had destroyed their marriage. This is what she told Andrew Morton in 1992, and repeated on television in 1994. But it is not what those people who were around at the time remember. In the early years of the marriage, Diana did not make particular mention of Camilla's name at all. Her constant complaint at that time was that she was not getting enough attention, not being taken seriously, that the Prince seemed more interested in his work than dealing with her problems, and that she was bored and lonely.

After 1986, however, when the Prince had started seeing Camilla again, her name was very much on the Princess's lips, and it was very clear that she hated and resented Camilla. She knew that her husband was in love with her, and that they were having an affair. She would rant and rave about her and kick the furniture, and call her 'that woman' through clenched teeth. But this was not the case in the early part of their marriage. Her tantrums then were not about Camilla – they were about her life.

It was true that the Prince did have a very heavy workload, more than most men. He was the Queen's representative, the Colonel-in-Chief of seven British regiments, the patron or president of innumerable charities and organisations, and as heir to the throne, had a duty not only to attend receptions, investitures, banquets for visiting foreign dignitaries, but to keep himself abreast of affairs of state, and in addition, take part in ceremonial occasions. He had always taken his duties as Prince of Wales seriously, always worked long hours, and always worked his staff hard. He had also always played hard, hunting in the winter months, playing polo in the summer. They were both a valuable release from the stress and frustrations of his work, and with polo there was often the added bonus of making money for charity in the process – he has raised millions of pounds this way over the years. In between times, he had great need for solitude, which he found walking in the countryside, settling down for a couple of hours in a lonely spot with his watercolours or standing thigh deep in a cold river, fishing. Apart from socialising as a couple in future, he had imagined life would go on very much as before. His friends had also been an important part of his life, and it never occurred to him that he might have to stop seeing them so much after his marriage. He imagined Diana would enjoy seeing them as much as he did. But the Princess resented the time he spent working, resented the horsy activities for which she had no love, resented the time Charles spent on his own, and resented his friends who were always around. She wanted him to concentrate on her.

Despite having appeared to get on so well with the Prince's friends when they first met, in reality she disliked and mistrusted most of them. In some cases, not without some justification. He listens to their advice, which is not always what his official advisers over the years have considered the wisest, and they enjoy the power they have. They did not want it diluted by a wife. Some were wonderful and went out of their way to help and to make Diana feel at ease. Emilie van Cutsem was one in particular, and the Princess was touched by her kindness. She wrote to thank her on one occasion, saying that she was like the mother she had never had. Lady Susan Hussey was another who was thanked in the most loving tones.

There were polo friends too, not so close, but whose company the Prince enjoyed from time to time. They were a highly sexed lot, loud and vulgar and after one dinner party with them all, Diana refused to go to another. Another group that he partied with occasionally were members of the Beaufort Hunt, less brash than the polo crowd, but still highly-sexed, loud and horsy. Diana felt very uncomfortable and out of her depth in their company. She made it clear that she did not want anything to do with them.

But as time passed, Diana turned against all of the Prince's friends, including the two who had been so solicitous and to whom she had initially been so grateful. While writing warm and tender letters to them, she would in the same breath be saying terrible things about them behind their backs and sowing seeds of dissension amongst friends and colleagues. 'You wouldn't say that about so and so, if you knew what she told me about you,' she would say, and then repeat a conversation which would turn out to be complete fabrication but which sounded plausible. She accused friends of disloyalty, staff of dishonesty, and caused a lot of harm and uncertainty amongst people who no longer knew whom to trust.

When friends started to realise that something was amiss, they dropped discreet hints, which the Prince did not want to hear. His parents also made it clear that they thought Diana was less than perfect, but he was not prepared to listen to criticism, even from the Queen. He was fiercely loyal to Diana – he wouldn't discuss her moods or her tantrums with anyone – and he was desperate to make her happy, desperate to make her well. At one time she was so thin and ill he was afraid she was going to die. And he thought he was responsible. He thought maybe he had done something to make her like this, that maybe marriage to him was just too awful, and he had destroyed her by bringing her into this bizarre way of life. He was thoroughly depressed and despondent.

In an attempt to please her, and to try and bring back the lovely girl he had fallen in love with, he did everything she asked. He reluctantly cut his friends out of his life. One by one he stopped all contact with them. He didn't telephone, didn't write and didn't visit. He said nothing to explain to them what had happened and they were all too reticent to telephone and ask why they had not heard from him. They had valued their friendship with the Prince; they had protected him, been there for him when he needed them, and were very deeply hurt. Some went earlier than others. The Romseys were one of the last to go. In the midst of an ornament-throwing, screaming match one day, the Prince lost his cool with Diana and said, 'I should have listened to Norton. He said I should never have married you.' That was the end of the Romseys. They were no longer allowed in the house, banished like all his other friends.

Charles not only gave up his friends in an effort to please Diana, he also gave up his dog at her behest. Harvey was a big yellow Labrador, whom he had had for many years. He travelled everywhere with him, living in Kensington Palace during the week and at Highgrove at weekends. When he went shooting at Sandringham, Harvey went too, as he did to Balmoral for the summer. Diana said the dog was associated with his past and with his friends and she couldn't have him around. Sadly, Harvey was sent off to live with the Prince's comptroller, Lt.Col. Philip Creasey, who had a house in Kent. Diana was never particularly moved by animals, despite having had pets as a child. Animal charities always left her cold and, when presented with an animal, as she occasionally was, she would never reach out and touch it as she would a child. But the Prince loved dogs, having grown up with them, and in time filled the space in his life left by Harvey with a Jack Russell terrier from Lady Salisbury, an old friend who had known the Prince since he was a child and helped create the garden at Highgrove.

By the summer of 1982 Charles and Diana were using Highgrove on a regular basis. At the Prince's instigation, Diana had overseen the interior, employing a designer called Dudley Poplak, whom her mother had used in the past and who had also decorated Kensington Palace. Both interiors were pretty, bright and colourful, quite unlike anything the Prince had known before. The Prince loved Highgrove. It was not overly grand or ostentatious, although it boasted nine bedrooms and domestic quarters. It was a comfortable family home, with a garden into which, over the years, the Prince poured heart and soul – with enthusiastic support in the early days from Diana. It had originally belonged to the Colonel Mitchell who founded a famous arboretum at Westonbirt just down the road. It was planted with magnificent trees, and it was this, principally, which attracted the Prince immediately. More recently the house had belonged to the Macmillan family and, when the Prince took it over, he kept on the couple who had looked after the Macmillans, Nesta Whiteland, who had been cook come housekeeper, and her Irish husband, Paddy, who worked as general factotum.

Mrs Paddy, as she was known, and the Princess didn't hit it off together. The housekeeper was frankly at a loss to understand what the Prince had seen in Diana. Having been used to aristocrats who understood their place in the house, she was disturbed to have Diana rushing into the kitchen to raid the fridge or to arrange flowers for the house, when there was a woman employed to do the flowers. Nesta was a shrewd judge of character and, although she never said anything, the Princess began to feel the vibrations. Paddy, meanwhile, kept out of it and devoted himself wholeheartedly to the Prince.

On 21 June 1982, soon after they had moved into Highgrove, Prince William was born in the private Lindo Wing of St Mary's Hospital in Paddington, London. Her obstetrician, George Pinker, had decided to induce the birth because he was concerned for Diana's health, and William Arthur Philip Louis came into the world at 9.03 p.m., after a sixteen-hour labour.

'Thrilled, everyone absolutely high as a kite – we had found a date where Charles could get off his polo pony for me to give birth. That was very nice, felt very grateful about that!' said Diana.

Her rancorous account was written ten years after the event. The Prince's letter to Patricia Brabourne, Lord Mountbatten's daughter, written days afterwards, indicates a very different attitude. 'The arrival of our small son has been an astonishing experience and one that has meant more to me than I could ever have imagined. As so often happens in this life, you have to experience something before you are in a true position to understand or appreciate the full meaning of the whole thing. I am *so* thankful I was beside Diana's bedside the whole time because by the end of the day I really felt as though I'd shared deeply in the process of birth and as a result was rewarded by seeing a small creature which belonged to *us* even though he seemed to belong to everyone else as well! I have never seen such scenes as there were outside the hospital when I left that night – everyone had gone berserk with excitement ... Since then we've been over-whelmed by people's reactions and thoroughly humbled. It really is quite extraordinary ... I am so pleased that you like the idea of Louis being one of William's names. Oh! How I wish your papa could have lived to see him, but he probably knows anyway ...'

The Prince was overwhelmed by the experience of becoming a father and watching his son being born was something he enthused about for long afterwards; but it brought no let up in Diana's condition, and only the briefest respite to the misery of their situation. After the initial elation, the Princess sank into severe post-natal depression, which she described herself. 'Boy, was I troubled. If he didn't come home when he said he was coming home I thought something dreadful had happened to him. Tears, panic, all the rest of it.'

The Prince was seriously worried, and that autumn he arranged for her to see a behavioural psychiatrist. He saw her for about six months at which point she signed herself off and refused to go back. He said she was not well, but no one could force Diana to be treated, and there was obviously nothing further he could do.

Friends in the Queen's household suggested Diana take it easy after William's birth and simply enjoy being a mother, cutting out the public side of her life for a while. But she wanted to work. Early in 1983, she and the Prince took William, then nine months old, on a six-week tour of Australia and New Zealand, which she found completely gruelling. The crowds and the fascination with Diana was unprecedented, and the Prince was hurt and depressed by the comments he couldn't help hearing, from people disappointed when they found he was taking their side of the street on their walkabouts rather than her. He was also desperately worried about her health again and the effect the stress of the cameras and the crowds was having on her, combined with his inability to persuade her to eat.

While they were away William learned to crawl. Charles wrote excitedly to Lady Susan Hussey, 'Your godson couldn't be in better form. Today he actually crawled for the first time. We laughed and laughed with sheer, hysterical pleasure and now we can't stop him crawling everywhere.' And to the van Cutsems he wrote, 'William now crawls over Government House at high speed knocking everything off the tables and causing unbelievable destruction.'

By 1983, before moving on to his friends and dog, Diana had seen off a number of the Prince's staff. The first to go was a policeman called Paul Officer, who had once saved the Prince's life and to whom he was as a result very close; Diana took against him for no apparent reason. Next went his valet, Stephen Barry, who had also been very close for many years, and was too intimately associated with the Prince's past sexual liaisons. He had cared for the Prince like a wife, and doubtless he resented the intrusion of a real wife who wanted her husband to herself, as much as she resented him. It was he who some years after his departure, bitter at the way life had treated him, started the rumour that the Prince had slept with Camilla Parker Bowles two nights before the Royal Wedding.

Saddest by far was the departure of Oliver Everett, Diana's private secretary, who left in December of that year. Oliver Everett was a charming, intelligent and sensitive man who had served the Prince well as an assistant private secretary between 1978 and 1980, and who had been recalled as the perfect person to look after Diana. It was he who had taken her down to join *Britannia* for Cowes Week in the summer of 1980, and reported back to the office that this one looked serious. He was married with a young family and lived in Oxford and, having to commute, was never in the office quite as early as the Princess would have liked. She was an early riser, and after a swim in the Buckingham Palace pool and breakfast at whatever time it was brought, she sat impatiently awaiting his arrival. Initially this was not a problem – nothing was a problem, he could do no wrong. They got on very well together, and the relationship was warm and friendly. She was always popping into his office for a chat. They were even described as being more like conspirators and friends than private secretary and Princess. Then quite suddenly and for no reason that anyone could fathom, she went off him. She said she didn't like him fussing over her, it drove her demented. She completely cut him out of her life. She wouldn't speak to him, didn't return his phone calls, and if they were in a room together, ignored him. She talked to other people in the office who said that if she felt that strongly about Oliver Everett, she must talk to the Prince. The Prince was mortified. Everett had given up his career at the Foreign Office to join his office at the Prince's request, and although a job was found for him as Librarian at Windsor Castle, many regard it as a shocking waste of talent; and the whole episode offended the Prince's sense of justice. But yet again, he went along with what Diana wanted.

Instead of bringing in a replacement, Anne Beckwith-Smith and Michael Colborne both took over Everett's responsibilities. It was a good solution. Anne, slightly older than the Princess, and a motherly figure, was much more informal; and Colborne – so Diana told the

Prince – was the only person she could really get on with. But it was not long before he grew tired of being caught in the cross-fire between the Prince and Princess. Matters reached a head on their tour of Canada in 1983.

The Prince by this time had become uncharacteristically moody. Gone was the man Colborne had known in his bachelor years, a man thirsty for life, who was ready to have a go at anything and everything, who worked hard and drove himself hard, but who was fun to be with. The joy seemed to have gone out of his life, and the serious side to his nature, which had always been there, appeared to have taken over.

They were on board *Britannia* in Canada. It was a beautiful afternoon and the Prince had gone off to visit his regiments. Colborne had just gone into the office to prepare for a reception that evening for President Trudeau, when he was told that the Princess wanted to see him up on the sun deck. She told him to get a chair and, as the afternoon passed, it became clear all she wanted was someone to talk to. The Prince wanted to speak to the editor of *The Times* when he came back, which Colborne organised for him via satellite. All went well, the Prince made the phone call and the two men then went into the Duke of Edinburgh's cabin for a drink, as they always did on board the royal yacht if they had a chance. The moment the cabin door was closed, the Prince went berserk. He paced round and round the cabin, kicking the furniture and shouting at Colborne. He said he had upset him greatly recently by spending more of his time looking after the Princess than after him. Colborne struggled to explain that he thought he had been helping the Prince by looking after Diana, but the boss was not in the mood to listen. After about fifteen minutes of ranting and raving the Prince suddenly looked at his watch and said, 'We'd better go and get changed.' He flung open the door, and there standing in the doorway was the Princess, who had been listening to everything that had been said, and was in tears. Charles wrapped her in his arms and, after a few moments, the two of them disappeared to their cabin to change into evening dress and be ready to greet the President.

Such was the pace of life that there was never any time for either of them to deal with problems properly. Duty dictated they were always on to the next engagement, the next photo call, the next handshake and, ever professional, they stitched the smiles on to their faces and tucked the inner turmoil away.

Michael Colborne had had enough. He was tired of being piggy in the middle. He recognised there was some truth in what the Prince had said. He had recently been devoting more attention to the Princess but because he felt so sorry for her. She was becoming quietly intoxicated with the extraordinary effect she was having. She was operating too much on impulse, enjoying the glitter more than she ought and beginning to flirt. Wherever she went, whatever room she walked into she was the centre of attention and she could see men fall like ninepins in her thrall, with no more than a coquettish tilt of the head or a teasing laugh. It would have been enough to turn even the strongest head, let alone a girl who was still only twenty-two. She was, he felt, in danger of becoming an unguided missile.

That evening he sat down and wrote a note to the Prince. He said that the one thing he had always tried to do during his ten years of service was look after the Prince. It was something which Lord Mountbatten had asked him to do. And he felt the Prince had been unfair to accuse him of looking after the Princess more than him because he thought that by helping her he would be helping him.

That was the Tuesday and the Prince didn't speak to him again until the Friday, their last day in Canada. That night the Prince and Princess went along to the mess to say goodbye and thank you to the crew, as they always did at the end of a stay on *Britannia*. As they were walking along, the Prince dropped back and said, 'Thanks for your note, Michael. I realise what you meant and I'm sorry for that evening.'

It was too late. Those fifteen minutes on the receiving end of the Prince's blistering wrath, unable to do anything but stand and take it, sowed the seeds that would mark the end of their relationship – the longest the Prince has had with anyone in his office. Colborne had had one earful too many. He had given the Prince ten years of his life. He had loved most of it, and he loved the man – he would have walked through fire for the Prince – but the man he knew had changed and he couldn't see how the situation was going to improve. The Princess was becoming more and more demanding and he was being pulled in two directions at once and couldn't go on.

The Prince was shocked when he read Colborne's letter of resignation. Colborne was important to him: he was a link with the real world, in tune with his thinking, and where the more traditional courtiers were cautious about the areas he was becoming involved in, like inner city deprivation and young people, Colborne was encouraging. He understood the man in the street in a way that the establishment around him couldn't begin to. The Prince tried repeatedly to persuade Michael to change his mind, and even telephoned his wife, Shirley, several times at home to try and get her to persuade him. Several other people tried, including the Queen's former private secretary, Sir Martin Charteris, and Colborne finally agreed to stay on until the end of 1984, having handed in his notice in the spring, but that was it.

He was still a member of the household when Prince Henry, known as Harry, was born on 15 September 1984 – like his brother in St Mary's Hospital, Paddington. The Princess later said that six weeks before his birth she and the Prince were closer than they had ever been, or ever would be. 'Then suddenly as Harry was born it just went bang, our marriage, the whole thing went down the drain.' She had known her second child was a boy from the scan, but had not told her husband because she knew he had been hoping for a girl. 'Harry arrived, Harry had red hair, Harry was a boy. First comment was "Oh, God, it's a boy", second comment "and he's even got red hair". Something inside me closed off.'

Those around them at the time knew Diana had been worried that the Prince would be disappointed; however, they say that if he was, he certainly showed no trace of it. In fact he appeared to be thrilled to have a second son, and was once again overwhelmed by the miracle of childbirth. It put life into perspective again.

But Harry's birth was no miracle cure for the relationship. The Prince's moodiness and temper were getting worse, and although Diana didn't go through the same terrifying post-natal depression that she had suffered after William was born, she was by now in the grip of bulimia, and still experienced frighteningly violent mood swings. She was also growing ever more demanding, and the Prince continued to do what she wanted in a desperate effort to make her happy. One of the things she insisted upon was that he spend more time with the children. Diana sent a note to Edward Adeane saying that in future her husband would not be available for meetings in the early mornings or evenings because he would be upstairs in the nursery. Adeane could not believe it. He was a bachelor. He had no children and no understanding of what it was like to change a nappy, bath a baby, or read a little boy a bedtime story. He was a courtier in the best old school tradition. New man he certainly was not, and he was not happy for his boss to become one either. His best times of day with the Prince were first thing in the morning and last thing at night. They were the two moments in a normally very busy day when there was some peace in which to talk and to go through vital briefings for the day ahead. It was yet another of the irritants which made his departure at the end of the year inevitable.

They had also clashed over the Prince's plans to deliver a damning speech to the Royal Institute of British Architecture earlier in the year, and put a bomb under an institution which had enjoyed uncritical royal approval for 150 years. When Adeane saw what Charles had drafted in cahoots with one or two architectural advisers, including an art historian called Jules Lubbock, he tried hard to persuade the Prince to tone the speech down. Even as they drove to Hampton Court for the dinner he was still suggesting amendments; but the Prince was not to be moved. The speech was delivered as written and, predictably, caused an almighty row.

It offended many of the architects present at the dinner that night, and delighted a small minority of highly unfashionable community architects and, as a result, quite unintentionally, launched a crusade, which is still just about alive today. It is widely known in the Prince's office as 'the nightmare brief', the one that no private secretary wholly enjoys dealing with. And of all the issues that the Prince has taken to heart, architecture is the one which even his greatest fans question.

Sir Edward Adeane, the Prince's private secretary, was shocked when he heard that Michael Colborne was leaving, but Colborne had failed to realise how much Adeane had also been suffering. He was particularly unaware of how much he had been affected by the tension between the Prince and Princess. During a farewell lunch on the Friday of Michael's departure, Adeane was clearly very depressed. Shirley Colborne asked him if he was all right. 'I'm going to really miss Michael,' he said. 'He's been taking the personal things off my shoulders, he's been looking after everybody.'

The following day, Adeane went down to Windsor where he and the Prince had a blazing row, very similar to the one the Prince had had with Colborne. Right there and then, Adeane resigned.

SEVEN

A State of Mind

'Almost any human being would have found
[being the Princess of Wales] absolutely intolerable.'
Aide to Prince Charles

The Princess of Wales saw a great many doctors and psychiatrists as well as holistic and alternative practitioners during the course of her marriage. Most of them she dismissed after a while when it became apparent that they could do nothing for her. The condition she talked about openly was bulimia, but most experts agree that the bulimia was merely a symptom of a far greater problem. Psychiatrists are generally loath to put labels on patients, understanding that the mind is a very inexact science. Individuals vary in the symptoms they display, and no two doctors are likely to come up with the same diagnosis, far less agree on a treatment. It is reasonably safe to say, however, that Diana had severe, clinical depression. Given her childhood history and the behaviour patterns, several experts suggest that she was suffering from a well-recognised, if controversial, condition called Borderline Personality Disorder.

The condition was first described by an American psychiatrist, Adolf Stern, in 1938. He used it to categorise patients who had low self-esteem and difficulty in sustaining relationships. According to the manual of mental disorders, published by the American Psychiatric Association for diagnostic purposes, these were patients who showed 'a pervasive pattern of instability of mood, interpersonal relationships, and self-image, beginning in early adulthood and present in a variety of contexts, as indicated by at least five of the following:

(1) a pattern of unstable and intense interpersonal relation-ships characterised by alternating between extremes of over-idealisation and devaluation

(2) impulsiveness in at least two areas that are potentially self-damaging, e.g., spending, sex, substance use, shoplifting, reck-less driving, binge eating

(3) affective instability: marked shifts from baseline mood to depression, irritability, or anxiety, usually lasting a few hours and only rarely more than a few days

(4) inappropriate, intense anger or lack of control of anger, e.g. frequent displays of temper, constant anger, recurrent physical fights

(5) recurrent suicidal threats, gestures, or behaviour, or self-mutilating behaviour

(6) marked and persistent identity disturbance manifested by uncertainty about at least two of the following: self-image, sexual orientation, long-term goals or career choice, type of friends desired, preferred values

(7) chronic feelings of emptiness or boredom

(8) frantic efforts to avoid real or imagined abandonment.'

It was several years before anyone around the Princess realised that she had a serious problem. They all thought for a very long time that the incidents of strange behaviour were unconnected, and that stress was the main factor. Stress certainly can't have helped and it is impossible for anyone who has never been with the Princess when she was in public or on tour to understand how stressful it was. As one of the Prince's private secretaries says, 'I've never succeeded in describing to anybody, who wasn't in the middle of it, the pressures of that life and that relationship, and looking as she looked and being who she was. Almost any human being would have found it absolutely intolerable. Wherever you happened to be, every look, every gaze, every smile, every scowl, every hand you held or touched, under the microscope every time, front page news in the tabloids day after day, sometimes of your own volition, I know, but everybody after you. It was the most extraordinary pressure. I did the same sort of work for politicians. It was utterly different. There was a clearish divide between public and private life, and I didn't need to cross any of those dividing lines.

'Here the whole thing was a great big ball of wax, the job, the public life, the private life, it was all indistinguishable, not just for them, but for us too. The phone calls would come at any time of the day or night, wherever you were in the world, your involvement with them was twenty-four hours a day and you couldn't distinguish because they didn't distinguish. How could they distinguish between what was public and private, what was work and what was play? It was all part of the same thing. There wasn't much respite and that clearly took its toll on her. It takes its toll on him too, but he's been brought up to it and developed his own defence mechanisms, his own thick skin.'

Charles and Diana had scarcely been married six months before everyone was so worried about Diana's state of mind that the Queen called in Fleet Street editors to Buckingham Palace, as she had only done once in her reign before – at the end of Prince Charles's first term at Cheam preparatory school in 1957 – to appeal for privacy. On this occasion she asked the editors to give Diana a break. The poor girl couldn't even go into the local Gloucestershire town of Tetbury to buy a packet of wine gums without being on the front page of the newspapers, and the strain was having a very bad effect on her. They had assumed the Palace was worried she might be in danger of a miscarriage. That was not the worry. The then editor of the *News of the World*, Barry Askew, said that if the Princess had a craving for wine gums, she ought to send a servant out to get them.

'That,' retorted the Queen famously, 'is the most pompous thing I've ever heard.'

For many of the people who worked most closely with the Princess, the discovery that she had some kind of psychiatric disorder made it easier to handle. As the Prince of Wales said about schizophrenia, when launching the SANE Appeal in 1991, 'Physical disability, illness, accidents which break bones or upset the functions of the body are painful, yet can be overcome by strength of personality, good medical care and will-power. Schizophrenia is different: we are talking about an illness which changes the way people think, understand and perceive the world around them and relate to others – the very essence of their personality – so that they are isolated from all sources of comfort and reason. I believe we have to accept that accidents can happen to the mind as they can to the body, and that the consequences can sometimes be even more devastating.'

Charles was not interested in labels. He knew what symptoms Diana displayed and sought out the best doctors and psychiatrists to relieve them. He was angered by her behaviour at times, and thoroughly depressed by it, but deep down he felt desperately sorry for her, and although it didn't making coping any easier, he was eventually convinced that Diana had an illness and could no more be blamed for her actions than she could be blamed had she bled all over the carpet from an open wound.

What puzzles some experts who knew her is that she never crashed or had a breakdown. She came close to it, they reckon, one day when, leaving therapist Susie Orbach's north London home, she burst into tears in front of waiting photographers and ran away. She also cried in public during her first engagement after Andrew Morton's book was published, when someone stroked her cheek. As one expert in psychiatric disorders said, 'If all sufferers were royal there might be no more mental illness, because if you are in control you have power and can use your fantasies and manipulations.'

What is universally acknowledged is that Borderline Personality Disorder is one of the most difficult conditions to cure. It is treated with anti-depressants, tranquillisers and intensive care and support, but the success rate is not encouraging. A recent Canadian study suggested that ten per cent of sufferers would, ultimately, commit suicide. It also takes its toll on the relatives who attempt to care and support, also on the psychiatrists who attempt to treat it, partly because the symptoms are only displayed in private. In public, sufferers are cheerful, outgoing, attractive, successful and often highly charismatic people, who give every indication of being quite well balanced. These people are generally so mesmerising that even the professionals, who are trained to keep a distance from the patients they treat, find themselves becoming sucked into their orbit and emotionally engulfed. When they fail to solve the problem, and are spewed out – as friends and relatives are too – they feel a colossal sense of failure and dejection. Many of them say that, although evil is not a word that should ever enter their vocabulary, they are tempted to use it in relation to these patients. It is because they feel frustrated that despite all their professionalism and understanding of the condition, they are allowing themselves to be so successfully manipulated by someone who on the face of it appears so rational.

A mental illness can, in theory, be treated with chemicals, as it is commonly the result of a chemical imbalance. A disorder is different. It is like a jigsaw puzzle that has had some of the pieces mixed up: the personality traits which go together to make up every individual are put together in a way that is abnormally balanced. Minor personality disorders are common, seen in people who need attention or adoration. Provided they can keep them under control there is no problem. The people who have them very often find their way into politics or on to the stage. Indeed most people don't begin to know there is any kind of abnormality. When the disorder is serious, it is particularly difficult for everyone concerned because sufferers need attention, but at the same time repel and repudiate anyone who offers it. They are unable to engage in proper relationships or feel any real emotion. It is all copied from watching others, as if through glass. The only emotion which is genuine is the sense of despair and frustration at being unable to have the relationships that they see others having.

Quite unprompted, one of Diana's closest friends at the end of her life described her as having terrible problems exactly fitting the medical description of Borderline Personality Disorder. 'She is like someone who has her nose pressed to the glass looking at the world outside, but never feeling that she is part of it. She can't emotionally, psychologically cope with it.'

Did Diana have this disorder before she became engaged to the

Prince of Wales, or was it what she called his uncaring and indifferent attitude towards her which brought it on? One of the most common causes of Borderline Personality Disorder is said to be 'unstable or disruptive early childhood relationships', which Diana was certainly not short of; and there are indications that she was showing signs of being difficult and manipulative when she was quite young.

A very senior member of the royal household, who had a daughter at Riddlesworth Hall prep school with Diana until the age of twelve, volunteered long before things became bad with the Princess that he had made specific enquiries about where Diana would next be going to school, so that he could choose somewhere different for his daughter. They were a local family and he didn't think his daughter's friendship with Diana Spencer was having a good effect on her.

Diana's grandmother, Ruth, Lady Fermoy, described her as 'a dishonest and difficult girl' and, less than a month before she died, in July 1993, said that she could have kicked herself for not screwing up her courage to warn the Prince of Wales about Diana before he married her. Diana's father, who died in March 1991, also said he had been wrong not to say something. The Prince therefore went into the marriage wholly unprepared. It is doubtful that any man could have helped Diana, and probable that Charles stuck with it longer than most husbands would have, because of the man he is and because of the position he holds.

The Prince behaved as best he knew how, unaware until the relationship had very nearly destroyed him that he had been handed an almost impossible task.

EIGHT

The Offices of a Prince

'The day you think I'm not useful, tell me.'
Charles

The mid-eighties were difficult for the Prince. He felt that Michael Colborne had deserted him – and he found his departure particularly tough; Edward Adeane had also left him; his marriage was not working; the press was critical; his father was unsympathetic; he was uncertain about what he should be doing with his life and torn about whether he should be following his instinct or listening to his cautious courtiers.

His friends were reaching senior position in their chosen professions while he was still waiting in the wings to fulfil the role he had trained for since birth. As a sensitive man, he knew he had no business feeling sorry for himself. Looking at the shattered and demoralised young people he met in the inner cities, he knew he had more than they could ever hope for. But knowing this didn't help. People listened to him, did what he asked, and came to see him when he opened a building or visited a factory. Yet it was not because of *who* he was, but because of *what* he was. He had been born with a silver spoon in his mouth and had never been able to do any real job that made him feel he had earned respect and admiration. He was desperate to be of some use, and to understand the purpose of life and his role within it.

He became temperamental and depressed and hugely demanding of everyone around him. He cut back on his engagements and spent many a contemplative hour digging the garden at Highgrove or riding hard, pushing himself physically to the limits.

Diana, trying to come to terms with her own problems, was the last person who could help. She was too young to understand the tortuous soul-searching Charles was going through; too preoccupied with the maelstrom of her own life. In the last four years it had been turned completely upside down. She had shot from unremarkable teenager to international superstar, recognised in every corner of the globe, watched and photographed everywhere she went. She had married into the most extraordinary family in Britain – one of the most extraordinary families in the world – and in doing so taken on a title that set her apart from everyone she had ever known. She had a job and a life she had had no training for. And to top it all she had become a mother of two small boys. Even the most well-balanced, level-headed, secure and self-confident young woman would have found it difficult to cope. For Diana it was impossible.

The press began to notice that all was not well. They calculated that in a three-month period, Charles had carried out just fifteen engagements, compared with his sister's fifty-six, Prince Philip's forty-five, and the Queen's twenty-eight. Meanwhile he seemed to have plenty of time for polo. The criticism stung, but polo was one of the few things that was keeping him sane. He once said, 'If I can have a game of polo I feel five hundred times better in my mental outlook. But without some form of exercise I'm afraid to say I get terribly jaded and, well, not depressed, but below par.'

By 1985 he was not just below par, he was seriously, chronically depressed, almost suicidal, and his friends were so worried about him they decided something had to be done to restore his spirits. They knew he had always got on well with Camilla Parker Bowles; they knew she was sitting at home while her charming husband philandered his way around London and Wiltshire, and they suggested the two of them contact one another.

Charles and Camilla had had virtually no contact since 1981. They had been at the same social gathering from time to time, but had not met to talk since the time of his engagement, with one exception, when he gave Camilla the bracelet. They had spoken on the telephone a few times during his engagement, but since then he had only telephoned once to tell Camilla that Diana was expecting a baby.

It was Patti Palmer-Tomkinson who organised it, and at first they wrote long letters to each other. Then they started to speak on the telephone, and this went on for several months. Finally they met at Patti's house in Hampshire. The Prince was enormously relieved to have someone to talk to whom he trusted and who was so sympathetic. Camilla took him out of his gloom and despondency, listened to his worries and concerns, understood him and cared in a way that is only possible when two people have once been lovers. For years he had spoken to no one about the difficulties of his life with Diana for fear that to do so would be disloyal. But their former intimacy meant that Camilla was someone from whom he needed to keep no secrets, someone who he knew beyond doubt would keep his confidence. Gradually their friendship turned into something deeper and more physical. The Prince always felt guilty about this but, to his astonishment, discovered years later that while he had been feeling so guilty about Camilla, the Princess had been having an affair many months before he and Camilla had even made contact.

Camilla's friendship brought Charles back from the brink of the abyss, but it was a long climb back, and many of his friends think that he was irreparably damaged by the experiences of his marriage. Camilla bolstered his confidence, took an interest in his work and encouraged him to believe that he had a contribution to make.

One of the areas in which no one can deny his contribution to society is the Prince's Trust. It began with a few ideas scribbled on the back of an envelope in 1972, and since then all of the ideas that have driven the Trust, in outline if not in detail, have been the Prince's. He has taken enormous pleasure and pride in watching it grow and become a success. He was originally moved by hearing a probation officer talking on the radio about young offenders, and felt the urge to try and help. If young people could be given something positive to do with their time and energy, he reasoned, it might keep them out of trouble. And so he gave his naval allowance of £3,000 a year, in its entirety and quite anonymously, to young people. In the early days that was how the Trust was funded.

The facts and figures that drive the Prince's Trust today are simple. There are nearly 120,000 young people unemployed long-term in Britain, and many of them have no skills to take up jobs even if they could find them. More and more children are being excluded from school, particularly amongst the ethnic minorities. Young black men are twice as likely to be unemployed as their white counterparts. And, according to studies commissioned by the Prince's Trust, crime committed by unemployed youth costs the nation over £7 billion a year. So the three areas the Trust now focuses on are targeted directly at those people. It helps children do their homework outside school hours, by way of Study Support Centres, of which there are now 800. It sets up young people in their own small businesses: 4,618 were launched last year, and a total of 44,000 since the Trust began. Sixty per cent of those people the Trust helps are still trading three years later; the top ten now turn over £38.7 million per annum; the top 100 turn over a total of £80 million per annum, and employ 1,600 people between them. The Trust's third activity is training the unemployed in the community on a mixture of courses, some of them residential, some of them dedicated to particular skills, all of them involving teamwork in the community. Seventy per cent of those people who take part move from unemployment to either work or training within three months of completing the programme.

Charles has employed some unfortunate people over the years. Equally, there have been some very remarkable people in his orbit. Tom Shebbeare, who runs the Prince's Trust, was one of his best appointments. He is an ex eurocrat and, since his arrival in 1987, has turned it from an amateurish charity with plenty of good ideas into an organisation that will spend £30 million on young people this year. As a consequence it is rapidly having its clothes stolen by the government. While the general public may still think all the Trust does is hold pop concerts, they are beginning to recognise the

Prince's part in all of it. When he arrived at a Prince's Trust concert in London's Hyde Park in the summer of 1998 and made his way to the grandstand, the crowd of over 100,000 people turned to face him, clapping and cheering for five minutes, before singing an early 'Happy Birthday'. For a while, actor Stephen Fry, who was on stage trying to introduce the Prince, seemed almost lost for words.

There have been a number of figures in the Prince's life who have played a central role for a while, and by whom he has been impressed and influenced. The South African born writer, explorer and philosopher Laurens van der Post was one, who first entranced the Prince in the mid-seventies, and encouraged him to listen to his instincts and explore the 'old world of the spirit'.

'We suffer from a hubris of the mind,' he wrote in one of his books, every one of which the Prince devoured with a passion. 'We have abolished superstition of the heart only to install a superstition of the intellect in its place.'

Another more down to earth influence, and one about whom no one had any qualms, was Stephen O'Brien, who in late 1984 brought the Prince into an organisation called Business in the Community (BitC). The combination of the man and the mission he was engaged in, which immediately struck a chord with the Prince of Wales, unleashed a whole new interest in life. BitC is now one of his principal interests, and although Stephen O'Brien has moved on, his successor, Julia Cleverdon, is another remarkable and inspirational individual, who works very closely with the Prince. The idea that drives BitC is simple: involve companies in the communities in which they operate, persuade them to invest, train and recruit from within those communities, and you solve unemployment, thereby improving the whole depressed inner city environment.

O'Brien had initially approached the Prince for support with a project for young unemployed black people in the inner cities called Fullemploy, knowing of the Prince's Trust work in that area. Out of their meeting came a daring event, known as the Windsor Conference, which people involved in race relations still talk about today. For two days the chairmen of sixty major companies in the UK were brought face to face with a crowd of bright, articulate members of the black community in a hotel in Windsor. They mixed, talked and ate together, and discussed the problems of unemployment among black youths. Racism, Charles told the assembled gathering, was a problem of the white society and not the black. It was a failure to recognise the potential of the black community and a failure to use it. By the end of the conference both black and white participants had discovered that their preconceptions about each other were entirely false. The exercise was widely regarded as one of the most significant advances ever made in race relations. Nothing of the kind had ever been done before and without the Prince of Wales it would almost certainly never have happened. But there is no doubt it was a highly risky experiment, which could have gone badly wrong.

His courage was not lost on Stephen O'Brien; and the following year, 1985, the Prince was invited to become President of BitC. He accepted with alacrity. Here was a man and a group of people with a real determination to make things happen, who appeared to share his concerns about society and his ideals, who had the financial support of government and industry, unlike his own endeavours which were so reliant on the begging bowl. Also, it was young enough, having been in existence for just four years, for him to be able to make a positive contribution.

'The day you think I am not useful,' he told one of BitC's directors, 'tell me. I want to be involved in the growth of something. I don't just want to open things and be seen trundling around. I can go to all the dinners and banquets on earth, but it's not going to make any difference to the world. What I want to do is be part of something that does.'

This was exactly what he needed to stop him brooding about his marital problems, and the Prince threw himself into what was the closest he had yet come to a real job. He quickly realised that his presence made an impact on BitC, that he was adding real value, and he found in Stephen O'Brien a man off whom he could bounce ideas that were not immediately condemned as ill advised, as they would have been by the cautious courtiers.

Whatever else may be said of the Prince of Wales, courage is never something that he has lacked. He has seldom listened to the advice of worried courtiers or royal protection officers who would wrap him up in cotton wool. Physically he has always pushed himself to the limit – he rides fast and fearlessly, he skis dangerously off piste, and has brushed with death on many occasions. He courts danger and thrives on the adrenalin of living close to the edge.

He constantly needs to push himself to the limit to prove that he in some way merits the position he was born to. During his Action Man days in the Navy he chose to do a Royal Marine commando training programme, including the drill for escaping from a sunken vessel, which in the following two years killed two men, and which he admitted he found quite terrifying. During his spell in the RAF, he made a parachute jump and got his legs caught in the rigging. And when he was later appointed Colonel-in-Chief of the Parachute Regiment, he insisted on doing the notoriously testing training course, on the grounds that he should 'be able to do some of the things one expects others to do for the country'. It enabled him, he said, to look the other men in the eye.

It was for much the same reason that during the year of the Queen's Silver Jubilee, against all advice, he stepped out of the security of his crested limousine, to find out what demonstrators corralled inside police barricades in Lewisham were so angry about. The answer, he discovered from one, sporting a badge saying, 'Stuff the Jubilee', was police harassment of the black community. Twenty-four black youths had recently been arrested for mugging and it was felt that the police were randomly, without due evidence, picking black men in particular from the street to take the rap. The Prince called over the police commander responsible and suggested the two groups should get together to sort out the matter. Eight days later, under the auspices of the Prince's Trust, the Prince invited both groups to Buckingham Palace. As a result the situation was defused, but not before the Prince was roundly rebuked by the press for having interfered in a matter which was none of his business, an opinion his father reinforced. He retired hurt, but not defeated; and through the Prince's Trust continued to work towards improving relations between police forces and minority communities in Britain 'to dampen down a potentially disastrous situation'. His instincts were right about the mounting tensions. A year later violent race riots broke out in inner cities all over the country.

It takes nerve to go ahead when the whole of Fleet Street, your father and your most senior advisers are telling you that what you have said or done is stupid. But since then, the Prince has continued to say what he believes, sticking his head recklessly above the parapet, when he has felt something needed to be done, and he has continued to be battered by the press for doing so. He has attacked architecture, medicine, farming, industry, education, religion – not one of our hallowed institutions has escaped a princely swipe – and he has been roundly criticised for meddling in things his critics claim he knows nothing about. Sometimes his critics have been right; he hasn't had the facts to support him, and has followed nothing more scientific than instinct. Yet after each and every assault, he has been flooded with mail from ordinary people thanking him for what he has said.

Time has shown, again and again, that the wacky, crackpot Prince, who went tilting at windmills, has become a man of vision, ahead of his time. And those issues that he spoke out about when no one else would, those causes which seemed obscure and unfashionable at the time, have all, several years down the line, become mainstream.

It was pure intuition that drove Charles to attack the medical establishment fifteen years ago. He caused outrage by suggesting that drugs were becoming 'the universal panacea for all our ills', and that in dismissing complementary medicine the British Medical Association was, 'like the celebrated Tower of Pisa, slightly off-balance'. The BMA immediately set up an inquiry into alternative medicine, which concluded that there was no scientific proof that any of the treatments worked. Today, however, alternative medicine is widely recognised and used by doctors as enthusiastically as the rest of the population. There is a growing mistrust of drugs; and some general practices even offer alternative treatments on the National Health Service.

It was also fifteen years ago that he horrified the farming establishment by condemning conventional high-yield methods of agriculture which relied on chemicals. In supporting the National Organic Food Production conference, he said he was 'convinced that any steps that can be taken to explore methods of production which make better and more effective use of renewable resources are extremely important'. The hugely powerful agrochemical industry thought it could ignore him, and was delighted when he apparently shot himself in the foot shortly afterwards. He confessed in an ITN documentary that he talked to his plants, and was mercilessly ridiculed by the press as 'the loony prince' who had clearly joined the beard and beads brigade. Yet today, not only are the major supermarkets stocking organic produce, they are in fierce competition with one another to find more lines and bigger and better suppliers. Farmers all over the world are converting to organic methods as they discover that the public is prepared to pay a premium price for purer food.

But nothing made him more unpopular with the powers-that-be than his attack on the architectural establishment in the famous Hampton Court speech in the summer of 1984, when he talked of 'monstrous carbuncles' and 'giant glass stumps'. Yet he seemed to be articulating what thousands of ordinary people felt. He accused architects of building houses for the approval of fellow architects and critics, not for the people who have to live in them. Community architecture was the way forward, in his view, and housing co-operatives where the tenants were consulted about the sort of environment they wanted to live in. '... Architects and planners do not necessarily have the monopoly of knowing what is best about taste, style and planning ...' he said, and ordinary people 'need not be made to feel guilty or ignorant if their natural preference is for the more "traditional designs" – for a small garden, for courtyards, arches and porches ...' There was a growing number of architects prepared to listen and to offer imaginative ideas.

The Prince still has some serious detractors about his views on modern architecture, and with some justification. Many people believe his interference in this area is an abuse of his power on a matter which is nothing more than personal preference. 'It has taken fifty years to destroy the accumulated architectural wisdom of thousands of years. I am quite prepared for it to take at least as long to rebuild it – even if I have to be sent to a taxidermist in order to see it through,' he once declared. But on the subject of urban design and development, which he put into practice with Poundbury, his model village on Duchy land outside the town of Dorchester, today even his harshest critics appear to be singing a remarkably similar tune.

Of all the areas in which the Prince has taken a stand, architecture has always been the most difficult, not least because housing is a highly political issue. He plunged in not just because of his preference for classical buildings, but because he was convinced that insensitive design, and ugly high-rise tower-blocks were responsible for a great deal of inner-city despair, and that if you design a community as opposed to a series of rabbit hutches, a happier, more civilised society will follow. Once drawn in, he was encouraged by those architects whose ideas he championed to get more and more involved. It is the curse of the Prince to be used by people who see him as a vehicle for their own advancement, and he is usually the last person to see what is going on. In challenging the development and construction industry he was challenging one of the major players in the British economy, an area riven by vested interest where vast sums of money are at stake. The classicists and community architects very much enjoyed their royal patronage, while the modernists likened him to Stalin, Hitler and Pol Pot. The architectural practice responsible for designing the National Gallery extension – which the Prince had denounced in that first speech as 'a monstrous carbuncle on the face of a much loved and elegant friend' – went to the wall.

He relishes his role as David against Goliath. When a small cheese maker in Scotland was prosecuted by his local health authority because tiny traces of listeria had been found in his cheese, the Prince, as patron of the Specialist Cheese Makers, came racing to the rescue. He brought together the cheese makers with the Ministry of Agriculture, Fisheries and Food, the Department of Health and the Department of Trade and Industry – not just officials but the ministers from each department – so they could hear at first hand the problems that the small producers faced. As he said, 'Every French farmer would go to prison if they enforced those rules in France.' They are EC rules, he said, which only the British appear to be concerned about.

When Charles opened the new Dyson vacuum cleaner factory in the Wiltshire town of Malmesbury, he learned that James Dyson had been forced to take his first invention, the ball barrow, to Japan because he couldn't get the funding he needed in the UK. The local MP, Richard Needham, was in tow the day Charles opened the factory. 'This is a marvellous example of government supporting industry,' Needham said as they left.

'Richard,' said the Prince, 'this has got nothing to do with government. All government has done is put obstacles in the way.'

During the visit, Needham had tried to get the Prince photographed pushing a vacuum cleaner, but he wasn't have any of it, knowing what the headlines would be. 'Richard, I'm sure you're much more used to doing this than I am.'

Rules, regulations and red tape are the plague of the Prince's life: a life that is inevitably bound by all three. He longs for people who will say 'yes' and not give him a hundred and one reasons why something cannot be done. Edward Adeane was conservative, in the mould of old-style courtiers who understood perfectly the purpose and role of monarchy, and did everything in their power to discourage enterprise. The Prince felt shackled by him, partly, no doubt, because while Adeane was advising caution, Michael Colborne was telling him to listen to his instincts, to look about him and see how the world was changing, and how he, the Prince of Wales, could provide some badly needed leadership and make a difference.

The man he found to replace Edward Adeane as private secretary came not from the traditional Foreign Office or Armed Forces pool, but from a high-powered job in the City. The Prince had been very specific about the sort of person he was looking for: someone of high calibre, with business and administrative skills, who could sort out the chaos that was his office, who would fit in with the old guard but not be like them and, most important of all, be sympathetic to his views.

Sir John Riddell could not have been better suited. He was a successful investment banker in his early fifties with a young family and a delightful attitude to life. Ace administrator he was not, and the office continued to be as chaotic as ever, but he was universally liked and he guided the Prince through some difficult times with unfailing good humour. As one of his staff said of him, 'I cannot count the number of times I have been into John's office with a disastrous problem to solve, to come out again with the problem still unsolved but feeling that the world was a much nicer place.'

John was in many ways a most unlikely candidate for courtier. The Prince chose him from three men who were presented by a head hunter because he was determined to have someone who would be sympathetic to his ideas. This prerequisite was the cause of considerable apprehension at St James's Palace, and there was much relief when Riddell arrived wearing a pinstriped suit rather than a beard and sandals.

His humour did wonders for the office, which by this time was not always the happiest of places. As thirteenth Baronet from an old Northumberland family, educated at Eton and Oxford, he was not used to dancing attendance on anyone. Nor, despite his City career, was he used to working round the clock. He gave the Prince his wholehearted support and enthusiasm, and admired what he was trying to do, but when his day was finished he wanted to go home to his wife and children. As a complete newcomer to the royal circle, Riddell was much less hidebound than his predecessor, yet sensitive to the niceties of court, and was generally acknowledged to have been another of the Prince's best appointments.

In some ways he gave the Prince a new lease of life. He was much less anxious about the Prince's interests than Adeane had been, particularly with regard to the inner cities and his involvement with BitC. Over the next five years the Prince's public life began to flourish. Having been tortured and uncertain of where he was going or what his role in life should be, he began to see a way forward.

In the same year, Richard Aylard arrived in the office as equerry to the Princess of Wales, replacing Michael Colborne, and three years later joined the Prince's staff as an assistant private secretary. He also played an important part in the Prince's new direction. Aged thirty-three, he had been a naval commander, and latterly worked in naval public relations.

It was the first time Diana had needed an equerry. She had been approached by over 150 charities when she became Princess of Wales and had agreed in her first year to affiliate herself to just five. Now she felt ready to expand her activities, but in her own way and on her own terms, which was sometimes hard for the Lord-Lieutenants who had become used to the punishing schedules prepared for other senior female royals. If she was doing a day in Yorkshire, for example, they would expect Diana to travel overnight on the royal train so that she could start early and fit in six engagements during the day – as the Queen, Princess Margaret or the Princess Royal would do, probably before going home for a reception or a dinner in the evening. In the early days, this was the kind of model that everyone was working to. It didn't cross the minds of any of the people advising Diana on how to handle the public side of her life that a royal schedule could be planned any other way.

However, by this time the Princess had discovered what she enjoyed and felt able to handle and what she hated, and everyone around her knew how best she liked her days to be organised. A day in Yorkshire would begin later in the morning because she was not prepared to spend the night away from home. Ideally she would want to take William and later Harry to school before she set off on her engagements, although that was not always possible if they were far afield. During the course of the day she would do maybe three engagements rather than six, so that she was home again in time for the children's bath and bedtime. Often she would stop at a super-market on the way home and buy some of their favourite biscuits for tea. She wanted her engagements to be short and she wanted to meet real people. If she visited a hospital, she insisted, as indeed the Prince always did, on sitting on every bed in the ward and speaking to every patient, which meant tours invariably overran. She wanted the simplest possible briefing notes, which left out anything technical and emphasised the human element of any visit. And she conducted conversations on her own terms, never afraid to ask questions, however ignorant they made her look. The more confident she became, the more coquettish she grew, and the result was very powerful. Strong men melted under her gaze and became her devotees.

Anne Beckwith-Smith and Richard Aylard ran her life between them and because they were both new recruits to royal life, neither had any preconceptions about what other members of the Family did or how they behaved on days out. Under their management the Princess felt happy. They knew she did not like formal line-ups and that she hated eating in public. If she had to, she would never want to sit next to anyone who was very clever, or who was old. So they would organise small groups or one-to-one meetings, and instead of lunch they would arrange for her to have a plate of sandwiches in a back room somewhere, so she could unwind and laugh and joke and tell stories with her entourage, before being back on parade.

As time passed, Diana's eating habits became noticeably odd, and they could no longer be put down to post-childbirth dieting, nerves, or any of the excuses her staff had found to explain her behaviour to themselves. One day she would eat her own and everyone else's tea on the way home from a day out. The next, she would eat nothing; then suddenly wolf down four Kit-Kat bars and disappear into the lavatory. No one knew quite what to do about it, and so they said nothing. It was simply accepted as part of a manic day out with the Princess.

The press was fascinated by her weight loss, and her state of health was a national preoccupation. Anorexia had been suggested at various times, and she always said how much it made her laugh. Had these people not seen her appetite, she would say? It was not until about 1986 that her household fully appreciated the problem. By then it was no longer anorexia, but bulimia.

Diana was demanding to work for but she could be very good fun, and she would always make a point, for instance, of asking about people's family – Richard Aylard had a wife and child at home – and of saying thank you at the end of a day out. On a Friday, she would often want to be finished by lunchtime so she could go home to the children, and would say she was sure the others would want to get home early too. She would very rarely telephone staff at the weekend. The Prince, on the other hand, often rang his staff at weekends, and would frequently forget the niceties of thanking the people who made his life work.

Diana, however, was quick to criticise if she felt something hadn't been done properly, or if she thought one of her charities was taking advantage of her or asking too much. She would swing from a situation where there wasn't enough she could do for a charity to cutting it completely dead and refusing to do anything. Organisers were left wondering what on earth had gone wrong. Sometimes it was justified; at other times not. She would never let a charity down if she had already agreed an engagement – she was always one hundred per cent professional in honouring her commitments – but at the next programme meeting their proposals would be ignored. There were only two occasions in fifteen years when the Princess failed to show for an engagement, and they were both when her children took precedence. The first occasion was in May 1988 when Prince Harry was rushed into Great Ormond Street Children's Hospital for an emergency hernia operation. The other was after Prince William had been hit on the head by a school friend with a golf club in June 1991 and he too was taken into Great Ormond Street.

The Princess would also swing in her treatment of friends. She blew hot and cold with them, and caused a great deal of distress. One minute a friend would be her closest possible confidant: she would telephone them ten times a day – and several of those calls might be an hour long – she would lunch with them several times a week, tell them the most intimate details of her life, and shower them with gifts. The next minute, for no apparent reason, she would cut them out of her life entirely, refusing to take their calls. Those who had known her since childhood, in particular, were left hurt and wondering what they could possibly have done to offend. If pressed, she would say they were taking advantage of her. In reality, she panicked because she thought she had told them too much and allowed them to get too close to her.

She was the same with her staff, as Oliver Everett, her private secretary, had discovered. One minute she could not do enough to help them: she would send their mothers flowers on their birthdays, give them presents, be pally and informal and open her heart to them. The next she would cut them dead and might not speak to them for a month, for no reason that they could possibly fathom.

As one of them said, 'I would have given up all the flowers, all the niceness if only we could have avoided the sheer bloody-minded sarcasm, the silences, and sending to Coventry that went with it.'

When either Richard Aylard or Anne Beckwith-Smith had offended her – maybe by allowing photographers to get too close at an engagement, or giving her advice that she didn't like – she would freeze them out for days. If the one she wasn't talking to sent her a memo, she would reply to the other.

She was never entirely comfortable with the press *en masse*, but she had one or two favourites – of which James Whitaker was one for many years; also Arthur Edwards of the *Sun*. In the last four years of her life she developed an entirely different relationship with Richard Kay of the *Daily Mail*, spending hours on the telephone to him and baring her soul in a way she had never done with a journalist before. She was always scrupulously polite to all journalists, calling them by their names, saying 'Good morning', teasing them, flirting with them, and it worked wonders, as she knew it would. She read what they wrote about her avidly and loved to see nice photographs of herself. She learnt very quickly what they wanted and in later years she used the press effectively when she was waging war on her husband. Yet it entirely depended upon what mood she was in. If she felt amenable she would give them the picture they wanted, she would dangle a child on her knee or give them a dazzling smile. If she felt they had taken advantage of her, or crowded in too closely, or been taking photographs for too long, she would simply raise her shoulder to obscure her face or ruin the shot and put an end to it. In the early days she was worried about being accused of upstaging the Queen or the Prince. By the end, when the gloves were off, she delighted in it.

NINE

Marriage and the Media: After Morton

'She thinks he is a bad father ...'
James Gilbey in Andrew Morton's Diana – Her True Story

It was clear to their staff that the Prince was a victim of the Princess's mood swings just as much as everyone else. The shouting that they heard behind closed doors was commonplace, and he would be on the receiving end of sarcastic remarks, no less than the cook or the chambermaid. On greeting one of his staff in full uniform one morning before going off to a formal engagement, the Prince said, 'You only have one medal. We'll have to do something about that.' Whereupon the Princess, following her husband down the stairs said, 'Yes, but at least he earned his.'

Though such remarks were awkward for everyone, no one really knew how serious the situation was. At times they would appear to be very happy together, and in public they were always very civil to one another, but it was growing obvious at programme meetings that the Princess didn't want to do engagements with the Prince, and in private she was gradually cutting herself off from him, not wanting to go to Balmoral with him, refusing to see his friends, cutting short her weekends at Highgrove and, when she was there, spending her time indoors talking to friends on the telephone, never going into the garden – which she had at one time enjoyed – and never going to see the farm.

Many of her friends, like Tally, Duchess of Westminster, née Phillips, were from her teens, and there were those she had shared her flat with before her marriage, like Carolyn Bartholomew, née Pride,

Sophie Kimball and Laura Greig. Sarah Ferguson, who married Prince Andrew, introduced her to several people too, including Kate Menzies, Julia Dodd Noble and the Marchioness of Douro, with whom Diana played tennis at the fashionable Vanderbilt Racquet Club in London's Shepherd's Bush. Julia Samuel, Angela Serota and Catherine Soames, former wife of the Prince's friend Nicholas, were also close for a time. Male friends included James Gilbey, George Plumtre, Rory Scott, two Fergie introductions, Philip Dunne and David Waterhouse, via whom she met James Hewitt.

In later years friends included the Lucia Flecha de Lima, Rosa Monckton, and Mara and Lorenzo Berni, the proprietors of San Lorenzo, her favourite London restaurant.

As well as the moods and the rows, there were rumours that she was being unfaithful to her husband. By 1985 Diana's staff were aware that there was something going on between her and Sergeant Barry Mannakee, her personal protection officer. He was displaying signs of intimacy, which she clearly encouraged; but there was very little gossip because everyone was frightened of the Princess getting to hear what was being said, and they feared for their jobs.

In July 1986, shortly before the Yorks' marriage, the Prince was told that Barry Mannakee had to go. He was given no reason, and told he didn't need to know why. Curiously, he asked no questions but accepted the advice, and Mannakee was moved to the diplomatic protection group and thus out of Diana's orbit. Those near him at the time assumed the Prince must have guessed the reason, but he hadn't. Like most observers, he found the idea incredible, and it was not until some years later that he learned the truth. But Mannakee was not the only affair he knew nothing about until much later.

The Prince never played the jealous husband, and apparently never wanted to know what his wife did when she was out of his sight. If he had thought she might be being disloyal, he never challenged her and never shared his suspicions with anyone. Even during the darkest periods of their marriage, when life, as a friend puts it, 'was one long whinge, it was not always directed at Diana and even at the worst times he did show understanding and sympathy for her position'.

In July 1987 Mannakee was killed in a motorcycle accident. He was riding pillion on a bike which collided with a car in the East End of London. The news reached the Prince at Kensington Palace moments before he and Diana were due to leave for the Cannes Film Festival. He decided it would be better to tell her immediately rather than risk a question shouted from a journalist in the crowd, so he broke the news to her in the car *en route* to RAF Northolt. The Princess was distraught, and spent the journey and much of the trip in floods of tears, with the Prince and Anne Beckwith-Smith both desperately trying to console her. In her despair, she slashed herself, and the dress she wore in Cannes had to be adjusted to hide the damage.

By this time Diana had formed an attachment to Major David Waterhouse, whom she had met along with banker Philip Dunne when the Waleses and the Yorks went skiing together in Klosters in February.

The arrival of Fergie into the royal circle was a mixed blessing for the Princess. On the one hand she was someone closer to her own age and an ally. But she was also a rival. In the early days, Fergie was popular. She was like the girl next door, undaunted by protocol, relaxed, irreverent and determined to have fun: people talked about her being a breath of fresh air. Diana, who had never been confident at the best of times, felt doubly insecure. As she later admitted, 'I got terribly jealous.'

Soon after the Yorks' wedding the Princess unexpectedly announced that she wanted to do some more engagements and gave Richard Aylard and Anne Beckwith-Smith three dates when she specifically wanted them to find something for her to do. It was an odd request and quite out of character. Nevertheless, they fixed things for her to do, and it was only when they had organised it all that the policeman pointed out that they were the precise dates when the Duchess of York had her first three public engagements. Diana upstaged her new rival to perfection.

Diana tried for a while to be like Fergie. She went to pop concerts and out to the cinema and dinner parties and restaurants with friends, including David Waterhouse and Philip Dunne; and at Royal Ascot she poked her husband's equerry in the backside with her rolled up umbrella. She took off in her car without telling anyone or taking a detective. On one occasion, driving herself across London late at night, she was followed by photographers, but it could so easily have been terrorists.

The gossip columnists began to comment, and the press began to speculate, that the marriage was in trouble. One night, as the Princess was emerging with friends from Kate Menzie's mews house in the early hours of the morning, a waiting photographer took some pictures of Diana with David Waterhouse indulging in some horse-play. Diana was distraught when she realised she had been caught on film and she and her detective pleaded with the photographer to hand over his film and say nothing of what he had seen. The photographer duly obliged with the film but went straight back to his newspaper with the story. The next morning it was headline news.

In March 1987 the Prince left for a walk in the Kalahari Desert with Sir Laurens van der Post, and was no sooner back from that than he was off for a week's painting holiday in Italy. By the end of the summer, when he had done his usual stint at Balmoral while Diana had stayed firmly put in London, the press calculated that they had spent one day together in six weeks.

Yet during this period in the mid- and late-1980s, when their private life was so troubled, the Prince and Princess were in many ways a formidable double act.

The Prince had set himself up as a controversial figure, and although some people were clearly bemused by some of his interests and concerns, many of his speeches had struck a chord, as the hundreds of letters that arrived in his office made clear. The Prince's Trust was beginning to have an impact, he was busily importing ideas from America to help solve inner-city problems, and was making waves on the environmental front.

The Princess, meanwhile, although looking ever more glamorous, was making it clear that she had more to offer than her looks. She had taken on unglamorous causes like drug abuse, marriage guidance and Aids, and was proving to be quite unparalleled in her ability to charm, communicate and empathise with ordinary people.

Abroad, they were a sensation and on every trip – to Australia, America, the Gulf States, Italy, Japan – the reception was rapturous. At home the combination was never more successful than as joint patrons of the Wishing Well Appeal. Great Ormond Street Children's Hospital needed £30 million to rebuild, and in well under the two-year target, had raised a total of £54 million with a further £30 million promised by the government.

While everyone who worked for the Prince and Princess knew there were problems, heard the rows and felt the brunt of the changes of mood that affected them both on a daily basis, no one appreciated that there was ever a danger of the marriage breaking down irreparably. While fending off questions from the media about the state of the relationship, those running the press office at Buckingham Palace were far more concerned about how best to manage the run-away success of the royal couple. In terms of providing the perfect foundation for the future of the monarchy, this was a marriage made in heaven. The problem was how to pace the success: not to allow too much exposure, not to allow them to give too many interviews, not to let too much light in on the mystery of monarchy. The popularity needed to be kept going for another twenty or thirty years; because unlike politics or show business or any other career in which fame and popularity are a measure of success, the monarchy is a long-term game. There is no stepping out of public life when the going gets tough, no retreating into anonymity or even retiring at sixty. The work goes on remorselessly and the exposure with it, and as every celebrity knows, the greater the adulation, the faster it can disappear. The danger at that time was too much too quickly.

There was also the danger that if anyone talked too openly about the state of the marriage it might precipitate disaster, when disaster was far from certain. Most of those closest to the couple were aware that there were other people in both their lives. The men who had basked in the Princess's affections were comparatively well known. After David Waterhouse, James Gilbey, who had known Diana since the age of seventeen, had featured briefly. James Hewitt was the one with whom she said she had been very much in love, but there were several men over a period who all seemed to have a claim on her affections, and who came and went from Kensington Palace at all hours of the day and night. She appeared to enjoy the power she had over them, telephoning and having them arrive at her bidding, and dismissing them when she wanted them gone.

Most of the Prince's staff knew he was seeing Camilla Parker Bowles, although he was always painstakingly discreet about it, but none of them assumed that this meant that the marriage was in danger of breaking up. Extra-marital affairs were a traditional part of aristocratic marriages and had been for centuries. Who was to say that this would be any different? Indeed, both Lord Mountbatten and the Duke of Edinburgh had told the Prince of Wales that if his marriage didn't work out, the solution was to find a married woman with whom he could quietly conduct an affair.

Divorce was seldom the solution for couples who had tired of one another in this stratum of society, and many couples lived with great civility, and even affection, under one roof, displaying a united front in public, while pursuing love affairs elsewhere. It meant stability for the children and security for the future of the family estate. Both the Prince and Princess had grown up witnesses to this sort of marital behaviour, and although each was as idealistic as the other and determined at the outset to make their marriage different, they recognised that it was the way people coped. But there was a difference. In previous generations, although their social peers knew who was bedding whom, no one ever broke rank and the gossip seldom went further than their own circle of friends. If ever a whisper reached the newspapers, the proprietors, all themselves members of the establishment, made sure the story never surfaced.

But times, society and newspaper proprietors had changed, and by the late 1980s and early 1990s there was protection for no one, and high prices were paid for information.

The Prince and Princess had already suffered from members of their domestic staff selling the odd story, but no one, not even in their wildest dreams, could have foreseen that the person who would tell the world about the most intimate details of their married life and the Prince's love for Camilla Parker Bowles would be Diana herself. When Andrew Morton's book, *Diana – Her True Story*, was serialised in *The Sunday Times* in June 1992, the Prince and his staff were taken completely by surprise. And for the Prince, the embarrassment, hurt and humiliation was total.

'Diana driven to five suicide bids by "uncaring" Charles', ran the front-page headline on the first day of serialisation. It went on to talk about Diana's bulimia, her husband's indifference towards her, his obsession with his mistress, his shortcomings as a father, and the loneliness and isolation she had felt for so many years, trapped in a loveless marriage within a hostile court and cold and disapproving Royal Family. The book had a compelling authority, and many of the Princess's closest friends were openly quoted. For example, 'James Gilbey explains: "She thinks he is a bad father, a selfish father, the children have to tie in with what he's doing. He will never delay, cancel or change anything which he has sorted out for their benefit.'

At first, Diana denied any involvement with the book and Sir Robert Fellowes believed her. The result of Fellowes's appeal to Lord McGregor, chairman of the Press Complaints Commission, was the issue of a statement condemning the serialisation as an 'odious exhibition of journalists dabbling their fingers in the stuff of other people's souls in a manner which adds nothing to the legitimate public interest in the situation of the heir to the throne'. Having given her word to Fellowes that she had not contributed to the book, the Princess then put on a deliberate and public show of affection for Carolyn Bartholomew, her former flatmate, and one of the most quoted sources in the book. She telephoned in advance to make sure that the press photographers were in place outside Carolyn's London house when she went to visit and the friends greeted one another warmly on the doorstep. The message that Diana approved of what her friend had said on her behalf could not have been clearer. Robert Fellowes realised at once that he had been taken in by the Princess, and that it had caused everyone, including Lord McGregor and the Prince of Wales, acute embarrassment. He promptly handed in his resignation – which the Queen rejected.

It was not until after her death five years later, however, that the full extent of Diana's co-operation with Andrew Morton was known. It transpired that she had spoken into a tape recorder at Kensington Palace during the summer and autumn of 1991, and the tapes were then delivered to Morton via an intermediary, Dr James Colthurst, a friend of Diana who also happened to be a squash-playing partner of Morton. What had puzzled the Prince and those close to him was that much of the book was accurate in some respects, and there were stories told that only Diana or at most only a handful of people could possibly have known about, or memos leaked that nobody else could have seen. But most of the stories had a spin on them, which made them not quite as anyone else who had been present remembered.

There was a memo, for example, which, according to Morton, Richard Aylard had written to the Prince of Wales to encourage him to see more of his children. He had recently been badly censured by the press for his apparently cavalier attitude to William after he had been hit on the head by a golf club. 'At the conclusion of his missive,' said Morton, 'he [Aylard] heavily underlined in red ink and printed in bold capitals a single word: "TRY".'

In actual fact the Prince had sent Aylard a memo saying that William and Harry had said they wanted to do a few things with their father and could Aylard please look in the diary and pick out a few engagements that would be suitable for the boys to go along to. Aylard wrote back with three or four suggestions, including a trip to a naval ship, and said that the next step was to speak to the Princess to make sure she was happy about the plan. It would be best, wrote Aylard, if the Prince could speak to her about it himself. Failing that, he would speak to Patrick Jephson, the Princess's private secretary. The Prince sent the memo back, annotated in his red pen – and he was the only person in the office allowed to use red ink. Against the suggestion that he should speak to his wife, he wrote, 'I will TRY!'

In the immediate aftermath of the serialisation, the office at St James's Palace was a very unsettled and unhappy place. No one knew who was responsible for the leaked information. There were one or two suspects, but they were trusted members of the team and it was deeply uncomfortable not knowing who had betrayed them and therefore might betray them again.

Even before she gave Carolyn Bartholomew such public endorsement, several people suspected the Princess. A number of stories which were clearly very well sourced had been appearing in *The Sunday Times* and other newspapers for some time. One such story was the dismissal of Sir Christopher Airy as private secretary to the Prince of Wales.

In his late fifties, Sir Christopher Airy had taken over from Sir John Riddell in 1990, and from the outset it was apparent that he was not going to fit. As a former Major-General commanding the Royal Household Division, he was not the man to take over a highly disorganised, under-staffed, over-worked office working for an impatient and demanding man with the most disparate collection of interests. One of Airy's first edicts was that everyone should wear their jackets in the office. He never fully understood the difference between the Prince's various organisations, never quite grasped where the Prince's Trust ended and Business in the Community began, or what the Prince's Youth Business Trust had to do with either of them, or where the Prince's interest in organic farming or wildlife fitted into the picture. And when, after a year, he was still very much at sea, the Prince was persuaded that, delightful man though he was, the time had come to part company.

The crunch had come at the end of a tour of Brazil in April 1991, when the Prince hosted a top-level international seminar on development and the environment on board the royal yacht half-way up the Amazon. As private secretary, Airy had insisted on being there although he had no real role to play because three assistant private secretaries, Peter Westmacott, Guy Salter and Richard Aylard, had every aspect of the two-day event covered – Westmacott, the Foreign Office angle, Salter, business, and Aylard, the environment. Nothing irritates the Prince more than supernumeraries on a tour and to see his private secretary left with nothing better to do than hand round the coffee was the final straw. On the night flight back to London, the Prince told Richard Aylard that he wanted him to change jobs with Sir Christopher, having first told the Princess about his plans.

Aylard had been equerry to the Princess for three years from 1985 to 1988. He had then become an assistant private secretary with responsibility for the environment brief, and comptroller to the Prince and Princess.

The Prince's idea was that Airy should run the household and Aylard the office, but was persuaded that this would be unpalatable to all concerned. Better to say the time had come for both Prince and Princess to have their own private secretaries, which up to that time they had shared, and to have a senior figure, namely Airy, to run the household. This was the formula which the Prince put to Airy on their return to London, but the older man saw it as a plot to oust him and refused the offer.

At this point they became aware that *The Sunday Times* was planning to run a story that Sir Christopher Airy had been sacked by the Prince of Wales. It would have to be confirmed or denied, which forced the Prince's hand. He offered Aylard the job of private secretary and determined to sack Airy on the Friday after a meeting of the Prince of Wales Co-ordinating Committee at Highgrove. The Prince is deeply loyal by nature and telling people he likes that they have to go is something he hates doing and is very bad at. He liked Airy and he recognised that the fault had been his own in asking the man to do the job in the first place. When he tackled him, Airy once again refused to accept what he was hearing, so the Prince brought in reinforcements. He asked Allen Sheppard, chief executive of Grand Metropolitan and a member of the Co-ordinating Committee, to take Airy into the garden and tell him that the time had come to hand in his letter of resignation. It was a difficult and highly emotional end to the afternoon, brought to a rather comical conclusion by the Princess arriving at the house, apparently unaware of what was going on, and starting to pour gin and tonics for everyone. In fact, Airy was left so confused by everything that Peter Westmacott found it necessary to explain the situation to him later that afternoon.

The story subsequently appeared in *The Sunday Times*, written by Andrew Morton, with detail of the afternoon at Highgrove that could only have come from one of two people in the room at the time – either the Princess or Sir Christopher Airy. Other stories had had Diana's fingerprints on them too, but no one knew how the stories were reaching Morton. It could quite easily have been that one of her friends, possibly without her knowledge, was passing on gossip that she had told them over lunch or in one of her endless telephone conversations.

There were several people at the time who thought Richard Aylard might have been responsible for the original leak about Sir Christopher Airy's downfall, ambitious as he was for the post and wanting to force the indecisive Prince's hand. Much as he wanted the job of private secretary, Aylard did not want Airy to go yet. He wanted Sir Christopher to handle the household, to be the figurehead and take care of the pomp and ceremony which he was so good at. Aylard himself wanted to be left to get on with writing speeches and pulling together all the different strands of the Prince's interests, and turning his ideas into reality.

There was another possible contender for the job of private secretary in 1991: Peter Westmacott. Of the two candidates he was the more heavyweight. Slightly older than Aylard, he was a senior Foreign Office secondee, who also wrote well and, like Aylard, was responsible for some of the Prince's best speeches, particularly on education. He was a very important influence during his time at

St James's Palace. Like Aylard, he was devoted to the Prince. They got on very well together and it would have been a good team. Unhappily for Westmacott, however, he and the Princess also got on very well together. They became very close; so close that many, possibly even including the Prince, thought they were having an affair.

They were not. But Diana did flirt outrageously, as she did with many men, and did spend many hours confiding her innermost thoughts and fears to him. He had joined the team in March 1990 and first met the Princess when they all went off on a tour of Hungary together. She was on very good form, relaxed and happy, flirtatious as ever and obviously pleased to have a new and good looking face around. Having come from the Foreign Office he was not highly attuned to the finer details of the marriage. At one stage in the tour Diana was being driven around in a horse and cart, and needing to stop quite frequently to go to the loo. The press started saying she must be pregnant, and Westmacott asked Sir John Riddell whether perhaps he should let the Princess know what they were writing.

'Dangerous stuff, Peter,' said Riddell. 'It would take a braver man than you or me to raise that subject.'

At lunch that day, which was a barbecue in the woods, the Princess told Westmacott to sit next to her. They chatted for a while, then he decided she ought to know what was being said. She didn't bat an eye-lid.

'Me pregnant?' she said. 'Chance would be a fine thing!'

Probably like every court that ever was, St James's Palace is a place of camps, a hotbed of internal politics and jealousies, where everyone is jockeying for positions of favour with the Prince and, given the slightest opportunity, will gleefully drop poison into his ear about friends or colleagues. Peter Westmacott was aware that people were talking, and the Princess did indeed seem to regard him as a friend, but he felt that since he was working for both the Prince and Princess he had to speak to them both. If he could help inject a little balance into the way in which the Princess perceived what was going on around her, and be in a position to tell her when something was nonsense – stop her running away with crazy ideas – it might be helpful for everyone. But he was only on loan from the Foreign Office, and was not, therefore, a good long-term bet for the Prince. It was hardly surprising that, in the event, Richard Aylard was given the top job and Westmacott was given the newly created title of deputy private secretary.

Many men found themselves in Diana's thrall, and it was always the Princess who was in control of the situation. She picked them up and put them down at whim, and if she chose to telephone late at night and speak for more than an hour at a time, or plead for someone to drop everything and come and visit, there was no easy way of refusing her. Even Sir Christopher had been entranced by her in his time. On one occasion he was waiting at Highgrove for the Prince, who was late as usual in returning from an engagement. He had just heard that the helicopter was in range, and would therefore be arriving shortly, when the Princess invited him for a drive in her brand new Mercedes soft-top. When the Prince arrived his first question was 'Where's Christopher?' and he was incensed to be told he had gone for a drive with the Princess.

Richard Aylard never found himself caught in the middle, as so many others had been, because after 1988, when he started working principally for the Prince, the Princess looked upon him as an enemy. She accused him of 'defecting to the other side' when his three-year secondment as her equerry came to an end. She began to talk about there being two camps, and wanted to have her own staff and be independent from her husband.

Soon after he had become comptroller and was therefore working for both camps, Aylard was in Switzerland trying to sort out the press in advance of the annual skiing trip. The Princess telephoned from London and acidly asked what her comptroller was doing on the ski slopes. 'Why aren't you back here running the office?'

Aylard explained that he was in Switzerland because the Prince had asked him to go across to organise the press. 'Well that's not good enough,' she said. 'You're needed here,' and slammed the phone down. Having been fond of Diana while working for her he was hurt that she should have turned on him. They had been through a lot together in three years and he was disappointed that she took his departure so personally.

Anne Beckwith-Smith also came to be regarded with suspicion and was eased out as private secretary in 1990. Anne had never allowed herself to get too close to Diana; she wished to keep the relationship professional. Diana was her boss, and Anne kept herself out of Diana's personal life as much as possible. She was unhappy with the way things were going and had a number of fallings out with the Princess. In the past Diana had been receptive to advice, but latterly the advice Anne had to give was not to her liking. Diana had changed and Anne was no longer able to read her or judge how to play things. She tried to persuade her to keep the marriage going, and to make the marriage work, but realised that the Princess was determined to go her own way, and viewed Anne as a stick in the mud. They agreed to a parting of the ways, but Anne remained an extra lady-in-waiting and saw her thereafter about once a month.

Most conversations with anyone who has been involved with the Prince and Princess, either as friends or employees, are categorised as Before or After Morton. There is no doubt that his book spelt the beginning of the end, although at the time, the Prince's immediate reaction was not that he wanted a separation. Despite what the book had said about him, much of which was so devastatingly untrue and unjust, the Prince clung to the hope that Diana had not been involved. He was still desperately keen to keep the marriage going, just as he had always been. He knew separation would cause so much hurt – to the Queen, the monarchy, the country and, most of all, William and Harry – and he thought it was unnecessary. He and Diana both had their own groups of friends, their own interests, their own private lives, and could put on a good public show together for the sake of the country. He did not understand why that shouldn't continue. Before he discovered the truth about the Morton book, he had even cherished the hope that one day he and Diana could be friends.

Curiously, Charles never replied to the accusations against him in Morton's book and gave very firm instructions to his staff and his friends not to reply or offer any kind of defence on his behalf. He didn't want to do anything that would hurt Diana, and he didn't want the degeneration of his marriage to become a tit for tat exercise. He couldn't bear to see the intimate details of their troubled marriage played out on the front covers of the tabloid press for a moment longer. He thought it damaging for his children and damaging for the monarchy. Understandably, the man in the street was left with little alternative but to believe Diana's shocking account of his callous behaviour.

There was another reason why he was loath to retaliate. He had grown bitterly disillusioned about the media during the course of his marriage. He felt, not without some justification, that it had short-changed him. In the early days he had been ignored in favour of his wife. Since their problems first started being talked about in 1987, the newspapers had chipped away remorselessly. They had printed story after story which condemned or ridiculed him; they had analysed his body language, counted the days spent away from his wife, speculated on the identity of mystery blondes seen boarding aeroplanes or spied through long lenses at Balmoral.

During the course of that time he had introduced initiatives to inner city schools which were proving highly successful, he had raised thousands of pounds for the Prince's Trust, he had developed a Volunteer Scheme to give young people a reason for getting out of bed in the morning, he had ensured the future of Shakespeare in our language, he had put architecture into the hands of the people for whom buildings were built, he had raised £5 million for charity on the polo field. The list was endless. Yet all of this, and more, had been largely ignored by the press.

There are a number of theories about why Diana spoke to Morton. It was known in certain circles that some of her telephone conversations had been recorded and were being touted around Fleet Street. There would have been a persuasive argument that she should get her story out and gain public sympathy before a newspaper published any intimate late-night chat she may have had with a man who was not her husband. She had always thought that people were talking behind her back and watching her, and became obsessed with the idea that the Buckingham Palace switchboard was spying on her and listening in to her telephone calls. She was reassured by a member of the Queen's household that this was impossible, but because Diana was insistent, she was given a mobile phone to use instead. Ironically, it was the mobile phone, not the landline, that was tapped.

Diana had been living a charmed existence as far as the newspapers were concerned. Given the number of men who came to visit her by day and night at Kensington Palace, the number of letters she wrote to James Hewitt when he was fighting in the Gulf War in January 1991 – any one of which could have been opened or seen by someone else – the number of phone calls she made, the restaurants she openly ate in with male friends, her late-night hospital visits to see a doctor on the pretext of visiting patients, there was surprisingly little gossip about her in the press. She was firmly advised it was highly dangerous to write to James Hewitt in the Gulf, but took no notice. During the course of their relationship she sent over a hundred affectionate, loving hand-written letters to him, which he still cherishes. Sixty-two of her letters were taken from him by a girlfriend who tried to sell them to the *Daily Mirror* after Diana's death. Piers Morgan, the editor, honourably handed them over to the Spencer family without publishing any, although what should become of them is hotly disputed. Diana also wrote to David Waterhouse, who was also serving in the Gulf. She was frightened that both men might be killed.

The fact that she was never seriously exposed by the press was very largely the result of a concentrated charm-offensive on a number of key figures, not least the late Sir David English, who ran the *Mail* titles, whose daily and Sunday papers accounted for the biggest middle-market circulation in Britain. Sir David was charmed and entranced by Diana, as all men who met the Princess face to face invariably were. But he was also a tough and experienced newspaper man, who could see that in a black and white world, taking Diana's side against the Prince in two newspapers with a high proportion of female readers was sound business. Many suspect there was an understanding between the two that in return for stories, and photo opportunities, unflattering aspects of Diana's personal life would remain out of the newspapers. The *Mail* did have a remarkably constant flow of positive stories about the Princess and demonstrated no very great support or affection for the Prince. But Diana targeted other editors too, plus one or two influential journalists, and rang them with stories, invited them to lunch and flattered their male egos.

Despite the show she put on to the outside world, in the early 1990s, the Princess was at a very low ebb. Years of anorexia and bulimia had played havoc with her system and she not only saw a constant stream of conventional doctors but also dabbled in some extreme and strange alternative treatments. One of the problems was a bad back – ironically, a problem shared by both the Prince of Wales and Camilla Parker Bowles. She saw therapists of every sort: she had aromatherapy, reflexology, colonic irrigation, acupuncture, massage, chiropractic treatment, and consulted an astrologer and a medium, and a doctor who runs magnetic pulses through the body. She was also working out at the gym at the Harbour Club in Chelsea on a regular basis. She was spending an alarming amount of money on all of this – and with clothes and holidays thrown in, it was working out at about £3,000 per week.

Whether she believed deep down that as a result of all this therapy she had grown into a strong woman is questionable. She certainly had the vocabulary. She also had the anger. She felt that despite the best efforts of her husband and his family to destroy her, she had managed to pull herself back from the brink of disaster, and she wanted to prove that she had done it by herself. She had cried for help and her cries had been ignored. She had coped with the difficulties, coped with the stress, survived the despair of post-natal depression and bulimia, she had learnt to rely on her own resources, and she had come out the other side, high in the opinion polls, a star in the royal firmament and doing the job better than any other member of the Royal Family – giving the public what they wanted.

Now it was payback time. Whether psyched up by counselling and therapy, or simply angry on her own account, she was determined to have her revenge, and *Diana – Her True Story* was it. The puzzling aspect of the exercise was the effect she must have known it would have on the children she adored. She did subsequently regret what she had done, and told her friends it had been a terrible mistake, but not for some time.

In the immediate aftermath, Diana was elated, and in her triumph she became more and more difficult. The children would not be where they were supposed to be, or she would change her mind at the last minute about arrangements, making life very awkward for the Prince, whose days are tightly scheduled. She became even more reluctant to carry out joint engagements, which made it hard to send positive messages about the health of the marriage to the outside world. Even before Morton there had been an embarrassing trip to India, when the Princess had posed forlornly in front of the Taj Mahal, taking practically every press photographer in India with her, while her husband delivered two speeches and launched a new charity with scarcely one. The potent symbolism of the Princess sitting alone in front of the world's greatest monument to love was enough to wipe anything the Prince did off the map. It was only a couple of days later, when Diana reluctantly agreed to present the trophies at a polo match, that Charles got a mention. And only then because when the Prince came to give her a very public kiss on the cheek as he collected his prize, she turned her head away so as to leave him awkwardly kissing the air. The stories in the newspapers were all about the state of the marriage and that was some four months before Morton's book appeared.

On 25 August 1992 any elation Diana had felt from the publication of the Morton book completely disappeared. Transcripts of a tape-recorded amorous late-night telephone conversation allegedly between her and James Gilbey were published in the *Sun* newspaper. He called her 'Darling' fifty-three times, and 'Squidgy' or 'Squidge' fourteen times, which led to the scandal being dubbed 'Squidgygate'. Once upon a time Diana had used the same sort of vocabulary about Charles. She had said things like, 'My gorgeous sqwunchy man, I love you, I love you, I love you.' And he had gone weak at the knees.

Aside from romantic endearments, Diana also talked about how her husband made her life 'real, real torture', and described a lunch at which the Queen Mother had given her a strange look. 'It's not hatred, it's sort of interest and pity ... I was very bad at lunch and I nearly started blubbing. I just felt really sad and empty and thought "Bloody hell, after all I've done for this fucking family" ... It is just so desperate. Always being innuendo, the fact that I'm going to do something dramatic because I can't stand the confines of this marriage.'

The recording had been made illegally on New Year's Eve in 1989 when Diana was at Sandringham and Gilbey in a car parked in Oxfordshire. Her distress at its publication was excruciating.

Another foreign tour was coming up, to Korea, which had like everything been planned far in advance. Late in the day, the Princess announced that she was not prepared to go. After much persuasion, including intervention by the Queen, she finally agreed to stick to her original plan, but the trip was a disaster. The only angle the press was interested in was the marriage, and for the first time, the Princess made no attempt to disguise her feelings. Normally the master of self-control and a performer of the first order, she looked sad and miserable and frequently on the verge of tears. The Prince looked no happier, and although he worked hard to cover up for her by doing all the talking and smiling, nothing could salvage the situation.

In private there was nothing left between them, not even the enforced civility they had become accustomed to faking for the sake of their staff. To be in the same room with them both, trying to talk to one or other of them, was quite frightful. Meanwhile, journalistic coverage of the Korean tour was confined to obituaries of the marriage and ignored in its entirety the trade deals and governmental ties which had been secured. Peter Westmacott, the deputy private secretary with the unenviable task of accompanying the Prince and Princess, took aside James Whitaker, royal correspondent of the *Daily Mirror*, to complain about the coverage. Whitaker was sympathetic, but commented, 'Peter, you really can't say this is a marriage made in heaven.'

'I am not saying it is,' said Westmacott. 'What I am saying is that you guys are getting it so grossly wrong, you're mis-reporting what's going on and ignoring the substance of the visit.'

Two hours later Sky News was interrupting broadcasts to say 'Palace official confirms marriage is on the rocks.' Whitaker's defence was that he had had a duty to relay what he had been told to the rest of the journalists who were covering the tour, because Westmacott had 'sought him out for conversation'. By the next day the tabloid press was full of the story: 'Palace official in gaffe.' 'Palace official confirms marriage over.'

At the end of the tour the Prince and Princess flew on to Hong Kong. He was staying there; she was to fly back to London. By the time they arrived in Hong Kong, just three hours later, the storm had broken. Shortly after their arrival Westmacott went into the Prince's bedroom with the newspapers to break the bad news. The Prince had been quite unaware of what had happened the night before, but listened to Westmacott's tale and apology with a wan smile. The Prince is always unfailingly gracious if people take problems to him rather than leaving him to hear bad news through back channels. In this case, he was understanding when Westmacott explained what had happened. The Prince had always felt 'it was a waste of time trying to talk sense to these people'.

During the flight to Hong Kong Westmacott had tried hard to talk the Princess out of separation. He tried to persuade her that it would be best for everyone if they could find a *modus vivendi*. She had her own friends, her own life, the children had the stability of two parents and she was good at her job. Why did she want to destroy it all?

It was to no avail. By the time the Prince was looking at the morning papers, the Princess was on a plane bound for London, determined that she was going to end the sham of their marriage.

TEN

The Beginning of the End

'I hope you find it in your hearts to understand ...'
Diana's 'resignation' speech, 1993

On the afternoon of 9 December 1992, John Major, the then Prime Minister, stood up at the dispatch box in the House of Commons before a packed but silent House and read aloud the following statement:

> 'It is announced from Buckingham Palace that, with regret, the Prince and Princess of Wales have decided to separate. Their Royal Highnesses have no plans to divorce and their constitutional positions are unaffected. This decision has been reached amicably and they will both continue to participate fully in the upbringing of their children.
>
> 'Their Royal Highnesses will continue to carry out full and separate programmes of public engagements and will, from time to time, attend family occasions and national events together.'

The Prince was on a Business in the Community visit to Holyhead on the day the separation was announced, followed by a Prince's Trust board meeting in the afternoon. The news had started to leak, and there were shouts from the press 'Give us a statement, Charlie.' Julia Cleverdon, chief executive of BitC, was with him and, much to her amusement, photographed as 'an unknown woman in green' as they boarded the aircraft together. She had been blissfully ignorant about the announcement, and it was only on the flight home that she realised what was going on. They had been working together closely for nearly ten years and shared a lot of the same ideas, frustrations and enthusiasms. That afternoon he told her about the separation and, in all the years she had known the Prince, she had never seen him so deeply miserable.

The crunch had come during a weekend at Sandringham, soon after the disastrous Korean trip. Every year the Prince and Princess had hosted a shooting party at Sandringham for sixteen friends who came to stay for three days with their children, and the Prince had organised it around the Princes' exeat from Ludgrove, their preparatory school, so they could be there and see their friends. Less than a week beforehand, the Prince discovered that Diana had decided to take the children to stay with the Queen at Windsor instead. He explained the situation to the Queen who then spoke to Diana, but the Princess announced that if she couldn't go to Windsor she would take the boys to Highgrove. Charles asked whether she might not at least let the boys come, even if she was determined to stay away herself, but she refused. The Prince's patience finally snapped.

He had put up with years of tantrums and abuse, he had given up his friends to try and please her, he had given up his dog, he had given up shooting for a while, he had sacked perfectly innocuous members of staff because she took against them, he had had no comfort, no companionship in recent years, he had been embarrassed and humiliated by the Andrew Morton book, upstaged by her in the press on more occasions than he cared to think of, she had flaunted boyfriends quite openly, and she had caused acute difficulty in Korea by appearing to be there under sufferance, hardly able to be in his presence. Now she was embarrassing him in front of his friends and making life difficult for their sons. Painful though it would be for everyone, there was no alternative but to call a halt to the marriage.

After the announcement, the Prince's staff had quickly to divide the household in two. He wanted to have the smallest most loyal staff he could reasonably get away with, so that the danger of people selling stories or gossiping would be minimised. He decided to keep Bernie Flannery, the number-three butler, for himself, and let Diana have the two senior butlers, Paul Burrell, from Highgrove, and Harold Brown, who was already at Kensington Palace.

The office at St James's Palace remained intact, and although there was much talk about warring factions, the two teams were remarkably united. They continued to share the same rooms, the same coffee-making facilities, the same secretaries and fax machine, and they continued to talk to one another as they always had done. But there is no doubt there were difficulties, which were never truly resolved until the divorce four years later.

The principal problem remained that the Princess would frequently go off and do things without telling anyone, or change the arrangements for the children at the last minute. It was at the eleventh hour, for example, that Charles's staff discovered she was planning to take Prince William to Wales on St David's Day. This was quite against the spirit of their agreement about the children doing public engagements, which was essentially that they would not do any. However, if there was to be an exception, they would discuss it in advance. The Prince's private secretary heard about this particular outing by chance, and with luck was able to alter Charles's arrangements so that he could be there with them. Diana had not been intending to tell him. Conversely, on the day when the Prince had been planning to take Harry to visit the aircraft carrier HMS *Invincible*, the Princess announced that he had a dental appointment and would not be available. Rather than risk a high-profile row with his estranged wife, the Prince let it go, and Harry missed the excitement of seeing Harrier jump jets take off and land.

On the whole, however, Charles and Diana were scrupulously fair with the children and in total agreement about how they should be treated and educated. They never argued about them, and they never argued in front of them. Both wanted the very best for the young Princes. They had chosen Ludgrove as a prep school for them together, and were both delighted by the choice of Eton as a public school, where William started at the age of thirteen, Harry following in September 1998. Diana's brother had been at Eton, and Dr Eric Anderson, Head Master up until the year William arrived, had been the Prince's English and drama teacher at Gordonstoun. Tom Parker Bowles, the Prince's godson, had also recently left the school and there were plenty of sons of friends either there already or due to go who would make the Princes welcome.

Before making their final decision, Charles and Diana had spoken at length to people connected with the school, such as Douglas Hurd, the then Foreign Secretary, who is an Old Etonian, a fellow of the school and a friend of the Head Master. They both asked the same kind of questions about the teachers (known at Eton as 'beaks'), the people there, and most particularly the privacy.

'I was struck,' Hurd says, 'that they were both, separately, singing from the same hymn sheet.'

There are no dormitories at Eton. Boys all sleep in their own study bedrooms from the day they arrive, in one of twenty-five individual houses of about fifty boys each. The town in which the school is situated is dominated by the school, and it is well used to coping with high-profile boys. William entered historian Dr Andrew Gailey's house, where Harry joined him, and Gailey was instrumental in helping William through some of the most difficult times, when his parents were waging a very public war against each other. He was also there to help William after his mother's death and spent a lot of time talking to him. William and Harry's protection officers have also been a great help to both boys. They were carefully chosen for the job and are very much a cross between friend and uncle.

The Princess was acutely conscious of living in a gilded cage, and saw it as part of her duty as a royal parent to expose her children to real life and give them an understanding of how ordinary people lived. The Prince was in full agreement. He felt that the Palace system had made a mess of him and he was determined that it was not going to wreck his sons too – the very thing that Earl Spencer so unkindly suggested would happen if Diana's blood relatives were not there to save them. Consequently, Charles approved of most of what the boys did with Diana, though he was uneasy that she chose to take them to visit hostels for the homeless, and didn't quite understand why she was doing it. He felt it would have been better to let them be carefree children while they still could. They would have the rest of their lives to carry out public engagements. Why burden them with the plight of the disadvantaged when they were still so young? But he never tried to stop her. She was their parent, he reasoned, just as much as he was, and her point of view about how William and Harry should be brought up was every bit as legitimate as his own.

Charles and Diana unquestionably had very different styles. With their father, William and Harry were typical sons of the landed gentry. They loved hunting, albeit as followers, shooting and fishing, and spent hours on the Highgrove farm with the animals, or on bikes or tractors. More recently, they have both taken up polo, and are mad about skiing, which Diana also loved. When they were with her, they became urban kids. They dressed in jeans and baseball caps and ate in McDonald's hamburger restaurants, went to the movies and hurtled down the scariest runs at all the major theme parks. These were private trips, but Diana always made certain that the newspapers knew about them, which helped to reinforce the perception that she was a loving mother who did fun things with her children, in stark contrast to their father, who looked cold and stiff, with hands clasped firmly behind his back, a picture of distant old-fashioned formality.

If they are at home, Charles's philosophy is they can do exactly as they please and have fun; but when they are doing anything remotely public as royal princes, he expects something a little different. The sight of Prince Harry, aged thirteen, dressed in a suit at the World Cup football match in France in July 1998, when England played Argentina, was typical. Prince Charles was criticised for making him dress up in a suit, when it was so obvious what his mother would have dressed him in. What the commentators failed to recognise was that Prince Charles and Prince Harry both met the President of France while they were at the match. They were not there as anonymous punters, and it would have been discourteous to President Chirac to dress in any other way. Whether he likes it or not, Harry is not a normal teenager, and never can be. He is third in line to the throne of England and, as he discovered long ago, this sets him apart from his peers.

In reality, Diana wasn't the only one who handed out the laughter and the hugs. The Princess was very often warmer and more demonstrative in public than in private. Away from the cameras, the boys saw the extremes of her moods as clearly as everyone else, and were often quite frightened and bewildered by what they saw. She had taken no effort to spare them her emotions. When a friend once suggested it was unwise to have hysterics in front of Prince William, who was at that time in a cot, Diana said he was too young to notice, and anyway he would have to learn the truth sooner or later.

The Prince's private persona is also completely different from his public one. He fools around with the boys, they tease each other, laugh, joke, rough and tumble, and even hug and kiss. On the last night of their skiing holiday in Klosters in 1997, there was a big farewell dinner party in their hotel restaurant. In the middle of dinner Harry got to his feet and, in front of a table full of people, made a little speech to thank 'Papa', as both boys call him (to rhyme with 'supper'), for giving him such a wonderful holiday. He then walked smartly up to his father and smothered his face in kisses until, in mock embarrassment, the Prince begged for mercy. It was a touching scene.

When William and Harry were small, one of the biggest problems Charles's valets had was keeping his suits clean. Whenever Charles arrived home at Highgrove by helicopter, it would land in the front field, where sheep graze. As soon as William and Harry heard it overhead, they would come running out to meet him. Once it had landed safely, they would race across the field and jump up into his arms for a hug, smearing one suit after another with the sheep droppings they had trodden in on the way. He built them a massive tree house in a holly tree, affectionately known as Holyroodhouse, after Holyroodhouse Palace, the Queen's official residence in

Edinburgh. They share the same silly sense of humour, as Diana did too, and they are great practical jokers – another of their mother's legacies. They are also both very funny mimics, like the Prince, and take him off better than anyone. These days, William is taller than his father so any physical horse-play invariably ends in cries of 'Get off, you great big enormous lout.'

After the separation Charles recognised he was going to need some practical help looking after the boys when they were with him. They were too old for a nanny but needed someone who could be around to do things with them, drive them to their friends', take them shopping or shooting and, being a hopeless disciplinarian himself, exert some discipline over them. Alexandra Legge-Bourke, known as Tiggy, was the twenty-eight-year-old daughter of a family friend, and perfectly qualified. She was a delightful, dizzy nursery school teacher, who had a brilliant rapport with children of all shapes and sizes, who were known as her Tiggywigs.

William and Harry took to her instantly. She was like an over-grown child, very good fun to be with. She treated them as a big sister might, rather than as a nanny or a parent would. She loved doing all the outdoor things they enjoyed, like shooting and following the hunt, she told jokes, liked the same kind of music, watched the same videos, yet at the same time she managed to get them to do what they were told, without ever being officiously strict. If their father tells them to go to bed, they ignore him or wheedle him round. If Tiggy tells them to, they call her a 'Bossy Old Bat' but go.

The Princess looked on the blossoming relationship between her sons and Tiggy Legge-Bourke with horror; and this was the one area in which Camilla Parker Bowles was entirely sympathetic. As a mother herself, she could understand how painful it must have been for the Princess to see her children fooling around and enjoying themselves with another woman, who was allowing them to do things she might not have done, and to whom they were inevitably growing closer emotionally. She was angry and jealous, and the Prince was not overly sensitive to her feelings.

These years of separation were not happy ones for the Princess.

She developed a passion for Oliver Hoare, an art dealer friend of the Prince of Wales, whom she had met through her husband. He was often seen arriving at Kensington Palace and there was much gossip. Hoare was married, with no intention of leaving his wife and, when he realised that the situation was getting out of control, he tried to cool the relationship. The Princess was not happy about it. She liked to be in control. As a result she started telephoning Hoare's wife, Dianne, at the family home. When Dianne picked up the receiver there would be a long silence, or the caller would hang up. Eventually she reported the matter to the police and a trace was put on the calls, which all seemed to have emanated from Kensington Palace. When the story appeared in the press, Diana was livid, and to their complete fury, accused one of the Prince's staff and her husband of leaking it. She was convinced that her husband's office was running a campaign to discredit her, and was certain that this was yet one more example of their treachery. The leak had actually come from a boy who was at school with one of the Hoare children.

There was no campaign to discredit Diana. In fact, in August 1993, when Charles declared independence from Buckingham Palace and, with the Queen's agreement, set up his own press office at St James's Palace, he had given specific instructions to his staff to say and do nothing to reflect badly upon Diana. Constitutionally the Monarch and Prince of Wales do very different jobs, and for some time it had seemed common sense that they each should have a dedicated team to handle the media. What is more, there had been a great deal of bad feeling between the press and Buckingham Palace in the latter part of the marriage. The more it became apparent that there were serious difficulties, the less the Palace press office would say. At best, the information they gave was misleading, with the result that most of the papers had stopped talking to the press office at all. The Princess, meanwhile, was talking privately to journalists and editors, and the whole situation was a mess. Much as he despised the press, the Prince was well aware that it was important to him.

He recruited two highly experienced press officers, both from solid civil service jobs: Allan Percival, from the Northern Ireland Office, and Sandy Henney, as his number two, who was with the Crown Prosecution Service. The Prince said he wanted no games and no spinning; and he wanted nothing going out of his office that might be even mildly damaging to the Princess. He left them in no doubt about his views. No matter what she did or said, she would always be the mother of his children, and anything that hurt the Princess would hurt them.

Nonetheless, Diana saw conspiracies everywhere. She left disturbing messages on a number of people's pagers and answering machines. They were all unsigned but there was no doubting where they came from. Patrick Jephson, her private secretary, was a regular recipient, with messages like, 'We know where you are and so does your wife. I know you're being disloyal to me.' Richard Aylard was another target, and there were others in the office. But some of the most poisonous messages were reserved for Tiggy. In the late-1980s Camilla also had a number of threatening and unnerving telephone calls in the middle of the night. Diana would never say who she was, but would say things like, 'I've sent someone to kill you. They're outside in the garden. Look out of the window; can you see them?' For a woman alone at night in a large house in the country and no protection, it was frightening.

No one dared confront the Princess about the messages, for fear of provoking a scene and, in the case of staff, being sacked. Diana's sackings had cost the Prince a lot of money over the years. With modern employment law it was not possible to dismiss people without warnings and good reason, and most of the people she took against had done nothing wrong. Diana had decided, sometimes quite arbitrarily, that she no longer wanted them around. On each occasion the office had to work out what that person would have been awarded by an industrial tribunal and add twenty per cent. Awards for unfair dismissal in those days were a maximum of about £11,000, depending upon length of service. As the succession of cooks, housemaids, dressers, secretaries and butlers left, each one cost between £12,000 and £14,000.

One person dismissed for no good reason was Steve Davies, a thirty-two-year-old chauffeur who had been having an affair with Helen Walsh, one of the Princess's pretty young dressers, who lived in a grace and favour cottage at the back of Kensington Palace. The Princess didn't like the relationship, and thought that they were taking advantage of their position and having fun when they shouldn't be. As a result the chauffeur was paid off, and the dresser told that her boyfriend wasn't to come on the premises again. Furious that the Princess should be interfering in her personal life, the dresser consulted the Personnel Department, who told her that she was perfectly entitled to have any guest she wanted in her home, provided the police on the gate knew they were coming. When the Princess heard this she got someone to check the rules and discovered that, technically, visitors had to be off the premises by midnight. At ten past midnight she banged on the girl's front door, like a woman possessed, shaking with rage and shouting, 'I know he's in there, I want him out now!'

Another victim of Diana's erratic behaviour towards friends and staff was Victoria Mendham. She was the Princess's secretary for seven years, and was totally devoted to her. The relationship was exceptionally close – she even began dressing like her employer – and was treated by Diana as a friend and a confidante. It was a measure of their friendship that Diana asked Victoria to go on holiday with her four years running. For the first two, one to America and the other to the Caribbean, Diana paid the full cost. When they went to the Caribbean again at Easter in 1996, Victoria assumed she was there as a guest once again. It was a great treat and all was going well until half way through the holiday when the Princess suddenly said, 'Oh, Victoria, I've written a note to Tony Burrows to make sure you get your share of the bill. I think it's about £5,000.'

'But, Ma'am,' spluttered Victoria, 'you asked me to come.'

'Yes,' said the Princess, 'but you always knew you would have to pay your way.'

Victoria telephoned the office in London in floods of tears, saying she didn't have £5,000 in the world and not knowing what on earth to do. The Prince paid.

Nine months later it happened again. This time Victoria said she could pay the airfare to the Caribbean, which had been economy class, but they had stayed at the K Club where beach-side villas cost £1,700 a night, and paying that kind of money was out of the question. When the Princess learnt that her husband had footed the previous bill she 'went through the roof' and Victoria was frozen out as others had been before her. On her anti-landmines campaign to Angola, Diana took Paul Burrell with her instead of Victoria, who was very upset. On Diana's return, they had a confrontation, which resulted in Victoria tending her resignation. She was told to clear her desk and leave at once without serving her four weeks' notice.

The Prince picked up a lot of Diana's casualties. He also picked up Diana herself. She drove him to distraction in many ways. He was angered by some things she did – not least her decision to retire from public life, which she did dramatically on a public platform, despite pleas from him, the Queen and the Duke of Edinburgh to withdraw if she liked, but to do it quietly so that she could change her mind at a later date if ever she wanted to. She ignored them all. At a charity luncheon on 3 December 1993, she said, 'Over the next few months I will be seeking a more suitable way of combining a meaningful public role with, hopefully, a more private life. I hope you can find it in your hearts to understand and give me the time and space that has been lacking in recent years ... Your kindness and affection have carried me through some of the most difficult periods, and always your love and care have eased the journey.'

Charles was in Kentish Town in north London the day before the announcement and in a filthy mood, which his private secretary thought must have been because of something he had done. Colin Trimming, Charles's policeman, reassured him. 'It's nothing you've done,' he said. 'Wait until you get back to the office and all will be revealed.'

The Prince was furious with Diana. He saw it as her job to support all the institutions and charities she had taken on, and the faxes that arrived in the office in the aftermath of her speech indicated just how much they would miss her. The one from the Welsh National Opera was typical. 'Your Royal Highness, it is just so helpful to be able to use your name. We only ask you to do one engagement a year, which is a reception followed by an opera, but twenty per cent or so of all our fundraising is achieved that night. What are we going to do now?'

The Prince found conversations with Diana very difficult and upsetting, but he never felt she was entirely responsible for what she did. He regarded her as an injured soul, a poor damaged creature who needed help. He had come to learn that he wasn't the person to give that help. Everything he had tried had failed, and he seemed to do nothing more than provide a focus for her anger, but he did care very much that she should be looked after. He worried about her, and was always there at the end of a telephone, right up until the time of her death, when things went wrong with a love affair or the children or even the press. She would ring him up in tears, and he would do whatever needed to be done to sort out the problem.

ELEVEN

Camillagate

'There were three of us in this marriage.'
Diana on 'Panorama'

For a man obsessed about his privacy, the publication in January 1993 of a highly intimate late-night telephone conversation with Camilla Parker Bowles was the ultimate humiliation. Known as the Camillagate tapes, they were recordings said to have been made four years before, which left no one in any doubt that these were two people who were very much in love, and who enjoyed a close physical relationship. Everything that the Princess of Wales had told Andrew Morton appeared to be confirmed.

A full transcript of the eleven-minute tape was first published in an Australian magazine, but swiftly reproduced in the British press, where millions of people digested it with their breakfasts. What they read was allegedly the heir to the throne's wish that he could be with the woman he adored, and musing on the possibility of turning into a tampon in order to be closer to her. It was a conversation which should never have been overheard – the sort many lovers might have in bed, after a bottle of wine, when they are tired, relaxed and entirely alone – and of toe-curling embarrassment for the two participants.

The puritanical outburst that followed was hysterical and out of all proportion. The widespread feeling was of a nation in crisis. There were lurid headlines and cartoons, wide condemnation of the Prince, questions about his fitness to be king and, in the mounting fever, demands from Cabinet ministers that the Prince give up Mrs Parker Bowles.

Charles: ...He thought he might have gone a bit far.

Camilla: Ah, well.

Charles: Anyway, you know, that's the sort of thing one has to beware of. And sort of feel one's way along with, if you know what I mean.

Camilla: Mmmmm. You're awfully good at feeling your way along.

Charles: Oh, stop! I want to feel my way along you, all over you and up and down you and in and out.

Camilla: Oh!

Charles: ...particularly in and out.

Camilla: Oh, that's just what I need at the moment.

Charles: Is it?

Camilla: I know it would revive me. I can't bear a Sunday night without you.

Charles: Oh, God.

Camilla: It's like that programme 'Start the Week'. I can't start the week without you.

Charles: I fill up your tank!

Camilla: Yes, you do!

Charles: Then you can cope.

Camilla: Then I'm all right.

Charles: What about me? The trouble is I need you several times a week.

Camilla: Mmmmm. So do I. I need you all the week, all the time.

Charles: Oh, God, I'll just live inside your trousers or something. It would be much easier!

Camilla: (Laughs) What are you going to turn into? A pair of knickers? (Both laugh) Oh you're going to come back as a pair of knickers.

Charles: Or, God forbid, a Tampax, just my luck! (Laughs)

Camilla: You're a complete idiot! (Laughs) Oh, what a wonderful idea!

Charles: My luck to be chucked down the lavatory and go on and on for ever swirling round on the top, never going down!

Camilla: (Laughing) Oh, darling!

How the conversation, which went on in a similarly ridiculous vein, demonstrated in any way that Charles was unfit to be king was a mystery. What it revealed, in the silliness and crudity of the jokes as well as the rest of their sleepy ramblings, was that the Prince had found in Camilla what he had so much hoped to find in Diana. It was clearly a loving, friendly, familiar relationship, with no suspicion or tension or jealousy. They took pleasure in hearing each other's voice, they had fun in their friendship, and they made each other laugh. And as his staff will say, no matter what sort of a day he has had, a conversation with Camilla last thing at night – which he will try and have wherever he is in the world – will always cheer him up.

The Prince likes people who are fun to be with, and one of the greatest disappointments in his marriage was that the sense of fun which had so attracted him to Diana when he first met her, quickly vanished. But it was more than her sense of humour that attracted him to Camilla; and some of the other elements that made her so important to him were evident in that tape. Camilla was interested in the Prince: she boosted his ego, she wanted to hear about his work, she was straightforward, she made no demands on him, she was happy to see him but understanding when he had to be elsewhere. She was sexy and giggly and pulled his leg when he was angry or pompous, but didn't criticise or put him down. She asked to read his speeches, wanted to hear about his plans and schemes, and on the rare occasions that she met someone from one of his organisations, said she had heard so much about them and wanted to know more. She was friend as well as lover; and shared many of his enthusiasms.

How the conversation was taped that night is unknown, and the Prince would still dearly love to get to the bottom of. It mystifies them both to this day. The tape was not one single conversation, but a compilation of many, which they worked out they had had over several months around Christmas 1989. The original notion that it was some radio buff accidentally tuning into the Prince's mobile phone signal was quickly dismissed, and an official government inquiry into MI5 and other intelligence agencies dismissed their involvement too. The Princess was one of very few people who knew the Prince's mobile telephone number, and it was known that she had been worried about bugging on her own account and had installed some sophisticated equipment at Kensington Palace.

The real agony of the tape is that it will haunt Charles for ever. He knows that it will be recalled at his coronation and all the serious moments in his life, and his humiliation and that of his parents and two sons, also of Camilla and her family and children, will go on indefinitely.

He was in Liverpool the morning the tape was published, and had seriously to steel his courage to climb out of the car and face the crowds, not knowing what kind of reception awaited him. He behaved as though nothing had happened, and the crowd, in turn, behaved similarly. There were no sniggers, no shouts, no catcalls, and no absence of people. Throughout all the difficulties and revelations, no one who accompanied the Prince on any engagements ever saw so much as a single placard or heard the faintest jeer. Despite the brave exterior that day, it was nonetheless one of the very worst days of his life: he was excruciatingly embarrassed on a personal level, extremely annoyed with the media for having published the tape, terrified for his children, and miserable that yet again he had managed to drag the monarchy through the mire. The Queen had called 1992 an 'annus horribilis' and 1993 was obviously going to be no improvement.

Charles was also devastated for Camilla. The Morton book had turned the spotlight on Mrs Parker Bowles for the first time in all the years of their friendship. The press took up residence outside her house in Wiltshire, making her a prisoner in her own home, and she was on the receiving end of some unpleasant mail, which accused her of breaking up the royal marriage. But the Camillagate tapes were infinitely worse, and effectively brought an end to her marriage to Andrew Parker Bowles by making his position untenable. Having the explicit nature of her relationship with the Prince of Wales all over every newspaper made life extremely unpleasant for her children and elderly parents too. She was the butt of jokes up and down the country. She was never pelted with bread rolls by a bunch of abusive women shoppers in a car park in Chippenham, although the story has been told time and again; but she did get dozens of abusive letters and telephone calls, which she found enormously upsetting, and even quite scary. She scarcely went out, and when she did it was always with the protection of friends. Friends shopped for her and delivered supplies to her home, and were her lifeline.

Her children were innocent victims, and it was deeply unfair that her husband should have had to run the gauntlet of media scrutiny as a result of someone illegally bugging the phone line to his home. But Andrew Parker Bowles was by no means the poor cuckold, stepping aside dutifully for the heir to the throne to exercise his *droit de seigneur*. The very qualities which had attracted Camilla to him in the early 1970s, and made him such an exciting catch, had not diminished. Good looking, charming, slim and fit, he was still the womaniser he had always been. Camilla liked Andrew; they were good friends despite the infidelity, and have remained so. Having been brought up by her mother to have a strong sense of family and to put the children of a marriage before the wants of their parents, Camilla had settled for the life she had, put up with Andrew's behaviour which she couldn't stop, and happily devoted herself to her house and garden, her children and her horses. When the Prince of Wales reappeared in her life, he brought excitement, which had been missing for a long time. She, likewise, brought light into his life, which had been steadily closing in on him in dark despair.

The Prince loved Camilla. She had rescued him from the depths and brought laughter and sunshine into his life, but it didn't mean he wanted to marry her or escape from his marriage to the Princess. The separation from Diana in December had been a desperate and difficult time. What distressed him as much as anything was the feeling that he had let so many people down. It had taken a severe toll and left him at a very low ebb. He knew he had tried as hard as was humanly possible to keep his marriage together, but whatever the excuses, whatever the reasons, the fact was that he had failed. It was no comfort to know that his marriage was no different from a high percentage of the population's. He had known from the outset that his marriage was different and must be for life, which is why he had been at such pains to find the right bride. As the man who would be king as well as Defender of the Faith, he couldn't easily walk away from the vows he had made before God 'to love and to cherish, for better or worse, in sickness and in health'.

He felt, in admitting defeat, that he had disappointed many people, the Queen, the Queen Mother, his children, not to mention all the millions of strangers who had watched his marriage to Diana, heard the spine-tingling notes of the Trumpet Voluntary and Dame Kiri te Kanawa, seen the pomp and ceremony, the glass coach, the kiss on the balcony, and had believed in the fairytale.

The Queen and the Duke of Edinburgh had been shocked and appalled by the Andrew Morton book. They were shocked still further by the publication of the Squidgygate tapes, and were deeply disappointed by the separation.

Yet despite their disappointment, the Queen and Prince Philip were not unsympathetic. They had seen the difficulties at first hand, particularly over the recent Sandringham weekend when Diana had been so awkward about the children attending, and although over the years they had tried hard to resist taking sides, now that the crunch had come, they recognised he had had no alternative. The Duke, normally sparing in the extreme with any kind of praise or support for his eldest son, wrote him a long and sympathetic letter saying that in his opinion, Charles had displayed the fortitude of a saint.

In the summer of 1992, before the Andrew Morton book, the Squidgy tapes, and Camillagate, the writer and broadcaster Jonathan Dimbleby began working on a double project: a television documentary about Charles and an authorised biography. Both were timed to coincide loosely with the twenty-fifth anniversary of his Investiture as Prince of Wales in July 1994. What began as an innocent and well-intentioned exercise had unimaginable consequences, and was ultimately responsible for Camilla's divorce from Andrew Parker Bowles, terrible ructions within the Royal Family,

Diana's devastating 'Panorama' interview, Richard Aylard's downfall, and the fiercest controversy yet about the Prince's fitness to be king.

The moving force behind the exercise was Richard Aylard, who chose Dimbleby for the task and convinced the Prince that he should give maximum co-operation. Dimbleby was experienced, distinguished, and sufficiently heavyweight to appeal to the Prince and be trusted by his friends. Having never previously written about the Royal Family he was also suitably neutral. He was a passionate country-lover, with a small organic farm near Bath, married to the writer Bel Mooney with whom he had two children. In all sorts of ways there was a useful synergy between the two men and they got on well.

The producer for the film was Christopher Martin, who had made the Prince's two previous films, 'A Vision of Britain', about architecture, and 'The Earth in Balance', on the environment. It was a winning combination of people whom the Prince liked and trusted, and the crew became part of his life over the next year and a half, as they filmed at Highgrove and St James's Palace, at Windsor, Balmoral and Sandringham, abroad, at work and play. The result was a sensitive and illuminating film called 'Charles: The Private Man, the Public Role', which ran for two and a half hours and attracted an audience of fourteen million viewers, many of whom understood for the first time what the Prince of Wales actually did when he was not playing polo.

What most people remembered of the film, however, ran to no more than three minutes.

Dimbleby asked the Prince about his infidelity. 'Were you,' he said, 'did you try to be faithful and honourable to your wife when you took on the vow of marriage?'

'Yes,' said the Prince, and after a brief and rather anguished pause said, 'until it became irretrievably broken down, us both having tried.'

When asked about Camilla in the film, he said she was 'a great friend of mine ... she has been a friend for a very long time.'

At a press conference the next day Aylard confirmed that the adultery to which the Prince had confessed was indeed with Mrs Parker Bowles.

The question had had to be asked. By the time the programme was shown in June 1994, the Prince and Princess had separated, Morton and both sets of tapes had been published, as had a series of prominent articles in a variety of publications, which talked quite openly about the Prince having been unfaithful to his wife. There was serious discussion between Aylard and Dimbleby about whether in the light of all of this the project should be abandoned, but they decided that would give quite the wrong signals to the outside world, and it was important to go ahead. However, given what had happened, it would have been impossible for Dimbleby to have ignored the one topic that was fascinating people up and down the country. It would have entirely destroyed his credibility as a serious journalist. So although no one doubted that the question had to be asked, what the Prince's friends, colleagues and advisers still disagree violently about was whether the Prince should have answered it. At the time, many thought his answer might cost him the throne.

As the author of it all, Aylard was convinced that the Prince did the right thing, and was deeply cynical about the moralistic and hypocritical tabloid outcry. As one tabloid journalist said to Jonathan afterwards, 'You shot our fox.' They didn't want this coming out in the programme because there was a million pounds worth of exclusive in this story for someone, which they weren't going to get.

Aylard was also convinced that if the Prince had said 'No' and denied he had been unfaithful, it would only have been a matter of time before someone intercepted another telephone call or came up with photographs, or the evidence of a disaffected housemaid, which would have proved he had lied. He knew the *News of the World*, in particular, was spending a vast amount of money in having both the Prince and Camilla Parker Bowles followed, day and night.

The other option would have been to bat the question away, to say that he was not prepared to answer personal questions, but that would have done nothing to kill the speculation, nor indeed the determination to find evidence of an affair. And since most people who either watched television and read the tabloids were already pretty sure he had been unfaithful to Diana, he would simply have looked as though he was not prepared to be honest with the people who would one day be his subjects.

'It wasn't being honest to Jonathan that was the problem,' Aylard said when accused of allowing the Prince of Wales to make what many people regard as one of the most serious mistakes of his life. 'If you want to start placing blame, the fault was getting into the relationship in the first place.'

But it was the book that followed that, in the view of most of the Prince's friends, did the real damage. Not the book itself, which few people will have read from cover to cover, but its serialisation in *The Sunday Times*. It was a formidable tome, running to 620 pages, meticulously annotated and painstakingly detailed, which the Prince had been over with a fine-tooth comb checking facts, and which is now widely used as a handbook amongst 'the rat pack', as the tabloid royal reporters are known. For the first time in his life, Charles had made every source available to a writer. Dimbleby had a free run of everything, including his personal letters, diaries and journals, and his archives at St James's Palace and Windsor Castle. Furthermore, the Prince had positively encouraged friends and relatives to talk about him, many having never previously done so. Each one spent many taped hours talking about the man they knew, in the belief that this definitive, comprehensive and authoritative book would do him good and put right the injustices they felt he had endured for so long. When they saw what happened, they recoiled in horror and felt that the blood was partly on their hands. They had helped destroy the man they had all so wanted to help.

The deal Aylard struck with Dimbleby was quite extraordinary and left the Prince dangerously exposed. While Dimbleby undertook 'to take into account any comments made by HRH with respect to factual inaccuracies', he had the final say and 'sole discretion about the contents' of what he produced. In other words, Dimbleby could write whatever he liked and, provided it was accurate, the Palace was powerless to remove it from the book, no matter how much embarrassment or damage it might cause. In fact, Dimbleby took quite a lot out that would have been awkward for the Prince, but there were other details which he thought important to retain.

The Prince's relationship with his parents and other members of the Royal Family was one damaging element, which was deeply illuminating about the personality, but not enormously helpful in terms of the continuing relationships. Also, Aylard had no control over serialisation. *The Sunday Times* inevitably sensationalised the book, and the lasting impression, once the headline writers had finished, was of a whinging Prince, whose parents had never shown him any affection, who had loved Camilla for most of his adult life, and never loved the wife that his father had bullied him into marrying. All the juiciest bits were picked up by the tabloids and by columnists, and the Prince was given another very sound kicking.

Initially, the Prince had been rather pleased with the whole exercise. He had been over the book and watched the film, and was comfortable that he had made the right decision in answering Dimbleby's question about adultery. And then his telephone started ringing and one friend after another said, 'Oh, sir, what a ghastly programme. Wasn't that awful? You were led up the garden path, weren't you? What was Richard Aylard thinking of? Why on earth did you let him persuade you to do it?' And all the resolve and the certainty began to evaporate.

The decision had been his own, albeit with a strong recommendation from Aylard, who had been convinced by Dimbleby that he should tell the truth. They had discussed the pros and cons, and he had been given the advice. But the Prince is the boss, he was the one facing the camera, and he could have simply said 'No.' One of his constant complaints is that he is always made to do things he doesn't want to do by the people he pays to advise him. A stronger character would stand up for what he believes himself and let his advisers advise, and not dictate.

Aylard had not consulted with anyone else over the Dimbleby deal. He played the whole project very close to his chest, as he did most things, and his critics say that was his big mistake. When it all began to unravel, he had no supporters. No one was prepared to fight his corner because they had not been involved in the process, and many were angry that it had been sprung on them. There were plenty of people he could have gone to for advice, even within the office at St James's Palace. Belinda Harley, for example, an assistant private secretary, had been a PR in the publishing world but she had not even been asked to have a look at the contract. She felt the Prince could have had a much better deal and been properly safeguarded. Tom Shebbeare, chief executive of the Prince's Trust, and Julia Cleverdon of BitC, both of whom featured heavily in the film as key players in the Prince's two major activities, knew nothing about the venture until it was underway.

'We all tried to say it was a frightfully good idea to the outside world once we heard about it,' says Shebbeare, 'but it was all happening before anyone could have any influence on it. The first thing I knew about it was when television cameras started wandering into everything we did.'

The film could not have come at a worse time for Camilla, and she blames herself for not having taken a greater interest in what the Prince was telling Dimbleby. In the wake of his admission that they had had an affair, an assortment of friends and relatives appeared in print to condemn the Prince on her behalf.

'Frankly,' said one, 'he has behaved like an absolute pig and landed Camilla right in it. She has done absolutely nothing to deserve this after all the support she has given him over the years through difficult times.'

They said she had begged him not to talk to Dimbleby, but that he had ignored her pleas and selfishly exposed her to public vilification. This was not true. She never begged him not to talk to Jonathan. She was too busy with her own problems to worry about what Prince Charles might or might not say to Jonathan Dimbleby. Her life was a mess. Her marriage had virtually fallen apart thanks to the

Morton book and the Camillagate tapes. Her children were being teased and tormented. She couldn't go out of her house; and there were photographers camped on her doorstep. On top of everything, her mother was dying. Her lively, lovely, sparky mother, the Hon. Rosalind Shand, the much-adored bedrock of her tightly knit family, was slowly and painfully dying of osteoporosis. She had had the disease for some years, and as her spine gradually collapsed in on itself, she lost a foot in height. To have to stand by, feeling so helpless, and watch her mother suffer was more distressing to Camilla than anything the media could throw at her. She died on 14 July 1994 in hospital in Brighton, with Camilla and the rest of the family by her side, and was buried in the Sussex village of Plumpton, where she had lived throughout her married life. To add to the family's distress, the number of photographers that day almost outnumbered the mourners.

Though still married, Camilla and Andrew had been leading separate lives for years. However, the horrors of Morton and the tapes had made his position impossible. After Dimbleby, there was absolutely no way they could carry on as man and wife, and by January the following year the Parker Bowleses were divorced and a line finally drawn under their twenty-one-year-old marriage. Although it was precipitated by the Prince's confession, the truth was that Andrew had been wanting a divorce from Camilla for some time. He was keen to marry his own long-standing love, one of Camilla's friends, Rosie Pitman, who lived nearby in Wiltshire. The grounds for the divorce were that the couple had been living apart for more than three years, and it went through uncontested.

Knowing that the divorce would cause a sensation in the tabloid press, and could rake up the tapes and everything else all over again, Alan Kilkenny, the PR consultant who had masterminded the publicity for the immensely successful Great Ormond Street Wishing Well Appeal, was brought in by the Prince to help manage the publicity. Since Great Ormond Street, Kilkenny had helped with a number of projects, which included organising the Symphony for the Spire, a spectacular open-air event in the precinct of Salisbury

Cathedral, to raise money for the crumbling edifice. He had also been involved in the Prince of Wales's Charities Trust, and given advice on the Institute of Architecture. After the Parker Bowles's divorce he assisted Camilla in handling the press on an informal basis for almost three years, but that role came to an end shortly before Diana's death, when the Prince's office at St James's Palace took Mrs Parker Bowles under its protective wing.

The plan was that on the day the divorce was heard, Camilla's lawyer, Hilary Browne-Wilkinson, would make an announcement to the Press Association, and all enquiries would be directed to Simon Elliot, Camilla's brother-in-law. The day before the announcement, Andrew Parker Bowles went to see the woman who lived in a tied cottage at the end of their driveway in Wiltshire to tell her what was happening. Margaret Giles worked as a housekeeper and looked after the property when the Parker Bowleses were away. Andrew wanted to warn her that she might be pestered by the press. The plan backfired dramatically. Mrs Giles immediately contacted the South West News Agency – where the editor of the *Sun*, Stuart Higgins, once worked – and within minutes he was on the phone to Simon Elliot to say he had heard the Parker Bowleses were about to divorce. Unable to deny the story, it was all over the next day's newspaper, followed by some personal photographs. Some had come from the Parker Bowles's private family photograph album which was subsequently found at the *Sun*'s offices in Wapping. Others, such as a photograph of the four-poster bed in which Camilla slept, had been taken by someone with access to the house. Mrs Giles had a key to the Parker Bowles's house and subsequently admitted having agreed to sell the photographs for £25,000. The money was never paid. The Parker Bowleses sued the *Sun* and the newspaper settled out of court for the same sum it had offered Mrs Giles. The money went to charity.

When the interest in Camilla's divorce was past, the fuss over Dimbleby long gone, and life was pleasantly uneventful, the Princess of Wales released another Exocet which took everyone back to square one. It shattered the Prince, shattered Camilla, and dealt yet another serious body blow to the monarchy.

Diana gave a theatrical performance on the BBC's flagship current-affairs programme 'Panorama'. Sitting forlornly in a chair at Kensington Palace, occasionally pausing to recover her composure or wipe a tear that threatened, she told journalist Martin Bashir about her life. The scene could not have been more dramatic. With black kohl lining her eyes, Diana looked vulnerable and wretched, but talked about being a strong woman, and other phrases straight from the counsellor's couch. Much that was said echoed what she had told Andrew Morton. She talked about her bulimia, her cries for help, the Prince's friends who waged a war in the media against her, his obsession with Camilla, 'the enemy' within the Palace. She confessed that she had been unfaithful to her husband, with James Hewitt, whom she had adored, but who had also let her down. She talked about her desire to be 'a Queen in people's hearts ... someone's got to go out there and love people and show it.'

The most memorable moment of the whole broadcast was her simple description of what had destroyed her marriage. 'There were three of us in this marriage,' she said, 'so it was a bit crowded.'

The most damaging remark, however, was her doubt that the Prince of Wales should ever be king.

The programme had been filmed and prepared in total secrecy, and announced at the last minute. The BBC governors had not even been told about it, for fear that the establishment mafia would interfere and have it stopped. Until the opening credits rolled at 9.30 p.m. on Monday 20 November 1995, no one at either St James's or Buckingham Palace had any idea of what was about to follow.

A group of courtiers gathered in the Buckingham Palace press office to watch it together. They included Charles Anson and Philip Mackie, from the Queen's press office, Richard Aylard, Allan Percival and Sandy Henney from the Prince's press office, and Geoff Crawford, who was Diana's press officer and as much in the dark as anyone else present. He resigned as a direct result, as did Patrick Jephson, her private secretary. Both had been taken entirely by surprise and felt they couldn't carry on.

Philip Mackie, a genial Scot, who was always telling people he had the inside track on a story, and that he had his sources, said reassuringly, 'I've been doing a bit of ringing around, and there's nothing to worry about. It'll be a damp squib – I bet you a bottle of Champagne.'

About fifteen minutes into the film, Aylard said, 'Philip, we're up to a whole case by now!'

On the notoriously tough discussion programme, 'Newsnight', immediately after 'Panorama', Nicholas Soames – clearly one of the 'enemies' the Princess had been referring to, and not the most sensitive of men – explained that Diana had endured 'a period of unhappiness [that] led to instability and mental illness'. Her theories about her telephone being tapped, which she had talked about in the interview, exhibited 'the advanced stages of paranoia'. While some people might have agreed with him, it was not the most helpful remark under the circumstances. He had gone into the studio quite unprepared. The script that the BBC had promised to send him hadn't arrived. The programme had asked for Charlie Palmer-Tomkinson but, being a politician – the Armed Forces Minister – Soames, who was used to being put on the spot, seemed a safer bet.

'What shall I do?' he asked of one of the Prince's staff, who was as much in the dark.

'Just be careful!' were the memorable parting words.

The Prince was at Highgrove that evening and chose not to watch the 'Panorama' programme himself, but was soon told about it; also about the remarks his friend had made on 'Newsnight'. Despite speculation in the newspapers the next day that it might end their friendship, that was not the case. Rather, the Prince was worried that Soames might have damaged his own career by going out on a limb on his behalf.

Camilla watched the programme at home with her family and laughed at the sheer theatricality of it, as did many people who knew Diana.

Martin Bashir, 'Panorama' and the BBC were all being expertly manipulated in just the same way as Andrew Morton had been. The

Princess was using them to inflict maximum hurt on the Prince, and she could not have been given a better platform from which to do it. But it was still essentially a very private battle, and in her determination to make the Prince pay for having failed to make her happy, she hurt her sons and also the monarchy, which was not just about the Queen and the Prince of Wales. It was the throne that William would one day inherit.

The Queen had had enough. She was concerned about William and Harry, and thought the tit for tat nonsense that had been going on through the media was undignified and damaging. The time had come to bring the marriage that had caused such grief and heartache to an end. After consulting with the Prime Minister and the Archbishop of Canterbury, she wrote formally and privately to her son and daughter-in-law asking them to divorce as early as could practicably be done. Negotiations began, but while they were still in the very early stages, to everyone's surprise, on what Diana called 'the saddest day of my life', she put out a statement to the press.

'The Princess of Wales,' it said, 'has agreed to Prince Charles's request for a divorce. The Princess will continue to be involved in all decisions relating to the children and will remain at Kensington Palace with offices in St James's Palace. The Princess of Wales will retain the title and be known as Diana, Princess of Wales.'

The Queen was furious and issued an immediate response. 'The Queen was most interested to hear that the Princess of Wales had agreed to the divorce. We can confirm that the Prince and Princess of Wales had a private meeting this afternoon at St James's Palace. At this meeting details of the divorce settlement and the Princess's future role were not discussed. All the details on these matters, including titles, remain to be discussed and settled. This will take time. What the Princess has mentioned are requests rather than decisions at this stage.'

Richard Aylard handled the divorce for the Prince, and on top of the other demands on his time, including a marriage of his own that was falling apart, he was closeted with lawyers for several hours almost every day for many months. The Princess had engaged

Anthony Julius, a high-profile divorce lawyer from the well-established firm Mishcon de Reya, and the Prince was represented by Fiona Shackleton, from the royal solicitors, Farrer and Co. Negotiations could not have been more difficult or acrimonious, but by July they had agreed a settlement, widely perceived as generous towards the Princess in terms of money, which was the Prince's express intention and instruction from the outset.

It was a financial package thought to be worth more than £17 million, although both parties signed a confidentiality agreement about it and the precise deal was never known. They retained equal access to their sons, and equal responsibility in the children's upbringing. Diana was still to be regarded by the Queen and the Prince of Wales as being a member of the Royal Family and would receive invitations to some state and national public occasions. She would carry on living in Kensington Palace, but her office would be there rather than at St James's Palace, as she had wanted. There was one detail in the settlement that was widely perceived as petty, and which rankled. She was stripped of the title Her Royal Highness. It was not a detail that the Prince had wanted, it was a decision for the Queen. In public relations terms, it turned out to be a blunder, as her brother made so painfully obvious in his funeral address at Westminster Abbey.

TWELVE

Difficulties at Work

'It's not you I'm cross with, it's the situation.'
Charles

'Matthew, you work in public relations,' said the Prince, taking him by surprise, 'what do you think I should be doing differently?' They had been looking at ways of streamlining the Prince's Trust. 'How can I do it better?'

Matthew Butler had joined the Prince of Wales's office on secondment from Allied Dunbar as an assistant private secretary in July 1993, to look after the UK side of things in terms of the Prince's relationships with the business world. On appointment, like all secondees, his salary was frozen.

'Remember,' said Sir James Mellon, former ambassador to Denmark, who knew the Prince, 'the worst thing that can possibly happen to you is you get sent back to your £40,000 a year job in PR.'

With this advice in mind, plus a little reckless courage, Butler began to tell the Prince what he thought. He was not employed to do PR for the Prince but that was his field. Few people dare say what they really think to the Prince of Wales, even when asked, and the new recruit rapidly realised why. After he had proffered some advice to the Prince on the subject of his public image, Charles quite suddenly flew into a towering rage. 'I'm sorry, it's not you I'm cross with,' he said, mid rant, 'it's the situation.'

Butler retreated, shaken, and immediately telephoned Sir James. 'I've just had a rather interesting conversation,' he said, and told him what his advice had been. He believed that the Prince needed to be more focused in his activities, with a far greater distinction between what was public and what was private – not in the marital or extra-marital sense, but in terms of his private interests. It was not easy to explain to the outside world what relevance organic farming had to unemployed young people on peripheral housing estates in Glasgow, and it would be better if he kept the farming, likewise the architecture, as private interests.

Sir James reassured Butler that he had given exactly the right advice. 'The only thing I would have done differently is make the point about why his sister gets a better press than he does.'

'I'm afraid I did,' said Butler. 'That was when he really got agitated!'

The Princess Royal has been hugely successful. She may not have achieved as much as the Prince has in his scatter-gun way, but no one has ever suggested that she is neither hard working nor professional and everyone knows what she does. An image of the Princess in a sensible head scarf visiting African children as president of Save the Children is indelibly etched on the national psyche – not cuddling them, as the Princess of Wales did, but observing, making sure no one forgot their plight. And she is ever present on formal occasions: never glamorous, seldom smiling but a dependable pillar of respectability. Her private life has been no more saintly than his. She has been through a divorce, and there were rumours of affairs during her first marriage, but she has managed to keep her private life entirely private and earn the respect of the public and, more importantly, the media. It is a remarkable recovery since the 1970s, when she was one of the most unpopular members of the Royal Family, with a reputation for telling photographers to 'Naff off.' She is still surly and bad mannered on occasion, and quite capable of snapping people's heads off if they annoy her, but she has always been much more straightforward than her eldest brother, and has managed her public image with great skill.

Ask people what the Prince of Wales does and, even today, not many have a clear idea. It has not been helped by the fact that since 1981 the scandals, rumours and revelations about his private life were infinitely more fascinating to the public than anything he ever did in the line of work. Furthermore, to his intense frustration, the opportunity to have a photograph of Diana on any given occasion was instantly guaranteed to drive him off the pages of almost every newspaper – as she was well aware. In the five years after the separation, Diana was engaged in a PR war with Charles and the Royal Family, and in the black and white world of the media, she held all the cards.

It is only since Diana's death that the press has begun to take an interest in Charles again. When he visited Canada in 1996 only one press photographer went on the trip. When he went to the Gulf States before her death in 1997, there were two photographers and one journalist. An ITN crew happened to go because they were making a film about the royal yacht, not because they were interested in the Prince. Yet when he visited South Africa with Harry in early 1998, all forty seats on the aircraft were taken and many more photographers made their own way. It was the same in Sri Lanka when he was on his own, and again in Nepal and Bhutan.

Having hardly changed one iota in style or substance in the last ten years, the Prince was less than enthused to hear that the press were saying, 'This guy's great. Why haven't we seen him like this before?' The answer was that for the last sixteen years no one had really looked.

His involvement with the Prince's Trust is well known, although not many people understand what the Trust does, apart from hold pop concerts. Most people associate him with architecture. Some know about the organic farming and Duchy biscuits; and much of the business world is aware of his activity in the inner cities. But the overall impression is of a butterfly, moving from one random issue to another, most of them slightly off-beam.

John Major, when he was Prime Minister, used to worry about the Prince's lack of focus, and the two men frequently talked about trying to find some kind of role which would establish him firmly in the public consciousness. 'Although The Prince's Trust ought to fit the bill,' he says, 'it does it by stealth, and does not have sufficient public impact; it is, by its very nature, a series of small packets. There is nothing immediate about the work it does, nothing photogenic that generates the publicity to fix in the public mind: Prince's Trust, Prince of Wales, Good Thing. He deserves more public recognition of the work he does.'

The ideas, though not always good, have been the easy bit. Raising the money and making the ideas work is the tricky part. The only reason the Prince's Trust has succeeded is because the Prince has worked tirelessly on its behalf, hosting lunches, nobbling likely donors, bringing groups together to find solutions to problems, lobbying government to cut the red tape, and taking an interest in the young people it helps. Without him, several thousand people might never have had a chance to make something of their lives.

Business in the Community was not the Prince's idea, although he has contributed plenty of ideas to it since he joined forces with Stephen O'Brien in 1984. It has grown immeasurably since then, and succeeded in altering the face of many of Britain's inner cities. Once again, much of this is due to the Prince of Wales, with his determination and energy to keep pushing and pushing until he gets what he wants. But it hasn't been without the odd complaint.

'Oh, Julia,' he will say in a pained voice, when he has been up working on his official paperwork until two o'clock in the morning. 'So much paper, Julia, I can't cope. I spent two and a half hours on it yesterday.'

The ideas often arrive on what Julia Cleverdon calls Black Spider Memos. When the Prince is on form, she gets about one a week, as does Tom Shebbeare. They are impassioned notes about some campaign he wants to run, some person one of them ought to do something about, or organise some event with, or some opportunity that he thinks they should not miss.

'I remember getting one saying could we please help resettle the Army. The Army was being flung out of various regiments all over the place. Could we take the project on of resettling them? And some reasonably mad character inside BitC said, "Oh, frightfully good idea," and I said, "Absolutely not. We are not resettling the Army; it's the Army's problem. Of course, we'd be interested to talk to them about ways in which young soldiers could be helped to set up their own businesses – send them off to Tom at the Prince's Trust." You have to be reasonably firm about knowing what is the mission and what isn't the mission.'

More frequently, the Prince will telephone. 'Do you know, I sat next to a Swiss gnome at dinner last night who appears to run that confectionery company and he knew nothing at all about anything we did. I've got his phone number here, will you ring him up?'

The ideas and thoughts come at any hour of the day or night, and the Prince will track down who ever of his staff is appropriate for the particular thought.

'Last night, on the train going home,' says Tom Shebbeare, 'something to seven, the Prince just back from Canada, rings me up: "I've just met the Poet Laureate, Ted Hughes. He has some ideas about how he might help young people with their writing and I would love to involve him. Would you mind terribly meeting Ted Hughes?"'

His work has been a lifeline throughout the years of personal anguish, and it has been a real boost to see some obvious benefit, but nothing thrills him more than when either of his parents notice what he has achieved. Recently the Queen was due to visit Hull and Buckingham Palace rang Julia Cleverdon to see if there was anything the Prince had been involved in nearby, which the Queen might be able to visit. There was, said Cleverdon, a staggeringly good Compact running in Hull, the idea for which the Prince had brought back from America.

A Compact is a bargain between companies and school children in the community in which they operate. If the children keep their literacy skills up, the company rewards them with, perhaps, tickets to the local football match. The idea is for business to talk to the schools to make sure that they are teaching the kind of skills the companies need from their workforce, so that the children are working towards the goal of potential jobs at the end of their education. Business provides the incentives for the children to go to school and succeed, and the schools provide a supply of skilled employees for the local businesses. Everyone benefits.

The Queen was given a presentation by a group of children who told her what they had achieved and came away impressed and enthusiastic about what she had seen and heard. But did she pick up the phone and tell her son? The news that she had been impressed filtered its way down on paper to Julia, who passed it on to the Prince of Wales. He telephoned straight away. 'I gather it went terribly well,' he said.

'Yes, sir, the children were stunning.'

The Prince used to agonise over the problem of having no role, of seeing no positive benefits from his toils at the end of a long working day. It was one of the reasons why he became so passionate about his garden. He enjoyed the physical exertion of digging because he could see the results of his labour and felt gratifyingly tired when he had finished. It was also one of the reasons why he hunted and played polo so obsessively. Pushing himself to the limit physically made him feel alive. It is also, he says, 'one of the best cures for jet-lag'. To be told he had raised thousands of pounds by shaking a lot of hands was thoroughly unsatisfactory, and the curse of people born to his position, where fame and esteem come from an accident of birth rather than hard work or achievement.

Nowadays, the Prince knows he is making a real contribution to society. The frustration is people not making his ideas happen fast enough, or people telling him something can't be done. What he enjoys so much about Business in the Community, almost more than any of the other organisations he is involved with, is that when he has a good idea, not only is it put into practice, the results are immediate and there for everyone to see.

Typical is the Seeing is Believing programme which he dreamt up in 1990. His idea was that if, instead of telling chief executives about the problems of poor housing, drugs, crime and racism, you could let them actually see for themselves what was going on in run-down parts of the country, and meet some of the people who lived there, they would have a far better understanding of the problem and might be more inclined to help. His instinct was absolutely right. In the last seven years more than 700 business leaders have been taken to the inner cities, to community projects, prisons, housing estates – about three tours a year led by the Prince himself. At the end of it the businesspeople are asked to write reports for him on what they've seen and, over lunch at either Highgrove or St James's Palace, discuss what they might be able to contribute. Most of them have found the experience shocking, the more so because they were so unaware of the deprivation that was often on their own doorsteps. They have given not just money, but equipment, property, secondees and volunteers, and many have created work experience, training and job opportunities for the unemployed.

The Prince reads the reports and follows them up. 'He's got a memory like a bloody elephant,' says Cleverdon. 'He cares very much whether any grass came off the mowing machine, and he's an absolute stickler for "What happened as a result of that? Did that hostel for thirty-four homeless people get built after we'd been given 40,000 square feet in Liverpool by Ladbroke Hotels?"'

The answer was, 'Yes.' Forte equipped it with beds from one of its hotels and the hostel was built and ready for business within five months of the Seeing is Believing visit. Another astounding success was Great Yarmouth. After a visit, which the Prince attended, the local business support group produced £1 million to run a re-generation programme called SeaChange. And in Manchester, Charles Allen, the chief executive of Granada Television, was so impressed by what he had seen that he announced he wanted to go one step further and produce a Seeing is Doing programme. He twinned five companies with five housing estates where there was heavy unemployment amongst young people, got each company to give five middle managers for five hours a week, and filmed what happened over a five month period. It was hugely successful. The companies and their suppliers gave the project £7.5 million, which built five community centres on the five housing estates, several of which the Prince opened.

Realising that his intervention and ideas could make a difference, particularly to the young, was one of the things that really gave Charles the confidence to keep going through the darkest patches, and still gives him an enormous sense of fulfilment. He also gets pleasure from the people he meets in the course of his travels. Occasionally he hears remarks that make him roar with laughter, and sees a side of life that others miss.

One day Charles was visiting an Indian family at a housing association in Smethick, near Birmingham. Once the press had gone, he said how nice it was to meet the whole family. The man of the house said, 'Yes, we are all here apart from my father who is out at work.'

'What?' said the Prince. 'You must be fifty, and your father is still working?'

'Yes, he's seventy-four, but he still goes out to work every day.'

'How's that?' asked the Prince.

The man looked very worried and said, 'You are my future king, I cannot tell a lie. In India there is no provision for old age and so my father and his friends, when he came over to Britain in the 1950s, he was forty-six, but on his form he said he was aged thirty-six, so he can go on working for ten more years and earn a lot more pension.'

Once he was back in the car, the Prince picked up the mobile phone and with a mischievous grin asked if he should call the Home Secretary.

The Prince has tramped around more inner-city streets and spoken to many more tenants in high-rise blocks than any politician, and what he understood early on is that to be effective, change must come from the bottom and work its way upwards. Government initiatives alone won't work. You have to help the community entrepreneurs in the housing estates, so that they can fight the crime, vandalism and drugs. But as well as pouring money into projects, they need to learn how to tackle the problems. So in collusion with Anne Power, an expert in housing at the London School of Economics, who is a great advocate of two-storey back-to-back housing, he had the idea of setting up a National Tenants Resource Centre, to teach local

The Prince of Wales in his element, with his faithful dog, Harvey. Charles cut his friends out of his life at Diana's insistence, and even gave away the dog he loved in an effort to make Diana happy.

The fateful trip to Korea in November 1992, when the marriage was all but over and the pretence gone.

The PR war was on, and photographers were telephoned and told where they should go if they wanted a good picture. The laughter and enthusiasm Diana put on for the cameras were not always in evidence at home.

Diana's father, Johnnie Spencer, died in March 1992 while she, the Prince and the boys were skiing in Austria. She was determined to go home alone, but the Prince insisted on accompanying her. When Jane, Sarah, Charles and Diana took the ashes to the family crypt, interestingly, it was Diana who carried them.

In 1993 Diana announced her retirement from public life. Charles saw it as a dereliction of duty, and was furious.

Diana became obsessed about Camilla, who after 1986 was a regular visitor to Highgrove and occasionally with others to Balmoral. Anonymously, Diana would make threatening telephone calls to her in the middle of the night.

Charles with his arm in a sling after falling from his horse during a polo match in 1990. Pushing his horses to the limit was an outlet for his frustration.

A hug for Carolyn Bartholomew, who had talked to Andrew Morton, told the world that Diana approved of his book.

iana's dramatic
rformance on 'Panorama'
November 1993 prompted
e Queen to insist she and
harles seek a divorce.

Diana wearing a
deliberately sensational
dress on the night the
Dimbleby documentary was
shown in June 1994. She
knew which picture would
make the front page.

Camilla taking a break while out hunting with the Beaufort. She's her own woman; she smokes, drinks and enjoys life.

After her divorce from Andrew Parker Bowles, Camilla went to ground for several months. This was the first time she was seen again, in a Hampshire village. It was the start of a slow process towards making her acceptable to the British public.

Camilla arriving at Highgrove for her fiftieth birthday party in July 1997 in one of the Prince's cars. Diana went berserk when she heard about the party; so did Sir Robert Fellowes.

July 1997. Diana, William and Harry with Mohamed al Fayed and his daughter Jasmin on the St Tropez holiday which turned into a media circus. Diana was heavily criticised for exposing her sons to it all, and Charles feared she was being sucked into the al Fayed publicity machine.

Prince Charles in Manchester in September 1997. It was his first public engagement since Diana's death and he was terrified. He was touched and relieved by the warmth of the crowds.

There is a spring in his step as Charles begins to enjoy life once again. In March 1998 he took William and Harry to Canada.

Camilla with her daughter, Laura. All she wants is to be a legitimate part of the Prince's life. William and Harry approve – they can see how happy he is when she's around.

committees how to manage their estates. They found a building in Cheshire, which Grand Metropolitan gave to the Prince for the project; Richard Rogers – the modern architect who had once been the Prince's most vociferous critic – ran an appeal. Money came in from business leaders, Laings did the work for free, Sir John Riddell became chairman and, despite a certain amount of scepticism, the centre has been busy ever since. It is just one example of many.

'At heart, he's a campaigner and a world-changer,' says Cleverdon, 'and driven with passion. "It's the primary schools, Julia, that we have to focus on. Do you take in that, it's the primary schools?" "Yes, sir, oddly enough I do." "Yes, but what can we *do*?" "Why not have a reception for the primary head teachers who have been a beacon of achievement?" "Oh, that's a good idea, we'll have a reception. But that's not enough. What else can we do?" So we have a drive on literacy and get all the Seeing is Believing teams to go and visit primary schools and report back on what they've seen.'

And all the while he is power-brokering behind the scenes. Hundreds of computers, for example, will go into the community because of the pressure he brought to bear on the Treasury about charging VAT on gifts in kind.

Matthew Butler believes that the Prince has a problem in reaching Mr and Mrs Average Briton, living in their three-bedroomed, detached Barratt home in Didcot, catching the train to London every day, both out working because they need the money for the mortgage. 'What does monarchy mean for them?' he asks. 'At the top end of the social scale and the bottom end the Prince is very much in touch. It's the middle where there's a problem. If ever it came to a referendum on the monarchy, it would be the husbands and wives in the Barratt homes in Didcot that settled the matter. It's not going to be the kids on the inner city estates, sadly.'

He feels there are flaws in the way the Prince's diary is planned. 'There are a number of formal events, which will increase as time goes on. The remainder of his time is up for grabs, which encourages all his patronages and interests to compete for it, instead of driving the process proactively. He very seldom carries out engagements over weekends, which is the obvious time to attract crowds. If he turns up at Cardiff, for example, on a wet Wednesday morning, it is hardly surprising if there are only a handful of old-age pensioners to greet him. Everyone else is at work. Go at the weekend, as he did to Llandudno on the Sunday night of his twenty-fifth anniversary trip – organised deliberately over a weekend – and the promenade was jammed as far as the eye could see. It's not rocket science,' he says. But being the son of a Bradford and Bingley branch manager from Yorkshire, he knows more about how ordinary people live than many a private secretary before him.

The magic touch has not worked as smoothly as Charles might have hoped in the architectural world. The Prince of Wales's Institute of Architecture was opened to students in 1992, following on the success of a couple of pilot summer schools held in Oxford, Rome and a glorious villa lent to the Prince by the Italian government near Viterbo. The Institute had brave new ideas, and was going to provide an alternative architectural education. Launching it, the Prince said, 'We are told that our contemporary built environment must reflect the "spirit of the age". But what concerns me most of all is that we are succeeding in creating an "age without spirit" … What I would like to be taught and explored and studied in my Institute, is the fact that the architecture which nourishes the spirit is not so much a traditional architecture, which resembles or apes the past, but rather a particular kind of architecture whose forms, plans, materials, are based on human feeling.

'At the end of their course, I would like the students to leave my Institute with a feeling that they have experienced something rather special in their lives; that a new dimension of life has been revealed to them which has struck a chord in their hearts that will never stop resonating. I hope this will enable them to have the true vision to see that although styles may vary, proportion is in itself a reflection of the order inherent in the Universe. They will need to discover these great truths, I believe, in order themselves to provide the beacons of civilised values in a world increasingly in need of real meaning and of that most precious of commodities – hope.'

Alas, hope was not enough. The students who left the Institute may indeed have experienced something rather special in their lives, but they did not leave with a qualification that would ensure them a job – in as much as any qualification ever can. Good as the idea that drove it and the architects and academics connected with it were, the venture was nonetheless little short of a fiasco. Jules Lubbock, the art historian who had helped write the Prince's famous Hampton Court speech, ran the first summer school, organised the second, and was to have run the Institute as director. But he resigned and went back to his job in Essex because he could not agree the terms of his contract. He had identified the flaw that has dogged the Institute ever since. He thought it imperative that one person should be responsible for running the Institute; but the governing council wanted a division of power – a director to oversee the academic side of life and an administrator to oversee the director. The man who picked up the reins was Dr Brian Hanson, an architectural historian, who, like Jules Lubbock, had formed part of the Prince's advisory group on architecture, and had been shaping his views and speeches since 1987. He became Director of Studies, and Keith Critchlow, who was not by nature a team player, became Director of Research. In the late-1980s, these people had direct access to the Prince and could push his ideas forward, but once Richard Aylard became private secretary in 1991 he took a much tighter grip on things and the direct line they had enjoyed was considerably weakened. By the time the Institute finally opened, the Prince seemed to have lost his appetite for a fight and was wanting to pull in his horns.

Without strong support, a venture of this sort, which challenged conventional wisdom, had no chance of survival; and those involved felt badly let down. The Prince didn't stand up for the principles he believed in. He allowed his teaching staff to be overruled and undermined by the council, and failed miserably to back the people he had put in place. The Institute had four directors in six years, which was hardly an encouraging start. The first two were Brian Hanson, who lasted until March 1994, and went on to run the Prince's Urban Design Task Force programme, and a young and fanatical classicist, Richard John, who was another architectural historian. Richard John lasted a year before he was removed and replaced by Richard Hodges, an archaeologist with no particular view on architecture at all; and finally, Adrian Gale stepped into the musical chair as Head of School. Gale was one of the team of architects at Ludwig Mies van der Rohe, the company which designed the 'glass stump' proposed for No. 1 Poultry in the City of London, which the Prince had lambasted so famously in 1984. It was the final irony, and yet another example, some felt, of the Prince being manoeuvred into betraying his ideals.

The foundation course students were unaffected by the less than solid administrative base and went on to places like the Mackintosh School, in Glasgow, widely recognised as the best in the country, where they were welcomed as quality students. However, the changes in directors meant that most of the graduate course students were seriously disrupted in their studies. The Institute failed to get the Royal Institute of British Architects to agree that the graduate course could qualify as a Part II exemption for architects. The RIBA had been receptive in early discussions and it was assumed there would be no problems, but the Institute did not keep up the rapport, and when the RIBA saw such instability at the helm, it refused the qualification. Changes and political in-fighting at the RIBA did not help.

The Institute swallowed up vast sums of money, much of it from the Sultan of Brunei, and Arab sheikhs, and constantly lived in a state of under funding. To avoid any accusations of élitism, it opened its doors to anyone it felt right for the course, so there was an extensive system of student bursaries, which led to the accusation that the Institute paid students to attend. Students came from all corners of the globe, and they were careful not to turn anyone down simply because they couldn't afford the fees. The fees were too low to start with, set at a level to match other foundation courses in the arts, but other schools offering courses had a high level of public funding. The Institute had none.

At the end of 1996, in an attempt to put an end to the internal intrigue and bickering, the Prince sacked the entire governing council and appointed a group of lawyers in their place, chaired by Lady Browne-Wilkinson, Camilla Parker Bowles's divorce lawyer, who openly admitted having neither knowledge nor interest in architecture. Many people in the know have been predicting doom for the Institute for some time, and are not impressed by the latest reorganisation. In August 1998, the Prince announced that he was launching a new Foundation for Architecture and the Urban Environment. It was to be an umbrella for a number of schemes that have been spawned around the urban design theme in recent years, and would include the Institute – renamed the Prince of Wales's School of Architecture and the Building Arts – the Urban Villages Forum, Regeneration through Heritage and the Phoenix Trust; and the whole lot would be housed at a cost of £4.6 million in a former fur warehouse in the East End of London.

'So, once again, in a triumph of hope over experience,' wrote Giles Worsley in the *Daily Telegraph*, 'Prince Charles rides forward in his architectural quest. Perhaps this time it will work. But if the new Foundation turns out merely to be a presentational device to paper over the failure of the institute, if it has been cobbled together to give the appearance of action because nobody dares tell the Prince that it is time to close down, then the old flaws are doomed to re-emerge.

'One longs to be proved wrong, for the Foundation to work. But the suspicion lurks that this is just the Institute mark two. Same trustees, same confusion of purpose, just a new building, a new name and a few new victims to be sucked into the maelstrom.'

Giles Worsley was himself a victim, having been made redundant as editor of architecture magazine *Perspectives* on its demise in January 1998. The magazine had been set up to widen the architectural debate, and attract lay readers. It struggled on for four troubled years, accumulating debts of almost £1.8 million – money it borrowed from the Institute. Apart from the debts, there were irregularities over advertising. Space had been sold on wildly exaggerated sales figures, which had been falling dramatically since its launch. The first issue, with articles by the Prince, Clive James and Lucinda Lambton, sold around 20,000 copies, but that figure steadily declined. In April 1997 it was as low as 2,109 copies. What infuriated many of Charles's friends in the architectural world was that, although the magazine was set up by the Prince to promote his ideas, his own favourite projects – like Poundbury in Dorset and Paternoster Square in London – were scathingly knocked, while modern schemes, by far Charles's least favourite architectural projects, were lavishly praised.

Arguably, it was an area into which the Prince of Wales should never have ventured. He expects too much of his staff, depending on them to have expertise in areas where they have none. Publishing is a specialist industry, and difficult at the best of times. When he first said he wanted a magazine, someone should have had the courage to say 'no'.

The Prince's ideas on architecture have not changed since he made his first speech on the subject in 1985, but he has allowed himself to be pushed around yet again, and he has failed to support the people whose ideals he shares. He would doubtless say it wasn't his fault, it was the fault of those who advised him. Some of his once staunchest supporters are very critical. Mira Bar-Hillel, planning corre- spondent of the London *Evening Standard*, says, 'The Prince could have made a real difference to the way architecture is viewed and practised in this country, giving a voice to millions. But he has allowed himself to be compromised, marginalised and ultimately silenced altogether. His direct influence is now negligible.

'What is both ironic and tragic is that the Prince's own views have never changed. He loathes the Millennium Dome every bit as pas- sionately as he hates other buildings by Lord Rogers, Sir Norman Foster, Sir Michael Hopkins and others who have flourished regardless of his views of them.

'But we can no longer expect him to add his weight to any future anti-modernist campaigns. His success in defeating "a monstrous carbuncle on the face of a much-loved friend" and the "glass stump more suitable to Manhattan" will, tragically, not be repeated.

'This is all very sad, but we must now accept that, while his views have not changed at all, we can no longer expect the Prince to voice them in defence of his architectural realm.'

THIRTEEN

Organic Highgrove

'We live in an age of rights – it seems to me that it is
time our Creator had some rights too.'
Charles

If Camilla has been Charles's emotional lifeline throughout the
darker moments, and work a mental escape, Highgrove has always
been his spiritual refuge. All the while his marriage was disin-
tegrating, he was creating, ever more furiously, a garden which,
whether by accident or design, is an uncanny reflection of the man
who made it. It became a sanctuary where he could clear his mind,
feel close to the natural world, pause briefly from the demands of the
job, and escape from the torment of the media and the failure of his
marriage. Today, it is simply home.

'The garden at Highgrove really does spring from my heart,' he
wrote in the introduction to a book about the estate published in
1993, 'and, strange as it may seem to some, creating it has been
rather like a form of worship.'

It is still his passion, and he spends many happy hours there, no
matter what the weather. He has five full-time and four part-time
gardeners, but he knows every square metre of the ground
intimately, and planted most of the trees and plants himself. He
notices every spurt of growth, every weed, and is constantly
changing and improving and dreaming up new ideas, adapting
schemes he has seen in other gardens and in other parts of the world,
and experimenting with different materials. The latest addition is a
stumpery, a faintly surreal, almost sculptured area of vast and aged
tree stumps that he has collected from different parts of the country

and arranged to extraordinary effect. He likes nothing more than the opportunity to show it all off, and watch the surprise on people's faces as they move from one part of the garden to another, like rooms in a house, each one quite different from the last.

There is sculpture in the gardens too, and a fountain, and giant Ali Baba pots. Poignantly, outside the walled vegetable garden, there is a figure of Diana the Huntress. He is genuinely pleased when people take an interest, and time and again, he has had letters from quite hard headed people saying that they felt something almost spiritual there.

'In some strange way, when I took on Highgrove,' he wrote, 'I knew what I wanted to do even though I had absolutely no experience of gardening or farming and the only trees I had planted had been official ones in very official holes! I experienced no sudden conversion to a new way of thinking, but merely developed an almost unconscious train of thought that seemed, now I reflect upon it, like some powerful echo that arose, inexplicably, from within.

'I knew I wanted to take care of the place in a very personal way and to leave it, one day, in a far better condition than I had found it.'

After Diana's death the Prince was thrilled to have back an album of photographs she had taken of the garden during its transformation in the early years of their marriage. It had gone missing from Highgrove some years before. She had captioned each photograph – 'Charles digging the Rose Garden', for instance – and it was a record that he treasured as an indelible memory of happier times. The Prince had realised it was missing when he wanted to include some of the photos in the book about the estate, written after the separation, and finally learnt the album was at Kensington Palace, and that was where it was staying.

Though he loves the garden, he feels no less passionately about the land. The Prince regularly takes the dogs up to Broadfield, and roams the fields and woods of the Home Farm with a little pruning saw in his pocket, which he uses to tidy up the lower branches of saplings. While Tigger, the remaining Jack Russell, whose daughter Pooh was lost down a rabbit hole, and William's black Labrador bitch, Wigeon, snuffle around after rabbits, he makes notes about things he has spotted, like a dead tree which needs to be removed, an untidy bit of hedgerow, a damaged stone wall, or some other detail, and fires off memos either to David Wilson, the farm manager, or to Nick Mould, the deputy land steward for the Eastern Region of the Duchy of Cornwall.

Sometimes the Prince and Wilson will walk round together and exchange stories, the Prince talking about ideas he has had, things that he has heard during the course of his travels, or things that have excited or troubled him. Recently a butcher they deal with in Essex told David a horror story, which he passed on to the Prince of Wales. A friend of his has steers which graze on the Essex marshes that had started to grow udders, from drinking the water. Oestrogen-mimicking chemicals had evidently seeped into the marshes. Stories like this serve to convince them that what they are doing at Highgrove is the only responsible way of farming for the future. There have been wild quail nesting on a particular block of land for the last two summers and that has been a thrill for everyone. It is important to the Prince that the land is managed in a way that encourages wildlife, and the arrival of quail, not normally seen so far north, is a compliment.

The farm is now fully organic, and Charles is adamant that it must be an example of best practice, and on the principle that Seeing is Believing, has regular tours for visiting groups of interested people, like farmers, researchers and agricultural students. The result is an estate which looks beautiful. Where he has had to replace buildings, he has never gone for the practical and economic option. He has brought in architects. He has a cowshed that commanded more work and expense than many a modern house. He has planted copses and mixed hedges to enhance the landscape, and to encourage birds – skylarks sing above; there are wild poppies growing through the fields of wheat, gates that hang properly on their hinges, and smart wooden fencing that sits well with the landscape. For many years there was not even a strand of barbed wire on the estate.

This pastoral idyll is not just personal vanity; it is at the root of the man. 'In farming, as in gardening,' he wrote, 'I happen to believe that if you treat the land with love and respect (in particular, respect for the idea that it has an almost living soul, bound up in the mysterious, everlasting cycles of nature) then it will repay you in kind. But if you fail to respect the complex, universal laws to which every living creature is ultimately subject, and if you discard that essential humility which recognises the subtle balance that has to be struck between Man's ambition and the finite nature of the physical world, in the end the consequences could be painful and deeply destructive.'

In David Wilson, the Prince found a kindred spirit, in total agreement with him about the environment and future sustainability of the planet. However, the men in suits who were running the Duchy of Cornwall at the time when the Prince decided he wanted to farm organically were another matter. They thought he was about to make a fool of himself by getting involved with some wild and wacky loss-making enterprise that was better left to oddballs.

Highgrove is owned by the Duchy of Cornwall, which, since its creation for the Black Prince in 1385, has been providing an income for successive Princes of Wales, and it has a duty, enshrined by an Act of Parliament, to continue doing so. The Prince's council of eight men, chaired by the Prince himself, has a statutory obligation, therefore, to make enough money for the Prince of Wales to live on, without diminishing the capital assets. No major projects can be undertaken at Highgrove without consulting the council and, although the Prince finds it intensely frustrating at times, it has a tempering effect on some of his more impulsive schemes. But on this matter the Prince was adamant: 'If the Duchy of Cornwall can't afford to try organic farming, then who the hell can?' he argued.

The conversion was gradual, and not entirely free from anxious moments. They experimented first with an eighty-acre block in 1986 and, three years later, after much consultation and visits to other organic pioneers, decided to go with their convictions and convert all 1,080 acres. But in the early 1990s, when the conversion was about half way, they had a succession of very poor harvests, like everyone in the Cotswolds, and the books began to look decidedly wobbly. The Prince's preference for post and rail fencing everywhere instead of barbed wire, and wooden tree guards instead of the plastic sleeves most farmers use, and even stone and wood state of the art cowsheds, did not help. They have not been cheap, but where once the cost would have had to be written off over five years, there is now no need. The final block of land was converted in 1996, the farm is fully organic, and to everyone's delight, it has now been in profit for five years running. Even the council has come round to thinking that organic farming is rather a good wheeze.

One of the farms the Prince took comfort and inspiration from when so many people seemed to be telling him he was mad, was Kite's Nest near the Cotswold town of Broadway. It is farmed by a remarkable family: Mrs Mary Young, who is a disarmingly forthright woman, and her son and daughter, Richard and Rosamund. Mary Young's husband, Harry, was alive at the time of the Prince's visit, but died in 1993.

'Are you a graduate of English literature?' she said, greeting Charles Clover, who was writing the Highgrove book, on his arrival at the house. 'They're the only people I have time for.' And when the Prince's staff were going over plans for his visit in 1989, and said they wanted him to drive round in his own Range Rover, Mary Young said, 'If he's not prepared to drive round in our Range Rover then you can tell him not to bother coming!' And so it was that the Prince was driven around in a battered old blue Range Rover – albeit newly serviced and freshly polished in his honour – and had a highly entertaining day.

This unusual turn of events was not dictated by pride, it was simply Mary Young's concern for her cattle, which happily roam the pastures in family groups, each one, in a herd of 200, individually named with something suitably literary. She thought they would be frightened if they saw a vehicle they didn't recognise. She cares about her animals' welfare in a most commendable way – right through to the end. When the time comes for any of the animals to be slaughtered, Richard and Rosamund take them to the abattoir and comfort the creatures until the bolt strikes. This is not simply sentimentality: there is strong evidence that the meat tastes better from animals which have been slaughtered without the stress and fear normally associated with abattoirs. The Youngs are practically self-sufficient: they grow their own vegetables, mill their own flour, make their own bread and sell their meat in their own shop.

The Prince didn't go quite as far as the Young family, but he came away with plenty of ideas. He has a herd of Aberdeen Angus beef cattle, which live in family groups; also a dairy herd – Ayrshires because he likes their brown and white colouring – and sheep. There are also three glossy brown Gloucester heifers, and a few other rare breeds dotted around the farm, which the Prince, as patron of the Rare Breeds Trust, keeps to provide a gene base. In 1998 they tried outdoor pigs for the first time, in a share-farming arrangement, where a local pig farmer runs his business on Highgrove land – also vegetables, as an experiment. The Prince already has five rather special pigs, which are extremely friendly and pleased to see people. The boys love them. Three are Large Blacks, a breed in danger of extinction, which were a birthday present to the Prince from some friends last year, and two rare Gloucestershire Old Spots, which were also presents, one for a birthday, the other for Christmas. They are supposed to live in the woods in an area specially fenced off, but are forever escaping and coming back to the farmyard in search of company.

The Gloucestershire Old Spots will have to go to the abattoir shortly. They have failed to breed, and in the practical world of farming that means they are no longer of any use alive. There is no boar at Highgrove, so they were sent off to be mated with the Princess Royal's Old Spot boar at Gatcombe. Sadly, they both appear to be barren.

The Prince lives about six miles from his sister, but seldom sees her; although her children, Peter and Zara, have become close to William and Harry recently. The Queen Mother came once to

Highgrove to look at the Prince's herd of Aberdeen Angus. She has a herd of her own at the Castle of Mey and sold Charles a few heifers in 1988. The Queen has also visited Highgrove, but she is very unaware of what her eldest son does. A visitor invited to afternoon tea at Sandringham not long ago complimented the Queen on the Prince's delicious Duchy Original biscuits. The Queen appeared not to know of their existence, and yet the Prince has been marketing his own biscuits made with organic oats grown on the Home Farm for more than six years.

Although they have not done much riding for a few years, the boys have recently become keen on polo. When they were younger, they both rode on ponies loaned by a local horsewoman, Marjorie Cox, who used to teach them – indeed James Hewitt also taught them. The ponies went when the marriage was in trouble, because the children were spending so much time in London, but they are great enthusiasts for the hunt. They love to follow it in a four-wheel drive vehicle, or on the back of one of the terrier men's quad bikes. They also spend hours on the estate shooting and roaring around the fields on trial bikes. They are fascinated by the animals; at lambing time, they spend hours in the lambing pens with Fred Hartles, the shepherd.

The Prince is delighted that William and Harry get so much pleasure from the countryside, which he loves so much, and is keen to let them enjoy themselves in any way they like.

Hunting is still one of the Prince's greatest passions, and he views the move to ban it with great sadness. He sees it as a natural part of the management of nature and an extension of man's involvement in the countryside. It is also a great leveller. As a fellow member of the Beaufort says, 'There's very little protocol on the hunting field, particularly when you're covered in mud and being hauled out of a ditch!' The killing of the fox is almost incidental. What Charles enjoys is the danger, the adrenalin and the challenge and the fact that in the process of trying to stay alive, it's very difficult to worry about anything else. As Trotsky once said, 'Hunting works on the mind like a poltice on a sore.' The danger, however, is very real. Many people, even the most skilled horsemen and horsewomen, have been killed, maimed or confined to a wheelchair as a result of an accident on the hunting field.

Charles didn't start hunting until 1974, when he was twenty-five, because he was never brought up to it. The Queen was a supporter, but never participated. Her father, King George VI, had hunted with great enthusiasm, and was fully supported by Queen Elizabeth, although she never hunted herself. Before George became king they rented a house in the Pytchley country, a hunt in Northumberland, where he hunted regularly. Princess Anne made her name as a three-day eventer, but at one time she hunted frequently, especially when she was married to Mark Phillips. But Charles had only ever played polo, and had therefore never done any jumping. It was one of Mark's horses that the Prince of Wales rode when he hunted for the first time. The late Duke of Beaufort laid on a special meet with some friends, specially for his benefit and, on that one day out, Charles was hooked.

It was not easy starting so late in life, and in the early days he fell off a lot, but he was remarkably brave and always went for the biggest and most difficult jumps. To the Queen's concern, he still rides fast and fearlessly, and she has said that she wished he wouldn't be quite so daring on the hunting field. He tests himself against every obstacle, and pushes himself and the horse to the absolute limit. Like all who wish to stay out to the end of the day, which he does whenever possible, he has a second horse in reserve. Most people who ride at Charles's pace get rid of a horse after a few seasons, but he gets desperately fond of his horses and puts great pressure on his head groom, Tom Normington, to keep his favourites going.

Camilla has a very different style. She takes the day at a much gentler pace and jumps when necessary, but does not leap blindly over every hedge, ditch and five-bar gate that presents itself. She was brought up hunting – her father, Bruce Shand, a wildly popular man, who won two Military Crosses during the Second World War, was joint Master of the Southdown Foxhounds. The social side of hunting is important. There is enormous camaraderie amongst the hunting fraternity, like any group who regularly face danger together, and they have a lot of fun. It is predominantly a sport for the rich, who have the time and money to do it, although there can be a surprising mix. For the Prince, it's an ideal opportunity to meet locals, particularly farmers. He always stops and chats to farmers whose land the hunt crosses, and every year holds a lunch at Highgrove for them by way of thanks.

The Prince is not a regular at the annual Hunt Ball, but he did enjoy a couple of very blue evenings laid on in recent years by the hunt at Badminton, home of the Duke of Beaufort.

'Matthew,' said the Prince after the first of these, 'I was at this marvellous hunt dinner last night and they had a wonderful comedian, a man called Jethro.'

'What?' said Matthew Butler in disbelief. 'I thought Jethro was for people who found Bernard Manning too subtle!'

Jethro is a Cornish comedian, whose act is extraordinarily crude: 'My pal Denzel got a Hoover stuck up his bum and I took him to hospital. When I phoned the hospital next day to see how he was getting on, they said, "He's picking up nicely."

'Denzel's dog swallowed a condom. The vet agreed to come over. Ten minutes later, Denzel rang back saying, "Don't bother. We found another one."'

Jethro had the hunt audience falling off their chairs with laughter. At the end of what was a very drunken evening the Prince swore everyone present to secrecy, then proceeded to tell a very filthy joke himself.

In the summer of 1998 there was a second Jethro evening, which members of the Beaufort were fighting to get tickets for. It was every bit as funny, and every bit as rude and, once again, at the end the Prince told a joke that was not out of keeping. He was telling it, he said, as a reward because everyone had been so good in keeping his last one out of the press. Most had actually been too drunk to remember it, but members of the Beaufort Hunt are entirely discreet.

The young of the Gloucestershire set are now doing much the same for Will, as he is known locally. He regularly goes to parties, often with his friend Mark Tomlinson, who is the son of polo playing neighbours, and he has already made such an impression on the local youth that even sixteen-year-olds close ranks and shield him with a protective wall of silence – sometimes against their own mothers' curiosity.

The Prince's impatience, and his desire to see his ideas implemented before the ink has dried on the page, makes him highly vulnerable. He doesn't want to hear good reasons why it might be ill advised to leap into a new venture without first thinking through all the possible consequences. He wants immediate action. So when people come along promising they can deliver, he takes them into his embrace as the answer to all his problems. But in every area that an idea takes him, there are groups and individuals waiting to hi-jack his name and exploit his enthusiasms for their own ends.

In 1989 he delivered a strong message of support to the organic movement. He also charged David Landale, secretary of the Duchy of Cornwall, with finding ways of giving added value to farm produce. David met a man called Michael Silverman, a management consultant who had contacts with Tesco, the giant super-marketing chain. They approached Tesco with the idea of selling Duchy produce and, spotting a marketing opportunity, Tesco was interested. The Prince was delighted. He had toyed with the idea of selling produce from Highgrove for years. He had thought it might be fun to sell apples and put them in carrier bags with the Prince of Wales's feathers on the side, but everyone wrote it off as another of his impractical ideas. Tesco promised to deliver.

Thus, in the summer of 1990, bread made from Highgrove's very first organic wheat crop went on sale in a selected number of stores in the south-east of England. It was called the Highgrove loaf, but couldn't be labelled organic because it didn't meet the Soil Association's strict guidelines: the palm oil used 'to give good loaf volume' was not organic. The loaf sold well initially, but in the recession of the early 1990s demand fell off and the loaf was discontinued.

In the meantime, still capitalising on the Prince's organic credentials, Silverman was hatching a plan to sell lamb reared by Duchy tenants to Tesco. But there was a problem. Wheat from the Home Farm for the bread had been organic; Duchy lamb was not. So Silverman set about writing a new set of guidelines for lamb production which lamb from Duchy farms would be able to meet sooner than the normal three-year period needed to qualify under the Soil Association guidelines.

Richard Young, from Kite's Nest farm, was then deputy director of British Organic Farmers, and number two at the Soil Association. He was asked to come to London to give them some advice, but told not to talk to anyone about it. Silverman wanted Richard to give the organic movement's seal of approval to a non-organic farming regime, and had drawn up detailed standards which allowed the use of chemicals. Richard flicked through a weighty volume Silverman put on the table in front of him and told him there was no chance of this being accepted. It completely missed the point of organic farming. Silverman then showed him a Code of Practice for free-range lamb production.

The draft, drawn up by Silverman, was a masterpiece of writing, with reassuring phrases about sustainability and the environment, but nothing of any real substance. Young asked whether he might consult Patrick Holden, director of the Soil Association, or Lawrence Woodward of the Elm Farm Research Centre, and was told he couldn't consult anyone: the project had to be confidential. It was only when Young protested that he was told he could discuss the broad principles with Patrick and Lawrence, but he was not to show them the Code of Practice. His instinct was to write, 'This is crap – an appalling dilution of organic standards'; but having the clear impression that the Prince wanted this code to be approved, Richard sat down and wrote a seven-page diplomatic critique of the draft. His major criticism was that it allowed the use of nitrogen fertiliser. It banned pesticides, which sounded good, but the sort they were banning, namely insecticides, were rarely used on grassland in that area anyway, while herbicides, which were used, were to be allowed. He then wrote a second letter putting his reservations more forcefully: the code was not acceptable to the organic movement, it would create big problems for the movement, and it would not achieve what the Prince wanted in terms of sustainable production.

'I think I had been identified,' said Richard, 'as someone who was a bit naïve and sufficiently involved with the organic movement to carry some weight, but not so involved that I was battle-hardened like Patrick, who would have seen through it straightaway.'

David Landale was on the telephone to Young at 7.30 a.m. to say that things now had to be done in a great hurry, and that he was sending Silverman to visit him at Kite's Nest. Silverman arrived in a Rolls Royce on 17 December 1990. Thinking he had been sent by the Prince, the Young family entertained him politely. Silverman wanted approval for the Duchy lamb initiative, and would not take no for an answer. In the end, Richard agreed to sign a hand-written statement, drafted in front of him, which said he would give limited backing to the scheme – his 'broad sympathy' – subject to a number of conditions being satisfied.

The Young family did not take to Silverman. They put up with him because they believed the Prince had sent him. During the course of his visit, Silverman twice said that he was worried the Queen would abdicate, which would be hopeless because once the Prince of Wales became King, he would no longer be able to use him in this way. He said this in a very direct manner, with a lot of impatience and nervous energy. Richard had the impression he was dealing with someone who was single-mindedly intent on exploiting the Prince of Wales's concern about the environment and animal welfare in an unpleasant and mercenary way.

He also felt within minutes of Silverman leaving that he had made a terrible mistake in signing the statement of support. Silverman, he felt, had used every trick to win his confidence and allay his concerns. He rang Silverman as soon as he arrived back in London that evening and told him he had had a change of heart. Silverman was not at all pleased and said he had already spoken to the Prince of Wales and everything was going ahead.

It was only at this point that Young broke his vow of silence and sent a fax to Richard Aylard, who unfortunately was in the Gulf at the time and didn't see the note for some days. Aylard was appalled when he read what had been going on, as was the Prince. Charles was furious that his name was being used in this way, and telephoned Richard Young to say how uneasy he was about the scheme, and that he shared all his reservations. He assured Richard that it would be dropped.

A few weeks later, Richard Young happened to be having lunch at Highgrove with the Prince and a group of people, including Patrick Holden. The Prince sought them both out. 'I can't get out of it,' he said with pent-up frustration. 'It's gone too far down the road.' The argument from Silverman that he had been presented with – which had not pleased him one jot – was that because of his initial support for the idea, the Duchy tenants had invested such time and energy, as well as money in starting to modify production, that it would cause major problems if the Prince pulled out. This was not entirely true: many Duchy tenants were extremely unhappy. They bitterly resented being presented with a set of guidelines telling them how to farm by 'a blue-suited bugger from London', as one referred to Silverman.

'Prince sells 3,000 stress-free lambs, humanely reared on a vegetarian diet from his own Good Life farm' was the story in the *Today* newspaper as the first lamb hit Tesco's shelves in March 1991, shortly after the Prince had made another big speech about organic farming; 'Baa Royal Appointment', the headline. Although the labels did not make any false claims, the link between the Prince of Wales and organic production was already established in the public's mind.

The farming press was quick to react. 'The Prince of Wales's Duchy of Cornwall Estate is trying to pull the wool over consumers' eyes with marketing gimmicks that could lead people to believe Duchy lamb is produced organically,' said *Farming News*, under the headline 'Royal woolly lamb fools buyers'. Use of his crest was giving the Duchy a fifteen per cent premium for the lamb.

'Real organic farmers are livid. It is unfortunate that Tesco has begun marketing the Duchy lamb so soon after the Prince's speech on organic farming last week,' said British Organic Farmers' chairman Bill Starling. The Prince had delivered a major speech to the Royal Agricultural Society of England in which he called for wholesale reform of farming methods and better labelling of foods.

After some heated debate at Highgrove, the Soil Association managed to convince the Duchy that there was a serious problem in labelling this product 'Duchy Lamb'. It was stopped. The meat thereafter was known as Cornwall Quality Lamb, and later still, West Country Lamb.

The Prince was still convinced that the basic idea had been good. It was a question of finding the right way of making it happen. It was John Lister who runs Shipton Mill, a couple of miles down the road from Highgrove, who came up with the answer. He suddenly said to David Wilson one day, 'I think I could make a biscuit with your oats.' David Wilson presented the idea at a management committee, and the Prince snapped it up.

The Duchy was not so enthusiastic, but after a certain amount of argument, Guy Salter, the Prince's then assistant private secretary with the business brief, was given the go-ahead to develop a product. Salter was a maverick who didn't obey the rules, and was dangerously cavalier in using the Prince's name, but much liked by the Prince. He had useful connections in the media and was good company. He also had extraordinary energy and a capacity to make things happen. It was he who set up the Prince of Wales's Business Leaders Forum, through which Business in the Community ideals were extended into a global context. He organised a highly successful conference, which involved getting the Prince of Wales, plus 200 business leaders, their wives and luggage, to Charleston, South Carolina, just eight weeks after a fearsome hurricane had all but flattened the town. He was one of a rare breed of 'can do' men who have passed through the Prince's office, who brooked no opposition. When told there were no longer any tiles on the roofs in Charlston, he said, 'Well get some,' and when told that the Prince could no longer stay in the very large beautiful house that Salter had found for him, because the garden had disappeared, he said, 'Well just deliver 4,000 tons of top-soil plus some cactuses by Tuesday and I don't want to hear any more nonsense about this.' After that, developing a biscuit was child's play.

Knowing that the key to success was not what you know but who, he immediately brought in some experts to develop the idea of Duchy Originals. What the Prince liked about the idea was three-fold: use of his name would give added value to Duchy produce and help his tenant farmers, it would encourage his tenants to go properly organic by providing an outlet for their produce, for which the market would pay a premium, and by running the company as a charitable trust, it would make money for his charities. Unlike Richard Aylard, who had a tendency to go for the less high profile characters, Salter went straight to the top. He recruited the head of the country's leading advertising agency and the head of the country's leading market research company to form the Duchy Marketing Advisory Group, chaired by Keith Holloway of Grand Metropolitan. The group then recruited Chris Nadin, a secondment from Grand Met, to run the business. Things couldn't have been going better. The first product was an oaten biscuit, made with organic oats, mostly from the farm, milled at Shipton. It went on sale in 300 independent retail outlets in 1993, and a year later, that number had doubled. The result was stupendous. Most people who tasted it agreed it was a delicious biscuit. Then followed a ginger biscuit, equally good, apart from a few minor setbacks with shelf-life, and Duchy organic bread. The future looked promising.

Then Nadin left, his secondment over, and was replaced by Mike Cornish, marketing manager of VW-Audi, who was of a much more conventional mould. He knew nothing about organics but a great deal about marketing. If the business was going to make real money, he said, it needed volume, and since there wasn't enough organic produce available to create volume with the biscuits and the bread, he struck a deal, first mooted by his predecessor, with Coca-Cola Schweppes bottling to produce a range of fizzy drinks. Before anyone had really caught up with what was happening, Coca-Cola Schweppes was churning out more fizzy drinks than anyone could possibly handle or sell. They were a disaster. There was nothing organic about the drinks, and most people thought they tasted like cough mixture. Furthermore, so that they could have some tenuous claim to the Duchy label, estate workers had to pick elder flowers from the farm, which amounted to no more than two per cent of the drinks' ingredients, and could have been bought dried, for a fraction of the cost, from the Eastern Bloc with a much stronger aroma than they were able to produce by improvising a drying system in the grain store.

For a while the drinks traded on the integrity of the biscuits, but it didn't last. By 1996 the business was in a parlous state. It had accumulated huge overheads, and spent a lot of money developing products, which it never recouped. In six years of trading it had lost £373,180 and reached the point where it either had to stop trading entirely, or expand at speed so that it made money quickly.

In 1996 the Prince thought he had found the person who could rescue Duchy Originals from the mess it had got itself into – the latest in a long line of people who he hoped might provide the answer to the problems that none of his advisers seemed able to do. Sue Townsend was a marketing wizard, who had had great success with Crabtree & Evelyn, the up-market toiletries and jam firm, which she co-founded. He had met her through Robert Kime, the interior designer who had redecorated Highgrove after the separation. She was an engaging blonde, with lots of energy, a husky voice and plenty of charm, which the Prince immediately fell for. He announced that he wanted her to take over Duchy Originals and, although her references were not encouraging for this particular job, the Prince didn't care and was deaf to advice; he was adamant she should be appointed.

Like her predecessor, Townsend knew nothing about organics, although she went to the Home Farm often to glad-hand and talk to visitors. She appeared to be more interested in the garden at Highgrove and in the domestic arrangements than in the produce she was marketing. She worked slavishly for the bottom line, and had a good eye for an appealing image, introducing smart designs to all the packaging, but she set about it in a way that irritated almost everyone with whom she had dealings. The direct access she enjoyed to the Prince caused jealousies, and she created extra work throughout the Duchy, the gardens and the house. She failed to appreciate that the Prince of Wales was not like any other commodity or brand name that could be prettily packaged and sold in bulk for maximum profit. The departure into fizzy drinks had started the compromise, but Sue Townsend went further and introduced a whole range of products which had no pretence to be organic in any way. They included soap, bath oil, perfume, chocolates, tea – twenty-three products in all, and most of them made by well-known conventional companies, like Crabtree & Evelyn, Fortnum & Mason and Floris. Even the pork sausages and jams were no different from any other you could buy in an upmarket food shop. All that was different was the label and the price.

The labels did not make any claim to be organic, so there was no suggestion of any deception. Nevertheless, for the last ten years the Prince of Wales had been widely viewed as a champion of the organic movement, and consumers seeing a Duchy Original product could have been forgiven for assuming that it would be organic. Even the biscuits, which once *were* organic, were no longer. Yet they were still being sold in what was basically the same packaging. All that had changed was the wording, which consumers who had been buying the biscuits from the beginning would have been unlikely to notice.

The situation was causing great nervousness all round, not least at the Soil Association, but Sue Townsend's position seemed unassailable, until a meeting at Highgrove in the summer of 1997. The Prince was confronted by all the big names in the organic movement who all told him that Duchy Originals was heading for catastrophe, and would take the Prince with it, if it was allowed to continue on its present course. Sue Townsend stoutly defended herself, but in so doing made it clear that her commitment to marketing and developing the image of Duchy Originals took precedence over the product pedigree and organic integrity of the production system. 'There was blood on the carpet that day,' said one of the participants, 'but it wasn't arterial.'

At the next meeting a couple of months later, it was. Sue Townsend had a set-to with Helen Browning, chairman of the Soil Association, which was said to have been 'like putting a couple of cats into a cardboard box'. In the heat of the moment, Townsend accused organic farmers of being 'a bunch of hillbillies' – not the most sensible remark to make in front of the Prince of Hillbillies himself. 'It was a watershed meeting,' is the deliberate under-statement of one of those present. The Prince recognised that the situation could not continue, and Sue Townsend departed as swiftly as she had arrived. She was replaced by her deputy, Fiona Gately, and in January 1998 Guy McCracken, a senior if unexciting director of Marks & Spencer, was hired as non-executive chairman, charged with the task of trying to restore the company's integrity.

Patrick Holden, who has watched in dismay the rise and fall of Duchy Originals, has every sympathy. 'It was a brilliant aspiration, and he was exactly right to create the company in the first place,' he says. 'What went wrong was the people running the company were tempted by the commercial element, because they were wanting to create profit for the Prince's Trust and run a viable business. And they were right: all their training, their mindsets, said volume equals profit. You can't make profit instantly on tiny volumes of expensive, high integrity product. Where they were wrong was compromising the story, which is the essence of what it's all about. In the long run it would be an own goal, because ultimately you lose the trust of the consumer and the mechanism for that is exposed by journalists.'

It was what they all feared could happen at any time, but it wasn't until January 1998, ironically the very month that Guy McCracken arrived to put things right, that Sheila Dillon, producer of Radio 4's 'Food Programme', who had been such an admirer of the project when it first began, could stand her disillusion no longer.

Food writer Henrietta Green, amongst others, was interviewed.

'When Duchy Originals was founded in 1990,' she said, 'I, and I think lots of other people, got very excited about it because what it was setting out to do was very, very different. It was unique. It was all about sustainable farming and linking the farmer right the way through to the product. And also, I think one of the intentions, although perhaps they didn't express it, was to use themselves as a model, so that other farmers could see how it could be done, how they too could get into a niche market. And I think it's fair to say that over the years they have, well, perhaps, drifted a little from their intention to ... what they have ended up with now is, in essence, no more than a range of gift foods.

'Prettily packaged, taste good, fine. But they've just been brought in from other manufacturers, other producers. Nothing particularly interesting about them. I mean, take, say, Ackermans chocolates. Well, Ackermans chocolates do very nicely, thank you ... What is there about these chocolates that could possibly help the British farming community? I mean, the cocoa solids are imported, the orange flavours ... Similarly, what's satsuma marmalade got to do with the British farmer? What have fine teas blended by Taylors of Harrogate? ...'

As the presenter, Derek Cooper, commented, 'Even more depressingly, in the last eight years, only two Duchy farmers have gone organic.'

The whole sorry saga of Duchy Originals was typical of so many of the Prince's good ideas. His interest is just as keen as it ever was, his principles are intact and he is just as radical as he ever was, but he allows himself to be led by anyone whose star is currently in the ascendant.

Nonetheless, as Patrick Holden is the first to acknowledge, Charles's influence on the organic movement cannot be overstated. He helped make organic farming respectable, and his involvement has persuaded a lot of influential people to take it more seriously than they would otherwise have done. Organic production in Britain is still smaller than in any other country in Europe – about 1,000 farms account for 0.4 per cent of total production – and consumer demand is far greater and growing all the time. The people who once mocked the organic movement are now queuing up at their local supermarket to pay over the odds for chemical-free food. Conventional farmers, who have been propping up the agro-chemical industry for years, are seeing that organics are good business, and are busy converting. Organic production is likely be up to two per cent by the millennium.

Charles has been most powerful in the work he does behind the scenes, bringing together people who would not normally meet, very often people of opposing views, and exerting gentle pressure on government. It is the way he operates in all his areas of interest. One of his concerns is 'greening' the Common Agricultural Policy. To this end a seminar was organised in Brussels in October 1996 for seventy-five people, including both agricultural and environment commissioners, and five people from each member state, which the Prince attended. He spent a morning listening to the debate, spoke himself, and hosted a dinner. At Sandringham he has hosted three seminars for environmentalists, organic and conventional farmers, to try and move farming in a greener direction.

But there is still work to be done, and anyone who thinks that the Prince of Wales has lost his campaigning edge is mistaken. The latest danger in the environmental world is the encroachment of genetically modified crops, which threaten the very heart of sustainable agriculture. They are plants which have been given genes from bacteria, which make them resistant to a broad-spectrum weed-killer, available from the manufacturer that supplies the GM seed. When the crop is sprayed with this weed-killer, every other plant in the field is killed. The result is an essentially sterile field, providing neither food nor habitat for wildlife. More frightening yet, these crops are capable of interbreeding with their wild relatives, creating new weeds with built-in resistance to weed-killer. They have also been found to have spread more than a mile away from their own field, which poses a threat to other methods of farming, both conventional and organic. GM production is owned by half a dozen giant multi-national companies, and if things continue unchallenged, within ten years everyone's staple food, whether they like it or not, will come from genetically engineered plants.

Since 1995, the Prince has chosen to write newspaper and magazine articles on matters of importance as a safer way of communicating his thoughts and ideas than via speeches, where he was prone to being quoted out of context. Genetic modification had been a concern for some years and it was a question of finding the right moment to launch an attack. The moment was deemed right in June 1998, and the *Daily Telegraph* carried a powerful leader-page piece calling for a moment's pause to consider the consequences of crops that take 'mankind into realms that belong to God, and to God alone. Apart from certain highly beneficial and specific medical applications, do we have the right to experiment with, and commercialise, the building blocks of life? We live in an age of rights – it seems to me that it is time our Creator had some rights too.'

FOURTEEN

The Prince's People

'I wouldn't go on advising him if I didn't think he
was doing very, very important work.'
Adviser to the Prince of Wales

In October 1993 Charles's cousin, Viscount Linley, married. The
Prince was entertaining a group of overseas businessmen, called
British Invisibles, on board *Britannia*, in an attempt to drum up
trade abroad. The appointment had been fixed at a programme
meeting before the Linleys even announced their engagement, let
alone the date of their wedding. He was going to have to miss the
church service, because he couldn't be back in England in time, but
would make it to the reception. It would have to be a life or death
situation for the Prince to let down someone who had been
expecting him. James Whitaker, then writing for the *Mirror*, decided
this was nonsense; the real reason he wouldn't be at the wedding was
because he couldn't bear to be seen near an altar with the Princess of
Wales.

'This is total crap, James,' said Sandy Henney, as she patiently
explained the chronology. 'You would be the first to bark if he said,
"Sod the country, I'm going to a family wedding."'

The next day the front-page story in the *Mirror* was all about the
Prince not wanting to be seen in church with Diana.

In July 1994 the crescendo of his twenty-five years as Prince of
Wales celebrations was a return to Caernarvon Castle, where
Charles had been invested by the Queen in 1969. There he had won
the hearts of millions of Welsh people, not all of whom were pleased
to have an English prince foisted on them, by taking the trouble to

learn the language and giving the Loyal Address in a mixture of English and Welsh. He had returned in 1981 to present his new bride on their first tour together. The Welsh people once again fell in love, this time with Diana. In July 1994, just a month after the Dimbleby film, in which he had admitted being unfaithful in his marriage, there was no certainty the visit would go so well. In fact, *Daily Mail* readers the following day were given the impression that the Prince was very badly snubbed when the paper published a photograph with a small gathering of people behind a police barricade and the headline, 'Welsh stay away in their droves'. According to the article, between 200 and 300 people had turned up. According to the police, an estimated 5,000 were there – so many people that they had to mobilise their strategic reserve for crowd control.

It was the kind of negative press coverage that drove the Prince to distraction.

More damaging yet were sensational revelations in the *News of the World* by Ken Stronach, the Prince's valet for fifteen years, about the Prince's affair with Camilla Parker Bowles. Stronach was tricked into selling his story, although, in the end, he never received any payment. The newspaper had first contacted his son, also named Ken, who persuaded his father to come with him to meet a reporter from the *News of the World* in a pub. With a bit of encouragement and a few drinks inside him, Stronach began to talk, but the following day he had decided he was not interested in saying anything for the record or for any money. Neither he nor his son had realised that the reporter had a tape recorder hidden during their conversation which had picked up everything.

The *News of the World* was not slow to point out the tricky situation he was in. It was going to publish the material it had whatever Stronach's views on the matter. He was trapped, so when the newspaper asked for photographs too, he obliged.

The story ran under the headline, 'Charles Bedded Camilla As Diana Slept Upstairs', with photographs he had taken himself in the Prince's bedroom. It was as damaging as it could possibly be, particularly given the timing. The newspaper had had the story for some time, but sat on it until the Parker Bowles's divorce was announced in January 1995, when it was guaranteed maximum impact.

In the wake of this, an informal media advisory group was set up chaired by Richard Aylard, with Alan Kilkenny, the PR consultant, Jonathan Dimbleby, Allan Percival and Sandy Henney from the press office, and Stephen Lamport, Aylard's assistant, to discuss ways of improving the situation. Everyone agreed that their strongest asset was the Prince himself. No one who meets him face to face is ever unimpressed. So, in the absence of sympathetic media coverage, why not go on the offensive and invite opinion formers down to Highgrove to meet the Prince and get to know him in a social context? There could be newspaper editors amongst those chosen, MPs, and influential people in all his fields of interest, like medicine, architecture, farming and business. But the real problem he faced, they all acknowledged, was the incompatibility of being both heir to the throne and a public figure in a media age.

Some months later a larger and more formal Media Advisory Group was set up at Matthew Butler's suggestion, to discuss how to put over more effectively what the Prince did. The group included people like Charles Allen, head of the Granada Media Group, a number of eminent journalists, several leading PR consultants, including Alan Kilkenny, Simon Mayo, the Radio One disc jockey, also Tom Shebbeare from the Prince's Trust, Julia Cleverdon from BitC, and Richard Aylard.

The first meeting was hugely invigorating and professional, and produced a number of good ideas and observations – also questions, which Matthew Butler undertook to convey to the Prince for feedback to the Group. He duly sent the Prince a memo detailing the meeting, which the Prince annotated liberally, clearly enthused by some of the ideas.

The Group never got to see the Prince's notes. Matthew was on the point of circulating them but was stopped by Richard. As a result, with no feedback from the Prince, the second meeting proved to be a complete waste of time, and a significant part of Aylard's downfall. In the months when he was working on the Prince's divorce settlement, plus coping with the normal office load and the collapse of his own marriage, his behaviour became increasingly puzzling. 'It was a terrible existence, poor chap,' says one of his former colleagues, 'and because he couldn't share a lot of the stuff with anyone else – the stuff he was dealing with ten hours a day, when he was locked in with the solicitors – I think he got into a mindset that spilt over into nobody could know anything else either.'

It became clear as a result of that second meeting that Aylard wanted to keep aspects of the Prince to himself. He felt that the private Prince and the Prince who was heir to the throne was his responsibility, and wanted the Group to concern itself with the Prince's charitable activities and nothing else. 'But don't let's forget,' he said, 'that there are two quite separate Princes here. The Prince I am dealing with, and the Prince's Trust Prince.'

The Group pointed out that they couldn't be marketing two separate Princes. As one of them said, 'Richard saw this as a bit of a threat and the issue really was, are we going to have someone who, however talented and devoted to the Prince, is going to do all of this on his own? Or are we going to have someone who's a bit more of a team player with a single message coming out? Richard wasn't very good at working with other people and, when things went wrong, he got in his bunker and managed as best he could on his own. These people, some of whom were quite distinguished, clearly wanted it to be done in a different way.' Their voices joined the chorus that was already telling the Prince it was time for Aylard to go.

Another voice in the chorus was Camilla's divorce lawyer, Hilary Browne-Wilkinson, who had become a good friend. More significantly, she had a suggestion about who might strengthen the team. Over dinner at St James's Palace she judiciously brought the subject up while Aylard was present.

Also at the table were Hilary's husband, Law Lord Nico Browne-Wilkinson, and former Head of the Bar Council, Lord Alexander, and his wife, Marie. The party had reached the coffee without anyone saying anything very alarming, when Lord Browne-Wilkinson cleared his throat and launched into a fearsome attack on the way the Prince's staff had handled the media and the legal profession's collective view that the situation could not be worse, nor more damaging for the monarchy. As the man responsible for the office, Richard Aylard found himself in an uncomfortable position.

Hilary Browne-Wilkinson was also on the board of the Press Complaint's Commission, and therefore probably knew better than most how St James's was regarded by the press.

'Have you come across a man called Mark Bolland?' she asked. 'He works for the Press Complaints Commission,' and proceeded to describe this Canadian-born, comprehensive-school educated, bright, entertaining thirty-year-old from Middlesbrough, who had been director of the PCC for the last five years. 'You should hire him,' she said, 'and see if he can do anything to help.'

The Prince leapt at the suggestion, said he must have him at once, and would arrange a meeting. Here was a new wonder man who would solve all his problems.

Sure enough, a couple of days later Aylard invited Bolland to lunch and offered him a job as Sandy Henney's assistant, on terms which Bolland thought rather peculiar for an assistant press secretary. He had been warned the job he would be offered would be 'crap' but had been told to take it; there would be better things to come. He accepted.

Soon afterwards he was following Richard Aylard up the stairs at St James's Palace on his way to meet the Prince, when they bumped into Allan Percival, who was then press secretary. 'Oh, Allan,' said Aylard, 'this is Mark Bolland. We've just offered him a job in the press office.' Neither Percival nor Henney had been told of Bolland's appointment. Sensing what was coming, Percival opted for a post in Downing Street.

'I've heard lots of rumours about you from people,' said the Prince to Bolland. 'If you could bear to do this ...'

Bolland said that he could certainly bear to do the job; what is more, he intended to have some fun doing it. 'If you don't have fun in a job, there's no point in it,' he said. 'It doesn't all need to be so terrible. Things can get better.'

'If you say so,' said the Prince.

'Well, I do, actually.'

The two men struck an instant rapport and in July 1996 he took up his unlikely and lowly post in the press office, where he spent his first month poring over the file on Dimbleby, reading all the notes and memos, wanting to understand how it had all come about, and taking calls from the Prince, which he enjoyed. Whilst not being the greatest admirer of Aylard, and believing Dimbleby to have been a mistake – easier with the benefit of hindsight – he acknowledges that 'Richard became a lightning rod for quite a lot that was wrong.'

It soon became obvious that Richard Aylard and Mark Bolland could not continue in tandem. While Stephen Lamport, who was then Aylard's deputy, Mark Bolland and Colin Trimming, the Prince's protection officer, were on a recce to Central Asia, a plot was hatched to remove Aylard. The Prince had to be the one to tell Aylard to go, however. This was one conversation he could not duck or pass on to someone else. He did it in a typically clumsy way, at the end of a week's fishing on the Duchess of Westminster's Scottish estate, Lochmore. He was deeply fond of Richard and knew the conversation would be more painful than he could bear, and had postponed it all week. As one observer said philosophically, 'Richard is a classic case of that S-Level cliché: "The victims always get a bad press because the victors write the history books".'

Apart from Sir James Mellon's reminder that if the worst came to the worst he could go back to his well-paid job in PR, the other good piece of advice that Matthew Butler was given on joining the Prince's office in July 1993 came from Robert Fraser, the equerry, who had been in the job a while. Matthew was off for a fortnight to Birkhall, one of the Queen Mother's homes on the Balmoral estate, which was regarded as one of the best parts of the job. The five people in the office did a two-week stint each, staying in a little cottage on the estate.

'The Prince will ask you to go and have dinner with him most nights,' said Fraser. 'He will say, "Oh, you will come for dinner, won't you?" My advice is to plead a previous engagement, because he's only doing it out of old-fashioned courtesy. He's there with his friends and doesn't really want someone from the office there. Do it once, but otherwise stay clear.'

It is a shame for Richard Aylard that he was never given the same advice. Although he would say he never presumed upon a friendship with the Prince of Wales, he became so close over the seven years he worked for him that, to everyone who watched the relationship at first hand, it seemed almost symbiotic. Aylard gave one hundred and ten per cent of himself and his time to the Prince, and in the end it cost him his job, and his marriage.

He worked long hours, and was with the Prince over many weekends as well, sometimes fishing or shooting with him, but there was scarcely a day when the Prince would not do some work at some point. Whatever recreation he is engaged in, whether fishing, painting, gardening, or even reading a book, his mind never stops. As an idea occurs or a worry clouds his day, he wants someone to bounce it off. He is also a great writer of memos. If he has a sudden thought, or notices something he's not happy about, or decides there's someone he ought to see who might be able to help solve a problem or raise some money, he commits it to paper for his private secretary to action. There are even memos from the Prince dated 25 December, written from Sandringham, the one date in the year when perhaps even the Prince thought twice about telephoning.

If ever there were three people in a marriage, it was in Richard Aylard's. Because the Prince never stops working himself, it doesn't occur to him that his staff might need a break, and unless something is pointed out to him, he is curiously blind to what is going on in other people's lives. The Princess was always very acute at picking up vibrations from the people around her, and solicitous for their well-being. Once alerted, the Prince could not be more concerned, but his antennae are poor. For all the time spent together, and the obvious closeness, the Prince was unaware that his private secretary's home life was in serious difficulty. Aylard had two young children at home and a wife who had suffered severe post-natal depression, whom he seldom saw. She lived in Surrey, and he lived in a grace-and-favour apartment at Kensington Palace. On the rare occasions when he was at home, he would be interrupted by the telephone. It was not the formula for a happy marriage.

'I don't know what I would do without Richard,' the Prince said to Belinda Harley, an assistant private secretary, one day. 'He's helping me so much through this difficult situation.'

'Yes, sir,' said Belinda, 'and it's difficult for Richard, as you probably know. His own marriage is in difficulty at the moment as well, so he's getting it at home as well as at work.'

'I had no idea,' said the Prince. 'Why didn't anyone tell me?'

The following morning Aylard came storming into the office. 'Well, thank you very much, Belinda,' he said. 'Thanks to you, the Prince was on the phone from a quarter past ten until midnight last night sympathising with me.' Though he feigned anger, he was clearly quite touched.

Everyone who has worked for the Prince has experienced the pressure. He is demanding and if allowed will take over every waking hour. Whether others were more determined, or simply more successful than Aylard in making sure they kept a life for themselves, it is difficult to know. There is no doubt Aylard saw the Prince through infinitely more difficult times than any other private secretary, and perhaps felt that he needed the extra support. He was with him when Andrew Morton's book came out, he was with him through both the Squidgy and Camillagate tapes, and the 'Panorama' interview, and he was with him through the painful process of separation, and divorce – times when the Prince was desperately low, and his confidence all but gone. There were days when it took a real effort to motivate him, and Richard gave his life over to keeping the Prince going.

He was also with the Prince in Klosters on 10 March 1988, when his friend Major Hugh Lindsay was killed by an avalanche, which must rank as one of the very worst days in the Prince's life. Nothing since the death of Lord Mountbatten had distressed him more. Hugh Lindsay had been his guest, he was newly married and his wife, Sarah, who worked in the press office at Buckingham Palace, was pregnant with their first child. They had been skiing off-piste, down a particularly difficult run known as the Wang, which runs below the Gotschivagrat cable car. They were skiing with Charlie and Patti Palmer-Tomkinson and a local guide called Bruno Sprecher. Fergie had fallen and hurt herself that morning, and Diana had stayed behind with her in the chalet. As the party paused at the top of a steep and narrow gully, there was suddenly a great roar, a noise the Prince has never forgotten, and they looked up to see giant blocks of snow tumbling down the mountain towards them at terrifying speed. The guide shouted 'Jump!' and, trained to move when he is told, the Prince jumped, escaping death by no more than a couple of seconds. Patti had been caught under the falling wall of snow. She had appalling injuries and was initially thought unlikely to live, or at least unlikely to recover fully. It took many months and countless operations but, miraculously, not only did she recover, she was able to ski again. Hugh Lindsay was not so lucky.

The Prince blamed himself for his friend's death, even though he was in no way responsible. Everyone understood the risks they were taking in skiing off-piste. The situation was not helped by the media, which blamed him too. The *Sun*'s headline read, 'ACCUSED. Official: Charles DID cause the killer avalanche'. There were stories that the Prince had led the party down a 'closed' run, despite warning signs to stay away, and had thereby triggered the avalanche. An official enquiry, however, found him in no way culpable: the run was not closed, and there were no warning signs.

Sarah Lindsay, whose baby, Alice, was born two months later, went through some very black times after Hugh's death, but amongst the welter of support and kindness from friends and strangers alike, both the Prince and Princess were memorable. She was desperate for details of what precisely had happened, what precise time he had died, how he must have felt as he looked up and saw the avalanche, and Charles talked to her endlessly. Unlike so many people who tried to avoid mentioning Hugh's name, Charles understood Sarah's need to talk about him. It was important to her to know that wherever he was, he was all right, which he also understood. She tried mediums and automatic writers, who claim to write what they are instructed from the spirit world, and the Prince suggested a number of people who could help her, including Mervyn Stockwood, the former Bishop of Southwark, who put her on to the Institute of Psychic Studies. Diana's support was even more exceptional. For three years after Hugh's death, she telephoned Sarah every Sunday night or Monday morning, which were always difficult times; and on Alice's first birthday, she invited her to Kensington Palace, where they had a birthday cake with the boys.

The Princess told Sarah she would never go back to Klosters, and she kept her word. The Prince, however, has been back many times, and was accused by the media of great insensitivity. But he has never been there since without thinking of Hugh Lindsay. As Patti Palmer-Tomkinson explained, 'We all agreed that we would never go anywhere else ... It would have been like turning our back on him and leaving him there. We can't ski together, the three of us, without remembering Hugh.'

The Klosters disaster happened soon after Richard Aylard had become assistant private secretary, and a bond was formed in the mountains, and an understanding and admiration for the Prince, which never diminished. Although from quite different backgrounds, they shared a lot of common interests. Aylard was sympathetic to all the Prince's ideas and ideals, and keen to push forward and find ways of achieving what the Prince wanted. What he lacked was confidence. He was deluged with work, which he refused to delegate, and tried to handle himself. There was pressure coming from every direction. He even had a furious telephone call from Tiggy Legge-Bourke's father blasting him because his daughter was always in the newspapers, but resisted the temptation to say she was in the newspapers because she did such stupid things. The more he did, the more the Prince asked for, and Richard found it difficult to say 'No.' Meanwhile, all semblance of a home life, or any other kind of life, disappeared.

To others watching the relationship develop, watching the hours he put into the job, and knowing about the tensions at home, it was clear that the situation was going to end in disaster. Julia Cleverdon discussed her fears with John Riddell. 'This is awful,' she said; 'you must stop him working like this or he's going to ruin another marriage.'

Riddell looked at Julia in complete astonishment and said, 'Of course he will. Everything he does has to be one hundred and ten per cent dedicated to the Prince, so of course he will. It's quite impossible. That's what will happen.' Sure enough it did. He subsequently went through a very acrimonious divorce.

By 1996 he had been fatally wounded by the Dimbleby exercise, and, although he was the last person to see it, his days as the Prince's right hand man were numbered. The all-powerful friends thought the Prince had been wrong to confess adultery and blamed Aylard. He might have survived the initial furore, but too many things followed that kept reminding them all about the fatal question, and St James's Palace constantly seemed to be caught on the wrong foot. It was a period of intense fire fighting, with the media perpetually having the upper hand. As horror heaped on horror and the Prince's popularity plummeted, his friends all said it would never have happened if it hadn't been for Aylard. Gradually their influence chipped away the Prince's confidence in his trusted private secretary and, exposing his own fundamental weakness, he gave in to them. He knew that it was not fair, and he knew that Aylard had served him loyally and well, and helped him get through the most traumatic years of his life, up to and including sorting out his impenetrable divorce settlement. Yet he bowed to pressure and agreed he had to go. He is now, however, working as an environmental consultant to the Prince and is happily remarried.

Stephen Lamport was asked to take over as private secretary, and Mark Bolland was pulled out from under the cloak as his deputy. Bolland is an immensely charming but dangerous man, another maverick, whom the Prince finds stimulating and fun to have around. Bolland creates as many enemies as friends, and has caused havoc in St James's Palace, and suspicion at Buckingham Palace. He places stories in the press which unnerve his colleagues, but he is a skilled operator and, after five years at the PCC, his contacts in Fleet Street are second to none. He has built on the work done by Alan Kilkenny in making Camilla acceptable to the British public. And it is a measure of their joint success that just nine months after Diana's death a story which appeared in the *Sun* that Camilla was spending nights with the Prince at St James's Palace scarcely raised an eyebrow.

Stephen Lamport had been in the Prince's office since 1993, and as a much more traditional courtier, was a good antidote to Bolland. Educated at Winchester and Cambridge, he arrived at St James's from the Foreign Office, where he had worked for Douglas Hurd when he was Foreign Secretary. He took over foreign tours and the architectural brief from Peter Westmacott. He is highly orthodox, cautious and discreet. Where Bolland is prepared to stick his neck out, Lamport is loath to take decisions, as a colleague says, 'lest the gun-boats come over the hill'. Bolland makes decisions then worries about how he's going to break the news of what he has done to the Boss. Recently, Bolland presented the Prince with a *fait accompli* that he wasn't overjoyed by. The *Sun* newspaper had agreed to sell prints of a watercolour he had painted on a trip to Bhutan in 1998, and in return promised to make a £50,000 donation to a local charity running a home for girls rescued from prostitution, which the Prince had been impressed by during a visit there. Believing the *Sun* to be a rag from the lower reaches of the tabloid sewer, the Prince was deeply reluctant, and the marmalade wasn't the only thing that flew on the morning he was told, but since no other newspaper was prepared to pay the money, his private secretary was insistent. The money was raised, but his friends would say at what price? He shouldn't have had to go begging to a newspaper which had caused him such torment with intrusive and negative coverage of his marriage.

Lamport has a first class brain, but is generally thought a bit rarefied. 'Take him a completely insoluble, knotty problem,' say colleagues, 'and he will think a way through it.' Bolland is very clever, and he's the one you go to if you really want to know what the Prince thinks and what is going on. Lamport is tougher than he looks and is more than happy to play the nice guy while Bolland attracts the flak; and while Bolland may not be the most reverent man on earth, nor the closest timekeeper, nor even the best keeper of appointments or returner of phone calls, he has not yet put a foot wrong as far as the Prince is concerned. He gets on famously with the Prince's women friends; he loves intrigue, lunches regularly at the Caprice, drinks Champagne with enthusiasm, has friends in high places – including Lord Wakeham, chairman of the Press Complaints Commission, and Peter Mandelson, Secretary of State for Trade and Industry – and is, as he promised the Prince he would, having the greatest fun.

There are people who predict Mark Bolland is riding for a fall, and many more who will enjoy watching it happen – a few of them across the road at Buckingham Palace – but the Prince is entranced; he enjoys his company, recognises that he has been good for his public image, and believes that he has finally found the man who can solve his problems. He came in at a time when the Prince needed above all to have his confidence and his courage restored – emotional needs, for which Bolland, with his exuberant manner and reassuring optimism, was well suited.

Whatever the manner of Richard Aylard's departure, it was time for a change, as with hindsight he would be the first to admit. Seven years was too long and he had become so involved that he had lost his sense of perspective. Inevitably he was also tarred with the brush of the most difficult days of the past, when nothing that came out of the press office could be believed. No matter what he did, the situation was not going to change until the man at the helm changed. His departure and the arrival of a new team sent powerful signals to the outside world that, post-divorce, this was a brand new beginning for the Prince of Wales. It also sent signals to the team in St James's Palace, where from the dark days of bunker mentality, three emotions prevailed: a hatred of the media, a hatred of Camilla Parker Bowles, and a hatred of the Princess of Wales, who terrified most people in the office.

Bolland's attitude was that if Mrs Parker Bowles was a non-negotiable fixture in the Prince's life, which she clearly was, then a way had to be found of making her acceptable to the British public. As for the Princess, he rather liked her. Despite her divorce from the Prince, she still took a lively interest in his office, and she had been to inspect the new recruit on his third day and invited him for tea, to try and establish whether or not he might be an ally. She knew one or two people who knew him and they had obviously been talking. After tea she took him to his car, parked on the gravel outside. 'Oh, Mark, you'd better be quick,' she said mischievously, pointing to Richard Aylard's house across the courtyard. 'He'll probably clamp it!'

With his fiftieth birthday approaching, there was an imperative to improve the Prince's image, not just because he preferred to read nice things about himself, but because it has a serious bearing on the future security of the monarchy, which Bolland understands very well. The fundamental purpose of monarchy is to be a symbol of unity, to represent the nation to itself. If it is a source of division, it loses its purpose. Therefore to have a figure accede to the throne who was as controversial as Prince Charles then was – and to a lesser extent still is – would have been highly dangerous. If the Queen lives as long as her mother, it could still be a very long time before the Prince becomes sovereign, but it would clearly be foolish to presuppose such certainty. Unless fifty years of preparation and dogged devotion to duty were to be wasted, it was time to get the scandal off the front page, and present the Prince of Wales as less of a crazed crusader lashing out at farmers and architects and all the other orthodox establishments he had had in his sights, and more as a king in waiting.

The Prince has moaned and complained about the press to his staff and friends for years, and some of them have been too sympathetic for his own good, encouraging his self-pity. He didn't understand why they turned against him, why they ignored the things he tried to do, why they were so dishonest, as he saw it, in their reporting, why they were so intrusive when he had asked them not to be, why they were concerned all the time with the trivia of his personal life. At one time he read nothing but *The Times*. Now he reads no newspaper regularly and listens instead to Radio 4's early morning news programme, 'Today', and relies upon others to tell him anything he needs to know.

Some of the people he works with find his capacity for self-pity quite irritating. As one who has been advising for years says, 'There are times when all I want to do is say "For God's sake, just get a grip, stop going on about it. We know what it's like out there. Yes, the media are ghastly; yes, things have been rough, but you still have an enormous amount to do. You've still got a huge amount to contribute to this stuff, so just stop banging on about how awful it is and settle down to the things you can do, and go on doing them, and go on doing them, and go on doing them." Eventually people will respond to the deeds and not to anything else. That's what you've got to keep coming back to. I wouldn't go on advising him if I didn't think he was doing very, very important work and keeping things moving on a host of progressive agenda issues which I think are crucial, as he does.'

The press has circumscribed his life for a very long time. The Prince would love to be able to hunt with Camilla, for example, but he doesn't. She keeps her horse at Highgrove, and, very often, will go hunting for the morning, then go home. He will then go out in the afternoon, because they still have a horror of being seen and photographed together. It is the one picture every newspaper and magazine in the world wants, and which every photographer knows he would get big money for. Members of the Prince's staff are regularly offered bribes for a tip-off about when they will be together, but so far there have been no takers.

The closest they have come was in August 1995, when the Prince and Camilla were photographed with their friends Nic and Sukie Paravicani at their house in South Wales where they sometimes spend the weekend. Nic was previously married to Mary Ann Parker Bowles, Camilla's former sister-in-law.

It is no longer a secret that Charles and Camilla spend time together, including nights together, but they are damned if the media are going to get a photograph until they are good and ready. And so they forgo simple pleasures like hunting or even just going for walk with each other. A night spent with friends in the North Country, where the Prince had engagements the next morning, was typical. They woke up to the most glorious day, in the most glorious countryside. Camilla suggested a walk. 'We can't,' said the Prince, 'there will be photographers out there.' And he was right. Yet to his frustration, the photographers never appeared to be interested in taking photographs when he was doing anything useful. How could people possibly know what he did if the newspapers didn't tell them?

The Prince is well aware of his problem relationship with the press and desperately worried for his children. How, he wonders, are they ever going to be able to have girlfriends or find wives if they are subjected to the sort of personal intrusion he had been? Their lives will be completely insupportable, and the only sort of girls who will be able to endure the media attention would be quite the wrong sort. He is deeply fearful for them.

FIFTEEN

'Mrs PB'

'Do you really think I will do you any good?'
Camilla to the National Osteoporosis Society

A good relationship between St James's Palace and Buckingham Palace is hugely important. Both incumbents work for the same 'firm', and although they go about their work in very different ways, it is crucial for the people of Britain to recognise that they are two parts of a whole. The institution of monarchy is above individuals and above governments. It is part of the history and heritage of Britain and can be a force for great good; but it has to embrace the people because it is here to serve the people. It is also here by the consent of the people. Yet ever since the Prince set up camp in St James's Palace, across the Mall from Buckingham Palace, the relationship between the two private offices has been strained, and is possibly worse today than it has ever been. While they just recognise Stephen Lamport as one of them, the Queen's courtiers do not share the Prince's enthusiasm for his number two, Mark Bolland, and sense that private discussions are probably safer held in his absence. So blackened is his name, that even leaks from the Prime Minister's office in Downing Street are likely to be attributed to Bolland. The Prince puts such remarks down to jealousy.

It is not hard to see why the two offices clash. It is a matter of age and style. The Queen's private secretary, Sir Robert Fellowes, who took over from Sir William Heseltine in 1990, is the nicest of men and very able, but he comes from a highly privileged background. His father was the Queen's land agent at Sandringham for nearly thirty years, he was educated at Eton, was an officer in the Scots Guards before spending fourteen years in the City, and is much more aware of what the burning issues are around the polished mahogany bars of the gentlemen's clubs in St James's, than what is being said in the pubs and clubs of Bristol, Birmingham or Bolton. At fifty-seven he has already announced his retirement after twenty-one years in service, and will be succeeded by his deputy, Sir Robin Janvrin, in February 1999. Aged fifty-two, Janvrin is another immigrant from the Foreign Office, but has a much more realistic view of the modern world, and an understanding that the monarchy must be seen to adapt to it. Having begun his career at the Palace in the press office, he has a better feel for the media too.

Buckingham Palace has often been blamed when the Prince's plans have been thwarted, and not always quite fairly. It has been easy for his staff to stir up trouble. 'Sir, your idea was so good,' they might say, 'but I couldn't get those people over there to listen.' Charles is predisposed to believe that the Queen's courtiers are out to scupper him, and is easily encouraged to launch into an attack, when the truth is that a private secretary just doesn't dare disagree with the Prince and tell him outright that an idea wouldn't work.

'Those people over there are getting in the way of me doing my job as Prince of Wales,' he will say. 'Why don't they get on with looking after the Queen and let me do my thing?'

'The private secretaries ought to be building bridges all the time,' says one former private secretary. 'It was the right thing for the Prince to have his own office and press office, because what he does is so specialised and so different. You've got two people who are from different generations, doing different jobs with different personal styles. To try and run the whole thing from Monarchy plc in one office isn't the answer. The answer is to have separate offices but have very good communications, and to operate on an absolutely "no surprises" basis. It will never be a relationship of equals because the Queen's team will always be senior. On the other hand, they have to recognise that the Prince's team must have autonomy on a great deal of issues relating to him. When a problem is Monarchy plc, as it was when the Princess died, they should all get together and sort out the best solution. Unless both sides are trying constantly to bring it together, they can drift apart, and what the media wants is, "Buckingham Palace says this, St James's says something else." That is what creates and fuels stories. You have to be constantly bending over backwards to talk to Buckingham Palace, and realise you can have honest disagreements about things without falling out.'

As the Queen slows her pace, and the Prince takes over more and more of the formal tasks which will eventually all fall to him, communication between the two offices becomes even more relevant.

Foreign tours are one of the most obvious tasks that he is taking on; and former Foreign Secretary, Douglas Hurd, who saw him in action on many occasions, has no doubt that he is 'a unique asset to this country in its dealing with foreigners'. One of the most memorable occasions was the half-centenary celebrations in Hamburg, the German city which fifty years before had been virtually destroyed by the British during the Second World War. The reception could have been cool. 'He had mugged up a twenty-minute speech in German – he doesn't speak German but he had learnt it specially. And I said, "You must do a bit in English, because this is a big story at home", and he said, "Oh, do you really think I need to do that?" His whole mind was focused on making a success of the occasion, in the open in the big square in Hamburg, surrounded by thousands and thousands of Germans. He didn't have to do it, and that he should have gone and taken such trouble – they thought it remarkable.'

Stephen Lamport was also there. 'The impact there was electrifying. And it is important because he helps define what German people think of this country, and helps open doors and arouse sympathy and helps others who have to do business there. The same is true in Italy and much of Europe and even to a degree in France. His impact is more emotional and deeper than that of a politician.'

Neither is that difference lost on the British public. The Prince was visiting the scenes of the Paisley floods in Scotland some years ago, accompanied by Tom Farmer, chairman and chief executive of Kwik-Fit, also the Prince's Trust in Scotland. A crabby old woman in the crowd, obviously mistaking Tom Farmer, who was fifty-five if he was a day, for a local councillor, waved at him. 'Hey you, boy,' she shrieked. 'Come here.' Then stabbing the air with her finger in a menacing way, said, 'You're here because you *have* to be here. He's here,' she said pointing at the Prince, 'because he *wants* to be here.'

Vernon Bogdanor, the constitutional historian and Oxford don, believes that most of the conflict between the two Palaces is fundamentally generational. 'The Queen's formative period was during the war and afterwards,' he says, 'with the transformation of the Empire to the Commonwealth. She grew up in a period when social obligations were taken for granted. That broke down under the pressures of affluence in the 1960s, which was when the Prince of Wales grew up, and he is therefore more conscious of rebuilding communities, and the fact that the Commonwealth isn't the Empire; and whatever one's attitude to European integration, the most important relationship for Britain is with the Continent and not the far away Commonwealth. These generational differences are very fundamental and there is a danger that his view of monarchy could be seen to be in conflict with her view of monarchy. But in a way they complement one another, because her role is primarily symbolic, and his can be slightly different. He can go into areas where she cannot tread. But it is not easy for the Queen to keep in touch with the modern world, and very important for her advisers to keep her in touch.'

The simple fact is that the Queen doesn't live in the modern world as most of her subjects know it. When Matthew Butler arrived in 1993 his predecessor told him that if he fancied it, he could get lunch at Buckingham Palace. He decided to give it a try and, expecting a staff canteen, was astonished to find four tiers of eating, and men in tail coats. The Queen and the Duke of Edinburgh ate in one dining room, members of the household in a second – which included private secretaries, keepers of the royal stamp collections and chaplains; and then below stairs – in the basement – were the senior officials' dining room and the junior officials' and lady clerks' dining room. The year he arrived, the Palace was opened to the public for the month of August for the first time, and one of the rooms that could be seen was the household dining room. The result was some very unpopular rearrangement, which offended the natural order of things. The senior officials had to double up with the junior and lady clerks, and the members of the household were sent below stairs, which caused chaos. Half of them had never been into the basement and so many got lost they had to put up signs to direct them.

All the Queen's residences feel as though they belong to another age. They are run by uniformed staff, they have antiquated heating systems and are short on creature comforts – but so are most houses belonging to the British upper classes, particularly in the country. The Royal Family are great lovers of fresh air, and even in the midst of winter the Prince will have a window open. At Sandringham he works in a little room with a primitive three-bar electric heater, which he rarely turns on, and visitors freeze. When the heating is working, the Victorian system that has never been replaced in either Sandringham or Balmoral pumps out so much heat that everyone boils.

Highgrove is different. The Princess was a perfectionist and she liked to be comfortable and although the décor was changed when she moved out, it is still smart and visitors don't feel they are stepping into a 1950s time-warp as they do in most of the Queen's residences.

Camilla's house is very largely given over to her dogs, which sleep on the furniture and cover everything with paw prints and hair. Muddy wellington boots clutter up the doorway, and the furnishings are worn and comfortable. There is a slightly chaotic feel to her house, which is in perfect keeping with the woman. She has no interest in designer clothes, manicures, smart salons, shopping or doing lunch. She is a strong, practical, independent woman who doesn't particularly care what she looks like, and unless she is going somewhere special, doesn't bother with her hair or with make-up. She has dozens of friends, and a few who are very close. Patti Palmer-Tomkinson, Candida Lycett-Green, Frances Shelburne, Amanda Ward, Emilie van Cutsem and Jilly Cooper are amongst them, but her sister Annabel, two years her junior, is probably closer to her than anyone. She is less conventional than Camilla: while Camilla came out as a debutante, Annabel did the hippy trail in her youth and now runs an antique business in Dorset. They have similar features, the same husky voice, laughing eyes and earthy sense of humour; and they have a brother, Mark Shand, two years younger than Annabel, who is less conventional still. He writes about travel and is married to Cleo Goldsmith. Their children are all good friends and it is a close and mutually supportive family.

The children often come to stay, and bring friends, which she enjoys, but Camilla is perfectly happy alone. She has the dogs for company and she gardens and paints. She is not the least bit house proud, and not the greatest cook – but she does know about wine, having had a father in the trade, and has taken the Prince's wine cellar in hand at Highgrove, much to the relief of his friends.

The Prince, like all of his family, is quite ignorant about wine – the Queen drinks martinis, and if she must drink wine it will be mostly sweet, white and German. For preference Charles drinks strong gin martinis and Manhattans, even with a meal.

Dinner is the main meal of his day which he usually has at about nine o'clock, and he will choose the week's menus. He usually skips lunch or at most will have a sandwich – a favourite is egg mayonnaise on wholemeal bread – with fruit juice to drink. Breakfast is also light, usually a bowl of odd looking cereals, nuts and wheat. On the royal train one morning one of the stewards, a Liverpudlian, asked the Prince whether he would like yoghurt on his cereal as usual. 'No,' said the Prince, uncorking a large bottle of black liquid. 'I'd like this rather splendid date oil I was given in the Middle East last week. It's very good.'

The steward, rather more doubtful, replied, 'It looks like sump oil to me, Your Royal Highness.'

When the Prince goes to Sandringham he takes his own staff, who also dress in uniform – as they do at Highgrove and York House, where he stays when in London. There is a minimum of formality, although the way in which he lives in any of his houses still bears no relation to the way in which normal people live their lives. But then nothing about the Royal Family is normal. The Queen thinks and reacts how she is told to by her advisers, as, to a lesser extent, does the Prince of Wales – and friends say he is retreating ever more into a world of his own and leaving his staff to run the detail of his life.

When, in the spring of 1998, the Prince gave a weekend party for a group of friends at Sandringham he took advice about inviting Camilla. Stephen Lamport and Mark Bolland both said, 'Invite her. It will be a two-day wonder in the press and then it will go away. It won't be a problem.' The weekend was important in terms of defining what Camilla's future role in the Prince's life would be, and what was private and what was not. There was another consideration. Camilla was becoming increasingly fed up with being abandoned like a piece of left luggage, and it was important from the point of view of their relationship that they spend some time together. When he knew the story would be in the newspapers, Bolland rang Sir Robin Janvrin and told him there would be an issue in the press of whether the Queen had known about the weekend, and whether she had given her permission for the Prince to invite Camilla.

Robin Janvrin said he would deal with it and, on his advice, the Queen's reaction was that this was a private party, it was up to Charles to invite who he wanted, and she would not have expected to be consulted. They say that if Sir Robert Fellowes had made the call to the Queen, her reaction would have been entirely different. 'There would have been rows, hysteria, battles.'

Robert Fellowes was absolutely furious when he heard that the Prince had plans to give a fiftieth birthday party for Camilla at Highgrove in the July of 1997. He said that if the party went ahead he would have to advise the Queen to tell the Prince that he must give up Camilla for good. In his view, all the difficulties that had befallen the monarchy in the previous ten years had been because of the Prince of Wales and his relationship with Camilla Parker Bowles, and he wanted rid of her. There is a view that Robert Fellowes doesn't much like the Prince, a view shared by his mentor, Lord Carnarvon, the Queen's close friend and racing manager. Robin Janvrin and Mary Francis, his deputy, were appalled by his attitude over the birthday party, and horrified by his lack of simple humanity. They told him in no uncertain terms that if he advised the Queen as he intended, then they would have to offer very different advice. He backed down.

The Queen has not seen Camilla for some years and does not choose to discuss her. A couple of days after Camilla crashed her car on her way to Highgrove shortly before her fiftieth birthday, the Prince was at Sandringham with the Royal Family. Everyone asked whether Camilla was all right, including the Duke of Edinburgh. The Queen said nothing. At one time she was very much a part of the royal scene, and the family were very fond of her, particularly the Queen Mother. She had grown up in that circle. She, her sister and brother all went to all the same parties together as children, and after she married Andrew Parker Bowles, she was ever present. He still is, as Commanding Officer of the Household Cavalry, with the improbable title of Silver Stick in Waiting. It is a title from Tudor times – the incumbent kept close to the Sovereign to protect him or her from danger, and carried a staff of office, topped in silver.

Andrew Parker Bowles was amongst the guests at the birthday party, also Camilla's father Bruce Shand, her children Tom and Laura, and all her closest friends. Camilla was the first to arrive at Highgrove. She came with her sister Annabel and her husband, driven by one of the Prince's drivers. She looked quite radiant, in a black dress with a diamond and pearl necklace, and there were glowing reports and photographs in the press the next day. The evening had been a triumph.

Appearances aside, Robert Fellowes was cross about the party because he knew that the Princess was unhappy about it. Diana had gone completely berserk when she heard about the party and put around all sorts of stories that Camilla was about to start writing newspaper articles and coming out into society in a big way. These stories circulated for three days, and then the Princess telephoned Bolland.

'Mark, I'm very cross,' she said. 'What on earth's going on?' This was the Princess's usual phraseology to indicate that there was trouble. 'I don't know what's going on. People keep telling me all these things, I don't know what to think. I'm really cross.'

Diana had seen the headlines and read the reports. The *Daily Mail*'s write-up of the evening began with the line, 'She was the first to arrive, sweeping into Highgrove last night with all the confidence of a queen.' That particular headline did little for Diana's blood pressure.

Bolland reassured the Princess that nothing untoward was about to happen, and that Camilla was not on the verge of launching herself as a public figure; indeed nothing could have been further from the truth.

In April there had been an announcement that Camilla had become a patron of the National Osteoporosis Society, which was accompanied by the first glamorous portrait of her that had ever been seen, taken specially by Sir Geoffrey Shakerley. There were reports then that this was the start of a PR push to bring Camilla out into the open, raise her profile and make her acceptable to the British public as a companion to the Prince of Wales. Diana had been incensed.

It was true that there was a move to make Camilla acceptable, but only so that she didn't have to skulk around like a criminal. She had no desire to be a public figure in any way. She hates publicity and shies away from any kind of exposure, as Diana was quickly reassured. She had become a patron of the National Osteoporosis Society only after much persuasion, having been approached by the charity in 1994, just as her life seemed to be crashing around her ears. Linda Edwards, the director, had read an article about Camilla, which mentioned that her mother had osteoporosis, and wrote at once enclosing some literature, which she thought might help, and inviting her to get in touch if she wanted any further information. After a while, Camilla wrote back to say that her mother had sadly died since the article was published, but how she wished she had known about the society earlier. Could she please come and see them? In due course she arrived at their new headquarters and research centre near Bath and after seeing round and chatting to Linda Edwards, said that she would like to do something help. She had known nothing about the disease during the years of her mother's illness, and if anything could be done to educate people and prevent others suffering the way her mother and every other member of the family had, she wanted to do it. There was one condition: she didn't want any publicity. That, said Linda, was no problem at all.

What the charity needed most of all was money, and it was not long before donations started arriving as Camilla talked to friends. When the charity was formed in 1986, very few people knew about osteoporosis, and even doctors tended to dismiss it as nothing more than the normal ageing process, a disease suffered by little old ladies. However, it can also strike young women, and is now affecting an increasing number of teenagers because of their obsession with slimming. More women die from osteoporosis than from cancer of the ovaries, cervix and uterus combined, but it is not the sort of disease that has people instantly reaching for their wallets – as child or animal charities do – and raising funds to improve diagnosis, treatment and prevention, as well as support for sufferers, had always been a very uphill struggle.

The first thing Camilla did was donate her half of the £25,000 settlement from the *Sun* for the photos published from the family album at the time of her divorce.

While she looked for a house to live in after her divorce from Andrew, she was staying with friends, the Earl and Countess of Shelburne, at Bowood House, and it was there in September 1995 that she held a private soirée. The setting could not have been bettered, nor the weather more perfect. There was Champagne, music, sculpture and theatre, and in front of 200 guests, including her ex-husband, despite great nerves, Camilla gave a touching speech about her mother's illness, which Tom, her son, recorded on video. In one night, Camilla raised £20,000 and was absolutely thrilled.

Some months later, Linda Edwards wrote to Camilla, inviting her to become a patron of the society. 'Do you really think I will do you any good?' Camilla asked. She was under no illusions about just how unpopular she was; and she recognised that her association with the charity could even be positively harmful. Linda was adamant.

'Look,' she said, 'your mother died of osteoporosis, your grand-mother, you now realise, died of osteoporosis. You have spoken from time to time about the devastating effect it had on your family, so you are very aware of how osteoporosis can destroy someone's quality of life. You've learnt that at first hand. Inevitably, people want to read about you, and if at the same time they are reading about osteoporosis and putting osteoporosis on the map, then you are helping an awful lot of people. We can make it a household word and give it the recognition it needs to get something done about it.'

By the time of Camilla's fiftieth birthday party Diana had actually become quite relaxed about her as a presence in the Prince's life, although she hated the idea of Camilla becoming acceptable as a public figure. She had met Dodi Fayed by this time, and no longer seemed to mind so much. Importantly, she had never seen Camilla as a threat to William and Harry, which undoubtedly would have caused problems, because she knew the Prince had always kept them apart. She had even become slightly more relaxed about Tiggy, about whom she had at one time been vitriolic. At the staff Christmas lunch at the Lanesborough Hotel in Knightsbridge in 1995, which the Prince and Princess continued to attend together even after their divorce, Diana couldn't resist the temptation to wreak her revenge on the woman she thought had not only stolen her children, but was possibly having an affair with her ex-husband too. She had seen the photographs of Tiggy and Charles kissing on the ski slopes, and believed the innuendo she'd read in the newspapers. There was nothing sexual in the relationship. Tiggy is a girl with a big heart who gives everyone great hugs, including the Prince of Wales whom she has known since she was a child.

Tiggy had recently been in hospital for a minor operation, and at the lunch Diana had sidled up to her and said, 'So sorry to hear about the baby.' The clear indication was that Tiggy had been in hospital having an abortion. Tiggy was devastated and rushed out of the room in tears, with Michael Fawcett, the Prince's valet, by her side. Everyone else went on to have a very jolly party with lots of drink, which degenerated into a crazy foam fight, which the Princess enjoyed as enthusiastically as anyone. It was only when they read about it in the press, and libel lawyer Peter Carter-Ruck was instructed by Tiggy four days later, that anyone realised what had happened. She decided to drop the action.

The two boys found life with Tiggy relaxed and uncomplicated and, at times, they found their mother's mood swings very unsettling. They hated the press, hated photographers and disliked being put on show in theme parks. They were also well aware of what the Princess thought about their father. There was nothing she told Andrew Morton that she had not confided in them, particularly William, many times over, and the emotional burden was considerable.

The Prince took the boys on an outing to the Royal Shakespeare Company at Stratford about three years ago, along with Julia Cleverdon and her daughter, Emilie van Cutsem and her youngest son, Bel Mooney and her daughter. Sitting around the table for a pre-performance supper, the Prince started to talk about the Goons and, being of the same generation, Bel Mooney fell into the famous 'Ying tong, ying tong' routine.

'God, aren't parents embarrassing!' said her daughter turning to Prince William by her side.

'Papa doesn't embarrass me,' he replied. 'Mama does.' Gradually he was beginning to see that his father was not as black as he had been painted over the years.

Camilla had become a patron of the National Osteoporosis

Society and her sister Annabel had also become involved. After the success of the soirée at Bowood, Camilla suggested holding another fundraising extravaganza at Talisman Antiques, Annabel's business in Dorset, which was housed in a former brewery. The date was fixed for 13 September 1997, the invitations were specially designed by a leading illustrator, Julia Whatley, and promised 'an evening of enchantment, fascination and the unexpected'. Tickets were £100 each and, although they originally planned to stop when they had sold 500, so many people wanted tickets they eventually stopped at 700. The acts were booked, the ticket money was in, donations had arrived, the cheques had been banked, the catering was organised and, as the excitement of the day grew nearer, there was mounting speculation in the press about whether the Prince of Wales would be there. It was a private event, all the guests were friends, and since the birthday party at Highgrove had been so successful, and the cause of minimal outrage, this could have been another step in the direction of making Camilla a legitimate part of the Prince's life.

Then Dodi and Diana's car ploughed into the tunnel beneath the Seine, and as the fateful news arrived from Paris in the early hours of Sunday 31 August, Charles and Camilla both knew that things would never be the same for them again. Their relationship was forced deeper underground. Dearly though Charles loves Camilla, his sons have always come first, which she understands entirely. She would not have it any other way. Love him as she does, she has always believed that children have to come first.

One of the first repercussions of the accident was the cancellation of the party. Linda Edwards telephoned Camilla the moment she heard and said she felt they ought not to go ahead. Camilla was in a state of shock – desperately sad for Diana, and desperately worried for the Prince, William and Harry. She was concerned that cancelling would mean they wouldn't raise the money they had hoped for, but she agreed there was absolutely no question about it, the event must not merely be postponed, but cancelled, and it would be a long time, she thought, before anyone could think of doing something so light-hearted again.

The staff at the NOS had spent the Saturday getting the tickets and thank-you notes for the donations, each one individually signed by Camilla and Annabel, ready to post first thing on Monday morning. Instead the first thing they did on Monday morning was throw all the tickets in the bin, and start writing to all 700 people to explain why the event had been cancelled and offering to repay ticket money and donations. Very few asked for their money back, and many more donations arrived when people heard the event had been cancelled out of respect for the Princess. It raised £80,000 in all.

The following week was a living hell for everyone. Charles and Camilla spoke at length on the telephone each day – as they do most days, wherever they both might be – and she was a tower of strength. After the funeral he took the boys home to Highgrove, where Tiggy was again on hand to look after them and keep them occupied, but they were both in remarkable control. On the Monday she took them out to follow the hunt by car. On seeing them arrive, Captain Ian Farquhar, Master of the Beaufort, went over to them and, speaking on behalf of the entire meet, said very simply, 'It's good to see you, sirs. I just want you to know that we are all very, very sorry about your mother. You have our deepest sympathy and we were all incredibly proud of you on Saturday. That's all I'm going to say, and now we're going to get on with the day.'

'Thank you,' said William. 'Yes, you're right. We all need to get on with the day.'

The Prince found it harder to continue with normal life. He was very despondent for many weeks and loath to re-engage. When he did finally get back on the road, he was less certain that the crowds he met would be as sympathetic to him as members of the Beaufort had been to his sons. It was a day out in Manchester during the last week of September, and he rang Julia Cleverdon to seek her advice on whether or not he should go. 'Julia, there's the most frightful row going on about Manchester. Half the world says I should do it, the other half says I shouldn't do it. I don't know what to do. If I don't then I'm away, and I've got to face it some time.'

'If you want my advice,' said Julia, 'you should do it, because it's always better to get out there and be seen rather than to stay hidden behind closed doors.'

Julia's advice came from painful experience. By an extraordinary coincidence, her husband had died very suddenly and unexpectedly on a family holiday in Greece, two weeks before the Princess's death. She had made her way back home with the children in a terrible state, and when she arrived her mother said, 'I've had the Prince on the phone four times, he says he must be the first person you speak to as you come in through the door.' At that moment the phone rang again. It was Charles.

'There are not very many people who would care enough to do that,' she says. 'And there was endless support and love and organising life to come to the memorial service to support me.' It touched her deeply.

She had planned to take two months away from the office, but agreed at once to go on the Prince's day out in Manchester, and face the world together.

Julia is also one of the select few to have met Camilla. She had been with the Prince to a Tesco golf tournament to collect a cheque they were giving to the Prince's Trust for a quarter of a million pounds in 1996. He had complained bitterly, which is his standard procedure before going anywhere, almost as if it is his way of combating his natural shyness and getting his adrenalin going. 'Yes, I do agree,' she said. 'Sunningdale is a very way from Highgrove, but you're only going to be there for fourteen minutes. Let's divide fourteen into a quarter of a million. It's probably a rather higher rate than the Spice Girls earn.' And as usual he giggled and his temper was restored.

She was staying at Highgrove overnight, and on the way back the Prince said, 'Julia, I've got a very good friend coming to dinner tonight.'

'Oh, don't worry about that,' said Julia, realising immediately who he was talking about. 'I'll have scrambled egg in the kitchen and go to bed. I'd like an early night.'

'No, I'd very much like you to meet her. It's Mrs Parker Bowles.'

What she found in Mrs Parker Bowles – known by most of the Prince's staff as 'Mrs PB' – was a great giggler, someone who makes life fun, and has a capacity to make Charles talk and laugh about what has happened during the day, while being quite clear that doing what he may not always enjoy is duty. It was clear she was interested in him as a campaigner and that she cared about the causes he cares about. But above all, she was funny and a good raconteur.

The day in Manchester had been very carefully thought through. For six hours, from ten until four, Charles would have to endure the scrutiny of press and public. What mattered most was the backdrop for his first words, which the whole world would be waiting for and judging him by. Julia chose a Salvation Army drop-in centre on one of the most problematic estates in Manchester, which had been built as a result of the Granada community challenge regeneration programme. The estate had been twinned with British Nuclear Fuels, which had built not only the centre, but also an all-weather sports facility with a lot of new equipment.

The Prince was terrified, and so were Julia, Tom Shebbeare, Mark Bolland and Sandy Henney, all of whom had come with him for moral support. None of them had any idea what to expect. They had all had a hand in writing a speech for him, but he had discarded it and scribbled his own notes in the plane on the way up. When they arrived, he straightened his tie in front of the mirror, for perhaps a second or two longer than usual, took a very deep breath, and stepped out to face cameras flashing furiously. At the Salvation Army centre, Julia had deliberately arranged for him to be on his own for a few minutes with ten locals who knew just how much he had done in the area, and what a difference his interest in their problems had made to their lives. It was perfect. They were all loving and anxious about him and he suddenly knew exactly what he had to say when he went into the hall to face the cameras. In the most touching, brave, tear-jerking tribute to the courage of his sons, and to the public who had shown such kindness in what had been an unbelievably difficult time, he won the respect and sympathy of millions.

'I think they are handling a very difficult time with enormous courage and greatest possible dignity,' he said. 'I also want to say how particularly moved and enormously comforted my children and I were, and indeed still are, by the public's response to Diana's death. It has been really quite remarkable and indeed in many ways overwhelming. I think, as many of you will know from experiences of family loss in your own lives, it is inevitably difficult to cope with grief at any time. But you may realise, it is even harder when the whole world is watching at the same time. But obviously the public support, and the warmth of that support, has helped us enormously. I can't tell you how enormously grateful and touched both the boys and myself are.'

Slowly the tide of public opinion began to turn in his favour.

SIXTEEN

Visions of the Monarchy

'It's 1,500 years of breeding. It comes from being
descended from Vlad the Impaler.'
Charles

Every Christmas, the Prince's last engagement before the holiday is
at the two hospices local to Highgrove of which he is patron: the Sue
Ryder Home in Leckhampton and the Cotswold Care Centre in
Minchinhampton. The visit is entirely private and he will not hear
of photographers. 'Absolutely not,' he will say. 'It would be intruding on private grief. These people are terminally ill. I won't have it.'

One year, when his private secretary went to look round one of
the hospices, a fortnight before the visit, so that he could brief the
Prince on the people he would meet, he met a patient who looked as
though he was unlikely to last the night. 'It's a bit unlikely Mr Smith
will still be alive in a couple of weeks' time, isn't it?' he asked the
matron.

'Oh, no,' she replied. 'He's said he's going to meet the Prince of
Wales.'

A fortnight later when the Prince came to visit, Mr Smith was still
alive and did meet the Prince of Wales – and died that night.

For most people it is *what* he is that is so potent. They are excited
by the prospect of meeting the Prince of Wales, the Queen's son, the
heir to the throne of England, Scotland, Wales and Northern
Ireland, a senior member of the Royal Family. But having met him,
what people remember is *who* he is. He may be fundamentally weak
and spoilt, and have a bad temper and be a lousy judge of character;
he may surround himself with people who tell him what he wants to

hear, and cast out those who try and tell him the truth; he may be self-absorbed and self-pitying and have a terrible tendency to whinge. But he has a very big heart, and those that love him do so because, in their view, the goodness of his heart and the integrity of his intentions outweigh any negative aspects of his character.

When Paddy Whiteland – the groom turned odd job man whom Charles had inherited with Highgrove – became ill with cancer, he took care of him. Paddy was in and out of Tetbury hospital, and Charles visited often. The remainder of the time Paddy lived with Joan and Mary Baker, two sisters in the town, who had been his neighbours and once ran the local laundry. When Paddy was home the Prince organised and paid for nurses to look after him, sent Maureen, the housekeeper from Highgrove, to help, and came to see him regularly himself. Paddy died, aged eighty-four, during one night in 1997, and the Prince saw him and paid his last respects the very next morning. He arranged the funeral, a Roman Catholic service in Tetbury Church, swallowing his pride as he did so – the vicar had publicly condemned his adultery, but the local RC church was too small for the sort of numbers expected. Three hundred and sixty people came to the service, including Paddy's eighty-three-year-old sister from Ireland, whom the Prince took under his wing both in the church and at the reception he held for family and friends at Highgrove afterwards.

Paddy had come from very humble origins. 'Fancy me finishing up with the Prince of Wales!' he would say, and adorned his house with signed photographs of the Prince who had done him proud.

On Christmas Eve, 1993, Marjorie Wallace, chief executive of SANE, of which the Prince had been patron since its inception seven years earlier, was told she had cancer. In January, a few weeks into treatment, she wrote to him. Virtually by return post she received a twelve-page, hand-written letter full of love and encouragement, which ended, 'With lots of love, Charles.' In the meantime, he had arranged for Marjorie to be treated, at his expense, by Dr Mohammed Ali, the Indian practitioner of alternative medicine who had treated Dale Tryon some years previously. The Prince had given strict instructions that no bill was to go to Marjorie. Whenever she went through a particularly bad patch of chemotherapy, he would send a huge bouquet of flowers to her home or some other gift like bath oil. When she rang and thanked him, he said, 'Oh, did you like the lilies?' Or the purple and white flox, or whatever it was that he had obviously chosen specially himself.

Then one day he telephoned at nine o'clock in the morning and said, 'I had bad dreams last night and I was really worrying about you so much. How are you?'

She confessed she was not very good at that particular moment. She had huge ulcers all over her mouth, she had no hair and looked dreadful. 'I've been so worried about you,' he said again. 'Would you like to come and have tea? Are you well enough? Don't come if you're not.'

Marjorie said, 'But I look awful,' and he said, 'I don't mind.'

So Marjorie went to Highgrove for tea, where there was just the two of them, and while she sat with her feet curled up on the sofa, with a scarf covering her bald head, they talked of their feelings about death, life and love. Then he said, 'I've got to give you something.' So they wandered through to his office, which was a complete mess, and he started climbing up on a little step ladder to look for things, and he found more bath oil for her and the book on Highgrove – *Portrait of an Estate*, which he had written with Charles Clover – and said, 'I don't suppose you want to read that, do you?' She replied, 'Yes, if you'll sign it.'

Finally he said, 'Who looks after you? Is there anyone to look after you? What do you do when you get home? Would you like some biscuits?' which made her laugh. He then gave her a big cuddle and she set off for home, laden with gifts. But that was not the end to it. Throughout a whole year of treatment, hand-written letters would arrive every few weeks, in which he wrote about philosophy, about life and death, his concerns and sometimes his own frustrations.

In the course of conversation he suggested a visit to see the film *Shadowlands* which he had just seen. It was about the death of C. S.

Lewis's wife Joy from cancer. It was only when Majorie pointed out that she might be a little nervous of the death element that Charles realised what he had been suggesting. Both of them collapsed into giggles.

'Most people,' says Marjorie, 'send a bunch of flowers and a card and then they leave it and hope for the best. The warmth of his friendship and endurance of it really was way beyond the bounds of duty, and he really did help me keep going.' Whether or not it was the ministrations of Dr Ali, or maybe the integrated healthcare she received, Marjorie recovered and is still campaigning as enthusiastically as ever for SANE. In the summer of 1998 she held a big fundraising twelfth anniversary dinner in the new Orchard Rooms at Highgrove, attended by the great, the good and the seriously rich from all over the world. The Prince came and spoke, not only supporting Majorie, but fighting eloquently for the mentally ill and their families.

Such stories are legion, and very little known. As are the scores of lengthy hand-written letters that have gone out to soldiers in his regiments who have had accidents, or the families of people killed in the line of duty. Although he and the Princess went about it in very different ways, and the public perception is therefore quite different, they both expressed great empathy with those who were suffering, and both had an almost magic ability to lift the spirit of those who, for whatever reason, were scraping along the bottom.

The night before a visit to Teeside in March 1994, Charles was persuaded to stop at a school in Middlesbrough on the way, where a child had been brutally murdered the previous day. His private secretary thought it was a good idea; his valet, Michael Fawcett – who very often behaved more like the private secretary than the valet – advised against it. The Prince went to the school, complaining nonetheless that he didn't like intruding on private grief and that was all he was really doing. He was told quite firmly that this was what was expected of monarchy, which of course in his heart of hearts he knew very well. There is nothing the Prince of Wales does not know about the job, but he has always been self-deprecating, and never keen to thrust himself forward on the assumption that people are going to be pleased to see him. Equally, he is genuinely delighted and surprised when they are. The school children in Middlesbrough were no exception. The press was there in force, and he talked to the headmaster and the parents of the murdered girl, as arranged, and then quite unexpectedly, the headmaster asked whether he would go and have a few words with the girl's classmates who had witnessed the attack. Unprepared, but unable to say no, the Prince spoke to the children, privately and most movingly, about what the death of Lord Mountbatten had meant to him and how he had learned to cope, which they clearly appreciated.

He drew on personal experience again when he visited Omagh in Northern Ireland, the scene of the terrible IRA atrocity in August 1998 – the worst outrage in the province since the Troubles began. Twenty-nine people, many of them women and children, were blown apart by a bomb planted by the self-styled 'Real IRA', and over 200 people were injured, many seriously. One of the doctors performing amputations afterwards said he had done so many he had lost count. The Prince spent five and a half hours in the small town, talking to the injured and to the relatives of the dead, meeting doctors, nurses and the people from the emergency services who had had the grim task of collecting the pieces, and visiting the scene where the twenty-nine had died. It was a gruelling day, which he found tremendously emotional and upsetting. Yet he has an ability to soak up the most shocking and appalling grief without cracking up himself. He has his grandmother's strength in these situations. His mother is less good at it. When asked how he does it, he says, 'It's 1,500 years of breeding. It comes from being descended from Vlad the Impaler!' Again, he was doubtful about being there. Wasn't it intruding on people's private grief? he kept asking. But about a thousand people came to see him, and said again and again how grateful they were that he had come. It was clear that there was something healing in his presence.

Monarchy has always had a role to play in national disasters and human tragedy. The Queen Mother, visiting the East End of London during the Second World War, where whole streets had been destroyed during the Blitz, meeting survivors, sent a powerful message that generations of Londoners have never forgotten. The Queen's visit in 1966 to the Welsh mining village of Aberfan, where 144 people, mostly children, were killed when a slag heap collapsed on the primary school, is another picture indelibly etched. Each time the Queen visits a scene of grief, it is an indication that she cares, not just personally, but on behalf of the nation.

The Prince appreciates the value of that role, but he doesn't take the institution of monarchy for granted. He questions its purpose in the modern world. Ten years ago he would never have talked about his thoughts and ideas for the future, believing that it was tantamount to wishing his mother dead; but he has recognised that change can't wait for his succession. It has been becoming increasingly clear to him that modernisation is essential for the monarchy now, if it is to continue to have relevance; and the public reaction to Diana's death made those discussions even more urgent.

Vernon Bogdanor is one of a group which has been advising on these matters for some time. He is worried about making irreversible changes to appease criticism of the monarchy which is based on ignorance about what the Monarch and the Prince of Wales actually do. The real problem with the monarchy, he says, is that it was unable to cope when society began to question the relevance of all its hallowed institutions.

'When the Queen came to the throne in the 1950s, around a third of the population believed she had been chosen by God and there was a tremendous sense of deference. It was a magical institution and you didn't ask questions about it. It was like asking questions about Santa Claus. It was a fairytale, unreal world and when that illusion crashed, as all illusions crash, monarchy wasn't equipped to deal with it. We have moved away from being a society where magic, or even strong religious feelings or deference, play a role, partly as a result of Margaret Thatcher's premiership, although I think it would have happened anyway. We've developed a much more utilitarian attitude to all our institutions. We say, what's the point of it? The fact that something has existed for a long time isn't enough for many people, so the monarchy has to re-establish itself on new foundations. It seems to me that the only way that it can keep going to the twenty-first century is as a practical institution which does a lot of good to the country in a way which politicians can't.'

He is in no doubt at all that monarchy is 'a great benefit which we lose at our peril', pointing out that 'most countries who have become republics have not done so after intellectual argument, but after revolution'.

'The best way of summarising, is that the monarchy represents the nation to itself. There are all sorts of things a sovereign can do which are sullied if done by a politician, because people suspect their motives. The Queen is the only person who has no party history, who has been trained from early times to have no views. The Prince has been trained from birth that if he has views they are not to be publicly expressed. He is not a partisan. Then there are the constitutional functions of the sovereign, in choosing a Prime Minister and deciding whether to dissolve Parliament. Those could be very important if we had proportional representation, because we'd have more coalition governments. It's very important the person who exercises those functions is neutral.

'People talk as if you could have a non-political figure as President. They mention Richard Branson [founder of Virgin records and a host of companies under the same brand] but in practice, the parties would get hold of it, because you couldn't afford to run for election unless you had support of a party, you wouldn't be able to canvas, or get television programmes together. For that you need an organisation and that's best supplied by a party. It is a salutary defence against politicians that the person who is head of state has no political power, has never had it nor is able to seek it or get it, and has no party political motives.'

The Queen is politically very astute and meets her Prime Minister formally for an hour once a week. The Prince of Wales is less so, although he does go to greater lengths than any previous heir to the throne to keep himself informed. He used to see John Major about once every two months, and the two men got on well together. The Prime Minister admired much of what the Prince was trying to do – they were of like mind on many issues – but the Prince did not take account of the intricacies and restraints of government. Over a cup of tea and a plate of Duchy Originals at St James's Palace, he was quite likely to suggest some scheme for dealing with the unemployed, which would involve the government in a fresh commitment of one sort or another, and was frustrated when it could not be done. If there was a famine, a flood, or some sort of disaster around the world, it frustrated him to be told that it would not be possible to send EC surpluses. Lynda Chalker, the former Overseas Minister, was one close contact in the last government whom he would ring, or Douglas Hurd, the former Foreign Secretary, who had delicately to explain why his suggestion about how to stop the shelling in Bosnia, or the despoliation of Romanian monasteries, was not going to work.

The former Tory government did adopt some of the Prince's ideas, but New Labour has gone further, particularly with a scheme for youth unemployment. There has been a lot of contact between the Prince and Tony Blair, and other ministers like Peter Mandelson, since the new government came to power in May 1997. The Prime Minister would like to be thought of as the man who modernised the Royal Family after the death of the Princess, or even as the man who saved it in the week before the funeral. He was certainly the one who created 'the People's Princess'.

Stephen Lamport is well aware of this, and with the diplomacy one would expect from a man of his pedigree, suggests that because the government was so new, it was still learning. 'It may have taken some time for government to understand the rather special and not always self-evident relationship between itself and the sovereign. Government doesn't own the monarchy. They are complementary parts of a system which goes back a very long way and whose history is an important part of why we are what we are. It would be a mistake of any government to think that it could use, own and trade on the monarchy as part of a common enterprise.'

His former boss at the Foreign Office, Lord Hurd, sees no danger in the Prince of Wales getting close to the government; in fact quite the reverse. 'I think one of the weaknesses with the Royal Family is they keep too far away from politicians because they are so worried about being thought to be involved in politics. They should be aware of what's going on. They don't know enough people. They didn't know enough Labour politicians when we [the Tory party] were in power. The whole story of the royal yacht [which was decommissioned, to the family's great sadness, in 1998] would have been different, in my opinion, if people like Robin Cook [Foreign Secretary], Margaret Beckett [Secretary for Trade and Industry] and Tony Blair had been invited on board *Britannia*, because they would have seen how important it was. The Prince ought to be in touch with the younger generation of all the political parties.'

One of the things that rankles most with the Prince, and indeed the rest of the Royal Family, is the notion that they have been pushed into modernising the monarchy by the death of Diana. This is demonstrably untrue, as the politicians, civil servants and expert advisers who have been involved in the process of modernising the monarchy over the years will confirm. Surprisingly, much of the momentum has come from the Duke of Edinburgh. It is true that the process has been given greater urgency by Diana's death, but the Way Ahead group – in which principal members of the family meet to discuss the future – was already in existence, and the Prince had his own groups that were looking at ways of making monarchy more relevant to the current climate. There is, however, an essential conundrum. The monarchy can't react until nearly one hundred per cent of the country wants it to react. Otherwise it will cause controversy and division, which as a symbol of unity it cannot do. Right now, several million people want the Royal Family to behave as Diana did, to wear their hearts on their sleeves, hug Aids patients and stride bravely through fields cleared of land-mines, irrespective of the political sensitivities. Several million want nothing of the sort. They like the dignity and majesty of a traditional monarchy. Several million more want to strip them of their palaces, trains and planes and cut the cost to the nation.

At the moment, the cost of keeping the Royal Family per year is about half the cost of running the vehicle licensing centre in Swansea. The financial benefits alone, in terms of business won abroad, money raised for charity, and tourism in Britain, are incalculable.

John Major's view is that 'We British do not want a bicycling monarchy. It doesn't matter what spin doctors might tell the press. I don't believe that's what they want in Little Rumblington on the Marsh. There was huge emotion at the time of the Princess's death, not surprisingly. This enormously beautiful, attractive young woman who had become an icon, dying in the most tragic and painful of circumstances. So it was an astonishing reaction. But the monarchy's roots are very deep, and to rush to the flip judgement that this has changed the House of Windsor for ever is reckless. The truth is that it is always changing and will continue to do so. But there will be many reasons for these changes, mainly the instincts and judgement of the Queen and Prince Philip.'

'People misunderstand,' says Vernon Bogdanor. 'The style of the Swedish monarchy is much more popular, it's a bicycling monarchy. It is said that the Swedish King was recently asked to provide evidence of his credit card viability in a store. I think people want a bit of glamour and a coach, and so on. What people don't understand is that the continental monarchies interfere much more in government than ours do, partly because of the proportional representation systems. The Belgian King plays a very heavy role in choosing governments. He consults with the equivalent of the Trades Union Congress and the Confederation of British Industry before choosing a Prime Minister.

'Ours is the only international monarchy. It gives a certain colour to Britain that it would otherwise lack. We'd just be a small island off the coast of Europe, but because of our history of Empire and Commonwealth, it gives a certain international flavour which the other monarchies don't have.'

The Prince's greatest fear for the future is the intrusion of the media. He doesn't see how William will ever have a chance of being happy. 'You have absolutely no idea of what it's like,' he will say again and again.

After Diana's death, Earl Spencer said the tabloid press had blood on its hands, and the industry took the message to heart. After some heated debate about whether a privacy law was called for, the outcome was self-regulation, and a strict new code of conduct binding on every editor and publisher in Britain was drawn up by the Press Complaints Commission. Published in November 1997, it was designed to prevent all the excesses of the previous ten years. Every aspect of intrusion that the Prince and Princess had suffered was covered, and the two boys were guaranteed privacy. For example:

Privacy
i) Everyone is entitled to respect for his or her private and family life, home, health and correspondence. A publication will be expected to justify intrusions into any individual's private life without consent.
ii) The use of long lens photography to take pictures of people in private places without their consent is unacceptable. Note – Private places are public or private property where there is a reasonable expectation of privacy.

Children
i) Young people should be free to complete their time at school without unnecessary intrusion.
ii) Journalists must not interview or photograph children under the age of sixteen on subjects involving the welfare of the child or of any other child, in the absence of or without the consent of a parent or other adult who is responsible for the children.
iii) Pupils must not be approached or photographed while at school without the permission of the school authorities.
v) Where material about the private life of a child is published, there must be justification for publication other than the fame, notoriety or position of his or her parents or guardian.

Listening devices
Journalists must not obtain or publish material obtained by using clandestine listening devices or by intercepting private telephone conversations.

It was a code, according to the introduction, which 'both protects the rights of the individual and upholds the public's right to know'. The Prince is thoroughly pessimistic, not least because of that very sentence which is supposed to reassure. It won't be long before William finds himself a girlfriend. Girls find him extremely attractive – as the youth of Canada demonstrated when Prince Charles and both boys went skiing in Whistler during the Easter holidays. If he had been any less well protected, the clothes would have been torn from his back by swooning, fainting, sobbing teenagers. At home he is already going to dances and discos in Gloucestershire. And when he finds someone special, the Prince reasons in his gloom, the newspapers could plead it was the public's right to know the identity of the girl who might one day be Queen of England.

William is utterly determined to protect himself. The *Mail on Sunday* published a speculative piece for his sixteenth birthday in July 1998, which was friendly but perhaps presumed too much. William immediately instructed his father's press office to complain to the Press Complaints Commission. He saw what happened to his mother and he is not about to let it happen to him.

William is showing every sign of being a stronger personality than his father. He has very firm ideas about what he wants and a determination to get it – some say there is more than a hint of his mother in him. On the anniversary of Diana's death he refused to go to church on the day, a Monday, unless his father's office issued an announcement calling for an end to the mourning. He agreed a text and Sandy Henney, the Prince's press secretary, read it out on his behalf on the first day of the Eton school term on 2 September 1998. Henney has developed a good rapport with the boys since their mother's death, and William is pleased to be able to use his father's

265

office. It was one of the rare occasions when, under the new privacy rules, the press are allowed to photograph the Princes, and an ideal opportunity.

'They have asked me to say that they believe their mother would want people now to move on – because she would have known that constant reminders of her death can create nothing but pain to those she left behind. They therefore hope very much that their mother and her memory will now finally be allowed to rest in peace.'

Despite his gloom about the future, the Prince has lost none of his fighting spirit. What he took on, with his fiftieth birthday in his sights, was the modification of his style so as to be less confrontational.

The early speeches of the 1980s had been right in establishing the Prince as a man who cared so passionately about issues that he was prepared to take on the giants in society. They had been right for a younger man. With the approach of fifty, it was time for subtler ways. The launch in October 1997 of his initiative for integrated healthcare – taking the best of orthodox and complementary medicine – was clearly different from anything he had done before. The Prince himself explained how he had gone about it in an article in the *Daily Telegraph*.

'Last year I asked a group of leading individuals from different scientific, educational and healthcare backgrounds for their advice on how we could make further progress. We established four working groups and produced a draft report on what seemed to be the main issues, which was circulated for comment to a large number of individuals and organisations with an interest in orthodox and complementary healthcare.

'The results of eighteen months' discussion and consultation are published today in a new report ... The report makes twenty-eight specific proposals for further consideration and development ... But the report is not a definitive blueprint for action. Its purpose is to stimulate a wider public and professional debate about the possible role of complementary medicine within the changing pattern of healthcare in this country.'

The belief that inspired this initiative was that the increased acceptance of complementary medicine 'reflects a growing concern with the use of more and more powerful drugs and a potentially rather impersonal approach to healthcare ... Health should be much more than the mere absence of disease or infirmity; and we should strive to ensure that everybody can fulfil the full potential and expression of their lives.'

The article was published to coincide with a conference at St James's Palace, and was followed in May by a conference at the Queen Elizabeth II Centre in Westminster at which the Prince spoke and quoted Plato:

'The cure of the part should not be attempted without treatment of the whole, and also no attempt should be made to cure the body without the soul, and therefore if the head and body are to be well, you must begin by curing the mind; that is the first thing ... For this is the error of our day in the treatment of the human body, that physicians separate the soul from the body.'

The Prince's views on medicine, 1998 style, took two years of research to prepare, and won admiration from very disparate quarters. It was a far cry from the reaction he had received fourteen years earlier, when he shared much the same thoughts at the BMA's 150th anniversary dinner, and was an indication of a new respect for the Prince of Wales.

SEVENTEEN

Charles and Camilla

'The press has dictated the last fifteen years of my life,
they're bloody well not dictating the next bit.'
Charles

Richard Kay wrote a speculative piece about the Prince and Camilla from New York, at the time Diana's dresses were auctioned, two months before her death. The *Daily Mail* turned it into a lead story, with the headline, 'Charles and Camilla will marry'. When Kay saw what the editor was planning to do with the piece he objected, and the headline was changed to read, 'Charles and Camilla could marry'. Kay was appeased, but when the Prince saw it he was furious. 'The press has dictated the last fifteen years of my life, they're bloody well not dictating the next bit.'

Technically, Charles and Camilla could marry. At one time it would have been impossible for a member of the Royal Family to marry a divorcee, as Edward VIII discovered in 1936. He had to choose between the crown and the American divorcee, Wallace Simpson, and chose marriage. But what made abdication essential then was convention, not law. Times have changed and divorcees are now not only acceptable, they can be remarried in church at the discretion of the bishop. Presbyterian churches are particularly accommodating, as the Princess Royal discovered when she married for the second time, because the Church in Scotland regards marriage as a contract, not a sacrament. Whether it would be acceptable for the man who is to become Supreme Governor of the Church of England to marry a divorcee is open to debate. The only person he would be barred legally from marrying is a Roman

Catholic, and that hasn't changed since the Act of Settlement in 1701. Camilla married a Roman Catholic – and, until he remarried, Andrew Parker Bowles was a member of the Sovereign Military Order of Malta, one of the oldest Catholic lay orders – and their children, Tom and Laura, are Roman Catholic. Camilla did not convert.

There is, therefore, no constitutional obstacle, although while he is still Prince of Wales, under the Royal Marriages Act of 1772, he would need the Queen's permission, which amounts to rather more than a mother telling her son he has her blessing – if ever that were likely to happen. The sovereign acts on the advice of her government of the day, and cannot constitutionally take decisions which might have a bearing on the country without it. The sovereign is the only member of the Royal Family who can marry without consulting or without the need for permission from ministers. If permission were not forthcoming while he was Prince of Wales, Charles could in theory wait until he became King. He could then marry Camilla, and she would automatically become Queen unless an Act of Parliament was passed to prevent this.

In practice, however, as the abdication of Edward VIII demonstrated, the government would still have the upper hand. If the King had decided to go ahead and marry someone he was told the country would find unacceptable, the Cabinet could have simply threatened to resign and refused to carry on as the monarch's constitutional advisers, making the King's position completely untenable. The key to it all is public opinion. Stanley Baldwin, the former Prime Minister, made the point appositely during the debate on the Abdication Bill in December 1936, by quoting from Polonius's speech in *Hamlet*:

> '... his will is not his own.
> For he himself is subject to his birth.
> He may not, as unvalu'd persons do,
> Carve for himself. For on his choice depends
> The safety and health of this whole state.'

If the government felt that public opinion had reached the point where Camilla was acceptable as a wife, but not as a queen, they could theoretically have a morganatic marriage, in which the wife and children, if any, have no claim on the sovereign's rights, status and privileges. Edward VIII had suggested this as a means of keeping the throne and still marrying Mrs Simpson, but his proposal was turned down. Ramsay MacDonald, the former Prime Minister, called it 'degrading to women, offensive to country'. In fact it is unheard of in Britain and in British law, although it happens occasionally on the continent, where sovereigns are required to marry from a narrowly specific range of royal families. If it were going to happen for Camilla, it would require an Act of Parliament, not just in Britain, but in all other monarchies of the Commonwealth. In 1936 they were not keen to support the King, and it is unlikely they would be any more enthusiastic today.

Most senior politicians agree that marriage to Camilla would still be too controversial. It was discussed at great length between the government and the Church, at the highest levels, at the time of the Prince's divorce, and the consensus was that it couldn't happen. As one authority describes it, 'Marrying comes under the heading "too difficult for the stability of the monarchy".'

Edward VIII's solution was abdication, which the Prince of Wales does not consider a possibility. The Princess of Wales hinted at it in her 'Panorama' interview, and as one senior minister at the time said, 'It was one of the most mischievous things that Diana ever did.' The Prince's sense of duty has driven him all his life. He was spoon fed it from birth, and repeatedly reminded of the shame his great uncle had brought upon the family and the misery he had caused. The Duke of Windsor, as he then became, had no more bitter critic than the Queen Mother, whose beloved husband, the then Duke of York, was obliged to step into his shoes to become King George VI. It wrecked his life and his health, and she never forgave Edward for his selfishness in putting a desire for personal happiness above his duty to the country.

Much as the idea of disappearing behind the gates of Highgrove with Mrs Parker Bowles to spend the rest of his life gardening, farming and painting might appeal, Prince Charles has never even allowed himself to dream. Camilla has, and sometimes the tug has been tough for him, but the reality is unthinkable. He is worried enough about William's future happiness as it is. If Charles were to abdicate, he would be exposing William, as next in line to the throne. If for no other reason, he will stay and carry out his duty to the bitter end, to protect his son for as long as he is able.

But there are other reasons. Like George V, George VI and Elizabeth II, he has studied *The English Constitution*, the great and oft-quoted work by Walter Bagehot, the Victorian economist, political analyst and man of letters, whose description of constitutional monarchy and its value to society has been the fundamental model for monarchy and its relationship with government and the people ever since. It was Bagehot who warned that if you let daylight in on the monarchy you ruin its magic.

The Prince of Wales understands the importance of the monarchy being hereditary. Succession is not a matter of choice, it is a duty. 'What suicide is to a man, abdication is to a king,' wrote the novelist Bulwer-Lytton in *The Last of the Barons* in 1843, and Prince Charles recognises that. If the sovereign treats the job as voluntary, then the idea of succession becomes nonsense, and the whole institution would very quickly disintegrate.

Marriage to Camilla, therefore, is not an option, until or unless public opinion changes even more radically than it already has. It is not even something they discuss. What they would dearly like, instead, is public acceptance of her as his companion. He is now fifty, she is fifty-one; they have been in love with one another for many years, their relationship is well known to everyone, and yet they have still not felt able to take a walk in the country together for fear of being photographed; they have not been able to eat in a restaurant, watch a play or an opera, or sit openly side by side in the Tuscan hills and paint together, which they long to do.

Camilla has to behave like an illicit lover, sliding surreptitiously in and out of houses, unable to go shopping or be seen in public places without the protection of friends, and elaborate plans being made in advance. Her life has improved in recent months, and she and the Prince of Wales will soon start spending time together at Birkhall when the Queen Mother is away, but their relationship is still by no means normal. She has all of the disadvantages of fame with none of the perks and pleasures.

Most weeks Camilla spends a couple of nights at Highgrove, and occasional nights at St James's Palace, but London is still a more difficult venue because of constantly being recognised. The Prince now lives in York House, which is attached to his offices, and was once the servants' quarters. The offices are where Edward VIII lived with Mrs Simpson when he was Prince of Wales, and what is now Stephen Lamport's office on the first floor, was once their bedroom. York House was done up by Robert Kime, the interior designer who did Highgrove after the separation. Highgrove is rather bohemian, and homely. York House feels more like a London base than home, although it is comfortable and there are plenty of photographs about to make it personal – snapshots as well as formal pictures of family and friends – and the odd painting of friends.

A surprising number of the photographs in the house are of Diana, including a beautiful black and white one in her wedding dress in the carriage that took her to St Paul's Cathedral, and many more of her with the children taken over the years. On the desk in the Prince's study, tucked into the corner of a photo frame, sits a little snap of Diana with William as a baby. He and the boys talk about Diana a lot; there is nothing forced about it, but if they see something she would have liked, or something that would have made her laugh, they say so. Her memory is being kept very much alive in a healthy and positive way – and it is the good times they remember, not the bad.

William has a self-contained flat at the top of the house, which he keeps locked – and he is the only one with a key – with a bedroom, bathroom, dressing room, sitting room, and his own kitchen, so that he can invite friends back for coffee. He has plenty of friends, in Gloucestershire and London, loves parties, goes to the cinema a lot, and leads a very active social life. Both boys have posters of pretty women and pop groups on their walls – which at one time included the Spice Girls, and All Saints – but, like all children's, their enthusiasms change from one day to the next.

When Harry met the Spice Girls in South Africa with his father early in 1998 he was thrilled. When his father then saw the band back in London at a film premier, he invited them to tea, thinking he had earned himself several brownie points with his children. The girls couldn't come immediately because they were off to Hong Kong but another date was fixed, and the five of them duly turned up in a helicopter at Highgrove, dressed in high platform heels which immediately sank into the sodden ground. They had tea with Harry, William and a couple of friends from Eton who had been given special permission to be out for the day. But by then ... 'After all the trouble I go to, to arrange the Spice Girls to come round to tea,' said the Prince in complete exasperation, 'they change their minds, fickle little devils. They've now gone on to the All Saints!'

Highgrove is their real home, and it too is filled with photographs of Diana. The Prince spends a lot of money on it, and he is a stickler for detail inside the house, just as much as in the garden. He bought new carpet recently, which was a major expense, and every bill he sees he questions. 'Who authorised that?' he will say accusingly, only to discover that *he* did. He knows precisely how much money he has and how much he spends on the different components of his life, and will always say, 'Good God, everything is so expensive', but it doesn't stop him spending. He is not unlike his grandmother in that respect. But, unlike some members of the family, he is punctilious about paying his bills.

It is an extravagant lifestyle by any standards. He has four valets, two of whom are on duty at any one time, three butlers, four chefs, two drivers, two large houses, and when he goes to Sandringham for ten days a huge container lorry arrives to take his luggage. He also has a Bentley, two Aston Martins, a fleet of Range Rovers and Vauxhall Omegas. He has a few horses too. The polo ponies are now kept at Fort Belvedere, courtesy of his polo playing friend, Galen

Weston, his host when he and the boys were skiing in Canada at the beginning of the year, who is as rich as he is generous. And he keeps three hunters at Highgrove: his, Camilla's and a spare. He also has the two dogs, Tigger and Wigeon.

Life at Highgrove is as relaxed as that kind of lifestyle, with its considerable support system, can be. If any of his friends or staff are staying overnight, the Prince will take them to their room himself, and will say, 'Is that all right? Sorry, but you'll have to use the children's bathroom.' The top floor of the house, the nursery floor, is very simple. It has a big landing and a table in the middle with fresh flowers on it, but the rooms are not huge. 'Oh, I'm so glad they put the lime bath oil in your bathroom,' he will say. 'I do think it's particularly good, but perhaps you'd like to try the rosemary. I'll go and get you some rosemary.'

After the death of the conductor Sir Georg Solti, the Prince wrote at once to his widow, Valerie, inviting her to stay. She readily accepted and enjoyed, she said, her first night's sleep and real relaxation since her husband's death. The Prince was genuinely delighted to have been able to provide some comfort. It is his home, and it's his children's home, and he wants other people to enjoy it and relax in it as much as he does.

Whenever Camilla comes to stay, she brings one of her dogs. She has two Jack Russells, Freddie and Tosca. Freddie is Tigger's son, and Tosca is Freddie's daughter, and sadly relationships between relatives are not all they might be. Tigger and Tosca fight so badly that Camilla usually has to leave Tosca behind. They make a comical sight when they leave: her car is brought to the front of the house, her kit is loaded into it for her and, as she gets into the driving seat, Freddie hops on to the seat beside her, and sits up, facing forward, waiting to be chauffeured home. Not long ago there was great drama in the household. Tosca was expecting puppies, so when Camilla and the Prince went to stay at Chatsworth with the Devonshires for a few days in the spring of 1998, the Prince took Tigger, she took Freddie and left the expectant mother at Highgrove with Kevin, the house manager, who by the end of the weekend had become midwife too. To everyone's huge excitement, the puppies were born in his airing cupboard.

After her divorce from Andrew, Camilla bought a new house in Wiltshire near the picturesque village of Lacock, south of the M4 motorway, which her father, Bruce Shand, moved into for a while, intending to convert the barn. Planning permission was refused, however, and he now lives in Dorset, next door to his other daughter, Annabel, and her husband, Simon Elliot. The Prince helped Camilla financially, paying for some of the alterations, including the installation of a security system, but he seldom visits Camilla at home because the security is still so much better in his own houses. For a while security for Camilla was a major concern. After the Princess died, emotions were running so high amongst the population at large that she was given some protection at her home in the country, and it was impossible for her to go anywhere alone. The Prince put a car and a driver at her disposal, and also sent one of his valets to shop for her and generally help around the house.

He was particularly worried after Camilla collided with an oncoming car while driving to dinner at Highgrove one night in June 1997. The roads between their two houses are very narrow and winding in places, and Mrs Parker Bowles is not known locally as the most cautious of drivers, much like the Prince of Wales, who pushes his Aston Martins almost as hard as he drives his horses.

The accident made the front page of every newspaper, but the details changed from day to day. The two cars hit with such force that Camilla's lost a wheel, and the other one ended up in the ditch. Although unhurt, the woman driving the other car was trapped inside and in need of help. According to one report, Camilla couldn't see the other car and assumed that it had hit her and kept on going. She tried to phone for help, but couldn't get a signal on her mobile phone, so ran up to the top of the hill where she could, and was able to telephone Highgrove. Two royal protection officers immediately set off to rescue her, while someone at Highgrove alerted the local Chippenham police. All arrived on the scene at much the same time. The Prince's protection officers took Camilla back to Highgrove, and the local police were left to find the second car and release the driver. For some time there was a possibility that Mrs Parker Bowles might be charged with dangerous driving or leaving the scene of an accident, but in the end no charges were brought.

At first the headlines read 'Camilla the heroine', who after the crash had helped the other woman out of her car. The next day, having realised for the first time who the driver of the other car had been, the woman corrected a few facts. Camilla had not been a heroine, she said. She had come at her like a torpedo, run her car into the ditch, left her trapped inside, failed to help, and run off never to be seen again. By day three the newspapers had it that Camilla had left the scene because she was responding to special anti-terrorist training, which was just as wide of the mark as the previous stories.

The true facts of the accident were never reported. The reason Camilla hit the other car was because she was momentarily distracted while travelling at speed. The cars struck with a tremendous banging and crashing of glass and metal. Camilla's first reaction was to speak to the Prince on her mobile phone and he immediately sent a car to the rescue. In a state of shock, Camilla then got out of her car and went over to the car she had collided with. She looked in through the window at the woman driver, screamed loudly, panicked and ran off. The Prince's policemen found her sitting by the side of her car in the road, crying. She was bruised and very severely shaken.

The Prince was also shaken, and the accident made him realise how vulnerable Camilla was. Although she has always been very resistant to the idea of protection, she was prevailed upon to agree to it, and to a little help from his office. From that day onward she was taken under the protective umbrella of St James's Palace and became a more acknowledged part of his life. She still values her independence and doesn't want to be wrapped up in cotton wool, but to have her life arranged for her, and to be protected from the media, is very seductive.

As well as giving financial help with the house, Charles also provided a personal assistant, Amanda McManus. The wife of a

Times newspaper executive, she worked part time, helping, amongst other things, with Camilla's correspondence. Amanda fell on her sword, however, in July 1998, when it emerged that she was responsible for a story which first appeared in the *Sun*, reporting that the long awaited meeting between Camilla and Prince William had finally taken place. Amanda made the fatal mistake of telling her husband, who had mentioned it inadvertently to a journalist.

The meeting had taken place at St James's Palace, when William, according to the original story, had arrived unexpectedly to change before going out with friends, and had found Camilla there with his father. The Prince of Wales was absolutely furious that the story should have appeared in the press. The details were such that it had to have come from someone inside St James's, and he wanted to know which member of his staff was the leak. His edict that no one should talk about his sons except to discuss travel and school arrangements had been breached and he was extremely angry.

There was another issue. The tabloid press had been particularly restrained in the year since Diana's death. They had each been fed stories, which were beneficial all round – good for the papers, good for the Prince of Wales – and, while they felt they were being treated fairly and honestly by the Palace, there was no need to play dirty. This was a big story. It looked as though a source was favouring the *Sun*, which enraged the other papers. Suspicion immediately fell on Mark Bolland, as the man with the best contacts in the media, and unless he was to lose the goodwill that had been built up in the previous year, it was essential his innocence be demonstrated.

In fact, it had been no accidental encounter. Prince William had said he would like to meet Camilla, and happened to telephone and say he was coming to London one day at a time when Camilla was staying for a couple of nights. The Prince told Camilla of William's imminent arrival and she immediately said she would leave. 'No, stay,' said the Prince. 'This is ridiculous.'

He then rang William and said Mrs Parker Bowles would be in the house, would that be a problem? To which William replied, 'No.'

By this time William had met Camilla's children, and reckoned that Camilla couldn't be as bad as she had been made out to be if she had produced such nice offspring. They had met during the Easter holidays. The Prince had decided William and Harry should meet Tom and Laura to see if they got on with each other, so while the three of them were staying at Birkhall, he invited the Parker Bowles children to join them for the weekend. Ted Hughes, the Poet Laureate, was also a guest that weekend. The meeting could not have been more successful. William clearly thought Tom at twenty-three was pretty cool, and both Princes, but especially Harry, thought Laura at nineteen was very beautiful. William had seen Laura fleetingly at parties before, but this was the first time they had really spoken and, despite the differences in age, the four of them got on famously. After that meeting they continued to see each other every few weeks or so, either in London or at home in the country.

At about the same time, William and Harry began plotting a surprise party for their father's fiftieth birthday. It started out as a party for the Prince's godchildren and their parents. Tom was his godson, and William therefore wanted to invite Camilla, but he first wanted to meet her in more private circumstances. The Prince had only once spoken to his sons about Camilla. It was in June 1997, when he sat them both down together and tried to explain a bit about the situation, but the boys were very quiet and William was not receptive. He told Tiggy afterwards that William didn't want to know about it.

The Prince had always deliberately kept them away from Camilla – the more so after that experience – hoping that one day they might feel differently and it might be possible to introduce them, but knowing that the initiative would have to come from the boys. He was not sure how much anti-Camilla conditioning William had had from his mother, so he didn't want to force anything, not knowing what he was pushing against. Camilla understood entirely. She had had all of this to go through with her own children, and knew that you had to be patient and wait until the time was right, and then when it was, to just get on and deal with it.

William had heard a lot of terrible things about Camilla from his mother, as he had about his father too – she had spared him little – but he had been beginning to realise that not everything he had heard was true, and his holiday with Diana on board al Fayed's yacht in the South of France in July had been an eye-opener.

Everyone was extremely nervous about the proposed meeting on the afternoon of Friday 12 June. Prince William had said he would arrive at 7 p.m., but typically turned up at York House at about 3.30 p.m. and went straight up to his flat at the top of the house. The Prince went to find Camilla, who was with Amanda McManus, and said, 'He's here. Let's just get on with it. I'm going to take you to meet him now.' So he took her up to William's flat, introduced them to each other and left them alone to talk for about half an hour. At the end of the encounter Camilla came out saying 'I need a drink', but it had been remarkably easy. William was friendly, and Camilla was sympathetic and sensitive and understood the need to let things go at his pace. They met again for lunch a few days later, and since then William has stayed at York House several times when Camilla has been there for the night and they have all had breakfast together the following morning.

The snub to Camilla that afternoon came not from Prince William, who might have been excused, but from Sir Robin Janvrin, the Queen's private secretary designate. Earlier in the afternoon the Prince had interviewed Simon Lewis, the new communications supremo at Buckingham Palace, who took up his post in September 1998. Stephen Lamport and Mark Bolland had been with him, and at the end of the interview, Robin Janvrin came in to chat about how it had gone. When they were done, Stephen and Mark stayed on with the Prince to talk about another matter, and Robin went and sat in the waiting room. When they had finished talking, the Prince said, 'Stephen, before you go, why don't you get Robin back in and I'll introduce him to Camilla because I'm tired of all this nonsense.'

The meeting between William and Camilla had already happened, William had left, and the Prince was feeling rather euphoric. They had talked before about Robin Janvrin meeting Camilla, and he decided to seize the opportunity while they were both in the same building. Stephen went downstairs to the waiting room and said, 'Robin, the Prince of Wales would like you to come back up because he'd like to introduce you to Mrs Parker Bowles.'

Janvrin said, 'I can't possibly do that. I couldn't do it without asking the Queen's permission and making sure it was the right thing to do.' He was not to be budged, and Stephen had no alternative but to go back to the Prince, in a state of some shock, and tell him that the Queen's deputy private secretary was refusing to meet Mrs Parker Bowles.

The language that came from the Prince when he heard this is unrepeatable – he was completely and utterly furious, outraged and affronted – and the hope that the relationship between St James's Palace and the Queen's household would become easier when Robin Janvrin took over from Robert Fellowes became highly questionable. 'In my house …' he said. 'How dare he be so rude in my house?' However, when the Prince knew that the news of the meeting between William and Camilla was about to appear in print, he telephoned Robin personally and told him to speak to his mother and tell her that it was not a problem, not an issue. Robin complied and there was no fuss from Buckingham Palace when the story appeared.

The Prince is fed up with the hostility from the Queen and her advisers towards Camilla. He is fifty, he has been through a lot, he works extremely hard, and feels it is time his mother showed him a little understanding. His fiftieth birthday party was to be something of a watershed in the relationship. The Queen planned to give an official party for Charles at Buckingham Palace on the night of 13 November for a thousand people to celebrate his public work, at which she would speak. It was for all the people who have been involved in his charities and organisations, and Camilla, quite rightly, was not included. What people wondered all summer, however, was whether the Queen would accept Camilla's invitation to the private family birthday party, which she and a group of the Prince's friends had organised for him at Highgrove on the night of 14 November, his actual birthday. It really mattered to Charles that the Queen should be there.

What is not known is that Harry also met Camilla before the boys' surprise party. Harry is a much less complicated child than William. As someone who knows him well says, 'Harry is just Harry.' He just gets on with life. Being younger, he also appears to have taken in much less of what Diana told him than his brother. He had no qualms about meeting Camilla. About two weeks before the party, after consulting with both boys, the Prince invited Camilla to bring Tom and Laura over to Highgrove for tea one Sunday afternoon. Once again, it was very easy and they liked one another.

The surprise party for their father, held on the night of 31 July, was brought about entirely by William and Harry. It was their own idea, and the Prince was immeasurably touched that they should have gone to such trouble. Sadly the surprise was spoilt by the *Sunday Mirror*, which got wind of what was happening, inadvertently, from one of the guests, and published details the Sunday before. It was an incident which didn't improve the Prince's feelings about the media, but the party was a huge success nonetheless. The boys had wanted to do something special for their father and, since his birthday fell during the school term, fixed a date during the holidays before the family went up to Balmoral. They enlisted the help of Tiggy and Michael Fawcett, the Prince's former valet, in planning the party, but they knew exactly what and who they wanted. They recruited the actors Stephen Fry, Emma Thompson and Rowan Atkinson – all the Prince's friends because, like many entertainers, they have done work for the Prince's Trust over the years – to help them write and put together a revue, along the lines of Atkinson's television comedy series 'Blackadder', in which they appeared themselves, in front of a hundred of the Prince's family and friends. What touched the Prince most of all was that the boys arranged the seating plan themselves, and placed Camilla in the front row of the audience between their father and William's godfather, King Constantine, former King of the Hellenes.

The Queen and the Duke of Edinburgh, though invited, were not able to attend. It was the Queen Mother's ninety-eighth birthday the following day and they were all at Sandringham, but this was no great disappointment because the boys had intended it to be a younger party. Prince Andrew and Prince Edward both came, and also Princess Anne, none of whom had met Camilla for many years. The meeting with Anne was the trickiest. Camilla finds her terrifying, and was very nervous at the prospect, but Anne was quite friendly.

The Prince was incredibly moved – moved to tears – that his children should have gone to so much trouble for him, and Camilla was thrilled to have been invited and touched that William and Harry should both have wanted her to be there. They could not have given their father a more welcome or perfect birthday present, and he stood up at the end of the evening and thanked them both profusely. According to those who were there, he thanked everyone who had had a hand in the evening, with one notable omission – Tiggy.

Tiggy has been posing an increasing problem to the Prince. He recognises the huge debt he owes her for all she has done over the years, and the abuse and vilification from the press she has had to put up with. She was completely invaluable at the time of Diana's death and helped William and Harry in a way that left everyone marvelling and overcome with gratitude. Like the rest of his family, he adores Tiggy, but she does drive him mad at times. She has been hopelessly irresponsible at times and repeatedly found her way into the newspapers, both in her private life and in the course of looking after William and Harry. Whenever they have been in any sort of trouble, Tiggy has not been far away. There were photographs in the press, for example, of Tiggy driving along in a car with a cigarette hanging out of her mouth, while Harry shot at rabbits out of the open window. She had accepted William's invitation to take a picnic to Eton's fourth of June parents' event in 1997, without consulting either the Prince or Princess, who had both been asked by William to stay away because he didn't want the day turned into a media circus. More recently, under Tiggy's supervision, Harry abseiled face outwards down a 150-foot dam wall in Wales, without either a hard hat or a safety line, which the experts immediately condemned as extremely dangerous. The Prince only discovered what had been going on when he saw the photographs published in the press, and he hit the roof. His dilemma is that the boys are very fond of Tiggy, and the last thing he wants to do is take away the emotional support she provides, but she is not the most steadying influence, and she encourages their already rather wild and hedonistic instincts. As the daughter of one of the Prince's friends says of her, corrupting a famous pre-war instruction for country cooks, 'Tiggy shoots a rabbit, stuffs it, skins it, and eats it.'

Diana thought Tiggy was a bad influence on her sons, and there are many people around the Prince who share that view. Whenever he confronts her about some idiocy she bursts into tears and he gets no further. So instead of doing something decisive, he keeps her on and, according to those around him, treats her badly. She wanted to give him a spaniel puppy as an early fiftieth birthday present in July. He told her quite bluntly that he didn't want one.

The Prince is a much easier man when he is at Highgrove. In London he feels hemmed in. There's nowhere for him to walk that's not overlooked by offices. In the country he goes out first thing in the morning with the dogs and it sets him up for the day. For preference, he works from Highgrove, which makes life difficult for all the people who have to drive back and forth from London along the M4 on a regular basis, and tricky for his private secretaries. As one senior politician, who knows the family well, says, 'The difficulty is access. The difficulty for all royal servants is access. They lead these extraordinary lives. They don't operate like a minister where the private secretary sits outside and is the filter, the person who sifts what you see and who you see, which can be maddening. But provided you've got the right people in your team outside in the anti-chamber, it is fine. But the Royal Family doesn't operate like that. The Prince of Wales goes to Highgrove and there's no control, nobody quite knows what or whom he's seeing. None of them is easy to work for because the machine is not smooth running and the co-ordination is not adequate. He's not easy to work for, but none of the important ones are.'

'He's a man of great integrity and great loyalty,' says someone who worked with the Prince of Wales for several years, 'but someone described him to me before I knew him at all as intellectually lazy, and there is a bit of that to him. He sails along, motoring on two or three cylinders instead of everything going properly, he won't always stop and think through all the angles, won't always stop and really get it right. He'll follow his instincts, which he trusts, and bugger the critics. He's a creature of his upbringing, a bit self-centred and a bit inconsiderate, he doesn't really stop and put himself in someone else's shoes. Hugely courteous and well mannered and apparently considerate, but deep down, actually, he knows what he wants out of life, and that is what makes him comfortable.'

Another adviser, who has been working for the Prince in an unpaid capacity, as many do, for well over ten years, finds the inefficiency of his office a serious frustration. 'There was a time when you were trying to do something you just put up with it because they're different from other organisations. They're not a business, not a non-governmental organisation, and not a conventional charity in any sense. It was just one of those endearing hangovers of royalty that they ran an office in this way. Richard [Aylard] improved things and brought it half way into the twentieth century, but I think it's got worse since he left. They are so unprofessional and so unhelpful in terms of managing relationships with the outside world, you wonder what they think the rest of the world expects of them.

'And for people trying to organise activities which involve the Prince, whether it is for a meeting or getting him to write something or just say "yes" or "no", and you go into this absolutely insane system, where you don't get an answer for months and then you're told you'll have to wait, then it's the diary meeting, and we don't do the diary meeting until June, even when you're waiting for a "yes" or a "no" for something in September. It's archaic, and it doesn't seem to make any difference who you are. I, and others, have been battering away at them for years to try and sort it out and they just won't. It's gross exploitation. And there's a slight sense of who needs whom around the place from time to time. Talk to any organisation that has to run itself professionally and use basic standards of administration and good partnership and they just say, forget it, his office is hopeless.'

Julia Cleverdon has a monthly meeting with the Prince of Wales. Looking at her diary on one occasion when Channel 4 was filming about Business in the Community in her office, she said to Bernie, her secretary, 'You're not telling me all these meetings are at Highgrove? It's absolutely impossible. Four hours down there, four hours back. The entire bloody day gone.' The crew had been around the office long enough for Julia to have grown used to the cameras.

The Prince, hearing that she had been on television, asked to see the tape. Julia complied, but knowing that it wasn't so much what she had said as the body language that went with it, she awaited his response with a certain apprehension. He rang her up immediately and said he had never laughed so much in his life. He'd had no idea it was so awful getting to Highgrove.

Although his staff complain about having to go to Gloucestershire all the time, most people relish an invitation to the Prince's home and will drop every other commitment at a moment's notice if an invitation should be extended. An invitation to Highgrove has proved invaluable over the years as a means of thanking people for some task they have undertaken on his behalf, a performance they have given for the Prince's Trust, perhaps, or for people he hopes will do something for him in the future. He holds discussion groups there, and working lunches. During the summer he opens the garden up to special interest groups, or charities, and has a pool of locals who come in to conduct the tours.

Functions at Highgrove were costing the Duchy tens of thousands of pounds per annum in marquee hire, so in 1997 the Prince built a magnificent function room in the park, called the Orchard Room. The Orchard Room was designed not by an architect but by a chartered surveyor called Charles Morris. The Prince was closely involved in the design and although some critics have unkindly likened it to a supermarket, most people think that in time it will blend in well. The Prince is very pleased with the result. It opened in May 1998 with a party the Prince gave for the builders, and he was astonished by the amount of beer they drank.

It was in the Orchard Room that William and Harry staged their father's surprise party but, in the main, it is used by his charities to hold fundraising dinners and receptions. He also has a shop, originally housed in a stable outside the back door, but which moved into the Orchard Room in 1998. Any guests who come to Highgrove find themselves escorted purposefully by their host to buy a few souvenirs before they leave. Since the shop is not open to the public, anyone who fails to buy their Highgrove jigsaw puzzle or place mats may not get a second chance; and not many have the temerity to leave empty-handed.

The shop was set up and run initially by Michael Fawcett, who was at that time the Prince's valet. It was intended as yet another way to raise money for charity – in this case, the Prince of Wales Charitable Foundation, which owns two companies: AJ Carrick, which deals with income from the Prince's children's books, lithographs and paintings, and Duchy Originals, which deals with all the produce. Asking people for money is not something Charles enjoys, but the need to raise money is never-ending and he knows that because of who he is, he has the power to do it.

Michael Fawcett is a man with influence beyond his intellect and extraordinary sticking power. He has been a valet to the Prince since the time of the engagement in 1981; before that he was a member of the Queen's household, which he joined when he was very young. In his spare time he has worked on the selling floor of a department store, but he dresses and behaves as though he were one of its better-bred customers. He is flamboyant, has great style and can be utterly charming and persuasive; he knows what the Prince likes, and is very good at making things happen. He can also be arrogant and domineering and is able to throw his weight about with anyone and everyone, because he knows he has the Prince's backing. He has the Prince's ear, and uses it to damn those people foolish enough to cross him. He is disliked and mistrusted by most people in the office, and over the years there have been suggestions that he was exploiting his friendship with the Prince, who always chose to turn a blind eye.

Early in 1998, it looked as though he had finally come unstuck, but the rejoicing throughout the office was short-lived. Although the Prince's lawyer, Fiona Shackleton, was one of a group who persuaded the Prince that Fawcett must be removed – and the story that he was leaving appeared in the press – he never went. The Prince changed his mind, and Fawcett was kept within the fold, no longer as a valet, but as a consultant organising functions.

'It is an area of weakness in the Prince,' says one of his staff, 'that he does put his trust and faith in people who can deliver what he wants delivered, and is prepared to ignore suggestions that they have cut corners to do it. There is an unspoken, "He's doing what I want. Don't let's make too much fuss about it."'

EIGHTEEN

Victim or Villain?

'How much worse if you happen to be
born into a public position.'
Charles

'The most peculiar thing is that here is this poor wronged creature, of whom I was very fond and a great fan, with a string of boyfriends. He was a man who, at worst, after his marriage was unfaithful with one woman. Yet he is the one who has been cast as the villain of the piece, and she as the poor wronged creature, who, poor little thing, had to go and find succour somewhere, didn't she?

'I've always felt it was rather an unfair perception that the wrong was all on one side.'

These are the words of someone who knew both the Prince and Princess well, who worked with them closely for several years, admired them both in different ways and, most unusually, never fell out seriously with either of them. Most people who knew them both did, and very quickly lost their objectivity. Yet even those people, for the most part, don't apportion blame. There were no villains in this tragedy, only victims, as anyone who saw and understood the reality will recognise. There is no blame or bitterness, despite the damage; simply terrible sadness.

The system played a big part in this whole sad story. The system required the Prince to find a wife and produce an heir, but not just any wife – a wife who was a member of the Church of England, who was pure, with no past experience of men, who was well-bred and who understood the protocol and would be able to share the duties of monarchy. The criteria were unrealistic for the 1980s, and had

Diana not set her sights on the Prince when she was still a schoolgirl, and pursued him with such determination, he might never have found a suitable bride over the age of consent.

Having found a bride, the system then dictated how they would spend their life together, as Charles knew it would, but having been brought up to it from birth, he had no real understanding of how difficult it might be for an ordinary person to handle. Diana should have known the system better than anybody, because she had been around it all her life, but she was little more than a child, in love with a dream. She didn't know the Prince any better than he knew her, but she didn't care. She wanted to marry him, and if anyone had sat her down and told her that she would have to share him with his staff, his family, the United Kingdom and half of the world, plus a diary of immovable dates that could be written in for the rest of their lives, she could not have begun to understand what that might mean. Any more than she could have realised what the loss of her freedom and privacy would mean.

If the system orchestrated an inevitably disastrous marriage, the perception that the Prince was responsible for it came from the media, which the Princess used unscrupulously in the war against her husband. The media took sides, which, in times of falling circulation and cut-throat competition, is not based on fairness and truth, but driven by sales. The public fell in love with a Princess of Wales that the newspapers created. She dressed for them, she performed for them. She was young and glamorous and the public appetite was insatiable. The Prince was balding and boring and predictable, and he'd been around for a very long time.

When Diana went to visit a hospice, she allowed the cameras to follow and the next day's newspapers were filled with photos of her holding a dying child's hand. Cynics would say it was self-promotion; alternatively, one could legitimately argue that it made people think about the dying and the less fortunate. The Prince also visited many a hospice, but out of the respect for the suffering only those who were there knew about it. Instead, he made speeches about the needs of the dying, which went unnoticed as the media focused its attention on his wife; and behind the scenes he worked to find ways of improving their care by bringing all the various professional bodies together who could have an influence on it, and making them find solutions.

These days, when so much of life is visual, most of Charles's words have gone unheard. Diana understood that the medium was the message. She was a child of the tabloid and television era and, although she found photographers too much at times, she knew that her ability to make the media follow her, listen to her and watch her, gave her immense power. She knew that one look could speak volumes. He was still caught in the traces of the past and, emotionally repressed, couldn't begin to engage in the contest. She enjoyed and needed the adulation, and as their relationship began to fall apart, she used the media to arouse sympathy for herself and to punish her husband and his family, whom she blamed for all her unhappiness. The marriage never worked, but in the end, it was Diana's manipulation of the media that killed it.

The irony is that it was a marriage brought about by the media in the first place. Had James Whitaker not been spying on the Prince with binoculars and long lenses in the summer of 1980, and spotted Diana on the riverbank beside him, there might have been no wedding. Once she had been seen, the media tracked her down, followed her, photographed her, telephoned her and built her up into a likely bride, and nothing she said led them to believe they were on the wrong track. She was no fool and quickly learnt that she could use the media to get what she wanted. The hype and the fever of speculation and the intrusion were so fierce that it seemed unimaginable it could continue.

But, of course, it did. An entire industry grew up around Diana. Still painfully young and impressionable, she became everybody's pin-up. Men of all ages fancied her, children thought she was the Princess from a fairytale, young women wanted to look like her, mothers thought she was everything they could have wished for in a daughter, and the media recognised that it could feed all of those interests if it got the photographs and the stories. Designers saw her as a swift passage to fame, as did hairdressers, make-up artists, photographers – their ambitions all achieved through the media. Even psychologists, astrologers and hand-writing experts found themselves caught up in the industry, as the media called on their services to explain what a particular gesture or a snatched remark to someone in the crowd had meant, whether she was healthy or happy or pregnant or what the future might hold.

To blame the media for destroying the marriage is clearly nonsense. The media did not make life easy or pleasant, and it has a great deal to answer for; but the fundamental problem was not the media. It was the fact that these were two people who should never have married. They were both tragic figures in the literal Greek definition of the word – each one brought down by flaws within their personalities, manipulated by forces beyond their control. Each was inadequate, and each needed something that the other was quite incapable of giving. If there had ever been a bond between them, it could have been strengthened by facing a common enemy, in the shape of the media, together. If there had been a bond, they would have given one another confidence, so that invidious comparisons about who did what better would never have wounded with the severity they did. If there had been a bond, they could have had the security to present a united front and use the media to convey whatever message they chose to the world.

But there was no bond. There was nothing more than brief patches of happiness in a morass of misery, and so, given the intrusion, given the comparisons, given the hero-building of Diana and the character-assassination of Charles, the relationship didn't stand a chance.

But what finally fixed the perception of Diana as the poor wronged creature who had to seek succour was the Andrew Morton book. Angry that the Prince had not been able to make her happy, she used a journalist to punish him, and didn't appear to mind that in punishing him she hurt her children too. Of all Diana's actions over the years, this is the most inexplicable – to have deliberately put the sons she adored through the pain of seeing their father attacked publicly, not once but twice, by following up the book with the 'Panorama' interview. Yet no one seemed to see the paradox. She accused the Prince of being a bad father in those attacks, and although she had some increasingly fierce critics in the media towards the end of her life, her adoring public believed everything she said. They didn't seem to question what vilifying Charles in public, and in front of their children, made her.

The Prince remained silent and let the public perception of him, unkind and unfair as it was, persist. He made no attempt to stand up for himself in any way. His staff and friends, who all knew the reality, knew Diana and had watched what went on, were desperate to speak up in his defence, but the Prince forbade it, and was very angry with anyone who attempted to. He was adamant that there should be no criticism of the Princess and no defence of himself or his reputation. And in the absence of a second side to the story, the public had no alternative but to believe that what the Princess of Wales told them about her husband and her marriage was true.

Right to the end, the Prince believed that any attempt to justify or explain could have made matters worse, harmed the boys, and done even greater damage to the monarchy. The 'Panorama' interview was generally thought to be a tit for tat response to Dimbleby. Yet Charles had said nothing in his defence and had in no way spoken disparagingly about Diana during that interview. In admitting his infidelity, without attempting to address any of the other accusations Diana had made via Morton, he merely compounded the problem. The whole undignified business could have gone on indefinitely, and the only winners would have been the media, feasting gluttonously on the seamier intricacies of their lives.

After Diana's death, the opportunity, had he ever wanted to take it, was lost for ever. To tell his side of the story when she was no longer there to answer back, however truthful, however well corroborated by other witnesses, would have been unthinkable. He would rather look forward than dwell on the past, get on with his life and let his children get on with theirs. If he must go to his grave with some people believing that he was to blame for the failure of his marriage and Diana's sadness, that is the way it must be. He knows in his heart that he was no villain. He didn't intend to hurt Diana, any more than she ever intended, at the outset, to hurt him.

The tragedy is that in their own way they did love each other, and in an inexplicable way he still does love her. He still wears her wedding ring, he still kneels down at night and prays for her. She hurt him very deeply and she almost destroyed him, but he knows she was no villain either. She was a victim of the system, as he was. She married him because she craved security, because she didn't want her children to experience what she had as a child. The Prince of Wales, she thought, was the one man for whom divorce would be impossible. He believed the same. He had wanted a companion who would share his life for the next fifty years, and his disappointment that they failed was no less acute than hers.

His attitude is almost impossible for an outsider to understand. If people think him a villain, that's something he will have to live with. His concern is how he will be judged in the next world, and his conscience is clear. He believes that one day history will vindicate him. He knows that the facts – the documentation – papers, diaries, letters, medical reports and tapes are safely stored for the future. When he is dead, and possibly when his children are dead too, historians will discover the truth about his marriage.

But sadly, the documentation will be incomplete. The Prince has discovered that all Diana's papers, which she meticulously kept in a number of safes inside Kensington Palace, have been destroyed since her death.

The Prince was utterly incredulous when he heard that Diana's mother and sister, Lady Sarah McCorquodale, as executors, had instructed Paul Burrell – who was the only person alive who knew the combinations to the safes – to open them and hand over the contents. He did so, and the two women destroyed the lot – letters, medical records, everything.

The Prince's lawyer, Fiona Shackleton, who is acting on the boys' behalf over their mother's will, advised him to have a full inventory of Diana's possessions at Kensington Palace drawn up the day after her death. A number of items had been loaned to Diana following the divorce settlement and it was important to get those back – also to ensure that none of her possessions went missing, as some have. He thought going in so soon was unnecessarily brutal and delayed the process, with the result that these papers, which could have been so illuminating, have been lost for ever.

Much as one can sympathise with the Spencer family for wanting to protect Diana's memory, and for trying to reclaim a little of her for their own, she was a public figure, she belonged to the people, she walked on the world stage, and will go down in history as one of the greatest phenomena of the twentieth century. To have destroyed material that could give future generations an insight into that phenomenon is both misguided and irresponsible.

Diana's will was drawn up in 1993, shortly after the separation but before the £17 million divorce settlement, and the executors were Diana's mother and sister Sarah. She left over £21 million gross, from which inheritance tax of over £8.5 million was deducted. The original will named Patrick Jephson, her private secretary, as an executor with Mrs Shand Kydd. But Diana had amended the will after she fell out with Jephson in 1995, and replaced him with Sarah. She had left no bequests to her mother, brother and sisters, or any of her nephews and nieces, although she left instructions that if she and Prince Charles were both to die before the boys reached the age of eighteen, her mother and brother should be their guardians.

On Fiona Shackleton's advice, and with the agreement of the Queen and the Prime Minister, the Prince of Wales invited John Major, the former Prime Minister, to be guardian to William and Harry, which, on the face of it, seemed a sensible idea. In December 1997, he was involved in a complicated but successful application to Sir Richard Scott, the Vice-Chancellor and Head of the Chancery Division, to vary the will. Not least of their reasons was to protect the unique Intellectual Property aspects of Diana's image; also to give a larger proportion of Diana's inheritance to Harry, who unlike William, will not inherit an income from the Duchy of Cornwall when his father becomes monarch. A third executor was added at the same time, the Bishop of London, the Rt. Revd Richard Chartres, an old college friend of the Prince of Wales, who conducted William's confirmation service. Although Major's role has been to act as honest broker, given the friction between the Spencers and the Royal Family, and with tabloid criticism of the legal costs involved, there must have been times when it made his nightmare years in government feel like a holiday.

Other amendments secured in the High Court, which her mother and sister thought the Princess would have wanted, provided a bequest of £50,000 for Paul Burrell, whom she had described as her rock, 'the only man I can trust', and who was the only outsider present at Diana's burial. He had not been mentioned in the will. Her seventeen godchildren had been mentioned: she had left them one fifth of the value of her chattels shared between them, but the executors decided Diana would have preferred them instead to have something to remember her by, and allocated each one a trinket of sentimental rather than monetary value. Since her chattels today are worth many millions of pounds more than they were in 1993, it was a sensible decision, which none of the godchildren's parents would argue with, but the trinkets that have been chosen are a poor substitute – they include pieces of crockery, and porcelain, a decanter, a carriage clock, hunting figures and a couple of watercolours. The whole business has caused a great deal of bitterness. The chattels belong to William and Harry, who inherited the bulk of their mother's estate, but many of them, including the famous David and Elizabeth Emanuel wedding dress, are currently on display in Earl Spencer's memorial museum at Althorp.

Looking ahead to the future, having watched helplessly as all this happened to Charles and Diana, one member of the Royal family has serious concerns.

'It is probably impossible, I now realise, for a Prince of Wales to have a happy marriage. Charles was handicapped from day one. It is as much to do with the position and the pressures put upon the Prince of Wales and Princess in the modern world, mostly the media, enquiring about every tiny thing in their life. The media will destroy the children too, I have no doubt about that. William can never be a really happy man.'

William seems to have remarkable resilience. Both he and Harry have so far coped with their mother's death very well indeed, and are flourishing. No one can begin to comprehend the pain and confusion they have been through in their short lives, but they do have an elaborate support group of friends and family, and, free from the strain of having constantly to divide their loyalty between warring parents, they have both started to come out of their shells and develop into much more confident, carefree boys. They have grown very close to their father since Diana died, and have made it clear that he is the only blood relative they need.

What is particularly heart-warming for the Prince is that his sons have accepted his love for Camilla Parker Bowles, and are pleased to see him happy at last. The day after William and Harry went back to school in September 1998, Charles and Camilla flew to Greece on their first ever holiday together. There was a great deal of subterfuge involved. The Prince flew back to Balmoral on the Wednesday to lay a false trail, then flew down to RAF Lyneham the following day to collect Camilla. They flew on to Greece in a friend's private plane. The week before, the Prince had almost called it off because he was unnerved by the paparazzi who had followed Camilla to Corfu, where she had been with Candida Lycett-Green as a guest of Jacob Rothschild. Charles and Camilla had been planning a similar holiday in 1997, when Diana, William and Harry were on board the al Fayed yacht in the South of France. But when he saw what was going on there, he called it all off. He feared it would come out in the press, and provide an alternative seemy, seedy spectacle to what was happening in the South of France.

They had planned to go with Candida and her husband, Rupert, also the artist Derek Hill, who helps the Prince with his painting, and was going to give Camilla some tips too. This year Charles was persuaded to stick to his guns and for five days they cruised around the Greek islands, dodging the bad weather, on a small but powerful boat that belonged to another friend. It was a closely guarded secret and the best birthday present the Prince could have asked for. Even better than the sheer joy of being able to spend time with Camilla away from the cameras and prying eyes, was the fact that they went with William and Harry's blessing.

How long the Princes remain carefree remains to be seen. The older they grow, the more interesting their lives will become, and the more legitimate the public interest will be. The Prince once said that Tony Blair, when he was Leader of the Opposition, had told him that the House of Commons had become a bear pit, and that if he was thinking of going into politics today he would probably decide against it.

'How much worse, therefore,' said the Prince, 'if you happen to be *born* into a public position in these intolerable circumstances. My guess is, before long – especially when William leaves school – the press will call for him to become king rather than me. And they will go on doing so until *he* puts a foot wrong – poor chap! And then they'll start on another tack.'

Perhaps the Royal Family are all destined to be victims, and maybe it is we, who demand too much from them, who are the villains.

Index